# THE ROUGH GUIDE TO
# THAILAND'S
# BEACHES & ISLANDS

ROUGH
GUIDES

This seventh edit
Paul Gray an

# Contents

# Introduction to
# Thailand's
# Beaches & Islands

Despite myriad cultural attractions, sand and sea are what most Thailand holidays are about, and with over three thousand kilometres of tropical coastline there are plenty of stunning white-sand beaches to choose from. In addition, the peculiar shape of the country – which is often likened to an elephant's head, with Bangkok as the eye, the east coast as the chin, and the peninsular Andaman and Gulf coasts forming the trunk – means you can dive, swim and sunbathe all year round, for when the monsoon rains are battering one coast you merely have to cross to the other to escape them.

Geographical differences have given distinctive character to each of the coasts. The **Andaman coast** is the most dramatic, edged by sheer limestone cliffs carved by wind and water into strange silhouettes, and interleaved with thick bands of mangrove forest. The **Gulf coast** begins and ends quietly with relatively flat, featureless stretches to the south of Bangkok and down towards the Malaysian border, but peaks at its midpoint, where the peninsular mountains march into the sea to form the wildly varied landscapes of the Samui archipelago and the Ang Thong National Marine Park. A fair chunk of the **east coast** is dominated by the rigs of offshore oil and gas exploration, but the islands that lie further out have forested spines and gorgeous strands. In short, you'll find great beaches on all three coasts: idyllic confections of clear turquoise waters at invitingly balmy temperatures, sand so soft that it squeaks underfoot, and palm trees laden with coconuts.

The Thai royal family started the craze for seaside holidays by making regular trips to Hua Hin in the early 1900s, and the subsequent construction of the Southern Railway Line soon opened up the region to the rest of the population. Inspired by American GIs who'd discovered Thailand's attractions during their R&R breaks from Vietnam, it

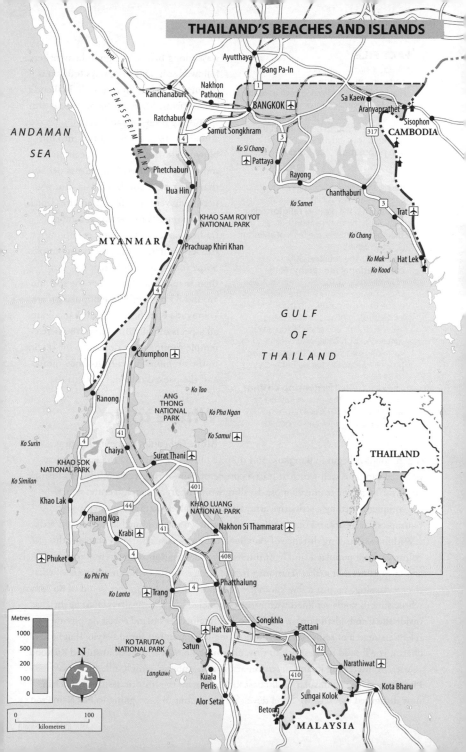

## FACT FILE

- Divided into 76 provinces or *changwat* and one special administrative area (Bangkok), Thailand was known as **Siam** until 1939 (and again from 1945 to 1949); some academics suggest changing the name back again, to better reflect the country's Thai and non-Thai diversity.
- The **population** of 69 million is made up of ethnic Thais (75 percent) and Chinese (14 percent), with the rest comprising mainly immigrants from neighbouring countries as well as hill-tribespeople.
- Buddhism is the national **religion**, Islam the largest minority religion, but nearly all Thais also practise some form of animism (spirit worship).
- Since 1932 the country has been a **constitutional monarchy**. At the time of his death in 2016, King Bhumibol, also known as Rama IX (being the ninth ruler of the Chakri dynasty), was the world's longest-ruling head of state, having been on the throne since 1946; he was succeeded by his son, who became King Vajiralongkorn (Rama X), though, at the time of writing, the coronation had yet to be held.
- The world record for **nonstop kissing** was set by two Thai men in Pattaya on Valentine's Day, 2012, at a gobsmacking 50 hours, 25 minutes and 1 second.

wasn't long before foreign holidaymakers followed suit, and these days **tourism** is the main industry in nearly all Thailand's coastal areas. Many of the most beautiful spots have been well and truly discovered, and a number have developed into full-blown high-rise resorts that seem to have more in common with the Costa del Sol than the rest of Southeast Asia. But you need only venture a few kilometres from such anomalies to encounter a more traditional scene of fishing communities, rubber plantations and Buddhist temples. Some forty percent of Thais still earn their living from the land or the sea, and around 85 percent of the population are **Theravada Buddhists**, a faith that colours all aspects of daily life – from the tiered temple rooftops that dominate the skyline, to the omnipresent saffron-robed monks and the packed calendar of festivals.

# Where to go

Airline schedules decree that many beach holidays begin in **Bangkok**, and despite initial impressions, Thailand's crazy, polluted capital is well worth at least a couple of days of your time. Within its historic core you'll find the country's most dazzling works of art and architecture, which are complemented by a seductive array of traditional markets and contemporary boutiques, cool bars and outstanding restaurants, in the fashionable downtown area.

Within easy striking distance of Bangkok, the east-coast resort of **Pattaya** is the country's most popular – and least interesting – destination, a concrete warren of hotels and strip joints that makes its money from package tourists who are unaware of what they're missing. Yet just a few kilometres beyond sits the diminutive island of **Ko Samet**, whose superb sands are lined with more conducive beach bungalows. East again, just inside the Cambodian border, **Ko Chang** has retained its upland forest despite the relentless march of resort-style facilities along its shores; but for old-style Thai beach charm, you'll need to press on, to tiny, charming **Ko Mak** and wild, unsullied **Ko Kood**.

After an interesting inland diversion at the atmospheric, temple-filled town of **Phetchaburi**, the peninsular Gulf coast kicks off with the historic resort of **Hua Hin**, now disfigured by excessive hotel development; better to keep going to **Pak Nam Pran**'s arty boutique hotels or unspoilt **Prachuap Khiri Kan**, with its handsome promenade and shady sands. The main draw on this side of the peninsula, though, is the Samui archipelago to the south: **Ko Samui** itself is the most developed of the three main islands here, but has largely kept its good looks and offers an appealing variety of beachside accommodation, restaurants and facilities; **Ko Pha Ngan**, with its small resorts and desolate coves, is still firmly backpacker territory, drawing party people – to **Hat Rin** – and solitude seekers in equal parts; and **Ko Tao** is the remotest outcrop of the three, but has established itself as one of the world's leading centres for scuba-diving courses. On the mainland to the south, **Nakhon Si Thammarat** is a great place to recharge your cultural – and culinary – batteries.

Across the peninsula, there's extraordinary drama and beauty all along the Andaman coast. Underwater highlights include the polychromatic reefs of the **Ko Similan** island chain, while above water there's the islet-studded bay of **Ao Phang Nga**, the curvy white-sand shores of party-island **Ko Phi Phi** and the primeval cliffs of **Krabi's Railay peninsula**. There's grandeur inland, too, in the lofty tropical rainforests of **Khao Sok National Park**. Sadly, the big resort island of **Phuket** is increasingly denuded of its natural beauty, but five million visitors a year are still drawn to its dozen different beaches, which offer everything from luxurious five-star seclusion to seedy nightlife. **Ko Lanta** is, for the moment at least, a calmer alternative for families, while independent

---

**RAT OR RAJA?**

There's no standard system of **transliterating** Thai script into Roman, so you're sure to find that the Thai words in this book don't always match the versions you'll see elsewhere. Maps and street signs are the biggest sources of confusion, so we've generally gone for the transliteration that's most common on the spot; where it's a toss-up between two equally popular versions, we've used the one that helps best with pronunciation. However, sometimes you'll need to do a bit of lateral thinking, bearing in mind that a classic variant for the town of Satun is Satul, while among street names, Thanon Rajavithi could come out as Thanon Ratwithi – and it's not unheard of to find one spelling posted at one end of a road, with another at the opposite end.

---

travellers will much prefer the uncommercial islands of **Ko Jum**, **Ko Yao Noi**, **Ko Chang** and **Ko Phayam**.

Spectacular limestone backdrops continue down the Andaman coast into the provinces of the deep south, where the main attractions are teeming sea life and unfrequented sands. The quietest spot of all is the beautiful national park of **Ko Tarutao**, though **Ko Lipe** is a rather rowdy neighbour, with the fastest development on this stretch of littoral; half a dozen other varied islands down here offer an appealing balance of remoteness and facilities. There's now the intriguing possibility of **island-hopping** your way down through them – in fact, all the way from Phuket to Penang in Malaysia – without setting foot on the mainland.

# When to go

The **climate** of most of Thailand is governed by three seasons (see page 56): **rainy** (roughly May–Oct), caused by the southwest monsoon dumping moisture gathered from the Andaman Sea and the Gulf of Thailand; **cool** (Nov–Feb); and **hot** (March–May). The rainy season is the least predictable of the three, varying in length and intensity from year to year, but it's never a case of the heavens opening in May and not closing again till October: there'll be rain most days, but often only for a few hours in the afternoon or at night. The rains usually gather force between June and August, coming to a peak in September and October, when unpaved roads are reduced to mud troughs and some islands become inaccessible.

Within this scheme, slight variations are found from region to region. In southern Thailand, temperatures are more consistent throughout the year, with less variation the closer you get to the Equator. The rainy season hits the **Andaman coast** harder than anywhere else in the country: rainfall can start in April and usually persists until November. The **Gulf coast** of the southern peninsula lies outside this general pattern – with the sea immediately to the east, this coast and its offshore islands feel the effects of the northeast monsoon, which brings rain between October and January, especially in November, but suffers less than the Andaman coast from the southwest monsoon.

Overall, the cool season is generally the **best time** to come to Thailand, and the most popular: as well as having more manageable temperatures and less rain, it offers waterfalls in full spate and the best of the flowers in bloom.

# Author picks

Having finally settled down in Thailand after twenty years of toing and froing, our author, Paul, has plenty to write home about. Here are some of his personal favourites.

**Messing about in boats** It's hard to beat a short, richly diverse boat trip around Ko Tao (see page 263) and the causeway beaches of Ko Nang Yuan (see page 269).

**Kneads must** A good pummelling at the massage pavilions amid the historic, kaleidoscopic architecture of Wat Pho is one of Bangkok's unmissable experiences (see page 85).

**Best view** Among dozens of contenders along Thailand's vast coastline, in the end it has to be the implausible concentration of limestone turrets in Phang Nga bay (see page 345).

**Laid-back islands** Ko Mak and Ko Phayam lack the spectacular scenery of some of their neighbours, and their beaches, though beautiful, are not quite as stunning, but they both have a lovely, laid-back atmosphere for chilling out and just enough facilities to keep most beach bums happy (see pages 191 and 293).

**Aaaaaah-roy** "Delicious" food is never far away in Thailand, be it fluffy deep-fried catfish with a tangy mango salad, toothsome beef green curry, or mango with sticky rice and coconut milk (see page 39).

**Sundowners** Anywhere along Ko Lanta's (see page 378) vast swathe of west-facing beaches is great for watching the sun set with an ice-cold beer – the restaurant at *Lanta Coral Beach* (see page 388), on a small promontory at Hat Khlong Nam Jud, particularly sticks in the mind.

Our author recommendations don't end here. We've flagged up our favourite places – a perfectly sited hotel, an atmospheric café, a special restaurant – throughout the Guide, highlighted with the ★ symbol.

THAI BEEF GREEN CURRY
KO PHAYAM

# things not to miss

It's not possible to explore every inch of Thailand's coastline in one trip – and we don't suggest you try. What follows, in no particular order, is a selective taste of the highlights: beautiful beaches, outstanding national parks, exuberant festivals and thrilling activities. All highlights have a page reference to take you straight into the guide, where you can find out more.

1

### 1 DIVING AND SNORKELLING

See page 51

There's another world of teeming colours under the water, and Thailand's coastline offers hundreds of opportunities to explore it.

### 2 NIGHT MARKETS

See page 41

After-dark gatherings of dramatically lit pushcart kitchens, which are usually the best-value and most entertaining places to eat.

### 3 SEA-CANOEING

See pages 182, 250 and 316

Low-impact paddling is the best way to explore the natural beauty of the Ko Chang, Ang Thong and Ao Phang Nga archipelagos.

### 4 ANG THONG NATIONAL MARINE PARK

See page 249

This dense cluster of jungle-clad islands set in the deep-blue Gulf of Thailand offers stunning vistas and some truly remote accommodation.

### 5 PHETCHABURI

See page 207

Many of the temples in this charming, historic town date back three hundred years and are still in use today.

### 6 SEAFOOD
See page 39
Fresh fish, curried with
vegetables, steamed whole
with ginger and mushrooms
or simply barbecued…the
only problem is knowing
when to stop.

### 7 FULL MOON PARTY AT HAT RIN, KO PHA NGAN
See page 258
*Apocalypse Now* without
the war…

### 8 KO TAO
See page 263
Take a dive course, or just
explore this remote island's
contours by boat or on foot.

### 9 SONGKHRAN
See page 47
Thai New Year is the excuse
for a national water fight –
and tourists are definitely
fair game.

### 10 ROCK-CLIMBING
See pages 340, 365 and 361
Even novice climbers can
scale the cliffs at Ko Yao
Noi, Phi Phi or the Rallay
peninsula for an unbeatable
perspective on the
Andaman seascape.

9

10

### 11 THE GRAND PALACE, BANGKOK
See page 75
No visitor should miss this huge complex, which encompasses the country's holiest and most beautiful temple, Wat Phra Kaeo, and its most important image, the Emerald Buddha.

### 12 KO KOOD
See page 195
An untamed beauty, fringed by very pretty beaches.

### 13 KO PHA NGAN
See page 252
The island is dotted with beautiful beaches, so head out to secluded Bottle Beach or Thong Nai Pan, or gear up for the fun at Hat Rin.

### 14 KO TARUTAO NATIONAL MARINE PARK
See page 408
Spectacular islands, with a surprising variety of land- and seascapes.

### 15 CHATUCHAK WEEKEND MARKET, BANGKOK
See page 110
Thailand's top shopping experience features over ten thousand stalls selling everything from cooking pots to designer lamps.

11

12

13

14

15

16

17

# Itineraries

The following itineraries cover Thailand's coastline in all its diversity, from snorkelling the Similans to beach-bumming your way through the Andaman archipelagos. Whether you want to feel the buzz of adventure in the great outdoors, feast on the never-ending variety of Thai cuisine, or find the nearest thing to a desert island paradise, these will point the way.

## FOR ADVENTURE-SEEKERS

Thailand offers an astonishing range of good-value adventure sports, especially in, on and over the teeming tropical seas.

**❶ Ko Tao dive courses** The best place to hone your skills, whether you're a beginner, advanced or speciality diver. See page 263

**❷ Khao Sok National Park** Halfway between the southern peninsula's two coasts, Khao Sok offers guided and self-guided hikes, caving, tubing and kayaking. See page 301

**❸ Diving and snorkelling off Ko Similan** Camp out on this remote chain of national park islands or take a live-aboard trip to make the most of the spectacular turquoise waters and shallow reefs. See page 312

**❹ Sea-canoeing in Ao Phang Nga** Day, night or multi-day paddling trips are the best way to explore the secret caves and mangrove swamps of this extraordinary bay. See page 345

**❺ Ko Yao Noi** This relaxing island on the edge of Phang Nga bay is a low-key hub for active visitors, who kayak, snorkel, dive and climb rocks. See page 340

**❻ Rock-climbing on the Railay peninsula** Offering courses for beginners, as well as equipment rental and guides, this is Thailand's premier site for climbers, with over seven

hundred bolted routes amid awesome scenery. See page 361

## FOR FOOD-LOVERS

The seafood's great all around Thailand's coastline, but the places mentioned below are at least one notch above your average bungalow kitchen: they're all locally famous restaurants serving a wide range of regional specialities, where you can eat extremely well.

**❶ Bangkok** Among fifty thousand places to eat in the capital, a couple of restaurants can be singled out for special mention: *Taling Pling* (see page 135), with a long list of dishes from the four corners of the country praised by Thai food critics; and *Bolan* (see page 133) for its meticulous commitment to traditional recipes and the "Slow Food" philosophy.

**❷ Hua Hin** Long the favourite seaside retreat of Bangkok's food-loving middle classes, Hua Hin has built up a thriving culinary scene – standouts include the super-fresh, reasonably priced seafood dishes at *Sopa Seafood* (see page 218) and *Baan Itsara*'s (see page 217) creative plates.

**❸ Phuket** An antidote to the bland restaurants of Phuket's resorts, *Kopitiam by Wilai* is a typical southern coffee house serving authentic local dishes such as *muu hong* (pork stewed with Chinese herbs). See page 321

**④ Krabi** You may have to queue for a table at *Ko Tung*, but it's worth the wait for the fresh, southern-style seafood such as delicious sweet mussels and baked crab. See page 355

**⑤ Nakhon Si Thammarat** *Krua Thale* is almost reason in itself to go to Nakhon – don't miss the chunky mussels in herb soup. See page 278

## FOR ISLAND-HOPPERS

Ferries now join up the karst islands of the southern Andaman coast, so it's possible to travel from Phuket to Penang in Malaysia without setting foot on the mainland. You can easily avoid the crowds, and save yourself money and hassle, by bypassing the kiss-me-quick resorts of Phuket, Ko Phi Phi and Ko Lipe in favour of these alluring island beauties.

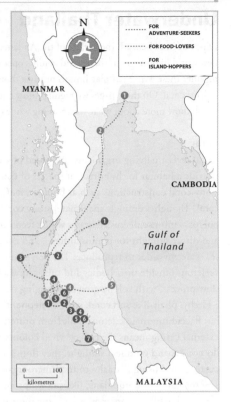

**❶ Phuket Town** Base yourself among the Sino-Portuguese architecture of the island capital, which has better-value and more interesting places to stay and eat than the big-name beaches, and much better transport links. See page 317

**❷ Ko Jum** Half a dozen wild and lonely beaches facing the sunset, with boat trips to enjoy, a small mountain to climb, and paraffin lamps in some of the resorts. See page 374

**❸ Ko Lanta** With around 20km of tempting, west-facing sandy beaches and a laid-back, family-friendly atmosphere, Ko Lanta offers a wide range of affordable accommodation. See page 378

**❹ Ko Hai** A variety of good resorts for all budgets and a gorgeous panorama of jagged limestone islands. See page 402

**❺ Ko Mook** The main draw here is the stunning Emerald Cave, with its inland beach of fine sand

at the base of a spectacular natural chimney. See page 403

**❻ Ko Kradan** A remote island that's uninhabited apart from its half-dozen resorts, with a long, powdery, east-facing strand, crystal-clear waters and a reef for snorkellers to explore. See page 404

**❼ Ko Tarutao** Huge national park island with mangroves and jungle tracks to discover, and the most unspoilt beaches in the area. See page 408

# Underwater Thailand

Dip your head beneath the surface of the Andaman Sea or the Gulf of Thailand and a whole new world of outrageous shapes and colours opens up. The figures speak for themselves: together these two tracts play host to nearly a thousand species of fish and some 270 species of hard coral. On these pages we highlight just a few of the most fascinating examples, so you'll know more about what you're seeing while out diving or snorkelling (see page 51).

## Coral

Coral reefs are living organisms composed of a huge variety of marine life forms, which provide a habitat for hundreds of species of fish, but the foundation of every reef is its stony coral constructions such as **boulder, leaf, table, mushroom, staghorn** and **brain coral**. Though seemingly inanimate, stony coral is actually composed of colonies of polyps – minuscule invertebrates which feed on plankton, generally depend on algae and direct sunlight for photosynthesis, and extract calcium carbonate (limestone) from sea water in order to reproduce. The polyps use this calcium carbonate to build new skeletons outside their bodies and this is how a reef is formed. It's an extraordinarily slow process, with colony growth averaging between 0.5cm and 2.8cm a year.

Fleshy, plant-like **soft coral**, such as **elephant's ear**, is also composed of polyps, but has flaccid internal skeletons built from protein rather than calcium. The lack of an external casing means the polyps' vivid colours are much more visible and, as they do not depend on direct sunlight, they flourish at greater depths, swaying with the currents and using tentacles to trap microorganisms.

**Horny coral**, or **gorgonians**, like **sea whips** and **sea fans**, are a cross between stony and soft coral, while **sea anemones** have the most obvious, and venomous, tentacles of any member of the coral family, using them to trap fish and other large prey.

## Reef fish

The algae and plankton that accumulate around coral colonies attract a catalogue of fish known collectively as **reef fish**. Most are small in stature, with vibrant and exotically patterned skins for camouflage against the coral, and flattened bodies, broad tails and specially adapted fins for easy manoeuvring around the tiniest of reef crannies.

**Butterfly fish** are typically well designed: named for the butterfly-like movements of their thin, flat, yellow-white-and-black bodies, they can swim backwards, and some also have elongated snouts for nosing into crevices; a number even sport eye-like blotches near the tail to confuse predators.

Vibrantly coloured with flattened bodies that are well adapted for reef-dwelling, **angelfish** are distinguished from the similar butterfly fish by the strong spines on their gill flaps. **Emperor angelfish**, with their tangerine and blue stripes, make a clicking sound when disturbed and can grow up to 30cm in length.

There are approximately one hundred different species of **surgeonfish**, each with its own distinctive markings, but they all share the feature that gives them their name

– a sharp blade on either side of their tail-base that becomes erect when antagonized and can inflict serious damage. More innocuous is the distinctive long pennant fin that trails from the dorsal fin of the **moorish idol**, which is also recognizable by its pronounced snout and dramatic bands of colour.

Among the most impressive reef fish that school are the huge shoals of silvery **fusilierfish**, which move as one, changing direction in an eye-catching flash of rippling silver. Growing up to 60cm in length, they have extensible upper jaws, adapted for picking plankton. Some reef fish, among them the ubiquitous **parrotfish**, eat coral. With the help of a bird-like beak, which is in fact several teeth fused together, the parrotfish scrapes away at the coral, leaving characteristic white scars, and then grinds the fragments down with another set of back teeth – a practice reputedly responsible for the erosion of a great deal of Thailand's reef.

**Anemonefish** are so called because, having covered themselves in the sea anemone's mucus, they are able to move among and gain protection from the anemone's venomous tentacles, which would paralyse other fish on contact. Since the film *Finding Nemo* came out, their most famous species, the **clown anemonefish**, is generally just referred to as "Nemo".

Equally as predictable as sightings of anemonefish is the presence of cleaner fish, or **cleaner wrasse**, on the edges of every shoal of reef fish. Streamlined, with a long snout and jaws that act like tweezers, a cleaner fish spends its days picking parasites off the skins of other fish, such as the normally voracious **grouper fish** – a symbiotic relationship essential to both parties. A close but more colourful relative of the grouper is the commonly sighted **coral hind**, which is often found among staghorn coral.

Larger, less frequently spotted visitors to Thailand's offshore reefs include the **moray eel**, whose elongated jaws of viciously pointed teeth make it a deadly predator; it hunts mainly at night and often holes up in coral caves during the day. The similarly befanged **barracuda** can grow to 2m and is one of the world's fastest-swimming fish, using its speed – up to 40kmh – to prey on other fish of any size.

## Sharks and rays

One of the few shark species – along with the white-tip shark – that can breathe while stationary, the **leopard shark** is often found on sand bottoms, camouflaged by its grey-to-brown body with dark spots and blotches. Sometimes found up to 3m in length, they're completely harmless to humans and live off such things as fish, shellfish and worms.

Curious but very rarely aggressive unless provoked, small **white-tip reef sharks** are named for the white tips on their dorsal and tail fins. They hunt, mostly at night, for fish, crustaceans and octopus. With its white belly and greyish back with light spots and stripes, the **whale shark** is quite harmless, feeding on plankton and small fish that are filtered into its huge mouth as it cruises the seas. The largest fish in the world, at up to 18m long, the whale shark lives for around seventy years and migrates every spring to feed on the abundant plankton off the west coast of Australia.

MOORISH IDOL

You have to keep your distance if you encounter a stingray (see page 24), but it is sometimes possible to swim with a graceful **manta ray**, whose extraordinary flatness, strange wing-like fins, and massive size – up to 6m across and weighing some 1600kg – make it an astonishing presence.

## Turtles

Occasionally seen paddling around reef waters, turtles come in four local species, all of them endangered: the green, the leatherback, the olive ridley and the hawksbill (critically endangered). The loggerhead turtle also once swam in Thai waters, until the constant plundering of its eggs rendered it locally extinct. Most of the beaches favoured by turtles for egg-laying are now protected as marine parks and are off-limits to visitors.

Of the remaining four species, the **green turtle** is the commonest, a mottled brown creature named not for its appearance but for the colour of the soup made from its flesh. Adults weigh up to 180kg and are herbivorous, subsisting on sea grass, mangrove leaves and algae.

The **leatherback**, encased in a distinctive ridged shell, is the world's largest turtle, weighing between 250kg and 550kg; it eats nothing but jellyfish. Weighing up to 50kg and feeding mainly on shrimps and crabs, the small **olive ridley** is named partly after its olive-green, heart-shaped carapace (no one knows who or what "ridley" was).

Named for its peculiar beak-like mouth, the **hawksbill** is prized for its spectacular carapace (the sale of which was banned by CITES in 1992), with light and dark streaks

## OTHER BITERS AND STINGERS

Thailand is home to 25 species of **sea snake**, whose tails are flattened to act as an efficient paddle in water. Most sea snakes are venomous, though not aggressive. Of the venomous ones, the commonest and most easily recognized is the banded sea snake, which is silvery grey with thirty to fifty black bands and a slightly yellow underside at its front end. It grows to 1.5m and inhabits shallow coastal waters, coming onto land to lay its eggs.

Other harmful creatures to be avoided include the highly camouflaged sea-bed-dwelling **stonefish** and **scorpionfish**, both of which can be very hard to spot but have extremely venomous spines which are dangerous when trodden on. The magnificent **lionfish** should also be admired from afar as its impressive plumes are venomous if brushed against, as are the tentacles of the **jellyfish**.

The **blue-spotted ray** or **stingray** has two venomous spines on its long tail with which it lashes out when threatened; as it tends to bury itself with almost complete disguise in the mud or sand near reefs, it can be a particular hazard to unwary divers. Another thing to be wary of is so-called **fire coral** (not actually a true coral but a coral-like brownish encrustation), which is found in shallow waters on the edge of the reef and is covered in a mass of tiny, fuzz-like tentacles that can inflict a painful burn.

on an amber background and a serrated appearance towards the tail; it weighs up to 75kg and lives off a type of sea sponge.

### Invertebrates

Thailand's reefs support countless species of **invertebrates**, including spiral-feathered **Christmas-tree worms**, also sometimes evocatively known as bottle-brush worms, which embed their lower bodies in coral heads; all sorts of multi-celled, multi-hued **sponges**, both encrusting and free-standing; neon-bright squamose **giant clams**, which burrow into the reef, exposing only their soft, flamboyantly coloured mantle; and a thousand-plus species of hermaphroditic, shell-less mollusc known as **nudibranchs** or sea slugs, which come in an arresting array of patterns and shapes and live in shallow waters.

Of the reef's numerous spiny echinoderms, the commonest **sea urchins**, which also tend to live in shallow areas near shore, are those with evil-looking black spines up to 35cm in length, though some varieties are covered in short, blunt spines or even excruciatingly painful flower-like pincers.

The magnificent **crown-of-thorns starfish** is also protected by highly venomous spines, which sheath the twenty or so "arms" that extend from a body that can measure up to 50cm in diameter. Disastrously for many reefs, the crown-of-thorns starfish feeds on coral, laying waste to as much as fifty square centimetres of stony coral in a 24-hour period. The much more benign **feather stars** also have multiple feather-like arms arranged in star formations and come in many versions; they feed at night, crawling along reef surfaces with the help of tiny jointed limbs, or cirri, to sway in the current.

Though hideous, the **sea cucumber**, which looks like a large slug and lies half-buried on the sea bed, is quite harmless. Deceptively slothful in appearance, sea cucumbers are constantly ingesting and excreting so much sand and mud that the combined force of those in a three-square-kilometre area can together redistribute one million kilograms of sea-bed material a year.

LONGTAIL BOAT ON A BANGKOK CANAL

# Basics

GETTING THERE **BASICS** | 27

# Getting there

**There are international airports in Bangkok (Suvarnabhumi and Don Muang), Hat Yai, Krabi, Phuket, Ko Samui and Pattaya (U-Tapao). The vast majority of travellers fly into Suvarnabhumi Airport.**

Air fares to Thailand generally depend on the **season**, with the highest being approximately mid-November to mid-February, when the weather is best (with premium rates charged for flights between mid-Dec and New Year), and in July and August to coincide with school holidays. You will need to book several months in advance to get reasonably priced tickets during these peak periods.

The cheapest way of getting to most **regional Thai airports** is usually to buy a flight to Bangkok and then a separate domestic ticket. However, there are dozens of potentially useful, mostly seasonal, international routes into **Phuket**, including direct flights with several airlines from Australia. Most international flights into Krabi, Ko Samui, Pattaya and Don Muang are from Malaysia, Singapore and China (including Hong Kong and Macau). Krabi also handles seasonal, mostly charter flights from Scandinavia, while Qatar Airways has recently started nonstop flights from Doha to Chiang Mai, Krabi and Pattaya airports.

## Flights from the UK and Ireland

The fastest and most comfortable way of reaching Thailand **from the UK** is to fly nonstop from London to Bangkok with Thai Airways (W thaiairways.com), British Airways (W ba.com) or Eva Airways (W evaair.com), a journey of about eleven and a half hours. These airlines sometimes have special promotions, but a typical fare in high season might come in at around £800–900. Fares on indirect scheduled flights to Bangkok are always cheaper than nonstop flights – starting at about £450 in high season if booked many months in advance with Qatar Airways (W qatarairways.com), for example – though these journeys can take anything from two to twelve hours longer.

There are no nonstop flights from any **regional airports** in Britain or from any **Irish airports**, but rather than routing via London, you may find it convenient to fly to another hub such as Frankfurt (with Lufthansa; W lufthansa.com), Doha (with Qatar Airways; W qatarairways.com), Abu Dhabi (with Etihad; W etihadairways.com) or Istanbul (with Turkish Airlines; W turkishairlines.com), and take a connecting flight from there. Return flights from Newcastle upon Tyne with Emirates (W emirates.com), for example, currently start at around £500 in high season if booked far in advance, from Dublin with Qatar, at around €550.

## Flights from the US and Canada

At the moment, Thai Airways is no longer offering nonstop flights from the West Coast to Bangkok, though it's considering restarting them, either from Seattle or, possibly, San Francisco. Plenty of other airlines run to Bangkok from East and West Coast cities with one stop en route; it's generally easier to find a reasonable fare on flights via Asia than via Europe, even if you're departing from the East Coast – if you book far in advance, you can get a flight from LA or New York for as little as US$700 return in high season, including taxes. Air Canada (W aircanada.com) has the most convenient service to Bangkok from the largest number of Canadian cities; from Vancouver, expect to pay around Can$1250 in high season if booked in advance; from Toronto, Can$1500. Cheaper rates are often available if you're prepared to make two or three stops and take more time.

Minimum **flying times** are around twenty hours from New York or Toronto (westbound or eastbound), including stopovers, twenty hours from LA, and eighteen hours from Vancouver.

## Flights from Australia and New Zealand

There's no shortage of **scheduled flights** to Bangkok and Phuket **from Australia**, with direct services from major cities operated by Thai Airways (W thaiairways.

**A BETTER KIND OF TRAVEL**

At Rough Guides we are passionately committed to travel. We believe it helps us understand the world we live in and the people we share it with – and of course tourism is vital to many developing economies. But the scale of modern tourism has also damaged some places irreparably, and climate change is accelerated by most forms of transport, especially flying. All Rough Guides' flights are carbon-offset, and every year we donate money to a variety of environmental charities.

com), Qantas (**W** qantas.com) and half a dozen others (around 9hr from Sydney, Melbourne and Perth), and plenty of indirect flights via Asian hubs, which take at least eleven and a half hours. There's often not much difference between the fares on nonstop and indirect flights with the major carriers, nor between the fares from the major eastern cities. From Melbourne, if you book far in advance, you can get a ticket to Bangkok in high season for as little as Aus\$450, on a low-cost carrier such as Jetstar; nonstop flights with the major airlines from the east coast more typically cost from Aus\$900 if booked ahead. Fares from Perth and Darwin can be up to Aus\$200 cheaper.

From **New Zealand**, Thai Airways runs nonstop twelve-hour flights between Auckland and Bangkok, costing from around NZ\$1300 (including taxes) in high season with advanced booking. Qantas flights from Auckland make brief stops in Sydney, adding about three hours to the trip, and other major Asian airlines offer indirect flights via their hubs (from 13hr, but more typically 17hr); fares for indirect flights booked far in advance can start as low as NZ\$1000 in high season.

## Flights from South Africa

Thai Airways' nonstop, code-sharing flights with South African Airways (**W** flysaa.com) from Johannesburg to Bangkok have been discontinued, so you'll be making a stop in East Africa, the Middle East, Singapore or Hong Kong, with fares starting at around ZAR7000 for an advance booking in high season, and a journey time of fourteen hours (via Singapore) or more.

### AGENTS AND OPERATORS

**All Points East** UK **T** 023 9225 8859, Thailand **T** 081 885 9490; **W** allpointseast.com. Southeast Asia specialist operating small-group adventure holidays with off-the-beaten-track itineraries.

**Andaman Discoveries** Thailand **W** andamandiscoveries.com. Award-winning, village-based homestay community tourism programmes around Khuraburi on the north Andaman coast, which allow visitors to experience daily activities such as cooking and batik-making, cultural activities and the local flora and fauna. Other tours include trips to Ko Surin National Park to snorkel and learn about Moken life and to Khao Sok.

**Asian Trails** Thailand **W** asiantrails.travel. Western-run company that offers cycling adventures, plus more typical package tours.

**Backpackers Thailand Travel** Thailand **W** backpackersthailandtravel.com. Activities and accommodation packages in Ko Pha Ngan and the south.

**Eastern & Oriental Express** UK **T** 0845 077 2222, US **T** 800 524 2420; **W** belmond.com/eastern-and-oriental-express. Tours by luxury train between Bangkok and Singapore.

**Grasshopper Adventures** Australia **T** 03 9016 3172, Thailand **T** 02 280 0832, UK **T** 020 8123 8144, US **T** 818 921 7101; **W** grasshopperadventures.com. Half- and full-day cycling trips around Bangkok, as well as multi-day tours to the south of Thailand.

**Hivesters** Thailand **W** hivesters.com. This social enterprise and sustainable travel company offers interesting tours mostly in Bangkok, but also with the chance to be a fisherman for a day on Ko Yao Noi, plus runs a project, APPEAR, to revivify six of the capital's neighbourhoods.

**Local Alike** Thailand **W** localalike.com. Online marketplace that gives access to responsible tourism activities in communities from Trat to Trang.

**North South Travel** UK **T** 01245 608 291, **W** northsouthtravel. co.uk. Friendly, competitive travel agency, offering discounted fares worldwide. Profits are used to support projects in the developing world, especially the promotion of sustainable tourism.

**Nutty's Adventures** Thailand **W** nutty-adventures.com. Fascinating, multi-day, community-based tourism trips going off the beaten track all over the country, many with homestays and farmstays, including island-hopping on the Andaman coast.

**Origin Asia** Thailand **W** alex-kerr.com. Cultural programmes that teach and explain living Thai arts such as dance, music, martial arts, textiles, flower offerings and cooking. Courses in Bangkok last from a day to a week.

**Responsible Travel** UK **T** 01273 823700, **W** responsibletravel. com. One-stop shop for scores of fair-trade, ethically inclined holidays in Thailand, including trips that focus on cycling, cuisine and family activities.

**Spice Roads** Thailand **W** spiceroads.com. Escorted day and multi-day bike tours – including mountain biking – through all regions of Thailand.

**STA Travel** UK **T** 0333 321 0099, US **T** 800 781 4040, Australia **T** 134 782, New Zealand **T** 0800 474 400, South Africa **T** 0861 781 781, Thailand **T** 02 236 0262; **W** statravel.co.uk. Worldwide specialists in independent travel (with branches in Bangkok); also student IDs, travel insurance, car rental and more. Good discounts for students and under-26s.

**Take Me Tour** Thailand **W** takemetour.com. Online marketplace for one-day tours with local guides all over Thailand.

**Telltale Travel** UK **T** 0800 011 2571, US **T** 866 211 5972, **W** telltaletravel.co.uk. Tailor-made, upscale company that offers off-the-beaten-track wildlife, cultural, family, homestay and cooking tours.

**Thailand Birdwatching** Thailand **W** thailandbirdwatching.com. Specialist birdwatching tours in national parks and nature reserves.

**Trailfinders** UK **T** 020 7368 1200, Ireland **T** 01 677 7888; **W** trailfinders.com. One of the best-informed and most efficient agents for independent travellers.

**Travel CUTS** Canada **T** 800 667 2887, **W** travelcuts.com. Canadian youth and student travel firm.

**USIT** Ireland **T** 01 602 1906, Australia **T** 1800 092 499; **W** usit.ie. Ireland's main student and youth travel specialists, with a branch in Sydney.

# Travel via neighbouring countries

Sharing land borders with Myanmar, Laos, Cambodia and Malaysia, Thailand works well as part of many **overland itineraries**, both across Asia and between Europe and Australia. Bangkok is also one of the major regional flight hubs for Southeast Asia. Cross-border links in Southeast Asia have improved considerably recently and are likely to continue to do so in the next few years.

The main restrictions on overland routes in and out of Thailand are determined by where the permitted land crossings lie and by **visas**. All **Asian embassies** are located in Bangkok (see page 144), where many Khao San tour agents offer to get your visa for you, but beware: some are reportedly **faking the stamps**, which could get you into pretty serious trouble, so it's safer to go to the embassy yourself.

The right paperwork is also crucial if you're planning to **drive your own car or motorbike** into Thailand; see the Golden Triangle Rider website (Wgt-rider. com) for advice.

## Myanmar (Burma)

There are now several overland access points between **Myanmar (Burma)** and Thailand that are open to non-Thais, including at Kaw Thaung (Victoria Point) near Ranong. At these borders Western tourists forearmed with a Burmese tourist visa can enter Myanmar, and at most of them you can get a temporary US$10 (or B500) **border pass**, which will allow you to make limited-distance trips into Myanmar, usually just for the day. The crossing at Dan Singkhon near Prachuap Khiri Khan is currently open only to Thai tourists.

## Cambodia

At the time of writing, six overland crossings on the **Thai–Cambodia border** are open to non-Thais; see the relevant town accounts for specific details on all the border crossings.

Most travellers use the crossing at Poipet, which has transport connections with Sisophon, Siem Reap and Phnom Penh and lies just across the border from the Thai town of Aranyaprathet (see page 151), with its transport to Bangkok and to Chanthaburi; there are now also direct public buses that run all the way between Bangkok and Siem Reap and between Bangkok and Phnom Penh, which should help you dodge the scams and touts at this frontier post. The second most popular travel route is from Sihanoukville in Cambodia via Koh Kong (Cham Yeam) and Hat Lek to Trat, which is near Ko Chang on Thailand's east coast. There are also two little-used crossings in Chanthaburi province, with transport to and from Pailin in Cambodia.

Tourist **visas** for Cambodia are issued to travellers on arrival at all the above-listed overland border crossings. If you want to buy an advance thirty-day visa, you can do so online at Wevisa.gov.kh. Of the land borders discussed here, these "e-visas" can be used only at Poipet and Koh Kong, but they should help you to avoid the more excessive scams at these two frontier posts.

## Laos

There are seven main points along the **Lao border** where tourists can cross into Thailand: Houayxai (for Chiang Khong); between Nam Ngeun and Huai Kon in Thailand's Nan province; on the Nam Heuang River at the Thai settlement of Tha Li (Loei province); Vientiane (for Nong Khai); Khammouan (aka Thakhek, for Nakhon Phanom); Savannakhet (for Mukdahan); and Pakse (for Chong Mek). Increasing numbers of direct, long-distance public buses, such as between Bangkok and Vientiane, use these crossings to link major towns in the two countries. All these borders can also be used as exits into Laos, with tourist **visas** available **on arrival.**

## Malaysia

Travelling between Thailand and **Malaysia** has in the past been a straightforward and very commonly used overland route, with plentiful connections by bus, minibus, share-taxi and train, most of them routed through the southern Thai city and transport hub of Hat Yai. However, because of the ongoing **violence in Thailand's deep south** (see page 396), all major Western governments are currently advising people not to travel to or through Songkhla, Pattani, Yala and Narathiwat provinces, unless essential (and consequently most insurance companies are not covering travel there). This encompasses Hat Yai and the following border crossings to and from Malaysia: at Padang Besar, on the main rail line connecting Malaysia (and, ultimately, Singapore) with Hat Yai and Bangkok; at Sungai Kolok, terminus of a railway line from Hat Yai and Bangkok, and at adjacent Ban Taba, both of which are connected by road to nearby Kota Bharu in Malaysia; and at the road crossings at Sadao, south of Hat Yai, and at Betong, south of Yala. (The routes towards Kota Bharu and Betong pass through particularly volatile territory, with martial law declared in Pattani, Yala and Narathiwat provinces; however, martial law is not in effect in Hat Yai itself.)

Nevertheless, the provinces of Trang and Satun on the west coast are not affected, and it's still perfectly possible to travel **overland via Satun**: by ferry between Satun's Thammalang pier and the island of Langkawi, or overland between Satun and Kangar (see page 415); or by boat between Ko Lipe and Langkawi (see page 410). For up-to-the-minute advice, consult your government travel advisory (see page 58).

Most Western tourists can spend thirty days in Malaysia without having bought a visa beforehand, and there are Thai embassies or consulates in Kuala Lumpur, Kota Bharu and Penang (see page 61).

# Getting around

**Travel in Thailand is inexpensive and comparatively efficient, if not always speedy. Unless you travel by plane, long-distance journeys in Thailand can be arduous, especially if a shoestring budget restricts you to hard seats and no air conditioning.**

Nonetheless, the wide range of transport options makes travelling around Thailand easier than elsewhere in Southeast Asia. **Buses** are fast, cheap and frequent, and can be quite luxurious. **Trains** are slower but safer and offer more chance of sleeping during overnight trips; moreover, if travelling by day you're likely to follow a more scenic route by rail than by road. Inter-town **songthaews** and **air-conditioned minibuses** are handy, and **ferries** provide easy access to all major islands. Local transport comes in all sorts of permutations, both public and chartered.

Online bookings in English on trains, private "join" buses (see below) and ferries in Thailand are now offered by Ⓦbusonlineticket.co.th and Ⓦ12go. asia, which seems to have a wider choice of ferries and buses.

## Inter-town buses

**Buses**, overall the most convenient way of getting around the country, generally come in four main categories. In ascending order of comfort, speed and cost, they are **ordinary** buses (*rot thammadaa*; not air-conditioned, often orange-coloured) and three overall types of **air-conditioned** bus (*rot*

*ae – "air"* – or *rot thua*; often blue or partly blue): second-class, first-class and VIP first-class. Many ordinary and air-conditioned buses are operated by the government-controlled Baw Khaw Saw (borisat khon song or the "Transport Company"); fairly up-to-date schedules and fares to and from Bangkok can be seen in English at Ⓦtransport.co.th, while the English-language pages on its official booking site, Ⓦpns-allthai.com, may reappear – you should still be able to book tickets in English over the phone on ☎02 872 1777. Privately owned buses that are licensed by the Baw Khaw Saw (*rot ruam*, usually translated as "join buses"), some of which operate from Baw Khaw Saw terminals, also ply most routes; on many short-distance routes, air-conditioned minibuses are replacing buses.

Be warned that long-distance overnight buses, on which some drivers are rumoured to take amphetamines to stay awake, seem to be involved in more than their fair share of accidents; because of this, some travellers prefer to do the overnight journeys by train and then make a shorter bus connection to their destination.

### Ordinary and second-class

**Second-class** (*baw sawng*; often with a "2" on the side of the vehicle) air-conditioned buses have now replaced **ordinary buses** as the main workhorses of the Thai bus system on shorter routes, though you'll still see plenty of the latter in more remote parts of the country. Whether air-conditioned or not, these basic buses are incredibly inexpensive, generally run frequently during daylight hours, pack as many people in as possible and stop often, which slows them down considerably.

It's best to ask locally where to catch your bus. Failing that, designated **bus stops** are often marked by *sala*, small, open-sided wooden structures with bench seats, located at intervals along the main long-distance bus route through town or on the fringes of any decent-sized settlement, for example on the main highway that skirts the edge of town. Where there is only a bus shelter on the "wrong" side of the road, you can be sure that buses travelling in both directions will stop there for any waiting passengers; simply leave your bag on the right side of the road to alert the bus driver and wait in the shade. But if you're in the middle of nowhere with no *sala* in sight, any ordinary or second-class bus should stop for you if you flag it down.

### First-class and VIP

Express services on longer routes, with fewer stops, are mostly operated by **first-class** (*baw neung*;

often with a "1" on the side of the vehicle) and **VIP** (usually written in English on the side) buses. These are your best option for long-distance journeys: you'll generally be allotted specific seats, there'll be a toilet, and on the longest journeys you may get blankets, snacks and nonstop DVDs, though you might want a sweater to cope with excessive air conditioning. The first-class services have fewer seats than second-class and more leg room for reclining, VIP services fewer seats again. Other nomenclature for the top-of-the-range services is also used, especially by the **private "join" companies**: "999", "super VIP" (with even fewer seats), "Gold Class" and, confusingly, sometimes even "First Class" (in imitation of airlines, with just eighteen huge, well-equipped seats).

On a lot of long-distance routes private "join" buses are indistinguishable from government ones and operate out of the same Baw Khaw Saw bus terminals. The major private companies, such as Nakhon Chai Air (📞 1624, 🌐 www.nakhonchaiair. com with an English-language booking facility) and Sombat Tour (📞 02 792 1456 at Mo Chit Bus Terminal in Bangkok, 🌐 sombattour.com – which shows timetables in English, with an English-language booking facility "coming soon") have roughly similar fares, though naturally with more scope for price variation, and offer comparable facilities and standards of service. The opposite is unfortunately true of a number of the smaller, private, unlicensed companies, which have a poor reputation for service and comfort, but gear themselves towards foreign travellers with bargain fares and convenient timetables. The long-distance tour buses that run **from Thanon Khao San** in Banglamphu to Surat Thani are a case in point; though promised VIP buses, travellers frequently complain about shabby furnishings, ineffective air conditioning, unhelpful (even aggressive) drivers, lateness and a frightening lack of safety awareness – and there are frequent reports of theft from luggage on these routes, too, and even the spraying of "sleeping gas" so that hand luggage can be rifled without interruption. Generally it's best to travel with the government or licensed private bus companies from the main bus terminals (who have a reputation with their regular Thai customers to maintain and now operate a handy ticket office near Bangkok's Thanon Khao San – see page 115) or to go by train instead – the extra comfort and peace of mind are well worth the extra baht.

## Tickets and timetables

**Tickets** for all buses can be bought from the departure terminals, but for ordinary and second-class air-conditioned buses it's normal to buy them on

board. First-class and VIP buses may operate from a separate station or office, and it's best to book tickets for the more popular routes at least a day in advance. As a rough indication of **fares**, a trip from Bangkok to Phuket, a distance of 870km, on the Baw Khaw Saw's own buses costs B913 for VIP and B587 for first-class air conditioned.

Long-distance buses often depart in clusters around the same time (early morning or late at night, for example), leaving a gap of five or more hours during the day with no services at all. Local TAT offices occasionally keep up-to-date bus **timetables**, and there's a useful downtown information and booking office in Banglamphu in Bangkok (see page 115). Bus company websites and general transport booking sites are detailed above. Thai Ticket Major's website (🌐 thaiticketmajor. com) offers timetables and booking in English for many Baw Khaw Saw and "join" company routes. Ticketing options include buying them online by credit card through the site; reserving them online or by phone on 📞 02 262 3456, then making your payment at designated outlets around the country, including banks, supermarkets, cinemas and scores of affiliated major post offices (as listed on the site), including the Ratchadamnoen post office, just north of Thanon Rajdamnoen Klang in Banglamphu, and the Thanon Na Phra Lan post office opposite the entrance to the Grand Palace in Ratanakosin.

## Songthaews, share-taxis and air-conditioned minibuses

In rural areas, the bus network is often supplemented by **songthaews** (literally "two rows"), which are open-ended vans (or occasionally cattle-trucks) onto which the drivers squash as many passengers as possible on two facing benches, leaving latecomers to swing off the running board at the back. As well as their essential role within towns (see page 33), songthaews ply set routes from larger towns out to their surrounding suburbs and villages, and occasionally, where there's no call for a regular bus service, between small towns: some have destinations written on in Thai, but few are numbered. In most towns you'll find the songthaew "terminal" near the market; to pick one up between destinations just flag it down. To indicate to the driver that you want to get out, the normal practice is to rap hard with a coin on the metal railings as you approach the spot (or press the bell if there is one).

In the deep south (see page 394) they have traditionally done things in a little more style, with **share-taxis** – sometimes antique Mercedes – connecting

## TRAIN INFORMATION

The State Railway of Thailand (SRT) offers 24hr **train information and booking** in English on its free hotline ☎ 1690 and publishes free **timetables** in English, detailing types of trains available on each route (the best place to get hold of them is over the counter at Bangkok's Hualamphong Station). Its main website (ⓦ railway.co.th) carries English-language timetables, while the affiliated ⓦ thairailwayticket.com now accepts credit card bookings in English. For more comprehensive information and advice, go to ⓦ seat61.com/thailand.htm, which includes a link to download Dave Bernstein's compendious Thai Rail Guide.

the major towns, but they are now being inexorably replaced by more comfortable **air-conditioned minibuses** (*rot tuu*, meaning "cupboard cars"). Scores of similar private air-conditioned minibus services are now cropping up all over the country, either operating out of small offices or pavement desks in town centres or from the bus terminals – or even their own *rot tuu* terminals. Some of these services have a timetable, but many just aim to leave when they have a full complement of passengers; then again, some companies publish a timetable but depart when they're full – whether before or after the published time. They cover the distance faster than buses, but often at breakneck speed, and they can be uncomfortably cramped when full – they're not ideal for travellers with huge rucksacks, who may be required to pay extra. In some areas, GPS devices are now used to regulate the driver's speed, often with a "GPS" sticker on the back of the vehicle. *Rot tuu* services are usually licensed and need to keep up their reputation with their regular Thai passengers but, as with full-sized buses (see page 30), you should be wary of unlicensed private companies that offer minibuses solely for farangs from Bangkok's Thanon Khao San.

In many cases, long-distance songthaews and air-conditioned minibuses will drop you at an exact address (for example, a particular guesthouse) if you warn them far enough in advance. As a rule, the **cost** of inter-town songthaews is comparable to that of air-conditioned buses, that of air-conditioned minibuses perhaps a shade more.

## Trains

Managed by the State Railway of Thailand (SRT), the **rail** network consists of four main lines and a

few branch lines, mostly radiating out of Bangkok's Hualamphong Station. In the area covered by this book is the little-used **Eastern Line** (slow, third-class only) with two branches, one of which runs from Bangkok to Aranyaprathet on the Cambodian border, the other of which connects Bangkok with Si Racha and Pattaya. The **Southern Line** extends from Bangkok via Hua Hin, Chumphon and Surat Thani, with spurs off to Trang and Nakhon Si Thammarat, to Hat Yai (see page 416), where it branches: one line continues to Padang Besar on the Malaysian border, where you can change trains for Butterworth (for Penang) and the west coast of Malaysia; the other heads down the eastern side of the peninsula to Sungai Kolok on the Thailand–Malaysia border (20km from Pasir Mas on Malaysia's interior railway). The Southern Line also carries a few slow trains from Bangkok's Thonburi Station, as far as Nam Tok and Chumphon.

**Fares** depend on the class of seat, whether or not you want air conditioning, and on the speed of the train; those quoted here include the supplements for the various "speed" types of train (see below). Hard, wooden or thinly padded third-class seats are much cheaper than buses (Bangkok–Surat Thani's Phunphin station B217 on the Rapid train), and are fine for about three hours, after which numbness sets in; a few trains have air-conditioned third-class carriages. For longer journeys you'd be wise to opt for the padded and usually reclining seats in second class (Bangkok–Surat Thani B358 on the Rapid train, or B608 on the Special Express with a/c for example). On long-distance trains, you also usually have the option of second-class berths (Bangkok–Surat B458–508 on the Rapid service, or B718–808 with a/c on the Express, for example), with pairs of day seats facing each other that convert into comfortable curtained-off bunks in the evening; lower bunks, which are more expensive than upper, have a few cubic centimetres more space, a little more shade from the lights in the carriage, and a window. Travelling first class (Bangkok–Surat B1139–1339 per person on the Express) generally means a two-person sleeping compartment, complete with washbasin and fierce air conditioning.

There are several different types of train, most of which incur various "**speed**" supplements: slowest of all is the third-class-only Ordinary service, which is generally (but not always) available only on short and medium-length journeys, including Bangkok commuter trains, and has no speed supplement. Next comes the misleadingly named Rapid train, a trip on which from Bangkok to Surat Thani, for example, can take over twelve hours; the equally euphemistic Express, which does the Surat journey in a little under twelve hours; and the Special Express which covers the ground in around nine to eleven hours. The fastest services are usually the daytime Special Express trains, which can usually be relied on to run roughly on time (most other services pay only lip service to their timetables and are sometimes an hour or two late). Nearly all long-distance trains have **dining cars**, and rail staff will also bring meals to your seat.

**Booking** at least one day in advance – longer if possible, especially in high season and over national holidays – is strongly recommended for second- and first-class seats on all lengthy journeys, while sleepers should be booked as far in advance as you can (reservations open sixty days before departure). You can make bookings for any journey in Thailand in person (bring your passport) at Hualamphong Station in Bangkok (see page 114) or at the train station in any major town. You can now book online and print your ticket (note that tickets on mobile phones are not acceptable) through the SRT's ⓦ thairailwayticket.com or general Thai transport booking sites (see page 31).

## Ferries

Regular **ferries** connect all major islands with the mainland, and for the vast majority of crossings you simply buy your ticket on board. Safety standards are generally just about adequate but there have been a small number of sinkings in recent years – avoid travelling on boats that are clearly overloaded or in poor condition. In tourist areas competition ensures that prices are kept low, and fares tend to vary with the speed of the crossing: thus Surat Thani–Ko Pha Ngan costs between B350 (around 4hr) and B700 (2hr 30min).

On the east coast and the Andaman coast boats generally operate a reduced service during the monsoon season (May–Oct), when the more remote spots may become inaccessible. Ferries in the Samui archipelago are fairly constant year-round. Details on island connections are given in the relevant chapters.

## Flights

Thai Airways (ⓦ thaiairways.com) now concentrates more on international routes, leaving Bangkok Airways (ⓦ bangkokair.com) as the major full-service airline on the internal **flight** network, which extends to all parts of the country, using some two-dozen airports. Air Asia (ⓦ airasia.com), Nok Air (ⓦ nokair.com), which is part-owned by Thai

Airways, Thai Smile (ⓦ thaismileair.com), a subsidiary of Thai Airways, Thai Lion Air (ⓦ lionairthai.com) and VietJet (ⓦ vietjetair.com) provide the main "low-cost" competition. In a recently deregulated but ever-expanding market, other smaller airlines come and go with surprising frequency – and while they are operating, schedules tend to be erratic and flights are sometimes cancelled.

In some instances a flight can save you days of travelling: a flight from Chiang Mai to Phuket with Bangkok Airways, Thai Smile or Air Asia, for example, takes two hours, as against a couple of days by meandering train and/or bus. Book early if possible – you can reserve online with all companies – as fares fluctuate wildly. For a fully flexible economy ticket, Bangkok to Phuket costs over B2500 with Thai Airways, but you'll find flights on the same route with the "low-cost" carriers for around B1000 (with restrictions on changes), if you book online far enough in advance.

## Local transport

Most sizeable towns have some kind of **local transport system**, comprising a network of buses, songthaews or even longtail boats, usually with set fares and routes but not rigid timetabling – in many cases vehicles wait until they're full before they leave.

### Buses and songthaews

A few larger cities such as Bangkok have a **local bus** network that usually extends to the suburbs and operates from dawn till dusk (through the night in Bangkok). Most vehicles display route numbers in Western numerals – see the relevant accounts for further details.

Within medium-sized and large towns, the main transport role is often played by **songthaews**. The size and shape of vehicle used varies from town to town – and in some places they're known as "tuk-tuks" from the noise they make, not to be confused with the smaller tuk-tuks, described below, that operate as private taxis – but all have the tell-tale two benches (*sawng thaew*) facing each other in the back. In some towns, songthaews follow fixed routes; in others, they act as communal taxis, picking up a number of people who are going in roughly the same direction and taking each of them right to their destination. To hail a songthaew just flag it down, and to indicate that you want to get out, either rap hard with a coin on the metal railings, or ring the bell if there is one. Fares within towns are B10–30, depending on distance, usually payable when you disembark.

## Taxi services

**Taxis** also come in many guises, and in bigger towns you can sometimes choose between taking a tuk-tuk, a samlor and a motorbike taxi. The one thing common to all modes of chartered transport, bar metered and app-based taxis such as Uber and Grab in Bangkok, is that you must establish the **fare** beforehand: although drivers nearly always pitch their first offers too high, they do calculate with traffic and time of day in mind, as well as according to distance – if successive drivers scoff at your price, you know you've got it wrong.

### Tuk-tuks

Named after the noise of its excruciatingly unsilenced engine, the three-wheeled, open-sided **tuk-tuk** is the classic Thai vehicle. Painted in primary colours, tuk-tuks blast their way round towns and cities on two-stroke engines, zipping around faster than any car and taking corners on two wheels. They aren't as dangerous as they look though, and can be an exhilarating way to get around, as long as you're not too fussy about exhaust fumes. Fares come in at around B60 for a short city journey (over B100 in Bangkok) regardless of the number of passengers – three is the safe maximum, though six is not uncommon. It's worth paying attention to advice on how to avoid getting ripped off by Bangkok tuk-tuk drivers (see page 121).

### Samlors

Tuk-tuks are also sometimes known as samlors (literally translates to "three wheels"), but the original **samlors** are tricycle rickshaws propelled by pedal power alone. Slower and a great deal more stately than tuk-tuks, samlors still operate in one or two towns around the country.

A further permutation is the motorized samlor, where the driver relies on a motorbike rather than a bicycle to propel passengers to their destination. They look much the same as cycle samlors, but often sound as noisy as tuk-tuks.

### Motorbike taxis

Even faster and more precarious than tuk-tuks, **motorbike taxis** feature both in towns and in out-of-the-way places. In towns – where the drivers are identified by coloured, numbered vests – they have the advantage of being able to dodge traffic jams, but are obviously only really suitable for the single traveller, and motorbike taxis aren't the easiest mode of transport if you're carrying luggage. In remote spots, on the other hand, they're often the only alternative to hitching or walking, and are especially useful for getting between bus stops on main roads, around car-free islands and to national parks or ancient ruins.

Within towns motorbike-taxi fares can start at B10 for very short journeys, but for trips to the outskirts the cost rises steeply – reckon on around B300 for a 20km round trip.

## Longtail boats

Wherever there's a decent public waterway, there'll be a **longtail boat** ready to ferry you along it. Another great Thai trademark, these elegant, streamlined boats are powered by deafening diesel engines – sometimes custom-built, more often adapted from cars or trucks – which drive a propeller mounted on a long shaft that is swivelled for steering. Longtails carry up to between eight and twenty passengers: generally, you'll have to charter the whole boat, but on popular fixed routes – between small, inshore islands and the mainland, for example – it's cheaper to wait until the boatman gets his quorum.

# Vehicle rental

Despite first impressions, a high road accident fatality rate, especially involving motorcycles, and the obvious mayhem that characterizes Bangkok's roads, **driving** yourself around Thailand can be fairly straightforward. Many roads, particularly in the south, are remarkably uncongested. Major routes are clearly signed in English, though this only applies to some minor roads.

Outside the capital, the eastern seaboard and the major tourist resorts of Ko Samui and Phuket, local drivers are generally considerate and unaggressive; they very rarely use their horns for example, and will often indicate left and even swerve away when it's safe for you to overtake. The most inconsiderate and dangerous road-users in Thailand are bus drivers and lorry drivers, many of whom drive ludicrously fast, hog the road, race round bends on the wrong side of the road and use their horns remorselessly; worse still, many of them are tanked up on amphetamines, which makes them quite literally fearless.

Bus and lorry drivers are at their worst after dark (many of them only drive then), so it's best **not to drive at night** – a further hazard being the inevitable stream of unlit bicycles and mopeds in and around built-up areas (often driving on the wrong side of the road), as well as poorly signed roadworks, which are often not made safe or blocked off from unsuspecting traffic. Orange signs, or sometimes just a couple of tree branches or a pile of stones on the road, warn of hazards ahead.

As for local **rules of the road**, Thais drive on the left, and the speed limit is usually 60km/h within built-up areas and 90km/h outside them. Beyond that, there are few rules that are generally followed – smaller vehicles usually have to give way to larger ones, and you'll need to keep your concentration up and expect the unexpected from fellow road-users. Watch out especially for vehicles pulling straight out of minor roads, when you might expect them to give way. An oncoming vehicle flashing its lights or beeping its horn means it's coming through no matter what; a right indicator signal from the car in front usually means it's not safe for you to overtake, while a left indicator signal usually means that it is safe to do so.

Theoretically, foreigners need an international **driver's licence** to rent any kind of vehicle, but most car-rental companies accept national licences, and the smaller operations have been known not to ask for any kind of proof whatsoever; motorbike renters very rarely bother. However, if you don't have the correct licence, your travel insurance may not cover you if there's an accident. (There have been occasional reports of particularly brazen police asking motorcyclists for international driving licences at roadblocks, in an attempt to extort money.) A popular rip-off on islands such as Ko Pha Ngan is for small agents to charge renters exorbitant amounts for any minor damage to a jeep or motorbike, even paint chips, that they find on return – they'll claim that it's very expensive to get a new part shipped over from the mainland. Be sure to check out any vehicle carefully before renting.

For **petrol** (*nam man*, which can also mean oil), most Thais use gasohol, which can generally be used in rental cars (though it's worth checking) and currently costs around B27 a litre. The big fuel stations (*pam nam man*) are the least costly places to fill up (*hai tem*), and many of these also have toilets, minimarts and restaurants, though some of the more decrepit-looking fuel stations on the main highways only sell diesel. Most small villages have easy-to-spot roadside huts where the fuel is pumped out of a large barrel or sold in litre bottles.

## Renting a car

If you decide to **rent a car**, go to a reputable dealer, such as Avis, Budget or National, or a rental company recommended by TAT, and make sure you get insurance from them (and check the level of insurance included). There are international car-rental places at many airports, including Bangkok's Suvarnabhumi, which is not a bad place to kick off, as you're on the edge of the city and within fairly easy, signposted reach of the major regional highways.

Car-rental places in provincial capitals and resorts are listed in the relevant accounts in this book. The price of a small car at a reputable company can start as low as B900 per day if booked online. In some parts of the country, you'll still be able to rent a car or air-conditioned minibus with driver, which will cost from around B1200 for a local day-trip, more for a longer day-trip, up to about B3000 per day for a multi-day trip, including the driver's keep and petrol.

**Jeeps** or basic 4WDs are a lot more popular with farangs, especially on beach resorts and islands like Pattaya, Phuket and Ko Samui, but they're notoriously dangerous; a huge number of tourists manage to roll their jeeps on steep hillsides and sharp bends. Jeep rental usually works out somewhere around B1000–1200 per day.

International companies will accept your credit-card details as surety, but smaller agents will usually want to hold on to your passport.

## CAR RENTAL AGENCIES

**Avis** ⓦ avisthailand.com
**Budget** ⓦ budget.co.th
**Master** ⓦ mastercarrental.com
**National** ⓦ nationalcarthailand.com
**Thai Rentacar** ⓦ thairentacar.com

## Renting a motorbike

One of the best ways of exploring the countryside is to **rent a motorbike**. You'll almost never be asked for a driving licence, but take it easy out there – Thailand's roads are not really the place to learn to ride a motorbike from scratch. Bikes of around 100cc, either fully automatic or with step-through gears, are best for inexperienced riders, but aren't really suited for long slogs. If you're going to hit the dirt roads you'll certainly need something more powerful, like a 125–250cc trail bike. These have the edge in gear choice and are the best bikes for steep slopes, though an inexperienced rider may find these machines a handful; the less widely available 125–250cc road bikes are easier to control and much cheaper on fuel.

Rental **prices** for the day usually work out at somewhere around B150–200 for a small bike and B500 for a good trail bike, though you can bargain for a discount on a long rental. Renters will usually ask to hold on to your passport as surety but will generally accept a deposit instead; vehicle insurance is not often available (and some travel insurance policies won't cover you for motorcycle mishaps).

Before signing anything, **check the bike** thoroughly – test the brakes, look for oil leaks, check the treads and the odometer, and make sure the chain isn't stretched too tight (a tight chain is more likely to break) – and preferably take it for a test run. As you will have to pay an inflated price for any damage when you get back, make a note on the contract of any defects such as broken mirrors, indicators and so on. Make sure you know what kind of fuel the bike takes as well.

As far as **equipment** goes, a helmet is essential – most rental places provide poorly made ones, but they're better than nothing. Helmets are obligatory on all motorbike journeys, and the law is often rigidly enforced with on-the-spot fines in major tourist resorts. You'll need sunglasses if your helmet doesn't have a visor. Long trousers, a long-sleeved top and decent shoes will provide a second skin if you go over, which most people do at some stage. Pillions should wear long trousers to avoid getting nasty burns from the exhaust. For the sake of stability, leave most of your luggage in baggage storage and pack as small a bag as possible, strapping it tightly to the bike with bungy cords – these can usually be provided. Bag snatches from the front baskets of small motorbikes have recently been reported in some tourist resorts, so try to keep any valuables on your person. Once on the road, oil the chain at least every other day, keep the radiator topped up and fill up with oil every 300km or so. Be especially careful when there's water or loose gravel on the roads.

For expert **advice** on motorbike travel in Thailand, check out David Unkovich's website (Ⓦ gt-rider.com).

# Cycling

The options for **cycling** in Thailand are numerous, and most Thai roads are in good condition and clearly signposted; although the western and northern borders are mountainous, most of the rest of the country is surprisingly flat. The secondary **roads** (distinguished by their three- or four-digit numbers) are paved but carry far less traffic than the main arteries and are the preferred cycling option. Traffic is reasonably well behaved but the largest vehicles unofficially have – or take – the right of way and there are a fair number of accidents involving cyclists, so you'll need to "ride to survive"; dogs can also be a nuisance on minor roads so it's probably worth having rabies shots before your trip. There are bike shops in nearly every town, and basic equipment and repairs are cheap. Unless you head into the remotest regions around the Burmese border you are rarely more than 25km from food, water and accommodation. Overall, the best time to cycle is during the cool, dry season from November to February.

The traffic into and out of Bangkok is dense so it's worth hopping on a bus or train for the first 50–100km to your starting point. Intercity buses (though sometimes there's a small charge), taxis and some Thai domestic planes will **carry your bike** free of charge. Intercity trains will generally transport your bike for a cargo fare (about the ticket price of a person), either in the luggage carriage, if there is one, or tucked out of the way at the end of your passenger carriage – or, of course, you can dismantle it and carry it as luggage in the compartment with you. Songthaews will carry your bike on the roof for a fare (about the price of a person).

Local one-day cycle tours and **bike-rental outlets** (from around B50/day for a sit-up-and-beg) are listed throughout this book. There are also a number of longer organized **cycle tours** (see page 28). A very helpful English-language resource, dealing with all aspects of cycling in Thailand, is the **website** Ⓦ bicy-clethailand.com.

## Cycling practicalities

Strong, light, quality **mountain bikes** are the most versatile choice; 26-inch wheels are standard throughout Thailand and are strongly recommended, with dual-use (combined road and off-road) tyres best for touring. As regards panniers and **equipment**, the most important thing is to travel light. Carry a few spare spokes, but don't overdo it with too many tools and spares; parts are cheap in Thailand and most problems can be fixed quickly at any bike shop.

Bringing your bike from home is the best option as you are riding a known quantity. **Importing** it by plane should be fairly straightforward, but check with the airlines for details. Most Asian airlines do not charge extra.

**Buying** in Thailand is also a possibility: Ⓦ bicy-clethailand.com and Ⓦ chiangmaicycling.org give plenty of advice and listings.

# Hitching

Public transport being so inexpensive, you should only have to resort to **hitching** in the most remote areas, in which case you'll probably get a lift to the nearest bus or songthaew stop quite quickly. On routes served by buses and trains, hitching is very rare, but in other places locals do rely on regular passers-by (such as national park officials), and you can make use of this "service" too. As with hitching anywhere in the world, think twice about hitching solo or at night, especially if you're female. Like bus drivers, truck drivers are notorious users of amphetamines, so you may want to wait for a safer offer.

# Accommodation

**For the very simplest double room, prices start at a bargain B200 in the outlying regions, around B300 in Bangkok, and B400–500 in the pricier resorts. Tourist centres invariably offer a tempting range of more upmarket choices but in these areas rates fluctuate according to demand, plummeting during the off-season, peaking over the Christmas and New Year fortnight and, in some places, rising at weekends throughout the year.**

## Guesthouses, bungalows and hostels

Most of Thailand's **budget accommodation** is in **guesthouses** and **bungalows**. These are small, traveller-friendly hotels whose services nearly always include an inexpensive restaurant, wi-fi and safe storage for valuables and left luggage, and often a tour desk. The difference between guesthouses and bungalows is mostly in their design, with "bungalows" – which are generally found on the beach and in rural areas – mostly comprising detached or semi-detached rooms in huts, villas, chalets or indeed bungalows, and "guesthouses" being either a purpose-built mini-hotel or a converted home. Showers and flush toilets, whether en-suite or shared, are common in both, but at the cheapest up-country places you might be bathing with a bowl dipped into a large water jar, and using squat toilets.

Many guesthouses and bungalows offer a spread of options to cater for all budgets: their **cheapest rooms** will often be furnished with nothing more than a double bed, a blanket and a fan (window optional, private bathroom extra) and might cost anything from B200–400 for two people, depending on the location and the competition. A similar room

with **en-suite** bathroom, and possibly more stylish furnishings, generally comes in at B300–700, while for a room with **air conditioning**, and perhaps a TV and fridge as well, you're looking at B400/500 and up. In the north of Thailand in the cool season, air conditioning is more or less redundant, but you might want to check your room has a hot shower.

In the most popular tourist centres at the busiest times of year, the best-known guesthouses are often full night after night. Some will take **bookings** and advance payment via their websites, but for those that don't it's usually a question of turning up and waiting for a vacancy. At most guesthouses **checkout time** is either 11am or noon.

Generally you should be wary of taking accommodation advice from a **tout** or tuk-tuk driver, as they demand commission from guesthouse owners, which, if not passed directly on to you via a higher room price, can have a crippling effect on the smaller guesthouses. If a tout claims your intended accommodation is "full" or "no good" or has "burnt down", it's always worth phoning to check yourself. Touts can come into their own, however, on islands such as Ko Lanta where it can be a long and expensive ride to your chosen beach, and frustrating if you then discover your bungalow is full; island touts may sweet-talk you on the boat and then transport you for free to view their accommodation, ideally with no obligation to stay.

With only a dozen or so registered **youth hostels** in the country, bookable via ⓦ tyha.org, it's not worth becoming a Hostelling International member just for your trip to Thailand, especially as card-holders get only a small discount and room rates work out the same as or more expensive than guesthouse equivalents. In addition, there are a growing number of smart, modern, non-affiliated **hostels**, especially in Bangkok. They usually work out more expensive than budget guesthouses but are good places to meet other travellers.

---

### ACCOMMODATION PRICES

Throughout this guide, the prices given for guesthouses, bungalows and hotels represent the **minimum** you can expect to pay in each establishment in the **high season** (roughly July, Aug and Nov–Feb in most parts of the country) for a typical **double room**, booked via the hotel website where available; there may however be an extra "peak" supplement for the Christmas–New Year period. If travelling on your own, expect to pay between sixty and one hundred percent of the rates quoted for a double room. Where a hostel or guesthouse also offers **dormitory beds**, the minimum price per bed is also given; where a place has both fan-cooled and air-conditioned rooms, we've given the minimum price for a double in each category. Top-end hotels will add **seven percent tax** (though this may increase to ten percent) and **ten percent service charge** to your bill; the prices given in the Guide are net rates after these taxes (usually referred to as "plus plus") have been added.

## BATHROOM ETIQUETTE

Although modern, Western-style bathrooms are commonplace throughout Thailand, it's as well to be forewarned about local bathroom etiquette.

Sit-down **toilets** are now the norm but at public amenities in bus and train stations, and in some homes and old-style guesthouses and hotels, you'll still find squat toilets. Thais traditionally don't use **paper** but wash, rather than wipe themselves, after going to the toilet. Modern bathrooms are fitted with a special hose by the toilet for this purpose, while more primitive bathrooms just provide a **bucket of water and a dipper**. Thais always use their left hand for washing – and their right hand for eating (see page 41). As Thai plumbing is notoriously sluggish, where toilet paper is provided, you're often asked to throw it in the wastebasket and not down the U-bend. If a toilet is not plumbed in, you flush it yourself with water from the bucket. In really basic hotel bathrooms with no **shower** facilities, you also use the bucket and dipper for scoop-and-slosh bathing.

## Budget hotels

Thai sales reps and other people travelling for business rather than pleasure rarely use guesthouses, opting instead for **budget hotels**, which offer rooms for around B200–600. Usually run by Chinese-Thais, these functional three- or four-storey places are found in every sizeable town, often near the bus station or central market. Beds are large enough for a couple, so it's quite acceptable for two people to ask and pay for a "single" room (*hawng thiang diaw*, literally a "one-bedded room"). Though the rooms are generally clean, en suite and furnished with either a fan or air conditioning, there's rarely an on-site restaurant and the atmosphere is generally less convivial than at guesthouses. A number of budget hotels also double as brothels, though as a farang you're unlikely to be offered this sideline, and you might not even notice the goings-on.

Advance reservations are accepted over the phone, but this is rarely necessary, as such hotels rarely fill up. The only time you may have difficulty finding a budget hotel room is during Chinese New Year (a moveable three-day period in late Jan or Feb), when many Chinese-run hotels close and others get booked up fast.

## Tourist hotels

The rest of the accommodation picture is all about **tourist hotels**, which, like anywhere in the world, come in all sizes and qualities and are often best booked via online accommodation booking services such as local outfit Ⓦsawadee.com. Other useful booking sites that specialize in Thailand include Ⓦtrue-beachfront.com, which carries all kinds of accommodation, as long as there's no road between it and the strand; and Ⓦsecret-retreats.com, a curated collection of independent accommodation, including some lovely boutique hotels, resorts and villas. One

way or another, it's a good idea to **reserve ahead** in popular tourist areas during peak season.

Rates for **middle-ranking hotels** fall between B600 and B2000. For this you can expect many of the trimmings of a top-end hotel – air conditioning, TV and minibar in the room, plus an on-site pool, restaurant and perhaps nightclub – but with dated and possibly faded furnishings and little of the style of the famous big names; they're often the kind of places that once stood at the top of the range, but were outclassed when the multinational luxury hotels muscled in. At these places, breakfast – often referred to as "**ABF**", short for "American Breakfast" – is usually included, as noted in our listings.

Many of Thailand's **expensive hotels** belong to the big international chains: Hilton, Marriott and Sofitel (and the rest of the Accor group) all have a strong presence in the country, alongside upmarket home-grown groups such as Amari, Anantara and Dusit. Between them they maintain premium standards in Bangkok and major resorts at prices of B3000 and upward for a double – far less than you'd pay for equivalent accommodation in the West.

Thailand also boasts an increasing number of deliciously stylish, independent **luxury hotels**, many of them designed as intimate, small-scale **boutique** hotels, with chic, minimalist decor, exceptional personal service and excellent facilities. A night in one of these places may start at prices as little as B2500, rising rapidly if indulgences such as private plunge pools and spas are laid on.

## Homestays

As guesthouses have become increasingly hotel-like and commercial in their facilities and approach, many tourists looking for old-style local hospitality are choosing **homestay accommodation** instead. Homestay facilities are often simple, and cheap at around B300 per person per night, with guests staying in a spare room and eating with the family. Homestays give an unparalleled insight into typical Thai (usually rural) life and can often be incorporated into a programme that includes experiencing village activities such as rice farming, squid fishing, rubber tapping or silk weaving. They are also a positive way of supporting small communities, as all your money will feed right back into the village. Many of Thailand's homestays are geared towards Bangkokians, so language might be a barrier for overseas visitors. However, as well as the listed homestays that are used to dealing with farangs in Ban Khiriwong (see page 278) and Khuraburi (see page 298), there are many others bookable through tour operators (see page 28).

## National parks and camping

Nearly all the **national parks** have accommodation facilities, usually comprising a series of simple concrete bungalows that cost at least B600 for two or more beds plus a basic bathroom. Because most of their custom comes from Thai families and student groups, park officials are sometimes loath to discount them for lone travellers, though a few parks do offer dorm-style accommodation from around B150 a bed. In most parks, advance booking is unnecessary except at weekends and national holidays.

If you do want to pre-book, you'll have to take on the National Park Office's new, but cumbersome, uninformative and deeply frustrating, website, ⓦnps.dnp.go.th. Bookings open sixty days ahead of a proposed stay, though hopefully it won't take quite that long to navigate through the maze to the payment page. If you turn up without booking, check in at the park headquarters, which is usually adjacent to the visitor centre. In a few parks, private operators have set up low-cost guesthouses on the outskirts, and these generally make more attractive and economical places to stay.

### Camping

You can usually **camp** in a national park for a nominal fee of B60 per two-person tent, and some national parks also rent out fully equipped tents from B150, though the condition of the equipment is sometimes poor. Unless you're planning an extensive tour of national parks, though, there's little point in lugging a tent around Thailand: accommodation everywhere else is very inexpensive, and there are no campsites inside town perimeters, though camping is allowed on nearly all islands and beaches, many of which are national parks in their own right.

# Food and drink

**Bangkok is the country's big culinary centre, boasting the cream of gourmet Thai restaurants and the best international cuisines. The rest of the country is by no means a gastronomic wasteland, however, and you can eat well and cheaply in even the smallest provincial towns, many of which offer the additional attraction of regional specialities. In fact you could eat more than adequately without ever entering a restaurant, as itinerant food vendors hawking hot and cold snacks materialize in even the most remote spots, as well as on trains and buses – and night markets often serve customers from dusk until dawn.**

**Hygiene** is a consideration when eating anywhere in Thailand, but being too cautious means you'll end up spending a lot of money and missing out on some real local treats. Wean your stomach gently by avoiding excessive amounts of chillies and too much fresh fruit in the first few days.

You can be pretty sure that any noodle stall or curry shop that's permanently packed with customers is a safe bet. Furthermore, because most Thai dishes can be cooked in under five minutes, you'll rarely have to contend with stuff that's been left to smoulder and stew. Foods that are generally considered high risk include salads, ice cream, shellfish and raw or under-cooked meat, fish or eggs.

Most restaurants in Thailand are open every day for lunch and dinner; we've given full opening hours throughout the Guide. In a few of the country's most expensive restaurants, mostly in Bangkok, a ten percent service charge and possibly even seven percent VAT (which may be increased to ten percent) might be added to your bill.

For those interested in **learning to cook Thai food**, short courses designed for visitors are held in Bangkok (see page 131) and dozens of other tourist centres around the country.

## Where to eat

A lot of tourists eschew the huge range of Thai **places to eat**, despite their obvious attractions, and opt instead for the much "safer" restaurants in guest-houses and hotels. Almost all tourist accommodation has a kitchen, and while some are excellent, the vast majority serve up bland imitations of Western fare alongside equally pale versions of common Thai dishes. Having said that, guesthouses do serve comfortingly familiar Western breakfasts.

# FRUITS OF THAILAND

You'll find **fruit** (*phonlamai*) offered everywhere in Thailand – neatly sliced in glass boxes on hawker carts, blended into delicious shakes and served as a dessert in restaurants. The fruits described here can be found in all parts of Thailand; with enhanced agricultural techniques – and imports – many of them can now be found year-round, but we've given the traditional seasons where applicable below, which is when they should be at their best and cheapest. The country's more familiar fruits include forty varieties of **banana** (*kluay*), dozens of different **mangoes** (*mamuang*), several types of **pineapple** (*sapparot*), **coconuts** (*maprao*), **oranges** (*som*), **limes** (*manao*) and **watermelons** (*taeng moh*).

To avoid stomach trouble, **peel all fruit** before eating it, and use common sense if you're tempted to buy it pre-peeled on the street, avoiding anything that looks fly-blown or seems to have been sitting in the sun for hours.

**Custard apple** (*noina*; July–Sept). Inside the knobbly, muddy green skin is a creamy, almond-coloured blancmange-like flesh, with a strong flavour of strawberries and pears, and a hint of cinnamon, and many seeds.

**Durian** (*thurian*; April–June). Thailand's most prized, and expensive, fruit has a green, spiky exterior and grows to the size of a football. Inside, it divides into segments of creamy, yellow flesh with a complex taste, which gives off a disgustingly strong stink that's been compared to a mixture of strong cheese and caramel. Not surprisingly, many hotels and airlines ban durians.

**Guava** (*farang*; year-round). The apple of the tropics has green textured skin and sweet, crisp pink or white flesh, studded with tiny edible seeds. Has five times the vitamin C content of an orange and is sometimes eaten cut into strips and sprinkled with sugar and chilli.

**Jackfruit** (*khanun*; year-round). This large, pear-shaped fruit can weigh up to 20kg and has a thick, bobbly, greeny-yellow shell protecting sweet yellow flesh. Green, unripe jackfruit is sometimes cooked as a vegetable in curries.

**Longan** (*lamyai*; July–Oct). A close relative of the lychee, with succulent white flesh covered in thin, brittle skin.

**Lychee** (*linjii*; April–May). Under rough, reddish-brown skin, the lychee has sweet, richly flavoured white flesh, rose scented and with plenty of vitamin C.

**Mangosteen** (*mangkut*; April–Sept). The size of a small apple, with smooth, purple skin and a fleshy inside that divides into succulent white segments that are sweet though slightly acidic.

**Papaya** (paw-paw; *malakaw*; year-round). Looks like an elongated watermelon, with smooth green skin and yellowy-orange flesh that's a rich source of vitamins A and C. It's a favourite in fruit salads and shakes, and sometimes appears in its green, unripe form in salads, notably *som tam*.

**Pomelo** (*som oh*; Oct–Dec). The largest of all the citrus fruits, it looks rather like a grapefruit, though it is sweeter; sometimes used in delicious salads.

**Rambutan** (*ngaw*; May–Sept). The bright red rambutan's soft, spiny exterior has given it its name – *rambut* means "hair" in Malay. Usually about the size of a golf ball, it has a white, opaque flesh of delicate flavour, similar to a lychee.

**Rose apple** (*chomphuu*; year-round). Linked in myth with the golden fruit of immortality; small and pear-shaped, with white, rose-scented flesh.

**Sapodilla** (sapota; *lamut*; Sept–Dec). These small, brown, rough-skinned ovals look a bit like kiwi fruit and conceal a grainy, yellowish pulp that tastes almost honey-sweet.

**Tamarind** (*makhaam*; Dec–Jan). A Thai favourite and a pricey delicacy – carrying the seeds is said to make you safe from wounding by knives or bullets. Comes in rough, brown pods containing up to ten seeds, each surrounded by a sticky, dry pulp which has a lemony taste; generally sour, but some parts of the country produce sweet tamarinds.

---

Throughout the country most **inexpensive Thai restaurants** and cafés specialize in one general food type or preparation method, charging around B40–50 a dish – a "noodle shop", for example, will do fried noodles and/or noodle soups, plus maybe a basic fried rice, but they won't have curries or meat or fish dishes. Similarly, a restaurant displaying whole roast chickens and ducks in its window will offer these sliced, usually with chillies and sauces and served over rice, but their menu probably won't extend to noodles or fish, while in "curry shops" your options are limited to the vats of curries stewing away in the hot cabinet.

To get a wider array of low-cost food, it's better to head for the local **night market** (*talaat yen*), a term for the gatherings of open-air night-time kitchens found in every town. Sometimes operating from 6pm to 6am, they are typically to be found on permanent patches close to the fruit and vegetable market or the bus station, and as often as not they're the best and most entertaining places to eat, not to mention the least expensive – after a lip-smacking feast of savoury dishes, a fruit drink and a dessert you'll come away no more than B150 poorer.

A typical night market has maybe thirty-odd "specialist" pushcart kitchens (*rot khen*) jumbled together, each fronted by several sets of tables and stools. Noodle and fried-rice vendors always feature prominently, as do sweets stalls, heaped high with sticky rice cakes wrapped in banana leaves or thick with bags of tiny sweetcorn pancakes hot from the griddle – and no night market is complete without its fruit-drink stall, offering banana shakes and freshly squeezed orange, lemon and tomato juices. In the best setups you'll find a lot more besides: curries, barbecued sweetcorn, satay sticks of pork and chicken, deep-fried insects, fresh pineapple, watermelon and mango and – if the town's by a river or near the sea – heaps of fresh fish. Having decided what you want, you order from the cook (or the cook's dogsbody) and sit down at the nearest table; there is no territorialism about night markets, so it's normal to eat several dishes from separate stalls and rely on the nearest cook to sort out the bill.

Some large markets, particularly in Bangkok, have separate **food court** areas where you buy coupons first and select food and drink to their value at the stalls of your choice. This is also usually the modus operandi in the food courts found in department stores and shopping centres across the country, though some of the more modern ones issue each diner with a plastic card, on which is recorded their expenditure, for payment at the end.

For a more relaxing ambience, Bangkok and the larger towns have a range of more upmarket **restaurants**, many of which serve regional specialities. Some specialize in **"royal" Thai cuisine**, which is differentiated mainly by the quality of the ingredients, the complexity of preparation and the way the food is presented. Great care is taken over how individual dishes look: they are served in small portions and decorated with carved fruit and vegetables in a way that used to be the prerogative of royal cooks, but has now filtered down to the common folk. The cost of such delights is not prohibitive, either – a meal in one of these places is unlikely to cost more than B500 per person.

## How to eat

Thai food is eaten with a **fork** (left hand) and a **spoon** (right hand); there is no need for a knife as food is served in bite-sized chunks, which are forked onto the spoon and fed into the mouth. Cutlery is often delivered to the table wrapped in a perplexingly tiny pink napkin: Thais use this, not for their lap, but to give their fork, spoon and plate an extra wipe-down before they eat. Steamed **rice** (*khao*) is served with most meals, and indeed the most commonly heard phrase for "to eat" is *kin khao* (literally, "eat rice"). **Chopsticks** are provided only for noodle dishes, and northeastern and northern sticky-rice dishes are usually eaten with the **fingers of your right hand**. Never eat with the fingers of your left hand, which is used for washing after going to the toilet.

So that complementary taste combinations can be enjoyed, the dishes in a Thai meal are served all at once, even the soup, and shared communally. The more people, the more taste and texture sensations; if there are only two of you, it's normal to order three dishes, plus your own individual plates of steamed rice, while three diners would order four dishes, and so on. Only put a serving of one dish on your rice plate each time, and then only one or two spoonfuls.

Bland food is anathema to Thais, and restaurant tables everywhere come decked out with **condiment sets** featuring the four basic flavours (salty, sour, sweet and spicy): usually fish sauce with chopped chillies; vinegar with chopped chillies; sugar; and dried chillies – and often extra bowls of ground peanuts and a bottle of chilli ketchup as well. Similarly, many individual Thai dishes are served with their own specific, usually spicy, condiment dip (*nam jim*). If you do bite into a **chilli**, the way to combat the searing heat is to take a mouthful of plain rice and/or beer: swigging water just exacerbates the sensation.

## What to eat

Five core tastes are identified in Thai cuisine – spiciness, sourness, bitterness, saltiness and sweetness – and diners aim to share a variety of dishes that impart a balance of these flavours, along with complementary textures. Lemon grass, basil, coriander, galangal, chilli, garlic, lime juice, coconut milk and fermented fish sauce are just some of the distinctive components that bring these tastes to life. A detailed food and drink glossary can be found at the end of "Contexts" (see page 443).

### Curries and soups

Thai **curries** (*kaeng*) have a variety of curry pastes as their foundation: elaborate blends of herbs, spices,

## VEGETARIANS AND VEGANS

Very few Thais are **vegetarian** (*mangsawirat*) but, if you can make yourself understood, you can often get a non-meat or fish alternative to what's on the menu; simply ask the cook to exclude meat and fish: *mai sai neua, mai sai plaa*. You may end up eating a lot of unexciting vegetable fried rice and *phat thai* minus the shrimps, but in better restaurants you should be able to get veggie versions of most curries; the mushroom version of chicken and coconut soup is also a good standby: ask for *tom kha hed*. Browsing food stalls also expands your options, with barbecued sweetcorn, nuts, fruit and other non-meaty goodies all common. The two ingredients that you will have to consider compromising on are the fermented **fish sauce** and **shrimp paste** that are fundamental to most Thai dishes; only in the vegan Thai restaurants described below, and in tourist spots serving specially concocted Thai and Western veggie dishes, can you be sure of avoiding them.

If you're **vegan** (*jay*, sometimes spelt "*jeh*") you'll need to stress when you order that you don't want egg, as they get used a lot; cheese and other dairy produce, however, don't feature at all in Thai cuisine. Many towns will have one or more **vegan restaurants** (*raan ahaan jay*), which are usually run by members of a temple or Buddhist sect and operate from unadorned premises off the main streets; because strict Buddhists prefer not to eat late in the day, most of the restaurants open early, at around 6 or 7am, and close by 2pm. Most of these places have a yellow and red sign, though few display an English-language name. Nor is there ever a menu: customers simply choose from the trays of veggie stir-fries and curries, nearly all of them made with soya products, that are laid out canteen-style. Most places charge around B40 for a couple of helpings served over a plate of brown rice.

---

garlic, shallots and chilli peppers ground together with pestle and mortar. The use of some of these spices, as well as coconut cream, was imported from India long ago; curries that don't use coconut cream are naturally less sweet, spicier and thinner, with the consistency of soups. While some curries, such as *kaeng karii* (mild and yellow) and *kaeng matsaman* ("Muslim curry", with potatoes, peanuts and usually beef), still show their roots, others have been adapted into quintessentially Thai dishes, notably *kaeng khiaw wan* (sweet and green), *kaeng phet* (red and hot) and *kaeng phanaeng* (thick and savoury, with peanuts). *Kaeng som* generally contains fish and takes its distinctive sourness from the addition of tamarind. Traditionally eaten during the cool season, *kaeng liang* uses up bland vegetables, but is made aromatic with hot peppercorns.

Eaten simultaneously with other dishes, not as a starter, Thai **soups** often have the tang of lemon grass, kaffir lime leaves and galangal, and are sometimes made extremely spicy with chillies. Two favourites are *tom kha kai*, a creamy coconut chicken soup; and *tom yam kung*, a hot and sour prawn soup without coconut milk. *Khao tom* and *jok*, starchy rice soups that are generally eaten for breakfast, meet the approval of few Westerners, except as a traditional hangover cure.

### Salads

One of the lesser-known delights of Thai cuisine is the *yam* or **salad**, which imparts most of the fundamental flavours in an unusual and refreshing harmony. *Yam* come in many permutations – with noodles, meat, seafood or vegetables – but at the heart of every variety is a liberal squirt of lime juice and a fiery sprinkling of chillies. Salads to look out for include *yam som oh* (pomelo), *yam hua plee* (banana flowers) and *yam plaa duk foo* (fluffy deep-fried catfish).

### Noodle and rice dishes

Sold on street stalls everywhere, **noodles** come in assorted varieties – including *kway tiaw* (made with rice flour) and *ba mii* (egg noodles) – and get boiled up as soups (*nam*), doused in gravy (*rat na*) or stir-fried (*haeng*, "dry", or *phat*, "fried"). Most famous of all is *phat thai* ("Thai fry-up"), a delicious combination of noodles (usually *kway tiaw*), egg, tofu and spring onions, sprinkled with ground peanuts and lime, and often spiked with tiny dried shrimps. Other faithful standbys include fried rice (*khao phat*) and cheap, one-dish meals served on a bed of steamed rice, notably *khao kaeng* (with curry).

### Desserts

**Desserts** (*khanom*) don't really figure on most restaurant menus, but a few places offer bowls of *luk taan cheum*, a jellied concoction of lotus or palm seeds floating in a syrup scented with jasmine or other aromatic flowers. Coconut milk is a feature of most other desserts, notably delicious coconut ice cream, *khao niaw mamuang* (sticky rice with mango), and a royal Thai cuisine special of coconut custard (*sangkhayaa*) cooked inside a small pumpkin, whose flesh you can also eat.

# Drinks

Thais don't drink water straight from the tap, and nor should you; plastic bottles of drinking **water** (*nam plao*) are sold countrywide, even in the smallest villages, for around B10 and should be used even when brushing your teeth. Cheap restaurants and hotels generally serve free jugs of boiled water, which should be fine to drink, though they are not as foolproof as the bottles.

Night markets, guesthouses and restaurants do a good line in freshly squeezed **fruit juices** such as lime (*nam manao*) and orange (*nam som*), which often come with salt and sugar already added, particularly upcountry. The same places will usually do **fruit shakes** as well, blending bananas (*nam kluay*), papayas (*nam malakaw*), pineapples (*nam sapparot*) and others with liquid sugar or condensed milk (or yoghurt, to make lassi). Fresh **coconut water** (*nam maprao*) is another great thirst-quencher – you buy the whole fruit dehusked, decapitated and chilled – as is **pandanus-leaf juice** (*bai toey*); Thais are also very partial to freshly squeezed **sugar-cane juice** (*nam awy*), which is sickeningly sweet.

Bottled and canned brand-name **soft drinks** are sold all over the place, with a particularly wide range in the ubiquitous 7-Eleven chain stores. Glass soft-drink bottles are returnable, so some shops and drink stalls have a system of pouring the contents into a small plastic bag (fastened with an elastic band and with a straw inserted) rather than charging you the extra for taking away the bottle. The larger restaurants keep their soft drinks refrigerated, but smaller cafés and shops add **ice** (*nam khaeng*) to glasses and bags. Most ice is produced commercially under hygienic conditions, but it might become less pure in transit so be wary (ice cubes are generally a better bet than shaved ice) – and don't take ice if you have diarrhoea. UHT-preserved **milk** and chilled **yoghurt** drinks are widely available (especially at 7-Eleven stores), as are a variety of soya drinks.

Weak Chinese **tea** (*nam chaa*) makes a refreshing alternative to water and often gets served in Chinese restaurants and roadside cafés, while posher restaurants keep stronger Chinese and Western-style teas. Instant Nescafé is the most widespread form of **coffee** (*kaafae*), even though fresh Thai-grown coffee – notably several excellent kinds of coffee from the mountains of the north – is now easily available. If you would like to try traditional Thai coffee, most commonly found at Chinese-style cafés in the south of the country or at outdoor markets, and prepared by filtering the grounds through a cloth, ask for *kaafae thung* (literally, "bag coffee"; sometimes known as

---

## SOUTHERN THAI FOOD

**Southern Thai** cuisine displays a marked Malaysian and Muslim aspect as you near the border and, as you'd expect in a region bounded by sea, the salty flavours associated with seafood are prevalent. Liberal use of **turmeric** is another distinctive feature, which gives many southern dishes a yellow hue, notably *plaa khluk khamin*, grilled fish rubbed with turmeric, garlic and salt.

A huge variety of very spicy **curries** is dished up in the south, many of them substituting shrimp paste for the fish sauce used elsewhere in Thailand. Two of the peninsula's most famous curries are *kaeng leuang* ("yellow curry"), which features fish, turmeric, pineapple, squash, beans and green papaya; and *kaeng tai plaa*, a powerful combination of fish stomach with potatoes, beans, pickled bamboo shoots and turmeric. Another very popular local dish, especially on the Andaman coast, is *nam prik kung siap*, a delicious relish of smoked, dried shrimps served with raw vegetables.

Satays feature more down here, as does delicious *hor mok* (sometimes known as *khai plaa mok*), a kind of seafood soufflé made with coconut milk and red curry paste. In Muslim areas, you'll come across *khao mok kai*, the local version of a biryani: chicken and rice cooked with turmeric, cinnamon, cloves and other Indian spices and served with clear chicken soup. Also popular, especially in Phuket, Nakhon Si Thammarat and Trang, is *khanom jiin* (literally, "Chinese pastry"), rice noodles topped with hot, sweet or fishy sauce (the latter Malay-style *naam yaa*, made with ground fish) and served with crispy raw vegetables.

Markets in the south often serve *khao yam* for breakfast or lunch, a deliciously refreshing salad of dried cooked rice, dried shrimp, grated coconut and lemon grass served with a sweet sauce. You'll find many types of **roti** in the south, too – pancake-like bread sold hot from pushcart griddles and, in its plain form, rolled with sickly sweet condensed milk and sugar. Other versions include *roti kluay* (with banana), *roti khai* (with egg), savoury *mataba* (with minced chicken or beef) and, served with curry sauce for breakfast, *roti kaeng*.

*kaafae boran* – "traditional coffee" – or *kopii*), which is normally served with sugar as well as sweetened condensed milk, alongside a glass of black or Chinese tea to wash it down with. Fresh Western-style coffee (*kaafae sot*) in the form of Italian espresso, cappuccino and other derivatives has recently become popular among Thais, so you'll now come across espresso machines in large towns all over the country (though some of these new coffee bars, frustratingly, don't open for breakfast, as locals tend to get their fix later in the day).

## Alcoholic drinks

The two most famous local **beers** (*bia*) are Singha (ask for "*bia sing*") and Chang, though many travellers find Singha's weaker brew, Leo, more palatable than either. In shops you can expect to pay around B35–40 for a 330ml bottle of these beers, B70 for a 660ml bottle. All manner of slightly pricier foreign beers are now brewed in Thailand, including Heineken and Asahi, and in the most touristy areas you'll find expensive imported bottles from all over the world.

**Wine** is now found on plenty of upmarket and tourist-oriented restaurant menus, but expect to be disappointed by both quality and price, which is jacked up by heavy taxation.

At about B150 for a hip-flask-sized 375ml bottle, local spirits are a lot better value, and Thais think nothing of consuming a bottle a night, heavily diluted with ice and soda or Coke. One of the most popular and widely available of these is Sang Som, a rum made from sugar cane, at forty percent proof. Mekhong, a whisky distilled from rice at 35 percent proof, is hard to come by these days as it's kept for the export market. Check the menu carefully when ordering a bottle of Sang Som from a bar in a tourist area, as they sometimes ask up to five times more than you'd pay in a guesthouse or shop. A hugely popular way to enjoy rum or whisky at beach resorts is to pick up a bucket, containing a quarter-bottle of spirit, a mixer, Red Bull, ice and several straws, for around B200–300: that way you get to share with your friends and build a sandcastle afterwards.

You can **buy** beer and whisky in food stores, guesthouses and most restaurants (according to a law that's spottily enforced, it's not meant to be for sale between 2pm and 5pm, when schools are finishing for the day); **bars** aren't strictly an indigenous feature as Thais traditionally don't drink out without eating, but you'll find plenty of Western-style drinking holes in Bangkok and larger centres elsewhere in the country, ranging from ultra-cool haunts in the capital to basic, open-to-the-elements "**bar-beers**".

# Culture and etiquette

**Tourist literature has marketed Thailand as the "Land of Smiles" so successfully that a lot of farangs arrive in the country expecting to be forgiven any outrageous behaviour. This is just not the case: there are some things so universally sacred in Thailand that even a hint of disrespect will cause deep offence.**

## The monarchy

It is both socially unacceptable to many Thais and a criminal offence to make critical or defamatory remarks about the **royal family**. Thailand's monarchy is technically a constitutional one, but pictures of King Vajiralongkorn, who acceded to the throne on the death of his much-loved father King Bhumibol in 2016, are displayed in many public places, and submissive crowds mass whenever the royals make a public appearance. When addressing or speaking about royalty, Thais use a special language full of deference, called *rajasap* (literally "royal language").

Thailand's **lese-majeste laws** are among the most strictly applied in the world and have been increasingly invoked since the 2014 coup. Accusations of lese-majeste can be levelled by and against anyone, Thai national or farang, and must be investigated by the police. As a few high-profile cases involving foreigners have demonstrated, they can be raised for seemingly minor infractions, such as defacing a poster or being less than respectful in a work of fiction. Article 112 of the Thai criminal code specifies insults to the king, the queen, the heir-apparent and the regent, but the law has been wielded against supposed slights to the king's dog and to kings who have been dead for centuries. Transgressions are met with jail sentences of up to fifteen years for each offence. We have had to take into account the lese-majeste laws in writing this guidebook.

Aside from keeping any anti-monarchy sentiments to yourself, you should be prepared to stand when the **king's anthem** is played at the beginning of every cinema programme, and to stop in your tracks if the town you're in plays the **national anthem** over its public address system – many small towns do this twice a day at 8am and again at 6pm, as do some train stations and airports. A less obvious point: as the king's head features on all Thai currency, you should never step on a coin or banknote, which is tantamount to kicking the king in the face.

# Religion

Almost equally insensitive would be to disregard certain **religious** precepts. **Buddhism** plays a fundamental role in Thai culture, and Buddhist monuments should be treated with respect – which basically means wearing long trousers or knee-length skirts, covering your arms and removing your shoes whenever you visit one.

All **Buddha images** are sacred, however small, tacky or ruined, and should never be used as a backdrop for a portrait photo, clambered over, placed in a position of inferiority or treated in any manner that could be construed as disrespectful. In an attempt to prevent foreigners from committing any kind of transgression the government requires a special licence for all Buddha statues exported from the country (see page 59).

**Monks** come only a little beneath the monarchy in the social hierarchy, and they too are addressed and discussed in a special language. If there's a monk around, he'll always get a seat on the bus, usually right at the back. Theoretically, monks are forbidden to have any close contact with women, which means that, as a female, you mustn't sit or stand next to a monk, or even brush against his robes; if it's essential to pass him something, put the object down so that he can then pick it up – never hand it over directly. Nuns, however, get treated like ordinary women.

See "Contexts" for more on religious practices in Thailand (see page 427).

# The body

The Western liberalism embraced by the Thai sex industry is very unrepresentative of the majority Thai attitude to the body. **Clothing** – or the lack of it – is what bothers Thais most about tourist behaviour. You need to dress modestly when entering temples (see page 79), but the same also applies to other important buildings and all public places. Stuffy and sweaty as it sounds, you should keep short shorts and vests for the real tourist resorts, and be especially diligent about covering up. Baring your flesh on beaches is very much a Western practice: when Thais go swimming they often do so fully clothed, and they find topless and nude bathing offensive.

According to ancient Hindu belief, the **head** is the most sacred part of the body and the **feet** are the most unclean. This belief, imported into Thailand, means that it's very rude to touch another person's head or to point your feet either at a human being or at a sacred image – when sitting on a temple floor, for example, you should **tuck your legs beneath you** rather than stretch them out towards the Buddha.

These hierarchies also forbid people from wearing **shoes** (which are even more unclean than feet) inside temples and most private homes, and – by extension – Thais take offence when they see someone sitting on the "head", or prow, of a boat. **Putting your feet up** on a table, a chair or a pillow is also considered very uncouth, and Thais will always take their shoes off if they need to stand on a train or bus seat to get to the luggage rack, for example. On a more practical note, the **left hand** is used for washing after going to the toilet (see page 38), so Thais never use it to put food in their mouth, pass things or shake hands – as a farang, though, you'll be assumed to have different customs, so left-handers shouldn't worry unduly.

# Social conventions

Thais rarely shake hands, instead using the **wai** to greet and say goodbye and to acknowledge respect, gratitude or apology. A prayer-like gesture made with raised hands, the *wai* changes according to the relative status of the two people involved: Thais can instantaneously assess which *wai* to use, but as a farang your safest bet is to raise your hands close to your chest, bow your head and place your fingertips just below your nose. If someone makes a *wai* at you, you should generally *wai* back, but it's safer not to initiate.

Public displays of **physical affection** in Thailand are more common between friends of the same sex than between lovers, whether hetero- or homosexual. Holding hands and hugging is as common among male friends as with females, so if you're caressed by a Thai acquaintance of the same sex, don't necessarily assume you're being propositioned.

Finally, there are three specifically Thai **concepts** you're bound to come across, which may help you comprehend a sometimes laissez-faire attitude to delayed buses and other inconveniences. The first, **jai yen**, translates literally as "cool heart" and is something everyone tries to maintain: most Thais hate raised voices, visible irritation and confrontations of any kind, so losing one's cool can have a much more inflammatory effect than in more combative cultures. Related to this is the oft-quoted response to a difficulty, **mai pen rai** – "never mind", "no problem" or "it can't be helped" – the verbal equivalent of an open-handed shoulder shrug, which has its basis in the Buddhist notion of karma (see page 428). And then there's **sanuk**, the wide-reaching philosophy of "fun", which, crass as it sounds, Thais do their best to inject into any situation, even work. Hence the crowds of inebriated Thais who congregate at waterfalls and other beauty spots on public holidays (travelling solo is definitely not *sanuk*), the reluctance to do almost anything without high-volume musical accompaniment, and the national waterfight which takes place during Songkhran every April on streets right across Thailand.

## Thai names

Although all Thais have a first **name** and a family name, everyone is addressed by their first name – even when meeting strangers – prefixed by the title "**Khun**" (Mr/Ms); no one is ever addressed as Khun Surname, and even the phone book lists people by their given name. In Thailand you will often be addressed in an anglicized version of this convention, as "Mr Paul" or "Miss Lucy" for example. Bear in mind, though, that when a man is introduced to you as Khun Pirom, his wife will definitely not be Khun Pirom as well (that would be like calling them, for instance, "Mr and Mrs Paul"). Among friends and relatives, **Phii** ("older brother/sister") is often used instead of Khun when addressing older familiars (though as a tourist you're on surer ground with Khun), and **Nong** ("younger brother/sister") is used for younger ones.

Many Thai **first names** come from ancient Sanskrit and have an auspicious meaning; for example, Boon means good deeds, Porn means blessings, Siri means glory and Thawee means to increase. However, Thais of all ages are commonly known by the **nickname** given them soon after birth rather than by their official first name. This tradition arises out of a deep-rooted superstition that once a child has been officially named the spirits will begin to take an unhealthy interest in them, so a nickname is used instead to confuse the spirits. Common nicknames – which often bear no resemblance to the adult's personality or physique – include Yai (Big), Uan (Fat) and Muu (Pig); Lek or Noi (Little), Nok (Bird), Nuu (Mouse) and Kung (Shrimp); and English nicknames like Apple, Joy or even Pepsi.

**Family names** were only introduced in 1913 (by Rama VI, who invented many of the aristocracy's surnames himself), and are used only in very formal situations, always in conjunction with the first name. It's quite usual for good friends never to know each other's surname. Ethnic Thais generally have short surnames like Somboon or Srisai, while the long, convoluted family names – such as Sonthanasumpun – usually indicate Chinese origin, not because they are phonetically Chinese but because many Chinese immigrants have chosen to adopt Thai surnames and Thai law states that every newly created surname must be unique. Thus anyone who wants to change their surname must submit a shortlist of five unique Thai names – each to a maximum length of ten Thai characters – to be checked against a database of existing names. As more and more names are taken, Chinese family names get increasingly unwieldy, and more easily distinguishable from the pithy old Thai names.

# The media

**There are several English-language newspapers in Thailand, though various forms of censorship (and self-censorship) affect all newspapers and the predominantly state-controlled media.**

## Newspapers and magazines

Of the hundreds of **Thai-language newspapers and magazines** published every week, the sensationalist daily tabloid *Thai Rath* attracts the widest readership, with circulation of around a million, while the moderately progressive *Matichon* is the leading quality daily, with an estimated circulation of 600,000.

Alongside these, the two main daily **English-language papers** are the *Bangkok Post* (Ⓦ bangkokpost. com) and the *Nation* (Ⓦ nationmultimedia.com), but you'll get a more balanced idea of what's going on in Thailand at Ⓦ khaosodenglish.com, which is owned by Matichon. Both the *Post* and *Nation* are still sold at many newsstands in the capital as well as in major provincial towns and tourist resorts; the more isolated places receive their few copies one day late. Details of local English-language newspapers, magazines, listings publications and websites are given in the relevant Guide accounts.

You can also pick up **foreign** magazines such as *Newsweek* and *Time* in Bangkok, Chiang Mai and the major resorts. English-language bookshops such as Bookazine and some expensive hotels carry air-freighted, or sometimes locally printed and stapled, copies of foreign national newspapers for at least B50 a copy; the latter are also sold in tourist-oriented minimarkets in the big resorts.

## Television

There are six government-controlled, terrestrial **TV channels** in Thailand: channels 3, 5 (owned and operated by the army), 7 (operated under license from the army) and 9 transmit a blend of news, soaps, sports, talk, quiz, reality and game shows, while the more serious-minded public-service channels are NBT, owned and operated by the government's public relations department, and the state-funded but more independent PBS. **Cable** networks – available in many guesthouse and hotel rooms – carry channels from all around the world, including CNN from the US, BBC World News from the UK and sometimes ABC from Australia, as well as English-language movie channels and various sports, music and documentary channels.

## Radio

Thailand boasts over five hundred **radio stations**, mostly music-oriented, ranging from Eazy (105.5 FM), which serves up Western pop, through *luk thung* on Rak Thai (90FM), to Cat (formerly Fat) Radio, which streams 24-hour Thai indie sounds on its website (🌐 thisiscat.com) and app. Met 107 on 107 FM is one of several stations that include English-language news bulletins.

By going **online** or with a **shortwave radio (BBC only)**, you can listen to the BBC World Service (🌐 bbc.co.uk/worldserviceradio), Radio Australia (🌐 radio-australia.net.au), Voice of America (🌐 voanews.com), Radio Canada (🌐 rcinet.ca) and a host of other international stations.

# Festivals

**Nearly all Thai festivals have a religious aspect. The most theatrical are generally Brahmin (Hindu) or animistic in origin, honouring elemental spirits and deities with ancient rites and ceremonial costumed parades. Buddhist celebrations usually revolve round the local temple, and while merit-making is a significant feature, a light-hearted atmosphere prevails, as the wat grounds are swamped with food and trinket vendors and makeshift stages are set up to show *likay* folk theatre, singing stars and beauty contests.**

Many of the **secular festivals** are outdoor local culture shows, geared specifically towards Thai and farang tourists. Others are thinly veiled but lively trade fairs held in provincial capitals to show off the local speciality, be it exquisite silk weaving or especially tasty rambutans.

Few of the **dates** for religious festivals are fixed, so check with TAT for specifics (🌐 tourismthailand.org). The names of the most touristy celebrations are given here in English; the more low-key festivals are more usually known by their Thai name (*ngan* – usually religious – and *tetsagaan* – usually organized by the municipality – are the words for "festival"). See the relevant town accounts for fuller details of the festivals below; some of them are designated as national holidays (see page 67).

## A festival calendar

### JANUARY– JUNE

**Chinese New Year** Nationwide, particularly Bangkok and Phuket (Truut Jiin; three days between mid-Jan and late Feb). The new Chinese year is welcomed in with exuberant parades of dragons and lion dancers, Chinese opera performances and colourful fireworks displays.

**Makha Puja** Nationwide (particularly Wat Benjamabophit in Bangkok and Wat Mahathat in Nakhon Si Thammarat; full-moon day usually in Feb). A day of merit-making marks the occasion when 1250 disciples gathered spontaneously to hear the Buddha preach, and culminates with a candlelit procession round the local temple's bot.

**Kite fights and flying contests** Nationwide, including a three-day festival in Hua Hin (late Feb to mid-April).

**Songkhran** Nationwide (particularly Bangkok's Thanon Khao San; usually April 13–15). The most exuberant of the national festivals welcomes the Thai New Year with massive waterfights, sandcastle building in temple compounds and the inevitable parades and "Miss Songkhran" beauty contests.

**Visakha Puja** Nationwide (particularly Bangkok's Wat Benjamabophit and Nakhon Si Thammarat's Wat Mahathat; full-moon day usually in May). The holiest day of the Buddhist year, commemorating the birth, enlightenment and death of the Buddha all in one go; the most public and photogenic part is the candlelit evening procession around the wat.

**Raek Na** Sanam Luang, Bangkok (early May). The royal ploughing ceremony to mark the beginning of the rice-planting season; ceremonially clad Brahmin leaders parade sacred oxen and the royal plough, and interpret omens to forecast the year's rice yield.

### JULY– DECEMBER

**Tamboon Deuan Sip** Nakhon Si Thammarat (Sept or Oct). Merit-making ceremonies to honour dead relatives accompanied by a ten-day fair.

**Vegetarian Festival** Phuket and Trang (Tetsagaan Kin Jeh; Oct or Nov). Chinese devotees become vegetarian for a nine-day period and then parade through town performing acts of self-mortification such as pushing skewers through their cheeks. Celebrated in Bangkok's Chinatown by most food vendors and restaurants turning vegetarian for about a fortnight.

**Tak Bat Devo and Awk Pansa** Nationwide (full-moon day usually in Oct). Offerings to monks and general merrymaking to celebrate the Buddha's descent to earth from Tavatimsa heaven and the end of the Khao Pansa retreat.

**Chak Phra** Surat Thani (mid-Oct). The town's chief Buddha images are paraded on floats down the streets and on barges along the river.

**Thawt Kathin** Nationwide (the month between Awk Pansa and Loy Krathong, generally Oct–Nov). During the month following the end of the monks' rainy-season retreat, it's traditional for the laity to donate new robes to the monkhood and this is celebrated in most towns with parades and a festival, and occasionally, when it coincides with a kingly anniversary, with a spectacular Royal Barge Procession down the Chao Phraya River in Bangkok.

**Cat Expo** Bangkok (over a weekend in Nov; details on Facebook near the time). Formerly Fat Festival, Thailand's biggest indie music event features over a hundred established and emerging bands on several stages, along with meet-the-band booths and film screenings.

**Loy Krathong** Nationwide (full moon in Nov). Baskets (*krathong*) of flowers and lighted candles are floated on any available body of water (such as ponds, rivers, lakes, canals and seashores) to honour water spirits and celebrate the end of the rainy season, and paper hot-air balloons are released into the night sky. Nearly every town puts on a big show, with bazaars, public entertainments and fireworks displays.

**Ngan Wat Saket** Wat Saket, Bangkok (nine days around Loy Krathong, Nov). Probably Thailand's biggest temple fair, held around the Golden Mount, with all the usual festival trappings.

**New Year's Eve Countdown** Nationwide (Dec 31). Most cities and tourist destinations welcome in the new year with fireworks displays, often backed up by food festivals, beauty contests and outdoor performances.

# Entertainment and sport

**Bangkok is the best place to catch authentic performances of classical Thai dance, though more easily digestible tourist-oriented shows are staged in some of the big tourist centres as well as in Bangkok. The country's two main Thai boxing stadia are also in the capital, but you'll come across local matches in the provinces too.**

## Drama and dance

**Drama** pretty much equals **dance** in classical Thai theatre, and many of the traditional dance-dramas are based on the *Ramakien*, the Thai version of the Hindu epic the *Ramayana*, an adventure tale of good versus evil that is taught in all schools – check out the wonderfully imaginative murals at Wat Phra Kaew in Bangkok. There are three broad categories of traditional Thai dance-drama – *khon*, *lakhon* and *likay* – described below in descending order of refinement.

## Khon

The most spectacular form of traditional Thai theatre is **khon**, a stylized drama performed in masks and elaborate costumes by a troupe of highly trained classical dancers. There's little room for individual interpretation in these dances, as all the movements follow a strict choreography that's been passed down through generations: each graceful, angular gesture depicts a precise event, action or emotion which will be familiar to educated *khon* audiences. The dancers don't speak, and the story is chanted and sung by a chorus who stand at the side of the stage, accompanied by a classical *phipat* orchestra.

A typical *khon* performance features several of the best-known **Ramakien** episodes, in which the main characters are recognized by their masks, headdresses and heavily brocaded costumes. Gods and humans don't wear masks, but the hero Rama and heroine Sita always wear tall gilded headdresses and often appear as a trio with Rama's brother Lakshaman. Monkey **masks** are wide-mouthed: monkey army chief Hanuman always wears white, and his two right-hand men – Nilanol, the god of fire, and Nilapat, the god of death – wear red and black respectively. In contrast, the demons have grim mouths, clamped shut or snarling; Totsagan, king of the demons, wears a green face in battle and a gold one during peace, but always sports a two-tier headdress carved with two rows of faces.

*Khon* is performed with English subtitles at Bangkok's Sala Chalermkrung (see page 139) and is also performed within the various cultural **shows** staged by tourist restaurants in Bangkok, Phuket and Pattaya. Even if you don't see a show, you're bound to come across finely crafted real and replica *khon* masks both in museums and in souvenir shops all over the country.

## Lakhon

Serious and refined, **lakhon** is derived from *khon* but is used to dramatize a greater range of stories, including Buddhist *Jataka* tales, local folk dramas and of course the *Ramakien*.

The form you're most likely to come across is *lakhon chatri*, which is performed at shrines like Bangkok's Erawan and at a city's *lak muang* as entertainment for the spirits and a token of gratitude from worshippers. Usually female, the *lakhon chatri* dancers perform as an ensemble, executing sequences that, like *khon* movements, all have minute and particular symbolism. They also wear ornate costumes, but no masks, and dance to the music of a *phipat* orchestra. Unfortunately, as resident shrine troupes tend to repeat the same dances a dozen times a day, it's rarely the sublime display it's cracked up to be. Bangkok's National Theatre stages the more elegantly executed *lakhon nai*, a dance form that used to be performed at the Thai court and often retells the *Ramakien*.

## Likay

**Likay** is a much more popular and dynamic derivative of *khon* – more light-hearted, with lots of comic interludes, bawdy jokes and panto-style over-the-top acting and singing. Some *likay* troupes perform *Ramakien* excerpts, but a lot of them adapt pot-boiler romances or write their own, and most will ham things up with improvisations and up-to-the-minute topical satire. Costumes might be traditional as in *khon* and *lakhon*, modern and Western as on TV, or a mixture of both.

*Likay* troupes travel around the country doing shows on makeshift outdoor stages wherever they think they'll get an audience, most commonly at temple fairs. Performances are often free and generally last for about five hours, with the audience strolling in and out of the show, cheering and joking with the cast throughout. Televised *likay* dramas get huge audiences and always follow romantic soap-opera-style plot-lines. Short *likay* dramas are also a staple of Bangkok's National Theatre, but for more radical and internationally minded *likay*, look out for performances by **Makhampom** (Ⓦmakhampom.org), a famous, long-established troupe that pushes *likay* in new directions to promote social causes and involve minority communities.

## Nang

**Nang**, or shadow plays (see page 276), are said to have been the earliest dramas performed in Thailand, but now are rarely seen except in the far south, where the Malaysian influence ensures an appreciative audience for *nang thalung*. Crafted from buffalo hide, the two-dimensional *nang thalung* puppets play out scenes from popular dramas against a backlit screen, while the storyline is told through songs, chants and musical interludes. An even rarer *nang* form is the *nang yai*, which uses enormous cut-outs of whole scenes rather than just individual characters, so the play becomes something like an animated film.

## Thai boxing

**Thai boxing** (*muay thai*) enjoys a following similar to football or baseball in the West: every province has a stadium and whenever a big fight is shown on TV you can be sure that large, noisy crowds will gather round the sets in streetside restaurants. The best place to see Thai boxing is at one of Bangkok's two main stadia, which between them hold bouts every night of the week (see page 140), but many tourist resorts also stage regular matches.

There's a strong spiritual and **ritualistic** dimension to *muay thai*, adding grace to an otherwise brutal sport. Each boxer enters the ring to the wailing music of a three-piece *phipat* orchestra, wearing the statutory red or blue shorts and, on his head, a sacred rope headband or *mongkhon*. Tied around his biceps are *phra jiat*, pieces of cloth that are often decorated with cabalistic symbols and may contain Buddhist tablets. The fighter then bows, first in the direction of his birthplace and then to the north, south, east and west, honouring both his teachers and the spirit of the ring. Next he performs a slow dance, claiming the audience's attention and demonstrating his prowess as a performer.

Any part of the body except the head may be used as an **offensive weapon** in *muay thai*, and all parts except the groin are fair targets. Kicks to the head are the blows that cause most knockouts. As the action hots up, so the orchestra speeds up its tempo and the betting in the audience becomes more frenetic. It can be a gruesome business, but it was far bloodier before modern boxing gloves were introduced in the 1930s, when the Queensbury Rules were adapted for *muay* – combatants used to wrap their fists with hemp impregnated with a face-lacerating dosage of ground glass.

A number of *muay thai* gyms and camps offer training **courses** for foreigners, including several in Bangkok, as well as Hua Hin, Ko Pha Ngan, Ko Tao and Ko Yao Noi – see the relevant accounts for details or go to Ⓦmuaythaicampsthailand.com

# Spas and traditional massage

**With their focus on indulgent self-pampering, spas are usually associated with high-spending tourists, but the treatments on offer at Thailand's five-star hotels are often little different from those used by traditional medical practitioners, who have long held that massage and herbs are the best way to restore physical and mental well-being.**

**Thai massage** (*nuad boran*) is based on the principle that many physical and emotional problems are caused by the blocking of vital energy channels within the body. The masseur uses his or her feet, heels, knees and elbows, as well as hands, to exert pressure on these channels, supplementing this acupressure-style technique by pulling and pushing the limbs into yogic stretches. This distinguishes Thai massage from most other massage styles, which are more concerned with tissue manipulation. One is supposed to emerge from a Thai massage feeling both relaxed and energized, and it is said that regular massages produce long-term benefits in muscles as well as stimulating the circulation and aiding natural detoxification.

Thais will visit a masseur for many conditions, including fevers, colds and muscle strain, but bodies that are not sick are also considered to benefit from the restorative powers of a massage, and nearly every hotel and guesthouse will be able to put you in touch with a **masseur**. On the more popular beaches, it can be hard to walk a few hundred metres without being offered a massage – something Thai tourists are just as enthusiastic about as foreigners. Thai masseurs do not traditionally use oils or lotions and the client is treated on a mat or mattress; you'll often be given a pair of loose-fitting trousers and perhaps a loose top to change into. English-speaking masseurs will often ask if there are any areas of your body that you would like them to concentrate on, or if you have any problem areas that you want them to avoid; if your masseur doesn't speak English, the simplest way to signal the latter is to point at the offending area while saying *mai sabai* ("not well"). If you're in pain during a massage, wincing usually does the trick, perhaps adding *jep* ("it hurts"); if your masseur is pressing too hard for your liking, say *bao bao na khrap/kha* ("gently please").

The best places for a basic massage are usually the government-accredited clinics and hospitals that are found in large towns all over the country. A session should ideally last at least one and a half hours and will cost from around B300. If you're a bit wary of submitting to the full works, try a **foot massage** first, which will apply the same techniques of acupressure and stretching to just your feet and lower legs. Most places also offer **herbal massages**, in which the masseur will knead you with a ball of herbs (*phrakop*) wrapped in a cloth and steam-heated; they're said to be particularly good for stiffness of the neck, shoulders and back.

The **science** behind Thai massage has its roots in Indian Ayurvedic medicine, which classifies each component of the body according to one of the four elements (earth, water, fire and air), and holds that balancing these elements within the body is crucial to good health. Many of the stretches and manipulations fundamental to Thai massage are thought to have derived from yogic practices introduced to Thailand from India by Buddhist missionaries in about the second century BC; Chinese acupuncture and reflexology have also had a strong influence. In the nineteenth century, King Rama III ordered a series of murals illustrating the principles of Thai massage to be painted around the courtyard of Bangkok's Wat Pho, and they are still in place today, along with statues of ascetics depicted in typical massage poses.

**Wat Pho** has been the leading school of Thai massage for hundreds of years, and it is possible to take courses there as well as to receive a massage (see page 85); it also has several satellite health centres scattered around Bangkok. Masseurs who trained at Wat Pho are considered to be the best in the country and masseurs all across Thailand advertise this as a credential, whether or not it is true. Many Thais consider blind masseurs to be especially sensitive practitioners.

While Wat Pho is the most famous place to take a **course** in Thai massage (see page 85), you will find others all over Thailand, including in Bangkok and at southern beach resorts.

All **spas** in Thailand feature traditional Thai massage and herbal therapies in their programmes, but most also offer dozens of other international treatments, including facials, aromatherapy, Swedish massage and various body wraps. Spa centres in upmarket hotels and resorts are usually open to non-guests but generally need to be booked in advance. Day-spas that are not attached to hotels are generally cheaper and are found in some of the bigger cities and resorts – some of these may not require reservations.

# Meditation centres and retreats

**Of the hundreds of meditation temples in Thailand, a few cater specifically for foreigners by holding meditation sessions and retreats in English. Novices as well as practised meditators are generally welcome at these wats, but absolute beginners might like to consider the regular retreats at Wat Suan Mokkh on Ko Samui and in Chaiya, which are conducted by supportive and experienced Thai and Western teachers and include talks and interviews on Buddhist teachings and practice. The meditation taught is mostly Vipassana, or "insight", which emphasizes the minute observation of internal sensations; the other main technique you'll come across is Samatha, which aims to**

calm the mind and develop concentration (these two techniques are not entirely separate, since you cannot have insight without some degree of concentration).

Longer **retreats** are for the serious-minded only. All the temples listed below welcome both male and female English-speakers, but strict segregation of the sexes is enforced and many places observe a vow of silence. Reading and writing are also discouraged, and you'll not be allowed to leave the retreat complex unless absolutely necessary, so try to bring whatever you'll need in with you. All retreats expect you to wear modest clothing, and some require you to wear white – check ahead whether there is a shop at the retreat complex or whether you are expected to bring this with you.

An average day at any one of these monasteries starts with a **wake-up call** at around 4am and includes several hours of **group meditation** and chanting, as well as time put aside for chores and personal reflection. However long their stay, visitors are expected to keep the eight main Buddhist precepts, the most restrictive of these being the abstention from food after midday and from alcohol, tobacco, drugs and sex at all times. Most wats ask for a minimal daily **donation** (around B200) to cover the costs of the simple accommodation and food.

Further details about many of the temples listed below – including how to get there – are given in the relevant sections in the Guide chapters. Little Bangkok Sangha (ⓦ littlebang.org) is a handy blog maintained by a British-born monk, Phra Pandit, which gives details of group meditation sessions and talks in Bangkok and retreats. Also in Bangkok, keep an eye out for events for English-speakers at the Buddhadasa Indapanno Archives in Chatuchak Park in the north of the city (ⓦ bia.or.th), a recently built centre in honour of the founder of Wat Suan Mokkh (see page 229).

### MEDITATION CENTRES AND RETREAT TEMPLES

In addition to those listed below, additional meditation centres and retreat temples are listed in the Guide chapters, including **Wat Mahathat** in Bangkok (see page 85) and **Wat Suan Mokkh** on Ko Samui (see page 235) and in Chaiya (see page 235).

**House of Dhamma Insight Meditation Centre** 26/9 Soi Lardprao 15, Chatuchak, Bangkok ☎ 02 511 0439, ⓦ houseofdhamma.com. Regular one- and two-day courses in Vipassana, as well as workshops in Metta (Loving Kindness) meditation for experienced practitioners upon request. Courses in reiki and other subjects available.

**Thailand Vipassana Centres** ⓦ dhamma.org. Frequent courses in a Burmese Vipassana tradition (ten days), in nine centres around Thailand.

# Outdoor activities

**Many beach itineraries include a stint snorkelling or diving, and the major resorts offer dozens of other watersports too. There are also plenty of national parks to explore and opportunities for rock climbing and kayaking.**

## Diving and snorkelling

Clear, warm waters (averaging 28°C), prolific marine life and affordable prices make Thailand a very rewarding place for **diving** and **snorkelling**. Most islands and beach resorts have at least one dive centre that organizes trips to outlying islands, teaches novice divers and rents out equipment, and in the bigger resorts there are dozens to choose from.

Thailand's three coasts are subject to different monsoon **seasons**, so you can dive all year round; the seasons run from November to April along the Andaman coast (though there is sometimes good diving here up until late Aug), and all year round on the Gulf and east coasts. Though every diver has their favourite reef, Thailand's **premier diving destinations** are generally considered to be Ko Similan, Ko Surin, Richelieu Rock and Hin Muang and Hin Daeng – all of them off the Andaman coast (see page 282). As an accessible base for diving, Ko Tao off the Gulf coast is hard to beat, with deep, clear inshore water and a wide variety of dive sites in very close proximity.

Whether you're snorkelling or diving, try to minimize your impact on the fragile reef structures by **not touching the reefs** and by asking your boatman not to anchor in the middle of one; **don't buy coral souvenirs**, as tourist demand only encourages local entrepreneurs to dynamite reefs.

Should you scrape your skin on coral, wash the wound thoroughly with boiled water, apply antiseptic and keep protected until healed. Wearing a T-shirt is a good idea when snorkelling to stop your back from getting sunburnt.

### Diving

It's usually worth having a look at several **dive centres** before committing yourself to a trip or a course. Always verify the dive instructors' and dive shops' PADI (Professional Association of Diving Instructors) or equivalent accreditations as this guarantees a certain level of professionalism. You can view a list of PADI dive shops and resorts in Thailand at ⓦ padi.com.

We've highlighted dive shops that are accredited Five-Star centres, as these are considered by PADI to offer very high standards, but you should always consult other divers first if possible. Some dive operators do fake their PADI credentials. Avoid booking ahead over the internet without knowing anything else about the dive centre, and be wary of any operation offering extremely cheap courses: maintaining diving equipment is an expensive business in Thailand so any place offering unusually good rates will probably be cutting corners and compromising your safety. Ask to **meet your instructor** or dive leader, find out how many people there'll be in your group, check out the kind of instruction given (some courses are over-reliant on videos) and look over the equipment, checking the quality of the air in the tanks yourself and also ensuring there's an oxygen cylinder on board. Most divers prefer to travel to the dive site in a decent-sized **boat** equipped with a radio and emergency medical equipment rather than in a longtail. If this concerns you, ask the dive company about their boat before you sign up; firms that use longtails generally charge less.

**Insurance** should be included in the price of courses and introductory dives; for qualified divers, you're better off checking that your general travel insurance covers diving, though some diving shops can organize cover for you. There are **recompression chambers** in Pattaya, on Ko Samui and on Phuket and it's a good idea to check whether your dive centre is a member of one of these outfits, as recompression services are extremely expensive for anyone who's not.

### Trips and courses

All dive centres run programmes of day and night **dives** starting at around B1000/dive (with reductions for subsequent dives and if you bring your own gear), and many of the Andaman-coast dive centres also do three- to seven-day **live-aboards** to the exceptional reefs off the remote Similan and Surin islands (from B12,000). Most dive centres can rent **underwater cameras** for about B1500 per day.

All dive centres offer a range of **courses** from beginner to advanced level, with equipment rental usually included in the cost; Ko Tao is now the largest, and most competitive, dive-training centre in Southeast Asia, with around fifty dive companies including plenty of PADI Five-Star centres. The most popular courses are the one-day **introductory** or resort dive (a pep talk and escorted shallow dive, open to anyone aged 10 or over), which costs anything from B2000 for a very local dive to B7000 for an all-inclusive day-trip to the Similan Islands; and the four-day **open-water course**, which entitles you to dive without an instructor (around B9800 on Ko Tao in high season). Kids' Bubblemaker courses, for children aged 8 and up, cost around B2000.

### Snorkelling

Boatmen and tour agents on most beaches offer **snorkelling** trips to nearby reefs and many dive operators welcome snorkellers to tag along for discounts of thirty percent or more; not all diving destinations are rewarding for snorkellers, though, so check carefully with the dive shop first. As far as

---

## THAILAND'S TOP DIVING SPOTS

**Ko Tao** Boasting a dozen great spots in deep, clear water close to shore – at least some of which can be accessed all year round – "Turtle Island" has established itself as Southeast Asia's largest dive-training centre. See page 263

**Ko Similan** National park archipelago that's rated as one of the best and most varied diving destinations in the world. Prolific reefs dominate the east-facing coasts while the west is all granite boulders, caves and tunnels. Visibility extends to 30m and the cast of celebrity visitors includes white-tip sharks, barracuda, giant lobster, enormous tuna and whale sharks. See page 312

**Ko Phi Phi** Fringing reefs of hard and soft corals that descend to 35m, plus wrecks and varied marine life mean there's plenty here for both snorkellers and divers, all within easy reach of Phi Phi's hotels, nightlife and beautiful beaches. See page 365

**Hin Daeng and Hin Muang** Two spectacular, and challenging, reef walls off the Andaman coast that attract lots of reef fish and pelagics. Hin Muang, at well over 50m, is the deepest drop in Thailand and reliable for stingrays, manta rays, tuna, jacks, silvertip sharks and whale sharks. See page 335

**Ko Lipe** Around forty sites, most of them nearby in the undisturbed Ko Tarutao National Park, notable for their colourful diversity of topography (including wrecks), of corals, both hard and soft, and of species, including rare surgeonfish, sailfish and demon stingers. See page 410

**Richelieu Rock** The sunken pinnacle at Richelieu Rock is considered the country's premier dive site, famed for its manta rays and whale sharks. See page 335

**A NOTE ON ELEPHANT RIDES**

Elephant rides are a popular attraction for tourists in Thailand; however, for **animal welfare** reasons Rough Guides doesn't want to encourage this practice. While we will not recommend elephant rides in this Guide, the situation in Thailand is not black and white. As such, we may list some places which offer elephant rides alongside other activities, many of which are wildlife sanctuaries – we'll always flag it up if so, so you can decide whether you'd rather go somewhere else. We would encourage you to learn more about the ethical implications before you decide whether to visit the sight and/or take an elephant ride. For more information, visit ⓦtourismconcern.org.uk/elephant-trekking-a-do-or-a-dont or ⓦroughguides.com/article/the-truth-about-elephant-tourism-in-asia (which also lists several ethical, reputable Thai elephant sanctuaries).

snorkelling **equipment** goes, the most important thing is that you buy or rent a mask that fits. To check the fit, hold the mask against your face, then breathe in and remove your hands – if it falls off, it'll leak water. If you're buying equipment, you should be able to kit yourself out with a mask, snorkel and fins for about B1500, available from most dive centres. Few places rent fins, but a mask and snorkel set usually costs about B150 a day to rent, and if you're going on a snorkelling day-trip they are often included in the price.

## National parks and wildlife observation

Thailand's hundred-plus **national parks**, including several marine parks in the south, are administered by the National Park, Wildlife and Plant Conservation Department, and are generally the best places to **observe wildlife**. Khao Sok (see page 301) is southern Thailand's most popular inland park, while birdwatchers consider Khao Sam Roi Yot (see page 220) to be one of the country's prime observation spots. Most parks charge an **entrance fee**, which for foreigners is usually B200 (B100 for children), though some charge B100 and a few charge B300, B400 or B500. Cars are usually B30 each; motorbikes B20. The parks' department has a website of sorts (ⓦnps. dnp.go.th) but you'll find ⓦthainationalparks.com much more helpful, covering thirty or so of the most popular parks, with useful species lists.

Waymarked hiking **trails** in most parks are generally limited and rarely very challenging, and decent park maps are hard to come by, so for serious national park treks you'll need to hire a guide and venture beyond the public routes. Nearly all parks provide **accommodation** and/or campsites (see page 39). Some national parks **close** for several weeks or months every year for conservation, safety or environmental reasons, as noted in the Guide.

There's an introduction to Thailand's coastal environment and wildlife in "Contexts" (see page 434).

## Rock climbing

The limestone karsts that pepper southern Thailand's Andaman coast make ideal playgrounds for **rock climbers**, and the sport has really taken off here in the past twenty years. Most climbing is centred round **East Railay** and **Ton Sai** beaches on Laem Phra Nang in Krabi province (see page 361), where there are dozens of routes within easy walking distance of tourist bungalows, restaurants and beaches. **Offshore Deep Water Soloing** – climbing a rock face out at sea, with no ropes, partner or bolts and just the water to break your fall – is also huge round here. Several **climbing schools** at East Railay and Ton Sai provide instruction (from B1000/half-day), as well as equipment rental (about B2400/day for two people) and guides. Ko Phi Phi (see page 365) also offers a few routes and a couple of climbing schools, as do Ko Tao (see page 263) and the quieter and potentially more interesting Ko Yao Noi (see page 340) and Ko Lao Liang (see page 407). For an introduction to climbing on Railay and elsewhere in south Thailand, see ⓦrailay.com, which features interactive route maps, while *King Climbers: Thailand Route Guide Book* is a fairly regularly updated guidebook that concentrates on Railay, Ton Sai and the islands.

## Sea kayaking

**Sea kayaking** is also centred around Thailand's Andaman coast, where the limestone outcrops, sea caves, *hongs* (hidden lagoons), mangrove swamps and picturesque shorelines of Ao Phang Nga in particular (see page 345) make for rewarding paddling. Kayaking day-trips around Ao Phang Nga can be arranged from any resort in Phuket, at Khao Lak, at all Krabi beaches and islands, and on Ko Yao Noi; multi-day kayaking expeditions are also possible. Over on Ko Samui, Blue Stars (see page 250) organizes kayaking trips around the picturesque islands of the Ang Thong National Marine Park, while Kayak Chang (see page 182) offers one- to twelve-day trips around Ko Chang. Many bungalows at other beach resorts have free kayaks or rent them out (from B100/hr) for casual, independent coastal exploration.

# Travelling with children

**Despite the relative lack of child-centred attractions in Thailand, there's plenty to appeal to families, both on the beach and inland, and Thais are famously welcoming to young visitors.**

Of all the **beach resorts** in the country, two of the most family-friendly are the islands of Ko Samui and Ko Lanta. Both have plenty of on-the-beach accommodation for mid- and upper-range budgets, and lots of easy-going open-air shorefront restaurants so that adults can eat in relative peace while kids play within view. Both islands also offer many day-tripping activities, from boat trips to snorkelling. Phuket is another family favourite, though shorefront accommodation here is at a premium; there are also scores of less mainstream alternatives. In many beach resorts older kids will be able to go kayaking or learn rock climbing, and many dive centres will teach the PADI children's scuba courses on request: the Bubblemaker programme is designed for kids of 8 and over, and the Discover Scuba Diving day is open to anyone 10 and over.

Inland, the many **national parks** and their waterfalls and caves are good for days out, and there are lots of opportunities to see and play with **elephants**. Bangkok has several child-friendly **theme parks** and activity centres.

Should you be in Thailand in January, your kids will be able to join in the free entertainments and activities staged all over the country on **National Children's Day** (Wan Dek), which is held on the second Saturday of January. They also get free entry to zoos that day, and free rides on public buses.

## Hotels and transport

Many of the expensive **hotels** listed in this guide allow one or two under-12s to share their parents' room for free, as long as no extra bedding is required. It's often possible to cram two adults and two children into the double rooms in budget and mid-range hotels (as opposed to guesthouses), as beds in these places are usually big enough for two. An increasing number of guesthouses now offer three-person rooms, and may even provide special family accommodation. Decent cots are available free in the bigger hotels,

and in some smaller ones (though cots in these places can be a bit grotty), and top- and mid-range rooms often come with a small fridge. Many hotels can also provide a **babysitting** service.

Few museums or transport companies offer student reductions, but in some cases children get **discounts**. One of the more bizarre provisos is the State Railway's regulation that a child aged 3 to 12 qualifies for half-fare only if under 150cm tall; some stations have a measuring scale painted onto the ticket-hall wall. Most domestic airlines charge ten percent of the full fare, or are free, for under-2s, but only Thai Airways and Thai Smile offer reduced fares for under-12s.

## Other practicalities

Although most Thai babies don't wear them, **disposable nappies** (diapers) are sold at convenience stores, pharmacies and supermarkets in big resorts and sizeable towns – Mamy Poko is a reliable Japanese brand, available in supermarkets; for stays on lonely islands, consider bringing some washable ones as back-up. A **changing mat** is another necessity as there are few public toilets in Thailand, let alone ones with baby facilities (though posh hotels are always a useful option). International brands of powdered milk are available throughout the country, and brand-name baby food is sold in big towns and resorts, though some parents find restaurant-cooked rice and bananas go down just as well. Thai women do not **breastfeed** in public.

For touring, child-carrier backpacks are ideal (though make sure that the child's head extends no higher than yours, as there are countless low-hanging obstacles on Thai streets). Opinions are divided on whether or not it's worth bringing a **pushchair** or three-wheeled **stroller**. Where they exist, Thailand's pavements are bumpy at best, and there's an almost total absence of ramps; sand is especially difficult for pushchairs, though less so for three-wheelers. Pushchairs and strollers do, however, come in handy for feeding small children (and even for daytime naps), as highchairs are provided only in some restaurants (and then often without restraints for smaller toddlers). You can buy pushchairs fairly cheaply in most towns, but if you bring your own and then wish you hadn't, most hotels and guesthouses will keep it for you until you leave. Bring an appropriately sized **mosquito net** if necessary or buy one locally in any department store; a mini **sun tent** for the beach is also useful. Taxis almost never provide baby **car seats**, and even if you bring your own you'll often find there are no seatbelts to strap them in with; branches of international car-rental companies should be able to provide car seats. Most department stores have dedicated kids' sections selling everything from bottles to dummies. There are even several Mothercare outlets in Bangkok.

## Hazards

Even more than their parents, children need protecting from the sun, unsafe drinking water, heat and unfamiliar **food**. Consider packing a jar of a favourite spread so that you can always rely on toast if all else fails to please. As with adults, you should be careful about unwashed fruit and salads and about dishes that have been left uncovered for a long time. As diarrhoea could be dangerous for a child, rehydration solutions (see page 63) are vital if your child goes down with it; sachets formulated specially for children are available in local pharmacies. Other significant **hazards** include thundering traffic; huge waves, strong currents and jellyfish; and the **sun** – not least because many beaches offer only limited shade, if at all. Sunhats, sunblock and water-proof suntan lotions are essential, and can be bought in the major resorts. Avoiding mosquitoes is difficult, but low-strength DEET lotions should do the trick. You should also make sure, if possible, that your child is aware of the dangers of **rabies**; keep children away from **animals**, especially dogs and monkeys, and ask your medical advisor about rabies jabs.

### INFORMATION AND ADVICE

**Bangkok Mothers and Babies International** ⓦ bambiweb.org. For expat mothers and kids, but some of the information and advice on the website should be useful.
**BKK Kids** ⓦ bkkkids.com. Especially good on activities for children in Bangkok, but also covers health matters and other services thoroughly.
**Thailand 4 Kids** ⓦ thailand4kids.com. Lots of advice on the practicalities of family holidays in Thailand.

# Travel essentials

## Charities and volunteer projects

Reassured by the plethora of well-stocked shopping plazas, efficient services and apparent abundance in the rice fields, it is easy to forget that life is extremely hard for many people in Thailand. Countless **charities** work with Thailand's many poor and disadvantaged communities: listed below are a few that would welcome help in some way from visitors. Longer-term placements and organized holidays that feature community-based programmes are also available (see pages 28 and 64, respectively).

**Andaman Discoveries** Khuraburi ⓦ andamandiscoveries.com. As well as community-based tourism programmes, this organization offers the chance to volunteer in rural schools, an orphanage, a Burmese learning centre or a special education centre.
**Children's World Academy** Kapong, near Khao Lak ⓦ yaowawit. com. Set in quiet countryside on the Takua Pa–Phang Nga road, Yaowawit School was set up for tsunami orphans and socially disadvantaged children. It accepts donations, sponsorships, volunteer teachers and guests who wish to stay at its lodge, a hospitality training centre.
**Human Development Foundation Mercy Centre** Klong Toey, Bangkok ⓦ mercycentre.org. Founded in 1973, Father Joe Maier's organization provides education and support for Bangkok's street kids and slum-dwellers. It now runs two dozen kindergartens in the slums, as well as one in Ranong for sea-gypsy children, among many other projects. Contact the centre for information about donations, sponsoring and volunteering. Father Joe's books, *Welcome to the Bangkok Slaughterhouse* and *The Open Gate of Mercy*, give eye-opening insights into this often invisible side of Thai life.
**Koh Yao Children's Community Center** Ko Yao Noi ⓦ koyao-ccc. com. Aims to improve the English-language and lifelong learning skills of islanders on Ko Yao Noi. Visitors, volunteers and donations welcome. See page 342.

---

### ADDRESSES IN THAILAND

Thai **addresses** can be immensely confusing, mainly because property is often numbered twice, first to show which real-estate lot it stands in, and then to distinguish where it is on that lot. Thus 154/7–10 Thanon Rajdamnoen means the building is on lot 154 and occupies numbers 7–10. However, neither of these numbers will necessarily help you to find a particular building on a long street; when asking for directions or talking to taxi drivers, it's best to be able to quote a nearby temple, big hotel or other landmark. There's an additional idiosyncrasy in the way Thai roads are sometimes named: in large cities a minor road running off a major road is often numbered as a soi ("lane" or "alley", though it may be a sizeable thoroughfare), rather than given its own street name. Thanon Sukhumvit, for example – Bangkok's longest – has minor roads numbered Soi 1 to Soi 103, with odd numbers on one side of the road and even on the other; so a Thanon Sukhumvit address could read something like 27/9–11 Soi 15, Thanon Sukhumvit, which would mean the property occupies numbers 9–11 on lot 27 on minor road number 15 running off Thanon Sukhumvit.

**The Students' Education Trust (SET)** ⓦ thaistudentcharity.org. High-school and further education in Thailand is a luxury that the poorest kids cannot afford so many are sent to live in temples instead. The SET helps such kids pursue their education and escape from the poverty trap. Some of their stories are told in *Little Angels: The Real-Life Stories of Twelve Thai Novice Monks*. SET welcomes donations.

**Thai Child Development Foundation** Pha To ⓦ thaichilddevelopment.org. This small Thai-Dutch-run village project near Ranong helps educate and look after needy local children. The foundation welcomes donations, takes on volunteers, and has an ecotourism arm.

**Tour de Thailand** ⓦ tourdethailand.com. Join a long-distance cycle tour through one of Thailand's five regions and raise money for Hua Hin Rotary Club's local projects and End Polio Now.

# Climate

There are three main **seasons** in most of Thailand: rainy, caused by the southwest monsoon (the least predictable, but roughly May–Oct); cool (Nov–Feb; felt most distinctly in the far north, but hardly at all in the south); and hot (March–May). The Gulf coast's climate is slightly different: it suffers less from the southwest monsoon, but is then hit by the northeast monsoon, making November its rainiest month.

# Costs

Thailand can be a very cheap place to travel. At the bottom of the scale, you can manage on a **budget** of about B650 (£15/US$20) per day if you're willing to opt for basic accommodation, eat, drink and travel as the locals do, and stay away from the more expensive resorts like Phuket, Ko Samui and Ko Phi Phi – and

you'd have to work hard to stick to this daily allowance in Bangkok. On this budget, you'll be spending around B200–250 for a dorm or shared room (more for a single room), around B200 on three meals (eating mainly at night markets and simple noodle shops, and eschewing beer), and the rest on travel (sticking to the cheaper buses and third-class trains where possible) and incidentals. With extras like air conditioning in rooms, taking the various forms of taxi rather than buses or shared songthaews for cross-town journeys, and a meal and beer in a more touristy restaurant, a day's outlay would be at least B1000 (£23/US$32). Staying in well-equipped, mid-range hotels and eating in more upmarket restaurants, you should be able to live comfortably for around B2000 a day (£46/US$64).

Travellers soon get so used to the low cost of living in Thailand that they start **bargaining** at every available opportunity, much as Thai people do. Although it's expected practice for a lot of commercial transactions, particularly at markets and when hiring tuk-tuks and unmetered taxis (though not in supermarkets or department stores), bargaining is a delicate art that requires humour, tact and patience. If your price is way out of line, the vendor's vehement refusal should be enough to make you increase your offer: never forget that the few pennies or cents you're making such a fuss over will go a lot further in a Thai person's hands than in your own.

It's rare that foreigners can bargain a price down as low as a Thai could, anyway, while **two-tier pricing** has been made official at government-run sights, as a kind of informal tourist tax: at national parks, for example, foreigners pay up to B500 entry while Thais pay just B20–100. A number of privately owned tourist attractions follow a similar two-tier system,

## AVERAGE MAXIMUM DAILY TEMPERATURES AND MONTHLY RAINFALL

|  | Jan | Feb | Mar | Apr | May | Jun | Jul | Aug | Sep | Oct | Nov | Dec |
|---|---|---|---|---|---|---|---|---|---|---|---|---|
| **BANGKOK** | | | | | | | | | | | | |
| Max temp (°C) | 26 | 28 | 29 | 30 | 30 | 29 | 29 | 28 | 28 | 28 | 27 | 26 |
| Rainfall (mm) | 11 | 28 | 31 | 72 | 190 | 152 | 158 | 187 | 320 | 231 | 57 | 9 |
| **PATTAYA** | | | | | | | | | | | | |
| Max temp (°C) | 26 | 28 | 29 | 30 | 30 | 29 | 29 | 28 | 28 | 28 | 27 | 26 |
| Rainfall (mm) | 12 | 23 | 41 | 79 | 165 | 120 | 166 | 166 | 302 | 229 | 66 | 10 |
| **KO SAMUI** | | | | | | | | | | | | |
| Max temp (°C) | 26 | 26 | 28 | 29 | 29 | 28 | 28 | 28 | 28 | 27 | 26 | 25 |
| Rainfall (mm) | 38 | 8 | 12 | 63 | 186 | 113 | 143 | 123 | 209 | 260 | 302 | 98 |
| **PHUKET** | | | | | | | | | | | | |
| Max temp (°C) | 27 | 28 | 28 | 29 | 28 | 28 | 28 | 28 | 27 | 27 | 27 | 27 |
| Rainfall (mm) | 35 | 31 | 39 | 163 | 348 | 213 | 263 | 263 | 419 | 305 | 207 | 52 |

---

### REPORTING A CRIME OR EMERGENCY

In the event of a crime, contact the English-speaking **tourist police**, who maintain a 24-hour toll-free nationwide line (📞1155) and have offices in the main tourist centres; getting in touch with the tourist police first is invariably more efficient than directly contacting the local police. The tourist police's job is to offer advice and tell you what to do next, but they do not file crime reports, which must be done at the nearest police station. In a medical emergency, call either the tourist police or the nationwide ambulance hotline (📞1669), which is likely to be quicker than calling an individual hospital for an ambulance.

---

posting an inflated price in English for foreigners and a lower price in Thai for locals.

Shoppers who are departing via an international airport can save some money by claiming a **Value Added Tax refund** (🌐vrtweb.rd.go.th/index.php/en), though it's a bit of a palaver for seven percent (the current rate of VAT, though this may increase to ten percent). The total amount of your purchases from participating shops needs to be at least B2000 per person. You'll need to show your passport and fill in an application form (to which original tax invoices need to be attached) at the shop. At the relevant airport, you'll need to show your form and purchases to customs officers before checking in, then make your claim from VAT refund officers – from which fees of at least B60 are deducted.

## Crime and personal safety

As long as you keep your wits about you, you shouldn't encounter much trouble in Thailand. **Pickpocketing** and **bag-snatching** are two of the main problems – not surprising considering that a huge percentage of the local population scrape by on under US$10 per day – but the most common cause for concern is the number of con-artists who dupe gullible tourists into parting with their cash. There are various Thai laws that tourists need to be aware of, particularly regarding passports, the age of consent and smoking in public.

### Theft

To **prevent theft**, most travellers prefer to carry their valuables with them at all times, but it's often possible to use a safe in a hotel or a locker in a guesthouse – the safest are those that require your own padlock, as there are occasional reports of valuables being stolen by guesthouse staff. **Padlock your luggage** when leaving it in storage or taking it on public transport. Padlocks also come in handy as extra security on your room, particularly on the doors of beachfront bamboo huts.

Theft from some long-distance **buses** is also a problem, with the majority of reported incidents taking place on the temptingly cheap overnight buses run by private companies direct from Bangkok's Thanon Khao San (as opposed to those that depart from the government bus stations) to destinations such as the southern beach resorts. The best solution is to go direct from the bus stations.

### Personal safety

On any bus, private or government, and on any train journey, never keep anything of value in luggage that is stored out of your sight and be wary of accepting food and drink from fellow passengers as it may be drugged. This might sound paranoid, but there have been enough **drug-muggings** for TAT to publish a specific warning about the problem. Drinks can also be spiked in bars and clubs; at full moon parties on Ko Pha Ngan this has led to sexual assaults against farang women, while prostitutes sometimes spike drinks so they can steal from their victim's room.

**Violent crime** against tourists is not common, but it does occur, and there have been several serious attacks on travellers in recent years, notably on Ko Pha Ngan and Ko Tao. However, bearing in mind that thirty million foreigners visit Thailand every year, the statistical likelihood of becoming a victim is extremely small. **Obvious precautions** for travellers of either sex include locking accessible windows and doors – preferably with your own padlock (doors in many of the simpler guesthouses and beach bungalows are designed for this) – and taking care at night, especially around bars. You should not risk jumping into an unlicensed taxi at the airport in Bangkok at any time of day: there have been some very violent robberies in these, so take the well-marked licensed, metered taxis instead.

Among hazards to watch out for in the natural world, **riptides** claim a number of tourist lives every year, particularly off Phuket, Ko Chang (Trat), Hua Hin, Cha-am, Rayong, Pattaya and the Ko Samui archipelago during stormy periods of the monsoon season, so always pay attention to warning signs and red flags, and always ask locally if unsure. **Jellyfish** can be a problem on any coast, especially just after a storm (see page 62).

## GOVERNMENTAL TRAVEL ADVISORIES

**Australian Department of Foreign Affairs** ⓦ smartraveller.gov.au.
**British Foreign & Commonwealth Office** ⓦ gov.uk/foreign-travel-advice/thailand.
**Canadian Department of Foreign Affairs** ⓦ travel.gc.ca.
**Irish Department of Foreign Affairs** ⓦ dfa.ie/travel.
**New Zealand Ministry of Foreign Affairs** ⓦ safetravel.govt.nz.
**South African Department of Foreign Affairs** ⓦ dirco.gov.za.
**US State Department** ⓦ travel.state.gov.

Unfortunately, it is also necessary for female tourists to think twice about spending time alone with a **monk**, as not all men of the cloth uphold the Buddhist precepts and there have been rapes and murders committed by men wearing the saffron robes of the monkhood.

Though unpalatable and distressing, Thailand's high-profile **sex industry** is relatively unthreatening for Western women, with its energy focused exclusively on farang men; it's also quite easily avoided, being contained within certain pockets of the cities and beach resorts.

As for **harassment** from men, it's hard to generalize, but most Western women find it less of a problem in Thailand than they do back home. Outside the main tourist spots, you're more likely to be of interest as a foreigner rather than a woman and, if travelling alone, as an object of concern rather than of sexual aggression.

### Regional issues

Because of the **violence in the deep south**, all Western governments are currently advising against travel to or through the border provinces of Songkhla, Yala, Pattani and Narathiwat, unless essential (see page 396). For up-to-the-minute advice on current political trouble-spots, consult your government's travel advisory (see above).

### Scams

Despite the best efforts of guidebook writers, TAT and the Thai tourist police, countless travellers to Thailand get scammed every year. Nearly all **scams** are easily avoided if you're on your guard against anyone who makes an unnatural effort to befriend you. We have outlined the main scams in the relevant sections of this guide, but con-artists are nothing if not creative, so if in doubt walk away at the earliest opportunity. The worst areas for scammers are the busy tourist centres, including many parts of Bangkok and the main beach resorts.

Many **tuk-tuk drivers** earn most of their living through securing **commissions** from tourist-oriented shops; this is especially true in Bangkok, where they will do their damnedest to get you to go to a gem shop (see page 144). The most common tactic is for drivers to pretend that the Grand Palace or other major sight you intended to visit is closed for the day (see page 75), and to then offer to take you on a round-city tour instead, perhaps even for free. The tour will invariably include a visit to a gem shop. The easiest way to avoid all this is to take a **metered taxi**; if you're fixed on taking a tuk-tuk, ignore any tuk-tuk that is parked up or loitering and be firm about where you want to go.

Self-styled **tourist guides**, **touts** and anyone else who might introduce themselves as **students** or **business people** and offer to take you somewhere of interest, or invite you to meet their family, are often the first piece of bait in a well-honed chain of con-artists. If you bite, chances are you'll end up either at a gem shop or in a gambling den, or, at best, at a tour operator or hotel that you had not planned to patronize. This is not to say that you should never accept an invitation from a local person, but be extremely wary of doing so following a street encounter in Bangkok or the resorts. Tourist guides' ID cards are easily faked.

For many of these characters, the goal is to get you inside a dodgy **gem shop**, nearly all of which are located in Bangkok (see page 144), but the bottom line is that if you are not experienced at buying and trading in valuable gems you will definitely be ripped off, possibly even to the tune of several thousand dollars.

A less common but potentially more frightening scam involves a similar cast of warm-up artists leading tourists into a **gambling** game. The scammers invite their victim home on an innocent-sounding pretext, get out a pack of cards, and then set about fleecing the incomer in any number of subtle or unsubtle ways. Often this can be especially scary as the venue is likely to be far from hotels or recognizable landmarks, and there have been stories of visitors being forced to withdraw large amounts of money from ATMs. You're unlikely to get any sympathy from police, as gambling is **illegal** in Thailand.

An increasing number of travel agents in tourist centres all over the country are trying to pass themselves off as official government tourist information offices, displaying nothing but "**Tourist Infor-mation**" on their shop signs or calling themselves names like "TAD" (note that the actual TAT, the Tourism Authority of Thailand, does not book hotels or sell any kind of travel ticket). Fakers like this are more likely to sell you tickets for services that turn out to be sub-standard or even not to exist. A word of warning also about **jet skis**: operators, who usually ask for a passport as guarantee, will often try to charge renters exorbitant amounts of money for any minor damage they claim to find on return.

### Age restrictions and other laws

Thai law requires that tourists **carry their original passports** at all times, though sometimes it's more practical to carry a photocopy and keep the original locked in a safety deposit. The **age of consent** is 15, but the law allows anyone under the age of 18, or their parents, to file charges in retrospect even if they consented to sex at the time. It is against the law to have sex with a prostitute who is under 18. It is illegal for **under-18s** to buy cigarettes or to drive and you must be 20 or over to **buy alcohol** or be allowed into a **bar or club** (ID checks are sometimes enforced in Bangkok). It is illegal for anyone to **gamble** in Thailand (though many do).

**Smoking** in public is widely prohibited. The ban covers all public buildings (including restaurants, bars and clubs), trains, buses, planes and popular beaches, and can even be extended to parks and the street; violators may be subject to a B2000–5000 fine. Possession of e-cigarettes is currently illegal, and several foreign nationals have been arrested. Dropping cigarette butts, **littering** and spitting in public places can also earn you a B2000–5000 fine. There are fines for **overstaying your visa** (see page 60), **working without a permit**, **not wearing a motorcycle helmet** and violating other **traffic laws**.

### Drugs

**Drug-smuggling** carries a maximum penalty in Thailand of death, and **dealing drugs** will get you anything from four years to life in a Thai prison; penalties depend on the drug and the amount involved. Travellers caught with even the smallest amount of drugs at airports and international borders are prosecuted for trafficking, and no one charged with trafficking offences gets bail. Heroin, amphet-amines, LSD and ecstasy are classed as Category 1 drugs and carry the most severe penalties: even **possession** of Category 1 drugs for personal use can result in a **life sentence**. Away from international borders, most foreigners arrested in possession of small amounts of cannabis are released on bail, then

fined and deported, but the law is complex and prison sentences are possible.

Despite occasional royal pardons, don't expect special treatment as a farang: you only need to read one of the first-hand accounts by foreign former prisoners (see page 437) or read the blogs at ⓦ thaiprisonlife.com to get the picture. The **police** actively look for tourists doing drugs, reportedly searching people regularly and randomly on Thanon Khao San, for example. They have the power to order a urine test if they have reasonable grounds for suspicion, and even a positive result for marijuana consumption could lead to a year's imprisonment. Be wary also of **being shopped** by a farang or local dealer keen to earn a financial reward for a successful bust (there are setups at the Ko Pha Ngan full moon parties, for example), or having substances slipped into your luggage (simple enough to perpetrate unless all fastenings are secured with padlocks).

**If you are arrested**, ask for your embassy to be contacted immediately (see page 144), which is your right under Thai law, and embassy staff will talk you through procedures; the website of the British government even includes a Prisoner Pack for Thailand (ⓦ gov.uk/government/publications/thailand-prisoner-pack). The British charity Prisoners Abroad (ⓦ prisonersabroad.org.uk) carries lots of useful information on its website, and may be able to offer direct support to a British citizen (and their family) facing imprisonment in a Thai jail.

## Customs regulations

The **duty-free** allowance on entry to Thailand is 200 cigarettes (or 250g of tobacco or cigars) and a litre of spirits or wine (visit ⓦ en.customs.go.th for more information).

To **export antiques** or newly cast **Buddha images** from Thailand, you need to have a licence granted by the Fine Arts Department (the export of religious antiques, especially Buddha images, is forbidden). Licences can be obtained for example through the Office of Archeology and National Museums, 81/1 Thanon Si Ayutthaya (near the National Library), Bangkok (☎ 02 628 5032). Applications take at least three working days in Bangkok, generally more in the provinces, and need to be accompanied by the object itself, some evidence of its rightful possession, two postcard-sized colour photos of it, taken face-on and against a white background, and photocopies of the applicant's passport; furthermore, if the object is a Buddha image, the passport photocopies need to be certified by your embassy in Bangkok. Some antiques shops can organize all this for you.

# Electricity

Mains **electricity** is supplied at 220 volts AC and is available at all but the most remote villages and basic beach huts. Where electricity is supplied by generators and/or solar power, for example on the smaller, less populated islands, it is often rationed to evenings only. If you're packing phone and camera chargers, a hair dryer, laptop or other appliance, you'll need to take a set of travel-plug adapters with you as several plug types are commonly in use, most usually with two round pins, but also with two flat-blade pins or three round pins.

# Entry requirements

There are three main entry categories for visitors to Thailand; for all of them, your passport should be valid for at least six months. As visa requirements are subject to frequent change, you should always consult before departure a Thai embassy or consulate, a reliable travel agent, or the Thai Ministry of Foreign Affairs' website at ⓦmfa.go.th. For further, unofficial but usually reliable, details on all visa matters – especially as the rules are not consistently enforced across all Thai border checkpoints and immigration offices – go to the moderated forums on ⓦthaivisa.com.

Most Western passport holders (that includes citizens of the UK, Ireland, the US, Canada, Australia, New Zealand and South Africa) are allowed to enter the country for thirty days without having to apply for a visa – officially termed the **tourist visa exemption** (not to be confused with "visas on arrival", another category of entry that's not available to citizens of the countries listed above); the period of stay will be stamped into your passport by immigration officials upon entry. You're supposed to be able to show proof of means of living while in the country (B10,000 per person, B20,000 per family), and you are also required to show proof of tickets to leave Thailand again within the allotted time, and, in theory, you may be put back on the next plane or sent back to get a sixty-day tourist visa from the nearest Thai embassy. However, the Thai immigration authorities do not appear to be consistent about checking these requirements (it seems to be more likely at land borders, especially Aranyaprathet). However, if you have a one-way air ticket to Thailand and no evidence of onward travel arrangements, it's best to buy a tourist visa in advance: many airlines will stop you boarding the plane without one, as they would be liable for flying you back to your point of origin if you did happen to be stopped.

If you're fairly certain you may want to stay longer than thirty days, then from the outset you should apply for a **sixty-day tourist visa** from a Thai embassy or consulate, accompanying your application – which generally takes several days to process – with your passport and one or two photos. The sixty-day visa currently costs B1000 or rough equivalent; multiple-entry versions are available, with more stringent requirements. Ordinary tourist visas are valid for three months; ie you must enter Thailand within three months of the visa being issued by the Thai embassy or consulate. Visa application forms can be downloaded from, for example, the Thai Ministry of Foreign Affairs' website.

Thai embassies also consider applications for **ninety-day non-immigrant visas** (B2000 or rough equivalent for single entry, B5000 for multiple-entry) as long as you can offer a reason for your visit, such as study, business or visiting family (there are different categories of non-immigrant visa for which different levels of proof are needed). As it can be a hassle to organize a ninety-day visa, it's generally easier to apply for a thirty-day extension to your sixty-day visa once inside Thai borders.

It's not a good idea to **overstay** your visa limits. Once you're at the airport or the border, you'll have to pay a fine of B500 per day before you can leave Thailand. More importantly, however, if you're in the country with an expired visa and you get involved with police or immigration officials for any reason, however trivial, they are obliged to take you to court, possibly imprison you, and deport you.

## Extensions, border runs and re-entry permits

Tourist visa exemptions, as well as sixty-day tourist visas, can be **extended** within Thailand for a further thirty days, at the discretion of immigration officials; extensions cost B1900 and are issued over the counter at immigration offices (*kaan khao muang* or *taw maw*; ☎1178 for information, ⓦimmigration.go.th) in nearly every provincial capital. You'll need to bring one or two photos, one or two photocopies of the main pages of your passport including your Thai departure card, arrival stamp and visa; you may be asked for proof of tickets to leave Thailand again within the proposed time and evidence of where you're staying, and it's possible that you'll be asked for proof of means of living while in Thailand. Many Khao San tour agents offer to get your visa extension for you, but beware: some are reportedly faking the stamps, which could get you into serious trouble. The Thai immigration authorities have recently clamped down on foreigners who stay in Thailand long-term by doing back-to-back **border runs** for tourist visa exemptions; however, it's still possible for ordinary travellers to get one new thirty-day tourist visa exemption by hopping **across the border** into a neighbouring country and back (the limit seems to be two tourist visa exemptions using a land border within a year). Immigration offices also issue **re-entry permits** (B1000 single re-entry, B3800 multiple) if you want to leave the country and come back again while maintaining the validity of your existing visa.

## THAI EMBASSIES AND CONSULATES ABROAD

For a full listing of Thai diplomatic missions abroad, consult the Thai Ministry of Foreign Affairs' website at ⓦ mfa.go.th; its other site, ⓦ thaiembassy.org, has links to the websites of most of the offices below.

**Australia** 111 Empire Circuit, Yarralumla, Canberra ACT 2600 ☎ 02 6206 0100; plus consulate at 131 Macquarie St, Sydney, NSW 2000 ☎ 02 9241 2542–3.

**Cambodia** 196 Preah Norodom Blvd, Sangkat Tonle Bassac, Khan Chamcar Mon, Phnom Penh ☎ 023 726306–8.

**Canada** 180 Island Park Drive, Ottawa, ON, K1Y 0A2 ☎ 613 722 4444; plus consulate at 1040 Burrard St, Vancouver, BC, V6Z 2R9 ☎ 604 687 1143.

**Laos** Vientiane: embassy at Avenue Kaysone Phomvihane, Saysettha District ☎ 021 214581–2, consular section at Unit 15 Bourichane Rd, Ban Phone Si Nuan, Muang Si Sattanak ☎ 021 453916; plus consulate at Khanthabouly District, Savannakhet Province, PO Box 513 ☎ 041 212373.

**Malaysia** 206 Jalan Ampang, 50450 Kuala Lumpur ☎ 03 2148 8222; plus consulates at 4426 Jalan Pengkalan Chepa, 15400 Kota Bharu ☎ 09 748 2545; and 1 Jalan Tunku Abdul Rahman, 10350 Penang ☎ 04 226 9484.

**Myanmar** 94 Pyay Rd, Dagon Township, Rangoon ☎ 01 226721.

**New Zealand** 110 Molesworth St, Thorndon, Wellington ☎ 04 476 8616.

**Singapore** 370 Orchard Rd, Singapore 238870 ☎ 6737 2158.

**South Africa** 248 Pretorius/Hill St, Arcadia, Pretoria 0083 ☎ 012 342 5470.

**UK and Ireland** 29–30 Queens Gate, London SW7 5JB ☎ 020 7589 2944. In Ireland, visa applications by post can be sent to the consulate in Dublin (ⓦ thaiconsulateireland.com).

**US** 1024 Wisconsin Ave NW, Suite 401, Washington, DC 20007 ☎ 202 944 3600; plus consulates at 700 North Rush St, Chicago, IL 60611 ☎ 312 664 3129; 611 North Larchmont Blvd, 2nd Floor, Los Angeles, CA 90004 ☎ 323 962 9574; and 351 E 52nd St, New York, NY 10022 ☎ 212 754 1770.

**Vietnam** 26 Phan Boi Chau St, Hanoi ☎ 04 3823 5092–4; plus consulate at 77 Tran Quoc Thao St, District 3, Ho Chi Minh City ☎ 08 3932 7637–8.

## Health

Although Thailand's climate, wildlife and cuisine present Western travellers with fewer health worries than in many Asian destinations, it's as well to know in advance what the risks might be, and what preventive or curative measures you should take.

For a start, there's no need to bring huge supplies of non-prescription medicines with you, as Thai **pharmacies** (*raan khai yaa*; typically open daily 8.30am–8pm) are well stocked with local and international branded medicaments, and they are generally much less expensive than at home. Nearly all pharmacies are run by trained English-speaking pharmacists, who are usually the best people to talk to if your symptoms aren't acute enough to warrant seeing a doctor. The British pharmacy chain, Boots, now has branches in many big cities (see ⓦ th.boots.com for locations). These are the best place to stock up on some Western products such as **tampons** (which Thai women do not use).

**Hospital** (*rong phayabaan*) cleanliness and efficiency vary, but generally hygiene and health-care standards are good and the ratio of medical staff to patients is considerably higher than in most parts of the West. As with head pharmacists, doctors speak English. Several Bangkok hospitals are highly regarded (see page 145), and all provincial capitals have at least one hospital: if you need to get to one, ask at your accommodation for advice on, and possibly transport to, the nearest or most suitable. For emergency numbers in Thailand, see page 57. In the event of a major health crisis, get someone to contact your embassy (see page 144) and insurance company – it may be best to get yourself transported to Bangkok or even home.

### Inoculations

There are no compulsory **inoculation** requirements for people travelling to Thailand from the West, but you should consult a doctor or other health professional, preferably at least four weeks in advance of your trip, for the latest information on recommended immunizations. In addition to making sure that your recommended immunizations for life in your home country are up to date, most doctors strongly advise vaccinations or boosters against tetanus, diphtheria, hepatitis A and, in many cases, typhoid, and in some cases they might also recommend protecting yourself against Japanese encephalitis, rabies and hepatitis B. There is currently no vaccine against malaria. If you forget to have all your inoculations before leaving home, or don't leave yourself sufficient time, you can get them in Bangkok at, for example, the Thai Red Cross Society's Queen Saovabha Institute or Global Doctor (see page 145).

### Mosquito-borne diseases

**Mosquitoes** in Thailand can spread not only malaria, but also diseases such as dengue fever and the very similar chikungunya fever, especially during the rainy season. The main message, therefore, is to **avoid being bitten** by mosquitoes. You should smother yourself and your clothes in **mosquito repellent** containing the chemical compound DEET, reapplying regularly (shops, guesthouses and department stores all over Thailand stock it, but if you want the highest-strength repellent, or convenient roll-ons or sprays, do your shopping before you leave home, or at a branch of Boots in Thailand). DEET is strong stuff, and if you have sensitive skin, a natural alternative is citronella (available in the UK as Mosi-guard), made from a blend of eucalyptus oils; the Thai version is made with lemon grass.

At night you should sleep either under a **mosquito net** sprayed with DEET or in a bedroom with **mosquito screens** across the windows (or in an enclosed a/c room). Accommodation in tourist spots nearly always provides screens or a net (check both for holes), but if you're planning to go way off the beaten track or want the security of having your own mosquito net just in case, wait until you get to Bangkok to buy one, where department stores sell them for much less than you'd pay in the West. Plug-in insecticide vaporizers, insect room sprays and mosquito coils – also widely available in Thailand – help keep the insects at bay; electronic "buzzers" are useless. If you are bitten, applying locally made yellow oil (see page 174) is effective at reducing the itch.

### Malaria

Thailand is **malarial**, with the disease being carried by mosquitoes that bite from dusk to dawn, but the risks involved vary across the country.

There is a significant risk of malaria, mainly in rural and forested areas, in a narrow strip along the **borders with Cambodia** (excluding Ko Chang), **Laos** and **Myanmar** (excluding, for example, resorts and road and rail routes along the Gulf coast). Discuss with your travel health adviser which anti-malarial drugs are currently likely to be effective in these areas, as prophylaxis advice can change from year to year.

Elsewhere in Thailand the risk of malaria is considered to be so low that anti-malarial tablets are not advised.

The **signs of malaria** are often similar to flu, but are very variable. The incubation period for malignant malaria, which can be fatal, is usually 7–28 days, but it can take up to a year for symptoms of the benign form to occur. The most important symptom is a raised temperature of at least 38°C beginning a week or more after the first potential exposure to malaria: if you suspect anything, go to a hospital or clinic immediately.

### Dengue fever

**Dengue fever**, a debilitating and occasionally fatal viral disease that is particularly prevalent during and just after the rainy season, is on the increase throughout tropical Asia, and is endemic to many areas of Thailand, with around 200,000 reported cases a year. Unlike malaria, dengue fever is spread by mosquitoes that can bite during daylight hours, so you should also use mosquito repellent during the day. Symptoms may include fever, headaches, fierce joint and muscle pain ("breakbone fever" is another name for dengue), and possibly a rash, and usually develop between five and eight days after being bitten.

If you think you may have contracted the disease, you should see a doctor: the treatment is lots of rest, liquids and paracetamol (or any other acetaminophen painkiller; not aspirin or ibuprofen), and more serious cases may require hospitalization.

### Rabies

**Rabies** is widespread in Thailand, mainly carried by dogs (between four and seven percent of stray dogs in Bangkok are reported to be rabid), but also cats and monkeys. It is transmitted by bites, scratches or even occasionally licks. Dogs are everywhere in Thailand, and even if kept as pets they're often not very well cared for; hopefully their mangy appearance will discourage the urge to pat them, as you should steer well clear of them. Rabies is invariably fatal if the patient waits until symptoms begin, though modern vaccines and treatments are very effective and deaths are rare. The important thing is, if you are bitten, licked or scratched by an animal, to vigorously clean the wound with soap and disinfect it, preferably with something containing iodine, and to seek medical advice regarding treatment right away.

### Other bites and stings

Thailand's seas are home to a few dangerous creatures that you should look out for, notably **jellyfish**, which tend to be washed towards the beach by rough seas during the monsoon season but can appear at any time of year. All manner of stinging and non-stinging jellyfish can be found in Thailand – as a general rule, those with the longest tentacles tend to have the worst stings – but reports of serious incidents are uncommon; ask around at your resort or at a local dive shop to see if there have been any sightings of venomous varieties. You also need to be wary of venomous **sea snakes**, **sea urchins** and a couple of less conspicuous species – **stingrays**, which often lie buried in the sand, and **stonefish**, whose potentially lethal venomous spikes are easily stepped on because the fish look like stones and lie motionless on the sea bed.

If **stung or bitten**, you should always seek medical advice as soon as possible, but there are a few ways of alleviating the pain or administering your own first aid in the meantime. If you're stung by a jellyfish, wash the affected area with salt water (not fresh water) and, if possible, with vinegar (failing that, ammonia, citrus fruit juice or even urine may do the trick), and try to remove the fragments of tentacles from the skin with a gloved hand, forceps, thick cloth or credit card. The best way to minimize the risk of stepping on the toxic spines of sea urchins, stingrays and stonefish is to wear thick-soled shoes, though these cannot provide total protection; sea urchin spikes should be removed after softening the skin with ointment, though some people recommend applying urine to help dissolve the spines; for stingray and stonefish stings, alleviate the pain by immersing the wound in hot water while awaiting help.

In the case of a **venomous snake bite**, don't try sucking out the venom or applying a tourniquet: wrap up and immobilize the bitten limb and try to stay still and remain calm until medical help arrives; all provincial hospitals in Thailand carry supplies of antivenins.

Some of Thailand's beaches are plagued by **sandflies**, tiny, barely visible midges whose bites can trigger an allergic response, leaving big red weals and an unbearable itch, and possible infection if scratched too vigorously. Many islanders say that slathering yourself in (widely available) coconut oil is the best deterrent as sandflies apparently don't like the smell. Applying locally made camphor-based yellow oil (see page 174) quells the itch, but you may need to resort to antihistamines for the inflammation. **Leeches** aren't dangerous but can be a bother when walking in forested areas, especially during and just after the rainy season. The most effective way to get leeches off your skin is to burn them with a lighted cigarette, or douse them in salt; oily suntan lotion or insect repellent sometimes makes them lose their grip and fall off.

## Worms and flukes

**Worms** can be picked up through the soles of your feet, so avoid going barefoot. They can also be ingested by eating undercooked meat, and liver **flukes** by eating raw or undercooked freshwater fish. Worms which cause schistosomiasis (bilharziasis) by attaching themselves to your bladder or intestines can be found in freshwater rivers and lakes. The risk of contracting this disease is low, but you should avoid swimming in most fresh-water lakes.

## Digestive problems

By far the most common travellers' complaint in Thailand, **digestive troubles** are often caused by contaminated food and water, or sometimes just by an overdose of unfamiliar foodstuffs (see pages 39 and 43).

Stomach trouble usually manifests itself as simple **diarrhoea**, which should clear up without medical treatment within three to seven days and is best combated by drinking lots of fluids. If this doesn't work, you're in danger of getting **dehydrated** and should take some kind of rehydration solution, either a commercial sachet of ORS (oral rehydration solution), sold in all Thai pharmacies, or a do-it-yourself version, which can be made by adding a handful of sugar and a pinch of salt to every litre of boiled or bottled water (soft drinks are not a viable alternative). If you can eat, avoid fatty foods.

**Anti-diarrhoeal agents** such as Imodium are useful for blocking you up on long bus journeys, but only attack the symptoms and may prolong infections; an antibiotic such as ciprofloxacin, however, can often reduce a typical attack of traveller's diarrhoea to one day. If the diarrhoea persists for a week or more, or if you have blood or mucus in your stools, or an accompanying fever, go to a doctor or hospital.

### HIV and AIDS

**HIV** infection is widespread in Thailand, primarily because of the sex trade (see page 112). **Condoms** (*meechai*) are sold in pharmacies, convenience stores, department stores, hairdressers and even street markets. Due to rigorous screening methods, Thailand's medical blood supply is now considered safe from HIV/AIDS infection.

## MEDICAL RESOURCES

**Canadian Society for International Health** ☎ 613 241 5785, ⓦ csih.org. Extensive list of travel health centres.
**CDC** ☎ 800 232 4636, ⓦ cdc.gov/travel. Official US government travel health site.
**Hospital for Tropical Diseases Travel Clinic** UK ⓦ thehtd.org/travelclinic.aspx.
**International Society for Travel Medicine** US ☎ 404 373 8282, ⓦ istm.org. Has a full list of travel health clinics.
**MASTA (Medical Advisory Service for Travellers Abroad)** UK ⓦ masta-travel-health.com.
**The Travel Doctor** ⓦ traveldoctor.com.au. Lists travel clinics in Australia, New Zealand and South Africa.
**Tropical Medical Bureau** Ireland ☎ 01 271 5200, ⓦ tmb.ie.

## Insurance

Most visitors to Thailand will need to take out **specialist travel insurance**, though you should

## ROUGH GUIDES TRAVEL INSURANCE

Rough Guides has teamed up with WorldNomads.com to offer great travel insurance deals. Policies are available to residents of over 150 countries, with cover for a wide range of adventure sports, 24hr emergency assistance, high levels of medical and evacuation cover and a stream of travel safety information. Roughguides.com users can take advantage of their policies online 24/7, from anywhere in the world – even if you're already travelling. And since plans often change when you're on the road, you can extend your policy and even claim online. Roughguides.com users who buy travel insurance with WorldNomads.com can also leave a positive footprint and donate to a community development project. For more information, go to ⓦ roughguides.com/travel-insurance.

check exactly what's covered. Insurers will generally not cover travel in Songkhla, Yala, Pattani and Narathiwat provinces in the deep south, as Western governments are currently advising against going to these areas unless it's essential (see page 397). Policies generally also exclude so-called **dangerous sports** unless an extra premium is paid: in Thailand this can mean such things as scuba diving, whitewater rafting and trekking, sometimes even riding a motorbike.

## Internet

Internet access is now almost ubiquitous in Thailand. The country is covered by 3G and 4G networks and wi-fi is available free in nearly all guesthouses, bungalow resorts and hotels; in cheaper places, the signal may not stretch to all bedrooms. Loads of cafés, restaurants, bars and other locations across the country, especially in big towns and tourist resorts, also provide wi-fi free of charge. Given all this, internet cafés are inexorably disappearing. If you're travelling without a mobile device, ask at your accommodation for advice or keep an eye out for online games centres, favourite after-school haunts that are easily spotted from the piles of orange schoolboy pumps outside the door.

## Laundry

Guesthouses and cheap hotels all over the country offer low-cost, same- or next-day **laundry** services, though in luxury hotels it'll cost an arm and a leg. In some places you pay per item, in others you're charged by the kilo (generally around B30–50/kg); ironing is often included in the price.

## Left luggage

Most major train stations have **left-luggage** facilities (around B30–80 per item per day); at bus stations you can usually persuade someone official to look after

your stuff for a few hours. Many guesthouses and basic hotels also offer an inexpensive and usually reliable service, while upmarket hotels should be able to look after your luggage for free. There's also left luggage at Phuket and both Bangkok airports (B75–200/day).

## Living in Thailand

The most common source of **employment** in Thailand is **teaching English**, and Bangkok and Chiang Mai are the most fruitful places to look for jobs. You can search for openings at schools all over Thailand on ⓦ ajarn.com (*ajarn* means "teacher"), which also features extensive general advice on teaching and living in Thailand. Another useful resource is the excellent ⓦ thaivisa.com, whose scores of well-used forums focus on specific topics that range from employment in Thailand to legal issues and cultural and practical topics.

If you're a qualified **dive instructor**, you might be able to get seasonal work at one of the major resorts – in Phuket, Khao Lak and Ao Nang and on Ko Chang, Ko Phi Phi, Ko Lanta, Ko Samui and Ko Tao, for example. Guesthouse noticeboards occasionally carry adverts for more unusual jobs, such as playing extras in Thai movies. A tourist visa does not entitle you to work in Thailand, so, legally, you'll need to apply for a **work permit**.

### STUDY, WORK AND VOLUNTEER PROGRAMMES

In addition to the programmes listed below, voluntary opportunities with smaller grassroots projects (see page 55) are available.

**AFS Intercultural Programs** Australia ☎ 1300 131736, Canada ☎ 800 361 7248, NZ ☎ 0800 600 300, South Africa ☎ 11 431 0113, US ☎ AFS INFO; ⓦ afs.org. Intercultural exchange organization with programmes in over fifty countries.

**Council on International Educational Exchange (CIEE)** US ☎ 207 553 4000, ⓦ ciee.org. Leading NGO that organizes paid placements for a semester or more as English teachers in schools in Thailand, for US citizens, among other programmes.

**Phuket Has Been Good To Us** Ⓦ phukethasbeengoodtous.org. Non-profit foundation that offers voluntary and paid teaching positions on its English-language programmes and after-school clubs in Phuket schools, with the aim to improve kids' standards of English so they can get jobs in Phuket's tourist industry.

**Volunteer Teacher Thailand** Ⓦ volunteerteacherthailand.org. Continuing the good work begun by the thousands of volunteers who came to Khao Lak to help rebuild lives and homes following the 2004 tsunami, this non-profit organization teaches English to kids in and around Khao Lak to enhance their future prospects. Teaching experience is appreciated but not essential.

**Volunthai** Ⓦ volunthai.com. Voluntary organization that invites volunteers to teach English in rural schools; the minimal fees help to cover homestay accommodation.

## Thai language classes

The most popular place to **study Thai** is Bangkok, where there's plenty of choice, including private and group lessons for both tourists and expats; note, however, that some schools' main reason for existence is to provide educational visas for long-staying foreigners. The longest-running and best-regarded courses and private lessons are provided by AUA (American University Alumni; Ⓦ auathailand.org), which has outlets in Bangkok and Pattaya.

# LGBTQ Thailand

Buddhist tolerance and a national abhorrence of confrontation and victimization combine to make Thai society relatively tolerant of **homosexuality**, if not exactly positive about same-sex relationships. Most Thais are extremely private and discreet about being gay, generally pursuing a "don't ask, don't tell" understanding with their family. The majority of people are horrified by the idea of gay-bashing and generally regard it as unthinkable to spurn a child or relative for being gay.

Hardly any Thai celebrities are out, yet the predilections of several respected social, political and entertainment figures are widely known and accepted. There is no mention of homosexuality at all in Thai law, which means that the **age of consent** for gay sex is fifteen, the same as for heterosexuals. However, this also means that LGBTQ rights are not protected under Thai law.

Although excessively physical displays of affection are frowned upon for both heterosexuals and homosexuals, Western gay couples should get no hassle about being seen together in public – it's much more acceptable, and common, in fact, for friends of the same sex (gay or not) to walk hand-in-hand, than for heterosexual couples to do so.

**Katoey** (which can refer both to transgender women and to effeminate gay men, so often trans-lated as "ladyboys") are also a lot more visible in Thailand than in the West. You'll find transgender women doing ordinary jobs, even in small upcountry towns, and there are a number of *katoey* in the public eye too – including national volleyball stars and champion *muay thai* boxers. The government tourist office vigorously promotes the transgender cabarets in Pattaya, Phuket and Bangkok, all of which are advertised as family entertainment. *Katoey* also regularly appear as characters in soap operas, TV comedies and films, where they are depicted as stereotyped but harmless figures of fun. Richard Totman's *The Third Sex* offers an interesting insight into Thai *katoey*, their experiences in society and public attitudes towards them.

## The scene

Thailand's LGBTQ scene is mainly focused on **mainstream venues** like karaoke bars, restaurants, massage parlours, gyms, saunas and escort agencies. For the sake of discretion, gay venues are often inter-mingled with straight ones. Bangkok, Phuket and Pattaya have the biggest concentrations of farang-friendly gay bars and clubs. For a detailed, though slightly outdated, guide to the gay and lesbian scene throughout the country, see the *Utopia Guide to Thailand* by John Goss.

Thai **lesbians** generally eschew the word lesbian, which in Thailand is associated with male fantasies, instead referring to themselves as either *tom* (for tomboy) or *dee* (for lady). There are hardly any dedicated *tom-dee* venues in Thailand, but we've listed established ones where possible; unless otherwise specified, gay means male throughout this Guide.

The farang-oriented gay **sex industry** is a tiny but highly visible part of Thailand's gay scene. With its tawdry floor shows and host services, it bears a dispiriting resemblance to the straight sex trade, and is similarly most active in Bangkok, Pattaya and Patong (on Phuket). Like their female counterparts in the heterosexual fleshpots, many of the boys working in the gay sex bars that dominate these districts are underage; note that anyone caught having sex with a prostitute below the age of 18 faces imprisonment. A significant number of gay prostitutes are gay by economic necessity rather than by inclination. As with the straight sex scene, we do not list commercial gay sex bars in the Guide.

## INFORMATION AND CONTACTS FOR LGBTQ TRAVELLERS

**Bangkok Lesbian** Ⓦ bangkoklesbian.com. Organized by foreign lesbians living in Thailand, Bangkok Lesbian posts general info and listings of the capital's few lesbian-friendly hangouts on its website.

**The Gay Passport** Ⓦ thegaypassport.com. Regularly updated listings for the main tourist centres.

**Gay People in Thailand** Ⓦ thaivisa.com/forum/forum/27-gay-people-in-thailand. Popular forum for gay expats.

**Travel Gay Asia** Ⓦ travelgayasia.com/destination/gay-thailand. Active, frequently updated site that covers listings and events all over the country.

**Utopia** Ⓦ utopia-asia.com. Lists clubs, bars, restaurants, accommodation, tour operators, organizations and resources for gay men and lesbians.

## Mail

Overseas airmail usually takes around seven days from Bangkok, a little longer from the more isolated areas (it's worth asking at the post office about its express EMS services, which can cut this down to about three days and aren't prohibitively expensive). **Post offices** in Thailand (Ⓦ thailandpost.com) have recently been quite successfully privatized, and many now offer money-wiring facilities (in association with Western Union), parcel boxes, long-distance bus tickets, amulets, whitening cream, you name it. They're generally open Monday to Friday 8.30am to 4.30pm, Saturday 9am to noon; some close Monday to Friday noon to 1pm and may stay open until 6pm, and a few open 9am to noon on Sundays and public holidays. Almost all main post offices across the country operate a **poste restante** service and will hold letters for one to three months. Mail should be addressed: *Name* (family name underlined or capitalized), Poste Restante, GPO, *Town or City*, Thailand. It will be filed by surname, though it's always wise to check under your first and middle names as well. The smaller post offices pay scant attention to who takes what, but in the busier GPOs you need to show your passport. Post offices are the best places to buy **stamps**, though hotels and guesthouses often sell them too.

## Maps

For most major destinations, the **maps** in this book should be all you need, though you may want to supplement them with larger-scale, hard-copy maps of Bangkok and the whole country. Bangkok bookshops are the best source of these; where appropriate, detailed local maps and their stockists are recommended throughout the Guide. Decent maps of the whole country include the 1:1,500,000 versions produced by Nelles and Bartholomew, and the bilingual 1:550,000 *Thailand Deluxe Atlas* published

by ThinkNet (Ⓦ thinknet.co.th). **Trekking maps** are hard to come by, except in the most popular national parks where you can usually pick up a free handout showing the main trails.

## Money and banks

Thailand's unit of currency is the **baht** (abbreviated in this guide to "B"), divided into 100 satang – which are rarely seen these days. Coins come in B1 (silver), B2 (golden), B5 (silver) and B10 (mostly golden, encircled by a silver ring) denominations, notes in B20, B50, B100, B500 and B1000 denominations, inscribed with Western as well as Thai numerals, and generally increasing in size according to value.

At the time of writing, **exchange rates** were around B31 to US$1 and B44 to £1. A good site for current exchange rates is Ⓦ xe.com. Note that Thailand has no black market in foreign currency.

**Banking hours** are generally Monday to Friday from 8.30am to 3.30 or 4.30pm, though branches in out-of-town shopping centres and supermarkets are often open longer hours and at weekends. Streetside exchange kiosks run by the banks in the main tourist centres are always open till at least 5pm, sometimes 10pm, and upmarket hotels change money (at poor rates) 24 hours a day. The Suvarnabhumi Airport exchange counters also operate 24 hours, while exchange kiosks at overseas airports with flights to Thailand usually keep Thai currency. Note that Scottish and Northern Irish sterling notes may not be accepted in some places.

Visa and MasterCard **credit and debit cards** are accepted at upmarket guesthouses and hotels as well as in posh restaurants, department stores, tourist shops and travel agents; American Express is less widely accepted. It's common for smaller businesses to add on a surcharge of three percent, which amounts to the fee that Visa and Mastercard charge them for the privilege. Beware theft and forgery – try not to let the card out of your sight, and never leave cards in baggage storage. With a debit or credit card and personal identification number (PIN), you can also withdraw cash from hundreds of 24hr **ATMs** around the country. Almost every town now has at least one bank with an ATM outside that accepts overseas cards (all the banks marked on our maps throughout the Guide have ATMs), and there is a huge number of standalone ATMs, in shopping malls and on the streets, often outside supermarkets and post offices. However, Thai banks now make a charge of B150–200 per ATM withdrawal (on top of whatever your bank at home will be charging you); the same goes for getting a cash advance inside the bank. Check with your bank before you come to Thailand – some overseas banks will not pass on to customers this levy.

## Opening hours and public holidays

Most shops **open** long hours, usually Monday to Saturday or Sunday from about 8am to 8pm, while department stores and shopping malls operate daily from around 10am to 9pm. Private office hours are generally Monday to Friday 8am to 5pm, plus perhaps Saturday 8am to noon, though in tourist areas these hours are longer, with weekends worked like any other day. Government offices work Monday to Friday 8.30am to 4.30pm (often closing for lunch between noon and 1pm), and national museums tend to stick to these hours too, but some close on Mondays and Tuesdays rather than at weekends. Temples generally open their gates every day from dawn to dusk.

Many tourists only register **national holidays** because trains and buses suddenly get extra-ordinarily crowded, especially if the holiday is moved from a Saturday or a Sunday to a Monday or a Friday as a substitution day, thus creating a long weekend: although government offices shut on these days, most shops and tourist-oriented businesses carry on regardless, and TAT branches continue to hand out free maps. (Bank holidays vary slightly from the government office holidays given below: banks close on May 1 and July 1, but not for the Royal Ploughing Ceremony nor for Khao Pansa.) Some national holidays are celebrated with theatrical festivals (see page 47). The only time an inconvenient number of shops, restaurants and hotels do close is during **Chinese New Year**, which, though not marked as an official national holiday, brings many businesses to a standstill for several days in late January or February. You'll notice it particularly in the south, where many service industries are Chinese-managed.

Thais use both the Western Gregorian **calendar** and a Buddhist calendar – the Buddha is said to have died (or entered Nirvana) in the year 543 BC, so Thai dates start from that point: thus 2019 AD becomes 2562 BE (Buddhist Era).

### NATIONAL HOLIDAYS

**Jan 1** Western New Year's Day.
**Feb (day of full moon)** Makha Puja. Commemorates the Buddha preaching to a spontaneously assembled crowd of 1250.
**April 6** Chakri Day. The founding of the Chakri dynasty, the current royal family.
**April (usually 13–15)** Songkhran. Thai New Year.
**May 5** Coronation Day.
**May (early in the month)** Royal Ploughing Ceremony. Marks the traditional start of the rice-planting season.
**May (day of full moon)** Visakha Puja. The holiest of all Buddhist holidays, which celebrates the birth, enlightenment and death of the Buddha.
**July (day of full moon)** Asanha Puja. The anniversary of the Buddha's first sermon.
**July (day after Asanha Puja)** Khao Pansa. The start of the annual three-month Buddhist rains retreat, when new monks are ordained.
**July 28** King Vajiralongkorn's birthday.
**Aug 12** Queen Mother's birthday and Mothers' Day.
**Oct 23** Chulalongkorn Day. The anniversary of Rama V's death.
**Dec 5** The late King Bhumibol's birthday and Fathers' Day. Also now celebrated as National Day (instead of Constitution Day).
**Dec 10** Constitution Day.
**Dec 31** Western New Year's Eve.

## Phones

Most foreign **mobile-phone** networks have links with Thai networks but you need to check on roaming rates, which are often exorbitant, before you leave home. To get round this, most travellers purchase a Thai pre-paid SIM card (providers include AIS, DTAC and True Move) either for their mobile phone (*moe thoe*), for an old phone brought from home or for a new set cheaply purchased in Thailand (which can most easily be done in a shopping centre, especially Mah Boon Krong opposite Siam Square in Bangkok – see page 132). Available for as little as B50 (sometimes free at airports) and refillable at 7-Elevens around the country, Thai SIM cards offer very cheap calls, both domestically and internationally (especially if you use low-cost international prefixes such as 008, 009 or DTAC's 004, rather than the standard 001 or 007 prefixes). They also offer data packages (4G is now available in most places), very cheap texting and are, of course, free of charge for all incoming calls. A data package or wi-fi on your own mobile device will also allow you to make free or very cheap video or voice calls via Skype or a similar service.

When **dialling** any number in Thailand, you must now always preface it with what used to be the area code, even when dialling from the same area. Where we've given several line numbers – eg ☎02 431 1802–9 – you can substitute the last digit, 2, with any digit between 3 and 9.

Mobile-phone numbers in Thailand have ten digits, beginning "06", "08" or "09". Note, however, that Thais tend to change mobile-phone providers – and

## INTERNATIONAL DIALLING CODES

Calling from abroad, the international **country code** for Thailand is **66**, after which you leave off the initial zero of the Thai number.

Calling from Thailand, you'll need the relevant country code (see page 67 for information on prefixes):

**Australia** 61
**Canada** 1
**Ireland** 353
**New Zealand** 64
**South Africa** 27
**UK** 44
**US** 1

therefore numbers – comparatively frequently, in search of a better deal.

One final local idiosyncrasy: Thai phone books list people by their first name, not their family name.

## Photography

Most towns and all resorts have at least one **camera shop** where you will be able to get your digital pictures downloaded from your memory card for around B150; new cards can be bought in electronic shops in shopping centres or in dedicated IT malls such as Panthip Plaza in Bangkok or Chiang Mai.

## Time

Thailand is in the same time zone year-round, with no daylight savings period. It's five hours ahead of South Africa, seven hours ahead of GMT, twelve hours ahead of US Eastern Standard Time, three hours behind Australian Eastern Standard Time and five hours behind New Zealand Standard Time.

## Tipping

It is usual to **tip** hotel bellboys and porters B20–40, and to round up taxi fares to the nearest B10. Most guides, drivers, masseurs and waiters also depend on tips. Some upmarket hotels and restaurants will add an automatic ten percent service charge to your bill, though this is not always shared out.

## Tourist information

The **Tourism Authority of Thailand**, or TAT (⊕ tourismthailand.org), maintains offices in several cities

abroad and has dozens of branches within Thailand (all open daily 8.30am–4.30pm, though a few close noon–1pm). Regional offices should have up-to-date information on local festival dates and perhaps transport schedules, but service varies widely; none of them offers accommodation, tour or transport booking. You can contact the helpful TAT tourist assistance phoneline from anywhere in the country for free on ☎ 1672 (daily 8am–8pm). In Bangkok, the Bangkok Tourism Division is a better source of information on the capital (see page 121). In some smaller towns that don't qualify for a local TAT office, the information gap is filled by a **municipal tourist assistance office**; some of these are very helpful, but at others you may find it hard to locate a fluent English-speaker.

### TAT OFFICES ABROAD

**Australia and New Zealand** Suite 2002, Level 20, 56 Pitt St, Sydney, NSW 2000 ☎ 02 9247 7549, ✉ info@thailand.net.au.
**South Africa** Contact the UK office.
**UK and Ireland** 1st Floor, 17–19 Cockspur St, London SW1Y 5BL ☎ 020 7925 2511, ✉ info@tourismthailand.co.uk.
**US and Canada** 61 Broadway, Suite 2810, New York, NY 10006 ☎ 212 432 0433, ✉ info@tatny.com; 611 North Larchmont Blvd, 1st Floor, Los Angeles, CA 94 ☎ 323 461 9814, ✉ tatla@tat.or.th.

## Travellers with disabilities

Thailand makes few provisions for its disabled citizens and this obviously affects **travellers with disabilities**, but taxis, comfortable hotels and personal tour guides are all more affordable than in the West and most travellers with disabilities find Thais only too happy to offer assistance where they can. Hiring a local tour guide to accompany you on a day's sightseeing is particularly recommended: government-licensed tour guides can be arranged through any TAT office.

Most **wheelchair-users** end up driving on the roads because it's too hard to negotiate the uneven pavements, which are high to allow for flooding, poorly maintained and invariably lack dropped kerbs. Crossing the road can be a trial, particularly in Bangkok and other big cities, where it's usually a question of climbing steps up to a bridge rather than taking a ramped underpass. Few buildings, buses and trains have ramps, but in Bangkok some Skytrain stations and all subway stations have lifts (though you might have to ask someone to unlock them).

Several **tour companies** in Thailand specialize in organizing trips featuring adapted facilities, accessible transport and escorts. The Bangkok-based Help and Care Travel Company (☎081 375 0792, ⓦwheelchairtours.com) designs **accessible holidays** in Thailand for slow walkers and wheelchair-users, as well as offering accessible taxis, vans and hotels, personal assistants, medical equipment and many other services. Mermaids Dive Center in Pattaya runs Disabled Divers International programmes and certifications for **disabled divers** and instructors (☎038 303 333, ⓦmermaids-divecenter.com).

# Bangkok

CHATUCHAK WEEKEND MARKET

# 1 Bangkok

The headlong pace and flawed modernity of Bangkok match few people's visions of the capital of exotic Siam. Spiked with scores of high-rise buildings of concrete and glass, it's a vast flatness that holds an estimated population of nearly fifteen million, and feels even bigger. Yet under the shadow of the skyscrapers you'll find a heady mix of chaos and refinement, of frenetic markets, snail's-pace traffic jams and hushed golden temples, of dispiriting, zombie-like sex shows and early-morning alms-giving ceremonies. Plenty of visitors enjoy the challenge of taking on the "Big Mango", but one way or another, the place is sure to get under your skin.

Most budget travellers head for the **Banglamphu** district, where if you're not careful you could end up watching films all day long and selling your shoes when you run out of money. The district is far from having a monopoly on Bangkok accommodation, but it does have the advantage of being just a short walk from the major sights in the **Ratanakosin** area: the dazzling ostentation of the **Grand Palace** and **Wat Phra Kaeo**, lively and grandiose **Wat Pho** and the **National Museum**'s hoard of exquisite works of art. Once those cultural essentials have been seen, you can choose from a whole bevy of lesser sights, including **Wat Benjamabophit** (the "Marble Temple"), especially at festival time, and **Jim Thompson's House**, a small, personal museum of Thai design.

For livelier scenes, explore the dark alleys of **Chinatown**'s bazaars or head for the water: the great **Chao Phraya River**, which breaks up and adds zest to the city's landscape, is the backbone of a network of **canals** that remains fundamentally intact in the west-bank Thonburi district. Inevitably the waterways have earned Bangkok the title of "Venice of the East", a tag that seems all too apt when you're wading through flooded streets in the rainy season. Back on dry land, **shopping** varies from touristic outlets pushing silks, handicrafts and counterfeit watches, through home-grown boutiques selling street-wise fashions and stunning contemporary decor, to thronging local markets where half

## ORIENTATION

Bangkok ("Krung Thep" in Thai) can be a tricky place to get your bearings as it's huge and ridiculously congested, with largely featureless modern buildings and no obvious centre. The boldest line on the map is the **Chao Phraya River**, which divides the city into Bangkok proper on the east bank, and **Thonburi**, part of Greater Bangkok, on the west.

The historical core of Bangkok proper, site of the original royal palace, is **Ratanakosin**, cradled in a bend in the river. Three concentric canals radiate eastwards around Ratanakosin: the southern part of the area between the canals is the old-style trading enclave of **Chinatown** and Indian **Pahurat**, connected to the old palace by Thanon Charoen Krung (aka New Road); the northern part is characterized by old temples and the **Democracy Monument**, west of which is the backpackers' ghetto of **Banglamphu**. Beyond the canals to the north, **Dusit** is the site of many government buildings and the nineteenth-century Vimanmek Palace, and is linked to Ratanakosin by the three stately avenues, Thanon Rajdamnoen Nok, Thanon Rajdamnoen Klang and Thanon Rajdamnoen Nai.

"New" Bangkok begins to the east of the canals and beyond the main rail line and Hualamphong Station, and stretches as far as the eye can see to the east and north. The main business district is south of **Thanon Rama IV**, with the port of Khlong Toey at its eastern edge. The diverse area north of Thanon Rama IV includes the sprawling campus of Chulalongkorn University and huge shopping centres around **Siam Square**. To the east lies the swish residential quarter of **Thanon Sukhumvit**.

RAMAYANA MURALS, WAT PHRA KAEO

# Highlights

**❶ The Grand Palace** The country's most iconic sight, incorporating its holiest and most dazzling temple, Wat Phra Kaeo. See page 75

**❷ Wat Pho** Admire the Reclining Buddha and the lavish architecture, and leave time for a relaxing massage. See page 83

**❸ The National Museum** The central repository of the country's artistic riches. See page 86

**❹ Thanon Khao San** Legendary hangout for Southeast Asia backpackers; the place for cheap sleeps, baggy trousers and tall tales. See page 91

**❺ The canals of Thonburi** See the Bangkok of yesteryear on a touristy but memorable longtail-boat ride along the city's labyrinthine canals. See page 98

**❻ Jim Thompson's House** An elegant Thai design classic. See page 106

**❼ Chatuchak Weekend Market** Over ten thousand open-air stalls selling everything from triangular pillows to faded Levi's. See page 110

**❽ 63rd-floor sundowner** Fine cocktails and jaw-dropping views, especially at sunset, at The Sky Bar and Distil. See page 138

**❾ Thai boxing** Nightly bouts at the national stadiums, with live musical accompaniment and frenetic betting. See page 140

**HIGHLIGHTS ARE MARKED ON THE MAP ON PAGE 74**

1

the fun is watching the crowds. Thailand's long calendar of festivals (see page 47) is one of the few things that has been largely decentralized away from the capital, but Bangkok does offer the country's most varied **entertainment**, ranging from traditional dancing and the orchestrated bedlam of Thai boxing, to cool bars, clubs, cafés and microbreweries, and beyond to the farang-only sex bars of the notorious Patpong district, a tinseltown Babylon that's the tip of a dangerous iceberg. Even if the above doesn't appeal, you'll almost certainly pass through Bangkok once, if not several times – not only is it Thailand's main port of entry, it's also the obvious place to sort out onward travel, with a convenient menu of embassies for visas to neighbouring countries.

# Ratanakosin

The only place to start your exploration of Bangkok is **Ratanakosin**, the royal island on the east bank of the Chao Phraya, where the city's most important and extravagant sights are located. When Rama I developed Ratanakosin for his new capital in 1782, after the sacking of Ayutthaya and a temporary stay across the river in Thonburi, he paid tribute to its precursor by imitating Ayutthaya's layout and architecture – he even shipped the building materials downstream from the ruins of the old city. Like Ayutthaya, the new capital was sited for protection beside a river and turned into an artificial island by the construction of defensive canals, with a central **Grand Palace** and adjoining royal temple, **Wat Phra Kaeo**, fronted by an open field, **Sanam Luang**; the Wang Na (Palace of the Second King), now the **National Museum**, was also built at this time. **Wat Pho**, which predates the capital's founding, was further embellished by Rama I's successors, who have consolidated Ratanakosin's pre-eminence by building several grand European-style palaces (now housing government institutions), as well as **Wat Mahathat**, the most important centre of Buddhist learning in Southeast Asia; the National Theatre; the National Gallery; and Thammasat and Silpakorn universities.

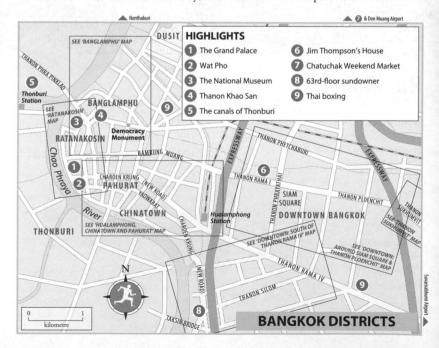

**HIGHLIGHTS**

1. The Grand Palace
2. Wat Pho
3. The National Museum
4. Thanon Khao San
5. The canals of Thonburi
6. Jim Thompson's House
7. Chatuchak Weekend Market
8. 63rd-floor sundowner
9. Thai boxing

**BANGKOK DISTRICTS**

### A WORD OF WARNING

When you're heading for the Grand Palace or Wat Pho, you may well be approached by someone, possibly pretending to be a student or an official, who will tell you that the sight is closed when it's not, or some other lies to try to lead you away from the entrance, because they want to take you on a shopping trip for souvenirs, tailored clothes or, if you seem really gullible, gems (see page 144). The opening hours of the Grand Palace – but not Wat Pho – are indeed sometimes erratic because of state occasions, but you can check the details out on its website, Ⓦ palaces.thai.net (click on "Annual Calendar for Visitor") – and even if it's closed on the day you want to visit, that's no reason to throw yourself at the mercy of these shysters.

Bangkok has expanded eastwards away from the river, leaving the Grand Palace a good 5km from the city's commercial heart, and the royal family has long since moved its main residence to Dusit, but Ratanakosin remains the ceremonial centre of the whole kingdom – so much so that it feels as if it might sink into the boggy ground under the weight of its own mighty edifices. The heavy, stately feel is lightened by traditional shophouses selling herbal medicines, pavement amulet-sellers and studenty canteens along the riverside road, **Thanon Maharat**; and by Sanam Luang, still used for cremations and royal ceremonies, but also functioning as a popular open park and the hub of the modern city's bus system. Despite containing several of the country's main sights, the area is busy enough in its own right not to have become a swarming tourist zone, and strikes a neat balance between liveliness and grandeur.

### ARRIVAL AND DEPARTURE                                           RATANAKOSIN

Ratanakosin is within easy walking distance of Banglamphu, but is best approached from the river, via the **express-boat piers** of Tha Chang (the former bathing place of the royal elephants, which gives access to the Grand Palace) or Tha Thien (for Wat Pho). At the time of writing, however, Tha Thien was being renovated and express boats were stopping on the opposite bank at Wat Arun, leaving you a cross-river ferry ride (or a 5min walk from Tha Chang) to get to Tha Thien. An extension of the **subway** line from Hualamphong is being built (its opening currently proposed for 2019), with a new station, called Sanam Chai, at the Museum of Siam, 5min walk from Wat Pho, 10min from Tha Thien express boat pier and 15min from the entrance to the Grand Palace.

## Wat Phra Kaeo and the Grand Palace

Thanon Na Phra Lan • Daily 8.30am–4.30pm, last admission 3.30pm (weapons museum, Phra Thinang Amarin Winichai and Dusit Maha Prasat interiors closed Sat & Sun) • B500, including a guide booklet and admission, within 7 days, to Dusit Park (if it's open – see page 101); 2hr personal audioguide B200, with passport or credit card as deposit • Ⓦ palaces.thai.net

Hanging together in a precarious harmony of strangely beautiful colours and shapes, **Wat Phra Kaeo** is the apogee of Thai religious art and the holiest Buddhist site in the country, housing the most important image, the **Emerald Buddha**. Built as the private royal temple, Wat Phra Kaeo occupies the northeast corner of the huge **Grand Palace**, whose official opening in 1785 marked the founding of the new capital and the rebirth of the Thai nation after the Burmese invasion. Successive kings have all left their mark here, and the palace complex now covers two acres, though very little apart from the wat is open to tourists.

The only **entrance** to the complex in 2km of crenellated walls is the Gate of Glorious Victory in the middle of the north side, on Thanon Na Phra Lan. This brings you onto a driveway with a tantalizing view of the temple's glittering spires on the left and the dowdy buildings of the Offices of the Royal Household on the right: this is the powerhouse of the kingdom's ceremonial life, providing everything down to chairs and catering, even lending an urn when someone of rank dies. Among these buildings, the hagiographic Queen Sirikit Museum of Textiles, which claims to show how she invented the Thai national dress in the 1960s, is included in the admission ticket but well worth missing, though you might want to check out the museum shop (see page 141). Turn left at the end of the driveway for the ticket office and entrance turnstiles.

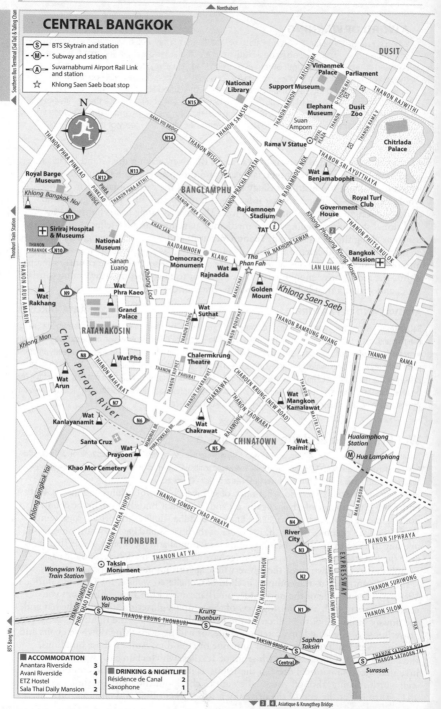

# CENTRAL BANGKOK

**(S)** BTS Skytrain and station
**(M)** Subway and station
**(A)** Suvarnabhumi Airport Rail Link and station
☆ Khlong Saen Saeb boat stop

| ■ ACCOMMODATION | |
|---|---|
| Anantara Riverside | 3 |
| Avani Riverside | 4 |
| ETZ Hostel | 1 |
| Sala Thai Daily Mansion | 2 |

| ■ DRINKING & NIGHTLIFE | |
|---|---|
| Résidence de Canal | 2 |
| Saxophone | 1 |

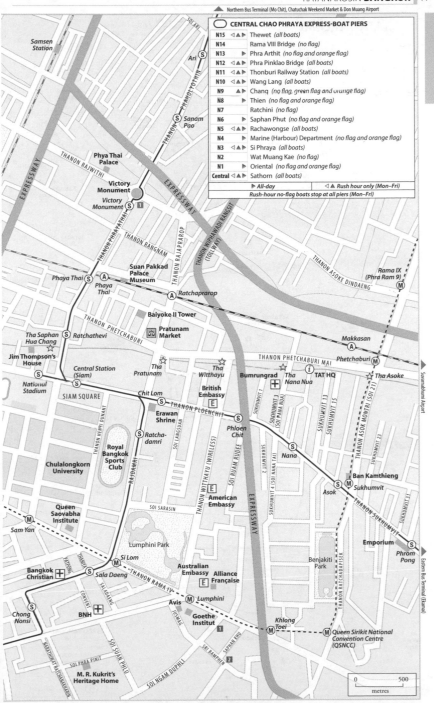

Northern Bus Terminal (Mo Chit), Chatuchak Weekend Market & Don Muang Airport

**CENTRAL CHAO PHRAYA EXPRESS-BOAT PIERS**

| | | |
|---|---|---|
| N15 | ◁▲▶ | Thewet (all boats) |
| N14 | | Rama VIII Bridge (no flag) |
| N13 | ▶ | Phra Arthit (no flag and orange flag) |
| N12 | ◁▲▶ | Phra Pinklao Bridge (all boats) |
| N11 | ◁▲▶ | Thonburi Railway Station (all boats) |
| N10 | ◁▲▶ | Wang Lang (all boats) |
| N9 | ▲▶ | Chang (no flag, green flag and orange flag) |
| N8 | ▶ | Thien (no flag and orange flag) |
| N7 | | Ratchini (no flag) |
| N6 | ▶ | Saphan Phut (no flag and orange flag) |
| N5 | ◁▲▶ | Rachawongse (all boats) |
| N4 | ▶ | Marine (Harbour) Department (no flag and orange flag) |
| N3 | ◁▲▶ | Si Phraya (all boats) |
| N2 | | Wat Muang Kae (no flag) |
| N1 | ▶ | Oriental (no flag and orange flag) |
| Central | ◁▲▶ | Sathorn (all boats) |

| ▶ All-day | ◁▲ Rush hour only (Mon–Fri) |
|---|---|

*Rush-hour no-flag boats stop at all piers (Mon–Fri)*

1

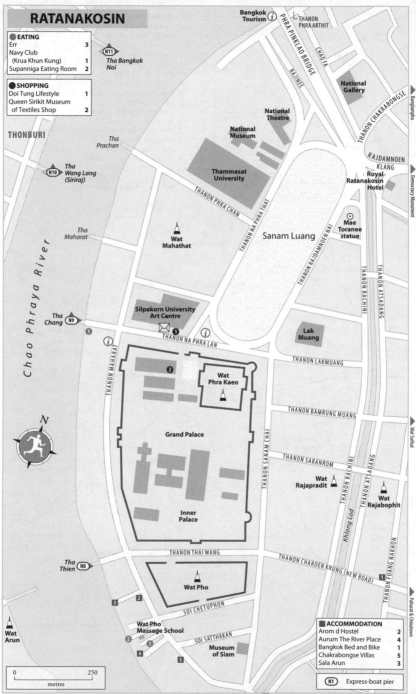

# RATANAKOSIN

**EATING**
| | |
|---|---|
| Err | 3 |
| Navy Club (Krua Khun Kung) | 1 |
| Supanniga Eating Room | 2 |

**SHOPPING**
| | |
|---|---|
| Doi Tung Lifestyle | 1 |
| Queen Sirikit Museum of Textiles Shop | 2 |

**ACCOMMODATION**
| | |
|---|---|
| Arom d Hostel | 2 |
| Aurum The River Place | 4 |
| Bangkok Bed and Bike | 1 |
| Chakrabongse Villas | 5 |
| Sala Arun | 3 |

N1 Express-boat pier

**1**

## CITY OF ANGELS

When **Rama I** was crowned in 1782, he gave his new capital a grand 43-syllable name to match his ambitious plans for the building of the city. Since then, 21 more syllables have been added. Kr ungthepmahanakhornbowornrattanakosinmahintarayutthayamahadilokpopnopparatratchatha niburiromudomratchaniwetmahasathanamornpimanavatarnsathitsakkathattiyavisnukamprasit is certified by the *Guinness Book of Records* as the longest place-name in the world, roughly translating as "Great city of angels, the supreme repository of divine jewels, the great land unconquerable, the grand and prominent realm, the royal and delightful capital city full of nine noble gems, the highest royal dwelling and grand palace, the divine shelter and living place of the reincarnated spirits". Fortunately, all Thais refer to the city simply as **Krung Thep**, "City of Angels", though plenty can recite the full name at the drop of a hat. **Bangkok** – "Village of the Plum Olive" – was the name of the original village on the Thonburi side; with remarkable persistence, it has remained in use by foreigners since the time of the French garrison.

As this is Thailand's most sacred site, you have to **dress in smart clothes**: no vests or see-through clothes; no flip-flops or open-back sandals; men must wear full-length trousers, women trousers or over-the-knee skirts. Suitable garments can be borrowed from the office to the right just inside the Gate of Glorious Victory (free, deposit of B200 per item).

### Wat Phra Kaeo

*It makes you laugh with delight to think that anything so fantastic could exist on this sombre earth.*
W. Somerset Maugham, *The Gentlemen in the Parlour*

Entering the temple is like stepping onto a lavishly detailed stage set, from the immaculate flagstones right up to the gaudy roofs. Reinforcing the sense of unreality, the whole compound is surrounded by arcaded walls, decorated with extraordinary murals of scenes from the *Ramayana*. Although it receives hundreds of foreign sightseers and at least as many Thai pilgrims every day, the temple, which has no monks in residence, maintains an unnervingly sanitized look, as if it were built only yesterday.

#### The approach to the bot

Inside the entrance turnstiles, you're confronted by 6m-tall **yaksha**, gaudy demons from the *Ramayana*, who watch over the Emerald Buddha from every gate of the temple and ward off evil spirits; the king of the demons, green, ten-faced Totsagan (labelled "Tosakanth"), stands to the left of the entrance by the southwest corner of the golden Phra Si Ratana Chedi. Less threatening is the toothless old codger, cast in bronze and sitting on a plinth immediately inside the turnstiles by the back wall of the bot, who represents a Hindu **hermit** credited with inventing yoga and herbal medicine. In front of him is a large grinding stone where previously herbal practitioners could come to grind their ingredients – with enhanced powers, of course. Skirting around the bot, you'll reach its **main entrance** on the eastern side, in front of which stands a cluster of grey **statues**, which have a strong Chinese feel: next to Kuan Im, the Chinese *bodhisattva* of mercy shown holding a bottle of *amritsa* (sacred elixir), are a sturdy pillar topped by a lotus flower, which Bangkok's Chinese community presented to Rama IV during his 27 years as a monk, and two handsome cows which commemorate Rama I's birth in the Year of the Cow. Worshippers make their offerings to the Emerald Buddha at two small, stand-in Buddhas here, where they can look at the main image through the open doors of the bot without messing up its pristine interior with gold leaf, candle wax and joss-stick ash.

#### The bot and the Emerald Buddha

The **bot**, the largest building of the temple, is one of the few original structures left at Wat Phra Kaeo, though it has been augmented so often it looks like the work of a

**1**

wildly inspired child. Eight *sema* stones mark the boundary of the consecrated area around the bot, each sheltering in a psychedelic fairy castle, joined by a low wall decorated with Chinese porcelain tiles, which depict delicate landscapes. The walls of the bot itself, sparkling with gilt and coloured glass, are supported by 112 golden garudas (birdmen) holding nagas (serpents), representing the god Indra saving the world by slaying the serpent-cloud that had swallowed up all the water. The symbolism reflects the king's traditional role as a rainmaker.

Of the bot's three doorways, the largest, in the middle, is reserved for the king himself. Inside, a 9m-high pedestal supports the tiny **Emerald Buddha**, a figure whose mystique draws pilgrims from all over Thailand – as well as politicians accused of corruption, who traditionally come here to publicly swear their innocence. Here especially you must act with respect, sitting with your feet pointing away from the Buddha. The spiritual power of the 60cm jadeite image derives from its legendary past. Reputed to have been created by the gods in India, it was discovered when lightning cracked open an ancient chedi in Chiang Rai in the early fifteenth century. The image was then moved around the north, dispensing miracles wherever it went, before being taken to Laos for two hundred years. As it was believed to bring great fortune to its possessor, the future Rama I snatched it back when he captured Vientiane in 1779, installing it at the heart of his new capital as a talisman for king and country.

Seated in the *Dhyana Mudra* (meditation position), the Emerald Buddha has three **costumes**, one for each season: the crown and ornaments of an Ayutthayan king for the hot season; a gilt monastic robe for the rainy season, when the monks retreat into the temples; this is augmented with a full-length gold shawl in the cool season. To this day it's the job of the king himself to ceremonially change the Buddha's costumes. The Buddha was granted a new set of these three costumes in 1997: the old set is now in the Wat Phra Kaeo Museum (see page 83) while the two costumes of the new set that are not in use are on display among the blinding glitter of crowns and jewels in the Royal Decorations and Coins Pavilion, which lies between the ticket office and the entrance to Wat Phra Kaeo.

Among the paraphernalia in front of the pedestal sits the tiny, silver **Phra Chai Lang Chang** (Victory Buddha), which Rama I always carried into battle on the back of his elephant for luck and which still plays an important part in coronation ceremonies. Recently covered in gold, it occupies a prestigious spot dead centre, but is obscured by the umbrella of a larger gold Buddha in front. The tallest pair of a dozen standing Buddha images, all made of bronze but encased in gold and raising both hands to dispel fear, are at the front: Rama III dedicated the one on the Emerald Buddha's left to Rama I, the one on his right to Rama II, and Rama IV enshrined relics of the Buddha in their crowns.

### The Royal Pantheon and minor buildings

On the north side of the bot, the eastern end of the **upper terrace** is taken up with the **Prasat Phra Thep Bidorn**, known as the **Royal Pantheon**, a splendid hash of styles. The pantheon has its roots in the Khmer concept of *devaraja*, or the divinity of kings: inside are bronze and gold statues, precisely life-size, of all the kings since Bangkok became the Thai capital. Constructed by Rama IV, the building is open only on special occasions, such as Chakri Day (April 6), when the dynasty is commemorated, and Coronation Day (May 5).

From here you get the best view of the **royal mausoleum**, the **porcelain viharn** and the **supplementary library** to the north (all of which are closed to tourists, though you can sometimes glimpse Thai Buddhists worshipping in the library), and, running along the east side of the temple, a row of eight bullet-like **prangs**, each of which has a different nasty ceramic colour. Described as "monstrous vegetables" by Somerset Maugham, they represent, from north to south, the Buddha, Buddhist scripture, the monkhood, the nunhood, the Buddhas who attained enlightenment but did not preach, previous emperors, the Buddha in his previous lives and the future Buddha.

**1**

### The Phra Mondop and Phra Si Ratana Chedi

In the middle of the terrace, dressed in deep-green glass mosaics, the **Phra Mondop** was built by Rama I to house the *Tripitaka*, or Buddhist scripture, which the king had rewritten at Wat Mahathat in 1788, the previous versions having all been lost in the sacking of Ayutthaya. It's famous for the mother-of-pearl cabinet and solid-silver mats inside, but is never open. Four tiny **memorials** at each corner of the mondop show the symbols of each of the nine Chakri kings, from the ancient crown representing Rama I to the present king's discus, while the bronze statues surrounding the memorials portray each king's lucky white elephants, labelled by name and pedigree. A contribution of Rama IV, on the north side of the mondop, is a **scale model of Angkor Wat**, the prodigious Cambodian temple, which during his reign (1851–68) was under Thai rule (apparently, the king had wanted to shift a whole Khmer temple to Bangkok but, fortunately, was dissuaded by his officials). At the western end of the terrace, you can't miss the golden dazzle of the **Phra Si Ratana Chedi**, which Rama IV erected, in imitation of the famous bell-shaped chedis at Ayutthaya's Wat Phra Si Sanphet, to enshrine a piece of the Buddha's breastbone.

### The murals

Extending for about a kilometre in the arcades that run inside the wat walls, the **murals of the Ramayana** depict every blow of this ancient story of the triumph of good over evil, using the vibrant buildings of the temple itself as backdrops, and setting them off against the subdued colours of richly detailed landscapes. Because of the damaging humidity, none of the original work of Rama I's time survives: maintenance is a never-ending process, so you'll always find an artist working on one of the scenes. The story is told in 178 panels, labelled and numbered in Thai only, starting in the middle of

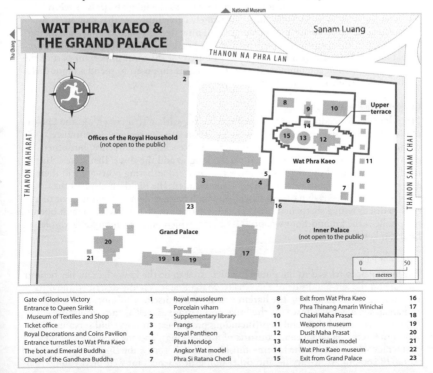

| | | | | | | |
|---|---|---|---|---|---|---|
| Gate of Glorious Victory | 1 | Royal mausoleum | 8 | Exit from Wat Phra Kaeo | 16 |
| Entrance to Queen Sirikit | | Porcelain viharn | 9 | Phra Thinang Amarin Winichai | 17 |
| Museum of Textiles and Shop | 2 | Supplementary library | 10 | Chakri Maha Prasat | 18 |
| Ticket office | 3 | Prangs | 11 | Weapons museum | 19 |
| Royal Decorations and Coins Pavilion | 4 | Royal Pantheon | 12 | Dusit Maha Prasat | 20 |
| Entrance turnstiles to Wat Phra Kaeo | 5 | Phra Mondop | 13 | Mount Krailas model | 21 |
| The bot and Emerald Buddha | 6 | Angkor Wat model | 14 | Wat Phra Kaeo museum | 22 |
| Chapel of the Gandhara Buddha | 7 | Phra Si Ratana Chedi | 15 | Exit from Grand Palace | 23 |

the northern side opposite the porcelain viharn: in the first episode, a hermit, while out ploughing, finds the baby Sita, the heroine, floating in a gold urn on a lotus leaf and brings her to the city. Panel 109 near the gate leading to the palace buildings shows the climax of the story, when Rama, the hero, kills the ten-headed demon Totsagan (Ravana), and the ladies of the enemy city weep at the demon's death. Panel 110 depicts his elaborate funeral procession, and in 113 you can see the funeral fair, with acrobats, sword-jugglers and tightrope-walkers. In between, Sita – Rama's wife – has to walk on fire to prove that she has been faithful during her fourteen years of imprisonment by Totsagan. If you haven't the stamina for the long walk round, you could sneak a look at the end of the story, to the left of the first panel, where Rama holds a victory parade and distributes thank-you gifts.

## The palace buildings

The exit in the southwest corner of Wat Phra Kaeo brings you to the palace proper, a vast area of buildings and gardens, of which only the northern edge is on show to the public. Though the king now lives elsewhere, the **Grand Palace** is still used for state receptions and official ceremonies, during which there is no public access to any part of the palace.

### Phra Maha Monthien

Coming out of the temple compound, you'll first of all see to your right a beautiful Chinese gate covered in innumerable tiny porcelain tiles. Extending in a straight line behind the gate is the **Phra Maha Monthien**, which was the grand residential complex of earlier kings.

Only the **Phra Thinang Amarin Winichai**, the main audience hall at the front of the complex, is open to the public. The supreme court in the era of the absolute monarchy, it nowadays serves as the venue for ceremonies such as the king's birthday speech. Dominating the hall are two gleaming, intricately carved thrones that date from the reign of Rama I: a white umbrella with the full nine tiers owing to a king shelters the front seat, while the unusual *busbok* behind is topped with a spired roof and floats on a boat-shaped base. The rear buildings are still used for the most important part of the elaborate coronation ceremony, and each new king is supposed to spend a night there to show solidarity with his forefathers.

### Chakri Maha Prasat

Next door you can admire the facade of the "farang with a Thai crown", as the **Chakri Maha Prasat** is nicknamed. Rama V, whose portrait you can see over its entrance, employed an English architect to design a purely Neoclassical residence, but other members of the royal family prevailed on the king to add the three Thai spires. This used to be the site of the elephant stables: the large red tethering posts are still there and the bronze elephants were installed as a reminder. The building displays the emblem of the Chakri dynasty on its gable, which has a trident (*ri*) coming out of a *chak* (a discus with a sharpened rim). The only part of the Chakri Maha Prasat open to the public is the ground-floor **weapons museum**, which houses a forgettable display of hooks, pikes and guns.

### The Inner Palace

The **Inner Palace** (closed to the public), which used to be the king's harem, lies behind the gate on the left-hand side of the Chakri Maha Prasat. Vividly described in M.R. Kukrit Pramoj's *Si Phaendin*, the harem was a town in itself, with shops, law courts and an all-female police force for the huge population: as well as the current queens, the minor wives and their children (including pre-pubescent boys) and servants, this was home to the daughters and consorts of former kings, and the daughters of the aristocracy who attended the harem's finishing school. Today, the Inner Palace houses a school of cooking, fruit-carving and other domestic sciences for well-bred young Thais.

Dusit Maha Prasat

On the western side of the courtyard, the delicately proportioned **Dusit Maha Prasat**, an audience hall built by Rama I, epitomizes traditional Thai architecture. Outside, the soaring tiers of its red, gold and green roof culminate in a gilded *mongkut*, a spire shaped like the king's crown, which symbolizes the 33 Buddhist levels of perfection. Each tier of the roof bears a typical *chofa*, a slender, stylized bird's-head finial, and several *hang hong* (swans' tails), which represent three-headed nagas. Inside, you can still see the original throne, the **Phra Ratcha Banlang Pradap Muk**, a masterpiece of mother-of-pearl inlaid work. When a senior member of the royal family dies, the hall is used for the lying-in-state: the body, embalmed and seated in a huge sealed urn, is placed in the west transept, waiting up to two years for an auspicious day to be cremated.

The Wat Phra Kaeo Museum

In the nineteenth-century Royal Mint in front of the Dusit Maha Prasat, the **Wat Phra Kaeo Museum** houses a mildly interesting collection of artefacts donated to the Emerald Buddha, along with architectural elements rescued from the Grand Palace grounds during restoration in the 1980s. Highlights include the bones of various kings' white elephants, and upstairs, the Emerald Buddha's original costumes and two useful scale models of the Grand Palace, one as it is now, the other as it was when first built. Also on the first floor stands the grey stone slab of the Manangasila Seat, where Ramkhamhaeng, the great thirteenth-century king of Sukhothai, is said to have sat and taught his subjects. It was discovered in 1833 by Rama IV during his monkhood and brought to Bangkok, where Rama VI used it as the throne for his coronation.

# Wat Pho (Wat Phra Chetuphon)

Soi Chetuphon, to the south of the Grand Palace • Daily 8am–6.30pm • B100 • ⓦ watpho.com

Where Wat Phra Kaeo may seem too perfect and shrink-wrapped for some, **Wat Pho** is lively and shambolic, a complex arrangement of lavish structures which jostle with classrooms, basketball courts and a turtle pond. Busloads of tourists shuffle in and out of the **north entrance**, stopping only to gawp at the colossal Reclining Buddha, but you can avoid the worst of the crowds by using the **main entrance** on Soi Chetuphon to explore the huge compound.

Wat Pho is the oldest temple in Bangkok and is older than the city itself, having been founded in the seventeenth century under the name Wat Photaram. Foreigners have stuck to the contraction of this old name, even though Rama I, after enlarging the temple, changed the name in 1801 to **Wat Phra Chetuphon**, which is how it is generally known to Thais. The temple had another major overhaul in 1832, when Rama III built the chapel of the Reclining Buddha, and turned the temple into a public centre of learning by decorating the walls and pillars with inscriptions and diagrams on subjects such as history, literature, animal husbandry and astrology. Dubbed Thailand's first university, the wat is still an important centre for traditional medicine, notably **Thai massage** (see page 85), which is used against all kinds of illnesses, from backaches to viruses.

## The eastern courtyard

The main entrance on Soi Chetuphon is one of a series of sixteen monumental gates around the main compound, each guarded by stone **giants**, many of them comic Westerners in wide-brimmed hats – ships that exported rice to China would bring these statues back as ballast.

The entrance brings you into the eastern half of the main complex, where a courtyard of structures radiates from the bot in a disorientating symmetry. To get to the bot, the principal congregation and ordination hall, turn right and cut through the two surrounding cloisters, which are lined with hundreds of Buddha images. The elegant **bot** has beautiful teak doors decorated with mother-of-pearl, showing stories from the *Ramayana* in minute detail. Look out also for the stone bas-reliefs around the base of

1

the bot, which narrate the story of the capture and rescue of Sita from the *Ramayana* in 152 action-packed panels. The plush interior has a well-proportioned altar with ten statues of disciples framing a graceful, Ayutthayan Buddha image, whose base contains some of the remains of Rama I, the founder of Bangkok (Rama IV placed them there so that the public could worship him at the same time as the Buddha).

Back outside the entrance to the double cloister, keep your eyes open for a miniature mountain covered in statues of naked men in tall hats who appear to be gesturing rudely: they are *rishis* (hermits), demonstrating various positions of healing massage. Skirting the southwestern corner of the cloisters, you'll come to two pavilions between the eastern and western courtyards, which display plaques inscribed with the precepts of traditional medicine, as well as anatomical pictures showing the different pressure points and the illnesses that can be cured by massaging them.

### The western courtyard

Among the 99 chedis strewn about the grounds, the four **great chedis** in the western courtyard stand out as much for their covering of garish tiles as for their size. The central chedi is the oldest, erected by Rama I to hold the remains of the most sacred Buddha image of Ayutthaya, the Phra Si Sanphet. Later, Rama III built the chedi to the north for the ashes of Rama II and the chedi to the south to hold his own remains; Rama IV built the fourth, with bright blue tiles, though its purpose is uncertain.

In the northwest corner of the courtyard stands the chapel of the **Reclining Buddha**, a 45m-long gilded statue of plaster-covered brick which depicts the Buddha entering Nirvana, a common motif in Buddhist iconography. The chapel is only slightly bigger than the statue – you can't get far enough away to take in anything but a surreal close-up view of the beaming 5m smile. As for the feet, the vast black soles are beautifully inlaid with delicate mother-of-pearl showing the 108 *lakshanas*, or auspicious signs, which distinguish the true Buddha. Along one side of the statue are 108 bowls: putting a coin in each will bring you good luck and a long life.

## Museum of Siam

Thanon Sanam Chai • Tues–Sun 10am–6pm • B200 • ☎ 02 225 2777, ⓦ museumsiam.org

The excellent **Museum of Siam** is a high-tech, mostly bilingual attraction that occupies the century-old, European-style, former Ministry of Commerce. It looks at what

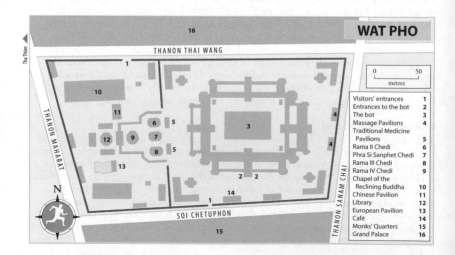

**WAT PHO**

THANON THAI WANG

0    50
metres

Visitors' entrances 1
Entrances to the bot 2
The bot 3
Massage Pavilions 4
Traditional Medicine
  Pavilions 5
Rama II Chedi 6
Phra Si Sanphet Chedi 7
Rama III Chedi 8
Rama IV Chedi 9
Chapel of the
  Reclining Buddha 10
Chinese Pavilion 11
Library 12
European Pavilion 13
Café 14
Monks' Quarters 15
Grand Palace 16

THANON MAHARAT

THANON SANAM CHAI

SOI CHETUPHON

Tha Thien

N

1

## TRADITIONAL MASSAGE AND SPAS IN BANGKOK

Thai massage sessions and courses are held most famously at Wat Pho, while luxurious and indulgent spa and massage treatments are available at many posh hotels across the city, as well as at the following stand-alone places.

**Asia Herb Association** 20 Soi 4 (Soi Nana Tai), Thanon Sukhumvit ☎ 02 254 8631, ⓦ asiaherbassociation. com. The speciality here is massage with heated herbal balls (phrakop), which are freshly made each day with ingredients from their organic farm in Khao Yai (B1100/90min). Also on offer are traditional Thai, aromatherapy and foot massages, plus body scrubs, with several other locations, mostly around Sukhumvit. Daily 9am–2am (last bookings midnight).

**Divana Massage and Spa** 7 Soi 25, Thanon Sukhumvit ☎ 02 661 6784–5, ⓦ divanaspa.com. Delightful spa serving up a variety of massages – Thai (B1100/70min), foot, aromatherapy and herbal – as well as facials, body scrubs and other treatments, with a number of other locations around Bangkok. Mon–Fri 11am–11pm, Sat & Sun 10am–11pm (last bookings 9pm).

**Health Land** 55/5 Soi 1, Thanon Asok Montri (Sukhumvit Soi 21) ☎ 02 261 1110, ⓦ healthlandspa. com. Very good Thai (B500/2hr) and other massages, Ayurvedic treatments, facials and body polishes, in swish surroundings, with several other locations around Bangkok. Daily 9am–11pm.

**Pimmalai** Thanon Sukhumvit, 50m east of BTS On Nut, exit 1, between sois 81 and 83 ☎ 02 742 6452, ⓦ pimmalai.com. In a nice old wooden house, Thai massages (B300/1hr), plus foot, herbal and oil massages, herbal steam treatments, body scrubs, masks and facials. Mon–Fri 9.30am–10pm, Sat & Sun 9.30am–10.30pm.

**Ruen Nuad** 42 Thanon Convent, near Thanon Sathon Nua ☎ 02 632 2662. Excellent Thai massages (B350/1hr, B650/2hr), as well as aromatherapy and foot massages and packages featuring herbal-ball massages and body scrubs, in an a/c, characterful wooden house, down an alley opposite the BNH Hospital and behind *Naj* restaurant. Daily 10am–9pm.

**Wat Pho** (see page 83). World-famous massages are available in two a/c buildings on the east side of Wat Pho's main compound; allow 2hr for the full works (B420/hr; foot reflexology massage B420/hr). There are often long queues here, however, so you might be better off heading over to the massage centre's other premises just outside the temple, at 392/33–4 Soi Pen Phat 1, Thanon Maharat (the soi is unmarked but look for signs for the *Riva Arun* hotel; ☎ 02 622 3533, ☎ 02 622 3550 or ☎ 02 622 3551, ⓦ watpomassage.com). Here you can also enrol on a 30hr massage training course in English, over five days (B9500), and foot-massage courses for B7500. Daily 8am–6pm.

it is to be Thai, with lots of humorous short films and imaginative touches such as shadow-puppet cartoons and war video games. In addition, the museum stages playful temporary exhibitions, which in the past have, for example, let visitors have a go at rice-growing, or explored the minds of Thai inventors. Generally, it's good fun for adults and kids, and there's a lovely indoor-outdoor **café-bakery-restaurant** in the grounds. The museum hosts the annual **Noise Market Festival**, usually over a weekend in November (ⓦ facebook.com/noisemarketfest), a great little free festival-cum-market of indie music, handicrafts and food.

The museum exhibition kicks off with the prehistory of Southeast Asia, or Suvarnabhumi (Land of Gold) as ancient Indian documents refer to it, and the legendary arrival of Buddhism via missionaries sent by the Indian emperor, Ashoka (Asoke). Much space is devoted to Ayutthaya, where we learn that during that kingdom's four-hundred-year history, there were no fewer than twenty outbreaks of war with the Burmese states, before the final annihilation in 1767. Beyond this, look out for a fascinating map of Thonburi, King Taksin's new capital between 1768 and 1782, as drawn by a Burmese spy. In the Bangkok period, under the banner of westernization, visitors can wind up cartoon peep-shows and dress up in colonial-style uniform shirts.

## Wat Mahathat

Main entrance on Thanon Maharat, plus a back entrance on Thanon Na Phra That on Sanam Luang

Eighteenth-century **Wat Mahathat** provides a welcome respite from the surrounding tourist hype, and a chance to engage with the eager monks studying at

**1**

Mahachulalongkorn Buddhist University here. As the nation's centre for the Mahanikai monastic sect (where Rama IV spent many years as a monk before becoming king in 1851), and housing one of the two Buddhist universities in Bangkok, the wat buzzes with purpose. It's this activity, and the chance of interaction and participation, rather than any special architectural features, that make a visit so rewarding. The many university-attending monks at the wat are friendly and keen to practise their English, and are more than likely to approach you: diverting topics might range from the poetry of Dylan Thomas to English football results.

### Vipassana Meditation Centre

Section Five, Wat Mahathat • Practice daily 1–4pm & 6–8pm • Donations welcome • ☎ 02 222 6011 or ☎ 02 222 4981

At the wat's **Vipassana Meditation Centre**, where the monk teachers speak some English, sitting and walking meditation practice, with chanting and dhamma talks, is available to drop-in visitors (there's now a competing "Meditation Study and Retreat Center", nearby in Section One of the wat, but this is less geared towards foreign meditators).

## The National Museum

Thanon Na Phra That, northwest corner of Sanam Luang • Wed–Sun 9am–4pm; free guided tours in English, French, German and Japanese Wed & Thurs 9.30am • Currently free because of the renovations, usually B200 • ☎ 02 224 1333

The **National Museum** houses a colossal hoard of Thailand's chief artistic riches, ranging from sculptural treasures in the north and south wings, through outlandish funeral chariots, to the exquisite Buddhaisawan chapel, as well as sometimes staging worthwhile temporary exhibitions. However, it's currently undergoing a massive, rolling renovation: at the time of research, all the decorative objects in the Wang Na and the first floor of the main collection's northern building were inaccessible due to refurbishment, while the Gallery of Thai History was closed for a temporary exhibition.

There's still more than enough on display to make a visit worthwhile, especially if you take one of the free guided tours run by the National Museum Volunteers (NMV): they're generally entertaining and their explication of the choicest exhibits provides a good introduction to Thai religion and culture. (The NMV organize interesting lectures and excursions, too; ☜mynmv.com.) There's also a museum shop and a café by the ticket office, as well as a simple outdoor restaurant inside the museum grounds, near the west end of the main collection's northern building, which dishes up decent, inexpensive Thai food.

### Gallery of Thai History

The first building you'll come to near the ticket office houses an overview of the authorized history of Thailand, illustrated by some choice artworks plucked from the main collection. Among them is the most famous piece of Srivijaya art, a bronze Bodhisattva Padmapani from around the twelfth century found at Chaiya (according to Mahayana Buddhism, a *bodhisattva* is a saint who has postponed his passage into Nirvana to help ordinary believers gain enlightenment). With its pouting face and lithe torso, this image has become the ubiquitous emblem of southern Thailand. Look out also for an elaborate eighth-century lintel from Ku Suan Tang, Buriram, which depicts Vishnu (aka Narayana) reclining on the dragon Ananta in the sea of eternity, dreaming up a new universe after the old one has been annihilated in the Hindu cycle of creation and destruction. Out of his navel comes a lotus, and out of this emerges four-headed Brahma, who will put the dream into practice.

This gallery houses a fascinating little archeological gem, too: a black stone **inscription**, credited to King Ramkhamhaeng of Sukhothai, which became the first capital of the Thai nation (c.1278–99) under his rule. Discovered in 1833 by the future Rama IV, Mongkut, it's the oldest extant inscription using the Thai alphabet. This, combined with the description it records of prosperity and piety in Sukhothai's

Golden Age, has made the stone a symbol of Thai nationhood. There's recently been much controversy over the stone's origins, arising from the suggestion that it was a fake made by Mongkut, but it seems most likely that it is indeed genuine, and was written partly as a kind of prospectus for Sukhothai, to attract traders and settlers to the underpopulated kingdom.

### The main collection: southern building

At the back of the compound, two large modern buildings, flanking an old converted palace, house the museum's **main collection**, kicking off on the ground floor of the **southern building**. Look out here for some historic sculptures from the rest of Asia (Room 301), including one of the earliest representations of the Buddha, in the Gandhara style (first to fourth centuries AD). Alexander the Great left a garrison at Gandhara (in modern-day Pakistan), which explains why the image is in the style of Classical Greek sculpture: for example, the *ushnisha*, the supernatural bump on the top of the head, which symbolizes the Buddha's intellectual and spiritual power, is rationalized into a bun of thick, wavy hair.

Upstairs, the **prehistory** room (302) displays axe heads and spear points from Ban Chiang in the northeast of Thailand, one of the earliest Bronze Age cultures ever discovered. Alongside are many roughly contemporaneous metal artefacts from Kanchanaburi province, as well as some excellent examples of the developments of Ban Chiang's famous pottery. In the adjacent **Dvaravati** room (303; sixth to eleventh centuries), there are several fine dharmachakras, while the pick of the stone and terracotta Buddhas is a small head in smooth, pink clay from Wat Phra Ngam, Nakhon Pathom, whose downcast eyes and faintly smiling full lips typify the serene look of this era. At the far end of the first floor, you can't miss a voluptuous Javanese statue of elephant-headed Ganesh, Hindu god of wisdom and the arts, which, being the symbol of the Fine Arts Department, is always freshly garlanded. As Ganesh is known as the clearer of obstacles, Hindus always worship him before other gods, so by tradition he has grown fat through getting first choice of the offerings – witness his trunk jammed into a bowl of food in this sculpture.

Room 305 next door is devoted to **Srivijaya** art (roughly seventh to thirteenth centuries), including an interesting ekamukhalinga from Nong Wai, Chaiya, a phallic stone lingam, carved with a sweet, almost plaintive bust of Shiva. The rough chronological order of the collection continues back downstairs with an exhibition of **Khmer** and **Lopburi** sculpture (seventh to fourteenth centuries), most notably some dynamic bronze statuettes and stone lintels. Look out for an elaborate eleventh- or twelfth-century lintel from Phanom Rung (308), which depicts Krishna subduing the poisonous serpent Galiya.

### The main collection: northern building

The second half of the survey, in the northern building, begins upstairs with the **Sukhothai** collection (thirteenth to fifteenth centuries; rooms 404–405), which features some typically elegant and sinuous Buddha images, as well as chunky bronzes of Hindu gods and a wide range of ceramics. An ungainly but serene Buddha head, carved from grainy, pink sandstone, represents the **Ayutthaya** style of sculpture (fourteenth to eighteenth centuries; rooms 405–406): the faintest incision of a moustache above the lips betrays the Khmer influences that came to Ayutthaya after its conquest of Angkor. A sumptuous scripture cabinet, showing a cityscape of old Ayutthaya, is a more unusual piece, one of a surviving handful of such carved and painted items of furniture.

Downstairs in the section on **Bangkok** or **Ratanakosin** art (eighteenth century onwards; 407), a small, stiffly realistic standing bronze in the posture of calling down the rain brings you full circle. In his zeal for Western naturalism, Rama V had the statue made in the Gandhara style of the earliest Buddha image displayed in the first room of the museum.

**1**

## The funeral chariots

To the east of the northern building stands a large garage containing the royal family's fantastically elaborate **funeral chariots**, which are constructed of teak and decorated with lacquer, gold leaf and mirrored glass. Pre-eminent among these is Phra Maha Pichai Ratcharot (the Royal Chariot of Great Victory), built by Rama I in 1796 for carrying the urn at his father's funeral. The 11m-high structure symbolizes heaven on Mount Meru, while the dragons and divinities around the sides – piled in five golden tiers to suggest the flames of the cremation – represent the mythological inhabitants of the mountain's forests. Weighing fourteen tonnes and requiring the pulling power of over two hundred soldiers, the chariot last had an outing in 2017, for the funeral of King Bhumibol (Rama IX).

## Wang Na (Palace of the Second King)

The sprawling central building of the compound was originally part of the **Wang Na**, a huge palace stretching across Sanam Luang to Khlong Lod, which housed the "second king", appointed by the reigning monarch as his heir and deputy. When Rama V did away with the office in 1887, he turned the palace into a museum, which now contains a fascinating array of Thai objets d'art and richly decorated musical instruments. The display of sumptuous rare gold pieces includes a well-preserved armlet taken from the ruined prang of fifteenth-century Wat Ratburana in Ayutthaya, while an intricately carved ivory seat turns out, with gruesome irony, to be a *howdah*, for use on an elephant's back. Among the masks worn by *khon* actors, look out especially for a fierce Hanuman, the white monkey-warrior in the *Ramayana* epic, gleaming with mother-of-pearl. The huge and varied ceramic collection includes some sophisticated pieces from Sukhothai, and nearby there's a riot of mother-of-pearl items, whose flaming rainbow of colours comes from the shell of the turbo snail from the Gulf of Thailand.

## The Buddhaisawan chapel

The second-holiest image in Thailand, after the Emerald Buddha, is housed in the **Buddhaisawan chapel**, the vast hall in front of the eastern entrance to the Wang Na. Inside, the fine proportions of the hall, with its ornate coffered ceiling and lacquered window shutters, are enhanced by painted rows of divinities and converted demons, all turned to face the chubby, glowing **Phra Sihing Buddha**, which according to legend was magically created in Sri Lanka in the second century and sent to Sukhothai in the thirteenth century. Like the Emerald Buddha, the image was believed to bring good luck to its owner and was frequently snatched from one northern town to another, until Rama I brought it down from Chiang Mai in 1795 and installed it here in the second king's private chapel. Two other images (in Nakhon Si Thammarat and Chiang Mai) now claim to be the authentic Phra Sihing Buddha, but all three are in fact derived from a lost original – this one is in a fifteenth-century Sukhothai style. It's still much loved by ordinary people and at Thai New Year in April is carried out to the nearby City Hall, where it sits for three days while worshippers sprinkle it with water as a merit-making gesture.

The careful detail and rich, soothing colours of the surrounding two-hundred-year-old **murals** are surprisingly well preserved; the bottom row between the windows narrates the life of the Buddha, beginning in the far right-hand corner with his parents' wedding.

## Tamnak Daeng

On the south side of the Buddhaisawan chapel, the gaudily restored **Tamnak Daeng** (Red House) stands out, a large, airy Ayutthaya-style house made of rare golden teak, surmounted by a multi-tiered roof decorated with swan's-tail finials. Originally part of the private quarters of Princess Sri Sudarak, elder sister of Rama I, it was moved from the Grand Palace to the old palace in Thonburi for Queen Sri Suriyen, wife of Rama II; when her son became second king to Rama IV, he dismantled the edifice again and

RIVERSIDE TEMPLE VIEWED FROM A LONGTAIL BOAT

**1**

shipped it here to the Wang Na compound. Inside, it's furnished in the style of the early Bangkok period, with some of the beautiful objects that once belonged to Sri Suriyen, a huge, ornately carved box-bed, and the uncommon luxury of an indoor bathroom.

# Banglamphu and the Democracy Monument area

Immediately north of Ratanakosin, **Banglamphu**'s most notorious attraction is **Thanon Khao San**, a tiny sliver of a road built over a canal in 1892, whose multiple guesthouses and buzzing, budget-minded nightlife have made it an unmissable way-station for travellers through Southeast Asia. There is plenty of cultural interest too, in a medley of idiosyncratic temples within a few blocks of nearby landmark **Democracy Monument**, and in the typical Bangkok neighbourhoods that connect them, many of which still feel charmingly old-fashioned.

## ARRIVAL AND DEPARTURE   BANGLAMPHU AND THE DEMOCRACY MONUMENT AREA

**By boat** Chao Phraya express-boat stops N13 (Phra Arthit), N14 (Rama VIII bridge) and N15 (Thewet) are nearby (see page 118). Banglamphu is also served by public boats along Khlong Saen Saeb to and from their Phan Fah

terminus, which are useful for Siam Square and the Skytrain, while Thewet to the north is connected by boat along Khlong Phadung Krung Kasem to Hualamphong Station.

**By Skytrain** In addition to connecting to the Skytrain via

---

## AMULETS

To invite good fortune, ward off malevolent spirits and gain protection from physical harm, many Thais wear or carry at least one **amulet** at all times. The most popular images are copies of sacred statues from famous wats, while others show revered monks, kings (Rama V is a favourite) or healers. On the reverse side, a yantra is often inscribed, a combination of letters and figures also designed to deflect evil, sometimes of a very specific nature: protecting your durian orchards from gales, for example, or your tuk-tuk from oncoming traffic. Individually hand-crafted or mass-produced, amulets can be made from bronze, clay, plaster or gold, and some even have sacred ingredients added, such as special herbs, or the ashes of burnt holy texts. But what really determines an amulet's efficacy is its history: where and by whom it was made, who or what it represents and who consecrated it. Stories of miracle cures and lucky escapes also prompt a rush on whatever amulet the survivor was wearing. Monks are often involved in the making of the images and are always called upon to consecrate them – the more charismatic the monk, the more powerful the amulet. Religious authorities take a relaxed view of the amulet industry, despite its anomalous and commercial functions, and proceeds contribute to wat funds and good causes.

The **belief in amulets** is thought to have originated in India, where tiny images were sold to pilgrims who visited the four holy sites associated with the Buddha's life. But not all amulets are Buddhist-related; there's a whole range of other enchanted objects to wear for protection, including tigers' teeth, rose quartz, tamarind seeds, coloured threads and miniature phalluses. Worn around the waist rather than the neck, the phallus amulets provide protection for the genitals as well as being associated with fertility, and are of Hindu origin.

For some people, amulets are not only a vital form of spiritual protection, but valuable **collectors' items** as well. Amulet-collecting mania is something akin to stamp collecting and there are at least half a dozen Thai magazines for collectors, which give histories of certain types, tips on distinguishing between genuine items and fakes, and personal accounts of particularly powerful amulet experiences. The most rewarding places to watch the collectors and browse the wares yourself are at Wat Rajnadda Buddha Centre (see page 94), the biggest amulet market and probably the best place in Bangkok; along "Amulet Alley" on Trok Mahathat, between Wat Mahathat (see page 85) and the river, where streetside vendors will have cheaper examples; and at Chatuchak Weekend Market (see page 110). Prices start as low as B50 and rise into the thousands.

**BANGLAMPHU'S BUS STOPS AND ROUTES**

The main bus stops serving Banglamphu are on Thanon Rajdamnoen Klang: with nearly thirty westbound and eastbound routes, you can get just about anywhere in the city from here. But there are some other useful pick-up points in Banglamphu for routes running out of the area. To make things simpler, we've assigned numbers to these **bus stops**, though they are not numbered on the ground. Where there are two stops served by the same buses they share a number. Bus stops are marked on the Banglamphu map (see page 92).

**Bus stop 1: Thanon Krung Kasem, north side**
#53 (clockwise) to Hualamphong train station

**Bus stop 2: Thanon Phra Sumen, south side; and Thanon Phra Arthit, east side**
#53 (anticlockwise) to the Grand Palace and Chinatown

**Bus stop 3: Thanon Phra Arthit, west side; and Thanon Phra Sumen, north side**
#3 to Chatuchak Weekend Market and Northern Bus Terminal
#15 to Jim Thompson's House, Siam Square and Thanon Silom
#53 (clockwise) to Hualamphong train station (change at Bus Stop 1, but same ticket)

**Bus stop 4: Thanon Chakrabongse**
#3 to Wat Pho, the Museum of Siam and Wongwian Yai train station
#15 to Jim Thompson's House, Siam Square and Thanon Silom

Khlong Saen Saeb boat, the other fast way to get on to the BTS system is to take a taxi from Banglamphu to BTS National Stadium.

**By bus** Dozens of useful buses serve Banglamphu (see pages 91 and 119).

## Thanon Khao San

At the heart of Banglamphu is the legendary **Thanon Khao San**, almost a caricature of a travellers' centre, its pavements lined with cheap backpackers' fashions, tattooists and hair-braiders. It's a lively, high-energy base: great for shopping and making travel arrangements – though beware the innumerable Khao San scams (see page 58) – and a good place to meet other travellers. It's especially fun at night when young Thais from all over the city gather here to browse the clothes stalls, mingle with the crowds of foreigners and squash into the bars and clubs that have made Khao San a great place to party. Even if you're staying elsewhere, the Khao San area is a cultural curiosity in its own right, a unique and continually evolving expression of global youth culture fuelled by Thai entrepreneurship.

## Democracy Monument

The megalithic yellow-tinged wings of **Democracy Monument** (*Anu Sawari Pracha Tippatai*) loom provocatively over Thanon Rajdamnoen Klang, the avenue that connects the Grand Palace and the new royal district of Dusit, and have since their erection in 1939 acted as a focus for pro-democracy rallies. Conceived as a testimony to the ideals that fuelled the 1932 revolution and the changeover to a constitutional monarchy, the monument's positioning between the royal residences is significant, as are its dimensions, which allude to June 24, 2475 BE (1932 AD), the date the system was changed. In the decades since, Thailand's leaders have promulgated numerous interim charters and constitutions, the more repressive and regressive of which have been vigorously challenged in demonstrations on these very streets.

## Thanon Bamrung Muang

**Thanon Bamrung Muang**, which runs east from Thanon Tanao to Sao Ching Cha and Wat Suthat, was an old elephant trail that, a hundred years ago, became one

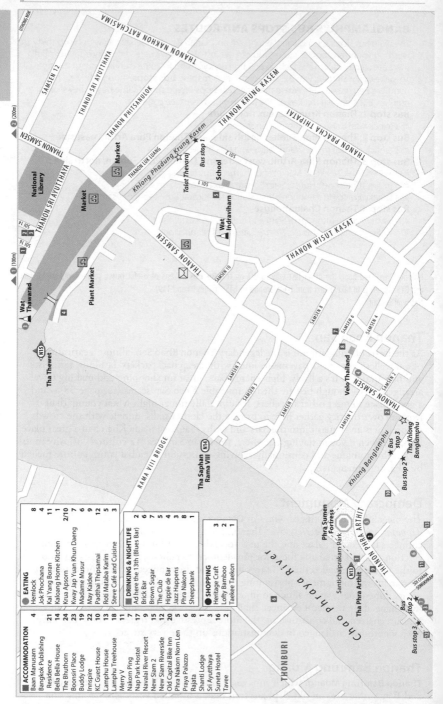

| ■ ACCOMMODATION | |
|---|---|
| Baan Manusarn | 4 |
| Bangkok Publishing Residence | 21 |
| Bella Bella House | 14 |
| The Bhuthorn | 24 |
| Boonsiri Place | 23 |
| Buddy Lodge | 19 |
| Innspire | 22 |
| KC Guest House | 10 |
| Lamphu House | 13 |
| Lamphu Treehouse | 18 |
| Merry V | 11 |
| Nakorn Ping | 7 |
| Nap Park Hostel | 17 |
| Navalai River Resort | 9 |
| New Siam 2 | 15 |
| New Siam Riverside | 12 |
| Old Capital Bike Inn | 20 |
| Phra Nakorn Norn Len | 5 |
| Praya Palazzo | 6 |
| Rajata | 8 |
| Shanti Lodge | 3 |
| Sri Ayutthaya | 16 |
| Suneta Hostel | 2 |
| Tavee | 1 |

| ● EATING | |
|---|---|
| Hemlock | 8 |
| Jok Phochana | 4 |
| Kai Yang Boran | 11 |
| Kaloang Home Kitchen | 1 |
| Krua Apsorn | 2/10 |
| Kway Jap Yuan Khun Daeng | 7 |
| Madame Musur | 6 |
| May Kaidee | 9 |
| Padthai Thipsamai | 12 |
| Roti Mataba Karim | 5 |
| Steve Café and Cuisine | 3 |

| ■ DRINKING & NIGHTLIFE | |
|---|---|
| Ad here the 13th (Blues Bar) | 2 |
| Brick Bar | 6 |
| Brown Sugar | 7 |
| The Club | 5 |
| Hippie de Bar | 4 |
| Jazz Happens | 3 |
| Phra Nakorn | 8 |
| Sheepshank | 1 |

| ■ SHOPPING | |
|---|---|
| Heritage Craft | 3 |
| Lofty Bamboo | 2 |
| Taekee Taekon | 1 |

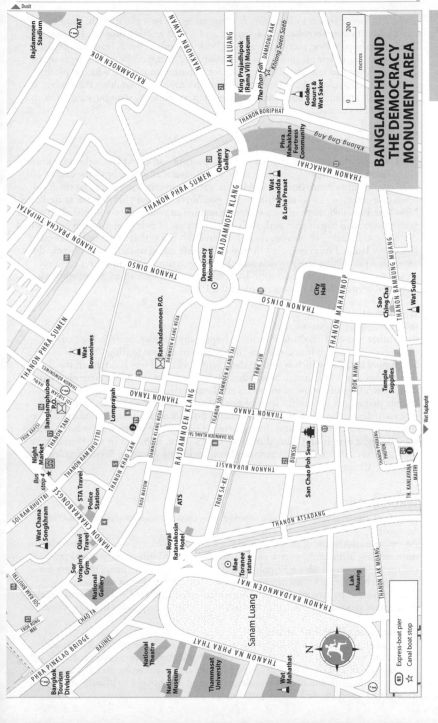

**BANGLAMPHU AND THE DEMOCRACY MONUMENT AREA**

Dusit

TAT

Rajdamnoen Stadium

RAJDAMNOEN NOK

NAKHORN SAWAN

LAN LUANG

King Prajadhipok (Rama VII) Museum

THE PHAN FAH    DAMRONG RAK

Klong Saen Saeb

Golden Mount & Wat Saket

THANON BORIPHAT

THANON PHRA SUMEN

Queen's Gallery

Phra Mahakhan Fortress Community

Klong Ong Ang

THANON MAHACHAI

Wat Rajnadda & Loha Prasat

THANON PRACHA THIPATAI

RAJDAMNOEN KLANG

THANON DINSO

Democracy Monument

THANON DINSO

City Hall

THANON MAHANNOP

THANON BAMRUNG MUANG

Sao Ching Cha

Wat Surthat

THANON PHRA SUMEN

Wat Bowoniwes

Ratchadamnoen P.O.

DAMNOEN KLANG NEUA

SOI SIBSAM BANG

THANON BOWONNIWES

Banglamphubon P.O.

THANON TANAO

TROK SIN

Temple Supplies

TROK NAWA

Lomprayah

THANON TANI

THANON RAM BHUTTRI

THANON KHAO SAN

RAJDAMNOEN KLANG

DAMNOEN KLANG NEUA

SOI DAMNOEN KLANG TAI

THANON SOI DAMNOEN KLANG TAI

THANON TANAO

TROK NAWA

TROK SIN

Night Market

Bus stop 4

STA Travel

Police Station

TROK MAYOM

TROK SA-KE

THANON BURANASIT

BUNSRI

San Chao Poh Seua

THANON PHRAENG PHUTON

TH. KANLAYANA MAITRI

Wat Rajabopit

SOI RAM BHUTTRI

Wat Chana Songkhram

Sor Vorapin's Gym

Olavi Travel

National Gallery

THANON CHAKRABONGSE

ATS

Royal Ratanakosin Hotel

THANON ATSADANG

Lak Muang

THANON LAK MUANG

SOI RAM BHUTTRI

TROK RONG MAI

PHRA PINKLAO BRIDGE

CHAO FA

RAJINEE

Bangkok Tourism Division

National Theatre

National Museum

Thammasat University

THANON NA PHRA THAT

Sanam Luang

Wat Mahathat

THANON RAJDAMNOEN NAI

Mae Toranee statue

N

Express-boat pier

Canal boat stop

0    200    metres

**1**

of the first paved streets in Bangkok. It's famous as the best place in Thailand to buy **Buddhist paraphernalia**, or *sanghapan*, and is well worth a browse. The road is lined with shops selling everything a good Buddhist might need, from household offertory tables to temple umbrellas and cellophane-wrapped Buddha images up to 2m high. They also sell special alms packs for donating to monks, which typically come in saffron-coloured plastic buckets (used by monks for washing their robes, or themselves), and include such necessities as soap, toothpaste, soap powder, toilet roll, candles and incense.

## Sao Ching Cha
Midway along Thanon Bamrung Muang, just in front of Wat Suthat

You can't miss the towering, red-painted teak posts of **Sao Ching Cha**, otherwise known as the **Giant Swing**, though it's likely to be swathed in scaffolding until the end of 2018 or so during renovation. Built in 1784, this strange contraption used to be the focal point of a ceremony to honour the Hindu god Shiva's annual visit to earth at Brahmin New Year, in which teams of young men competed to swing up to a height of 25m and grab a suspended bag of gold with their teeth. The act of swinging probably symbolized the rising and setting of the sun, though legend also has it that Shiva and his consort Uma were banned from swinging in heaven because doing so caused cataclysmic floods on earth – prompting Shiva to demand that the practice be continued on earth to ensure moderate rains and bountiful harvests. Accidents were so common with the terrestrial version that it was outlawed in the 1930s.

## Wat Suthat
Thanon Bamrung Muang • Daily 9am–4pm • B20

**Wat Suthat** is one of Thailand's six most important temples, built in the early nineteenth century to house the 8m-high statue of the meditating **Phra Sri Sakyamuni Buddha**, which is said to date from 1361 and was brought all the way down from Wat Mahathat in Sukhothai by river. It now sits on a glittering mosaic dais, which contains some of the ashes of Rama VIII, surrounded with surreal murals that depict the last 24 lives of the Buddha rather than the more usual ten. The encircling galleries contain 156 serenely posed Buddha images, making a nice contrast to the **Chinese statues** dotted around the temple courtyards, most of which were brought over from China during Rama I's reign, as ballast in rice boats; there are some fun character studies among them, including gormless Western sailors and pompous Chinese scholars.

# Wat Rajnadda
5min walk east of Democracy Monument, at the point where Rajdamnoen Klang meets Thanon Mahachai • **Loha Prasat** Daily 9am–5pm • B20

Among the assortment of religious buildings known collectively as **Wat Rajnadda**, the most striking is the multi-tiered, castle-like, early nineteenth-century **Loha Prasat**, or "Iron Monastery", whose 37 golden spires represent the 37 virtues necessary for attaining enlightenment. Modelled on a now-defunct Sri Lankan monastery, its tiers are pierced by passageways running north–south and east–west (fifteen in each direction at ground level) with small meditation cells at each point of intersection.

## Wat Rajnadda Buddha Centre
In the southeast (Thanon Mahachai) corner of the temple compound, Bangkok's biggest **amulet market**, the **Wat Rajnadda Buddha Centre**, shelters dozens of stalls selling tiny Buddha images of all designs. Alongside these miniature charms are statues of Hindu deities, dolls and carved wooden phalluses, also bought to placate or ward off disgruntled spirits, as well as love potions.

# Wat Saket

Easiest access is along Thanon Boriphat (the specialist street for custom-carved wooden doors), 5min walk south from the khlong bridge and Phan Fah canal-boat stop at the eastern end of Rajdamnoen Klang

Beautifully illuminated at night, when it seems to float unsupported above the neighbourhood, the gleaming gold chedi of late eighteenth-century **Wat Saket** actually sits atop a structure known as the Golden Mount. Being outside the capital's city walls, the wat initially served as a crematorium and then a dumping ground for sixty thousand plague victims left to the vultures because they couldn't afford funeral pyres. There's no sign of this grim episode at modern-day Wat Saket of course, which these days is a smart, buzzing hive of religious activity at the base of the golden hilltop chedi. Wat Saket hosts an enormous annual **temple fair** in the first week of November, when the mount is illuminated with lanterns and the compound seethes with funfair rides and travelling theatre shows.

## The Golden Mount

Daily 7.30am–7pm • B20

The **Golden Mount**, or **Phu Khao Tong**, dates back to the early nineteenth century, when Rama III commissioned a huge chedi to be constructed here, using building materials from the ruined fortresses and walls of the former capital, Ayutthaya. However, the ground proved too soft to support the chedi. The whole thing collapsed into a hill of rubble, but as Buddhist law states that a religious building can never be destroyed, however tumbledown, fifty years later Rama V simply crowned it with the more sensibly sized chedi we see today, in which he placed some relics of the Buddha's teeth from India, donated by the British government. These days the old rubbly base is picturesquely planted with shrubs and shady trees and dotted with memorials and cooling waterfalls. Winding stairways take you up to the chedi terrace and a fine view over Banglamphu and Ratanakosin landmarks, including the golden spires of the Grand Palace, the finely proportioned prangs of Wat Arun across the river beyond and, further upriver, the striking superstructure of the Rama VIII bridge.

# Chinatown

When the newly crowned Rama I decided to move his capital across to the east bank of the river in 1782, the Chinese community living on the proposed site of his palace was obliged to relocate downriver, to the **Sampeng** area. Two centuries on, **Chinatown** has grown into the country's largest Chinese district, a sprawl of narrow alleyways, temples and shophouses packed between Charoen Krung (New Road) and the river, bordered to the east by **Hualamphong** train station.

The **Chinese influence** on Thai culture and commerce has been significant ever since the first Chinese merchants gained a toehold in Ayutthaya in the fourteenth century. Following centuries of immigration and intermarriage, there is now some Chinese blood in almost every Thai citizen, including the king, and Chinese-Thai business interests play an enormous role in the Thai economy. This is played out at its most frantic in Chinatown, whose real estate is said to be among the most valuable in the country; there are over a hundred gold and jewellery shops along Thanon Yaowarat alone.

For the tourist, Chinatown is chiefly interesting for its **markets**, shophouses, open-fronted warehouses and remnants of colonial-style architecture, though it also harbours a few noteworthy **temples**. A meander through its most interesting neighbourhoods could easily fill up a whole day, allowing for frequent breaks from the thundering traffic and choking fumes. For the most authentic Chinatown experience, it's best to come during the week (before 5pm), as some shops and stalls shut at weekends.

1

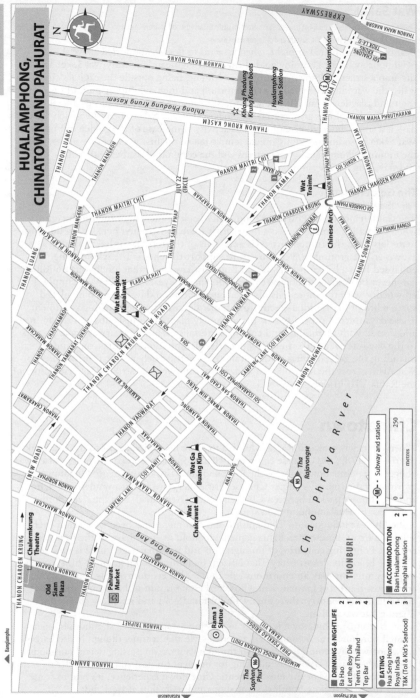

# HUALAMPHONG, CHINATOWN AND PAHURAT

Chao Phraya River

THONBURI

**Chinese Arch**

**Wat Traimit**

**Wat Mangkon Kamalawat**

**Wat Ga Buang Kim**

**Wat Chakrawat**

**Pahurat Market**

**Old Siam Plaza**

**Chalermkrung Theatre**

**Rama 1 Statue**

**Hualamphong Train Station**

**Khlong Phadung Krung Kasem boats**

Tha Rajavongse

Tha Saphan Phut

--- (M) --- Subway and station

0          250
    metres

■ ACCOMMODATION
Baan Hualamphong     2
Shanghai Mansion     1

● EATING
Hua Seng Hong            2
Royal India                  1
T&K (Toi & Kid's Seafood) 3

■ DRINKING & NIGHTLIFE
Ba Hao              2
Let the Boy Die     1
Teens of Thailand   3
Tep Bar             4

**Arrival** The easiest way to reach Chinatown is either by subway to Hualamphong Station, or by Chao Phraya express boat to Tha Rachawongse (Rajawong; N5) at the southern end of Thanon Rajawong. A westward extension of the subway is being built (with a proposed opening in 2019), with new stations at Wat Mangkon Kamalawat and near Pahurat. This part of the city is also well served by buses, with Hualamphong a useful and easily recognized place to disembark. Be warned that buses and taxis may take an unexpectedly circuitous route due to the many and complex one-way systems in Chinatown.

**Getting around** Orientation in Chinatown can be tricky: the alleys (often known as trok rather than the more usual soi) are extremely narrow, their turn-offs and other road signs often obscured by mounds of merchandise and thronging crowds, and the longer ones can change their names several times. For a detailed tour of the alleys and markets, use *Nancy Chandler's Map of Bangkok* (see page 113); alternatively, ask for help at one of the BMA tourist information booths, either just northwest of the Chinese Arch at the beginning of Thanon Yaowarat, beside Soi 5, or in front of Hualamphong Station (both Mon–Sat 9am–5pm).

# Wat Traimit

Thanon Mittaphap Thai-China, just west of Hualamphong train and subway stations (exit 1) • Daily 8am–5pm; exhibitions closed Mon • Golden Buddha only B40; Golden Buddha and exhibitions B100 • ⓦ wattraimitr-withayaram.com

The obvious place to start a Chinatown tour is on its eastern perimeter, with **Wat Traimit** and its famous Golden Buddha. You can see the temple mondop's golden spire from quite a distance, a fitting beacon for the gleaming treasure housed on its third floor, the world's largest solid-gold Buddha. It's an apt attraction for a community so closely linked with the gold trade, even if the image has nothing to do with China's spiritual heritage. A recent attempt has been made to bridge this gap, with the installation of exhibitions on the mondop's first two floors, covering the history of Chinatown and the Buddha image.

## The Golden Buddha

Over 3m tall and weighing five tonnes, the **Golden Buddha** gleams as if coated in liquid metal, seated on a white marble lotus-pad pedestal and surrounded with offerings of lotus flowers. It's a fine example of the curvaceous grace of Sukhothai art, slim-waisted and beautifully proportioned. Cast in the thirteenth century, the image was brought to Bangkok by Rama III, completely encased in stucco – a common ruse to conceal valuable statues from would-be thieves. The disguise was so good that no one guessed what was underneath until 1955 when the image was accidentally knocked in the process of being moved to Wat Traimit, and the stucco cracked to reveal a patch of gold. Just in time for Buddhism's 2500th anniversary, the discovery launched a country-wide craze for tapping away at plaster Buddhas in search of hidden precious metals, but Wat Traimit's is still the most valuable – it is valued, by weight alone, at around US$250 million.

## The exhibitions

The exhibition on the making and history of the Golden Buddha, on the second floor of the mondop, is fairly missable, but the **Yaowarat Chinatown Heritage Centre** on the floor below is rather more compelling. Interesting though sanitized, its display boards trace the rapid expansion of the Chinese presence in Bangkok from the late eighteenth century, first as junk traders, later as labourers and tax farmers. Enhancing the story are a diorama of life on board a junk, lots of interesting photos from the late nineteenth century onwards and a fascinating scale model of Thanon Yaowarat in its 1950s heyday, when it was Bangkok's business and entertainment hub.

# Sampeng Lane

From Wat Traimit, walk northwest from the big China Gate roundabout along Thanon Yaowarat, and make a left turn onto Thanon Songsawat to reach Sampeng Lane

One of Chinatown's most enjoyable shopping alleys, **Sampeng Lane** (also signposted as Soi Wanit 1) is where the Chinese community first settled in the area, when they were

**1**

moved from Ratanakosin in the late eighteenth century to make way for the Grand Palace. Stretching southeast–northwest for about 1km, it's a great place to browse, unfurling itself like a serpentine department store and selling everything from Chinese silk pyjama trousers to selfie sticks at bargain rates. Similar goods are more or less gathered in sections, so at the eastern end you'll find mostly cheap jewellery and hair accessories, for example, before passing through stalls specializing in Chinese lanterns, stationery, toys, then shoes, clothes (west of Thanon Rajawong) and, as you near Pahurat, fabrics, haberdashery and irresistibly girlie accessories.

## Soi Issaranuphap

Taking a right turn about halfway down Sampeng Lane will bring you into **Soi Issaranuphap** (also signed along its course as Yaowarat Soi 11, then Soi 6, and later Charoen Krung sois 16 and 21). Packed with people from dawn till dusk, this long, dark alleyway, which also traverses Charoen Krung, is where locals come in search of ginseng roots (essential for good health), quivering fish heads, cubes of cockroach-killer chalk and a gastronome's choice of dried mushrooms and brine-pickled vegetables. Alleys branch off to florid Chinese temples and tiny squares before Soi Issaranuphap finally ends at the Thanon Plaplachai intersection amid a flurry of shops specializing in paper **funeral art**. Believing that the deceased should be well provided for in their afterlife, Chinese people buy miniature paper replicas of necessities to be burned with the body: especially popular are houses, cars, suits of clothing and, of course, money.

## Wat Mangkon Kamalawat

Best approached via its dramatic multi-tiered gateway 10m up Thanon Charoen Krung from the Soi Issaranuphap junction

If Soi Issaranuphap epitomizes age-old Chinatown commerce, then **Wat Mangkon Kamalawat** (also known as **Wat Leng Noei Yee** or, in English, "Dragon Flower Temple") stands as a fine example of the community's spiritual practices. Built in 1871, it receives a constant stream of devotees, who come to leave offerings at the altars inside this important Mahayana Buddhist temple. As with the Theravada Buddhism espoused by the Thais, Mahayana Buddhism fuses with other ancient religious beliefs, notably Confucianism and Taoism, and the statues and shrines within Wat Mangkon cover the spectrum.

As you pass through the secondary gateway, under the glazed ceramic gables topped with undulating Chinese dragons, you're greeted by a set of forbidding statues of four guardian kings (one for each point of the compass), each symbolically clasping either a parasol, a pagoda, a snake's head or a mandolin. Beyond them, a series of Chinese-style Buddha images swathed in saffron netting occupies the next chamber, a lovely open-sided room of gold paintwork, red-lacquered wood, lattice lanterns and pictorial wall panels inlaid with mother-of-pearl. Elsewhere in the compound are booths selling devotional paraphernalia, a Chinese medicine stall and a fortune-teller.

# Thonburi

For fifteen years between the fall of Ayutthaya in 1767 and the founding of Bangkok in 1782, the west-bank town of **Thonburi**, across the Chao Phraya from modern-day Bangkok, stood in as the Thai capital, under the rule of General Phraya Taksin. Its time in the spotlight was too brief for the building of the fine monuments and temples that graced earlier capitals at Sukhothai and Ayutthaya, but some of its centuries-old **canals**, which once transported everyone and everything, have endured; it is these and the ways of life that depend on them that constitute Thonburi's main attractions. In

1

some quarters, life on this side of the river still revolves around these khlongs: vendors of food and household goods paddle their boats along the canals that crisscross the residential areas, and canalside factories use them to ferry their wares to the Chao Phraya River artery. Venture onto the backroads just three or four kilometres west of the river and you find yourself surrounded by market gardens and rural homes, with no hint of the throbbing metropolis across on the other bank. The most popular way to explore these old neighbourhoods is by **boat**, but joining a bicycle tour of the older neighbourhoods is also very rewarding (see page 116). Most boat trips also encompass Thonburi's imposing riverside Temple of the Dawn, **Wat Arun**, and often the **Royal Barge Museum** as well, though both are easily visited independently.

## ARRIVAL AND GETTING AROUND                                    THONBURI

**Arrival** Getting to Thonburi is generally just a matter of crossing the river. Either use Phra Pinklao or Memorial/Phra Pokklao bridge, take a cross-river ferry, or hop on one of the express boats, which make several stops on the Thonburi bank. The planned subway extension from Hualamphong, currently scheduled to open in 2019, will include a station near Wat Arun.

**Getting around** If you're not exploring Thonburi on a boat tour (see box opposite), getting around the district can be complicated as the lack of footbridges over canals means that walking between sights often involves using the heavily trafficked Thanon Arun Amarin. A more convoluted alternative would be to leapfrog your way up or down the river by boat, using the various cross-river ferries that connect the Thonburi bank with the Chao Phraya express-boat stops on the other side.

# Royal Barge Museum

Soi Wat Dusitaram, north bank of Khlong Bangkok Noi • Daily 9am–5pm • B100, plus B100 for a camera permit • Take the Chao Phraya express boat to Tha Phra Pinklao (N12), or cross-river ferry from under Pinklao Bridge in Banglamphu to Tha Phra Pinklao, then walk up the road 100m and take the first left down Soi Wat Dusitaram; if coming by bus from the Bangkok side (#507, #509 and #511 all cross the river here), get off at the first stop on the Thonburi side, which is at the mouth of Soi Wat Dusitaram – signs from Soi Wat Dusitaram lead you through a jumble of walkways and stilt-houses to the museum (10min)

Since the Ayutthaya era, kings of Thailand have been conveyed along their country's waterways in royal barges. For centuries, these slender, exquisitely elegant, black-and-gold wooden vessels were used on all important royal outings, and even up until 1967 the current king would process down the Chao Phraya to Wat Arun in a flotilla of royal barges at least once a year, on the occasion of Kathin, the annual donation of robes by the laity to the temple at the end of the rainy season. But the boats, some of which are a hundred years old, are becoming quite frail, so **royal barge processions** are now held only every few years to mark very special anniversaries. However, if your trip happens to coincide with one of these magnificent events, you shouldn't miss it (see ⓦ tourismthailand.org). Fifty or more barges fill the width of the river and stretch for almost 1km, drifting slowly to the measured beat of a drum and the hypnotic strains of ancient boating hymns, chanted by over two thousand oarsmen dressed in luscious brocades.

The most important vessels at the heart of the ceremony are suspended above their docks in the **Royal Barge Museum**, which often features as part of longtail-boat tours. Up to 50m long and intricately lacquered and gilded all over, they taper at the prow into imposing mythical figures after a design first used by the kings of Ayutthaya. Rama I had the boats copied and, when those fell into disrepair, Rama VI commissioned exact reconstructions, some of which are still in use today. The most important is *Sri Suphanahongse*, which bears the king and is graced by a glittering 5m-high prow representing the golden swan Hamsa, mount of the Hindu god Brahma; constructed from a single piece of timber, it's said to be the largest dugout boat in the world. In front of it floats *Anantanagaraj*, fronted by a magnificent seven-headed naga and bearing a Buddha image. The newest addition to the fleet is *Narai Song Suban*, which was commissioned by the current king for his golden jubilee in 1996; it is a copy of the mid-nineteenth-century original and is crowned with a black Vishnu (Narai)

1

## EXPLORING THONBURI BY BOAT

The most popular way to explore the sights of Thonburi is by **boat**, taking in Wat Arun and the Royal Barge Museum, then continuing along Thonburi's network of small canals. We've detailed some interesting, fixed-price tours below, but generally it's just a question of turning up at a pier on the Bangkok side of the Chao Phraya and chartering a longtail. At the pier beneath Phra Pinklao Bridge, behind the Bangkok Tourism Division head office in Banglamphu, a kiss-me-quick hour-long ride will cost from B700 for two people, while a two-hour trip, taking in an orchid farm deep among the Thonburi canals, costs from B1200. You can also charter your own longtail from Tha Phra Athit, River City shopping centre, Tha Sathorn and other piers.

Many tours include visits to one of Thonburi's two main **floating markets**, both of which are heavily touristed and rather contrived. **Wat Sai** floating market is very small, very commercialized and worth avoiding; **Taling Chan** floating market is also fairly manufactured but more fun, though it only operates on Saturdays and Sundays (roughly 8am–4pm). For a more authentic floating-market experience, consider heading out of Bangkok to Amphawa or Tha Kha, in Samut Songkhram province.

Arguably more photogenic, and certainly a lot more genuine than the floating markets, are the individual **floating vendors** who continue to paddle from house to house in Thonburi, touting anything from hot food to plastic buckets. You've a good chance of seeing some of them in action on almost any longtail boat tour on any day of the week, particularly in the morning.

**Mitchaopaya Travel Service** Tha Chang – on the left at the start of the pier, as you walk in from Thanon Na Phra Lan ☎ 02 225 6179. Licensed by TAT, offering fixed-price trips along the Thonburi canals of varying durations: in 1hr (B1000/boat, maximum 6 people, or B450/person if you can join in with other people), you'll pass Wat Arun and the Royal Barge Museum without stopping; in 90min (B1300), you'd have time to stop at either; while in 2hr (B1500) you'll have time to go right down the back canals on the Thonburi side and visit an orchid farm. On Saturday and Sunday, the 2hr trip takes in Taling Chan floating market. **Pandan Tour** 780/488 Thanon Charoen Krung ☎ 087 109 8873, ⓦ thaicanaltour.com. A selection of full-day tours of the Thonburi canals, the floating markets and beyond on an eco-friendly, natural-gas-powered teak boat, in small groups with a good English-speaking guide, starting from B2300/person, including lunch.

astride a garuda figurehead. A display of miniaturized royal barges at the back of the museum recreates the exact formation of a traditional procession.

# Wat Arun

Daily 8am–6pm • B50 • ⓦ watarun.org • Take the cross-river ferry from the pier adjacent to the Chao Phraya express-boat pier at Tha Thien (at the time of research, the Chao Phraya express-boat pier at Tha Thien was under renovation – for how long, it's not clear – and orange- and no-flag express boats were stopping instead at Wat Arun itself, across the river)

Almost directly across the river from Wat Pho rises the enormous, gleamingly restored five-spired prang of **Wat Arun**, the Temple of Dawn, probably Bangkok's most memorable landmark and familiar as the silhouette used in the TAT logo. It looks particularly impressive from the river as you head downstream from the Grand Palace towards the *Oriental Hotel*, but is ornate enough to be well worth stopping off for a closer look.

A wat has occupied this site since the Ayutthaya period, but only in 1768 did it become known as the Temple of Dawn – when General Phraya Taksin reputedly reached his new capital at the break of day. The temple served as his royal chapel and housed the recaptured Emerald Buddha for several years until the image was moved to Wat Phra Kaeo in 1785. Despite losing its special status after the relocation, Wat Arun continued to be revered, and its corncob prang was reconstructed and enlarged to its present height of 81m by Rama II and Rama III.

The prang that you see today is classic Ayutthayan style, built as a representation of Mount Meru, the home of the gods in Khmer cosmology. Both the **central prang** and the four minor ones that encircle it are studded all over with bits of broken porcelain, ceramic shards and tiny bowls that have been fashioned into an amazing array of polychromatic flowers. The statues of mythical *yaksha* demons and half-bird, half-human *kinnari* that support the different levels are similarly decorated. The crockery probably came from China, possibly from commercial shipments that were damaged at sea or used as ballast, and the overall effect is highly decorative and far more subtle than the dazzling glass mosaics that clad most wat buildings. On the first terrace, the mondops at each cardinal point contain statues of the Buddha at birth (north), in meditation (east), preaching his first sermon (south) and entering Nirvana (west). The second platform surrounds the base of the prang proper, whose closed entranceways are guarded by four statues of the Hindu god Indra on his three-headed elephant Erawan. In the niches of the smaller prangs stand statues of Phra Pai, the god of the wind, on horseback.

# Dusit

Connected to Ratanakosin via the boulevards of Rajdamnoen Klang and Rajdamnoen Nok, the spacious, leafy area known as **Dusit** has been a royal district since the reign of Rama V, King Chulalongkorn (1860–1910). The first Thai monarch to visit Europe, Rama V returned with radical plans for the modernization of his capital, the fruits of which are most visible in Dusit, notably at **Vimanmek Palace** and **Wat Benjamabophit**, the so-called "Marble Temple". Even now, **Rama V** still commands a loyal following and the statue of him, helmeted and on horseback, which stands in Royal Plaza at the Thanon U-Thong Nai/Thanon Sri Ayutthaya crossroads, is presented with offerings every week and is also the focus of celebrations on Chulalongkorn Day (Oct 23). On December 2, Dusit is also the venue for the spectacular annual **Trooping the Colour**, when hundreds of magnificently uniformed Royal Guards demonstrate their allegiance to the king by parading around Royal Plaza.

Today, the Dusit area retains its European feel, and much of the country's decision-making goes on behind the high fences and impressive facades along its tree-lined avenues: the building that houses the National Parliament is here, as is Government House and the king's residence, Amporn Palace, while the Queen Mother's home, Chitrlada Palace, occupies the eastern edge of the area. Normally a calm, stately district, in both 2008 and 2013 Dusit became the focus of **mass anti-government protests** by royalist yellow-shirts, who occupied Thanon Rajdamnoen Nok for several months on both occasions, creating a heavily defended temporary village in this most refined of neighbourhoods.

## ARRIVAL AND DEPARTURE                                    DUSIT

**By bus** From Banglamphu, you can get to Dusit by taking the #70 (non-expressway) bus from Rajdamnoen Klang and getting off near the Rama V statue for Wat Benjamabophit, or outside the zoo and Elephant Museum on Thanon U-Thong Nai. From downtown Bangkok, take one of the many buses (including #28) from the Skytrain stop at Victory Monument.

**By boat** From the express-boat pier at Tha Thewet, it's approximately a 30min walk to Dusit Park, to the zoo or to Wat Benjamabophit. There's also another pier near the Thanon Nakhon Sawan bridge on the Khlong Phadung Krung Kasem boat line that's convenient for Wat Benjamabophit.

## Dusit Park

Main entrance on Thanon Rajwithi, with another ticket gate opposite Dusit Zoo on Thanon U-Thong Nai • Currently closed for renovation – check ⓦ vimanmek.com for the latest

The outstanding feature of what's known as **Dusit Park** is the breezy, elegant **Vimanmek Palace**, which was originally built by Rama V as a summer retreat on Ko Si Chang in 1868; however, he realized that the palace was strategically too vulnerable, after the French briefly invaded the island in the 1890s, and had it transported here bit by bit in

**1**

1901. Among a dozen other specialist collections in Dusit Park, which include antique textiles, royal photographs, royal ceremonial paraphernalia and antique clocks, housed in handsome, pastel-painted, former royal residences, the most interesting are the Support Museum and Elephant Museum. Note that the same **dress rules** apply here as to the Grand Palace (see page 79), though T-shirts and sarongs are for sale for those who do not pass muster.

## Vimanmek Palace

Built almost entirely of golden teak without a single nail, the coffee-coloured, L-shaped **Vimanmek Palace** is encircled by delicate latticework verandas that look out onto well-kept lawns, flower gardens and lotus ponds. Not surprisingly, this "Celestial Residence" soon became Rama V's favourite palace, and he and his enormous retinue of officials, concubines and children stayed here for lengthy periods between 1902 and 1906. All of Vimanmek's 81 rooms were out of bounds to male visitors, except for the king's own apartments in the octagonal tower, which were entered by a separate staircase.

On display inside is Rama V's collection of **artefacts** from all over the world, including *bencharong* ceramics, European furniture and bejewelled Thai betel-nut sets. Considered progressive in his day, Rama V introduced many newfangled ideas to Thailand: the country's first indoor bathroom is here, as is the earliest typewriter with Thai characters, and some of the first portrait paintings – portraiture had until then been seen as a way of stealing part of the sitter's soul.

## The Support Museum

Immediately behind (to the east of) Vimanmek Palace, Dusit Park

The **Support Museum** is housed in a very pretty hundred-year-old building, the Abhisek Dusit Throne Hall, which was formerly used for meetings and banquets. It showcases the exquisite handicrafts produced under the Queen Mother's charity project, Support, which works to revitalize traditional Thai arts and crafts. Outstanding exhibits include a collection of handbags, baskets and pots woven from the *lipao* fern that grows wild in southern Thailand; jewellery and figurines inlaid with the iridescent wings of beetles; gold and silver nielloware; and lengths of intricately woven silk from the northeast.

## Chang Ton Royal Elephant National Museum

Just behind (to the east of) the Support Museum, inside the Thanon U-Thong Nai entrance to Dusit Park

These two whitewashed buildings once served as the stables for the king's white elephants. Now that the sacred pachyderms have been relocated, the stables have been turned into the **Royal Elephant National Museum**. Inside you'll find some interesting pieces of elephant paraphernalia, including sacred ropes, mahouts' amulets and magic formulae, as well as photos of the all-important ceremony in which a white elephant is granted royal status.

# Wat Benjamabophit

Corner of Thanon Sri Ayutthaya and Thanon Rama V: 200m south of the zoo's east entrance, or about 600m from Vimanmek's U-Thong Nai gate • Daily 7am–6pm • B20 • ⓦ facebook.com/watbencha

**Wat Benjamabophit** (aka Wat Ben) is a fascinating fusion of classical Thai and nineteenth-century European design, which features on the front of five-baht coins. The Carrara-marble walls of its bot – hence the tourist tag "**The Marble Temple**" – are pierced by unusual stained-glass windows, neo-Gothic in style but depicting figures from Thai mythology. Rama V commissioned the temple in 1899, at a time when he was keen to show the major regional powers, Britain and France, that Thailand was *siwilai* (civilized), in order to baulk their usual excuse for colonizing. The temple's sema stones are a telling example of the compromises involved: they're usually prominent markers of the bot's sacred area, but here they're hard to spot, decorative and almost

## THE ROYAL WHITE ELEPHANTS

In Thailand, the most revered of all elephants are the so-called **white elephants** – actually tawny brown albinos – which are considered so sacred that they all, whether wild or captive, belong to the king by law. Their special status originates from Buddhist mythology, which tells how the previously barren Queen Maya became pregnant with the future Buddha after dreaming one night that a white elephant had entered her womb. The thirteenth-century King Ramkhamhaeng of Sukhothai adopted the beast as a symbol of the great and the divine, decreeing that a Thai king's greatness should be measured by the number of white elephants he owns. A white elephant appeared on the Thai national flag until 1917, and the last king, Rama IX, had eleven white elephants, the largest royal collection to date.

Before an elephant can be granted official "white elephant" status, it has to pass a stringent assessment of its physical and behavioural **characteristics**. Key qualities include a paleness of seven crucial areas – eyes, nails, palate, hair, outer edges of the ears, tail and testicles – and an all-round genteel demeanour, manifested, for instance, in the way in which it cleans its food before eating, or in a tendency to sleep in a kneeling position. Tradition holds that an elaborate ceremony should take place every time a new white elephant is presented to the king, with the animal paraded with great pomp from its place of capture to Bangkok, before being anointed with holy water in front of an audience of priests and dignitaries. Rama IX, however, called time on this exorbitantly expensive ritual, and the royal white elephants now live in less luxurious, rural accommodation under the care of the Thai Elephant Conservation Centre.

The expression "white elephant" probably derives from the legend that the kings used to present certain troublesome noblemen with one of these exotic creatures. The animal required expensive attention but, being royal, could not be put to work in order to pay for its upkeep.

apologetic – look for the two small, stone lotus buds at the front of the bot on top of the white, Italianate balustrade. Inside the unusually cruciform bot, a fine replica of the highly revered Phra Buddha Chinnarat image of Phitsanulok contains some of Rama V's bones. The courtyard behind the bot houses a gallery of Buddha images from all over Asia, set up by Rama V as an overview of different representations of the Buddha.

Wat Benjamabophit is one of the best temples in Bangkok to see religious **festivals** and rituals. Whereas monks elsewhere tend to go out on the streets every morning in search of alms, at the Marble Temple the ritual is reversed, and merit-makers come to them. Between about 5.30 and 7 or 7.30am, the monks line up on Thanon Nakhon Pathom, their bowls ready to receive donations of curry and rice, lotus buds, incense, even toilet paper and Coca-Cola; the demure row of saffron-robed monks is a sight that's well worth getting up early for. The evening candlelight processions around the bot during the Buddhist festivals of Maha Puja (in Feb) and Visakha Puja (in May) are among the most entrancing in the country.

# Downtown Bangkok

Extending east from the main rail line and south to Thanon Sathorn and beyond, **downtown Bangkok** is central to the colossal expanse of Bangkok as a whole, but rather peripheral in a sightseer's perception of the city. In this modern high-rise area, you'll find the main shopping centres around **Siam Square**, though don't come looking for an elegant commercial piazza here: the "square" is in fact a grid of small streets, sheltering trendy fashion shops, cinemas and inexpensive restaurants. It lies to the southeast of **Pathumwan intersection**, the junction of Thanon Rama I (in Thai, "Thanon Phra Ram Neung") and Thanon Phrayathai, and the name is applied freely to the surrounding area. Further east, you'll find yet more shopping malls around the noisy and glittering **Erawan Shrine**, where Rama I becomes Thanon Ploenchit, an intersection known as **Ratchaprasong**. It was here that the opposition redshirts set up a fortified camp for several months in early 2010, before the Democrat Party government sent in the

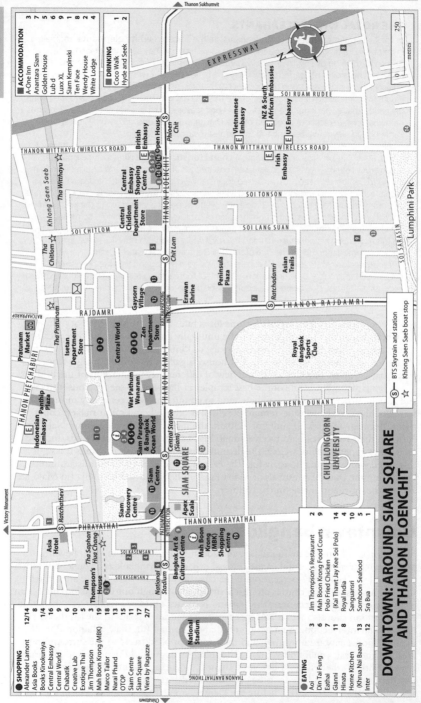

▲ Thanon Sukhumvit

| ■ ACCOMMODATION | |
|---|---|
| A-One Inn | 3 |
| Anantara Siam | 7 |
| Golden House | 5 |
| Lub d | 6 |
| Luxx XL | 9 |
| Siam Kempinski | 1 |
| Ten Face | 8 |
| Wendy House | 2 |
| White Lodge | 4 |

| ■ DRINKING | |
|---|---|
| Coco Walk | 1 |
| Hyde and Seek | 2 |

EXPRESSWAY

THANON WITTHAYU (WIRELESS ROAD)

Phloen Chit

British Embassy

Open House

Vietnamese Embassy

NZ & South African Embassies

US Embassy

SOI RUAM RUDEE

Irish Embassy

THANON WITTHAYU (WIRELESS ROAD)

Khlong Saen Saeb

Tha Witthayu

Central Embassy Shopping Centre

THANON PLOENCHIT

SOI TONSON

SOI LANG SUAN

Tha Chitlom

SOI CHITLOM

Central Chidlom Department Store

Chit Lom

Asian Trails

SOI SARASIN

Lumphini Park

Tha Pratunam

RAJDAMRI

RATCHAPRASONG

Gaysorn Village

Erawan Shrine

Peninsula Plaza

Ratchadamri

THANON RAJDAMRI

Pratunam Market

RATCHAPRAROP

THANON PHETCHABURI

Isetan Department Store

Central World

Zen Department Store

THANON RAMA I

Royal Bangkok Sports Club

BTS Skytrain and station

Khlong Saen Saeb boat stop

▲ Victory Monument

Tha Pratunam

Indonesian Embassy

Panthip Plaza

Wat Pathum Wanaram

THANON HENRI DUNANT

CHULALONGKORN UNIVERSITY

Siam Paragon & Bangkok Ocean World

Central Station (Siam)

Siam Centre

Asia Hotel

PHRAYATHAI

Ratchathevi

Jim Thompson's House

Tha Saphan Hua Chang

SOI KASEMSAN 1

SOI KASEMSAN 2

Siam Discovery Centre

PATHUMWAN INTERSECTION

Apex Scala

SIAM SQUARE

THANON PHRAYATHAI

National Stadium

Bangkok Art & Cultural Centre

Mah Boon Krong (MBK) Shopping Centre

THANON BANTHATTHONG

0 ____ 250 metres

| ● SHOPPING | |
|---|---|
| Alexander Lamont | 12/14 |
| Asia Books | 8 |
| Books Kinokuniya | 1/4 |
| Central Embassy | 16 |
| Central World | 9 |
| Chabatik | 6 |
| Creative Lab | 10 |
| Exotique Thai | 5 |
| Jim Thompson | 3 |
| Mah Boon Krong (MBK) | 19 |
| Marco Tailor | 18 |
| Narai Phand | 13 |
| OTOP | 15 |
| Siam Centre | 11 |
| Siam Square | 17 |
| Viera by Ragazze | 2/7 |

| ● EATING | |
|---|---|
| Aoi | 3 |
| Din Tai Fung | 6 |
| Eathai | 7 |
| Gianni | 11 |
| Hinata | 8 |
| Home Kitchen (Khrua Nai Baan) | 13 |
| Inter | 12 |
| Jim Thompson's Restaurant | 2 |
| Mah Boon Krong Food Courts | 9 |
| Polo Fried Chicken (Kai Thawt Jay Kee Soi Polo) | 14 |
| Royal India | 4 |
| Sanguansri | 10 |
| Somboon Seafood | 5 |
| Sra Bua | 1 |

# DOWNTOWN: AROUND SIAM SQUARE AND THANON PLOENCHIT

troops, leading to the deaths of 91 people. It's possible to stroll in peace above the cracked pavements, noise and fumes of Thanon Rama I, by using the elevated **walkway** that runs beneath the Skytrain lines all the way from the Siam Paragon shopping centre to the Erawan Shrine (further progress is blocked by Central and Chitlom Skytrain stations). East of Ratchaprasong, you pass under the expressway flyover and enter the farang hotel, shopping and entertainment quarter of **Thanon Sukhumvit**.

The area south of Thanon Rama I is dominated by Thailand's most prestigious centre of higher learning, Chulalongkorn University, and the green expanse of **Lumphini Park**. Thanon Rama IV (in Thai "Thanon Phra Ram Sii") then marks another change of character, with the high-rise, American-style boulevard of **Thanon Silom**, the heart of the financial district, extending from here to the river. Alongside the smoked-glass banks and offices, and opposite Convent Road, site of Bangkok's Carmelite nunnery, lies the dark heart of Bangkok nightlife, **Patpong**.

Surprisingly, among downtown's vast expanse of skyscraping concrete, the main attractions for visitors are three attractive museums housed in historic teak houses: **Jim Thompson's House**, the **Ban Kamthieng** and the **Suan Pakkad Palace Museum**.

**ARRIVAL AND DEPARTURE**        **DOWNTOWN BANGKOK**

**By Skytrain and subway** All of the sights reviewed here are within walking range of a Skytrain station; some are also served by the subway.

**By boat** The fastest way to head downtown from Banglamphu is by public boat along Khlong Saen Saeb, beginning near Democracy Monument. A slower but much more scenic route (and during rush hours, possibly quicker than a bus from Banglamphu downtown) is to take an express boat downriver, then change onto the Skytrain at BTS Saphan Taksin.

## Suan Pakkad Palace Museum

352–4 Thanon Sri Ayutthaya • Daily 9am–4pm • B100 • ☎ 02 246 1775–6 ext 229, ⊕ suanpakkad.com • 5min walk from BTS Phaya Thai

The **Suan Pakkad Palace Museum** stands on what was once a cabbage patch (*suan pakkad*) but is now one of the finest gardens in Bangkok. Most of this private collection of beautiful Thai objects from all periods is displayed in lovely traditional wooden houses on stilts, which were transported to Bangkok from various parts of the country.

In House no. 5, as well as in the modern Chumbhot-Pantip Center of Arts in the palace grounds, you'll find a very good collection of elegant, whorled pottery and bronze jewellery, axe- and spearheads, which the former owner of Suan Pakkad Palace, Princess Chumbhot, excavated from tombs at Ban Chiang, the major Bronze Age settlement in the northeast. Scattered around the rest of the museum are some fine ceramics, notably celadon and bencharong; attractive Thai and Khmer religious sculptures; an extensive collection of colourful papier-mâché *khon* masks; beautiful betel-nut sets; an impressive display of traditional musical instruments, including beautiful xylophones (ranat ek) inlaid with mother-of-pearl and ivory; and monks' elegant ceremonial fans.

### The Lacquer Pavilion

The highlight of Suan Pakkad is the **Lacquer Pavilion**, across the reedy pond at the back of the grounds. Set on stilts, the pavilion is actually an amalgam of two eighteenth- or late seventeenth-century teak temple buildings, a *ho trai* (library) and a *ho khien* (writing room), one inside the other, which were found between Ayutthaya and Bang Pa-In. The interior walls are beautifully decorated with gilt on black lacquer: the upper panels depict the life of the Buddha while the lower ones show scenes from the *Ramayana*. Look out especially for the grisly details in the tableau on the back wall of the inner building, showing the earth goddess drowning the evil forces of Mara. Underneath are depicted some European dandies on horseback, probably merchants, whose presence suggests that the work was executed before the fall of Ayutthaya in

**1**

1767. The carefully observed details of daily life and nature are skilful and lively, especially considering the restraints that the lacquering technique places on the artist, who has no opportunity for corrections or touching up.

## Jim Thompson's House

Just off Siam Square at the north end of Soi Kasemsan 2, Thanon Rama I • Daily from 9am, viewing on frequent 30–40min guided tours, last tour 6pm; shop 9am–8pm • B150 • ☎ 02 216 7368, ⓦ jimthompsonhouse.com • BTS National Stadium, or via a canalside path from the Khlong Saen Saeb pier at Saphan Hua Chang

**Jim Thompson's House** is a kind of Ideal Home in elegant Thai style, and a peaceful refuge from downtown chaos. The house was the residence of the legendary American adventurer, entrepreneur, art collector and all-round character whose mysterious disappearance in the jungles of Malaysia in 1967 has made him even more of a legend among Thailand's farang community.

Apart from putting together this beautiful home, completed in 1959, Thompson's most concrete contribution was to turn traditional silk-weaving in Thailand from a dying art into the highly successful international industry it is today. The complex now includes a **shop**, part of the Jim Thompson Thai Silk Company chain (see page 142), and an excellent **bar-restaurant** (see page 132).

Above the shop, the **Jim Thompson Center for the Arts** (ⓦ jimthompsonartcenter.org) is a fascinating gallery that hosts both traditional and modern temporary exhibitions on textiles and the arts, such as royal maps of Siam in the nineteenth century or *mor lam*, the folk music of the northeast. Ignore any con-men at the entrance to the soi looking for gullible tourists to escort on rip-off shopping trips, who'll tell you that the house is closed when it isn't.

### The house

The grand, rambling **house** is in fact a combination of six teak houses, some from as far afield as Ayutthaya and most more than two hundred years old. Like all traditional houses, they were built in wall sections hung together without nails on a frame of wooden pillars, which made it easy to dismantle them, pile them onto a barge and float them to their new location. Although he had trained as an architect, Thompson had more difficulty in putting them back together again; in the end, he had to go back to Ayutthaya to hunt down a group of carpenters who still practised the old house-building methods. Thompson added a few unconventional touches of his own, incorporating the elaborately carved front wall of a Chinese pawnshop between the drawing room and the bedroom, and reversing the other walls in the drawing room so that their carvings faced into the room.

The impeccably tasteful **interior** has been left as it was during Jim Thompson's life, even down to the place settings on the dining table – Thompson entertained guests most nights and to that end designed the house like a stage set. Complementing the fine artefacts from throughout Southeast Asia is a stunning array of Thai arts and crafts, including one of the best collections of traditional Thai paintings in the world. Thompson picked up plenty of bargains from the Thieves' Quarter (Nakhon Kasem) in Chinatown, before collecting Thai art became fashionable and expensive. Other pieces were liberated from decay and destruction in upcountry temples, while many of the Buddha images were turned over by ploughs, especially around Ayutthaya. Some of the exhibits are very rare, such as a headless but elegant seventh-century Dvaravati Buddha and a seventeenth-century Ayutthayan teak Buddha.

After the guided tour, you're free to look again, at your leisure, at the former rice barn and gardener's and maid's houses in the small, jungly **garden**, which display some gorgeous traditional Thai paintings and drawings, as well as small-scale statues and Chinese ceramics.

**1**

## Bangkok Art and Cultural Centre

Junction of Rama I and Phrayathai roads • Tues–Sun 10am–9pm • Free • ☏ 02 214 6630–8, ⓦ bacc.or.th • BTS National Stadium

A striking, white hunk of modernity, the prestigious **Bangkok Art and Cultural Centre** houses several galleries on its upper floors, connected by spiralling ramps like New York's Guggenheim, as well as performance spaces, cafés, boutiques and private art galleries on the lower floors. It hosts temporary shows by contemporary artists from Thailand and abroad across all media, from the visual arts to music and design, and there's usually something interesting on here – coming in from BTS National Stadium, there's a blackboard inside the entrance where the day's events and shows are chalked up in English. BACC will be one of the main venues for the first Bangkok Art Biennale in late 2018 and early 2019 (ⓦ bkkartbiennale.com), featuring over seventy Thai and international artists, cinema, music and performing arts.

## The Erawan Shrine

Corner of Thanon Ploenchit and Thanon Rajdamri • Daily 24hr • Free • BTS Chit Lom

For a glimpse of the variety and ubiquity of Thai religion, drop in on the **Erawan Shrine** (*Saan Phra Prom* in Thai). Remarkable as much for its setting as anything else, this shrine to Brahma, the Hindu creation god, squeezes in on one of the busiest and noisiest intersections in modern Bangkok. And it's not the only one: half a dozen other Hindu shrines and spirit houses are dotted around Ratchaphrasong intersection, most notably **Trimurti**, who combines the three main gods, Brahma, Vishnu and Shiva, on Thanon Rajdamri outside Central World near the intersection's opposite corner. Modern Bangkokians see Trimurti as a sort of Cupid figure, and those looking for love bring red offerings.

The *Grand Hyatt Erawan Hotel*, towering over the Erawan Shrine, is the reason for its existence and its name. When a string of calamities held up the building of the original hotel in the 1950s, spirit doctors were called in, who instructed the owners to build a new home for the offended local spirits, in the form of a shrine to Brahma (who had created the many-headed elephant, Erawan, as a vehicle for the god Indra): the hotel was then finished without further mishap. Ill fortune, however, has struck the shrine itself twice in recent years. In 2006, a young, mentally ill Muslim man smashed the Brahma statue to pieces with a hammer – and was then brutally beaten to death by an angry mob. An exact replica of the statue was quickly installed, incorporating the remains of the old statue to preserve the spirit of the deity. Then in 2015, a bomb exploded on the grounds of the shrine (which was largely undamaged), killing twenty people, the most deadly act of terrorism in Thailand's history. There were speculations that the device was planted by Uighur separatists, in retaliation for Thailand's forced repatriation of a planeload of their kinsmen to China.

Be prepared for sensory overload here: the main structure shines with lurid glass of all colours and the overcrowded precinct around it is almost buried under scented garlands and incense candles. You might also catch a group of traditional dancers performing here to the strains of a small classical orchestra to entertain Brahma – worshippers hire them to give thanks for a stroke of good fortune. People set on less abstract rewards will invest in a lottery ticket from one of the physically disabled sellers: they're thought to be the luckiest you can buy.

## Ban Kamthieng (Kamthieng House)

131 Thanon Asok Montri (Soi 21 off Thanon Sukhumvit) • Tues–Sat 9am–5pm • B100 • ⓦ siam-society.org • BTS Asok or Sukhumvit subway

A traditional northern Thai residence, **Ban Kamthieng** was moved in the 1960s from Chiang Mai to Thanon Sukhumvit and set up as an ethnological museum by the Siam Society, an august academic institution founded in 1904 to promote knowledge of Thailand. The delightful complex of polished teak buildings makes a pleasing oasis beneath the towering glass skyscrapers that dominate Sukhumvit. It differs from Suan Pakkad, Jim Thompson's House and M.R. Kukrit's Heritage Home in being the home of a rural family, and the objects on display give a fair insight into country life for the well-heeled in northern Thailand. In a traditional central Thai house at the front of the grounds, there's a nice little café-restaurant run by the Black Canyon chain.

The house was built on the banks of the Ping River in the mid-nineteenth century for local bigwigs, the Nimmanhaemins, and the ground-floor video will show you how to build your own northern Thai house. Also here are assorted looms and fish traps, which evoke the upcountry practice of fishing in flooded rice paddies to augment the supply from the rivers. Upstairs, the main display focuses on the ritual life of a typical Lanna household, explaining the role of the spirits, the practice of making offerings, and the belief in amulets, talismans, magic shirts and male tattoos. The rectangular lintel above the door is a *hum yon*, carved in floral patterns that represent testicles and are designed to ward off evil spirits. Walk along the open veranda to the authentically equipped kitchen, and to the granary to find an interesting exhibition on the ritual practices associated with rice farming.

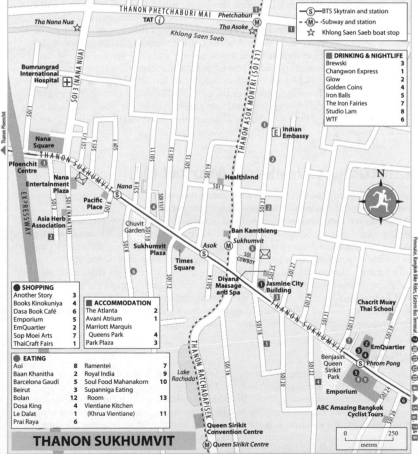

THANON SUKHUMVIT

**1**

## Patpong

Concentrated into two lanes running between the eastern ends of Thanon Silom and Thanon Suriwong, the neon-lit go-go bars of the **Patpong** district loom like rides in a tawdry sexual Disneyland. In front of each bar, girls cajole passers-by with a lifeless sensuality while insistent touts proffer printed menus and photographs detailing the degradations on show. Inside, bikini-clad women gyrate to Western music and play hostess to the (almost exclusively male) spectators; upstairs, live shows feature women who, to use Spalding Gray's phrase in *Swimming to Cambodia*, "do everything with their vaginas except have babies".

Patpong was no more than a sea of mud when the capital was founded on the marshy river bank to the west, but by the 1960s it had grown into a flash district of dance halls for rich Thais, owned by a Chinese millionaire godfather, educated at the London School of Economics and by the OSS (forerunner of the CIA), who gave his name to the area. In 1969, an American entrepreneur turned an existing teahouse into a luxurious nightclub to satisfy the tastes of soldiers on R&R trips from Vietnam, and so Patpong's transformation into a Western sex reservation began. At first, the area was rough and violent, but over the years it has wised up to the desires of the affluent farang, and now markets itself as a packaged concept of Oriental decadence.

The centre of the skin trade lies along the interconnected sois of **Patpong 1 and 2**, where lines of go-go bars share their patch with respectable restaurants, a 24-hour supermarket and an overabundance of pharmacies. Even the most demure tourists – of both sexes – turn out to do some shopping at the night market down the middle of Patpong 1, where hawkers sell fake watches, bags and designer T-shirts. By day, a relaxed hangover descends on the place. Farang men slump at the open-air bars on Patpong 2, drinking and watching videos, unable to find anything else to do in the whole of Bangkok. Running parallel to the east, **Soi Thaniya** is Patpong's Japanese counterpart, lined with hostess bars and some good restaurants, while the focus of Bangkok's gay scene, **Silom 2** (ie Soi 2, Thanon Silom) and the more mixed **Silom 4**, flank Thaniya.

# Chatuchak Weekend Market (JJ)

Occupies a huge patch of ground extending northwest from the corner of Phaholyothin and Kamphaeng Phet roads • Sat & Sun roughly 9am–6/7pm, though many stalls open earlier and some close later • Ⓦ chatuchak.org

With over ten thousand open-air stalls to peruse, 200,000 visitors each day and wares as diverse as Lao silk, Siamese kittens and designer lamps, the enormous **Chatuchak Weekend Market** (or **JJ** as it's usually abbreviated, from "Jatu Jak") is Bangkok's most enjoyable – not to mention hot and exhausting – shopping experience.

The market also contains a controversial pets section. In the past this has doubled as a clearing house for protected and endangered species such as gibbons, palm cockatoos and Indian pied hornbills, many of them smuggled in from Laos and Cambodia and sold to private animal collectors and foreign zoos. Crackdowns by the authorities, however, now seem to have driven this trade underground.

## Where to shop

Chatuchak is divided into 27 numbered **sections**, plus half a dozen unnumbered ones, each of them more or less dedicated to a particular genre, for example household items, plants and secondhand books. The demarcation is nothing like as clear-cut as the market's website would have you believe, but if you have several hours to spare, it's fun just to browse at whim. The market's primary customers are Bangkok residents in search of idiosyncratic fashions (try sections 2, 3 and 4), including used clothing (sections 5 and 6), and homewares (especially in sections A,

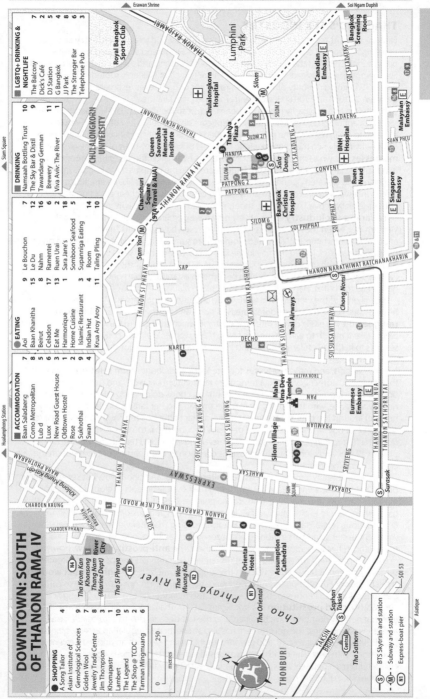

# DOWNTOWN: SOUTH OF THANON RAMA IV

● **SHOPPING**
| | |
|---|---|
| A Song Tailor | 4 |
| Asian Institute of Gemological Sciences | 9 |
| Golden Wool | 7 |
| Jewelry Trade Center | 8 |
| Jim Thompson | 3 |
| Khomapastr | 1 |
| Lambert | 10 |
| The Legend | 5 |
| The Shop @ TCDC | 2 |
| Tamnan Mingmuang | 6 |

■ **ACCOMMODATION**
| | |
|---|---|
| Baan Saladaeng | 7 |
| Como Metropolitan | 8 |
| Lub d | 5 |
| Luxx | 6 |
| New Road Guest House | 3 |
| Oldtown Hostel | 1 |
| Rose | 9 |
| Sukhothai | 2 |
| Swan | 4 |

● **EATING**
| | | | |
|---|---|---|---|
| Aoi | 7 | Le Bouchon | 9 |
| Baan Khanitha | 8 | Le Du | 15 |
| Beirut | 5 | Nahm | 8 |
| Celadon | 6 | Ramenti | 17 |
| Eat Me | 3 | Ruen Urai | 2 |
| Harmonique | 1 | Sara Jane's | 13 |
| Home Cuisine | 9 | Somboon Seafood | 1 |
| Islamic Restaurant | 3 | Supanniga Eating | |
| Indian Hut | 4 | Room | 14 |
| Krua Aroy Aroy | 11 | Taling Pling | 10 |

■ **DRINKING**
| | |
|---|---|
| Namsaah Bottling Trust | 10 |
| The Sky Bar & Distil | 9 |
| Tawandang German Brewery | 11 |
| Viva Aviv: The River | 1 |

■ **LGBTQ+ DRINKING & NIGHTLIFE**
| | |
|---|---|
| The Balcony | 7 |
| Dick's Café | 2 |
| DJ Station | 5 |
| G Bangkok | 4 |
| JJ Park | 8 |
| The Stranger Bar | 6 |
| Telephone Pub | 3 |

**BTS Skytrain and station**

**Subway and station**

**Express-boat pier**

**1**

## THAILAND'S SEX INDUSTRY

Bangkok owes its reputation as the carnal capital of the world to a **sex industry** adept at peddling fantasies of cheap thrills on tap. More than a thousand sex-related businesses operate in the city, but the gaudy neon fleshpots of Patpong and Sukhumvit's Soi Nana and Soi Cowboy give a misleading impression of an activity that is deeply rooted in Thai culture: the overwhelming majority of Thailand's prostitutes of both sexes (estimated at anywhere between 200,000 and 700,000) work with Thai men, not farangs.

Prostitution and polygamy have long been intrinsic to the Thai way of life. Apart from a few recent exceptions, Thai kings have always kept concubines, only a few of whom would be elevated to royal mothers. The practice was aped by the nobility and, from the early nineteenth century, by newly rich merchants keen to have lots of sons. Many men of all classes still keep **mistresses**, known as *mia noi* (minor wives), or have casual girlfriends (*gig*); the common view is that an official wife (*mia luang*) should be treated like the temple's main Buddha image – respected and elevated upon the altar – whereas the minor wife is like an amulet, to be taken along wherever you go. For less wealthy men, prostitution is a far cheaper option: at least two-fifths of sexually active Thai men are thought to visit brothels twice a month.

The **farang sex industry** is a relatively new development, having started during the Vietnam War, when the American military set up seven bases around Thailand. The GIs' appetite for "entertainment" attracted women from surrounding rural areas to cash in on the boom, and Bangkok joined the fray in the late 1960s. By the mid-1970s, the GIs had left, but tourists replaced them, lured by advertising that diverted most of the traffic to Bangkok and Pattaya. Sex tourism has since grown to become an established part of the Thai economy and has spread to Phuket, Hat Yai, Ko Samui and Chiang Mai.

The majority of the women who work in the country's go-go bars and "bar-beers" (outdoor hostess bars) come from the poorest areas of north and northeast Thailand. **Economic refugees**, they're easily drawn into an industry in which they can make in a single night what would take a month to earn in the rice fields. Many women opt for a couple of years in the sex bars to help pay off family debts and improve the living conditions of parents stuck in the poverty trap.

Many bar girls, and male prostitutes too, are looking for longer-term **relationships** with their farang customers, bringing a temporary respite from bar work and perhaps even a ticket out. A surprising number of one-night transactions do develop into some sort of holiday romance, with the young woman accompanying her farang "boyfriend" (often twice her age) around the country and maintaining contact after he's returned home. An entire sub-genre of novels and confessional memoirs (among them the classic *Hello, My Big Big Honey!: Letters to Bangkok Bar Girls and Their Revealing Interviews*) testifies to the role money plays in all this, and highlights the delusions common to both parties, not to mention the cross-cultural incomprehension.

Despite its ubiquity, prostitution has been **illegal** in Thailand since 1960, but sex-industry bosses easily circumvent the law by registering their establishments as clubs, karaoke bars or massage parlours, and making payoffs to the police and politicians. Sex workers, on the other hand, often endure exploitation and violence from pimps and customers rather than face fines and long rehabilitation sentences. Hardly surprising that many prefer to go freelance, working the clubs and bars in non-red-light zones such as Thanon Khao San. Life is made even more difficult because abortion is illegal in Thailand. The **anti-prostitution law**, however, does attempt to treat sex workers as victims rather than criminals and penalizes parents who sell their children. A high-profile voice in the struggle to improve the **rights of sex workers** is the Empower Foundation (Ⓦempowerfoundation.org), which not only organizes campaigns and runs education centres for bar workers but also manages its own bar in Chiang Mai.

Inevitably, **child prostitution** is a significant issue in Thailand, but NGOs such as ECPAT (Ⓦecpat.net) say numbers have declined over the last decade, due to zero-tolerance and awareness campaigns. The government has also strengthened legislation against hiring a prostitute under the age of 18, and anyone caught having sex with an under-15 can now be charged with rape. The disadvantaged are still targeted by traffickers however, who "buy" children from desperately poor hill tribe and other minority families and keep them as bonded slaves until the debt has been repaid.

B and C, behind the market's head office and information centre), but Chatuchak also has plenty of collector- and tourist-oriented **stalls**; best buys include antique lacquerware, unusual sarongs, traditional cotton clothing and crafts from the north, silver jewellery, and ceramics, particularly the five-coloured *bencharong*. For handicrafts (including musical instruments) and traditional textiles, you should start with sections 22, 24, 25 (which features textiles from northern Thailand) and 26, which are all in a cluster at the southwest (Kamphaeng Phet subway) end of the market. Section 7, meanwhile, at the north end of the market, is full of art galleries, which are often staffed by the artists themselves.

There are dozens of food stalls at Chatuchak, but foodies will want to check out **Talat Or Tor Khor** (the Agricultural Marketing Organization), a covered market that sells a fantastic array of fruit, veg and other produce from around the country, as well as prepared dishes to take away or to eat at the food court; it's on the south side of Thanon Kamphaeng Phet, next to Kamphaeng Phet subway station. The modern building next door to Talat Or Tor Khor, the Siam Orchid Centre, is a lovely market for orchids and other plants.

## ARRIVAL AND GETTING AROUND
### CHATUCHAK WEEKEND MARKET

**Arrival** Kamphaeng Phet subway station exits right into the most interesting, southwestern, corner of the market; on the northeast side of the market are Chatuchak Park subway and Mochit BTS stations. Coming from Banglamphu, either get a bus to BTS National Stadium or BTS Ratchathewi, or take the #503 (non-expressway version) or #509 bus all the way (about 1hr) from Thanon Rajdamnoen Klang; once the MRT extension has opened, it should be possible to catch an express-boat to Tha Tien, then walk 5min to Sanam Chai station, for subway trains to Chatuchak Park or Kamphaeng Phet stations.

**Getting around** A few very small electric trams circulate around the market's main inner ring road, transporting weary shoppers for free, though they always seem to be full.

## INFORMATION

**Maps** *Nancy Chandler's Map of Bangkok* has a fabulously detailed and informatively annotated map of all the sections in the market. Maps are also posted at various points around the market, including in the subway stations, or go to the more in-depth ⓦ jjmarketmap.com. For specific help you can ask at the market office, on the main inner ring road near Gate 1 off Thanon Kamphaeng Phet 2, which also has ATMs and currency exchange booths.

## ARRIVAL AND DEPARTURE
### BANGKOK

Unless you arrive in Bangkok by **train**, be prepared for a long trip into the city centre. Suvarnabhumi and Don Muang airports are both 25km out and the three **bus** stations are not much closer in, though at least the Eastern Terminal is next to a **Skytrain** stop.

### BY PLANE

When departing from Bangkok, leave plenty of time to get to Suvarnabhumi or Don Muang, as getting there by road can be severely hampered by traffic jams.

### SUVARNABHUMI

Bangkok's main airport (coded "BKK" and pronounced "soo-wanna-poom"; ⓦ suvarnabhumiairport.com) is situated 25km east of central Bangkok between highways 7 and 34. The large airport is well stocked with 24hr exchange booths, ATMs, places to eat, pharmacies and a post office. In the arrivals hall on Floor 2, TAT operates an official 24hr tourist information counter (near landside Gate 3) and the tourist police have an office; 24hr left-luggage depots (B100/item/day) can be found in arrivals and in the departures hall on Floor 4. There are a number of accommodation options near Suvarnabhumi (see page 129).

**Suvarnabhumi Airport Rail Link** The high-speed rail link (SARL; ⓦ srtet.co.th; daily 6am–midnight; B15–45) from the basement of the Suvarnabhumi terminal is generally the quickest means of getting downtown, though it also serves as an important link for commuters and can get very crowded. There's only one set of elevated tracks, ending at Phaya Thai station, with trains running roughly every 12–15min (26min), stopping at Makkasan, Ratchaprarop and four other stations. Makkasan is handy for Phetchaburi subway station and for Khlong Saen Saeb canal boats (see page 100) at Asoke (Petchaburi) pier, while Phaya Thai is an interchange with the Skytrain system, and is served by #59 buses (heading south on Thanon Phrayathai) to Thanon Rajadamnoen Klang, for Banglamphu.

**Taxis** Taxis to the centre are comfortable, a/c and reasonably priced, although the driving can be hairy. Walk past the pricey taxis and limousines on offer within the baggage hall and arrivals hall, and ignore any tout who may offer a cheap ride in an unlicensed and unmetered vehicle,

**1**

as newly arrived travellers are seen as easy prey for robbery and the cabs are untraceable. Licensed and metered public taxis are operated from clearly signposted and well-regulated counters, outside Floor 1's landside Gates 4 and 7. Including the B50 airport pick-up fee and around B70 tolls for the overhead expressways, a journey to Thanon Silom downtown, for example, should set you back around B400, depending on the traffic. Heading back to the airport, drivers will nearly always try to leave their meters off and agree an inflated price with you – say "*poet meter, dai mai khrap/kha?*" to get them to switch the meter on. If you leave the downtown areas before 7am or after 9pm you can get to the airport in half an hour, but at other times it's best to set off at least an hour and a half before you have to check in.

**Public Transportation Centre** Situated on the other side of the huge airport complex from the terminal building, the Public Transportation Centre is reached by a free 10min ride on an "Express" shuttle bus (every 10min) from Gate 5 outside arrivals or Gate 5 outside departures – be sure not to confuse these with the much slower "Ordinary" shuttle buses, which ferry airport staff around the complex.

**City buses and minibuses** The Bangkok Mass Transit Authority operates the S1 service to Thanon Khao San from outside Gate 7 of the terminal building's Floor 1 roughly every 45min (B60). The BMTA also runs other public a/c buses and minibuses out of the Public Transportation Centre, but they're really designed for airport staff. The route that's most likely to appeal to visitors is the #551 a/c minibus to Victory Monument (every 5–20min; B40), which starts at the Public Transportation Centre and picks up outside the terminal's Floor 1 (Gates 1 and 8); however, if they fill up at the Public Transportation Centre, there'll be no pick-up at the terminal. On departure, many travellers opt for one of the private minibus services to Suvarnabhumi (B130–150) organized through guesthouses and travel agents in Banglamphu and elsewhere around the city.

**Long-distance buses** From the Public Transportation Centre, there are public (Baw Khaw Saw) long-distance buses and minibuses to Hua Hin, Pattaya, Chanthaburi, Trat, Ko Chang and Aranyaprathet. Because of the inconvenience involved, many of these services also stop at Gate 8, Floor 1 of the terminal building (with information counters just inside the terminal); in the opposite direction, some of these buses continue to Bangkok's Eastern or Northern (Mo Chit) Bus Terminals.

**Car rental companies** The car-rental companies in the arrivals hall (Floor 2) near Gate 8 include Avis and Budget (see page 121).

### DON MUANG

The old Don Muang Airport (coded "DMK"; ⓦ donmueang airportthai.com), 25km north of the city, is now Bangkok's main base for low-cost airlines (though some still use Suvarnabhumi – check your booking carefully); its two

interconnected buildings effectively form one very long terminal. It shelters currency exchange booths, ATMs, car-rental outlets, a left-luggage depot (B75/item/day), a post office and plenty of places to eat.

**Taxis** The easiest way to get into the city centre is by licensed, metered taxi from outside the arrivals hall on Floor 1, costing about B400, including B50 airport fee and expressway fees (B110 to Banglamphu, for instance).

**Shuttle buses to/from Suvarnabhumi Airport** Operating between every 12min and every 30min (see ⓦ suvarnabhumiairport.com for times), an a/c shuttle bus that's free to passengers runs between the airports; at Suvarnabhumi, it picks up outside Gate 3, Floor 2, and drops off outside Gate 5, Floor 4. Allow at least 50min for the journey.

**Limo Buses** These small, a/c, wi-fi-enabled buses (ⓦ limobus.co.th) operate two circular routes from outside the arrivals hall on Floor 1 (both roughly every 30min–1hr; B150), one to Thanon Khao San and one to Silom.

**Public buses** The Bangkok Mass Transit Authority offers several special services from outside the arrivals hall (all a/c): A1 (every 5min; B30) to Mo Chit Skytrain and Chatuchak Park subway stations and the nearby Northern Bus Terminal (Mo Chit); A2 (every 10min; B30) to Victory Monument; A3 (every 30min; B50) to Lumpini Park; and A4 (every 30min; B50) to Thanon Khao San. You could also chance your arm on the regular city buses that stop on the main highway running north–south in front of the airport buildings: the a/c and non-a/c #59 bus, for example, will drop you off on Thanon Rajdamnoen Klang near Banglamphu.

**Minibuses from the centre** On departure, many travellers opt for one of the private minibus services to Don Muang (B130–150) organized through guesthouses and travel agents in Banglamphu and elsewhere around the city. Destinations Chumphon (2 daily; 1hr); Ko Samui (25 daily; 1hr–1hr 30min); Krabi (15 daily; 1hr 20min); Nakhon Si Thammarat (12 daily; 1hr 10min); Phuket (30 daily; 1hr 20min); Ranong (2 daily; 1hr 30min); Surat Thani (17 daily; 1hr 15min); Trang (5 daily; 1hr 30min); Trat (3 daily; 50min).

### BY TRAIN

Travelling to Bangkok by train from Malaysia and most parts of Thailand, you arrive at the main Hualamphong Station (note that an old plan to make Bang Sue to the north Bangkok's main station has recently resurfaced in the Thai news). A handful of slow, local trains on the Southern line pull in at Thonburi Station.

### HUALAMPHONG STATION

Centrally located at the edge of Chinatown, Hualamphong Station is on the subway line and is connected to Banglamphu by bus no 53. Station facilities include an exchange booth, several ATMs and a left-luggage office at the front of the main concourse (daily 4am–11pm; B20–80/

day). The State Railways (SRT) information booth in the main concourse, on the right (daily 4am–11pm), keeps English-language timetables, while tickets can be bought at nearby, clearly signed ticket counters (daily 4am–11pm). Train tickets can also be bought online or through almost any travel agent and some hotels and guesthouses for a booking fee of about B50. See "Basics" for more information on tickets and timetables (see page 31). The station area used to be known as fertile ground for con-artists with fake IDs, but it seems to have cleaned up its act; all the same, as at most major train stations across the world, it's as well to keep your wits about you.

Destinations Aranyaprathet (2 daily; 6hr); Cha-am (3 daily; 3hr 10min–3hr 50min); Chumphon (10 daily; 7hr–9hr 30min); Hua Hin (11 daily; 3hr 30min–5hr); Nakhon Si Thammarat (2 daily; 15hr 30min–16hr 30min); Padang Besar (for Malaysia; 1 daily; 17hr 45min); Pattaya (1 daily; 4hr); Phetchaburi (11 daily; 2hr 45min–3hr 45min); Prachuap Khiri Khan (8 daily; 5–7hr); Pranburi (1 daily; 5hr); Si Racha (1 daily; 3hr 30min); Surat Thani (10 daily; 9–12hr); Trang (2 daily; 15–16hr).

**THONBURI STATION**
Thonburi Station (sometimes still referred to by its former name, Bangkok Noi Station) is a short ride in a public songthaew or an 850m walk west from the N11 express-boat pier, just across the Chao Phraya River from Banglamphu and Ratanakosin.

Destinations Cha-am (2 daily; 3hr 30min–4hr 30min); Chumphon (1 daily; 9hr 30min); Hua Hin (2 daily; 4–5hr); Phetchaburi (2 daily; 2hr 45min–3hr 45min); Prachuap Khiri Khan (2 daily; 6–7hr); Pranburi (2 daily; 5hr–5hr 30min).

**BY BUS**
Bangkok's three main bus terminals, all of which have left-luggage facilities of some kind, are distributed around the outskirts of town. On departure, leave plenty of time to reach them, especially if setting off from Banglamphu, from where you should allow at least 1hr 30min (outside rush hour) to get to the Eastern Bus Terminal, and a good hour to get to the Northern or Southern terminals. On many shorter routes, buses have been wholly or partly replaced by *rot tuu* (a/c minibuses), which now depart from the same three terminals. Seats on the most popular long-distance a/c bus services (such as to Krabi, Phuket and Surat Thani) should be reserved ahead of time, most easily at the ATS (Advanced Technology Systems; Mon–Fri 8.30am–5pm) office near the *Royal Ratanakosin Hotel* on Thanon Rajdamnoen Klang in Banglamphu, the official seller of government bus tickets. Otherwise, go to the relevant bus station or use any of the ways described in Basics (see page 31), as guesthouses may book you on to one of the dodgy tourist services (see page 116).

**NORTHERN AND NORTHEASTERN BUS TERMINAL (MO CHIT)**
All services from the north and northeast terminate at Bangkok's biggest bus station, the Northern and Northeastern Bus Terminal (Mo Chit) on Thanon Kamphaeng Phet 2; some buses from the south and the east coast also use Mo Chit (there are plans to move Mo Chit to another site that's closer to the Skytrain and subway within the next few years, reportedly by 2023). The quickest way to get into the city centre from Mo Chit is to hop onto the Skytrain at Mo Chit Station on Thanon Phaholyothin, or the subway at the adjacent Chatuchak Park Station or at Kamphaeng Phet Station (at the bottom of Thanon Kamphaeng Phet 2), all of which are about a 15min walk from the bus terminal, and then change onto a city bus if necessary. Otherwise, it's a long bus or taxi ride into town: city buses from the Northern Bus Terminal include ordinary #3, and a/c #509 to Banglamphu. A/c minibuses for the Southern Bus Terminal depart every 20min.

Destinations Aranyaprathet (at least hourly; 4hr 30min); Chanthaburi (9 daily; 4hr); Pakse (Laos; 2 daily; 12hr); Pattaya (every 30min; 2hr 30min–3hr 30min); Phnom Penh (Cambodia; 1 daily; 11hr); Siem Reap (Cambodia; 2 daily; 7hr); Si Racha (every 40min; 2hr); Trat (hourly; 4hr 30min); Vientiane (Laos; 1 daily; 11hr).

**EASTERN BUS TERMINAL (EKAMAI)**
Most buses to and from east-coast destinations such as Pattaya, Ban Phe (for Ko Samet) and Trat (for Ko Chang) use the Eastern Bus Terminal (Ekamai) between sois 40 and 42 on Thanon Sukhumvit. This bus station is right beside the Ekamai Skytrain stop and is also served by lots of city buses, including a/c #511 to and from Banglamphu and the Southern Bus Terminal. Alternatively, you can use the Khlong Saen Saeb canal-boat service, which runs westwards almost as far as Banglamphu (see page 91); there's a pier called Tha Charn Issara, near the northern end of Sukhumvit Soi 63 (Soi Ekamai), which is easiest reached from the bus station by taxi.

Destinations Ban Phe (for Ko Samet; 14 daily; 3hr–3hr 30min); Chanthaburi (at least hourly; 4–5hr); Laem Ngop (for Ko Chang; 3–4 daily; 5hr 15min–6hr); Pattaya (every 30min; 2hr 30min–3hr 30min); Si Racha (every 40min; 1hr 30min–2hr 30min); Trat (6 daily; 4hr 30min–6hr).

**SOUTHERN BUS TERMINAL (SATHAANII SAI TAI)**
The huge, airport-like New Southern Bus Terminal, or Sathaanii Sai Tai Mai, handles transport to and from all points south of the capital, including Hua Hin, Chumphon (for Ko Tao), Surat Thani (for Ko Samui), Phuket and Krabi, as well as buses for destinations west of Bangkok. The terminal lies at the junction of Thanon Borom Ratchonani and Thanon Phutthamonthon Sai 1 in Taling Chan, an interminable 11km west of the Chao Phraya River and

**1**

## TOURS OF THE CITY

Unlikely as it sounds, the most popular organized **tours** in Bangkok for independent travellers are by bicycle, heading to the city's outer neighbourhoods and beyond; these are an excellent way to gain a different perspective on Thai life and offer a unique chance to see traditional communities close up. In addition to those listed below, other tour options include Thonburi canal tours (see page 100) and Chao Phraya Express tourist boats (see page 118).

**ABC Amazing Bangkok Cyclist Tours** 10/5–7 Soi Aree, Soi 26, Thanon Sukhumvit ☎02 665 6364, ⓦrealasia.net. ABC's popular, long-running and child-friendly bicycle tours last half a day or a full day, starting in the Sukhumvit area and taking you across the river to surprisingly rural khlong- and riverside communities (including a floating market at weekends); they also offer cycle-and-dine tours in the evening. Tours operate every day year-round, cover up to 24km depending on the itinerary, and need to be reserved in advance (B1300–2400 including bicycle).

**Bangkok Bike Rides (Spice Roads)** 45 Soi Pannee, Soi Pridi Banomyong 26, Soi 71, Thanon Sukhumvit ☎02 381 7490, ⓦbangkokbikerides. com or ⓦspiceroads.com. Bangkok Bike Rides runs a programme of half a dozen day and half-day tours

within Greater Bangkok (from B1450/person), including Ko Kred, as well as to the floating markets and canalside neighbourhoods of Damnoen Saduak and to Ayutthaya. Also offers multi-day trips, mountain biking and road biking out of the city.

**Bangkok Vanguards** Based at Innspire (see page 125) ⓦbangkokvanguards.com. Fun, educational and unconventional tours (from B1700), with a focus on social entrepreneurism, including walking tours of Chinatown and evening bike tours.

**Velo Thailand** Soi 4, Thanon Samsen ☎02 628 8628, ⓦvelothailand.com. Velo Thailand runs half a dozen different bike tours of the capital (and further afield) out of its cycle shop on the edge of Banglamphu, including an after-dark tour (6–10pm; B1100) that takes in floodlit sights including Wat Pho and Wat Arun.

Banglamphu, so access to and from city accommodation can take an age, even in a taxi. City buses serving the New Southern Bus Terminal include #124 for Banglamphu and #511 for Banglamphu, Thanon Sukhumvit and Ekamai, while a/c minibuses between the Southern and Northern Bus Terminals depart every 20min. Note that when arriving in Bangkok many long-distance bus services make a more convenient stop before reaching the terminus (via a time-consuming U-turn), towards the eastern end of Thanon Borom Ratchonani, much nearer Phra Pinklao Bridge and the river; the majority of passengers get off here and it's highly recommended to do the same rather than continue to the terminal. The above-listed city buses also cross the river from this bus drop, as do many additional services, and this is also a faster and cheaper place to grab a taxi into town. Nearly all a/c minibuses to points west and south of Bangkok now use the New Southern Bus Terminal, but when Bangkok's a/c minibuses were suddenly expelled from Victory Monument in 2016, a few companies set up shop (possibly temporarily) in the Old Southern Bus Terminal (Sathaanii Sai Tai Kao, aka Pinklao). On arrival in Bangkok, you may find yourself being deposited at the Old, rather than the New Southern Bus Terminal – handy, as it's much closer to the centre of town, although your drop-off point is entirely down to chance (you can't specify preferred terminal).

Destinations Cha-am (at least hourly; 2hr 45min–3hr 15min); Chumphon (roughly hourly; 7–9hr); Hua Hin (at least hourly; 3–4hr); Khao Lak (3 daily; 12hr); Ko Pha Ngan

(3 daily; 13hr–15hr 30min); Ko Samui (8–10 daily; 12–13hr); Krabi (12 daily; 12–14hr); Nakhon Si Thammarat (20 daily; 13hr); Phang Nga (5 daily; 13hr); Phetchaburi (at least every 30min; 2hr 15min); Phuket (21 daily; 12hr); Prachuap Khiri Khan (roughly every 30min; 4–5hr); Pranburi (every 30min; 3hr 30min); Ranong (15 daily; 9hr); Satun (4 daily; 16hr); Surat Thani (20 daily; 9–12hr); Trang (5 daily; 12hr).

### BY TOURIST BUS

Many Bangkok tour operators sell tickets for unlicensed budget tourist buses and minibuses to popular long-distance destinations such as Surat Thani (for Ko Samui) and Krabi (for Ko Phi Phi), and to places closer at hand such as Ko Samet and Ko Chang. Their only advantage is convenience, as they mostly leave from the Khao San area in Banglamphu. Prices, however, can vary considerably but rarely work out cheaper than licensed buses or a/c minibuses from the public terminals. The big drawbacks, however, are the lack of comfort and poor safety, which particularly applies to the long-distance overnight services. It is standard practice for budget tour operators, especially those on Thanon Khao San, to assure you that overnight transport will be in a large, luxury VIP bus despite knowing it's actually a clapped-out old banger. Security on overnight tourist buses is a serious problem, and because they're run by unlicensed private companies there is no insurance against loss or theft of baggage: don't keep anything of value in luggage that's stored out of sight, even if it's padlocked, as luggage sometimes gets slashed and rifled in the roomy baggage compartment. In addition, passengers sometimes find themselves dumped on the outskirts of their destination city, at the mercy of unscrupulous touts. Bear in mind that Khao San tour operators open up and go bust all the time; never hand over any money until you see the ticket. One tourist company that is licensed and reliable is Lomprayah, who operate catamarans to Ko Tao, Ko Pha Ngan and Ko Samui and connecting buses from Banglamphu to Chumphon. They have an office at 154 Thanon Ram Buttri (☏02 629 2569–70, ⊕lomprayah. com). Recommended travel agents are listed in the Directory (see page 145).

## GETTING AROUND

Getting around can undoubtedly be a headache in a city where it's not unusual for residents to spend 3hr getting to work. The main form of transport is **buses**, with a labyrinth of routes that reaches every part of the city, albeit slowly. Catching the various kinds of **taxi** is more expensive, and you'll still get held up by the daytime traffic jams. **Boats** are obviously more limited in their range, but they're regular and as cheap as buses, and you'll save a lot of time by using them whenever possible – a journey between Banglamphu and Saphan Taksin, for instance, will take around 30min by water, half what it would usually take on land. The **Skytrain** and **subway** each have a similarly limited range but are also worth using whenever suitable for all or part of your journey; their networks roughly coincide with each other at the east end of Thanon Silom, at the corner of Soi Asoke and Thanon Sukhumvit, and on Thanon Phaholyothin by Chatuchak Park (Mo Chit), while the Skytrain joins up with the Chao Phraya River express boats at the vital

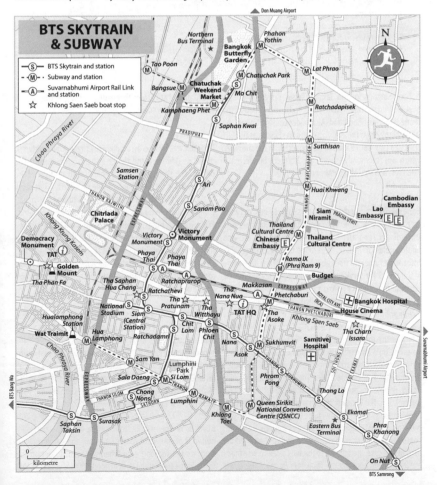

1

## CENTRAL STOPS FOR THE CHAO PHRAYA EXPRESS BOATS

**N15** Thewet (all express boats) – for Thewet guesthouses.

**N14** Rama VIII Bridge (no flag) – for Samsen Soi 5.

**N13** Phra Arthit (no flag and orange flag) – for Thanon Phra Arthit, Thanon Khao San and Banglamphu guesthouses.

**N12** Phra Pinklao Bridge (all boats) – for Royal Barge Museum.

**N11** Thonburi Railway Station (or Bangkok Noi; all boats) – for trains to Kanchanaburi.

**N10** Wang Lang (aka Siriraj or Prannok; all boats) – for Wat Rakhang.

**N9** Chang (no flag, green flag and orange flag) – for the Grand Palace, Sanam Luang and the National Museum.

**N8** Thien (no flag and orange flag) – for Wat Pho, and the cross-river ferry to Wat Arun (at the time of research, Thien express-boat pier was under renovation and express boats were stopping across the river at Wat Arun instead)

**N7** Ratchini (aka Rajinee; no flag).

**N6** Saphan Phut (Memorial Bridge; no flag and orange flag; boats sometimes stop at the adjacent Yodpiman pier, N6/1, instead) – for Pahurat and Wat Prayoon.

**N5** Rachawongse (aka Rajawong; all boats) – for Chinatown.

**N4** Harbour (Marine) Department (no flag and orange flag).

**N3** Si Phraya (all boats) – walk north past the *Sheraton Royal Orchid Hotel* for River City shopping complex; also for Thailand Creative & Design Center (TCDC).

**N2** Wat Muang Kae (no flag) – for TCDC.

**N1** Oriental (no flag and orange flag) – for Thanon Silom.

**Central** Sathorn (all boats) – for the Skytrain and Thanon Sathorn.

---

hub of Sathorn/Saphan Taksin (Taksin Bridge). At each Skytrain and subway station, you'll find a useful map of the immediate neighbourhood. Also under construction in the north of the city is the elevated metro line known as the SRT Dark Red Line from Bang Sue (to connect with the subway), which will (eventually) stop at the Northern Bus Terminal (Mo Chit) and Don Muang Airport.

### BY BUS

Bangkok has reputedly the world's largest bus network (see page 119), with two main types of bus service. On ordinary (non-a/c) buses, which are mostly red and white or blue and white, fares range from B6.50 to B9.50; most routes operate from about 5am to 11pm, but some maintain a 24hr service. Air-conditioned buses are mostly either blue, orange or yellow and charge between B10 and B23 according to distance travelled; most stop in the late evening, but a few of the more popular routes run 24hr services. As buses can only go as fast as the car in front, which at the moment is averaging 4km/h, you'll probably be spending a long time on each journey, so you'd be well advised to pay the extra for cool air – and use the a/c buses are usually less crowded, too. The main problem with using Bangkok's buses is getting reliable, up-to-date information. The Bangkok Mass Transit Authority keeps the Thai-language pages of its website (@bmta.co.th) current, but the English-language route descriptions (@bmta. co.th/?q=en/bus-lines) haven't been updated for a while, and, in any case, are difficult to follow. Easier-to-use maps are available in bookshops – Thinknet's *Bangkok Bus Guide*

– and online at @transitbangkok.com, but, at the time of research, neither had been updated for a few years.

### BY BOAT

Bangkok was built as an amphibious city around a network of canals (khlongs) and the first streets were constructed only in the second half of the nineteenth century. Many canals remain on the Thonburi side of the river, but most of those on the Bangkok side have been turned into roads. Longtail boats (*reua hang yao*) ply the canals of Thonburi like commuter buses, stopping at designated shelters (fares are in line with those of express boats), and are available for individual rental here and on the river (see page 118). The Chao Phraya River itself is still a major transport route for residents and non-residents alike, forming more of a link than a barrier between the two halves of the city.

#### CHAO PHRAYA EXPRESS BOATS

The Chao Phraya Express Boat Company operates the vital express-boat (*reua duan*; @chaophrayaexpressboat.com) services, using large water buses to plough up and down the river, between clearly signed piers (*tha*), which appear on all Bangkok maps. Tha Sathorn, which gives access to the Skytrain network, has been designated "Central Pier", with piers to the south of here numbered S1, S2, etc, those to the north N1, N2 and so on (see page 118 and map p.76). Boats do not necessarily stop at every landing – they only pull in if people want to get on or off, and when they do stop, it's not for long – so when you want to get off, be ready at the back of the boat in good time for your pier. No-flag, local-line boats call at every pier between Nonthaburi and Wat Rajsingkorn, 90min away to the south beyond Sathorn, but only operate during rush hour (Mon–Fri, departing roughly 6.45–7.30am & 4–4.30pm; B10–14). The only boats to run all day, every day, are on the limited-stop orange-flag service (Nonthaburi to Wat Rajsingkorn in about 1hr; departing roughly 6am–7pm or later, every 5–20min; B15). Other limited-stop services run during rush hour, flying either a yellow flag (between Nonthaburi and Tha Sathorn, in about 40min; Mon–Fri, departing Nonthaburi roughly 6.15–8.20am, and returning from Tha Sathorn roughly 4.45–8pm; B20) or a green flag (Pakkred to Tha Sathorn Mon–Fri 6.10–8.10am, Tha Sathorn to Pakkred Mon–Fri 4.05–6.05pm; about 50min; B13–32). Tickets can be bought on board; don't discard your ticket until you're off the boat, as the staff at some piers impose a B1 fine on anyone disembarking without one.

**CHAO PHRAYA TOURIST BOATS**
The Chao Phraya Express Boat service also runs tourist boats (⬆chaophrayatouristboat.com), distinguished by their light-blue flags, between Sathorn (departing every 30min, 9am–5.30pm) and Phra Arthit piers (departing every 30min, 9.30am–6pm). In between (in both directions), these boats call in at River City, Rachawongse, Yodpiman (adjacent to Memorial Bridge), Thien (under renovation at the time of writing, so boats were stopping at Wat Arun instead), Maharat (near Wat Mahathat, the

## USEFUL BUS ROUTES
In addition to those listed below, there are also bus routes from Suvarnabhumi Airport (see page 113) and Don Muang (see page 114). In Banglamphu, finding the right bus stop can sometimes be tricky (see page 91).
**#3** (ordinary)
Northern Bus Terminal–Chatuchak Weekend Market–Thanon Phaholyothin–Thanon Samsen–Thanon Chakrabongse/Thanon Phra Arthit (for Banglamphu guesthouses)–Thanon Sanam Chai (for Museum of Siam)– Memorial Bridge–Taksin Monument (for Wongwian Yai)–Krung Thonburi Skytrain station.
**#15** (ordinary)
Sanam Luang–Thanon Phra Arthit–Thanon Chakrabongse (for Banglamphu guesthouses)–Democracy Monument–Siam Square–Thanon Rajdamri–Thanon Silom–Thanon Charoen Krung (for Saphan Taksin and Asiatique).
**#16** (ordinary and a/c)
Northern Bus Terminal–Chatuchak Weekend Market–Thanon Samsen–Thewet (for guesthouses)–Thanon Phitsanulok–Thanon Phrayathai–Siam Square–Thanon Suriwong.
**#25** (ordinary)
Pak Nam (for Ancient City buses)–Thanon Sukhumvit–Eastern Bus Terminal–Siam Square–Hualamphong Station–Thanon Yaowarat (for Chinatown)–Pahurat–Wat Pho–Tha Chang (for the Grand Palace).
**#53** circular (also anticlockwise; ordinary)
Thewet–Thanon Krung Kasem– Hualamphong Station–Thanon Yaowarat (for Chinatown)–Pahurat–Thanon Maharat (for Wat Pho and the Grand Palace)–Sanam Luang (for National Museum)–Thanon Phra Arthit and Thanon Samsen (for Banglamphu guesthouses)–Thewet.
**#124** (ordinary and a/c)
Sanam Luang–Phra Pinklao Bridge–Southern Bus Terminal.
**#503** (a/c)
Sanam Luang–Democracy Monument (for Banglamphu guesthouses)–Thanon Rajdamnoen Nok (for TAT and boxing stadium)–Wat Benjamabophit–Thanon Sri Ayutthaya–Victory Monument–Chatuchak Weekend Market–Rangsit.
**#508** (ordinary and a/c)
Sanam Luang–Grand Palace–Siam Square–Thanon Sukhumvit–Eastern Bus Terminal–Pak Nam (for Ancient City buses).
**#509** (a/c)
Northern Bus Terminal–Chatuchak Weekend Market–Victory Monument–Thanon Rajdamnoen Nok (for TAT and boxing stadium)–Democracy Monument–Thanon Rajdamnoen Klang (for Banglamphu guesthouses)–Phra Pinklao Bridge–Thonburi.
**#511** (a/c)
Southern Bus Terminal–Phra Pinklao Bridge (for Banglamphu guesthouses)–Democracy Monument–Thanon Sukhumvit–Eastern Bus Terminal–Pak Nam (for Ancient City buses).

**1**

National Museum and the Grand Palace) and Thonburi Railway Station pier. On-board guides provide running commentaries, and a one-day ticket for unlimited trips costs B180; one-way tickets are also available, costing B50.

### CROSS-RIVER FERRIES

Smaller than express boats are the slow cross-river ferries (*reua kham fak*), which shuttle back and forth between the same two points. Found at or beside every express-boat stop and plenty of other piers in between, they are especially useful for exploring Thonburi. Fares are generally B3–4, payable at the entrance to the pier.

### KHLONG SAEN SAEB BOATS

On the Bangkok side, Khlong Saen Saeb is well served by passenger boats, which run at least every 20min during daylight hours (eastbound services start and end a little later; ⓦ khlongsaensaep.com). They start from the Phan Fah pier (Panfa Leelard) at the Golden Mount (handy for Banglamphu, Ratanakosin and Chinatown), and head way out east to Wat Sribunruang, with useful stops at Thanon Phrayathai, aka Saphan Hua Chang (for Jim Thompson's House and Ratchathevi Skytrain stop); Pratunam (for the Erawan Shrine); Soi Chitlom; Thanon Witthayu (Wireless Road); and Soi Nana Nua (Soi 3), Thanon Asok Montri (Soi 21, for TAT headquarters and Phetchaburi subway stop), Soi Thonglor (Soi 55) and Charn Issara, near Soi Ekamai (Soi 63), all off Thanon Sukhumvit. This is your quickest and most interesting way of getting between the west and east parts of town, if you can stand the stench of the canal. You may have trouble actually locating the piers as few are signed in English and they all look very unassuming and rickety; keep your eyes peeled for a plain wooden jetty – most jetties serve boats running in both directions. Once you've jumped on the boat, state your destination to the conductor when he collects your fare, which will be between B9 and B19. Due to the construction of some low bridges, all passengers change onto a different boat at Tha Pratunam – just follow the crowd. There's now also a tourist boat service (ⓦ bangkokcanal.com) on part of Khlong Saen Saeb and Khlong Banglamphu, running every 30min (10am–6pm) from Pratunam, via Saphan Hua Chang and Phan Fah, to Tha Khlong Banglamphu, which is near Thanon Samsen and handy for Thanon Khao San; the cost is B200 for a day-pass with unlimited rides.

### KHLONG PADUNG KRUNG KASEM BOATS

This new, little-publicized and possibly experimental service (Mon–Fri 6–9am & 4–8pm every 20min, daytime services may be added; Sat & Sun 8am–8pm every 30min; free) runs along the canal between Hualamphong Station and the pier at Talat Dhevaraj (Thewet Market), which is 10min walk from the Thewet guesthouses and the express-boat pier at Tha Thewet. The only intermediate stops that may be of interest to visitors are at Thanon Nakhorn Sawan and Thanon Rajdamnoen Nok, though there is talk of adding a pier that connects with Khlong Saen Saeb boats in the future.

### BY SKYTRAIN

Although its network is limited, the BTS Skytrain, or *rot fai faa* (ⓦ bts.co.th), provides a much faster alternative to the bus, and is clean, efficient and over-vigorously air-conditioned. There are only two Skytrain lines, which interconnect at Siam Square (Central Station). Both run every few minutes from around 6am to midnight, with fares of B15–59/trip depending on distance travelled (you'd really have to be motoring to justify buying a day pass at B140). Most of the ticket machines accept only coins, but you can change notes at staffed counters. The Sukhumvit Line runs from Mo Chit (stop N8) in the northern part of the city, via the interchange at Phayathai (N2) with the airport rail link, to Samrong way out on Thanon Sukhumvit (E15) in around 40min. This line is being extended southeast beyond Samrong towards Kheha station in Samut Prakan (currently scheduled for opening in 2019) and – more slowly – north beyond Mo Chit up Thanon Phaholyothin, running along the back of Don Muang Airport (currently slated for 2020). The Silom Line runs from the National Stadium (W1) via Saphan Taksin (Taksin, or Sathorn, Bridge; S6), to link up with the full gamut of express boats on the Chao Phraya River, to Bang Wa (S12) in Thonburi (on Thanon Phetkasem, Highway 4).

### BY SUBWAY

Bangkok's underground rail system, the MRT subway (or metro; in Thai, *rot fai tai din*; ⓦ bangkokmetro.co.th), has similar advantages to the Skytrain, though its main Blue Line goes to fewer places of interest for visitors (its other Purple Line running northwest from Tao Poon connects nothing of touristic interest). The Blue Line runs every few minutes between around 6am and midnight from Hualamphong train station, via Silom (near Sala Daeng Skytrain station), Sukhumvit (near Asoke Skytrain), Phetchaburi (near Makkasan station on the Suvarnabhumi Airport Rail Link), Chatuchak Park (near Mo Chit Skytrain) and Bang Sue train station, to Tao Poon in the north of the city. Building work is under way to continue the Blue Line westwards from Hualamphong to Wat Mangkon Kamalawat in Chinatown, Pahurat, Thanon Sanam Chai in Ratanakosin, then across to Thonburi, with a loop back to Tao Poon (currently due for completion in 2019). Pay your fare (B16–42) at a staffed counter or machine, where you'll receive a token to tap on the entrance gate and insert into the exit gate (the various stored-value cards available are unlikely to be worthwhile for visitors).

### BY TAXI

Bangkok taxis come in three main forms, and are so plentiful that you rarely have to wait more than a couple of minutes before spotting an empty one of some description. Neither tuk-tuks nor motorbike taxis have meters, so you should agree on a price before setting off, and expect to do a fair amount of haggling. App-based taxi services have recently come to Bangkok, of which the most popular are Uber, its Southeast Asian rival, Grab, and, in association with the Siam Taxi Co-operative, Line Man (Line is East Asia's equivalent to WhatsApp).

**METERED TAXIS**

For nearly all journeys, the best and most comfortable option is to flag down one of Bangkok's metered, a/c taxi cabs; look out for the "TAXI METER" sign on the roof, and a red light in the windscreen in front of the passenger seat, which means the cab is available for hire. Starting at B35, fares are displayed on a clearly visible meter that the driver should reset at the start of each trip (say "*poet meter, dai mai khrap/kha?*" to ask him to switch it on), and increase in stages on a combined distance/time formula; as an example, a medium-range journey from Thanon Ploenchit to Thanon Sathorn will cost around B60 at a quiet time of day. Try to have change with you as cabs tend not to carry a lot of money; tipping of up to ten percent is common, though occasionally a cabbie will round down the fare on the meter. If a driver tries to quote a flat fare (often the case with taxis that park outside tourist hotels waiting for business, or with any taxi for journeys to the airports) rather than using the meter, let him go, and avoid the now-rare unmetered cabs (denoted by a "TAXI" sign on the roof). Getting a metered taxi in the middle of the afternoon when the cars return to base for a change of drivers can sometimes be a problem. If you want to book a metered taxi by phone (B20–50 surcharge), try Siam Taxi Co-operative on ☏ 1661.

**TUK-TUKS**

Somewhat less stable though typically Thai, tuk-tuks in Bangkok have very little to recommend them. These noisy, three-wheeled, open-sided buggies, which can carry three medium-sized passengers comfortably, fully expose you to the worst of Bangkok's pollution and weather. You'll have to bargain very hard to get a fare lower than in a metered taxi; for a longer trip, for example from Thanon Convent to Siam Square, drivers will ask for as much as B200. Be aware, also, that tuk-tuk drivers tend to speak less English than taxi drivers – and there have been cases of robberies and attacks on women passengers late at night. During the day it's quite common for tuk-tuk drivers to try and con their passengers into visiting a jewellery, tailor's or expensive souvenir shop with them (see page 144).

**MOTORBIKE TAXIS**

Motorbike taxis generally congregate at the entrances to long sois – pick the riders out by their numbered, coloured vests – and charge from B10 for short trips down into the side streets. If you're short on time and have nerves of steel, it's also possible to charter them for hairy journeys out on the main roads (a short trip from Sanam Luang to Thanon Samsen will cost around B40). Crash helmets are compulsory on all main roads in the capital (traffic police fine non-wearers on the spot), though they're rarely worn on trips down the sois.

**CAR RENTAL**

You'd be mad to rent a self-drive car for getting around Bangkok, especially as taxis are so cheap, but you may want to start a driving tour around the country here.

**Avis** Branches are at 13 Soi 1, Thanon Sathorn (delivery and collection anywhere in Bangkok), as well as Suvarnabhumi and Don Muang airports (☏ 02 251 1131–2, ⊚ avisthailand. com).

**Budget** Branches can be found at the following locations: 19/23 Building A, Royal City Avenue, Thanon Phetchaburi Mai; Suvarnabhumi Airport; and Don Muang Airport (☏ 02 203 9222, ⊚ budget.co.th).

## INFORMATION

**Bangkok Tourism Division** The official source of information on the capital, whose head office is next to Phra Pinklao Bridge at 17/1 Thanon Phra Arthit in Banglamphu (Mon–Fri 8am–7pm, Sat & Sun 9am–5pm; ☏ 02 225 7612–4, ⊚ bangkoktourist.com). The head office is supported by about twenty strategically placed satellite booths around the capital; most open Mon–Sat 9am–5pm, though some open Sun too, including in front of the Grand Palace, on Thanon Maharat near Tha Chang, at Paragon and Mah Boon Krong shopping centres, and in front of Banglamphu's Wat Bowoniwes.

**Tourism Authority of Thailand** TAT (freephone tourist assistance 8am–8pm ☏ 1672; ⊚ tourismthailand.org) maintains tourist information counters at Suvarnabhumi Airport (see page 113); at its head office, which is rather inconveniently located at 1600 Thanon Phetchaburi Mai (daily 8.30am–4.30pm); and, within walking distance of Banglamphu, at the Ministry of Tourism and Sports, 4 Rajdamnoen Nok (daily 8.30am–4.30pm) – it's a 20min stroll from Thanon Khao San, or a short ride in a/c bus #503. Note, however, that the many other travel agents, shops and private offices across the capital displaying "TAT Tourist Information" signs or similar are not official Tourism Authority of Thailand centres and will not be dispensing impartial advice (they may be licensed by TAT to run their business, but that doesn't make them government information offices). The Tourism Authority of Thailand never uses the acronym TAT on its office-fronts or in its logo, and doesn't book hotels or sell transport tickets.

**Listings** The best of the current websites is *BK* (⊚ bk. asia-city.com), which gives a decent rundown of the art

**1**

and drama scenes, live music and club nights. If you're interested in Bangkok's contemporary art scene, go to ⓦfacebook.com/bangkokartmap for exhibition listings. **City maps** For a personal guide to Bangkok's most interesting shops, markets, restaurants and backstreets, look for the famously idiosyncratic hand-drawn *Nancy*

*Chandler's Map of Bangkok*. The map carries a mass of annotated city recommendations, is impressively accurate and regularly reissued; it's sold in most of the main tourist areas, and paper and digital copies and interim updates are also available to view or download at ⓦnancychandler.net.

## ACCOMMODATION

If your time in Bangkok is limited, you should think especially carefully about what you want to do in the city before deciding which part of town to stay in. Traffic jams are so appalling here that easy access to Skytrain, subway or river transport can be crucial. Advance reservations are recommended where possible during high season (Nov–Feb), though some guesthouses will only take cash deposits. For cheap sleeps, your widest choice lies on and around **Banglamphu's** Thanon Khao San. The most inexpensive rooms here are no-frills crash-pads – small and often windowless, with fans, thin walls and shared bathrooms – but Banglamphu also offers plenty of modern-style hostels and well-appointed mid-priced small hotels with a/c and swimming pools. Other, far smaller and less interesting travellers' ghettoes that might be worth bearing in mind are the generally dingy **Soi Ngam Duphli**, off the south side of Thanon Rama IV, which nevertheless harbours a couple of decent shoestring options; and **Soi Kasemsan I**, which is very handily placed next to Siam Square and firmly occupies the moderate range, though with a few rooms for around B700. Otherwise, the majority of the city's moderate and expensive rooms are scattered widely across the **downtown areas**, around Siam Square and Thanon Ploenchit, to the south of Thanon Rama IV and along **Thanon Sukhumvit**, and to a lesser extent in **Chinatown**. As well as easy access to transport links and shops, the downtown views from accommodation in these areas are a real plus, especially from the deluxe hotels that are scenically sited along the banks of the Chao Phraya River. In the reviews that follow, accommodation is a/c, unless specified.

### RATANAKOSIN

Several small, upmarket hotels and hostels have recently opened on the west side of Ratanakosin, which put you in a peerless location, in a quiet, traditional, heavily Chinese neighbourhood of low-rise shophouses, overlooking the river and on the doorsteps of Wat Pho and the Grand Palace. The restaurants and nightlife of Banglamphu are within walking distance if you fancy a bit more of a buzz, while the sights of Thonburi and Chinatown, and Saphan Taksin Skytrain station are just a public boat ride away.
**Arom d Hostel** 336 Thanon Maharat ☏02 622 1055, ⓦaromdhostel.com; map p.78. Meaning "good mood", this hostel and café overlooks Wat Pho from a century-old listed building with balconies and a roof terrace. The stylish, compact, a/c rooms include twins and doubles plus mixed

and women-only dorms with four bunk beds. Breakfast included. Dorms B800, twins B2250
**Aurum The River Place** 394/27–29 Soi Pansook, Thanon Maharat ☏02 622 2248, ⓦaurum-bangkok.com; map p.78. Modelled on a French townhouse, with wooden shutters and wrought-iron balconies, this spruce, four-storey hotel is set back very slightly from the river and four of the rooms are "City View" only, but the other eight offer at least partial views of the water. Splashed with colourful Thai fabrics and sporting heavily varnished wooden floors, the well-equipped rooms are a little on the small side, apart from those on the top floor. There's a daytime riverside café, *Vivi: The Coffee Place*, where complimentary breakfast is served. B3500
★ **Bangkok Bed and Bike** 19/6 Thanon Charoen Krung ☏094 487 8058, ⓦbangkokbedandbike.com; map p.78. Excellent hostel with a smart urban look, close to Wat Pho and the Grand Palace. Women's and mixed dorms are a/c with hot showers, and there are cycling tours, bikes for rent (with great hand-drawn maps of the area) and an impressive array of amenities, including a washing machine and drier. Good breakfast included. Dorms B600, doubles B1600
**Chakrabongse Villas** 396 Thanon Maharat ☏02 222 1290, ⓦchakrabongsevillas.com; map p.78. Upmarket riverside accommodation with a difference: seven tranquil suites, villas and compact rooms beautifully furnished in a choice of Thai, Chinese and Moroccan styles, set in the luxuriant gardens of hundred-year-old Chakrabongse House overlooking Wat Arun. All have a/c and cable TV, and there's a small, attractive swimming pool and a riverfront terrace restaurant for dinner (reservations required). B5620
**Sala Arun** 47 Soi Tha Thien, Thanon Maharat ☏02 622 2932–3, ⓦsalaarun.com; map p.78. At this riverside inn, the nine teak-floored rooms feature objets d'art from the owners' worldwide travels, DVDs, iPod docks and balconies (in most), while complimentary breakfast is served in the boldly coloured ground-floor café, which has a small terrace with armchairs facing Wat Arun (to get a view of the river and temple from your room, you'll have to pay B3800). B3200

### BANGLAMPHU AND DEMOCRACY MONUMENT AREA

Nearly all backpackers head straight for Banglamphu, Bangkok's long-established travellers' ghetto just north of the Grand Palace, location of the cheapest accommodation, the best traveller-oriented facilities and some of the most enjoyable bars and restaurants in the city. A growing number of Banglamphu guesthouses are reinventing themselves as good-value mini-hotels boasting chic decor, swimming pools, and even views from the windows, and have recently been joined by twenty-first-century hostels, which throw in a measure of style and sociability with your wi-fi-enabled bunk. The cheap guesthouses are still there, particularly immediately west of Khao San, around the neighbourhood temple Wat Chana Songhkram, and along riverside Thanon Phra Arthit – where you'll also find some upscale places offering prime views over the Chao Phraya. About a 10min walk north from Thanon Khao San, the handful of guesthouses and small hotels scattered among the shophouses of the Thanon Samsen sois enjoy a more authentically Thai environment, while the Thewet area, a further 15min walk in the same direction or a 7min walk from the Thewet express-boat stop, is more local still. Heading south from Khao San, across multi-laned Rajdamnoen Klang, to the upscale places in the area immediately south of Democracy also puts you plumb in the middle of an interesting old neighbourhood, famous for its traditional shophouse restaurants. Theft is a problem in Banglamphu, particularly at the cheaper guesthouses, so don't leave anything valuable in your room and heed the guesthouses' notices about padlocks and safety lockers.

### THANON KHAO SAN AND AROUND

**Buddy Lodge** 265 Thanon Khao San ☏ 02 629 4477, �ⓦ buddylodge.com; map p.92. Stylish hotel right in the thick of the action, whose charming, colonial-style rooms are done out in cream, with louvred shutters, balconies, marble bathrooms, a/c and polished dark-wood floors. There's a beautiful rooftop pool, a gym, sauna and several bars downstairs in the *Buddy Village* complex. Specify an upper-floor location away from Khao San to ensure a quieter night's sleep. B2300

**Nap Park Hostel** 5 Thanon Tani ☏ 02 282 2324, ⓦ nap park.com; map p.92. On a surprisingly untouristed street just north of Thanon Khao San, this lively hostel shelters smart dorm beds with lockers and hot showers (some with personal TVs), as well as plenty of space for lounging, either inside in front of the TV or outside in the tamarind-shaded front yard. Women-only dorm and laundry available. Dorms B399

**Suneta Hostel** 209–11 Thanon Kraisri ☏ 02 629 0150, ⓦ sunetahostel.com; map p.92. Welcoming, well-equipped hostel, 5min walk from Thanon Khao San, decked out with acres of wood to give a retro look, offering wide, souped-up bunk beds. Light breakfast included. Free weekly walking tours. Dorms B380, doubles B1180

### AROUND WAT CHANA SONGKHRAM AND PHRA ARTHIT

**Bella Bella House** Soi Ram Bhuttri ☏ 02 629 3090; map p.92. Above a plant-strewn café, the pastel-coloured rooms

here are no frills but well priced, and a few boast lovely views over Wat Chana Songkhram. The cheapest share cold-water bathrooms, a notch up gets you an en-suite hot shower, while the most expensive have a/c. Good prices for single rooms, especially the en-suite ones. Fan B320, a/c B530

**KC Guest House** 64 Trok Kai Chae, corner of Thanon Phra Sumen ☏ 02 282 0618, ⓦ kc64guesthouse.com; map p.92. Friendly, family-run guesthouse offering exceptionally clean, a/c bedrooms, with either en-suite or shared, hot-water bathrooms; try to get a room away from the noisy street. There's also a rooftop terrace and a decked eating area on the soi next to 7-Eleven. B500

**Lamphu House** 75 Soi Ram Bhuttri ☏ 02 629 5861–2, ⓦ lamphuhouse.com; map p.92. With smart bamboo beds, coconut-wood furniture and elegant rattan lamps in nearly all the rooms, this travellers' hotel set round a quiet courtyard has a calm, modern feel. Cheaper options (including good-value singles) share facilities and the cheapest fan rooms have no outside view; the more expensive options feature balconies overlooking the courtyard, with the triples and four-person rooms popular with families. Fan B480, a/c B600

**Merry V** Soi Ram Bhuttri ☏ 02 282 9267; map p.92. Large, utterly plain, but efficiently run, guesthouse offering some of the cheapest accommodation in Banglamphu. Bottom-end rooms are basic and small – many share bathrooms – and it's pot luck whether you get a window or not. Better en-suites with hot showers and a/c versions are also available. Good rates for singles. Fan B300, a/c B550

**Navalai River Resort** 45/1 Thanon Phra Arthit ☏ 02 280 9955, ⓦ navalai.com; map p.92. Style-conscious riverfront hotel, with an elegant rooftop pool, tastefully furnished bedrooms, and river views from the most desirable rooms. There's a/c, DVDs, bathtubs and private balconies, and the riverside *Aquatini* restaurant is at ground level. B2700

★ **New Siam 2** 50 Trok Rong Mai ☏ 02 282 2795, ⓦ newsiam.net; map p.92. Very pleasant and well-run small hotel whose en-suite rooms with fan and cold shower or a/c and hot shower stand out for their thoughtfully designed extras such as in-room safes, cable TV and drying rails on the balconies. Occupies a quiet but convenient location and has a small pool. Popular with families, and triple rooms are also available. Fan B790, a/c B890

**New Siam Riverside** 21 Thanon Phra Arthit ☏ 02 629 3535, ⓦ newsiam.net; map p.92. Occupying a prime spot on the Chao Phraya, the riverside branch of the *New Siam* empire offers well-designed, good-value rooms. Even the cheapest have a/c and full amenities, while the best of them boast fabulous river views from windows or private balconies. Also has a large riverside swimming pool and terrace restaurant. Breakfast included. B1590

★ **Praya Palazzo** 757/1 Soi 2, Thanon Somdet Phra Pinklao ☏ 02 883 2998, ⓦ prayapalazzo.com;

**1**

map p.92. A peaceful riverside sanctuary right opposite Banglamphu, this large, graceful, Italianate palace has been lovingly restored by an architecture professor, with great attention to detail – right down to the wallpaper and lampshades – to give the feel of its 1920s origins. Twenty-first-century luxuries have been overlaid, of course, such as DVDs and, in the bathrooms, big-head showers to go alongside the brass taps and swathes of coloured marble. There's a lovely pool in the lush waterfront garden, too. Access is by the free hotel boat, which shuttles across to Phra Arthit express-boat pier. No children under 13. Breakfast included. B3955

### SAMSEN SOIS AND THEWET

**Baan Manusarn** 8/11 Thanon Krung Kasem, Thewet ☎02 281 2976, ⓦbaanmanusarn.com; map p.92. A genuine B&B, friendly and helpful, in a pleasant white building near the pier, offering large a/c rooms with lovely polished wooden floors, some sharing hot showers, and access to a kitchen. Free showers after checkout. Breakfast included. B1330

**Lamphu Treehouse** 155 Saphan Wanchat, Thanon Phracha Thipatai ☎02 282 0991–2, ⓦlamphutreehotel. com; map p.92. Named after the *lamphu* trees that line the adjacent canal, after which Banglamphu ("the riverside village with mangrove apple trees") is named, this attractively turned-out guesthouse offers a pool and smart, a/c rooms, with plenty of polished wood fittings made of recycled golden teak, among other traditional Thai decorative elements; most have balconies, though the cheapest in the nearby annexe are windowless. It's in a quiet neighbourhood but just a few minutes' walk from Democracy. Breakfast included. B1300

**Nakorn Ping** 9/1 Soi 6, Thanon Samsen ☎02 281 6574, ⓦnakornpinghotel.com; map p.92. In a low-rise, orange building dotted with plants on a fairly quiet soi, this place sports some classic elements of a Thai-Chinese hotel: spittoons for waste baskets, gnarly wooden furniture and little natural light. However, it's very clean, efficiently run and good value, offering fridges, cable TV and bathrooms in all rooms, plus hot showers for an extra B100/room/day. Fan B530, a/c B630

**★ Phra Nakorn Norn Len** 46 Thewet Soi 1, Thanon Krung Kasem ☎02 628 8188, ⓦphranakorn-nornlen. com; map p.92. What was once a seedy short-time motel has been transformed into a leafy bohemian haven with genuine eco-conscious and socially engaged sensibilities and a tangible fair-trade philosophy. Every one of the comfortable, though not luxurious, rooms has been cheerily hand-painted to a different retro Thai design, and each has a cute bathroom, balcony and a/c. All kinds of workshops, such as soap-making and cooking, are offered to guests. Mostly organic vegetarian breakfast included. B2600

**Rajata** Soi 6, Thanon Samsen ☎02 281 8977–8, ⓦrajatahotel.com; map p.92. This traditional motel of large bedrooms and bathrooms around a quiet courtyard café has been subtly transformed with retro furniture, hundreds of plants and a friendly welcome. All of the shining white, spotlessly clean accommodation has a/c, satellite TV, hot showers and minibars. B1000

**Shanti Lodge** 37 Thanon Sri Ayutthaya (at Soi 16), Thewet ☎02 281 2497, ⓦshantilodge.com; map p.92. Colourful, old-school-hippy guesthouse with a yoga balcony and a mostly vegetarian restaurant festooned with pot plants. The cheapest "traditional" rooms (fan or a/c) are in a wooden building at the back with shared hot-water bathrooms, but it's worth paying a bit extra for a bright en-suite room in the main lodge with more space – or splash out B1990 for the penthouse with its big, leafy roof terrace. Dorms B250, fan doubles B500, a/c doubles B600

**Sri Ayutthaya** 23/11 Thanon Sri Ayutthaya (at Soi 14), Thewet ☎02 282 5942, ⓦfacebook.com/sriayuttaya; map p.92. The most attractive guesthouse in Thewet, where most of the good-sized rooms (choose between fan rooms without private bathroom and en suites with a/c) are elegantly done out with wood-panelled walls and beautiful polished wood floors; these have been augmented by a few modern, "Superior" rooms (B1200) done out in bright, fetching colours. Hot showers throughout. Fan B500, a/c B700

**★ Tavee** 83 Soi 14, Thanon Sri Ayutthaya, Thewet ☎02 280 1447, ⓦfacebook.com/taveeguesthouse; map p.92. *Tavee* is located down a pedestrian alley behind *Sri Ayutthaya* and is owned by the same family, but is the quieter and friendlier of the two options. Behind the stylish little café, the fan rooms sport attractive wood floors and share chic hot-water bathrooms, while the en-suite a/c options are larger and enjoy a few more decorative touches. Fan B500, a/c B750

### SOUTH AND EAST OF DEMOCRACY

**★ Bangkok Publishing Residence** 31/1 Thanon Lan Luang ☎02 282 0288, ⓦbpresidence.com; map p.92. Luxurious, friendly B&B in a beautifully converted printing house, which is also something of a museum to its most famous publication, the Bangkok Weekly magazine, scattered with old typewriters and printing blocks. The eight very comfortable rooms evoke a gentlemen's club, with leather armchairs and acres of polished wood, and there's a rooftop garden and Jacuzzi. B4800

**★ The Bhuthorn** 96 Thanon Phraeng Phuthon, just off Thanon Kanlayana Maitri ☎02 622 2270, ⓦthebhuthorn.com; map p.92. The architect-owners have beautifully converted this hundred-year-old shophouse into a B&B. Behind the small lobby lie just three elegant rooms (including a junior suite with a mezzanine for B5600), fitted with Chinese, Thai and Western dark-wood antique furniture, chandeliers, *khon* masks and other objets d'art, as well as modern comforts. Breakfast included. **B4500**

**Boonsiri Place** 55 Thanon Buranasart ☎02 622 2189–91, ⓦboonsiriplace.com; map p.92. Run by two charming sisters, this mid-sized hotel is notable for its good value, environmentally conscious policies and location in a lively, seedy old neighbourhood, just a 10min walk from the Grand Palace. Each of its 48 large a/c rooms with hot showers (an extra B300 buys you considerably more space in a "Deluxe" room) is painted in vibrant colours and hung with a different artwork commissioned from the late Thai traditional temple artist Chanok Chunchob. Buffet breakfast included. **B1400**

★ **Innspire** 4/4 Soi Trok Sin, Thanon Dinso ☎097 103 3836, ⓦwww.innspirebangkok.com; map p.92. Describing itself as a homestay and community space that aims to connect people to Thailand on a deeper level, Innspire is also home to unconventional tour company, Bangkok Vanguards (with discounts for guests; see page 121). Set in an attractive building in a quiet, very traditional neighbourhood, the bright, a/c, en-suite rooms, some with balconies, overlook a large, leafy courtyard. **B1250**

★ **Old Capital Bike Inn** 607 Thanon Phra Sumen ☎02 629 1787, ⓦoldcapitalbkk.com; map p.92. Formerly the Old Bangkok Inn, this chic little boutique guesthouse with an eco-friendly philosophy and a vintage bike theme has just ten a/c rooms, each of them individually styled in dark wood, with nostalgic murals, ironwork lamps and elegant contemporary-accented bathrooms. Most of the suites are split-level and some also have a tiny private garden. The guesthouse is located a 10min walk from Khao San. Sit-up-and-beg bicycles and thrice-weekly evening cycling tours are free to guests. Breakfast included. **B3690**

## HUALAMPHONG, CHINATOWN AND PAHURAT

Set between the Ratanakosin sights and downtown, Chinatown is among the most frantic and fume-choked parts of Bangkok – and there's quite some competition. If you're in the mood, however, it's got plenty of interest, sees barely any Western overnighters, and is handy for Hualamphong Station and the subway system. Another accommodation option that's handy for Hualamphong is the Oldtown Hostel (see page 129).

**Baan Hualamphong** 336/20 Soi Chalong Krung ☎02 639 8054, ⓦbaanhualampong.com; map p.96. Just 5min from Hualamphong, this wooden guesthouse offers a modicum of style and is the most welcoming of several similar places in the soi, with a traveller-friendly vibe. There are big, bright, twin rooms plus five-person dorms, but most bedrooms share bathrooms. It also has kitchen and laundry facilities and inviting lounging areas, and is open 24hr. Very good single rates. Dorms **B250**, fan doubles **B590**, a/c doubles **B700**

★ **Shanghai Mansion** 479 Thanon Yaowarat, next to Scala shark's fin restaurant ☎02 221 2121, ⓦshanghaimansion.com; map p.96. The most design-conscious accommodation in Chinatown has embraced the modern Chinoiserie look with gusto. It's not actually an historic mansion, but has been purpose-built on the site of a former Beijing opera house, with most bedrooms (and their windows and private terraces) facing onto an appealing, four-storey atrium, and thus cosily isolated from the Chinatown frenzy. Rooms are prettily done out in silks, lacquer-look furniture and lanterns, featuring a lot of sumptuous reds and purples, as well as a/c, hot showers, DVD players and complimentary minibars. **B2670**

## DOWNTOWN: AROUND SIAM SQUARE AND THANON PLOENCHIT

Siam Square and nearby Thanon Ploenchit are as central as Bangkok gets: all the accommodation listed here is within walking distance of a Skytrain or subway station. On hand are the city's best shopping possibilities – notably the phalanx of malls along Thanon Rama I – and a wide choice of Thai and international restaurants and food courts. There's no ultra-cheap accommodation around here, but a few scaled-up guesthouses complement the hotels. Concentrated in their own small "ghetto" on Soi Kasemsan 1, which runs north off Thanon Rama I, between the Bangkok Art and Cultural Centre and Jim Thompson's House, these offer typical travellers' facilities and basic hotel comforts – a/c and en-suite hot-water bathrooms – at moderate prices; the Khlong Saen Saeb canal-boat pier, Tha Saphan Hua Chang (easily accessed via Thanon Phrayathai), is especially handy for heading west to the Golden Mount and beyond, to Ratanakosin.

**A-One Inn** 25/13 Soi Kasemsan 1, Thanon Rama I ☎02 215 3029 or ☎02 216 4770, ⓦaoneinn.com; map p.104. The original upmarket guesthouse on this soi, and still justifiably popular, with plenty of facilities including a reliable left-luggage room. All bedrooms have fridges and cable TV and come in a variety of sizes, including triples; breakfast included. **B1750**

★ **Anantara Siam** 155 Thanon Rajdamri ☎02 126 8866, ⓦanantara.com; map p.104. The stately home of Bangkok's top hotels, formerly the *Regent*. Afternoon tea is still served in the monumental lobby, which is adorned with magnificent, vibrant eighteenth-century-style murals depicting the Thai cosmology, and flanked by acclaimed Thai, Italian and Japanese restaurants, a steakhouse, an opulent spa and lovely gardens. The large and luxurious rooms are decorated in warm Thai colours and dark wood and come with complimentary smartphones for use throughout your stay, and there's an excellent concierge service. **B7680**

**Golden House** 1025/5–9 Thanon Ploenchit ☎02 252 9535–7, ⓦgoldenhousebangkok.com; map p.104. A

1

very clean and welcoming small hotel in a peerless location, situated down a short soi by Chit Lom BTS. The colourful, parquet-floored bedrooms are equipped with a/c, hot water, cable TV and minibar – ask for one of the larger front rooms with bay windows, which leave just enough space for an armchair or two. **B1400**

**Lub d** 925/9 Thanon Rama I ☎ 02 612 4999, ⓦ lubd. com; map p.104. Branch of the popular, well-run Silom hostel (see page 128), with similar style and facilities (including women-only dorms). It's right on Thanon Rama I, under BTS National Stadium, so handy for just about everything but rather noisy. Dorms **B300**, doubles **B1300**

**Luxx XL** 82/8 Soi Lang Suan ☎ 02 684 1111, ⓦ stay withluxx.com; map p.104. Quietly set back behind *Thang Long* restaurant, this boutique hotel is the younger, but bigger, brother of the original Silom *Luxx*. It shelters large, balconied "Studio" rooms and suites in a seductive contemporary style, all red wood and grey stone, as well as a 13m, infinity-edge, slate pool in the leafy garden. **B2100**

**Siam Kempinski** 991/9 Thanon Rama I ☎ 02 162 9000, ⓦ kempinski.com/bangkok; map p.104. Though it's in downtown's throbbing heart, right behind Paragon shopping centre, this top-of-the-range offering from Europe's oldest luxury hotel group styles itself as a resort: all rooms turn in on an artfully landscaped triangular garden with three pools (some ground-floor rooms even have direct access to one of the pools). As the site used to be part of the "lotus-pond palace", Wang Sra Pathum, the interior designers have made subtle but striking use of lotus motifs, complemented by over two hundred specially commissioned paintings and sculptures by Thai artists, amid the Art Deco-inspired architecture. There's also a beautiful spa and an excellent contemporary Thai restaurant, *Sra Bua* (see page 133). **B8400**

**Ten Face** 81 Soi 2, Soi Ruam Rudee ☎ 02 695 4242, ⓦ tenfacebangkok.com; map p.104. The name comes from Totsagan, the ten-faced demon of the *Ramakien*, and this place ingeniously combines sleek, contemporary design with striking artworks inspired by the national myth, without being gimmicky. All the rooms are spacious suites with espresso machines and iPods, some with small kitchens; ask for a room at the back if you're worried about noise from the nearby expressway. There's a fusion restaurant, fitness centre, long, narrow "dipping" pool and shuttle service to Ploen Chit Skytrain, plus a special concierge, who DJs in the ultra-stylish *Sita Bar* and dispenses the lowdown on Bangkok parties and happenings. **B2080**

**Wendy House** 36/2 Soi Kasemsan 1, Thanon Rama I ☎ 02 214 1149, ⓦ wendyguesthouse.com; map p.104. Friendly and well-run guesthouse, with smart, clean and comfortable rooms, all with fridge and cable TV, most with queen-size double beds. Breakfast (included in the price)

is available in the ground-floor café, and there's reliable luggage storage among a host of useful facilities. **B1500**

**White Lodge** 36/8 Soi Kasemsan 1, Thanon Rama I ☎ 02 216 8867, ⓔ whitelodgebangkok@gmail.com; map p.104. The cheapest guesthouse on the soi, and not always the cleanest, with plain white cubicles and a lively, welcoming atmosphere – the best rooms, bright and quiet, are on the upper floors. **B700**

## THANON SUKHUMVIT

Thanon Sukhumvit is Bangkok's longest road – it keeps going east all the way to Cambodia – but for such an important artery it's far too narrow for the volume of traffic that needs to use it, and is further hemmed in by the Skytrain line that runs above it. Packed with high-rise office blocks and business hotels (though very little budget accommodation), an impressive array of specialist restaurants (from Lebanese to Lao), and stall after stall selling cheap souvenirs and T-shirts, it's a lively place that attracts a high proportion of single male tourists to its enclaves of girlie bars on Soi Nana Tai and Soi Cowboy. But for the most part it's not a seedy area, and is home to many expats and middle-class Thais. Even at the west end of Sukhumvit, many of the sois are refreshingly quiet, even leafy; transport down the longer sois is provided by motorbike-taxi (*mohtoesai*) drivers who wait at the soi's mouth, clad in numbered waistcoats. Odd-numbered sois run off the north side of Thanon Sukhumvit, even-numbered off the south side; some of the sois have become important enough to earn their own names, which are often used in preference to their numbers; many sois are long enough to have sub-sois running off them, which usually have their own numbers (or names).

**The Atlanta** At the far southern end of Soi 2 ☎ 02 252 1650, ⓦ theatlantahotelbangkok.com; map p.109. A Bangkok institution, this classic, five-storey budget hotel was built in 1952 around a famously photogenic Art Deco-style lobby and continues to emphasize an old-fashioned, conservative style of hospitality. It offers some of the cheapest accommodation on Sukhumvit: rooms are plain and simple, though they are all en suite and some have a/c and hot water; many have small balconies. There's a swimming pool and kids' pool in the garden, a good restaurant and a free left-luggage facility. Fan **B950**, a/c **B1050**

**Avani Atrium** 1880 Thanon Phetchaburi Mai ☎ 02 718 2000–1, ⓦ minorhotels.com/en/avani/atrium-bangkok; map p.109. Good-value, 600-room luxury hotel that's a little to the north of the Sukhumvit strip, but handy for the subway (Phetchaburi), the airport rail link (Makkasan) and Khlong Saen Saeb boats. Well-equipped, tasteful rooms enjoy great views of downtown, and there's a delicious and theatrical Japanese teppanyaki restaurant, Benihana. **B2090**

1

**Marriott Marquis Queens Park** 199 Soi 22 • 02 059 5555, ⓦmarriott.com; map p.109. This new 1400-room hotel overlooks and has direct access to Benjasiri Park (and its jogging track). Luxurious rooms offer subtly appealing hints of Thai style in their contemporary décor, and there are two pools and a lovely spa. A wide choice of eating outlets includes a Thai–Western tea room, a Chinese restaurant, a Japanese soba canteen and, on the rooftop, a clubby cocktail bar and a spectacular contemporary Asian restaurant that fuses Japanese, Korean and Western influences. B5530

**Park Plaza** 9 Soi 18 • 02 658 7000, ⓦparkplaza.com; map p.109. The quieter and newer of two nearby Park Plazas, this small hotel is topped by an appealing, open-air 20m pool, gym and bar-restaurant on the eighth floor. Fitted with DVD players, the rooms sport a perky contemporary look, with bright colours set against businessman's black. B2880

## DOWNTOWN: SOUTH OF THANON RAMA IV

South of Thanon Rama IV, the area sometimes known as Bangrak contains a full cross-section of accommodation. Tucked away at its eastern edge, there are a few cheap places that are worth recommending in the small travellers' haunt of Soi Ngam Duphli and adjacent Soi Sri Bamphen and Soi Saphan Khu. The neighbourhood is often traffic-clogged and occasionally seedy, but is close to Lumphini Park and subway station and fairly handy for Suvarnabhumi Airport. As well as a fair scattering of medium-range places, the arc between Thanon Rama IV and the river also lays claim to the capital's biggest selection of top hotels, which are among the most opulent in the world. Traversed by the Skytrain, this area is especially good for eating and for gay and straight nightlife, mostly near the east end of Thanon Silom (around which several LGBTQ-friendly hotels are scattered). Staying by the river itself in the atmospheric area around Thanon Charoen Krung, also known as New Road, has the added advantage of easy access to express boats.

★ **Anantara Riverside** 257 Thanon Charoennakorn • 02 476 0022, ⓦanantara.com; map p.76. A luxury retreat from the frenetic city centre, well to the south on the Thonburi bank, but connected to Taksin Bridge (for the Skytrain and Chao Phraya express boats), 15min away, by hotel ferries every 20min. Arrayed around a highly appealing, landscaped swimming pool, the tranquil, riverside gardens are filled with birdsong, while the stylish and spacious bedrooms come with varnished hardwood floors, balconies and complimentary smartphones. There's a fitness centre, tennis courts, kids' club, spa and, among a wide choice of places to eat, a good Japanese teppanyaki house. B5085

**Avani Riverside** 257 Thanon Charoennakorn • 02 365 9110, ⓦminorhotels.com/en/avani/riverside-bangkok. com; map p.76. Thoroughly modern luxury hotel with creative touches such as stylish work stations in the Long Bar and a deli-coffee bar. Though the hotel is set back a little from the Chao Phraya, towering views of the city and its riverscape are enjoyed from all of the rooms, the rooftop infinity-edge pool and the reputable bar-restaurant on the same floor, Attitude, which is staffed by fine chefs, mixologists and late-night DJs. Guests can use most of the facilities of the adjacent Anantara Riverside (see above), including its shuttle boats. B5600

**Baan Saladaeng** 69/2 Soi 3, Thanon Saladaeng • 02 636 3038, ⓦbaansaladaeng.com; map p.111. On a tiny, central alley, this chic, LGBTQ -friendly designer guesthouse offers sixteen individually styled and priced rooms, such as the Pop Art Mania Room and the Mediterranean Suite, some with bathtubs and balconies and one with its bath on the balcony. A/c, rain showers, minibars, cable TV and comfy beds throughout. Breakfast included. B1250

**Como Metropolitan** 27 Thanon Sathorn Tai • 02 625 3333, ⓦcomohotels.com/metropolitanbangkok; map p.111. The height of chic, minimalist urban living, where the spacious, Zen-like rooms are decorated in dark wood and creamy Portuguese limestone. There's a very seductive pool, a fine spa, a well-equipped fitness centre with bubbling hydro-pools, a yoga studio with free daily classes, and an excellent restaurant, Nahm (see page 135). B5000

**ETZ Hostel** 5/3 Soi Ngam Duphli • 02 286 9424, ⓦetzhostel.com; map p.76. Helpful and very clean, ETZ sports playful contemporary decor in primary colours, a popular roof terrace and a large, attractive lounge. It's very handy for Lumphini subway and Thanon Rama IV, though consequently a little noisy. The a/c dorms share hot showers and fit four to twelve people (one is women-only), or you could upgrade to a bright white double with large, en-suite, hot-water bathroom. Breakfast and luggage storage are available. Dorms B200, doubles B800

★ **Lub d** 4 Thanon Decho • 02 634 7999, ⓦlubd.com; map p.111. Meaning "sleep well" (lap dii), this buzzing, upmarket hostel has a/c and hot water throughout and an industrial feel to its stylishly lit decor. This crisp modernity extends to the bedrooms, among which the dorms (some women-only) and the bunk-bedded "Railway" private rooms ("Railway" twin B800) share large bathroom areas, while the top-of-the-range en-suite doubles boast TVs and iPod docks. The hostel lays on some interesting activities and tours, and there's a popular bar and café, a movie lounge, washing machines and free storage facilities, but no kitchen. Dorms B300, doubles B1300

**Luxx** 6/11 Thanon Decho • 02 635 8800, ⓦstaywithluxx.com; map p.111. Welcoming boutique hotel offering a good dose of contemporary style at reasonable prices. Decorated in white, grey and natural teak, the rooms feature DVD players and cute wooden baths surmounted by rain showers. B2500

★ **New Road Guest House** 1216/1 Thanon Charoen Krung, between sois 34 and 36 • 02 630 9371, ⓦnewroad guesthouse.com; map p.111. Thai headquarters of Danish backpacker tour operator, Go Beyond, offering a wide choice of accommodation around a courtyard off New Road, as well as a helpful service centre and travel agent, and interesting Thailand tours. There are mixed and women-only a/c dorms, as well as small "Backpackit" fan rooms with minibars and well-equipped, hot-water bathrooms; a/c rooms sport attractive wooden floors and Thai decorative touches. Guests can hang out in the restaurant, the sociable bar or the rooftop hammocks; free baggage storage available and free showers after checkout. Dorms B350, fan doubles B700, a/c doubles B1000

**Oldtown Hostel** 1048 Thanon Charoen Krung, between sois 26 and 28 ☎02 639 4879, ⓦoldtownhostelbkk. com; map p.111. Handy for Hualamphong Station, this hundred-bed hostel features a/c bunk beds and double beds, shared hot showers and extensive common areas, including a ground-floor café and pool table. Dorms B230, doubles B800

**Rose** 118 Thanon Suriwong ☎02 266 8268–72, ⓦrose hotelbkk.com; map p.111. Set back from the main road but very handy for the city's nightlife, the compact rooms here (all with bathtubs) boast a simple but stylish, modernist look, enhanced by paintings and silk cushions. The ground-floor public rooms are more elegant again, and there's a beautiful swimming pool, a small gym, saunas and a good Thai restaurant, *Ruen Urai* (see page 135), at the back. B1800

★ **Sala Thai Daily Mansion** 15 Soi Saphan Khu ☎02 287 1436, ⓔsalathai.guesthouse@hotmail.com; map p.76. The last and best of several budget guesthouses on this quiet, narrow alleyway, the first right off Soi Saphan Khu, coming from Soi Sri Bamphen. A clean and efficiently run place, with bright, cheerful rooms with wall fans, sharing hot-water bathrooms, and a large, leafy roof garden. Decent rates for single rooms. Fan B400, a/c B600

★ **Sukhothai** 13/3 Thanon Sathorn Tai ☎02 344 8888, ⓦsukhothai.com; map p.111. The most elegant

of Bangkok's top hotels, its decor inspired by the walled city of Sukhothai, offers low-rise accommodation, as well as a beautiful garden spa, all coolly furnished in silks, teak and granite. Service is of the highest standard and the architecture makes the most of the views of the surrounding six acres of gardens, lotus ponds and pools dotted with statuary. There's also a health club, a 25m Infinity pool and excellent restaurants, including *Celadon* (see page 134). B7650

**Swan** 31 Soi 36, Thanon Charoen Krung ☎02 235 9271–3, ⓦswanhotelbkk.com; map p.111. Next to the stately residence of the French ambassador, this good-value Chinese hotel is well run and welcoming. Arrayed around a 15m pool, the rooms are bright, clean and of a decent size (though bathrooms in the cheaper rooms are small), with a/c, hot water, cable TV, minibars and safes; some have balconies with armchairs. Good rates for singles. B1000

## SUVARNABHUMI AIRPORT

**Mariya Boutique Residence** 1627/2 Thanon Latkrabang ☎02 326 7854, ⓦmariyahotel.com. Five minutes' drive from the airport to the northeast (with pick-ups available 24hr), this well-organized hotel offers hot showers, a/c, double-glazed windows, minibars, cable TVs, microwaves, kettles and DVD players (on request) in all of the bedrooms, which feature some traditional Thai touches in the appealing decor. B1150

**Novotel Suvarnabhumi** ☎02 131 1111, ⓦnovotel. com. The official airport hotel, set within the complex and a 10min walk from arrivals via a walkway in the basement (or catch the shuttle bus from outside arrivals Gate 4). Offering smart, contemporary rooms with marble bathrooms, Thai, Japanese, Cantonese and international restaurants, a swimming pool and fitness centre, the eco-friendly *Novotel* operates on a 24hr basis – you can check in at any time, and check out 24hr later. Breakfast included. B5865

## EATING

As you'd expect, nowhere in Thailand can compete with Bangkok's diversity when it comes to food: it boasts an astonishing fifty thousand places to eat, almost one for every hundred citizens. Although prices are generally higher here than in the provinces, it's still easy to dine well on a budget. For **Thai** food, the best gourmet restaurants in the country operate from the downtown districts, proffering wonderful royal, traditional and regional cuisines that definitely merit a visit. At the lower end of the price scale, one-dish meals from around the country are rustled up at the **food courts** of shopping centres and department stores, as well as at **night markets** and **street stalls**. However in 2017 – just after CNN declared Bangkok the best city in the world for street food – the city authorities announced that they were going to rid the pavements of all vendors. They later backtracked, saying that the street stalls in Chinatown and Banglamphu

could stay and, at the time of research, it didn't seem that the ban was being rigorously enforced in the rest of the city. For the non-Thai cuisines, Chinatown naturally rates as the most authentic district for pure **Chinese** food; likewise neighbouring Pahurat, the capital's Indian enclave, is best for unadulterated **Indian** dishes, while there's a sprinkling of Indian and (mostly southern Thai) **Muslim** restaurants around Silom's Maha Uma Devi Temple and nearby Thanon Charoen Krung. Sukhumvit's Soi 3 is a hub for **Middle Eastern** cafés, complete with hookah pipes at the outdoor tables; good, comparatively cheap **Japanese** restaurants are concentrated, for example, on and around Soi Thaniya, at the east end of Thanon Silom; and there's a Korean enclave in Sukhumvit Plaza, at the corner of Soi 12. In the more expensive restaurants listed below you may have to pay VAT (currently seven percent) and a ten percent **service charge**.

**1**

## RATANAKOSIN

The places reviewed below are especially handy for sightseers, but there are also plenty of street stalls around Tha Chang and a load of simple, studenty restaurants off the north end of Thanon Maharat near Thammasat University, as well as a decent restaurant at *Arun Residence*.

★ **Err** Soi Maharat, Thanon Maharat ☎02 622 2291 / 02 622 2292, ⓦerrbkk.com; map p.78. A more basic offshoot of Bolan, one of Bangkok's finest restaurants (see page 133), Err rustles up "urban rustic" dishes, such as delicious *moo hong* (braised pork belly with pepper, B230), in a chic, retro space; wash it down with rice whisky. Tues–Sun 11am–10pm.

**Navy Club (Krua Khun Kung)** Tha Chang ☎02 222 0081; map p.78. This place is immediately on the south side of the express-boat pier, but a little tricky to get to: ignore the prominent but overpriced *Navy Club 77 Café* on the corner of Na Phra Lan and Maharat roads, walk down Thanon Maharat a short way and go in through the car park of the navy compound. The decor's deeply institutionalized but the real draw is the shaded terrace built over the river, where you can enjoy excellent dried prawn and lemon-grass salad (B130), *haw mok thalay* (seafood curry soufflé; B200) and other marine delights. Daily 11am–10pm; Mon–Fri kitchen closes 3–4pm & terrace closes 2–6pm (though you're welcome to finish your meal there after 2pm).

★ **Supanniga Eating Room** Riva Arun Hotel, 392/25–26 Thanon Maharat ☎02 714 7608; also at Soi 55 (Soi Thonglor), Thanon Sukhumvit ☎02 714 7508; and 28 Soi 10, Thanon Sathorn ☎02 635 0349, ⓦsupanniga eatingroom.com; maps p.78, p.109 and p.111. With head-on views of freshly renovated Wat Arun, the upstairs terrace at this riverside restaurant-coffee bar is a great place to try the distinctive cuisine of Chanthaburi, famous for its herbs and spices – the delicious mixed appetizer platter is a good place to start, followed by *moo cha muang* (B240), a mild red curry of stewed pork. The restaurant's other speciality is food from Isaan, where the family have a boutique hotel in Khon Kaen. Daily 11.30am–10.30pm (last orders 10pm).

## BANGLAMPHU AND THE DEMOCRACY MONUMENT AREA

Copycat entrepreneurship means that Khao San is stacked full of backpacker restaurants serving near-identical Western and (mostly) watered-down Thai food; there's even a lane, one block east, parallel to Thanon Tanao (behind *Burger King*), that's dominated by vegetarian cafés, following a trend started by *May Kaidee*. Hot-food stalls selling very cheap night-market snacks operate until the early hours. Things are more varied down on Thanon Phra Arthit, with its arty little café-restaurants favoured by Thammasat University students, while the riverside places,

on Phra Arthit and further north off Thanon Samsen and in Thewet, tend to be best for seafood with a view. For the real old-fashioned Thai taste though, browse southern Thanon Tanao, where traditional shophouses have been selling specialist sweets and savouries for generations.

### AROUND THANON KHAO SAN

**Madame Musur** Soi Ram Bhuttri; map p.92. Mellow bar-restaurant festooned with vines and paper lanterns, with good people-watching tables on the alley, serving a wide range of drinks, including excellent espressos, and authentic northern Thai food – try the *khantoke*, two kinds of chilli dip with pork scratchings and organic vegetables (B150). Daily 9am–midnight.

★ **May Kaidee** East off Thanon Tanao ⓦmaykaidee. com; map p.92. Simple, neighbourhood Thai vegetarian restaurant that still serves some of the best veggie food in Banglamphu despite having spawned several competitors on the same alley. Come for Western breakfasts or try the tasty green curry, the Vietnamese-style veggie spring rolls or the sticky black-rice pudding with mango or banana. Most dishes around B100. Also runs a variety of cookery courses (see page 131). Daily 9am–10pm.

### THANON PHRA ARTHIT

★ **Hemlock** 56 Thanon Phra Arthit ☎02 282 7507; map p.92. Small, stylish, a/c restaurant that's very popular with students and young Thai couples. Offers a long, mid-priced menu, including delicious *tom yam* (hot and sour soup) and green and *phanaeng* curries (around B150), as well as more unusual dishes such as several kinds of *laap* (spicy ground meat salad). The traditional *miang* starters (shiny green wild tea leaves filled with chopped vegetables, fish, prawn or meat) are also very tasty, and there's a good vegetarian selection. Worth reserving a table on Fri and Sat nights. Mon–Sat 5–11pm.

**Kway Jap Yuan Khun Daeng** Thanon Phra Arthit ☎085 246 0111; map p.92. This basic, bustling canteen does a roaring trade with Thammasat University students, who come for the delicious *kway jap yuan*, noodle soup similar to Vietnamese *pho* but a little starchier – go for the "extra" version with egg (B65) and you're set up for the day. Find it in an historic shophouse, unmistakably painted white and green – colours which the flamboyant owner often sports himself. Mon–Sat 11am–9.30pm.

**Roti Mataba Karim** 136 Thanon Phra Arthit ☎02 282 2119; map p.92. Famous 70-year-old outlet for the ever-popular fried Indian breads, or *rotis*, served here in lots of sweet and savoury varieties, including stuffed with meat and veg (*mataba*; from B44), served with vegetable and meat curries, or with bananas and condensed milk; biryanis (*khao mok*) are also on offer. Choose between pavement tables and a basic upstairs a/c room. Tues–Sun 10am–9pm.

## THAI COOKERY CLASSES IN BANGKOK

**Baipai** 8/91 Soi 54, Thanon Ngam Wongwan ☎02 561 1404, ⓦbaipai.com. Thorough, four-hour classes in an attractive garden house in northern Bangkok. The classes cost B2200, including transfers from central hotels. Closed Sun.

**Bangkok Bold Cooking Studio** 503 Thanon Phra Sumen ☎098 829 4310, ⓦbangkokbold.com. Three-hour classes (from B2500) in an old converted shophouse in Banglamphu, which also hosts chef's table dinners (B1500/person). Different dishes are taught at each class, according to a monthly schedule posted on their website.

**Cooking with Poo & Friends** Klong Toey ☎080 434 8686, ⓦcookingwithpoo.com. Set up by the ebullient Khun Poo with the help of a Christian charity, this culinary school offers a chance to experience the slums of Klong Toey and spend a morning learning to cook. The price of B1500 includes a market tour and free transfers from next to Phrom Pong BTS station. Classes also available on Phra Pradaeng, an undeveloped river island on the south side of Bangkok, including a short longtail trip and a bike ride.

**May Kaidee** East of Thanon Khao San, off Thanon Tanao ☎089 137 3173, ⓦmaykaidee.com. Banglamphu's famous vegetarian restaurant (see page 130) offers a huge variety of courses lasting anything from 2hr (B1000) to 10 days (B15,000), including raw food, desserts and fruit-carving classes.

### THANON SAMSEN AND THEWET

**Jok Phochana** On a side soi running between Soi 2 and Soi 4, Thanon Samsen; map p.92. This bare-basics, forty-year-old restaurant, which has featured on national TV, is about as real as you're going to get near Thanon Khao San; a green curry costs B80. The day's ingredients are colourfully displayed at the front of the shop, and the quiet pavement tables get more crowded as the night wears on. Daily 4pm–midnight.

**Kaloang Home Kitchen** Beside the river (follow the bend round) at the far western end of Thanon Sri Ayutthaya ☎02 281 9228; map p.92. Flamboyant service and excellent seafood attracts a largely Thai clientele to this open-air, no-frills, bare-wood restaurant perched on a stilted deck over the river. Dishes well worth sampling include the fried rolled shrimps served with a sweet dip and any of the host of Thai salads. Most mains are B100–150; expect to pay more for crab, shrimp and some fish dishes. Daily 11am–10pm.

★ **Krua Apsorn** Thanon Samsen, opposite Thanon Uthong Nok on the southwestern edge of Dusit ☎02 668 8788; map p.92; Thanon Dinso ☎02 685 4531. Very good, spicy and authentic food and a genteel welcome make this unpretentious, a/c restaurant popular with the area's civil servants – as well as the royalty whom they serve. Try the green fish-ball curry (B120) or the yellow curry with river prawns and lotus shoots, both recommended by the leading Thai restaurant guide, MacDang, and then put out the fire in your mouth with home-made coconut sorbet. Thanon Samsen Mon–Sat 10.30am–8pm (generally closes early on Sat); Thanon Dinso Mon–Sat 10.30am–8pm.

**Steve Café and Cuisine** Wat Thawarad ☎02 281 0915, ⓦstevecafeandcuisine.com; map p.92. In a lovely riverside setting with views of Rama VIII Bridge, come here for great service and a huge menu that encompasses southern, northern and northeastern Thai specialities and fusion dishes, including a very tasty and spicy salmon *laap* (B210). It's easy to see, right across the mouth of Khlong Krung Kasem from Tha Thewet express-boat pier, though harder to get there, walking round and right through the grounds of the temple. Daily 11am–10.30pm.

### SOUTH OF DEMOCRACY

In this area, there's also a branch of *Krua Apsorn* (see page 131).

**Kai Yang Boran** 474–476 Thanon Tanao, immediately to the south of the Chao Poh Seua Chinese shrine ☎02 622 2349; map p.92. Locally famous grilled chicken (B130 for half a bird) and *som tam* (green papaya salad; B80) restaurant (with a/c), wallpapered with photos of celebrities who have eaten here. *Nam tok* salad with roast pork and several kinds of *laap* round out the northeastern menu. Daily 8.30/9am–9pm.

**Padthai Thipsamai** 313 Thanon Mahachai, near Wat Rajnadda ☎02 221 6280; map p.92. The most famous *phat thai* in Bangkok, flash-fried by the same family since 1966. The "special" option is huge, comes with especially juicy prawns, and is wrapped in a translucent, paper-thin omelette. Best washed down with fresh coconut juice. Daily, except alternate Mon, 5pm–2am.

### HUALAMPHONG, CHINATOWN AND PAHURAT

Much of the fun of Chinatown dining is in the browsing of the night-time hot-food stalls that open up all along Thanon Yaowarat, around the mouth of Soi Issaranuphap (Yaowarat Soi 11) and along Soi Phadungdao (Soi Texas); wherever there's a crowd you'll be sure of good food.

**Hua Seng Hong** 371 Thanon Yaowarat ☎02 222 7053, ⓦhuasenghong.co.th; map p.96. Vibrant, ever-popular, few-frills restaurant with an open kitchen out

**1**

front, the original branch of what's now a citywide chain. Dishes from around B100, less for noodle soup, dim sum or roast duck on rice, more for delicacies such as braised geese's feet. Daily 9am–1am.

**Royal India** Just off Thanon Chakraphet at 392/1 📞 02 221 6565; map p.96; basement, Siam Paragon 📞 02 610 7667; map p.104; Floor 5, Emporium shopping centre 📞 086 973 8266; map p.109; 🌐 royalindiathailand.com. Great dhal, perfect parathas and famously good North Indian curries (from B125), with plenty of vegetarian options, served in a dark, basic little a/c restaurant in the heart of Bangkok's most Punjabi of neighbourhoods to an almost exclusively South Asian clientele. Daily 10am–10pm.

**T&K (Toi & Kid's Seafood)** 49 Soi Phadungdao, corner of Thanon Yaowarat 📞 02 223 4519, 🌐 facebook. com/tkseafood; map p.96. Hectic, rough-hewn street restaurant famous for its barbecued seafood, with everything from prawns and cockles (from B60 a serving) to whole fish and crab (from B300) on offer, as well as more complex dishes such as seafood *som tam*. Eat at crowded pavement tables by the busy road or inside in the basic a/c rooms. Daily 4.30pm–2am.

## DOWNTOWN: AROUND SIAM SQUARE AND THANON PLOENCHIT

In this neighbourhood, there are also branches of *Royal India* (see page 132), *Aoi* (see page 134) and *Somboon Seafood* (see page 135). Notable street food in this area includes delicious *khao man kai*, boiled chicken breast with broth, dipping sauces and rice cooked in chicken stock, served at a strip of late-night canteens on the south side of Thanon Phetchaburi, running east from the corner of Thanon Rajdamri.

**Din Tai Fung** Floor 5, Central Embassy 📞 02 160 5918, 🌐 dintaifung.com.sg; map p.104. At this attractive and efficient all-day dim sum place, the superb speciality is steamed pork dumplings with clear broth inside each one (B160), but other dishes such as spring rolls with duck and spring onion (B170) are also very tasty. Mon–Fri 11am–9.30pm, Sat & Sun 10.30am–9.30pm.

**Eathai** Basement, Central Embassy 🌐 centralembassy. com/eathai; map p.104. This upmarket food court – including a branch of *Krua Apsorn* (see page 131) – is a great place to learn about the huge variety of Thai food, with kitchens from the various regions rustling up their local dishes, plus seafood and vegetarian specialities, traditional drinks and dessert stalls and a section devoted to street food. Daily 10am–10pm.

**Gianni** 34/1 Soi Tonson, Thanon Ploenchit 📞 02 652 2922, 🌐 giannibkk.com; map p.104. Probably Bangkok's best independent Italian restaurant, offering a sophisticated blend of traditional and modern in both its decor and food. Twice-weekly shipments of artisan ingredients from the old country are used in dishes such as risotto with porcini

mushrooms and parmesan and squid-ink spaghetti with clams, prawns and asparagus. Best to come for lunch Mon–Fri when there's a good-value set menu (two courses for B490). Daily 11.30am–2pm & 6–10pm.

★**Hinata** Central Embassy, Thanon Ploenchit 📞 02 160 5935, 🌐 shin-hinata.com; map p.104. This branch of a famous Nagoya restaurant offers exquisite sushi (starting at B1000 for six pieces of nigiri sushi), good wines by the glass and great views over the leafy British Embassy grounds. Simpler rice dishes are available as part of lunchtime sets before 2pm (B500), or you could blow up to B6000 on a multi-course kaiseki meal, featuring appetizers, sushi, sashimi, seasonal dishes, soup and dessert. Daily 11am–11pm (last orders 9.30pm).

**Home Kitchen (Khrua Nai Baan)** 94 Soi Lang Suan 📞 02 255 8947, 🌐 khruanaibaan.com; map p.104. This congenial, unpretentious spot in an attractive a/c villa is like an upcountry restaurant in the heart of the city. On the reasonably priced Thai and Chinese picture menu, you're bound to find something delicious, including dozens of soups – try the *kaeng som*, with shrimp and acacia shoot omelette, for B200 – six kinds of *laap* and a huge array of seafood. Daily 8am–midnight.

**Inter** 432/1–2 Soi 9, Siam Square 📞 02 251 4689; map p.104. Honest, efficient Thai restaurant that's popular with students and shoppers, serving good one-dish meals from B68, as well as curries, soups, salads and fish, in a no-frills, fluorescent-lit canteen atmosphere. Daily 11am–9.30pm.

**Jim Thompson's Restaurant** Jim Thompson's House, 6 Soi Kasemsan 2, Thanon Rama I 📞 02 612 3601, 🌐 jimthompsonrestaurant.com; map p.104. A civilized, reasonably priced haven in the must-see house museum (see page 106), serving delicious dishes such as pomelo salad with prawns (B260) and *matsaman* curry with chicken (B200), as well as cakes and Thai desserts. Daily 11am–5pm & 6–10pm.

**Mah Boon Krong Food Courts** Corner of Rama I and Phrayathai rds 🌐 mbk-center.co.th; map p.104. Two decent food-courts at the north end of MBK: the long-running area on Floor 6 is a good introduction to Thai food, with English names and pictures of a huge variety of tasty, cheap one-dish meals from all over the country displayed at the various stalls (including vegetarian options), as well as fresh juices and a wide range of desserts; the slightly more upmarket version on Floor 5 is an international affair, spanning India, Italy, Vietnam, Lebanon, Indonesia, Mexico and Japan. Floor 6 daily 10am–roughly 9pm; Floor 5 daily 10am–9.30pm.

★**Polo Fried Chicken (Kai Thawt Jay Kee Soi Polo)** 137/13 Soi Polo, Thanon Witthayu 📞 02 655 8489; map p.104. On the access road to the snobby polo club, this simple restaurant is Bangkok's most famous purveyor of the ultimate Thai peasant dish: fried chicken. All manner of northeastern dishes, including fish, sausages and loads of salads, fill out the

## YELLOW-FLAG HEAVEN FOR VEGGIES

Every year, for nine days during the ninth lunar month (between late Sept and Nov), Thailand's Chinese community goes on a **meat-free** diet to mark the onset of the Vegetarian Festival (Ngan Kin Jeh), a sort of Taoist version of Lent. Though the Chinese citizens of Bangkok don't go in for skewering themselves like their compatriots in Phuket (see page 320), they do celebrate the Vegetarian Festival with gusto: some people choose to wear only white for the duration, all the temples throng with activity, and nearly every restaurant and food stall in Chinatown turns vegetarian for the period, flying small yellow flags to show that they are upholding the tradition and participating in what's essentially a nightly veggie food jamboree. For vegetarian tourists this is a great time to be in town – just look for the yellow flag and you can be sure all dishes will be one hundred percent vegetarian. Soya substitutes are a popular feature on the vegetarian Chinese menu, so don't be surprised to find pink prawn-shaped objects floating in your noodle soup or unappetizingly realistic slices of fake duck. Many hotel restaurants also get in on the act during the Vegetarian Festival, running special veggie promotions for a week or two.

menu, but it would be a bit perverse to come here and not have the classic combo of finger-licking chicken (B130 for a half), *som tam* and sticky rice. Daily 7am–9pm.

★ **Sanguansri** 59/1 Thanon Witthayu ☎ 02 251 9378; map p.104. The rest of the street may be a multi-storey building site but this low-rise, canteen-like old-timer, run by a friendly bunch of middle-aged women, clings on. And where else around here can you lunch on a sweet, thick and toothsome *kaeng matsaman* for B70? It goes well with *kung pla*, a tasty, fresh prawn and lemon-grass salad that can be spiced to order. The menu changes daily, and in the hot season they serve delicious *khao chae* (rice in chilled, flower-scented water) with delicate, fried side dishes. If possible, avoid the lunchtime rush between noon and 1pm. Mon–Sat 10am–3pm.

**Sra Bua** Siam Kempinski Hotel (see page 126); map p.104. Molecular gastronomy comes to Bangkok, with great success. Operated by Copenhagen's Thai Michelin one-star, *Kiin Klin*, this place applies some serious creativity and theatricality to Thai cuisine. Dishes such as frozen red curry with lobster salad (B650), which perfectly distils the taste of the *kaeng daeng*, match the dramatic decor, which encompasses two lotus ponds (*sra bua*). Daily noon–2.30pm & 6–10.30pm.

### THANON SUKHUMVIT

In this area, there are also branches of *Aoi* (see page 134), *Royal India* (see page 132), *Supanniga Eating Room* (see page 130) and *Ramentei* (see page 135).

**Baan Khanitha** 36/1 Soi 23 ☎ 02 258 4181; map p.109; also 69 Thanon Sathorn Tai, at the corner of Soi Suan Phlu ☎ 02 675 4200–1; ⓦ baan-khanitha.com. The big attraction at this long-running favourite haunt of Sukhumvit expats is the setting in a traditional Thai house and leafy garden. The food is upmarket Thai and fairly pricey, and includes lots of fiery salads (*yam*) and a good range of *tom yam* soups, as well as green, *matsaman* and seafood curries. Most mains cost B200–500. Daily 11am–11pm.

**Barcelona Gaudí** Ground floor, Le Premier 1 Condo, Soi 23 ☎ 02 661 7410, ⓦ facebook.com/barcelona gaudithailand; map p.109. This appealing Catalan café offers lovely outdoor tables under a broad, shady tree and a short menu of very good Spanish dishes, including salads, paellas and tapas, as well as tasty *crema catalana* (a bit like a crème brûlée) and on-the-money espressos. It's especially good value at lunchtime (Mon–Fri), when you can get four tapas and a soft drink for B290, and is also popular at weekends for watching Barcelona's football games, when the house wine at B95/glass goes down a storm. Mon–Fri 11am–11pm, Sat & Sun noon–11pm.

★ **Beirut** Basement, Ploenchit Centre, at the mouth of Soi 2 ☎ 02 656 7377; map p.109; also at 64 Silom Building, set back off Thanon Silom between Soi 4 and Soi Thaniya ☎ 02 632 7448; ⓦ beirut-restaurant.com. It's worth crossing the road from Bangkok's main Middle Eastern ghetto (Soi 3 and Soi 3/1) for the top-notch Lebanese food in this comfortable, a/c restaurant. Among dozens of salads and stuffed breads, the superb *motabel* (baba ganoush; B140) is fluffy and smoky, while the falafels are suitably moist inside and crunchy out. Good baklava, too. Ploenchit Centre daily 10am–10pm; 64 Silom Building daily 11.30am–midnight.

★ **Bolan** 24 Soi 53 (5min walk from BTS Thong Lo) ☎ 02 260 2961–2, ⓦ bolan.co.th; map p.109. Meticulous and hugely successful attempt to produce authentic traditional food in all its complexity, while upholding the "Slow Food" philosophy. It'll give you a lipsmacking education in Thai cuisine, best enjoyed on the "Bolan Balance" set dinner menu (B2680). Single-plate set lunches start at B420. Tues–Fri 6–10.30pm (last orders), Sat & Sun noon–2.30pm & 6–10.30pm.

**Dosa King** Soi 11/1, with a back entrance on Soi 11 ☎ 02 651 1700, ⓦ dosaking.net; map p.109. Usually busy with expat Indian diners, this vegetarian Indian restaurant serves good food from both north and south, including over a dozen different dosas (southern pancake dishes), tandooris and the like. It's an alcohol-free zone so you'll have to make do with sweet lassi instead. Most dishes B100–200. Daily 11am–11pm.

**Le Dalat** 57 Soi 23 (Soi Prasanmit) ☎ 02 664 0670, ⓦ facebook.com/ledalatrestaurant; map p.109. There's Indochinese romance aplenty at this delightful, recreated Vietnamese brick mansion decked out with pot plants, plenty of photos and eclectic curiosities. The extensive, high-class Vietnamese menu features favourites such as a *goi ca* salad of aromatic herbs and raw fish (B360) and *chao tom* shrimp sticks on sugar cane (B250 per piece). Daily 11.30am–2.30pm & 5.30–10.30pm.

**Prai Raya** 59 Soi 8 ☎ 02 253 5556; map p.109. Set in a grand, modern villa done out in Sino-Portuguese style, this branch of a famous Phuket Town restaurant brings that city's distinctive cuisine to the capital – with a welcome offer to spice things down if requested. Most dishes are B200–250, including *muu hong* (stewed pork belly with cinnamon), but it's worth forking out a bit extra for the yellow curry with coconut milk and big chunks of fresh crabmeat. A good selection of vegetarian southern Thai dishes is also available. Daily 11pm–10.30pm, last orders roughly 9.30pm.

**Soul Food Mahanakorn** 56/10 Soi 55 (Soi Thonglor; Exit 3 from BTS Thong Lo, then it's 100m up the soi on the right) ☎ 02 714 7708, ⓦ soulfoodmahanakorn.com; map p.109. If you already have your favourite stall for *som tam* or *laap*, this is not for you, but if not, this trim, welcoming, American–Thai bistro makes a great introduction to street food from around Thailand, using top-quality ingredients. The beef *khao soi* (curried noodle soup; B300) is thick and creamy, and the *som tam* (B150) is served with crispy chicken skin. Daily blackboard specials, and a wide selection of creative cocktails, craft beers and wines, including several by the glass. Daily 5.30pm–midnight (last food orders 11pm).

**Vientiane Kitchen (Khrua Vientiane)** 8 Soi 36, about 50m south off Thanon Sukhumvit ☎ 02 258 6171, ⓦ vientiane-kitchenbkk.com; map p.109. Just a 3min walk west then south from BTS Thong Lo (Exit 2) and you're transported into a little piece of Isaan, where the menu's stocked full of northeastern delicacies, a live band sets the mood with heart-felt, sometimes over-amplified *pong lang* folk songs, and there are even performances by a troupe of traditional dancers (daily from 7.30pm). The Isaan-accented menu (mostly B100–300) includes red ants' eggs salad, spicy-fried frog, jackfruit curry and grilled minced fish salad, plus there's a decent range of veggie options such as *som tam* and Thai desserts. With its airy, barn-like interior and mixed clientele of Thais and expats, it's a very enjoyable dining experience. Daily noon–11.30pm (last food orders 10.30pm).

### DOWNTOWN: SOUTH OF THANON RAMA IV

In this area, there are also branches of *Baan Khanitha* (see page 133), *Supanniga Eating Room* (see page 130) and *Beirut* (see page 133).

★ **Aoi** 132/10–11 Soi 6, Thanon Silom ☎ 02 235 2321–2; map p.111; ground floor, Siam Paragon ☎ 02 129 4348–50; map p.104; 3rd Floor, Emporium shopping centre; ☎ 02 664 8590–2; map p.109; ⓦ aoi-bkk.com. One of the best places in town for a Japanese blowout, justifiably popular with the expat community, with excellent authentic food and elegant décor. Prices are higher in the evening, when a superb sushi set will set you back B1200, but at lunchtime you can get a bento box for B500. Thanon Silom daily 11.30am–1.45pm (last orders) & 5.30pm–9.45pm; Siam Paragon Mon–Fri 11.30am–2.15pm & 5.30–9.30pm, Sat & Sun 11am–9.30pm; Emporium shopping centre daily 11/11.30am–1.45/2.30pm & 5/5.30–9.45pm.

★ **Celadon** Sukhothai Hotel, 13/3 Thanon Sathorn Tai ☎ 02 344 8888; map p.111. Consistently rated as one of the best hotel restaurants in Bangkok and a favourite with locals, serving outstanding traditional and contemporary Thai food from all over the country – try the delicious pomelo salad with chicken and prawns (B450) and the northern-style egg noodles in curry soup (*khao soi*) – in an elegant setting surrounded by lotus ponds. Expect nightly performances of classical Thai dancing (7.30 & 8.30pm). Daily noon–2.30pm (last orders) & 6.30–10.30pm.

★ **Eat Me** 1/6 Soi Phiphat 2, Thanon Convent ☎ 02 238 0931, ⓦ eatmerestaurant.com; map p.111. Justly fashionable art gallery and restaurant in a striking, white modernist building, with changing exhibitions on the walls and a temptingly relaxing balcony. The eclectic, far-reaching menu features such mains as grilled squid with fennel, pomegranate and white bean purée (B790), while the lemon-grass crème brûlée is not to be missed. There's an extensive wine list, too, with many available by the glass. Daily 3pm–1am.

**Harmonique** 22 Soi 34, Thanon Charoen Krung, on the lane leading to Wat Muang Kae express-boat pier ☎ 02 237 8175; map p.111. A relaxing, welcoming, moderately priced restaurant that's well worth a trip: tables are scattered throughout several converted shophouses, decorated with antiques and bric-a-brac, and a quiet, leafy courtyard, and the Thai food is varied and excellent, notably the house speciality crab curry (B240). Mon–Sat 11am–10pm.

**Home Cuisine Islamic Restaurant** 186 Soi 36, Thanon Charoen Krung ☎ 02 234 7911, ⓦ facebook.com/homecuisineislamic; map p.111. The short, cheap menu of Indian and Thai Muslim dishes here has proved popular enough to warrant a refurbishment in green and white, with comfy booths, pot plants, a/c inside and a few outdoor tables overlooking the colonial-style French embassy. The *khao mok kai* signature dish (B85), a typical hybrid version of a chicken biryani, served with pickled aubergine and *raita* (mint-infused yoghurt condiment), is delicious. Mon–Sat 11am–9.30pm, Sun 6–9.30pm.

**Indian Hut** 418 Thanon Suriwong ☎ 02 236 5672–3; ⓦ indianhutbangkok.com; map p.111. Bright, white-tablecloth, North Indian restaurant – look out for the Pizza Hut-style sign – that's justly popular with local Indians. For carnivores, tandoori's the thing (B375 for half a chicken), but there's also a wide selection of mostly vegetarian pakoras and other appetizers, as well as plenty of veggie main courses and breads, and a hard-to-resist house dhal (B250). Daily 11am–11pm.

★**Krua Aroy Aroy** 3/1 Thanon Pan (opposite the Maha Uma Devi Temple) ☎02 635 2365, ⓦfacebook.com/kruaaroyaroy; map p.111. Aptly named "Delicious, Delicious Kitchen", this simple shophouse restaurant stands out for its choice of cheap, tasty, well-prepared dishes from all around the kingdom, notably chicken *matsaman* curry (B90), *khao soi* (a curried soup with egg noodles from northern Thailand) and *khanom jiin* (rice noodles topped with curry). Daily roughly 10am–6pm, or earlier if the food runs out.

**Le Bouchon** 37/17 Patpong 2, near Thanon Suriwong ☎02 234 9109; map p.111. Cosy Lyonnais bar-bistro in the heart of the red-light district that's much frequented by the city's French expats, offering home cooking such as duck confit (B490) and a good-value lunch set menu (B450 for two courses); booking is strongly recommended. Mon–Sat noon–3pm & 6.30–10.45pm.

★**Le Du** 399/3 Soi 7, Thanon Silom ☎092 919 9969, ⓦledubkk.com; map p.111. Excellent new restaurant that takes authentic Thai flavours and ingredients and develops them creatively, and very successfully, with modern cooking techniques. The regularly changing menu is strong on fish and seafood, in dishes such as superb soft-shell crab with bitter gourd and pineapple in a southern-style curry, accompanied by fine wines, many available by the glass. Leave room for a delicious dessert – or push the boat out for one of the tasting menus (with wine pairings available). Mon–Sat 6–11pm.

★**Nahm** Como Metropolitan Hotel, 27 Thanon Sathorn Tai ☎02 625 3333, ⓦcomohotels.com/metropolitanbangkok; map p.111. Former flagship restaurant of Australian-born David Thompson, the doyen of foreign chefs of Thai cuisine, with a seductive Japanese-designed interior and poolside tables. Expect esoteric authentic dishes, such as oyster and Thai samphire salad, which are complex, intensely flavoured but well balanced, using the best of local ingredients. Go in the evening for the full effect, and book early; lunchtime sees a lighter, shorter menu that's more affordable and accessible

(main dishes from B560). Mon–Fri noon–2pm & 6.30–10.15pm, Sat & Sun 6.30–10.15pm.

★**Ramentei** 23/8–9 Soi Thaniya ☎02 234 8082; map p.111; Sukhumvit Soi 33/1 ☎02 662 0050; map p.109. Top-notch Japanese noodle café, bright, clean and welcoming, under the same ownership as *Aoi* (see page 134). The open kitchen turns out especially good, huge bowls of miso ramen (B230), which goes very well with the gyoza dumplings. Soi Thaniya daily 11am–2am; Soi 33/1 daily 11am–midnight.

**Ruen Urai** Rose Hotel, 118 Thanon Suriwong ☎02 266 8268–72, ⓦruen-urai.com; map p.111. Set back behind the hotel, this peaceful, hundred-year-old, traditional house, with fine balcony tables overlooking the beautiful hotel pool, comes as a welcome surprise in this full-on downtown area. The menu of varied Thai food, which includes a good *matsaman* curry (B350), is of a high quality. Daily noon–11pm.

**Sara Jane's** 55/21 Thanon Narathiwat Ratchanakharin, between sois 4 & 6 ☎02 676 3338; map p.111. Long-standing, basic, a/c restaurant, popular with Bangkok's Isaan population, serving good, simple northeastern dishes, including a huge array of *nam tok*, *laap* and *som tam*, as well as Italian food – and a very tasty fusion of the two, spaghetti with *sai krok*, spicy Isaan sausage (B260). Daily 11am–3.30pm & 5.30–10pm.

**Somboon Seafood** Thanon Suriwong, corner of Thanon Narathiwat Ratchanakharin ☎02 233 3104; map p.111; Floor 5, Central Embassy ☎02 160 5965–6; map p.104; ⓦsomboonseafood.com. Highly favoured, bustling seafood restaurant, known especially for its crab curry (from about B300, depending on weight), with functional, modern decor and an array of marine life lined up in tanks awaiting its gastronomic fate. Thanon Suriwong daily 4–11.30pm; Central Embassy daily 11am–10pm.

★**Taling Pling** 653 Building 7, Ban Silom Arcade, Thanon Silom ☎02 236 4829; map p.111. One of the best Thai restaurants in the city outside of the big hotels, specializing in classic dishes from the four corners of the kingdom. The toothsome green beef curry (B145) with *roti*, which is recommended by the leading Thai restaurant guides, goes well with the delicious and refreshing house deep-fried fish salad. The atmosphere's convivial and relaxing, too. Daily 11am–10pm.

## DRINKING AND NIGHTLIFE

For many of Bangkok's male visitors, nightfall is the signal to hit the city's sex bars, most notoriously in the area off the east end of Thanon Silom known as Patpong (see page 110). Fortunately, Bangkok's **nightlife** has thoroughly grown up in the past ten years to leave these neon sumps behind, and now offers everything from craft-beer pubs and vertiginous, rooftop cocktail bars to fiercely chic clubs and dance bars, hosting top-class DJs. The high-concept bars of Sukhumvit

and the lively, teeming venues of Banglamphu, in particular, pull in the style-conscious cream of Thai youth and are tempting an increasing number of travellers to stuff their party gear into their rucksacks. During the cool season, an evening out at one of the pop-up **beer gardens (usually Dec)** is a pleasant way of soaking up the urban atmosphere (and the traffic fumes); you'll find them in hotel forecourts or sprawled in front of dozens of shopping centres all over

**1**

the city. Among the city's **club nights**, look out for the interesting regular events organized by Zudrangma Record Store (ⓦzudrangmarecords.com), especially at their own bar *Studio Lam*, which mix up dance music from all around Thailand and from all over the world; Dudesweet's parties all over town, featuring Thai and international DJs and indie bands; and weekend DJ and band nights and creative events at Whiteline on Soi 8, Thanon Silom (ⓦfacebook.com/whitelinebangkok). Getting back to your lodgings should be no problem in the small hours: many bus routes run a (reduced) service throughout the night, and tuk-tuks and taxis are always at hand – though it's probably best for unaccompanied women to avoid using tuk-tuks late at night.

### BANGLAMPHU AND THE DEMOCRACY MONUMENT AREA

The travellers' enclave of Banglamphu takes on a new personality after dark, when its hub, Thanon Khao San, becomes a "walking street", closed to all traffic but open to almost any kind of makeshift stall, selling everything from fried bananas and buckets of "very strong" cocktails to share, to bargain fashions and one-off artworks. Young Thais come to the area to browse and snack before piling in to Banglamphu's more stylish bars and live-music clubs, most of which are free to enter (though some ask you to show ID first).

**Ad Here the 13th (Blues Bar)** 13 Thanon Samsen, opposite Soi 2, right by the start of the bridge over Khlong Banglamphu ☏089 769 4613; map p.92. Relaxed little neighbourhood live-music joint with sociable seats out on the pavement, where musos congregate nightly to listen to Thai and expat blues and jazz bands (from about 9.30pm). Well-priced beer and lots of cocktails. Daily 6pm–midnight.

**Brick Bar** Buddy Village complex, 265 Thanon Khao San ⓦbrickbarkhaosan.com; map p.92. Massive red-brick vault of a live-music bar whose regular roster of reggae, ska, rock'n'roll and Thai pop bands, and occasional one-off appearances, is hugely popular with Thai twenty-somethings and teens. Big, sociable tables are set right under the stage and there's food too. The biggest nights are Fri and Sat when there's sometimes an entry charge, depending on who's on. Daily 7pm–1.30am.

**Brown Sugar** 469 Thanon Phra Sumen ☏081 805 7759, ⓦbrownsugarbangkok.com; map p.92. Bangkok's best and longest-running jazz club moved in 2012 into smart, atmospherically lit premises in Banglamphu, which are hung with colourful modernist gig posters and include a leafy canalside terrace. It still has its famous Sun jam session, but is now allowing in a few early-evening acoustic sessions each week; music usually starts around 8.30pm. The prices of drinks are pumped up to pay for the talent, though they include imported beers on draught and in bottles. Tues–Thurs & Sun 5pm–1am, Fri & Sat 5pm–2am.

**The Club** 123 Thanon Khao San ☏02 629 1010, ⓦtheclubkhaosan.com; map p.92. Thumping electronic

dance music from an elevated, central DJ station with state-of-the-art lighting draw a young Thai and international crowd; check the website for upcoming events with imported DJs. Daily 10pm–late.

★**Hippie de Bar** 46 Thanon Khao San ☏081 820 2762; map p.92. Inviting courtyard bar set away from the main fray, with an indie-pop soundtrack and its own-brand fashion boutique. Attracts a mixed studenty/arty/high-society, mostly Thai crowd, to drink cheapish beer at its wrought-iron tables and park benches. Indoors is totally given over to retro kitsch, with plastic armchairs, Donny Osmond posters and floral prints. Daily 4pm–2am.

**Jazz Happens** 62 Thanon Phra Arthit ☏084 450 0505, ⓦfacebook.com/jazzhappens; map p.92. Typical Phra Arthit bar, full of students, with just one small room and a few sociable pavement tables, but what sets this place apart is that some of the students are from Silpakorn University's Faculty of Jazz, playing jazz here most nights. Tuck into a decent selection of well-priced cocktails and a narrower choice of food while you're listening. Daily (except Thurs) 5pm–1am.

**Phra Nakorn** 58/2 Soi Damnoen Klang Tai ☏02 622 0282, ⓦfacebook.com/phranakornbarandgallery; map p.92. Styles itself as "a hangout place for art lovers", and it successfully pulls in the capital's artists and art students, who can admire the floodlit view of the Golden Mount from the candlelit rooftop terrace, tuck into good food and reasonably priced drinks and browse one of the regular exhibitions on the first floor. Daily 6pm–1am.

**Résidence de Canal** 463/72 Thanon Luk Luang ☏02 061 8289, ⓦfacebook.com/residencebkk; map p.76. Situated on the eastern edge of Banglamphu by Khlong Krung Kasem, this is about as underground as Bangkok's clubs get, set in a gritty, minimally converted warehouse, with just a handful of chairs and tables scattered around the white walls to distract from the music. Trance, house, techno; everything's on offer – "Fuck Genres, Just Dance" is the motto – check out their Facebook page for line-ups, which currently include an open-decks night on Mon. Daily 9pm–1am.

**Sheepshank** Tha Phra Arthit express-boat pier ☏02 629 5165, ⓦsheepshankpublichouse.com; map p.92. Set in a former boat-repair yard overlooking the Chao Phraya and the riverside walkway, this cool bar-restaurant sports an industrial look that features black leather, silver studs, pulleys and girders. There's a wide selection of bottled craft beers from the US and Japan, as well as imaginative bar snacks and a long menu of more substantial gastropub dishes. Mon 5pm–1am, Tues–Sun 11am–1am.

### CHINATOWN

Chinatown has never had a reputation for its bars, but a handful of chic places, all affecting a rough-edged air of oriental mystique, have transformed Soi Nana into a small hub of nightlife, just 5min walk from Hualampong subway station.

1

## NIGHTLIFE HOURS, ID CHECKS AND ADMISSION CHARGES

Most bars and clubs in Bangkok are meant to **close** at 1am, while those at the east end of Silom and on Royal City Avenue can stay open until 2am. In previous years, there have been regular "social order" clampdowns by the police, strictly enforcing these closing times, conducting occasional urine tests for drugs on bar customers, and setting up widespread ID checks to curb under-age drinking (you have to be 20 or over to drink in bars and clubs). However, at the time of writing, things were more chilled, with some bars and clubs staying open into the wee hours on busy nights and ID checks in only a few places. It's hard to predict how the situation might develop, but you'll soon get an idea of how the wind is blowing when you arrive in Bangkok – and there's little harm in taking a copy of your passport out with you, just in case. Nearly all bars and clubs in Bangkok are free, but the most popular of them will sometimes levy an admission charge of a couple of hundred baht on their busiest nights (which will usually include a drink or two), though this can vary from week to week.

★ **Ba Hao** 8 Soi Nana, Thanon Maitri Chit ⓦfacebook. com/8bahao; map p.96. Illuminated by paper lanterns, friendly Ba Hao conjures up the spirit of old Chinatown with low red lighting and traditional, marble-topped tables and seats. As well as teas, ginseng shots and a short menu of Chinese food, it serves creative, Chinese-inspired cocktails – which Jamie Oliver likes, apparently – such as Opium, a Negroni using a ginseng and herb liquor. Tues–Sun 6pm–midnight.

**Let the Boy Die** 542 Thanon Luang ⓦfacebook.com/ ltbdbar; map p.96. At the time of research, Bangkok's pioneering craft-beer bar, under the same ownership as Goldencoins Taproom (see page 138), was about to reopen, offering a huge selection of the city's finest brews. Tues–Sun 5–11pm.

**Teens of Thailand (TOT)** 76 Soi Nana, Thanon Maitri Chit ⓦfacebook.com/teensofthailand; map p.96. The creaking of an ancient wooden door announces your arrival at this misleadingly named bar. Inside, old movie posters and a piano provide the setting for a cocktail menu that uses dozens of gins from around the world. Tues–Thurs & Sun 7pm–midnight, Fri & Sat 7pm–1am.

**Tep Bar** 69–71 Soi Nana, Thanon Maitri Chit ⓦfacebook.com/tepbarth; map p.96. Down a side alley off the main Soi Nana, Tep evokes the atmosphere of Bangkok of yore, with candles, distressed walls and a bar that looks like the base of a chedi, while a live group plays Thai classical music every evening. There's a long menu of local snacks, grilled meats and rice dishes, to be washed down with Thai rice whisky and herb liquor cocktails. Mon–Thurs & Sun 5pm–midnight, Fri & Sat 5pm–1am.

### DOWNTOWN: AROUND SIAM SQUARE AND THANON PLOENCHIT

Downtown, Siam Square has much less to offer after dark than Thanon Sukhumvit, further east. Out to the northeast, running south off Thanon Rama IX, lies RCA (Royal City Avenue). An officially sanctioned "nightlife zone" that's allowed to stay open until 2am, it's lined mostly with warehouse-like clubs that have a reputation as meat markets.

**Coco Walk** Thanon Phrayathai; map p.104. It would be hard not to enjoy yourself at this covered parade of loosely interchangeable but buzzing good-time bars, right beside Ratchathewi BTS. Popular with local students, they variously offer pool tables, live musicians, DJs and a small skateboarding ramp, but all have reasonably priced beer and food. Daily roughly 6pm–1am.

**Hyde and Seek** Ground floor, Athenée Residence, 65/1 Soi Ruam Rudee ☎02 168 5152, ⓦhydeandseek.com; map p.104. Classy but buzzy gastrobar, with nightly DJs and lots of attractive garden seating. Amid a huge range of drinks, there's a good selection of wines by the glass and imported beers on draught; the food menu features bar bites, pastas, salads and familiar dishes such as bangers and mash. Daily 4.30pm–1am (last food orders 11.45pm).

**Saxophone** 3/8 Victory Monument (southeast corner), just off Thanon Phrayathai ☎02 246 5472, ⓦsaxophonepub.com; map p.76. Lively, easy-going, spacious venue with decent Thai and Western food and a diverse roster of bands – acoustic from 7.30pm, then mostly jazz and blues, plus funk, rock and reggae, from 9pm (details on their website) – which attracts a good mix of Thais and foreigners. Daily 6pm–2am.

### THANON SUKHUMVIT

A night out on Thanon Sukhumvit could be subsumed by the girlie bars and hostess-run bar-beers on sois Nana and Cowboy, but there's plenty of style on Sukhumvit too, especially in the rooftop bars and craft-beer pubs. The scene has been gravitating eastwards over the last few years: the fashionable bars and clubs on and around Soi Thonglor (Soi 55) attract a "hi-so" (high-society) crowd, while those on Soi Ekamai (Soi 63) are perhaps a little more studenty.

**Brewski** Radisson Blu Plaza Hotel, Thanon Sukhumvit between sois 25 and 27 ⓦvenuesbkk.com; map p.109. Winning (though pricy) combination of views and brews: a thirtieth-floor rooftop bar (smoking allowed) with a 270-degree vista of all the other downtown skyscrapers; plus a dozen craft beers on tap (a hundred more in bottles),

1

with regular takeovers by the likes of Scotland's Brewdog. Daily 5pm–1am.

★ **Changwon Express** 37 Thanon Asoke–Din Daeng ⓦ facebook.com/changwonexpress; map p.109. Off-strip but right next to Phetchaburi subway station, this small, friendly, knowledgeable, Korean-owned bar brews its own excellent light stout and pale ale. Plenty of other Thai craft beers are on tap, as well as British and US imports – plus Korean fusion food. Mon–Sat 5pm–midnight.

**Glow** 96/4–5 Soi 23 ⓦ facebook.com/glowbkk; map p.109. This intimate, unpretentious, two-floor venue with a great sound system is one of Bangkok's best underground clubs, attracting an interesting roster of Thai and international DJs, such as Dubfire and Nakadia, to play mostly house and techno. Wed–Sun 9.30pm–roughly 3am.

**Goldencoins Taproom** Ekamai Mall, at the entrance to Soi 10, Soi Ekamai (Soi 63) ⓦ facebook.com/goldencoins taproom; map p.109. Small, brick-lined bar with rough-hewn wooden tables, serving its own craft beers on tap and pub grub from around the world. Daily 5pm–midnight.

**Iron Balls** Park Lane shopping mall, 5min walk up Soi Ekamai (Soi 63) from the Skytrain ⓦ facebook.com/ ironballsdistillery; map p.109. An unlikely spot for a gin distillery, but the product – using German juniper, ginger and lemon grass – is great; try their Negroni, with Campari and charred sandalwood bitters. The small, attached bar mixes clubbiness – leather armchairs, library lamps – with a low-tech, early industrial feel – bell jars, coils and lots of wrought iron. Daily 6pm–1am.

**The Iron Fairies** Just over 1km up Soi Thonglor (Soi 55) from BTS Thong Lo ☎ 099 918 1600, ⓦ theironfairies. com; map p.109. High-concept bar that's designed to evoke a magical fairytale factory, with low lighting, jars of glitter (fairy dust) lining the walls and windows, gargoyles and lots of wooden structures including higgledy-piggledy staircases. Nightly live music including an open-mike night on Monday. Daily 6pm–2am.

★ **Studio Lam** About 100m up Soi 51 on the left, on the corner of the first sub-soi, about 5min walk west of BTS Thong Lo ☎ 02 261 6661, ⓦ facebook.com/ studiolambangkok; map p.109. This friendly, cosy neighbourhood bar is the latest project of Zudrangma Records (see page 136), whose record shop is just up the sub-soi to the left. The soundproofing and massive, purpose-built sound system give the game away: the music's the thing here, with DJs and live musicians playing driving *mor lam* and an eclectic choice of world sounds nightly. Tues–Sun 6pm–late.

★ **WTF** 7 Soi 51 ☎ 02 662 6246, ⓦ wtfbangkok.com; map p.109. Small, Spanish-influenced bar-café and art gallery, which hosts occasional performance art, poetry and movie nights. Adorned with luridly coloured Thai film posters and a great soundtrack, it offers global tapas and a tempting variety of cocktails and wines. It's 5min walk west

of BTS Thong Lo, 100m up Soi 51, near the mouth of a small sub-soi on the left. Tues–Sun 6pm–1am.

## DOWNTOWN: SOUTH OF THANON RAMA IV

There are one or two mixed bars on the mostly gay Soi 4 at the east end of Thanon Silom – and, of course, a slew of go-go bars on Patpong – but otherwise the action in this area is widely scattered. If, among all the choice of nightlife in Bangkok, you do end up at one of Patpong's sex shows, watch out for hyper-inflated bar bills and other cons – plenty of customers get ripped off in some way, and stories of menacing bouncers are legion.

**Namsaah Bottling Trust** Soi 7, Thanon Silom ☎ 02 636 6622; map p.111. Playful gastro-pub in a century-old villa – now shocking pink – with dwarfing views of the new 300-metre MahaNakhon skyscraper from its leafy patio. Down creative cocktails with a Thai twist and feast on good fusion food (last orders midnight), amid the plush of velvet drapes, pink hogs' heads and suits of Samurai armour. Daily 5pm–2am.

★ **The Sky Bar & Distil** Floors 63 & 64, State Tower, 1055 Thanon Silom, corner of Thanon Charoen Krung ☎ 02 624 9555, ⓦ lebua.com; map p.111. Thrill-seekers and view addicts shouldn't miss forking out for an alfresco drink here, 275m above the city's pavements – come around 6pm to enjoy the stunning panoramas in both the light and the dark. It's standing-only at *The Sky Bar*, a circular restaurant-bar built over the edge of the building with almost 360-degree views, but for the sunset itself, you're better off on the outside terrace of *Distil* one floor up on the other side of the building (where bookings are accepted), which has a wider choice of drinks, charming service and huge couches to recline on. The bars have become very popular since featuring in *The Hangover II* movie and have introduced a strict, smart-casual dress code. Sky Bar daily 6pm–1am; Distil daily 5pm–1am.

★ **Tawandang German Brewery** 462/61 Thanon Rama III ☎ 02 678 1114–6, ⓦ tawandang.com; map p.111. A taxi-ride south of Chong Nonsi BTS down Thanon Narathiwat Ratchanakharin – and best to book a table in advance – this vast all-rounder is well worth the effort. Under a huge dome, up to 1600 revellers enjoy good Thai and German food, micro-brewed German beer and a mercurial, hugely entertaining cabaret, featuring live pop and luk thung, magic shows and dance numbers. Daily 5pm–1am.

**Viva Aviv: The River** Ground floor, River City shopping centre (free shuttle boat from Taksin Bridge) ☎ 02 639 6305, ⓦ vivaaviv.com; map p.111. With a lovely open deck right on the river and a gnarly interior decor of hide-bound chairs and ships' winches, this bar offers cool sounds, some serious cocktails, good coffees and smoothies, as well as comfort food such as gourmet hot dogs, pizzas and salads. Daily 11am–midnight.

## LGBTQ BANGKOK

Bangkok's gay bars, clubs and café-restaurants are concentrated around the east end of Thanon Silom, especially in the narrow alleys of Soi 2 and Soi 4. After a break of more than ten years, Bangkok Pride is scheduled to return to the city in 2018, with a parade, parties and social events across the city, workshops and film festivals, hosted by Out Bkk (ⓦfacebook.com/outinbkk). More general background on LGBTQ life in Thailand, plus contacts and sources of information, most of them concentrated in Bangkok, can be found in Basics (see page 65). Advice on opening hours, admission charges and ID is given in Drinking and Nightlife (see page 137) – Soi 2, for example, operates a strict ID policy.

**The Balcony** Soi 4, Thanon Silom ⓣ02 235 5891, ⓦbalconypub.com; map p.111. Unpretentious, fun place with plenty of outdoor seats, welcoming staff, reasonably priced drinks, upstairs karaoke and decent Thai and Western food. Happy hour till 8pm. Daily 5.30pm–2am.

**Dick's Café** Duangthawee Plaza, 894/7–8 Soi Pratuchai (aka Soi Twilight), Thanon Suriwong ⓣ02 637 0078, ⓦdickscafe.com; map p.111. Elegant day-and-night café-bar-restaurant, with a *Casablanca* theme to the decor (styling itself on *Rick's Café Americain*) and occasional art exhibitions. On a traffic-free soi of go-go bars off the north side of Suriwong, it's ideal for drinking, eating decent Thai and Western food or just chilling out. Daily 10.30am–2am.

**DJ Station** Soi 2, Thanon Silom ⓣ02 266 4029, ⓦdj-station.com; map p.111. Bangkok's most famous club, a highly fashionable but unpretentious three-storey venue, packed at weekends, attracting a mix of Thais and farangs, with a cabaret show nightly at around 11pm. Daily 9.30pm–2am.

**G Bangkok** 60/18–21 Soi 2/1, Thanon Silom, in a small pedestrianized alley between Soi Thaniya and Soi 2 ⓣ02 632 8033; map p.111. Large, full-on, three-level nightclub, somewhat more Thai-oriented than *DJ Station*, that's still often referred to by its former name, GOD (for Guys on Display). Popular venue, but it tends not to fill up until after *DJ Station* has closed. Hosts a big festival of parties over Songkran. Daily 11pm–3am, sometimes later on Sat.

**JJ Park** 8/3 Soi 2, Thanon Silom ⓣ02 235 1227; map p.111. Classy, Thai-oriented bar, for relaxed socializing among an older set rather than raving, with karaoke and live music. Daily 10pm–2am.

**The Stranger Bar** Soi 4, Thanon Silom ⓣ02 632 9425, ⓦfacebook.com/thestrangerbar; map p.111. Recently opened, stylish "pub theatre" with drag shows most nights at 10.30pm and good cocktails (happy hour till 9pm). Daily 5.45pm–2am.

**Telephone Pub** 114/11–13 Soi 4, Thanon Silom ⓣ02 234 3279, ⓦfacebook.com/telephonebkk; map p.111. Bangkok's first Western-style gay bar when it opened in 1987, this cruisy, dimly lit eating and drinking venue has a terrace on the alley and a restaurant and karaoke upstairs. Daily 6pm–2am.

## ENTERTAINMENT

On the cultural front, the most accessible of the capital's performing arts is **Thai dancing**, particularly when served up in bite-size portions in tourist shows. **Thai boxing** is also well worth watching: the raucous live experience at either of Bangkok's two main national stadiums far outshines the TV coverage.

### CULTURE SHOWS AND PERFORMING ARTS

Because of the language barrier, most Thai theatre is inaccessible to foreigners and so, with a few exceptions, the best way to experience the traditional performing arts is at shows designed for tourists, most notably at Siam Niramit. You can, however, witness Thai dancing being performed for its original ritual purpose, usually several times a day, at the Lak Muang Shrine behind the Grand Palace (see page 75) and the Erawan Shrine on the corner of Thanon Ploenchit (see page 108). Background information on Thai classical dance and traditional theatre can be found in Basics (see page 48). Meanwhile, more glitzy and occasionally ribald entertainment is the order of the day at the capital's ladyboy cabaret shows.

**Calypso Cabaret** Asiatique (see page 140), Thanon Charoen Krung, 2km south of Saphan Taksin BTS ⓣ02 688 1415–7, ⓦcalypsocabaret.com. Expect glamorous outfits and over-the-top song-and-dance routines twice a night. B1200, or B900 if booked online, including one drink.

**Chalermkrung Theatre (Sala Chalermkrung)** 66 Thanon Charoen Krung, on the intersection with Thanon Triphet in Pahurat, next to Old Siam Plaza ⓣ02 224 4499, ⓦsalachalermkrung.com or ⓦthaiticketmajor.com. This Art Deco former cinema, dating from 1933, hosts *khon* performances with English subtitles every Thurs and Fri at 7.30pm. Tickets from B800.

**National Theatre** Sanam Luang, Ratanakosin ⓣ02 224 1342. Hosts traditional performing arts such as *khon*, *lakhon* and medley shows of music and dancing roughly twice a month (not in the hot season), usually on Sun. However, it's difficult to get information about what's on in English – the nearby Bangkok Tourism Division (see page 121) often has a schedule.

**Siam Niramit** 19 Thanon Tiam Ruammit, 5min walk (or a free shuttle ride from Exit 1) from Thailand Cultural Centre subway, following signs for the South Korean embassy ⓣ02 649 9222, ⓦsiamniramit.com. Unashamedly tourist-oriented but the easiest place to get a glimpse of the variety and spectacle intrinsic to traditional Thai theatre. The show

1

presents a history of regional Thailand's culture and beliefs in a high-tech spectacular of fantastic costumes and huge chorus numbers, enlivened by acrobatics and flashy special effects. The complex also includes a kitschy handicrafts village, souvenir shops and a buffet restaurant (dinner plus show from B1850). Tickets (from B1500) can be bought on the spot, online or through most travel agents. Daily 8pm.

**Thailand Cultural Centre** Thanon Ratchadapisek ☎ 02 247 0028, ⓦ thaiticketmajor.com; Thailand Cultural Centre subway. All-purpose venue, under the control of the Ministry of Culture, that hosts mainstream classical concerts, traditional and contemporary theatre, and visiting international dance and theatre shows.

### THAI BOXING

The violence of the average Thai boxing match (see page 49) may be off-putting to some, but spending a couple of hours at one of Bangkok's two main stadiums, Rajdamnoen and Lumphini, can be immensely entertaining, not least for the enthusiasm of the spectators and the ritualistic aspects of the fights. Seats for foreigners cost B1000–2000 (cheaper, standing tickets are reserved for Thais). Sessions usually feature at least ten bouts, each consisting of five 3min rounds with 2min rests in between each round, so if you're not a big fan it may be worth turning up late, as the better fights tend to happen later in the billing.

**Lumphini Stadium** Thanon Ram Intra ⓦ muaythai lumpinee.net. This sixty-year-old stadium recently moved way out into the northern suburbs near Don Muang Airport, but will become more accessible once the northern extension of the Skytrain opens. The schedule of upcoming fights is posted on its website. Usually Tues 6.30pm, Fri 7pm, Sat 4pm.

**Rajdamnoen Stadium** Thanon Rajdamnoen Nok ⓦ rajadamnern.com. Thailand's oldest stadium (established in 1945) is handily located next to the TAT office near Banglamphu (and handily surrounded by restaurants selling northeastern food). Usually Mon, Wed, Thurs & Sun 6.30pm.

## SHOPPING

Bangkok has a good reputation for shopping, particularly for antiques, gems, contemporary interior design and fashion, where the range and quality are streets ahead of other Thai cities. Fabrics and handicrafts are good buys too, though shopping for these in Chiang Mai has many advantages. As always, watch out for **fakes**: cut glass masquerading as precious stones, old, damaged goods being passed off as antiques, counterfeit designer clothes and accessories, even mocked-up international driver's licences (though Thai travel agents and other organizations aren't that easily fooled). Bangkok also has the best English-language bookshops in the country. Downtown is full of smart, multi-storey **shopping plazas** like Siam Centre, Siam Paragon and Central World on Thanon Rama I, Central Embassy on Thanon Ploenchit and Emporium and EmQuartier on Thanon Sukhumvit, which is where you'll find the majority of the city's fashion stores, as well as designer lifestyle goods and bookshops. The plazas tend to be pleasantly air-conditioned and thronging with trendy young Thais, but don't hold much interest for tourists unless you happen to be looking for a new outfit. Shopping centres, department stores and tourist-oriented shops in the city keep late **hours**, opening daily at 10 or 11am and closing at about 9pm; many small, upmarket boutiques, for example along Thanon Charoen Krung and Thanon Silom, close on Sundays, one or two even on Saturdays. Monday is meant to be no-street-vendor day throughout Bangkok, a chance for the pavements to get cleaned and for pedestrians to finally see where they're going, but plenty of stalls manage to flout the rule.

### MARKETS

For travellers, spectating, not shopping, is apt to be the main draw of Bangkok's neighbourhood markets and the bazaars of Chinatown. The massive Chatuchak Weekend Market is an exception, being both a tourist attraction and a marvellous shopping experience (see page 110). With the notable exception of Chatuchak, most markets operate daily from dawn till early afternoon; early morning is often the best time to go to beat the heat and crowds.

**Asiatique** About 2km south of Taksin Bridge, between the river and Thanon Charoen Krung ⓦ www.asiatique thailand.com. Night-time market for tourists in ten rebuilt 1930s warehouses and sawmills that belonged to the Danish East Asiatic Company. Several of them are given over to souvenirs and to clothes stalls, which tend to morph into bigger, more chic and expensive fashion outlets the closer to the river you get. Warehouse 1, devoted to furniture and home decor is probably the most interesting section, featuring some creative contemporary designs. There's plenty to eat, of course, with the poshest restaurants, including a branch of *Baan Khanitha* (see page 133), occupying the pleasant riverside boardwalk, while attractions include a sixty-metre ferris wheel and *Calypso Cabaret* (see page 139). Free ferries shuttle back and forth from Tha Sathorn pier, though the queues are often very long. Currently, the Chao Phraya Express tourist boats leaving Phra Arthit between 4pm and 6pm are extending their route from Tha Sathorn to Asiatique. You could also catch an orange-flag express boat to Wat Rajsingkorn, leaving a 10min walk through the wat and down Thanon Charoen Krung to the shopping complex. Asiatique is planning to expand, introducing floating restaurants, five-star hotels and improved access by boat. Daily 4pm–midnight.

**Talat Rot Fai 2** Behind Esplanade Mall, Thanon Ratchadaphisek. Fun outdoor market that's the most accessible of several similar night-time operations in Bangkok, as it's 5min walk from Thailand Cultural Centre subway station. Among the nail bars, tattoo parlours and pop-up barbers, hundreds of stalls purvey all the cool stuff a twenty-something urbanite might want, including new and pre-loved clothes, caps, bags and general kitsch. Dozens of food stalls and vibrant outdoor bars, some with live music, round out the picture. Daily 5pm–midnight.

## HANDICRAFTS, TEXTILES AND CONTEMPORARY DESIGN

Samples of nearly all regionally produced handicrafts end up in Bangkok, so the selection is phenomenal. Many of the shopping plazas have at least one classy handicraft outlet, and competition keeps prices in the city at upcountry levels, with the main exception of household objects – particularly wickerware and tin bowls and basins – which get palmed off relatively expensively in Bangkok. Several places on and around Thanon Khao San sell reasonably priced triangular "axe" pillows (*mawn khwaan*) in traditional fabrics, which make fantastic souvenirs but are heavy to post home; some places sell unstuffed versions which are simple to mail home, but a pain to fill when you return. The cheapest outlet for traditional northern and northeastern textiles is Chatuchak Weekend Market (see page 110), where you'll also be able to nose out some interesting handicrafts. Most Thai silk, which is noted for its thickness and sheen, comes from the northeast and the north, where shopping for it is probably more fun. However, there is a decent range of outlets in the capital, including many branches of Jim Thompson. Bangkok also has a good reputation for its contemporary interior design, fusing minimalist Western ideals with traditional Thai and other Asian craft elements.

### RATANAKOSIN

**Doi Tung Lifestyle** Thanon Na Phra Lan (plus several other branches around town) ⓦ www.doitung.org; map p.78. Part of the late Princess Mother's development project based at Doi Tung near Chiang Rai, selling very striking and attractive cotton and linen in warm colours, made up into clothes, cushion covers, rugs and so on, as well as coffee and macadamia nuts from the Chiang Rai mountains. Daily 8am–8pm.

**Queen Sirikit Museum of Textiles Shop** Grand Palace (on the right just inside the Gate of Glorious Victory) ⓦ qsmtthailand.org/shop; map p.78. Not-for-profit shop under the auspices of the Queen Mother's Support Foundation, which is especially good for beautiful, top-quality *yan lipao*, traditional basketware made from delicately woven fern stems. Daily 9am–4.30pm (except when the Grand Palace is closed for royal events).

### BANGLAMPHU AND THE DEMOCRACY MONUMENT AREA

**Heritage Craft** 35 Thanon Bamrung Muang ⓦ heritage craft.org; map p.92. In an atmospheric old shophouse with a small café, a permanent outlet for the fair-trade products of ThaiCraft (see page 142), including jewellery, silk and indigo batiks made by the Hmong of northern Thailand. Mon–Fri 11am–6pm.

**Lofty Bamboo** Buddy Hotel shopping complex, 265 Thanon Khao San; map p.92; Floor 2, Mah Boon Krong (MBK) Centre, corner of Thanon Phrayathai and Thanon Rama I; ⓦ loftybamboo.com. Fair-trade outlet for crafts, accessories, clothes, bags and jewellery, including textiles and accessories made by Lisu people from northern Thailand. Buddy Hotel shopping complex daily 10.30am–7.30pm; Mah Boon Krong (MBK) Centre daily 10.30am–8pm.

## SHOPPING FOR EVERYDAY STUFF

You're most likely to find useful everyday items in one of the city's numerous **department stores**: seven-storey Central Chidlom on Thanon Ploenchit (daily 10am–10pm; ⓦ centralchidlom.com), which boasts handy services like watch-repair booths as well as a huge product selection (including large sizes), is probably the city's best. For **children's stuff**, Central Chidlom also has a branch of Mothercare (ⓦ mothercarethailand.com), as do the Emporium, Central World and Siam Paragon shopping centres. Meanwhile, the British chain of **pharmacies**, Boots (ⓦ th.boots.com), has scores of branches across the city, including on Thanon Khao San in Banglamphu, in Siam Paragon, in Central World, in EmQuartier and at the Thanon Suriwong end of Patpong 1.

The best place to buy anything to do with **mobile phones** (see page 67) is the scores of small booths on Floor 4 of Mah Boon Krong (MBK) Shopping Centre at the Rama I/Phrayathai intersection. For **computer** hardware and genuine and pirated software, as well as cameras, Panthip Plaza, at 604/3 Thanon Phetchaburi, is the best place; it's slightly off the main shopping routes, but handy for Khlong Saen Saeb boat stop Tha Pratunam, or a longer walk from BTS Ratchathevi. Mac-heads are catered for here, including authorized resellers, and there are dozens of repair and secondhand booths, especially towards the back of the shopping centre and on the upper floors.

1

**Taekee Taekon** 118 Thanon Phra Arthit ☎ 02 629 1473; map p.92. Tasteful assortment of handicraft gifts, souvenirs and textiles, plus a selection of Thai art cards and black-and-white photocards. Mon–Sat 9am–5pm.

### DOWNTOWN: AROUND SIAM SQUARE AND THANON PLOENCHIT

**Alexander Lamont** Floor 3, Gaysorn Village; Floor 2, Central Embassy; ⓦ alexanderlamont.com; map p.104. Beautiful lacquerware bowls, vases and boxes, as well as objects using bronze, glass, crystal, ceramic, parchment, gold leaf and petrified wood, all in imaginative contemporary, Asian-inspired styles. Daily 10am–8pm.

**Chabatik** Floor 2, River City ⓦ chabatik.com; map p.104. Gorgeous scarves, wraps, bags, accessories and hangings in a rainbow of colours, made from soft Khon Kaen silk, combining traditional weaving methods with contemporary designs. Daily 10am–8pm.

**Exotique Thai** Floor 4, Siam Paragon ⓦ siamparagon. co.th; map p.104. A collection of small boutique outlets from around the city and the country – including silk-makers and designers from Chiang Mai – makes a good, upmarket one-stop shop, that is much more interesting than Narai Phand (see below). There's everything from jewellery and beauty products to celadons and axe pillows. Daily 10am–10pm.

**Narai Phand** Ground floor, President Tower Arcade, just east of Gaysorn Village, Thanon Ploenchit ⓦ narai phand.com; map p.104. This souvenir centre was set up to ensure the preservation of traditional crafts and to maintain standards of quality, as a joint venture with the Ministry of Industry in the 1930s, and has a duly institutional feel, though it makes a reasonable one-stop shop for last-minute presents. It offers a huge assortment of reasonably priced, good-quality goods from all over the country, including silk and cotton, *khon* masks, *bencharong*, celadon, woodcarving, lacquerware, silver, brass, bronze, *yan lipao* basketware and axe cushions. Daily 10am–8pm.

**OTOP** Floor 4, Central Embassy ⓦ centralembassy.com/ brands/otop-heritage; map p.104. An attractive selection of the more high-end handicrafts made under the national OTOP (One Tambon, One Product) scheme, such as ceramics, bags and clothes, including silk. Daily 10am–8pm.

**Creative Lab** Siam Discovery, Thanon Rama I ⓦ siam discovery.co.th; map p.104. Recently renovated, Floor 3 of this mall is now an open-plan bazaar for all manner of contemporary Thai design, including lamps, vases, rugs, accessories, spa products and stationery. Daily 10am–10pm.

### THANON SUKHUMVIT

**Another Story** Floor 4, EmQuartier ⓦ facebook.com/ anotherstoryofficial; map p.109. This eclectic concept store shelters a bewildering anthology of cool stuff: lamps and interior décor; lovely leather bags and accessories by

Labrador; stationery and art books; sunglasses; and excellent breads, patisserie, cheese and wine at its deli-café. Daily 10am–10pm.

**Sop Moei Arts** 8 Soi 49 ⓦ sopmoeiarts.com; map p.109. If you're not going up to Chiang Mai, it's well worth checking out the lovely fabrics and basketware at this small branch shop. Tues–Sat 9.30am–5pm.

**ThaiCraft Fairs** Floor L, Jasmine City Building, corner of Thanon Sukhumvit and Soi 23 ⓦ thaicraft.org; map p.109. One-off craft sales and demonstrations, involving about fifty groups of artisans from all over the country, run on fair-trade principles by ThaiCraft, an independent development organization – check the website for dates.

### DOWNTOWN: SOUTH OF THANON RAMA IV

**Jim Thompson** 9 Thanon Suriwong, corner of Thanon Rama IV; map p.111; branches at the Jim Thompson House Museum (see page 106), the airports and many department stores, malls and hotels around the city; ⓦ jimthompson.com. A good place to start looking for traditional Thai fabric, or at least to get an idea of what's out there. Stocks silk, linen and cotton by the metre and ready-made items from shirts to cushion covers, which are well designed and of good quality, but pricey. They also have a home-furnishings section (daily 9am–7pm). Daily 9am–9pm.

**Khomapastr** 56–58 Thanon Naret, between Suriwong and Si Phraya roads ⓦ khomapastrfabrics.com; map p.111. Branch of the famous Hua Hin shop (see page 218), selling brightly coloured, hand-printed cotton in traditional Thai patterns. Mon–Sat 9am–5.30pm.

**The Legend** Floor 3, Thaniya Plaza, corner of Soi Thaniya and Thanon Silom ☎ 02 231 2170; map p.111. Stocks a small selection of well-made Thai handicrafts, notably wood, wickerware, celadon and other ceramics, at reasonable prices. Daily 10am–7pm.

**The Shop @ TCDC** Thailand Creative and Design Centre, Grand Postal Building, Thanon Charoen Krung ⓦ tcdc. or.th; map p.111. The retail outlet at Bangkok's design centre sells innovative products dreamt up by local creatives, mostly stocking-fillers, bags, T-shirts and art books, with more than a whiff of kitsch. Tues–Sun 10.30am–9pm.

**Tamnan Mingmuang** Floor 3, Thaniya Plaza, corner of Soi Thaniya and Thanon Silom ☎ 02 231 2120; map p.111. Subsidiary of *The Legend* (see above), which sells lovely basketry from all over the country: among the unusual items on offer are trays and boxes for tobacco and betel nut made from *yan lipao* (intricately woven fern vines), and bambooware sticky-rice containers, baskets and lampshades. Daily 10am–7pm.

### TAILORED CLOTHES

Inexpensive tailoring shops crowd Silom, Sukhumvit and Khao San roads, but the best single area to head for is the short stretch of Thanon Charoen Krung between Thanon Suriwong and Thanon Silom (near the Chao Phraya express-boat stops at Tha Oriental and Tha Wat Muang Kae, or a 10min walk from Saphan Taksin Skytrain station). It's generally advisable to avoid tailors in tourist areas such as Thanon Khao San, shopping malls and Thanon Sukhumvit, although if you're lucky it's still possible to come up trumps here.

**A Song Tailor** 8 Trok Chartered Bank, just round the corner from OP Place shopping centre off Thanon Charoen Krung, near the Oriental Hotel ⊕ 02 630 9708, ⓦ asongtailor.com; map p.111. Friendly, helpful small shop that's a good first port of call if you're on a budget. Men's and women's suits and shirts; preferably at least three to five days with two fittings, but can turn work around in a day or two. Tues–Sat noon–7pm.

**Golden Wool** 1340–2 Thanon Charoen Krung ⊕ 02 233 0149, ⓦ golden-wool.com; map p.111. A larger operation than nearby A Song, which can turn around decent work for men and women in two days, though prices are slightly on the high side. Mon–Sat 10am–8pm.

**Marco Tailor** Soi 7, Siam Square ⊕ 02 252 0689; map p.104. Long-established tailor with a good reputation, making men's suits in two or three weeks. Mon–Sat 10am–7pm.

### FASHION

Thanon Khao San is lined with stalls selling low-priced fashion clothing: the baggy cotton fisherman's trousers, elephant pants and embroidered blouses are all aimed at backpackers, but they're supplemented by cheap contemporary fashions that appeal to urban Thais as well. Downtown, the most famous area for low-cost, low-quality casual clothes is the warren-like Pratunam Market and surrounding malls such as Platinum Fashion Mall around the junction of Phetchaburi and Ratchaprarop roads (see map, p.77), but for the best and latest trends from Thai designers, you should check out the shops in Siam Square and across the road in the more upmarket Siam Centre. Prices vary considerably: street gear in Siam Square is undoubtedly inexpensive, while genuine Western brand names are generally competitive but not breathtakingly cheaper than at home; larger sizes can be hard to find. Shoes and leather goods are good buys in Bangkok, being generally handmade from high-quality leather and quite a bargain.

**Central Embassy** Thanon Ploenchit ⓦ centralembassy.com; map p.104. This recently built mall, constructed on land sold off by the British Embassy, is bidding to become the most chic of the city's shopping plazas: here you'll find Gucci and McQ – and gentlemen can get a very civilized haircut or shave at a branch of the London barber, Truefitt and Hill – while a few upmarket Thai names have made it to the party, notably Sretsis and Scotch & Soda. Daily 10am–10pm.

**Central World** Ratchaprasong Intersection, corner of Rama I and Rajdamri roads ⓦ centralworld.co.th; map p.104. This shopping centre is so huge that it defies easy classification, but you'll find plenty of Thai and international fashions on its lower floors and in the attached Zen department store at its southern end. Daily 10am–9/10pm.

**Emporium** Thanon Sukhumvit, between sois 22 and 24 ⓦ emporiumthailand.com; map p.109. Large and rather glamorous shopping plaza, with its own department store and a good range of fashion outlets, from exclusive designer wear to trendy high-street gear. Genuine brand-name shops include Prada, Chanel and Burberry, as well as established local labels such as Soda. Daily 10am–8/10pm.

**EmQuartier** Thanon Sukhumvit, opposite Emporium ⓦ emquartier.co.th; map p.109. Sprawled across three buildings, this mall runs the gamut from Miu Miu, Chanel and Jimmy Choo to Boots the chemist. Less exclusive brands such as Tommy Hilfiger also find space alongside Soda, Jaspal and other local names (and lots of good eating options). Daily 10am–10pm.

**Mah Boon Krong (MBK)** At the Rama I/Phrayathai intersection ⓦ mbk-center.co.th; map p.104. Vivacious, labyrinthine shopping centre which most closely resembles a traditional Thai market that's been rammed into a huge mall. It houses hundreds of small, mostly fairly inexpensive outlets, including plenty of high-street fashion shops. Daily 10am–9/10pm.

**Siam Centre** Thanon Rama I ⓦ siamcenter.co.th; map p.104. Particularly good for local labels – look out for Greyhound, Senada and Flynow, which mounts dramatic displays of women's party and formal gear – many of which have made the step up from the booths of Siam Square across the road, as well as international names like Superdry and Cath Kidston. Daily 10am–10pm.

**Siam Square** map p.104. It's worth poking around the alleys here and the "mini-malls" inside the blocks. All manner of inexpensive boutiques, some little more than booths, sell colourful street-gear to the capital's fashionable students and teenagers.

**Viera by Ragazze** Floor 2, Central World and in the attached Isetan and Zen department stores ⓦ vieraby ragazze.com; map p.104. Stylish, Italian-influenced leather goods. Daily 10am–9/9.30pm.

### BOOKS

English-language bookshops in Bangkok are always well stocked with everything to do with Thailand, and most carry fiction classics and popular paperbacks as well. The capital's secondhand bookshops are not cheap, but you can usually part-exchange your unwanted titles.

**Asia Books** Flagship store in Central World on Thanon Rama I, plus dozens of other branches around town ⓦ asia books.com; map p.104. English-language bookshop (and publishing house) that's especially recommended for its books on Asia – everything from guidebooks to cookery books, novels to art. Also stocks bestselling novels and coffee-table books. Daily 10am–9.30pm.

1

## GEM SCAMS

Gem scams are so common in Bangkok that TAT has published a brochure about it and there are lots of web pages on the subject, including ⓦ en.wikipedia.org/wiki/Gem_scam and the very informative ⓦ 2bangkok.com/2bangkok-scams-sapphire.html, which describes typical scams in detail. Never buy anything through a tout or from any shop recommended by a "government official"/"student"/"businessperson"/tuk-tuk driver who just happens to engage you in conversation on the street, and note that there are no government jewellery shops, despite any information you may be given to the contrary, and no special government promotions or sales on gems.

The basic **scam** is to charge a lot more than what the gem is worth based on its carat weight – at the very least, get it **tested** on the spot, ask for a written guarantee and receipt. Don't even consider **buying gems in bulk** to sell at a supposedly vast profit elsewhere: many a gullible traveller has invested thousands of dollars on a handful of worthless multicoloured stones, believing the vendor's reassurance that the goods will fetch at least a hundred percent more when resold at home.

If you're determined to buy precious stones, check that the shop is a member of the **Thai Gem and Jewelry Traders Association** by visiting their website, which has a directory of members (ⓦ thaigemjewelry.or.th). To be doubly sure, you may want to seek out shops that also belong to the TGJTA's **Jewel Fest Club** (look for the window stickers; ⓦ jewelfestclub. com), which guarantees quality.

**Books Kinokuniya** Floor 3, EmQuartier Shopping Centre, Thanon Sukhumvit; map p.104; Floor 6, Isetan, in Central World, Thanon Rama I; map p.109; Floor 3, Siam Paragon, Thanon Rama I; ⓦ thailand.kinokuniya.com. Huge, efficient, Japanese-owned, English-language bookshop with a wide selection of books ranging from bestsellers to travel literature and from classics to sci-fi; not so hot on books about Asia, though. All daily 10/10.30am–10pm.

**Dasa Book Café** Between sois 26 and 28, Thanon Sukhumvit ⓦ dasabookcafe.com; map p.109. Bangkok's best secondhand bookshop, Dasa is appealingly calm and intelligently, and alphabetically, categorized, with sections on everything from Asia to biography, and a large children's area. Browse its thrice-weekly updated spreadsheet of stock online, or enjoy coffee and cakes *in situ*. Daily 10am–8pm.

### JEWELLERY AND GEMS

Bangkok boasts the country's best gem and jewellery shops, and some of the finest lapidaries in the world, making this *the* place to buy cut and uncut stones such as rubies, blue sapphires and diamonds. However, countless gem-buying tourists get badly ripped off, so remember to be extremely wary.

**Asian Institute of Gemological Sciences** Jewelry Trade Center, 919 Thanon Silom ☎ 02 267 4325 (laboratory) or ☎ 02 267 4315 (school), ⓦ aigsthailand. com; map p.111. Independent professional advice and precious stones certification from its laboratory. Also runs reputable courses, such as a five-day introduction to gems and gemology (US$700). Mon–Fri 9am–6pm.

**Jewelry Trade Center** West end of Thanon Silom ⓦ jewelrytradecenter.com; map p.111. Dozens of members of the Thai Gem and Jewelry Traders Association have outlets in this shopping mall (and on the surrounding streets). Mon–Sat roughly 11am–8pm.

**Lambert** Floor 4, Shanghai Building, Soi 17, 807–9 Thanon Silom ☎ 02 236 4343, ⓦ lambertgems.com; map p.111. Thoroughly reputable, forty-year-old, American-owned outlet, offering a full service: loose stones and pearls, including collectors' stones, ready-made pieces, cutting, design, redesign and repairs. Mon–Fri 9am–5pm, Sat 9am–4pm.

## DIRECTORY

**Banks and exchange** The Suvarnabhumi Airport exchange desks are open 24hr, while many other exchange booths stay open till 8pm or later, especially along Khao San, Sukhumvit and Silom roads and in the major shopping malls. You can also withdraw cash from hundreds of ATMs around the city and at the airports.

**Embassies and consulates** Australia, 181 Thanon Witthayu ☎ 02 344 6300, ⓦ thailand.embassy.gov.au; Cambodia, 518/4 Thanon Pracha Uthit (Soi Ramkamhaeng 39) ☎ 02 957 5851–2 or ☎ 063 320 6370; Canada, 15th floor, Abdulrahim Place, 990 Thanon Rama IV ☎ 02 646 4300, ⓦ thailand.gc.ca; Ireland, Floor 12, 208 Thanon Witthayu ☎ 02 016 1360; Laos, 502/1–3 Soi Sahakarnpramoon, Thanon Pracha Uthit ☎ 02 539 6667–8 ext 106; Malaysia, 35 Thanon Sathorn Tai ☎ 02 629 6800; Myanmar (Burma), 132 Thanon Sathorn Nua ☎ 02 234 4789; New Zealand, 14th Floor, M Thai Tower, All Seasons Place, 87 Thanon Witthayu ☎ 02 254 2530, ⓦ nzembassy. com/thailand; South Africa, Floor 12A, M Thai Tower, All Seasons Place, 87 Thanon Witthayu ☎ 02 092 2900, ⓦ www. dirco.gov.za/bangkok; UK, 14 Thanon Witthayu ☎ 02 305 8333; US, 120 Thanon Witthayu ☎ 02 205 4000; Vietnam, 83/1 Thanon Witthayu ☎ 02 650 8979. For further details about Bangkok's diplomatic corps, go to ⓦ mfa.go.th/main/en/ information on the Thai Ministry of Foreign Affairs' website.

**Emergencies** For English-speaking help in any emergency, call the tourist police on their free 24hr phoneline ☎ 1155. The tourist police are based on the grounds of Suvarnabhumi Airport (⊛ touristpolice.go.th), or drop in at the more convenient Chana Songkhram Police Station at the west end of Thanon Khao San in Banglamphu (☎ 02 282 2323).

**Hospitals, clinics and dentists** Most expats rate the private Bumrungrad International Hospital, 33 Sukhumvit Soi 3 (☎ 02 066 8888, emergency ☎ 02 011 5222, ⊛ bumrungrad.com), as the best and most comfortable in the city, followed by the BNH (Bangkok Nursing Home) Hospital, 9 Thanon Convent (☎ 02 022 0700, emergency ☎ 02 632 1000, ⊛ bnhhospital.com); and the Bangkok Hospital Medical Centre, 2 Soi Soonvijai 7, Thanon Phetchaburi Mai (☎ 02 310 3000 or ☎ 1719, ⊛ bangkokhospital.com). You can get travel vaccinations and malaria advice, as well as rabies advice and treatment, at the Thai Red Cross Society's Queen Saovabha Memorial Institute (QSMI) and Snake Farm on the corner of Thanon Rama IV and Thanon Henri Dunant (Mon–Fri 8.30am–4.30pm, Sat 8.30am–noon; ☎ 02 252 0161–4 ext 125 or 132, ⊛ saovabha.com). Among general clinics, Global Doctor, Ground Floor, *Holiday Inn Hotel*, 981 Thanon Silom (corner of Thanon Surasak; ☎ 02 236 8444, ⊛ globaldoctorclinic.com), is recommended. For dental problems, try the Bumrungrad Hospital's dental department on ☎ 02 011 4100; the Dental Hospital, 88/88 Sukhumvit Soi 49 (☎ 02 260 5000–15, ⊛ dentalhospitalbangkok. com); or Siam Family Dental Clinic, Soi 3, Siam Square (☎ 081 987 7700, ⊛ siamfamilydental.com).

**Immigration office** North of the centre off Thanon Wiphawadi Rangsit at Floor 2, B Building, Government Complex, Soi 7, Thanon Chaengwattana (Mon–Fri 8.30am–noon & 1–4.30pm; ☎ 02 141 9889, ⊛ bangkok.immigration. go.th, which includes a map). When trying to extend your visa (see page 60), be very wary of any Khao San tour agents who offer to organize a visa extension for you: some are reportedly faking the relevant stamps and this has caused problems at immigration.

**Internet access** As well as 4G (see page 64), there's free wi-fi in nearly all hotels and guesthouses and most restaurants, bars and shopping centres in Bangkok. Internet cafés are now generally only found in the suburbs, full of schoolkids playing games, but most accommodation will have computers and printers for printing out boarding passes and the like.

**Laundry** Nearly all guesthouses and hotels offer same-day laundry services (about B40–50/kg at a guesthouse, much more at a hotel), or there are several self-service laundries on and around Thanon Khao San.

**Left luggage** Luggage can be left at Suvarnabhumi Airport (B100/day); Don Muang Airport (B75/day); Hualamphong train station (B20–80/day); the bus terminals and most hotels and guesthouses.

**Post offices** If you're staying in Banglamphu, it's probably most convenient to use the local postal, packing and poste restante services at Banglamphubon PO, Soi Sibsam Hang, Bangkok 10203 (daily 8am–5pm). Downtown, Nana PO, between sois 4 and 6, Thanon Sukhumvit, Bangkok 10112 (Mon–Fri 8am–6pm, Sat & Sun 9am–5pm), is handy for the BTS.

**Telephones** It's best to buy a Thai SIM card for both international and domestic calls (see page 67). Otherwise, you can easily access Skype or the like with your own device through Bangkok's plentiful wi-fi networks.

**Travel agents** If you are buying onward international air tickets, be warned that there are many dodgy, transient travel agents in Bangkok, particularly on and around Thanon Khao San, which is known for its shady operators who display fake TAT licences, issue false tickets and flee with travellers' money overnight. The best advice is to use one of the tried and tested agents listed here. Never hand over any money until you've been given the ticket and checked it carefully. Asian Trails, 9th Floor, SG Tower, 161/1 Soi Mahadlek Luang 3, Thanon Rajdamri (☎ 02 626 2000, ⊛ asiantrails.travel), does interesting Thailand tours and day-trips and runs airport transfers; *New Road Guest House* (see page 128) is a reliable agent for train and bus tickets, as well as their own unusual tours; Olavi Travel sells air, train and bus tickets and is opposite the west end of Thanon Khao San at 53 Thanon Chakrabongse, Banglamphu (☎ 02 629 4710, ⊛ olavi.com); and the Bangkok branches of the worldwide STA Travel (☎ 02 160 5200, ⊛ statravel.co.th) are reliable outlets for cheap international flights and local tours: Baan Chart Hotel, Thanon Chakrabongse, opposite Wat Chana Songkhram, Banglamphu, and Floor 3, Chamchuri Square Building, corner of Phrayathai and Rama IV roads, as well as at both Lub D hostels (see pages 126 and 128).

# The east coast

AO NOI BEACH, KO KOOD

**2**

# The east coast

Just a few hours' drive from the capital, the east-coast resorts attract a mixed crowd of weekending Bangkokians and sybaritic tourists. Transport connections are good and, for overlanders, there are several Cambodian border crossings within reach. Beautiful beaches aren't the whole picture, however, as the east coast is also crucial to Thailand's industrial economy, its natural gas fields and deep-sea ports having spawned massive development along the first 200km of coastline, an area dubbed the Eastern Seaboard. The initial landscape of refineries and depots shouldn't deter you though, as offshore it's an entirely different story, with beaches as glorious as more celebrated southern retreats and enough peaceful havens to make it worth packing your hammock.

The first worthwhile stop comes 100km east of Bangkok at the town of **Si Racha**, which is the point of access for tiny **Ko Si Chang**, whose dramatically rugged coastlines and low-key atmosphere make it a restful retreat. In complete contrast, nearby **Pattaya** is Thailand's number one package-tour destination, its customers predominantly middle-aged European men enticed by the resort's sex-market reputation, or snap-happy, package-tour groups, all undeterred by its lacklustre beach. Things soon look up, though, as the coast veers sharply eastwards towards Ban Phe, revealing the island of **Ko Samet**, the prettiest of the beach resorts within comfortable bus-ride range of Bangkok. East of Ban Phe, the landscape becomes lusher and hillier around **Chanthaburi**, the dynamo of Thailand's gem trade and one of only two eastern provincial capitals worth visiting. The other is **Trat**, 68km further along the highway, and an important hub for transport, both into **Cambodia** via Hat Lek – one of this region's two main border points, the other being Aranyaprathet (see page 151) – and to the 52 islands of the Ko Chang Marine National Park. The most popular of this island group is large, forested **Ko Chang** itself, whose long, fine beaches have made it an appealing alternative to Phuket or Ko Samui on the southern peninsula. A host of smaller, less-developed islands fills the sea between Ko Chang and the Cambodian coast, most notably temptingly diverse **Ko Mak** and **Ko Kood,** which lie outside the national park boundaries.

## GETTING AROUND                                                    THE EAST COAST

**By bus** Highway 3 extends almost the entire length of the east coast, beginning in Bangkok as Thanon Sukhumvit, and known as such when it cuts through towns, and hundreds of buses ply the route, connecting all major mainland destinations. It's also possible to travel between the east coast and the northeast and north without doubling back through the capital: the most direct routes into Isaan start from Pattaya, Rayong and Chanthaburi.

**By plane** Bangkok's Suvarnabhumi Airport (see page 113) is less than 50km from Si Racha, and there are two domestic airports along the east coast itself: at U-Tapao naval base, southeast of Pattaya, and just west of Trat.
**By train** Though a rail line connects Bangkok with Si Racha and Pattaya, it is served by just one slow train a day in each direction; a branch line makes two journeys a day to Aranyaprathet near the Cambodian border.

# Si Racha

The eastbound journey out of Bangkok is not at all scenic, dominated initially by traffic-choked suburban sprawl and then by the industrial landscape of the petrochemical and shipping industries that power Thailand's Eastern Seaboard. The first major population centre is the provincial capital of **Chonburi**, whose only notable

# Highlights

**❶ Ko Samet** This pretty little island, fringed with a dozen or so beaches of fine, dazzlingly white sand, is easy to get to and offers a wide choice of accommodation, though it's suffering a little for its popularity these days. See page 163

**❷ Chanthaburi** The atmospheric Chantaboon Riverfront, the town's gem market and absence of tour buses make this small town worth a visit. See page 171

**❸ Ko Chang** Head for Lonely Beach if you're in the mood to party, or take your pick from Hat Khlong Phrao, Ao Bang Bao and Hat Khlong Kloi for progressively more tranquil scenes. See page 178

**❹ Ko Mak** Lovely, lazy, palm-filled island with peaceful white-sand beaches, a welcoming atmosphere and some stylish accommodation. See page 191

**❺ Ko Kood** The real beauty of the east, with some great beaches, Thailand's fourth-largest island is untamed and, as yet, largely undeveloped. See page 195

**HIGHLIGHTS ARE MARKED ON THE MAP ON PAGE 150**

attraction is its annual October bout of buffalo racing. Twenty kilometres on, you reach the fast-growing town of **SI RACHA**, a prosperous residential and administrative hub for the Eastern Seaboard's industries and home to a sizeable population of expat families. The town is best known though as the source of *nam phrik Si Racha* (commonly known as Sriracha sauce), the chilli-laced ketchup found on every kitchen table in Thailand, and as the departure point for the island of **Ko Si Chang** (see page 152). Si Racha's only sights are a seafront public park and **Wat Ko Loy**, a gaudy hexagon presided over by a statue of the Chinese Goddess of Mercy, Kuan Im, and located on Ko Loy, an islet at the end of a 1500m causeway.

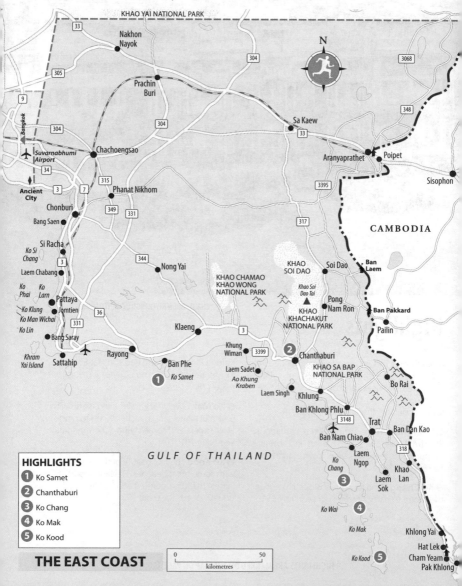

**HIGHLIGHTS**

1. Ko Samet
2. Chanthaburi
3. Ko Chang
4. Ko Mak
5. Ko Kood

**THE EAST COAST**

0    50
kilometres

**2**

## CROSSING THE CAMBODIAN BORDER VIA ARANYAPRATHET

The most commonly used overland crossing into **Cambodia** from Thailand is at **Poipet**, which lies just across the border from the Thai town of **Aranyaprathet (aka Aran)**, 210km due east of Bangkok. It's best to arm yourself in advance with an e-visa for Cambodia (see page 29) and to make the journey by regular public transport from Bangkok to Siem Reap and beyond. It's also possible to travel via Aranyaprathet and get a thirty-day visa on arrival at the border, though this can expose you to possible **scams**, including hustlers offering fake visas and rip-off currency exchange rates (it's not compulsory to buy riel before entering Cambodia, despite what some touts may say). Once you've walked across the border and entered Cambodia, it's about two hours in a taxi or bus to reach Siem Reap, 150km away. If you have the misfortune of getting stuck in Aranyaprathet, try the comfortable fan and a/c rooms at *Market Motel* at 105/30 Thanon Ratuthit (☎037 232302, ✆aranyaprathethotel.com; fan B300, a/c B400).

From **Bangkok**, you can travel to Aranyaprathet Station, 4km from the border post, by **train** (2 daily; 6hr); you'll need to catch the 5.55am if you want to get across the border the same day. Return trains depart Aranyaprathet at 6.40am and 1.55pm (5hr 25min–6hr). Alternatively, take a **bus** from Bangkok's Northern (Mo Chit) Bus Terminal to Aranyaprathet (at least hourly; 4hr 30min), or a faster, more expensive a/c minibus from Victory Monument. If you have an e-visa, you can catch one of Baw Khaw Saw's public buses that run from Mo Chit via Aranyaprathet all the way to Siem Reap and Phom Penh. To reach Aranyaprathet from east-coast towns, take a bus or minibus from **Pattaya or Chanthaburi** to Aranyaprathet.

It's also possible to buy a **through ticket to Siem Reap** from Thanon Khao San in Bangkok (B350–600), but this option is dogged by scams, can take longer than doing it independently, and often uses clapped-out buses or even pick-ups on the Cambodian side, despite the promised "luxury bus".

## ARRIVAL AND DEPARTURE
## SI RACHA

### BY BUS

Frequent buses pass through Si Racha on their journeys between Bangkok's Eastern (Ekamai) and Northern (Mo Chit) bus terminals, and Pattaya and Trat further east. They all drop off and pick up passengers near the huge Robinsons/Pacific Park shopping centre on Thanon Sukhumvit in Si Racha's town centre.

Destinations Bangkok (Eastern/Northern bus terminals; every 40min; 1hr 30min–2hr 30min); Chanthaburi (6 daily; 3hr 30min); Pattaya (every 20min; 30min); Trat (6 daily; 5hr).

### BY TRAIN

Though a rail line connects Bangkok with Pattaya and Sattahip via Si Racha, it is served by just one slow, third-class, often late, train a day in each direction. The train station is on the far eastern edge of town, a tuk-tuk ride from the pier for Ko Si Chang.

Destinations Bangkok (daily; 3hr 30min); Pattaya (daily; 30min).

### BY BOAT

Ferries to Ko Si Chang, which once left from Tha Ko Loy, now leave from Tha Jarin (Jarin pier), located about 1km south of Tha Ko Loy on Chermchompon Soi 14, or 2.5km from Robinsons shopping centre; a motorbike taxi or tuk-tuk ride will cost you around B40/B60. Boats run frequently to Ko Si Chang between 7am and 8pm (hourly; 40–50min; B50).

## ACCOMMODATION AND EATING

For **food**, Thanon Si Racha Nakhon 3 is a good place to browse, lined with restaurants and night-time street food stalls, or there's an official night market by the day market and clocktower, further south down Thanon Chermchompon.

**City Hotel** 6/126 Thanon Sukhumvit ☎038 322700, ✆citysriracha.com. This high-rise, two hundred-room hotel, 300m south of Pacific Place, offers smart a/c digs, with a gym, a spa, a tennis court, Japanese and international restaurants and a pool on site. B2825

**Mum Aroy** 16/4 Soi Laemket, about 1km north of Ko Loy ☎081 110 4567. Ideal spot for a sunset seafood feast with views out over the gulf. Dishes range from a simple crab fried rice (B100) to elaborate lobster preparations. Daily 10am–11pm.

**Samchai Resort** 3 Thanon Chermchompon, opposite Thanon Tessaban 1 ☎038 311800, ✆facebook.com/samchairesort. A range of simply furnished but clean and comfortable fan and a/c rooms on a jetty jutting out over the atmospheric waterfront. Fan B320, a/c B500

**2**

# Ko Si Chang

The unhurried pace and absence of consumer pressures make small, dry, rocky **KO SI CHANG** an engaging place to get away from it all for a day or two. Unlike most other east-coast destinations, it offers no real beach life – it's a populous, working island with a deep-sea port, rather than a tropical idyll – and there's little to do here but explore the craggy coastline by kayak or ramble up and down its steep, scrubby contours on foot or by motorbike. The island is famous as the location of one of Rama V's summer palaces, a few parts of which have been restored, and of a popular Chinese pilgrimage temple, as well as for its wild pigs and rare white squirrels, which live in the wooded patches inland.

## Phra Chudadhut Palace

Hat Tha Wang • Tues–Sun 9am–5pm • Free

The most famous sight on the island is the former summer palace of Rama V, now known as **Phra Chudadhut Palace**, which occupies a large chunk of gently sloping land midway down the east coast, behind pebbly **Hat Tha Wang**. It's an enjoyable place to explore and can be reached on foot from the middle of Thanon Asadang in about half an hour.

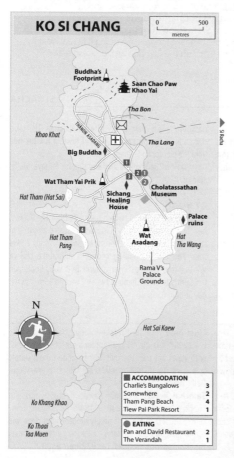

Built in the 1890s as a sort of health resort for sickly royals, the palace formed the heart of an extensive complex comprising homes for royal advisers, chalets for convalescents, quarters for royal concubines and administrative buildings. Within a few years, however, Rama V (King Chulalongkorn) was concerned about foreign incursions, particularly after the Franco-Siamese crisis of 1893 (see page 421), so in 1901 his golden teak palace was moved piece by piece to Bangkok, and reconstructed there as Vimanmek Palace; its foundations are still visible just south of the eye-catching Saphan Asadang pier. Following modern renovations, the elegant design of the palace grounds is apparent once more. They fan out around an elaborate labyrinth of fifty interlinked ponds and a maze of stone steps and balustrades that still cling to the shallow hillside. Close to the shore, four of the original Western-style **villas** have been reconstructed to house displays, of varying interest, on Chulalongkorn's relationship with Ko Si Chang; one of them also doubles as a weekend coffee shop. Inland, signs direct you up the hillside to the palace's unusual whitewashed shrine, **Wat Asadang**, whose circular walls are punctuated with Gothic stained-glass windows and surmounted by a chedi.

KO SI CHANG

0     500
metres

Buddha's Footprint
Saan Chao Paw Khao Yai
Tha Bon
Khao Khat
THANON ASADANG
Tha Lang
Big Buddha
Wat Tham Yai Prik
Hat Tham (Hat Sai)
Sichang Healing House
Cholatassathan Museum
Hat Tham Pang
Wat Asadang
Palace ruins
Hat Tha Wang
Rama V's Palace Grounds
Hat Sai Kaew
N
Ko Khang Khao
Ko Thaai Taa Muen
Si Racha

**■ ACCOMMODATION**
| Charlie's Bungalows | 3 |
| Somewhere | 2 |
| Tham Pang Beach | 4 |
| Tiew Pai Park Resort | 1 |

**● EATING**
| Pan and David Restaurant | 2 |
| The Verandah | 1 |

2

**KO SI CHANG FESTIVALS**

Ko Si Chang celebrates three particularly interesting festivals. **Songkhran** is marked from April 17 to 19 with sandcastle building, greasy-pole-climbing and kayak racing. At **Visakha Puja**, the full moon day in May when the Buddha's birth, death and enlightenment are honoured, islanders process to the old palace with hand-crafted Chinese lanterns. And on September 20, Ko Si Chang honours its royal patron **King Chulalongkorn**'s birthday with a sound and light show in the palace grounds and a beauty contest staged entirely in costumes from the Chulalongkorn era.

## Hat Tham Pang and Ko Khang Khao

The main beach on the west coast, and the most popular one on the island, is **Hat Tham Pang**. It's a tiny patch of sand, backed by shoulder-to-shoulder umbrellas and deckchairs belonging to the basic beach restaurants; you can rent snorkelling equipment and kayaks here too. The best **snorkelling** spots are further south, around the tiny islands off Ko Si Chang's southern tip, particularly off the north coast of **Ko Khang Khao**, forty minutes by kayak from Hat Tham Pang.

## Wat Tham Yai Prik

Accessible via a fork off Thanon Asadang opposite *Tiew Pai* (10min walk)

The **Wat Tham Yai Prik** temple and meditation centre is open to interested visitors and meditators, who can meditate in caves set into the mountain. Unusually, nuns as well as monks here wear brown (rather than white) and everyone participates in the upkeep of the splendid monastery: you can see some of the fruits of their labour in the extensive roadside orchard. Just west of the wat lies the pretty, rocky cove known as **Hat Tham** or **Hat Sai**, which is only really swimmable at low tide.

## Khao Khat

On the northwest trajectory of the ring road, you'll pass beneath the gaze of a huge yellow Buddha before reaching the rocky northwest headland of **Khao Khat**, a few hundred metres further on. The uninterrupted panorama of open sea makes this a classic sunset spot, and there's a stairway leading down to the rocky shore.

## Saan Chao Paw Khao Yai

The showy, multi-tiered Chinese temple of **Saan Chao Paw Khao Yai** (Shrine of the Father Spirit of the Great Hill) is stationed at the top of a steep flight of steps and commands a good view of the harbour and the mainland coast. Established here long before Rama V arrived on the island, the shrine was dedicated by Chinese seamen who saw a strange light coming out of one of the **caves** behind the modern-day temple. The caves, now full of religious statues and related paraphernalia, are visited by boatloads of Chinese pilgrims, particularly over Chinese New Year. Continue on up the cliffside to reach a small pagoda enshrining a **Buddha's Footprint**. A very long, very steep flights of stairs give access to the footprint from the main waterfront entrance to the Chinese temple, taking you past a cluster of monks' meditation cells, but there's also a steep paved road branching off the northern part of the ring road that motorbikes and samlors can climb. From the platform beside the footprint there are fantastic views looking south that take in both the east and west coasts of the island.

**ARRIVAL AND INFORMATION**                                                                 **KO SI CHANG**

**By boat** Ferries to Ko Si Chang leave from Tha Jarin in Si Racha (see page 148) from 6am to 8pm (hourly; 40–50min; B50), wending their way past the congestion of international cargo boats and Thai supply barges that

**2**

anchor in the protected channel between the mainland and Ko Si Chang. On arrival, boats dock first at Tha Lang (also signed as Tateawavong Bridge) in the island's main settlement, with many then continuing to Tha Bon a short distance up the east coast. Some hotels and guesthouses offer free pick-ups if you inform them which ferry you are on. Otherwise, samlor drivers meet the boats and charge B50 to most accommodation, or B80

to Hat Tham Pang. Boats to the mainland leave Tha Lang between 6am and 7pm (hourly; 40–50min; B50 except for the 7pm ferry B60); the same boats depart Tha Bon 15min earlier.

**Tourist information** ⊛ ko-sichang.com, a useful website compiled by in-the-know David of *Pan and David Restaurant* (see below), offers detailed coverage of the island and its attractions.

## GETTING AROUND

Both piers connect with Thanon Asadang, a small, concrete ring road on which you'll find the market, a bank and many shops. In town it's easy enough to walk from place to place, but to really enjoy what Ko Si Chang has to offer you'll need to either rent a motorbike or charter a samlor for a tour.

**By motorbike** Bikes can be rented from the pier or from

*Charlie's Bungalows* (see below) for B300 a day.

**By samlor** The island's trademark samlors are driven by distinctive, elongated 1200cc motorbikes and virtually monopolise the roads, as there are barely any private cars; a quick tour of the main sights on the island will set you back around B250, and takes just over an hour.

## ACCOMMODATION AND EATING

Though Ko Si Chang sees few Western visitors, there are now around 70 hotels and guesthouses that cater for weekenders from Bangkok, when rates are hiked up and booking ahead is advisable. There are plenty of cheap and cheerful eateries on Thanon Asadang.

**Charlie's Bungalows** Thanon Asadang, 2min walk south of Tiew Pai Park Resort in town ☎ 085 191 3863, ⊛ kohsichang.net; map p.152. A dozen or so attractive new bungalows, done out in a maritime theme and arranged around a small garden; all come with a/c, hot water, satellite TV and fridge. Prices increase a little at weekends. B1000

★ **Pan and David Restaurant** Thanon Asadang, 200m before the entrance to the old palace grounds ☎ 038 216 629, ⊛ ko-sichang.com; map p.152. Indisputably the best restaurant on the island, run by a sociable and well-informed American expat and his Thai wife. The long menu features a wide range of delicious dishes, including authentically fiery Thai salads, tasty home-made fettuccine (B320 with porcini mushroom sauce), fillet steak, Thai curries (B180 with free-range chicken), and home-made fresh strawberry ice cream. Thurs–Tues 7.30am–9.30pm.

★ **Somewhere** Off Thanon Asadang, just south of Tha Lang ☎ 038 109 400, ⊛ somewherehotel.com; map p.152. This cute, boutique hotel with a maritime theme has just twenty spacious rooms, some with sea views

from the upstairs balcony. There's a pool here too, and an excellent restaurant: *The Veranda* (see below). Breakfast included. B2500

**Tham Pang Beach** Hat Tham Pang ☎ 038 216 153, ⊛ tampangbeach.com; map p.152. Undergoing renovation at the time of writing, all rooms here have a/c and hot water bathrooms, though some rooms lack windows. The cheapest rooms are small for the price, and there's no breakfast included, but it's the only option if you want to be right on the beach. B1300

**The Veranda** At Somewhere Hotel, off Thanon Asadang ☎ 038 109 400 ⊛ somewherehotel.com; map p.152. The restaurant at this small resort serves some tasty pizzas and burgers as well as great Thai food. If you like spicy dishes, try the Southern Thai curry with salmon (B180). There's also a good range of wines and spirits and a cosy ambiance. Daily 6.30am–9.30pm.

**Tiew Pai Park Resort** Thanon Asadang, in town near Tha Lang ☎ 038 216 084, ⊛ tiewpai.net; map p.152. Very central and cheaper than the competition, this is most backpackers' first choice. Bungalows and rooms are crammed around a scruffy garden across the road from the restaurant and many don't have hot water; the best value are the en-suite fan bungalows, some of which have TV and fridge, and there are also some cheap single rooms with shared bathrooms (B200). No wi-fi. Fan B400, a/c B700

## DIRECTORY

**Massage** The charming little Sichang Healing House (☎ 081 572 7840; Thurs–Tues 9am–6pm; ⊛ ko-sichang.com/spa_welcome.html), west off Thanon Asadang on the way to the old palace, offers a menu of excellent Thai

massage (B500 for 90min) and herbal treatments, as well as five-day massage courses (B6000), at its cute little garden retreat. They have a couple of treatment rooms for rent too.

# Pattaya

With its streets full of high-rise hotels and hustlers on every corner, **PATTAYA** is the epitome of exploitative tourism gone mad, but most of the two million annual visitors don't mind that the place looks like the Costa del Sol bathed in smog because what they are here for is sex. The city swarms with male and female **prostitutes**, spiced up by

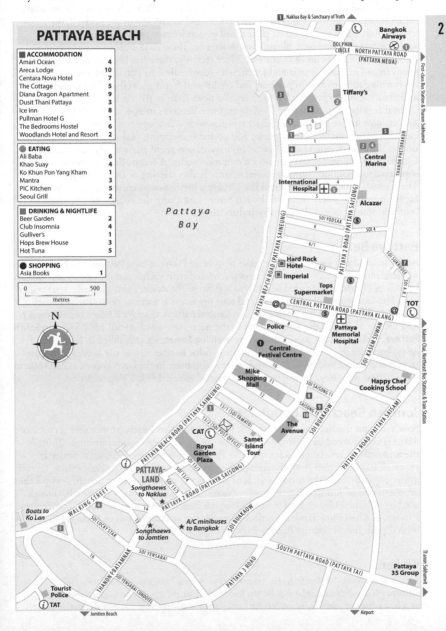

**PATTAYA BEACH**

**ACCOMMODATION**
| | |
|---|---|
| Amari Ocean | 4 |
| Areca Lodge | 10 |
| Centara Nova Hotel | 7 |
| The Cottage | 5 |
| Diana Dragon Apartment | 9 |
| Dusit Thani Pattaya | 3 |
| Ice Inn | 8 |
| Pullman Hotel G | 1 |
| The Bedrooms Hostel | 6 |
| Woodlands Hotel and Resort | 2 |

**EATING**
| | |
|---|---|
| Ali Baba | 6 |
| Khao Suay | 4 |
| Ko Khun Pon Yang Kham | 1 |
| Mantra | 3 |
| PIC Kitchen | 5 |
| Seoul Grill | 2 |

**DRINKING & NIGHTLIFE**
| | |
|---|---|
| Beer Garden | 2 |
| Club Insomnia | 4 |
| Gulliver's | 1 |
| Hops Brew House | 3 |
| Hot Tuna | 5 |

**SHOPPING**
| | |
|---|---|
| Asia Books | 1 |

*Pattaya Bay*

Thailand's largest population of *katoey* (transgender females), involved in sex work, and plane-loads of Western men flock here to enjoy their services in the rash of hostess bar-beers, go-go clubs and massage parlours for which "Patpong-on-Sea" is notorious. The signs trumpeting "Viagra for Sale" say it all. Pattaya also has the largest number of **gay services** (targeted mainly at foreigners) in Thailand, with several exclusively gay hotels and an entire zone devoted to gay sex bars.

Pattaya's evolution into sin city began with the Vietnam War, when it got fat on selling sex to American servicemen. When the soldiers and sailors left in the mid-1970s, Western tourists were lured in to fill their places, and ex-servicemen soon returned to run the sort of joints they had once blown their dollars in. These days, at least half the bars and restaurants in Pattaya are Western-run. More recently, there has been an influx of criminal gangs from Germany, Russia and Japan, who reportedly find Pattaya a convenient centre for running their rackets in passport and credit-card fraud, as well as child pornography and prostitution; expat murders are a regular news item in the *Pattaya Mail*.

Local tourism authorities try hard to improve Pattaya's **image**, and with surprising success now entice families and older couples with a catalogue of more wholesome entertainments such as theme parks, golf courses, shopping plazas and year-round diving. Russian, Chinese and Korean holidaymakers seem particularly keen, and Cyrillic and Chinese scripts are now a common sight. A recent flush of more sophisticated boutique hotels and restaurants is also starting to bring in a younger Thai crowd, which has brightened the picture a little. But in truth the beach here is far from pristine – way outshone by Ko Samet just along the coast – so after-hours "entertainment" is still the primary inducement.

## Pattaya Beach

At the heart of this ever-expanding adult playground is 4km-long **Pattaya Beach**, the noisiest, most unsightly zone of the resort, crowded with yachts and tour boats and fringed by a sliver of sand and a paved beachfront walkway. The densest glut of hotels, restaurants, bars, fast-food joints, souvenir shops and tour operators is halfway down Pattaya Beach Road (also signed as Pattaya Saineung), in **Central Pattaya** (Pattaya Klang), between sois 6 and 13, but after dark the action moves to the neon zone south of Soi 13/2. Here, in **South Pattaya**, and specifically along ultra-sleazy **Walking Street**, sex is peddled in hundreds of go-go bars, discos, massage parlours and open-sided bar-beers, and the hordes of visitors treat it as a tourist sideshow. The gay district is also here, in the lanes known as **Pattayaland** sois 1, 2 and 3 (or **Boyz Town**), but actually signed as sois 13/3, 13/4 and 13/5.

## Jomtien Beach and Buddha Hill

South around the headland from South Pattaya, **Jomtien Beach** (sometimes spelt Chom Tian) is also fronted by enormous high-rises, many of them condominiums. Though the atmosphere here is not as frantic as in Pattaya, Jomtien also flounders under an excess of bar-beers and shops flogging tacky souvenirs and, like its neighbour, is forever under construction. The nicest stretch of sand is the shady **Dongtan Beach**, beyond the northern end of Jomtien Beach Road, which is also Pattaya's main gay beach, though used by all. The bulge of land behind Dongtan Beach, separating Jomtien from South Pattaya, is Khao Phra Tamnak, variously translated as **Buddha Hill** or **Pattaya Hill**, site of several posh hotels and the Pattaya Park waterpark and funfair.

## Ko Lan

7km west of South Pattaya • Ferry from Bali Hai Pier at south end of Walking Street; 7 daily; B30 • ⓦ kohlarn.com

Pattaya's main beach might not be up to much, but things get considerably better at a few offshore islands, of which **Ko Lan**, just 4km long and 2km wide, is the most

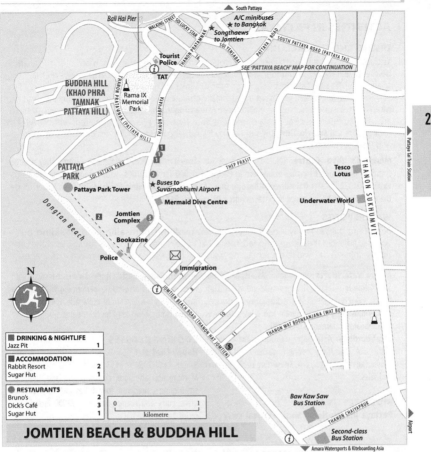

JOMTIEN BEACH & BUDDHA HILL

popular, attracting thousands of visitors each day. Several beaches on the west coast of the island boast powder-soft, white sand beaches and activities include glass-bottomed boat rides, banana boat rides, jetskis and parasailing. The last ferry returns to the mainland at 6pm, though it's also possible to arrange trips here and to other islands by speedboat; just ask at your resort.

## Underwater World

Thanon Sukhumvit, just south of the Thep Prasit junction near Tesco Lotus, behind Jomtien Beach • Daily 9am–6pm • B500 • ⓦ underwaterworldpattaya.com

If you've been disappointed with local reef life, the small and expensive but rather beautiful aquarium at **Underwater World** might make up for it, with its trio of long fibreglass tunnels that transport you through shallow rockpools to the ocean floor. There are touch pools and masses of reef fish, as well as a long roster of feeding times, detailed on the website.

## Sanctuary of Truth (Wang Boran)

Off the west end of Soi 12, Thanon Naklua, close to the Garden Sea View hotel, beyond the north end of Pattaya Beach • Daily 8am–6pm • B500 • ⓦ sanctuaryoftruth.com • From Central Pattaya take a Naklua-bound songthaew as far as Soi 12, then a motorbike taxi

2

## ACTIVITIES IN PATTAYA

### DIVING AND SNORKELLING

Though Pattaya's reefs are far less spectacular than those along the Andaman coast, they can be dived year-round, and underwater visibility is consistent. Most **dive trips** focus on the group of "outer islands" about 25km from shore, which include Ko Rin, Ko Man Wichai and Ko Klung Badaan where you have a reasonable chance of seeing barracuda, moray eels and blue-spotted stingrays. There are also three rewarding wreck dives in the Samae San/Sattahip area. Be careful when choosing a dive operator as there are plenty of charlatans around. All tour agents sell **snorkelling** trips to nearby islands, the majority of them going to the reefs and beaches of **Ko Lan**.

**Mermaid's Dive Centre** Thanon Tabphaya in Jomtien, plus three branches elsewhere in Pattaya ☏ 038 303333, ⊛ mermaidsdivecenter.com. One of the most reputable dive shops in Pattaya, with a PADI Five-Star Career Development Centre. They charge B3000 for two dives, with accompanying snorkellers paying B1000, while the four-day Open Water course costs B14,000.

### WATERSPORTS

Beachfront stalls in Pattaya and Jomtien offer **waterskiing**, **parasailing** and **jet-skiing**, but you should avoid the last-mentioned: the jet-ski jockeys are notorious for finding scratches on the machine at the end of the rental and trying to charge an exorbitant amount in damages.

**Amara Watersports** Blue Lagoon Watersports Club, Soi 14 Naa Jomtien, at the far south end of Jomtien Beach ☏ 099 239 3642, ⊛ amarawatersports.com. Windsurfing courses, rental and sales, as well as paddleboards, catamarans and kayaks.
**Kiteboarding Asia** Blue Lagoon Watersports Club, Soi 14 Naa Jomtien ☏ 085 134 9588, ⊛ bluelagoonpattaya.com. Kitesurfing courses, rental and sales.

### MUSIC FESTIVAL

**Pattaya International Music Festival** Every year in March, Pattaya hosts a three-day music festival, with live bands from across Asia performing from 6pm to midnight on the beachfront esplanade. Check with TAT (⊛ tourismthailand.com) for exact dates.

### COOKING CLASSES

**Happy Chef** 81/65 Soi 9, Nongpru, Thanon Pattaya Klang ☏ 080 809 4453, ⊛ learnthaicooking.net. Morning and afternoon classes (11am and 1pm) for small groups, preparing four dishes such as *phat thai*, green curry and *kaeng phanaeng*. B1000 including a recipe booklet.

---

The hugely ambitious **Sanctuary of Truth**, or **Wang Boran**, stands in a dramatic seaside spot behind imposing crenellated walls. Conceived by the man behind the Muang Boran Ancient City complex near Bangkok, it's a majestic 105m-high temple-palace built entirely of wood and designed to evoke the great ancient Khmer sanctuaries of Angkor. Though begun in 1981, it is ever-changing, its external walls covered in a growing gallery of beautiful, symbolic woodcarvings inspired by Cambodian, Chinese, Thai and Indian mythologies. Horse-drawn carriage and elephant rides are available in the grounds.

## ARRIVAL AND DEPARTURE PATTAYA

**By plane** Pattaya's U-Tapao Airport (☏ 038 245 595 ⊛ utapao.com) is located at the naval base near Sattahip, about 25km south of the resort. Air Asia currently operates a cheap connecting bus service between the airport and downtown Pattaya; alternatively a taxi will cost you about B1000. You can also use Bangkok's Suvarnabhumi Airport (see page 113), which is linked to Pattaya by bus. It's served by Air Asia and Bangkok Airways flights. The Bangkok Airways office is at Fairtex Arcade, North Pattaya Road (☏ 038 412 382).

Destinations Chiang Mai (3 daily; 1hr 10min); Hat Yai (daily; 1hr 20min); Ko Samui (1–2 daily; 1hr); Phuket (2 daily; 1hr 35min); Udon Thani (2 daily; 1hr 10min); Ubon Ratchathani (daily; 1hr 20min).
**By bus** All first-class and VIP Bangkok buses, and some Suvarnabhumi Airport buses, arrive at and depart from the bus station on North Pattaya Road. Slower second-class Bangkok buses and some Suvarnabhumi Airport buses use the station on Thanon Chaiyapruk in Jomtien, and there are also airport buses from a terminal on Thanon

Tabphaya in Jomtien. It's also possible to get to Pattaya direct from Isaan and the north: Nakorn Chai buses to and from Chiang Mai, Chiang Rai, Khorat and Ubon use a terminus on Thanon Sukhumvit, across from the Central Pattaya Road Intersection (☎038 424871); other Isaan buses can be found at two terminals on the opposite side of Thanon Sukhumvit and at the first-class bus station on North Pattaya Road, which has songthaews that take you south along one-way Pattaya Beach Road (B20), returning along Pattaya 2 Road. Coming by bus from Si Racha, Rayong or Trat, you'll probably get dropped on Thanon Sukhumvit, the resort's eastern limit, from where songthaews will ferry you into town (B40). If heading on to these towns, you need to pick up your bus from one of the drops on Thanon Sukhumvit (easiest at the junctions with North, Central and South Pattaya roads).

**Destinations** Bangkok (Eastern/Northern bus terminals; every 30min; 2hr 30min–4hr); Bangkok (Southern Bus Terminal; every 2hr; 3hr 30min); Bangkok (Suvarnabhumi Airport; every 30min; 2hr); Chanthaburi (4 daily; 3hr); Chiang Mai (8 daily; 12–14hr); Chiang Rai (2 daily; 15–17hr); Khorat (5 daily; 5hr); Rayong (every 30min; 1hr 30min); Si Racha (every 20min; 30min); Trat (4 daily; 4hr 30min); Ubon Ratchathani (6 daily; 10–12hr).

**By a/c minibus** In Bangkok, hostels near Khao San Road can arrange an a/c minibus service to the beach near Walking Street for B400/person; drivers pick you up from

your accommodation but may charge B100 to drop you off at your hotel or before the last stop. You can catch an a/c minibus to Bangkok's Victory Monument for B250 from several spots, including the east end of Central Pattaya Road near Foodland and South Pattaya Road in front of the Family Mart near Krung Thai Bank. Any hotel can arrange a ticket on a shared a/c minibus to Suvarnabhumi Airport for around B250/person (or about B800/car for a metered taxi). There are also tourist minibus services to Ko Samet and Ko Chang (tickets can also be booked through most tour agents): Samet Island Tour on Soi Yamato (☎038 427277, ☗malibu-samet.com) runs to the Ban Phe pier (for Ko Samet; B300 including transfer and boat but not B200 national park fee); and Pattaya 35 Group, opposite Big C on South Pattaya Road (☎038 423447 ☗35grouptour.com) goes to Ko Chang (B700 including ferry), via Ban Phe and Chanthaburi.

**By train** Pattaya is on a branch of the eastern rail line, and there's one slow train a day in each direction between the resort and Bangkok. Pattaya has two stations, both off the east side of Thanon Sukhumvit: the main one is about 500m north of the Central Pattaya Road intersection, while Pattaya Tai Station is in South Pattaya near the Thanon Thep Prasit junction. Songthaews (B30) wait at the main station to take passengers to Pattaya Beach Road; from Pattaya Tai Station a songthaew (B20) can take you along Thanon Thep Prasit to Jomtien Beach Road.

**Destinations** Bangkok (daily; 4hr); Si Racha (daily; 30min).

## INFORMATION

**Tourist information** There are municipal tourist service booths (daily roughly 8.30am–4pm) situated on the beach at the mouth of Walking Street, at City Hall on North Pattaya Road, at the north end of Jomtien Beach Road and opposite Thanon Chaiyapruk on Jomtien Beach. Note that

private tour companies also pose as "tourist information". The TAT office is inconveniently located at 609 Thanon Pratamnak between South Pattaya and Jomtien (daily 8.30am–4.30pm; ☎038 427667, ☗tatchon@tat.or.th).

## GETTING AROUND

**By songthaew** Public songthaews – known locally as baht buses, and also available to charter – circulate continuously around the resort from dawn until at least 11pm. Most follow a standard anticlockwise route up Pattaya 2 Road as far as North Pattaya Road and back down Pattaya Beach Road, for a fixed fee of B10/person; others run along the main east–west arteries of North, Central and South Pattaya roads. Songthaews to Jomtien start from next to the school on the south side of the junction of Pattaya 2 Road and South Pattaya Road and cost B10–20. Songthaews to Naklua, beyond north Pattaya, start from the north side of the same junction and head up Pattaya 2 Road (also B10–20).

**By mototaxi** Drivers in red or green vests are everywhere and offer a very open-air ride from the centre of Pattaya Beach Road to Walking Street for about B50. A helmet is not necessarily included; be sure to hold on to the rack behind you.

**By motorbike** Motorbike rental is available everywhere from B150/day, but beware of faulty vehicles, and of scams – sometimes rented bikes get stolen by touts keen to keep the customer's deposit, so you may want to use your own lock. Unpredictable drivers and a disregard for road rules makes Pattaya potentially dangerous for inexperienced riders, with frequent accidents and fatalities. Avoid wearing expensive-looking jewellery while riding a motorbike as ride-by snatchings sometimes occur.

**By taxi** Metered taxis in Pattaya often don't stop when flagged on the street, never use their meters, and charge excessive rates. You're better off downloading the Grab app and using them instead.

**By car** Avis car rental (☗avisthailand.com) has an office located inside the *Dusit Resort* (☎038 361627); many of the motorbike touts here also rent out jeeps for about B1300/day.

## ACCOMMODATION

The quietest and least sleazy end of town to stay in is **North Pattaya**, between Central Pattaya Road and North Pattaya Road (Thanon Hat Pattaya Neua) or just north of here in Naklua. There's not much in the way of budget accommodation, apart from a few hostels offering dorm rooms.

### PATTAYA BEACH AND NAKLUA

**Amari Ocean** 240 Pattaya Beach Road, North Pattaya ☎038 418418 ⓦamari.com/ocean-pattaya; map p.155. This long-standing, reliable, luxury hotel adding two new wings at the time of writing, which will offer guests a wider range of facilities. The location is ideal, at the top end of Beach Road, and the hotel boasts Pattaya's top restaurant: *Mantra* (see below). B3400

**Areca Lodge** 198/21 Soi Saisong 13 (aka Soi Diana Inn), Central Pattaya ☎038 410123, ⓦarecalodge.com; map p.155. An unusually stylish place for Pattaya, with pleasantly furnished a/c rooms in three wings built around two swimming pools. Most rooms have balconies, and all have king beds and hot showers. Buffet breakfast included. B2100

**Centara Nova Hotel** Soi 12 (aka Soi A.R. or Soi Sukrudee), Central Pattaya Road ☎038 725999, ⓦcentarahotelsresorts.com/centara/nvp; map p.155. Central, quiet and welcoming boutique hotel, done out in a plush contemporary style that features a lot of burnished gold. There's a large, attractive pool fed by an artificial waterfall, a spa that uses Dead Sea mud and salt, and a fitness centre. Breakfast included. B1600

**The Cottage** Off Pattaya 2 Road, North Pattaya ☎038 425650, ⓦthecottagepattaya.com; map p.155. Good-value, simply furnished semi-detached brick bungalows, all with a/c, hot water, TV and fridge, pleasantly set among tall trees within a mature tropical garden away from the main road but opposite the Central Centre. Facilities include two small swimming pools. B1200

**Diana Dragon Apartment** 198/16 Soi Saisong 13 (aka Soi Diana Inn), Central Pattaya ☎038 423928, ⓦdiana pattaya.co.th; map p.155. This long-running Pattaya institution has some of the cheapest doubles in town, just a few with fan and mostly a/c, and they're good value considering the competition: huge and quite light, with a breakfast included. Guests are left to their own devices, so expect a mild level of neighbour noise. Fan B400, a/c B750

**Dusit Thani Pattaya** 240/2 Pattaya Beach Road, North Pattaya ☎038 425611, ⓦdusit.com; map p.155. This luxury Thai chain hotel is one of only a few Beach Road hotels to be actually on the beach (the others are at the southern end). Sea-view rooms are worth paying extra for as the impressive panoramas take in the whole bay. Also on offer are two swimming pools, a spa and tennis courts. B2975

**Ice Inn** Corner of Saisong 12 and Pattaya 2 Road, Central Pattaya ☎038 720671, ⓦiceinnpattaya.com; map p.155. Cheap fan-cooled singles (B450) and reasonably priced a/c doubles in this small 28-room hotel behind a massage shop, a few metres from the busier bar-beer sois. Rooms are simple but are all en suite, making them some of the best value in town. B750

**Pullman Hotel G** 445/3 Moo 5, Wong Amat Beach, Thanon Pattaya-Naklua Soi 16 ☎038 411940-8, ⓦpullmanpattayahotelg.com; map p.155. Located on pretty Wong Amat Beach in Naklua, Hotel G is a chic, stylish hotel with two pools, a fitness centre and the relaxing Aisawan Spa. Rooms are equipped with all modern facilities and decorated in calming beige. Most rooms have balconies with sunset views. B4500

**The Bedrooms Hostel** 439/49 Pattaya Beach Road, near Soi 1 ☎063 395 5885, ⓦthebedroomshostelpattaya. com; map p.155. This smart hostel boasts a good location near the north end of Beach Road and a variety of rooms, including compact doubles, family bunk rooms (B2380) and well-equipped dormitories. All rooms share bathrooms. Dorms B750, doubles B1190

**Woodlands Hotel and Resort** 164 Thanon Pattaya-Naklua, North Pattaya ☎038 421707, ⓦwoodland-resort.com; map p.155. A quiet, unpretentious and welcoming family-friendly garden resort 100m north of the Dolphin Circle roundabout, and 400m from a scruffy but quiet thread of beach. The elegant, a/c rooms are in two storeys set round the pools and garden; the most expensive have direct access to the pool from ground-floor balconies. B3250

### JOMTIEN AND BUDDHA HILL

★ **Rabbit Resort** Dongtan beachfront, Jomtien ☎038 251 730, ⓦrabbitresort.com; map p.157. Beautiful place that's the most appealing option in Jomtien and located on the nicest stretch of Dongtan Beach. Most accommodation is in teakwood cottages that are elegantly furnished with Thai fabrics and antiques and have garden-style bathrooms; there are also some "forest rooms" in a two-storey block. All are set around a tropical garden and pool just metres off the beach. Breakfast included. Rooms B4900, cottages B5900

**Sugar Hut** 391/18 Thanon Tabphaya, midway between South Pattaya and Jomtien ☎038 251686, ⓦsugar-hut. com; map p.157. The most characterful accommodation in Pattaya comprises a charming collection of Ayutthaya-style traditional wooden bungalows set in a fabulously profuse garden with three swimming pools, saunas and steam rooms. The bungalows are decked out in tropical-chic style, with low beds, open-roofed shower rooms, mosquito nets and private verandas. There's a few eating options nearby, but you'll need your own transport for the 5min drive to Jomtien Beach Road or Pattaya Beach Road. B4500

## EATING

In among the innumerable low-grade Western cafés that dominate Pattaya's **restaurant scene** are a few much classier joints serving good, sophisticated cuisine – at top-end prices. For the cheapest, most authentic Thai food, just head for the nearest of Pattaya's myriad building sites and you'll find street stalls catering to the construction-site workers.

### PATTAYA BEACH

**Ali Baba** 1/13–14 Central Pattaya Road ☎038 361620 ⓦalibabarestaurantpattaya.com; map p.155. Look beyond the name and the wonderfully kitsch decor and waiters' uniforms, and you'll find some very good Indian food, which keeps many of Pattaya's visitors from the subcontinent happy. There's an authentically long menu of vegetarian dishes, featuring plenty of cheese and some interesting starters with okra; in addition, the butter chicken's a real winner (B280). Daily 11am–midnight.

**Khao Suay** Ground Floor, Central Marina, Pattaya 2 Road, North Pattaya; map p.155. A long menu of good modern Thai food (most mains B140–220) draws Thai families to this tiny café inside the shopping centre. The varied English menu includes *kaeng tai pla* (southern Thai fish stomach curry) and *nam prik pla thuu* (chilli relish with mackerel). The tasty one-meal rice dishes (B80) make for great solo dining. Daily 11am–9.45pm.

**Ko Khun Pon Yang Kham** North Pattaya Road, at Soi 6 ☎038 420571; map p.155. This garden restaurant offers Thailand's equivalent of wagyu beef, from pampered Pon Yang Kham cows that are bred (from French, Swiss and Thai breeds) and reared in Isaan. It's served northeastern-style too, so no chips or mustard, but it goes well with *som tam*, and the red wine is decent (B150/glass). B185 for a small but delicious portion of sirloin on a sizzling-hot plate. Daily 5.30pm–midnight.

★**Mantra** Amari Orchid Hotel, Beach Road, North Pattaya ☎038 429591, ⓦmantra-pattaya.com; map p.155. Setting the standard unexpectedly high for Pattaya, this large, beautifully designed bar-restaurant creates an ambience somewhere between a contemporary Shanghai hotel and a maharaja's palace. Downstairs there's an open-plan view of the seven different, equally eclectic kitchens specializing in Japanese, Chinese, Indian, Mediterranean and Western food, grills and seafood. A meal might begin with a California maki roll (B520), supplemented with Hong Kong barbecued duck (B320), continue with lamb shanks in Merlot sauce (B820), and end with a baked mango and glutinous rice parcel with coconut ice cream (B350). The dress code is no shorts, tank tops or sandals. Daily 6pm–1am; Sunday brunch 11am–3pm.

**PIC Kitchen** Soi 5, North Pattaya ☎038 428374, ⓦpic-kitchen.com; map p.155. Set in a simple, traditional, Thai house, this place serves up consistently delicious food, such as *matsaman* curry with chicken (B220). Daily 11am–10pm.

**Seoul Grill** The One Patio, next to Burger King, Pattaya 2 Road, North Pattaya ☎038 411982 ⓦthebimimbab. com; map p.155. Long streams of Korean visitors to Pattaya keep the dishes authentic at this clean, two-level spot with classics such as bibimbap (meat and vegetable rice bowls), hot pots and Korean barbecue. There are half a dozen other Korean and Japanese restaurants in the same outdoor plaza. Daily 11am–11pm.

### JOMTIEN BEACH

**Bruno's** 306/63 Chateau Dale Plaza, Thanon Tabphaya, Jomtien ☎038 364600–1, ⓦbrunos-pattaya.com; map p.157. A local institution that's a favourite with expats celebrating special occasions. The food is upmarket, expensive and European – rack of lamb, sirloin steak, chocolate soufflé with passion fruit sauce – and there's a cellar of some 150 wines. Main dishes from B290. Daily noon–2.30pm & 6pm–late.

**Dick's Café** 413/129 Thanon Tabphaya, Jomtien ☎038 252417, ⓦdickscafe.com; map p.157. Located on Jomtien's Walking Street beside the Jomtien Complex, Dick's serves excellent Thai and Western food such as chicken breast with garlic rice (B250) in a cosy atmosphere. They also offer sandwiches and cakes, as well as a good range of imported wines and spirits. Daily 10am–1am.

**Sugar Hut** 391/18 Thanon Tabphaya, Jomtien; map p.157. Attached to the charming hotel of the same name (see page 160), this restaurant gives you the chance to soak up the ambience and enjoy the tropical gardens without shelling out for a bungalow. Meals are served in an open-sided *sala* and the menu is mainly classy Thai; recommendations include roast duck in red curry (B280). Live music from 7pm–11pm. Daily 8am–11pm.

## DRINKING AND NIGHTLIFE

Pattaya's **nightlife** revolves around sex (see page 162). It is, however, just about possible to have a night out without getting entangled in sleaze, at one of the growing number of hostess-free **bars** listed below, a few of which are surprisingly style-conscious. However you choose to spend your evening, be warned that Pattaya is notorious for female and *katoey* (transgender female) **pickpockets**, who target drunk men walking home in the early hours: while one "distracts" the victim from the front, the other extracts the wallet from behind.

**Beer Garden** Central Marina, Pattaya 2 Road, North Pattaya; map p.155. Outdoor tables, draught beer and live music nightly (from about 8pm) from Thai singers and bands, doing mostly Thai pop and country. Also serves a full

**2**

## PATTAYA'S SEX INDUSTRY

Of the thousand-plus bars in Pattaya, the vast majority are staffed by women and men whose aim is to get bought for the night – depending on whom you believe, there are between six thousand and twenty thousand Thais (and quite a few Russians) working in Pattaya's **sex industry**; most depressing of all is that this workforce includes children as young as 10, despite fairly frequent high-profile paedophile arrests. The vast majority of Pattaya's bars are open-air "**bar-beers**", which group themselves in neon clusters all over North, Central and South Pattaya so that there's barely a 500m stretch of road without a rowdy enclave. The setup is the same in all of them: from mid-afternoon the punters – usually lone males – sit on stools around a brashly lit circular bar, behind which the hostesses (and their high-end versions, the "coyotes") keep the drinks, bawdy chat and well-worn jokes flowing. Where prices aren't established, this is open to a well-known scam of demanding an inflated bill at the end, with threats if the client doesn't cough up.

Drinks are a lot more expensive in the bouncer-guarded **go-go bars** on Walking Street in South Pattaya, where near-naked hostesses serve the beer and live sex shows keep the boozers hooked through the night. The scene follows much the same pattern as in Patpong, Nana and Soi Cowboy in Bangkok, with the women dancing on a small stage in the hope they might be bought for the night – or the week. Go-go dancers, "modelling competitions", shower shows and striptease are also the mainstays of the **gay scene**, centred on Pattayaland Soi 3 (Soi 13/5), South Pattaya.

menu of Thai food (dishes from about B120), with Isaan and seafood specialities. Daily 5pm–2am.

**Club Insomnia** Walking Street, South Pattaya ☎038 711322, ⓦclubinsomniagroup.com; map p.155. Currently Pattaya's most popular dance club, where you can get you in the mood at the downstairs iBar before heading upstairs to party untill late. It gets very crowded at weekends, so watch out for pickpockets. Daily 6pm–4am.

**Gulliver's** Pattaya Beach Road, near Soi 1 ☎038 416680, ⓦgulliverbangkok.com; map p.155. This large venue is more bar than restaurant – though there are plenty of tempting dishes on the menu – it's the place to go to watch sports on TV, have a game of pool, or just hang out people-watching while enjoying a cocktail (around B180) or pint of Guinness (B260). Choose between the spacious terrace and a/c interior. Daily 3pm–2am.

**Hops Brew House** Pattaya Beach Road, between sois 13/1 (Yamato) and 13/2 (Post Office), Central Pattaya ☎038 710653; map p.155. Cavernous and very popular a/c beer hall that brews its own beer, serves generous wood-fired pizzas and other Italian dishes, and stages live music nightly. Attracts a youngish crowd, including vacationing couples. Daily 2pm–1/2am.

**Hot Tuna** Walking Street, South Pattaya; map p.155. This open-sided bar hosts live music every night, with occasional appearances by Thai rock guitarist Lam Morrison. Most nights you'll hear covers of rock classics from bands like the Eagles and The Doors. Daily 6pm–3am.

**Jazz Pit** At the Sugar Hut Resort, 391/18 Thanon Tabphaya, Jomtien ☎038 364186; map p.157. Now moved from its location at PIC Kitchen, Pattaya's premier jazz bar is worth checking out in its new location, where Thai and Western musicians perform slick renditions of jazz classics. Weds–Mon 6pm–10pm.

## ENTERTAINMENT

### CINEMAS

There are several English-language screenings a day at the multiplex cinemas.

**Major Cineplex** The Avenue shopping centre, Pattaya 2 Road, Central Pattaya ⓦmajorcineplex.com.

**SF Cinema City** Central Festival, Pattaya Beach Road, Central Pattaya ⓦsfcinemacity.com.

### KATOEY CABARETS

Tour groups – and families – constitute the main audience at Pattaya's *katoey* cabarets. Glamorous and highly professional, each theatre has a troupe of sixty or more

transgender women who run through twenty musical-style numbers in fishnets and crinolines, ball gowns and leathers, against ever more lavish stage sets. Any tour agent can organize tickets or you can book at the venue.

**Alcazar** Opposite Soi 4 on Pattaya 2 Road in North Pattaya ⓦalcazarthailand.com. From B600. Daily 5pm, 6.30pm, 8pm & 9.30pm.

**Tiffany's** North of Soi 1 on Pattaya 2 Road in North Pattaya ⓦtiffany.cloudapp.net. Also hosts an annual international *katoey* beauty pageant over five days in March, Miss International Queen (ⓦmissinternationalqueen.com). From B800. Daily 6pm, 7.30pm & 9pm.

## SHOPPING

**Asia Books** Floor 3, Central Festival Centre, between Pattaya Beach and Pattaya 2 Roads; map p.155. This third-floor bookshop offers a good selection of English-language books. Daily 11am–11pm.

## DIRECTORY

**Emergencies** For all emergencies, call the tourist police on ☏ 1155 (free, 24hr) or contact them at their office (☏ 038 429 371) beside TAT on Buddha Hill, between South Pattaya and Jomtien; in the evenings, they also set up a post at the north end of Walking Street.

**Hospitals and dentists** The best-equipped hospital is the private Bangkok–Pattaya Hospital (☏ 1719 or ☏ 038 259 999, ⊚ bangkokpattayahospital.com) on Thanon Sukhumvit, about 400m north of the intersection with North Pattaya Road, which also has dental services.

**Immigration office** Soi 5, off Jomtien Beach Road, Jomtien (Daily 8.30am–4.30pm; ☏ 038 252751–4).

# Ban Phe

The small coastal town of **BAN PHE**, which lies 17km east of Rayong, its provincial capital, and about 200km from Bangkok, is the port for Ko Samet. Several piers for Samet boats compete for attention here, along with minimarkets, internet centres and tour desks selling onward bus tickets and private transfers. Ban Phe's main street runs from west to east behind the seafront, passing in turn the Chok Krisda pier and the nearby Taruaphe pier, before petering out a few hundred metres later at the municipal pier, Tha Reua Tessaban.

## ARRIVAL AND INFORMATION                           BAN PHE

When the time comes to leave Ko Samet, you can book tickets for any of the following direct buses and minibuses from Ban Phe through your hotel on the island.

**By bus** There are direct a/c buses operated by Cherdchai between Bangkok's Eastern (Ekamai) Bus Terminal and Ban Phe; on departure from Ban Phe, you can easily find them near the municipal pier. Coming by bus from Chanthaburi or Trat, you'll be dropped at a T-junction on Highway 3, from where a songthaew or motorbike taxi will take you the remaining 2km to the Ban Phe piers. Rayong has a wider choice of buses, including services to Chiang Mai and Isaan; the Ban Phe piers are served by frequent songthaews (about 30min) from Rayong bus station.

Destinations Bangkok (14 daily; 3hr); Chanthaburi (from Highway 3; 6 daily; 1hr 30min); Trat (from Highway 3; 6 daily; 3hr).

**By a/c minibus** A/c minibuses run between many locations in Bangkok, including Thanon Khao San (3–4hr; B250), Victory Monument (about 3hr 30min; B200) and Suvarnabhumi Airport (about 3hr; B500), and Ban Phe. There are also services from Pattaya (see page 158) and Ko Chang (see page 179). On departure, you'll find numerous a/c minibus companies in Ban Phe, including some at the municipal pier and in the two sois opposite Taruaphe (including Pattaya and Ko Chang services), on either side of a 7-Eleven, and a frequent Victory Monument service runs from 200m west of the municipal pier.

**By boat** Frequent boats run from Ban Phe to Ko Samet, leaving from various piers – Tha Reua Tessaban has the widest choice. Details are given in our Ko Samet coverage (see page 167).

**Tourist police** At the municipal pier ☏ 038 611 227 or ☏ 1155.

## ACCOMMODATION

**Ban Phe Hostel** In the lane next to the 7-Eleven opposite the Taruaphe pier ☏ 082 244 2241, ⊚ hostel world.com. This simple but clean hostel is a good choice for comfortable accommodation if you get stuck in Ban Phe, offering a couple of doubles and a couple of dorms, all with shared bathrooms. There's a sociable communal area and bar for guests to use, too. Doubles B400, dorms B200

# Ko Samet

B200 national park admission fee

Blessed with the softest, squeakiest sand within weekending distance of Bangkok, the tiny island of **KO SAMET**, which measures just 6km from top to toe, is a favourite escape for Thais, expats and tourists. Its fourteen small but dazzlingly white beaches

2

are breathtakingly beautiful, lapped by pale blue water and in places still shaded by coconut palms and occasional white-flowered cajeput (*samet*) trees, which gave the island its name and which are used to build boats. But they are also crowded – although on weekdays there's a lot more room to breathe and relax – and developed to full capacity with over fifty sprawling, albeit low-rise, bungalow developments, a disfiguring number of which pay scant attention to landscaping and rubbish disposal. It's a sobering state of affairs considering that much of the island's coastline has been protected as part of the Khao Laem Ya – Mu Ko Samet **national park** since 1981; all

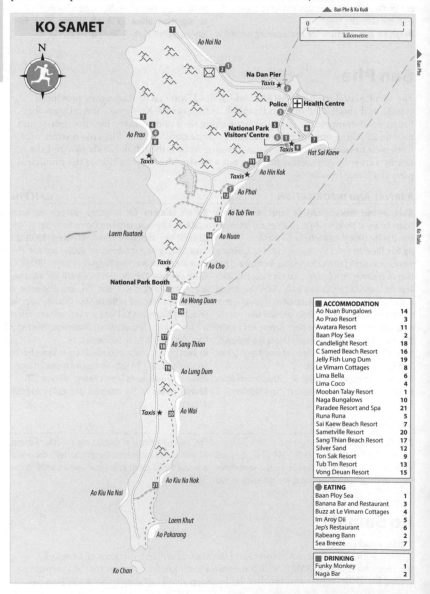

**KO SAMET**

Ban Phe & Ko Kudi

0          1
kilometre

Ban Phe

Ko Thalu

Ao Noi Na

Na Dan Pier
Taxis

Police    Health Centre

National Park
Visitors' Centre
Taxis

Ao Prao

Taxis

Hat Sai Kaew

Taxis

Ao Hin Kok

Ao Phai

Ao Tub Tim

Laem Ruataek

Ao Nuan

Taxis

Ao Cho

**National Park Booth**

Ao Wong Duan

Ao Sang Thian

Ao Lung Dum

Taxis

Ao Wai

Ao Kiu Na Nok

Ao Kiu Na Nai

Laem Khut

Ao Pakarang

Ko Chan

| ■ ACCOMMODATION | |
|---|---|
| Ao Nuan Bungalows | 14 |
| Ao Prao Resort | 3 |
| Avatara Resort | 11 |
| Baan Ploy Sea | 2 |
| Candlelight Resort | 18 |
| C Samed Beach Resort | 16 |
| Jelly Fish Lung Dum | 19 |
| Le Vimarn Cottages | 8 |
| Lima Bella | 6 |
| Lima Coco | 4 |
| Mooban Talay Resort | 1 |
| Naga Bungalows | 10 |
| Paradee Resort and Spa | 21 |
| Runa Runa | 5 |
| Sai Kaew Beach Resort | 7 |
| Sametville Resort | 20 |
| Sang Thian Beach Resort | 17 |
| Silver Sand | 12 |
| Ton Sak Resort | 9 |
| Tub Tim Resort | 13 |
| Vong Deuan Resort | 15 |

| ● EATING | |
|---|---|
| Baan Ploy Sea | 1 |
| Banana Bar and Restaurant | 3 |
| Buzz at Le Vimarn Cottages | 4 |
| Im Aroy Dii | 5 |
| Jep's Restaurant | 6 |
| Rabeang Bann | 2 |
| Sea Breeze | 7 |

| ■ DRINKING | |
|---|---|
| Funky Monkey | 1 |
| Naga Bar | 2 |

**WATERSPORTS AND BOAT TRIPS ON SAMET**

Samet has no decent coral reefs of its own, so you'll have to take a boat trip to the islands of Ko Kudi and Ko Thalu, off the northeast coast, to get good **snorkelling** (around B700 from most beaches) or **diving**. From the main beaches you can also organize **boat trips** around Samet itself (around B500), rent kayaks, jet skis and paddle boards, and arrange banana-boat rides and parasailing.

**Samed Resorts Diving Centre** Ao Prao ☎038 644100–3, ⊛ samedresorts.com. B2000 for one dive, and B17,000 for the four-day PADI Open Water course.

visitors to Ko Samet are required to pay the standard national park fee on arrival, and you should keep your ticket to show if you pass another checkpoint. Most hoteliers also pay rent to park authorities, but there's little evidence that this income has been used to improve the island's infrastructure.

Samet's best **beaches** are along the **east coast**, where you'll find nearly all the bungalow resorts, though there's one rather exclusive beach on the west coast, and the north-coast shoreline retains a pleasing village ambience. Most islanders and many resort staff live in the northeast, near the island's main pier, in the ramshackle, badly drained village of **Na Dan**, which has small shops and cheap food stalls as well as Samet's only school, health centre and wat. Na Dan's high street, which runs from the pier down to Hat Sai Kaew, is paved, as are the island's other main routes – heading south down the island's forested central ridge, west to Ao Prao and along the northwest coast. Much of the **interior** is dense jungle, home to hornbills, gibbons and spectacular butterflies. The evergreen vegetation belies the fact that there are no rivers on this unusually dry island, which gets only scant rainfall in an average year. Lack of rain is another plus point for tourists, though it means water is a precious and expensive commodity as it has to be trucked in from the mainland.

The most backpacker-oriented beaches are east-coast **Ao Hin Kok**, **Ao Phai** and **Ao Tub Tim**, with Ao Hin Kok and Ao Phai both quite lively in the evenings; the travellers' vibe at nearby **Ao Nuan** is more alternative, with **Ao Sang Thian** and north-coast **Ao Noi Na** also worth investigating. **Hat Sai Kaew** and **Ao Wong Duan** are the busiest beaches on the east coast, dominated by upper-scale accommodation aimed at families, package tourists and Bangkok trendies. Samet's super-deluxe accommodation is on west-coast **Ao Prao** and southern beauty **Ao Kiu**.

Shops and stalls in Na Dan (which has a pharmacy) and on all the main beaches sell basic travellers' necessities. Many bungalows have **safety deposits** and it's worth making use of them: theft is an issue on Samet and there are occasional instances of drinks being spiked by freelance bar-girls, and punters waking next day without their valuables.

## Na Dan and Hat Sai Kaew

From **NA DAN** pier, a ten-minute walk south along the high street brings you to **HAT SAI KAEW**, or Diamond Beach, named for its long and extraordinarily beautiful stretch of luxuriant sand, so soft and clean it squeaks underfoot – a result, apparently, of its unusually high silicon content. Unsurprisingly, it's the busiest beach on Samet, its shorefront packed with bungalows, restaurants, beachwear stalls, deckchairs and parasols, though the northern end is slightly more peaceful.

## Ao Hin Kok

Separated from Hat Sai Kaew by a low promontory on which sits a mermaid statue (a reference to the early nineteenth-century poem, *Phra Abhai Mani*, by famous local poet

Sunthorn Phu), **AO HIN KOK** is much smaller than its neighbour, and has more of a travellers' vibe. Just three sets of bungalows overlook the petite white-sand beach from the slope on the far side of the dirt road, and you can walk here from Na Dan in about fifteen minutes.

## Ao Phai

Narrow but sparkling little **AO PHAI**, around the next headland from Ao Hin Kok, is Samet's party beach, where the shoreside *Silver Sand* bar and disco is known for its late-night dance music (with a strong gay presence at weekends). Not everyone has to join in though, as the bungalows on the fringes of the bay are far enough away for a good night's sleep. There's a minimarket on the beach, and you can walk to Na Dan pier in twenty minutes.

## Ao Tub Tim

Also known as Ao Pudsa, **AO TUB TIM** is another cute white-sand bay sandwiched between rocky points, partly shaded with palms and backed by a wooded slope. It has just two bungalow operations and is only a short stroll from Ao Phai and the other beaches further north, and a half-hour hike from Na Dan pier.

## Ao Nuan

Clamber up over the headland from Ao Tub Tim (which gives you a fine panorama over Hat Sai Kaew) to reach Samet's smallest and most laid-back beach, the secluded **AO NUAN**, effectively the private domain of *Ao Nuan Bungalows* (see page 169). Because it's some way off the main track, the beach gets hardly any through-traffic and feels quiet and private. Although not brilliant for swimming, the rocky shore reveals a good patch of sand when the tide withdraws; the more consistent beach at Ao Tub Tim is only five minutes' walk to the north, and **Ao Cho**, which has some coral, is a five-minute walk south along the footpath.

## Ao Wong Duan

The crescent-moon bay of **AO WONG DUAN**, a ten-minute walk round the next-but-one point from Ao Nuan, is Samet's second most popular beach after Hat Sai Kaew, but the mood is calmer and more family oriented while the water is still clear and the backdrop of trees gives plenty of shade. It offers some attractive upmarket accommodation; most guests are either Chinese and Russian package tourists, Pattaya overnighters, or weekending Bangkokians. Although the beach is fairly long and broad, the central shorefront is almost lost under a knot of tiny bars (many with irresistibly comfy armchairs) and tourist shops, and the main stretch of beach all but disappears at high tide. Facilities include minimarkets and ATMs.

## Ao Sang Thian (Candlelight Beach) and Ao Lung Dum

A favourite with Thai students, who relish the beauty of its slightly wild setting, **AO SANG THIAN** ("Candlelight Beach") and contiguous Ao Lung Dum display almost none of the commerce of Wong Duan, a couple of minutes' walk over the hill, though the scenic shorefront is fronted by an unbroken line of bungalows. The narrow, white-sand coastline is dotted with wave-smoothed rocks and partitioned by larger outcrops that create several distinct bays; as it curves outwards to the south you get a great view of the island's east coast. At its southern end, Ao Sang Thian becomes **AO LUNG DUM**, and the various little bungalow outfits fringing the shore here are pretty similar.

## Ao Wai

A fifteen-minute walk along the coast path from Lung Dum brings you to **AO WAI**, a very pretty white-sand bay, partially shaded and a good size considering it supports just one (large) **bungalow** operation, *Sametville Resort* (see page 169), which also spills across on to neighbouring little Ao Hin Kleang.

## Ao Kiu

About a kilometre south of Ao Wai, the gorgeous little twin bays of **AO KIU** – Ao Kiu Na Nok on the east coast and Ao Kiu Na Nai on the west – are separated by just a few hundred metres of land. Both beaches are the domain of Samet's most exclusive hotel, the *Paradee Resort and Spa* (see page 169).

## Ao Prao (Paradise Bay)

On the upper west coast, the rugged, rocky coastline only softens into beach once, at **AO PRAO**, also known as Paradise Bay, some 4km north of Ao Kiu Na Nai. This is Samet's most upmarket beach, dominated by two expensively elegant resorts, plus one slightly more affordable option, and nothing else to lower the tone. A paved road branches off to here from the main road heading south down the island, passing a large reservoir along the way. If staying on Ao Prao, your hotel will arrange boat transfers to Ban Phe on the mainland.

## Ao Noi Na

West of Na Dan, the island's north coast – known simply as **AO NOI NA** even though it's not strictly a single bay – has a refreshingly normal village feel compared to the rest of Samet. There are an increasing number of places to stay along the narrow coastal road here, offering serene views across the water to the mainland hills behind Ban Phe, and just one white-sand beach of note at the far western end. Though this beach has been hogged by the luxurious *Mooban Talay Resort* (see page 170), it's not private and you can either walk there from Na Dan pier in about twenty-five minutes or ride by motorbike in five minutes, passing a good **restaurant** at Baan Ploy Sea (see page 170) en route.

---

### ARRIVAL AND DEPARTURE                                                              KO SAMET

The port of departure for Ko Samet is **Ban Phe** (see page 163). It helps to know where you are staying on your first night as this will determine your method of arrival; if you arrive without plans, you'll be besieged by touts and drivers looking for a commission. Once settled, all resorts, hotels and guest houses can help with onward travel, whether bus tickets to Bangkok or eastward travel towards Cambodia.

#### BY BOAT

#### RESORT BOATS

If you're staying in any of Samet's mid-range or expensive accommodation, ask the resort about boats when you book: many establishments have their own big boats or speedboats to ferry you direct from Ban Phe on reasonably priced shared transfers (usually at set times). Such transfers may be free, but a few resorts make their paid transfers compulsory. You might also want to look into the packages offered by many resorts, which is how most Thais travel to Ko Samet: as well as boats and accommodation, these might include things like dinners and massages.

#### PUBLIC BOATS

There are half a dozen competing piers in Ban Phe, offering a bewildering variety of speedboats and bigger, slower but much cheaper wooden boats; prices on the latter to Samet's main pier, Na Dan, are fixed (B50 one-way; 40min). Blue wooden boats direct to Ao Wong Duan are run by Malibu Travel (B70 one-way; 70min) from the Taruaphe pier. Watch out for rip-off touts in Ban Phe who try to sell boat tickets at inflated prices or falsely claim that visitors to Ko Samet have to buy a return boat ticket. The first boat from Ko Samet back to Ban Phe leaves Na Dan pier at 7am (from Ao Wong Duan at 8.30am, noon and 3.30pm), and in theory there's then an hourly service across to Ban Phe until 6pm, but if you have a plane to catch you should allow for boat no-shows and delays.

**Tha Reua Tessaban** The municipal pier at the east end of Ban Phe has a rather chaotic market hall of a dozen or so private booths which offer the widest choice of speedboats, as well as wooden boats (in high season, hourly to Na Dan, plus three daily to Ao Wong Duan for B70).

**Chok Krisda** About 500m west of Tha Reua Tessaban, this helpful pier (☎ 081 862 4067) offers speedboats (B1500/ boat to Na Dan; 15min) as well as wooden boats hourly to Na Dan (8am–6pm) and Ao Wong Duan (2 daily, 3 daily in the opposite direction; 70min; B70).

## GETTING AROUND

A good way to explore the island is by walking south along the east-coast beaches and the narrow trails over headlands that connect them. This allows you to check out the mood of each beach and decide which is best for you. Now that the main roads are paved, it's also easy to explore by motorbike, though the sidetracks to beaches are bumpy and hazardous, so take care. Otherwise, there are shared taxis that run up and down the main road on the east coast, and waiting at stops marked on the map (see page 164).

**By songthaew** Fleets of green songthaews wait for fares at the Na Dan pier and half a dozen other stands around the island, as marked on our map (see page 164); they will also pick up from accommodation if you get staff to phone them, but rates are high. You'll generally be charged for chartering the whole vehicle (Na Dan pier to Ao Sang Thian B350; Ao Wong Duan to Hat Sai Kaew B200). Only if there's a large group of people travelling, for example when boats dock at Na Dan, will you get the "shared" rates (B20–B100/person, depending where you are going and how many passengers there are).

**By motorbike** Motorbikes are available for rent all over the island for B300–B500/day. Check that things like brakes and lights work OK as there are several steep hills to negotiate, and side tracks are treacherous.

## ACCOMMODATION

The trend across the island is upmarket, and in high season you'll be hard pressed to secure an en-suite **bungalow** for under B800, though a few B400 dorm beds are available. All beaches get packed on weekends and national holidays, when booking ahead is advisable, though, unusually for Thailand, walk-in guests are often offered the best rates. Many bungalow managers raise their **prices** by sixty percent during peak periods and sometimes on weekends as well: the rates quoted here are typical weekday high-season rates. Keep in mind that on the far-flung beaches, your eating options are limited.

### HAT SAI KAEW AND NA DAN

Much of the accommodation on Hat Sai Kaew is crammed uncomfortably close together and prices are high. Cheaper rooms are available at places like Runa Runa on the main street from Na Dan.

**Lima Bella** Na Dan ☎ 038 644222, ⓦ limaresort.co.th; map p.164. This little garden haven occupies a quiet heliconia-filled plot with its own pretty swimming pool, on the semicircular road that arcs round behind and to the east of Na Dan high street. Its 26 design-conscious a/c rooms all have hot water, fridges, TVs and daybeds; some have separate mezzanine bedrooms or living areas and many have bathtubs. The ambience is more intimate and private than most hotels on Samet and it's popular with families. Breakfast included. B3000

**Runa Runa** On the west side of the main street from Na Dan to Hat Sai Kaew, about halfway along. ☎ 038 644306; map p.164. In the heart of the action and just a few minutes' walk from Na Dan pier, this hostel is a clean, cheap base if you're likely to be out most of the time. Smallish doubles and dorms with shared bathrooms, plus a small communal area. Dorms B500, doubles B750

**Sai Kaew Beach Resort** Hat Sai Kaew ☎ 038 644197, ⓦ samedresorts.com; map p.164. This popular and highly efficient resort has over 150 a/c rooms with hot water, TV and fridge, most of them in distinctive and thoughtfully designed bungalows in bright primary colours. Choose between the poolside villas in the 'hip zone', rooms with balconies/terraces in the 'hub zone', or the deluxe cottages in the 'hide zone' on the quiet Laluna beach. Free daily yoga classes. B6500

**Ton Sak Resort** Hat Sai Kaew ☎ 038 644314, ⓦ tonsak. com; map p.164. The timbered cabins here are packed very close together, but the surrounding borders of shrubs add a little privacy, and few are more than 100m from the water. Interiors are comfortable if a little old-fashioned, and have a/c and modern hot-water bathrooms. It's worth paying a bit extra for deluxe rooms, away from the frantic beachfront. Breakfast included. B2300

### AO HIN KOK

**Avatara Resort** Ao Hin Kok ☎ 038 644 112–3; map p.164. This stylish new resort has taken over the hillside formerly occupied by Jep's Bungalows, and perhaps more importantly, the hugely popular restaurant beachfront restaurant, which, for the moment at least, still bears Jep's name. A few of the old bungalows remain at the bottom of the hill, but the smart new rooms are in a block on the hillside, with a/c, hot water and efficient service. Bungalows B1200, rooms B3500

**Naga Bungalows** Ao Hin Kok ☎ 038 644035 ⓦ naga bungalows.com; map p.164. Long-running, basic resort, with a beachfront bar, a secondhand bookshop, and a currency exchange. Simple bamboo and wood huts are stacked in tiers up the slope, with decks, mosquito nets and shared bathrooms, as well as pricier concrete a/c rooms with their own adjacent hot-water bathroom. There is bar noise quite late and the compound's a bit scrappy, but the rooms are reasonably well maintained. Fan B600, a/c B1500

## AO PHAI
**Silver Sand** Middle of Ao Phai ☎038 644300–1, ⓦsilversandsamed.com; map p.164. This party hub has a spread of well-turned-out rooms, including whitewashed chalets set around a pretty garden; they all come with safety boxes, verandas and good modern hot-water bathrooms, and some have polished wooden floors. An ideal base if you plan to party, as it's not far to stagger from the bar to bed. B2500

## AO TUB TIM
**Tub Tim Resort** Ao Tub Tim ☎038 644 025–9, ⓦtubtim resort.com; map p.164. The most popular place to stay on Ao Tub Tim is a sprawling, well-run resort with over a hundred handsome chalet-style wooden bungalows of various sizes and designs, all with classy modern furnishings and outdoor space, plus a good restaurant. The cheapest rooms are in a concrete block on the hill; they're a decent size and have a shared veranda. Breakfast is included in a/c rooms. Fan B600, a/c B2000

## AO NUAN
★ **Ao Nuan Bungalows** Ao Nuan ☎038 644 334; map p.164. The octagonal restaurant and simple, idiosyncratic huts here hark back to a mellower, old-school island vibe, entirely removed from the commercialism and party-goers of the other beaches. The eleven sturdy timber huts are each built to a slightly different design and dotted across the tree-covered slope that drops down to the gorgeous, tiny bay, with a few hanging right over the beach, making it feel like just yours. Sharing bathrooms, the cheapest are large but spartan, with just a platform bed and a mosquito net; the most expensive boast a/c and hot water. What really makes this place, though, is the caring and competent family that run it. Wi-fi in restaurant area only. Fan B800, a/c B1500

## AO WONG DUAN
**Vong Deuan Resort** Middle of Ao Wong Duan ☎091 234 7770, ⓦvrresortkohsamed.com; map p.164. Ideally located in the middle of the beach, with attractive a/c bungalows in various designs set around a pretty tropical garden, including nice white cottages with thatched roofs, contemporary styled interiors and garden bathrooms (with hot showers). Service is efficient, attentive and hotel-like, which makes it a favourite with older guests. Breakfast included. B2700
**C Samed Beach Resort** Southern Ao Wong Duan ☎038 644260, ⓦthecsamed.com; map p.164. Occupying a big chunk of the bay's southern end, this resort features over fifty rooms, all of them with safes and a/c. The spacious cottages are whitewashed timber huts built on stilts, with

picture windows, decks and modern furnishings, divided into four types; standard, superior, seaview and beachfront, though interiors are all similar. There's also an attractive restaurant deck jutting out over the water, and kayaks and snorkelling equipment for rent. B2850

## AO SANG THIAN
**Candlelight Resort** Ao Sang Thian ☎098 979 7910; map p.164. Simple wooden bungalows strung out in a long line, each one facing the water. All have a/c, hot showers and TVs but not much in terms of furnishings; there's no restaurant here either. One of the quietest spots on the island, on weekdays at least. B1200
**Sang Thian Beach Resort** Towards Ao Sang Thian's northern end ☎038 644 255, ⓦsangthianbeachresort. com; map p.164. This efficiently-run complex, comprising a shop and an expansive waterfront restaurant area, stands in stark contrast to the minimalism of the neighbouring Candlelight Resort. It boasts tasteful a/c timber chalets built up the cliffside on a series of decks and steps – the decor is navy-and-white maritime chic. There's hot water, TVs and fridges, and views, mostly encompassing the sea, are above average for the area. B2500

## AO LUNG DUM
**Jelly Fish Lung Dum** Ao Lung Dum ☎081 458 8430 or ☎081 652 8056; map p.164. Friendly spot under the bougainvillaea with a decent waterside restaurant. Most of the twenty bungalows with hot showers are right on the rocky shore, practically overhanging the water; a few cheaper rooms and bungalows at the back are also available. Fan B900, a/c B1300

## AO WAI
★ **Sametville Resort** Ao Wai ☎038 651 681-2, ⓦsametvilleresort.com; map p.164. This sizeable resort actually occupies two bays, both Ao Wai and Ao Hin Kleang; since Ao Wai is one of Samed's prettiest beaches, it gets full at weekends. There's a large swimming pool and bungalows of all kinds, all surrounded by greenery and plenty of different designs to choose from, including a cute converted boat; there's a detailed map of the resort on their website. Fortunately there's also a decent restaurant, as it's a bit of a walk to anywhere else. Fan B1400, a/c B2000

## AO KIU
**Paradee Resort and Spa** Ao Kiu ☎038 644285–7, ⓦwww.samedresorts.com; map p.164. Top of the range on Samet, a very luxurious five-star resort where each of the forty villas stretches over more than 100 square metres and most have their own small private pools. There's also an infinity-edged main pool, a spa and fitness centre, plus lots of nice little extras like DVD players, free kayaks and snorkelling equipment. B17,500

2

### AO PRAO (PARADISE BAY)

**Ao Prao Resort** Ao Prao ☎038 644101, ⓦwww. samedresorts.com; map p.164. Fifty luxurious wooden chalets and rooms set in a mature tropical garden that slopes down to the beach, all with a/c, TVs and minibars. There's an infinity pool, a dive centre, windsurfing and kayaking, among lots of watersports, and a picturesquely sited restaurant with a live band most evenings in high season. The resort runs a shuttle boat from Ban Phe three times a day (11am, 1pm and 4pm; free for guests). B6850

**Le Vimarn Cottages** Ao Prao ☎038 644104, ⓦ www. samedresorts.com; map p.164. The most indulgent resort on this beach comprises charming, gorgeously furnished cottages, a delightful spa and an infinity pool. Its *Buzz* restaurant (see opposite) is highly regarded. B9000

**Lima Coco** Ao Prao ☎038 644068, ⓦlimaresort.co.th; map p.164. The youngest, trendiest and cheapest choice on the beach, with lots of white walls, brightly coloured cushions, day beds and decks. Rooms are built close together up the side of the hill, so most have some kind of a sea view. Kayaks, snorkels and sun beds for rent. Breakfast included. B3390

### AO NOI NA

**Baan Ploy Sea** Ao Noi Na ☎02 438 9771–2, ⓦwww. samedresorts.com; map p.164. Striking, brown contemporary building with an orange infinity pool, where bedrooms done out in dark wood and orange come with a/c, rain showers, TV and fridge. Pricier options come with a sea-view deck, and there's a good, relaxing seafood restaurant (see below) on the beachfront. Breakfast and boat transfers included. B4400

**Mooban Talay Resort** Northwestern Ao Noi Na ☎081 838 8682, ⓦmoobantalay.com; map p.164. At the far northwest end of Noi Na bay is one of the classiest resorts on the island, complete with its own pier. It's a secluded haven at the end of the road, set under the trees on a gorgeous, quiet white-sand beach. Accommodation is in large, attractive a/c bungalows, all with platform beds, garden bathrooms and outdoor seating: the priciest, seafront ones have enormous decks, and there's a beachside pool and a spa. Boat transfers and breakfast included. B3800

## EATING

One of the wonders of Ko Samet is that just when you're getting peckish while lazing on the beach, a grilled-chicken or fresh-fruit vendor comes strolling by. As for eating in restaurants, most resorts turn out reasonable food, so many visitors tend not to wander far from their base, but the following places are worth making the effort to get to.

### HAT SAI KAEW AND NA DAN

**Banana Bar and Restaurant** Na Dan high street, opposite the police station; map p.164. Tiny, welcoming establishment serving tastily authentic yellow, green and red curries (B90), as well as *tom yam* and spicy salads. Daily 8am–10pm.

**Im Aroy Dii** Na Dan high street, 10m from the National Park box on Hat Sai Kaew, on the west side of the road (no English sign); map p.164. There's not much to this basic but clean and bright restaurant, but its name, meaning "Full, Delicious, Good", says it all: tasty, cheap dishes on rice (from B60), as well as more interesting options such as squid with salted egg and chicken with cashew nuts (both B140). Fruit shakes and a cheery chef-owner, too. Daily 7am–9pm.

**Rabeang Bann** In front of Na Dan pier ☎038 644063; map p.164. Conveniently located if you're hungry on arrival or need somewhere to relax while waiting for a ferry to leave. They offer everything from rice soup (B70) to burger and fries (B120) and ice creams. Daily 8am–9pm.

### AO HIN KOK

★ **Jep's Restaurant** Ao Hin Kok ☎038 644 113; map p.164. Now run by the Avatara Resort, this popular all-rounder serves a great menu of authentic Thai dishes (including popular *som tam* sets for B190), seafood, Indian (with chicken biriyani for B190 and plenty of veggie dishes), Italian and Mexican food at tables on the sand, set under trees strung with fairy lights and given extra atmosphere by mellow music. Also does cappuccino and cakes. Daily 7am–12.30am.

### AO PHAI

**Sea Breeze** At the north end of Ao Phai ☎038 644 124; map p.164. Simple but satisfying seafood restaurant on the beach, with a BBQ every evening from 6pm, as well as dishes like seafood fried rice (B100). Wash it down with a cold beer or fresh-fruit smoothie as you wiggle your toes in the sand. Daily 8am–11pm.

### AO PRAO (PARADISE BAY)

**Buzz at Le Vimarn Cottages** Ao Prao ☎038 644 104, ⓦwww.samedresorts.com; map p.164. Very refined restaurant serving highly regarded Thai food, including a wide choice of salads, dips and curries (from B290), in its chic modern dining room and on the upstairs terrace. Daily 10am–11pm.

### AO NOI NA

**Baan Ploy Sea** Ao Noi Na ☎038 644 188–9; map p.164. Seafood restaurant belonging to the resort of the same name (see above), set in an impressive, open-sided wooden building supported on tree trunks, with low tables, sunken floors and axe cushions to recline on. The menu includes lots of tempting dishes such as the prawn green curry (B250). Daily 11am–9pm.

## DRINKING

### HAT SAI KAEW AND NA DAN

**Funky Monkey** Na Dan high street, just before the National Parks checkpoint ☎ 092 336 7843; map p.164. A bustling bar in the evening, serving large beers for B100, plus pizzas and all-day breakfasts. Worth checking out if you're heading into town. Daily 8.30am–11pm.

### AO HIN KOK

**Naga Bar** Ao Hin Kok ☎ 038 644 035; map p.164. Great place for drinking, dancing, body painting and meeting world travellers. B52 shots, Red Bull buckets and various beers are on offer. No live music but a good soundtrack. Daily 4pm–midnight.

## DIRECTORY

**Banks** There are ATMs at Na Dan pier, beside the Hat Sai Kaew national park office, and on all main beaches; the bigger resorts also change money, but at a poor rate.
**Emergencies** Ko Samet's health centre and police station

(☎ 038 644 111) are on Na Dan high street, but for anything serious you should go to the Bangkok–Rayong hospital in Rayong (☎ 038 611 104, ⓦ rayonghospital.net).
**Post office** On Ao Noi Na (see map p.165).

# Chanthaburi

For over five hundred years, the seams of rock rich in sapphires and rubies that streak the hills of eastern Thailand have drawn prospectors and traders of all nationalities to the provincial capital of **CHANTHABURI**, 80km east of Ban Phe. Many of these hopefuls established permanent homes in the town, particularly the Shans from Myanmar, the Chinese and the Cambodians. Though the veins of precious stones have now been all but exhausted, Chanthaburi's reputation as a gem centre has continued to thrive and this is still one of the most famous places in Thailand to trade in gems (most of them now imported from Sri Lanka and elsewhere), not least because Chanthaburi is as respected a cutting centre as Bangkok, and Thai lapidaries are considered among the most skilled – and affordable – in the world. Chanthaburi is also an exceptionally fertile province, renowned for its abundance of orchards, particularly durian, rambutan and mangosteen, which are celebrated with an annual **fruit festival** in the town, held in May or June.

The town is becoming a popular weekend destination for Bangkokians looking to slow down the pace of life, usually by strolling along the atmospheric Chantaboon Waterfront, a wonderfully preserved and regenerated riverside lane, while the nearby cathedral and gem market provide added attractions. There are few Western faces to be seen here, but some appealing sleeping and eating options, making it a good spot to get off the beaten track for a while. The nearby Chanthaburi coastline is barely developed for tourism, though it's popular with Thai visitors for its quiet, shady beaches. Chanthaburi is also a major transit point for east-coast bus services and a handy terminus for buses to and from the northeast.

## Chantaboon Riverfront

Chanthaburi's most interesting neighbourhood is along Thanon Sukhaphiban, which runs for a kilometre beside the Chanthaburi River and is often referred to as the Chantaboon Riverfront. It's been zealously protected by the Chantaboon Waterfront Community, who have banded together to create a **Community Learning Centre** in the middle of the street with photos and information boards about the street's preservation, and who own shares in the delightful **Baan Luang Rajamaitri Historic Inn** (see below), which is part-museum, part-hotel, towards the north end of the street. The rest of the street is a wonderful mix of pastel-painted, colonial-style housefronts and traditional wooden shophouses, many displaying finely carved latticework, and trendy cafés. This district is also home to a large Catholic Vietnamese community, most of whom fled here in waves following religious persecution between the eighteenth century and the late 1970s. The earliest refugees constructed what is now, following several revamps,

Thailand's largest cathedral, the **Cathedral of the Immaculate Conception**, located across the footbridge from the southern end of Thanon Sukhaphiban.

## The gem dealers' quarter

The **gem dealers' quarter** is centred around Trok Kachang and Thanon Sri Chan (the latter signed in English as "Gem Street") and packed with dozens of gem shops. Most lie empty during the week, but on Fridays, Saturdays and Sundays they come alive as local dealers arrive to sift through mounds of tiny coloured stones and classify them for resale to the hundreds of buyers who drive down from Bangkok.

## Taksin Park

Thanon Tha Chalaeb

Landscaped **Taksin Park** is the town's recreation area and memorial to King Taksin of Thonburi, the general who reunited Thailand between 1767 and 1782 after the sacking of Ayutthaya by the Burmese. Chanthaburi was the last Burmese bastion on the east coast – when Taksin took the town he effectively regained control of the whole country. The park's heroic bronze statue of Taksin is featured on the back of the B20 note.

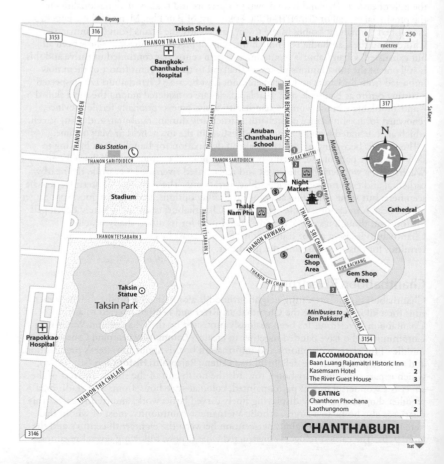

CHANTHABURI

ACCOMMODATION
Baan Luang Rajamaitri Historic Inn 1
Kasemsarn Hotel 2
The River Guest House 3

EATING
Chanthorn Phochana 1
Laothungnom 2

## CROSSING TO CAMBODIA VIA CHANTHABURI PROVINCE

Most foreigners use the Aranyaprathet–Poipet crossing to get into **Cambodia** (see page 151), with access possible by bus via Chanthaburi. There are also two less used crossings in Chanthaburi province, giving access to the Cambodian town of Pailin, just east of the border. Daung Lem Border Crossing at **Ban Laem** is 88km northeast of Chanthaburi and the Phsa Prom crossing is at **Ban Pakkard** (aka Chong Phakkat), 72km northeast of Chanthaburi. There's a minibus service in the morning from Chanthaburi (just south across the bridge from *The River Guest House*) to Ban Pakkard (1–2hr; B200) and one to Ban Laem (1–2hr; B200), that departs from south of the bridge. It's best to arm yourself in advance with an e-visa for Cambodia, but it's also possible to get a thirty-day visa on arrival at the border; if entering Thailand via this route you'll probably be obliged to show proof of onward travel from Thailand.

2

### ARRIVAL AND DEPARTURE

### CHANTHABURI TOWN

**By bus** Chanthaburi bus station (☎ 039 311299) is on Thanon Saritdidech, about 750m northwest of the town centre and Thalat Nam Phu market. Some services are operated by regular buses, others by minibuses, and yet others by both regular buses and minibuses. There's a regular minibus service to Aranyaprathet via Sa Kaew (see page 150).

Destinations Aranyaprathet (every hour; 3hr); Bangkok (Eastern Bus Terminal; at least hourly; 4hr); Bangkok (Northern Bus Terminal; 9 daily; 4hr); Khorat (9 daily; 6hr); Laem Ngop (for Ko Chang; 3 daily; 2hr); Phitsanulok (2 daily; 11hr); Rayong (Every 40min; 2hr); Trat (hourly; 1hr 30min).

### ACCOMMODATION

**Baan Luang Rajamaitri Historic Inn** 252 Thanon Sukhaphiban ☎ 088 843 4516, ⌨ baanluangrajamaitri. com; map p.172. If you've never slept in a museum, then here's your chance. You'll need to book in advance, as it's very popular. There are just ten well-equipped rooms in this beautifully restored, 150-year-old house that is run by the Chantaboon Waterfront Community, with the ground made up of historical relics and a tranquil riverside terrace. B1550
**Kasemsarn Hotel** 98/1 Thanon Benchamarachutit ☎ 039 311 100, ⌨ hotelkasemsarn.com; map p.172. Unexpectedly contemporary hotel, whose comfortable a/c

rooms, with hot showers, fridges and TVs, are built round a central atrium and done out in whitewash and dark wood; there is a smart coffee shop downstairs. Discounts frequently available. B1300
**The River Guest House** 3/5–8 Thanon Sri Chan ☎ 090 936 7499; map p.172. Recently refurbished, this traveller-oriented outfit offers good value. It's located on the edge of the gems quarter and features a breezy riverside terrace. The cheapest rooms are tiny and windowless and share hot-water bathrooms; it's worth forking out a bit more (B590) for a good-sized room, en-suite bathroom and view of the river. B500

### EATING

Food stalls in Thalat Nam Phu wet market (open dawn to dusk) and at the informal night market off the riverside sois sell Vietnamese spring rolls (*cha gio*) with sweet sauce. Locally made Chanthaburi rice noodles (*sen Chan*) are popularly used in *phat thai* throughout Thailand, but in Chanthaburi they're also crucial to the local beef noodle soup, *kway tiaw neua liang*, whose dark broth is flavoured with pungent herbs and spices, including the cardamom that the Chanthaburi mountains are famous for. Thalat Nam Phu is also a popular place for fresh seafood, and several street stalls along Thanon Sukhaphiban sell local delicacies, both sweet and savoury.
★ **Chanthorn Phochana** 102/5–8 Thanon Benchamarachutit; map p.172. By far the best of the

town's restaurants is this spot opposite the *Kasemsarn Hotel*, for which Thai foodies make a beeline. As well as selling Chanthaburi delicacies as souvenirs, it serves regional dishes such as *lon puu* (a kind of salad dip with crab; B150) and *kway tiaw neua liang,* and a delicious range of spicy *yam* salads, Thai curries and stir-fries, many of them using local herbs and vegetables. Daily 9am–9pm.
**Laothungnom** 141 Thanon Sukhaphiban ☎ 087 611 3582; map p.172. A simple but smart café with wooden stools round tables, serving everything from rice soup (B50) to *phat thai*, chicken nuggets and Italian sodas. A good spot to pause for refreshment while exploring the Chantaboon riverfront. Daily 8am–8pm.

# Coastal Chanthaburi

The barely developed **coastline** to the west of Chanthaburi is very pretty, popular with Thai visitors for its empty beaches and shady casuarina trees and worth exploring if you have your own transport.

**2**

> ## YELLOW OIL
>
> Trat is famous across Thailand for the **yellow herbal oil** mixture, *yaa luang*, invented by one of its residents, Mae Ang Ki, and used by Thais to treat many ailments: sniff it for travel sickness and blocked sinuses, or rub it on to relieve mosquito and sandfly bites, ease stomach cramps, or sterilize wounds. Ingredients include camphor and aloe vera. It's well worth investing in a lip-gloss-sized bottle of the stuff before heading off to the sandfly-plagued islands; you can buy it for about B70 and upwards at Trat market. There are now several imitations, but Mae Ang Ki's original product (ⓦ somthawinyellowoil.com) has a tree logo to signify that it's made by royal appointment.

## Hat Khung Wiman and Ao Khung Kraben

Just off Route 3399, about 30km southwest of Chanthaburi, or 80km east of Ban Phe, **HAT KHUNG WIMAN** is a quiet, shady, bronze-sand beach and has several places to stay. A couple of kilometres southeast of here and you're at the lip of **AO KHUNG KRABEN**, a deep, lagoon-like scoop of a bay that's occasionally visited by dugongs and is edged by dense mangrove forest. A wide swathe of this mangrove swamp is protected under a royal conservation project and crossed by a kilometre-long boardwalk; you can also rent double kayaks from a hut next to the observation tower for B150 an hour in the cool season and follow a signed riverine trail. Access is via Laem Sadet on the southern curve of the bay.

### KKB (Khung Kraben Bay) Aquarium

Across the road from the mangrove project on Laem Sadet's beach road • Tues–Fri 8.30am–4.30pm, Sat & Sun 8.30am–5.30pm • Free

The impressively stocked **KKB Aquarium** is a royal initiative and displays a multicoloured variety of reef fish, some sea horses and a few larger marine creatures, with informative English signage. It's possible to walk here from Chao Lao Beach (3km), and as there's no public transport your only other option would be to drive.

**ACCOMMODATION**                                                         **HAT KHUNG WIMAN**

**Al Medina Beach House** Hat Khung Wiman ☏ 085 334 3555, ⓦ almedinabeach.com. Nine very chic, Moroccan-inspired rooms, all with a/c, hot water and DVD players, some with rain showers and bathtubs. Bicycles and kayaks available. Breakfast included. B4950

★ **Faasai Resort** Khung Wiman ☏ 039 417404, ⓦ faasai.com. This New Zealand–Thai owned, environmentally conscious resort is an ideal base from which to explore the east coast. Its comfortable, family-friendly, a/c bungalows sit in a tropical garden with views to the Cardamom mountains on the Cambodian border and there's a swimming pool and Wat Pho-trained massage therapists on site. Very unusually, the resort also has its own private little wetland conservation area, where you can sit bird-watching, swim in the natural spring pool or kayak along the rivulet. Hat Khung Wiman is 10min walk away and *Faasai* rents bicycles and kayaks, and organizes interesting local tours. B1600

# Trat

The small and pleasantly unhurried provincial capital of **TRAT**, 68km southeast of Chanthaburi, is the perfect place to stock up on essentials, extend your visa, or simply take a break before striking out again. Most travellers who find themselves here are heading either for Ko Chang, for the outer islands, or for Cambodia, via the border at **Hat Lek**, 91km southeast of town. But Trat itself has its own distinctive, if understated, old-Thailand charm and there are lots of welcoming guesthouses to tempt you into staying longer.

Though there are no real sights in Trat, the historic neighbourhood down by Khlong Trat, where you'll find most of the guesthouses and traveller-oriented restaurants, is full of old wooden shophouses and narrow, atmospheric sois. The covered market in the heart of town is another fun place to wander. Out-of-town attractions that make enjoyable focuses for a leisurely cycle ride include the mangrove forest to the southeast near Ban Dan Kao, the ornate seventeenth-century **Wat Buppharam**, 2km west of Trat Department Store, and the nearby lake.

# Mangrove forest

5.5km southeast of town

In the **mangrove forest** near Ban Dan Kao, a boardwalk with informative English signs takes you through the swamp; after dark it's a good place to see twinkling fireflies too. The boardwalk access is unsigned in English; to get here with your own transport, head east from Trat towards Ban Dan Kao and after about 5.4km you'll pass dolphin statues on your left – the track to the mangroves is about 100m further on, on the right (if you get to the estuary and road's end you've gone about 500m too far).

## ARRIVAL AND DEPARTURE
TRAT

### BY PLANE

Tiny Trat airport (☎ 039 525767–8), served by Bangkok Airways, is about 16km from the Ko Chang piers at Laem Ngop. There's an airport shuttle minibus direct to Ko Chang hotels for B500/person, including ferry ticket, and a/c minibuses to Trat town (run by Bangkok Limousine; ☎ 039 516005) are also B500/person, for a ride of less than 30min (though at least you'll be dropped off at your hotel).
Destinations Bangkok (3 daily; 50min).

### BY BUS

All buses terminate at the bus station, 1.5km northeast of central Trat on Highway 318, from where songthaews

shuttle passengers into the town centre (B30, or about B100 if chartered) or on to the departure points for the islands (see page 176). A/c minibuses to Bangkok's Victory Monument leave from the 7-Eleven just off Thanon Vivatthana, on the north side of town; there are also minibuses that head to Hat Lek from the bus station (see page 178).
Destinations Bangkok (Eastern Bus Terminal; 6 daily; 4hr 30min–6hr); Bangkok (Northern Bus Terminal; hourly; 4hr 30min); Bangkok (Suvarnabhumi Airport; 6 daily; 4hr 10min); Chanthaburi (hourly; 1hr 30min); Korat (6 daily; 7hr); Pattaya (6 daily; 4hr 30min); Rayong (6 daily; 3hr 30min); Si Racha (6 daily; 5hr).

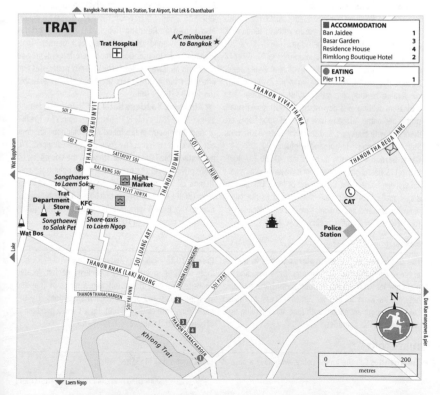

**2**

## BY BOAT

Details of boat services to Ko Chang, Ko Mak and Ko Kood are given in the relevant accounts. If you book your boat ticket through your guesthouse in Trat, they will help to arrange pick-up from the guesthouse. A useful reference for boat times is ⓦ kohchangferries.com.

### VIA LAEM NGOP

All ferries to Ko Chang and some services to Ko Mak leave from one of two piers to the west of the small port town of Laem Ngop, 17km southwest of Trat (see map, p.179): Tha Thammachat and Tha Centrepoint for the Ko Chang car ferries, and Tha Krom Luang (Naval Monument Pier) for speedboats to Ko Mak. These piers are served by songthaew share-taxis from Trat's bus station and by songthaew and a/c minibus share-taxis from Thanon Sukhumvit in the town centre, costing B50/person or B250–300 if chartered; if sharing, allow 60–90min before your boat leaves for the share-taxi to fill up and get you to the pier.

### VIA TRAT–SALAK PET SONGTHAEW

If you're going to the east coast of Ko Chang you can take a direct songthaew to Salak Pet (B200, including car ferry) from the temple compound behind *KFC* and Trat Department Store in Trat.

### VIA LAEM SOK

Some boats to Ko Mak and nearly all boats to Ko Kood depart from Laem Sok, 30km south of Trat; boat tickets bought in Trat should include free transfers to Laem Sok, but there's also a Laem Sok songthaew service (at least hourly, 8am–1pm; 30–60min) that leaves from the town centre.

## INFORMATION

**Tourist information** The Trat and Ko Chang TAT office (daily 8.30am–4.30pm; ☎039 597259, ✉ tattrat@tat. or.th) is out in Laem Ngop, but any guesthouse in the area will help you out with information on transport to the islands or into Cambodia. Alternatively, drop by *Ban Jaidee Guest House* and ask Sergy, the friendly and knowledgeable French owner, who can help out with most travel queries.

## ACCOMMODATION

Most **guesthouses** in Trat are small and friendly and are well used to fielding travellers' queries about the islands and Cambodia. All those listed here are within a 10min walk of the covered market on Soi Vijit Junya.

★ **Ban Jaidee** 67 Thanon Chaimongkon ☎039 520678 or ☎083 589 0839, ⓦ facebook.com/Ban-Jaidee-Guesthouse-153192208087626; map p.175. Very calm, good-value, inviting and rather stylish guesthouse with a pleasant seating area downstairs and just seven small, simple bedrooms. All rooms have polished wood floors, are decorated with quirky art, and share hot-water bathrooms. Staff are very knowledgeable and helpful. B300

**Basar Garden** 87 Thanon Thanacharoen ☎086 707 4688; map p.175. Decent-sized en-suite rooms in a lovely, atmospheric old wooden house at the greener end of town. Curtains and drapes made from faded batik sarongs add to the faintly bohemian ambience and all rooms have fans and mosquito nets. Free bicycles. They also offer cooking classes. B400

**Residence House** 87/1–2 Thanon Thanacharoen ☎039 510560, ⓦ trat-guesthouse.com; map p.175. Also known as Residang House, this is a comfortably appointed, good-value, four-storey German–Thai-managed guesthouse. Guest rooms are large, light and clean and all have windows, thick, comfy mattresses and hot-water bathrooms; there are family rooms available too. Fan B350, a/c B600

★ **Rimklong Boutique Hotel** 194 Thanon Lak Muang ☎081 861 7181, ⓦ bit.ly/Rimklong; map p.175. The five ground-floor rooms at this friendly, popular hotel are done out in a crisp contemporary style and well equipped: a/c, hot water, cable TV and fridge. Those on the side offer a bit more privacy than the two whose doors open right onto Thanon Lak Muang. There is also a nearly half-price single room (B600). The café in reception boasts a serious espresso machine, but you'll have to bring in your own food from outside for breakfast. B1100

## EATING

Two of the best and cheapest **places to eat** in Trat are at the covered day market on Thanon Sukhumvit, and the night market (daily roughly 5–10pm), which can be found between Rai Rung Soi and Soi Vijit Junya, east of Thanon Sukhumvit. Both are packed with food stalls serving up a wide range of Thai delicacies.

**Pier 112** 132/2 Thanon Thanacharoen ☎082 469 1900; map p.175. A stylish eatery in a leafy garden, located opposite Residence House, offering a range of Thai and Western dishes and several vegetarian options. Try the green curry with chicken (B100). There's also a good range of beers and cocktails. Daily 7.30am–10pm.

## DIRECTORY

**Emergencies** Call the tourist police, who have a base at Laem Ngop, on ☎1155 (free, 24hr).

SAAN CHAO PAW KHAO YAI TEMPLE, KO SI CHANG

2

**CROSSING THE CAMBODIAN BORDER VIA HAT LEK**

Many travellers use the **Hat Lek–Koh Kong border crossing** for overland travel into Cambodia. You can arm yourself in advance with an **e-visa** for Cambodia (see page 29) and make the journey by regular public transport, but it's also possible to buy a package all the way through to Sihanoukville and Phnom Penh (around B600 through Ban Jaidee Guest House in Trat) and get a thirty-day visa on arrival at the border, though Cambodian officials have a reputation for extorting extra fees when issuing visas and for getting visitors to buy a health certificate, which is not required.

The only way to get to **Hat Lek** under your own steam is by minibus from Trat bus station, 91km northwest (roughly every 45min; 1hr–1hr 30min; B120). Hat Lek (on the Thai side) and Koh Kong (in Cambodia) are on opposite sides of the Dong Tong River estuary, but a bridge connects the two banks. Once through immigration, expensive tuk-tuks ferry you into **Koh Kong** town for onward transport to Sihanoukville and Phnom Penh or for guesthouses should you arrive too late for connections (mid-afternoon onwards). **Vans, buses and share-taxis** to Phnom Penh and Sihanoukville take around 4–5hr.

**Hospital** The best hospital is the private Bangkok–Trat Hospital (☎039 552 777, ⓦbangkoktrathospital.com), part of the Bangkok Hospital group (not to be confused with the Trat Hospital), which has emergency facilities; it's on the Sukhumvit Highway, 1km north of the town centre. **Immigration office** Located in Laem Ngop, 100m west of the TAT office (Mon–Fri 8.30am–4.30pm; ☎039 597 261).

# Ko Chang

Edged with a chain of long, mostly white-sand beaches and dominated by a broad central spine of jungle-clad hills that rises sharply to over 700m, **KO CHANG** is developing fast but still feels green. It's Thailand's second-largest island, after Phuket, but unlike its bigger sister has no villages or tourist facilities within its steeply contoured and densely forested **interior**, just a few rivers, waterfalls and hiking trails that come under the auspices of the Mu Ko Chang National Park. Some of its marine environment is also protected, as the national park extends to over fifty other islands in the Ko Chang archipelago. Ko Chang's own coast, however, has seen major development over the past two decades, and the island is now well established as a mainstream destination, crowded with package tourists and the overspill from Pattaya, and suffering the inevitable inflated prices and inappropriate architecture. That said, it's still possible to find accommodation to suit most budgets, and though the beaches may be busy they're undeniably handsome, with plenty of inviting places to swim, stroll, or snooze under a palm tree.

At 30km north to south, Ko Chang has plenty of coast to explore. The western **beaches** are the prettiest and the most congested, with **White Sand Beach (Hat Sai Khao)** drawing the biggest crowds to its mainly upmarket and increasingly overpriced mid-range accommodation; smaller **Hat Kai Bae** is also busy. Most backpackers opt for so-called **Lonely Beach** (officially **Hat Tha Nam**), with its roadside village of travellers' accommodation and famous beachfront party scene; those in search of quiet choose the more laid-back **Hat Khlong Phrao**, a long and lovely sweep of sand that caters to most pockets, or **Bang Bao**, which has a village on a jetty with fine views, and its quiet neighbouring beach, **Hat Khlong Kloi**. Every beach has **currency exchange** and most have **ATMs**, along with minimarkets, tour agents, dive shops, clothes stalls and souvenir shops. White Sand Beach and Hat Kai Bae have the densest concentrations of facilities.

During **peak season**, accommodation on every beach tends to fill up very quickly, so it's worth booking ahead. The island gets a lot quieter (and cheaper) from June to October, when heavy downpours and fierce storms can make life miserable, though sunny days are common too; be especially careful of riptides on all the beaches during the monsoon season.

**Sandflies** can be a problem on the southern beaches (see page 63); watch out also for **jellyfish**, which plague the west coast in April and May, and for **snakes**, including surprisingly common cobras, sunbathing on the overgrown paths into the interior. The other hazard is **theft** from rooms and bungalows: use your own padlock on bags (and doors where possible) or, better still, make use of hotel safety boxes. After a local eradication programme, Ko Chang is no longer considered to be a malaria-risk area by health authorities in the US and the UK.

## ARRIVAL AND DEPARTURE KO CHANG

Access to Ko Chang from the **mainland** is by boat from the Laem Ngop coast, 17km southwest of Trat; details of transport to and from Laem Ngop are given on page 176. Tickets on tourist buses and minibuses to Ko Chang will often include the ferry crossing and transport to your hotel. During high season there are also boats to Ko Chang from Ko Mak and Ko Kood; a useful resource for island-hopping is ⓦ kohchangferries.com. On Ko Chang, **songthaew share-**

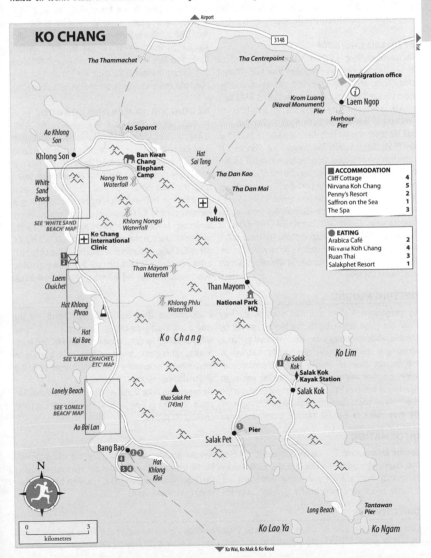

**KO CHANG**

Airport

3148

Tha Thammachat

Tha Centrepoint

Immigration office

ⓘ

Laem Ngop

Krom Luang
(Naval Monument)
Pier

Harbour
Pier

Ao Saparot

Ao Khlong
Son

Khlong Son

Ban Kwan
Chang
Elephant
Camp

Nang Yom
Waterfall

Hat
Sai Tong

Tha Dan Kao

Tha Dan Mai

White
Sand
Beach

SEE 'WHITE SAND
BEACH' MAP

Khlong Nongsi
Waterfall

Ko Chang
International
Clinic

Police

| ■ ACCOMMODATION | |
|---|---|
| Cliff Cottage | 4 |
| Nirvana Koh Chang | 5 |
| Penny's Resort | 2 |
| Saffron on the Sea | 1 |
| The Spa | 3 |

| ● EATING | |
|---|---|
| Arabica Café | 2 |
| Nirvana Koh Chang | 4 |
| Ruan Thai | 3 |
| Salakphet Resort | 1 |

Than Mayom
Waterfall

Laem
Chaichet

Hat Khlong
Phrao

Hat
Kai Bae

SEE 'LAEM CHAICHET,
ETC' MAP

Than Mayom

Khlong Phlu
Waterfall

National Park
HQ

Ko Chang

Ko Lim

Ao Salak
Kok

Salak Kok
Kayak Station

Salak Kok

Lonely Beach

SEE 'LONELY
BEACH' MAP

Ao Bai Lan

Khao Salak Pet
(743m)

Salak Pet

Pier

Bang Bao

Hat
Khlong
Kloi

Long Beach

Tantawan
Pier

N

0          3
kilometres

Ko Lao Ya

Ko Ngam

Ko Wai, Ko Mak & Ko Kood

Trat

2

2

taxis meet boats at the Tha Dan Kao and Ao Saparot ferry piers and transport passengers to west-coast beaches (B50 to White Sand Beach, 25min; B100 to Lonely Beach, 1hr; B150 to Bang Bao, 1hr 15min). On departure, either wait for a songthaew on the main road or ask your accommodation to book one for you (for a small extra fee, usually B20). If you're heading to Ko Chang's east coast, you can make use of the songthaew to Salak Pet from central Trat (see page 176).

### BY BOAT AND PLANE
Bangkok Airways (office in White Sand Beach, ☎039 551654) runs a shuttle-bus service from Ko Chang beaches via the ferry and on to Trat Airport (B500/person; see p.405).

### BY BOAT VIA LAEM NGOP
The main Laem Ngop–Ko Chang boat services are operated by two different car ferry companies from two different piers. Fares are competitive and change frequently: expect to pay B80/person one-way, and about B120 for a vehicle. Centrepoint Ferry (☎039 538196) runs from Tha Centrepoint, 3km west of Laem Ngop, to Tha Dan Kao; and the more popular Ferry Ko Chang (☎039 518588 or ☎039 555188) runs from Tha Thammachat, 9km west of Laem Ngop, to Ao Saparot. Departures are from 6/6.30am–6/7pm, hourly in high season, every 2hr rest of year. There's plenty of long-distance transport direct to Laem Ngop, bypassing Trat town: a/c buses from Bangkok (5hr 15min–6hr), either from the Eastern (Ekamai) Bus Terminal, via Suvarnabhumi Airport and Chanthaburi (3–4 daily), or from Thanon Khao San and Hualamphong Station (2 daily); and a/c minibuses from Bangkok's Victory Monument, Northern and Eastern bus terminals, Suvarnabhumi Airport and Thanon Khao San.

Destinations Tha Thammachat–Ao Saparot (25min); Tha Centrepoint–Tha Dan Kao (45min).

### BY BOAT AND BUS FROM KO CHANG
Every hotel and guesthouse on Ko Chang offers all manner of bus and a/c minibus packages (including ferries) from the island to other popular tourist destinations – we've listed the key ones. Most (it's worth checking) will include pick-up from your hotel either by songthaew, if you're going by big bus from the mainland ports, or by the minibus itself, which will then board the ferry and take you all the way through.
Destinations Bangkok (big bus to Khao San Road B400, not including songthaew to the ferry; minibus to Khao San Road B700; minibus to Sukhumvit Road hotels B850; 5–6hr); Bangkok Suvarnabhumi Airport (big bus B450; minibus B850; about 5hr); Ko Samet (minibus and ferries B750; about 5hr); Pattaya (minibus B650; about 4hr 30min); Siem Reap (Cambodia, changing at the border; minibus B600; about 10hr).

### BY BOAT VIA KO MAK AND KO KOOD
In high season, Bang Bao Boat (☎087 054 4300, ⓦkohchangbangbaoboat.com) runs wooden boats from Bang Bao on Ko Chang to *Koh Mak Resort* on Ao Suan Yai on Koh Mak (roughly Sept–June daily; 1hr 30min–2hr; B400), as well as speedboats to *Koh Mak Resort* (roughly Sept–June 2 daily; 1hr; B600) and on to the west coast of Ko Kood (about 1hr; B900 from Ko Chang). Prices include transfers to or from the west coast of Ko Chang. Several other companies run similar high-season inter-island speedboats, including Kai Bae and Leelawadee (ⓦkohmakboat.com), who sail from Hat Kai Bae on Ko Chang, via *Makathanee Resort* on Ao Kao on Ko Mak, to the west coast of Ko Kood. Hotels on on Ko Chang, as well as guesthouses on Ko Mak and Ko Kood, will have current details.

## GETTING AROUND

By songthaew A paved road runs nearly all the way round the island connecting all the beaches, served by plentiful, white songthaew share-taxis. They tend to charge according to how many passengers they have as well as the distance travelled (usually B50–150/person), but sometimes, especially on more remote beaches, you might have to wait until they fill up with enough passengers or the driver will ask you to charter the whole vehicle.
By motorbike or car You can rent motorbikes (from

B150) and cars (from B1000) on every beach, but the road is notoriously dangerous, with precipitously steep hills punctuated by sharp, unexpected hairpins, and many reckless, often drunk, drivers, so think twice if you're an inexperienced motorcyclist – accidents happen every day and fatalities are frequent.
By mountain bike Rental available at the bookshop just south of Ko Chang Gym in the VJ Plaza complex in Laem Chaichet (B150/day).

## INFORMATION

Tourist information The widely distributed, detailed free maps and quarterly Ko Chang guides published by Whitesands Publications (ⓦkoh-chang-guide.com) are a handy source of information for travellers, and the

website provides an accommodation-booking service, but for more intelligent insights and opinionated advice, check out ⓦiamkohchang.com, compiled by an in-the-know Ko Chang resident.

## DIRECTORY

Clinic The private 24hr Ko Chang International Clinic (☎1719 or ☎039 551 555, ⓦbangkoktrathospital.com)

is located beyond the south end of White Sand Beach, 1km south of *Plaloma Cliff Resort*; it has emergency ambulances and a dental service and will transfer seriously ill patients to its parent Bangkok–Trat Hospital in Trat.

**Post office** The Ko Chang post office is situated on the main road just beyond the southern end of White Sand

Beach (Monday–Friday 10am–noon & 1–6pm, Saturday 10am–1pm).

**Tourist police** At the north end of Hat Khlong Phrao (☎1155).

## White Sand Beach (Hat Sai Khao)

Framed by a band of fine white sand at low tide, a fringe of casuarinas and palm trees and a backdrop of forested hills, **Hat Sai Khao**, more commonly referred to as **White Sand Beach**, is, at 2.5km long, the island's longest beach and its most commercial, with scores of mid-range and upmarket hotel and bungalow operations packed together along the shore, plus dozens of shops, travel agents, bars and restaurants lining the inland side of the road. The vibe is much more laid-back and traveller-oriented at the far quieter northern end of the beach, however, beyond *KC Grande*, and this is where the most budget-priced accommodation squeezes in, some of it pleasingly characterful and nearly all of it enjoying its own sea view. An extra bonus is that the road is well out of earshot up here, and there's hardly any passing pedestrian traffic. There are some low-key beach **bars** up there too, and more along the shorefront in the central beach area – all of them quite different in feel from the rash of brash, Pattaya-style bar-beers inland from *Plaloma Cliff Resort* in southern Hat Sai Khao. Wherever you stay on White Sand Beach, be careful when swimming as the **currents** are very strong and there's no lifeguard service.

### ACCOMMODATION
### WHITE SAND BEACH

**Arunee Resort** Just across the road from White Sand Beach ☎039 551075, ⓦfacebook.com/aruneekohchang; map p.181. The cheapest rooms here are built in a partitioned wooden row-house; all are small and simple with a shared veranda, mattress, fan and tiny en-suite bathroom and are a good price for central Hat Sai Khao. There's also a newer block with compact, a/c rooms at a reasonable price. Fan **B500** a/c **B1500**

**Cookies Hotel** White Sand Beach ☎081 861 4227, ⓦcookieskohchang.com; map p.181. If you want hotel-style facilities at affordable prices this

2

## KO CHANG ACTIVITIES

Your accommodation should be able to obtain tickets for most of the **activities** described below. There are **spas** at Ao Bai Lan (see page 188) and Ao Salak Kok (see page 193); you can also **snorkel** and **dive** in the archipelago (see page 183).

### ELEPHANT CAMPS

Ko Chang or "Elephant Island" is named for its hilly profile rather than its indigenous pachyderms, but there are several **elephant camps** on the island that have brought in their own lumbering forest dwellers so that tourists can ride and help bathe them. Many people feel that riding elephants is unethical, because in order to be tame enough to be ridden, elephants are put through a cruel process that usually involves separation from their mothers, starvation, beating and sleep deprivation, among other methods. However, people have been riding elephants for centuries and this is a bit of a grey area (see page 53), so whether you decide to ride or not is up to you.

**Ban Kwan Chang** Khlong Son ☎ 081 919 3995 ⓦ facebook.com/ Ban-Kwan-Chang-100618275939 4224. Probably the best of the half dozen or so camps on the island. Rides cost between B800 and B1500 depending on duration, and visitors get to bathe the elephants too.

### KAYAKING

**Kayak Chang** At Amari Emerald Cove Resort, Hat Khlong Phrao ☎ 097 182 8319, ⓦ kayakchang.com. Well-organized, safety-conscious, British-run company offering full-day (B3700) up to seven-day (B43,000)

expeditions around the archipelago, as well as three-day kayaking courses (B14,000). Return transport from your accommodation is included.

### COOKING CLASSES

**KaTi Culinary Cooking School** Hat Khlong Phrao ☎ 039 557252, ⓦ facebook.com/katikhruathai. The amiable chef who runs the recommended *KaTi* restaurant (see page 186) teaches well-regarded cooking classes (Mon–Sat 11am; B1500, including recipe book and transfers as far as White Sand Beach and Hat Kai Bae).

is a good option, right in the middle of the beach. Rooms are in two locations, with the far less interesting site being across the road, with only shops and traffic to look at through the picture windows. Better to pay B800 extra and go for a ground-floor, sea-view "superior" room, set round the shorefront swimming pool. Rooms are large and comfortable and all include breakfast, a/c, hot water, TV, fridge and a veranda. B2000

**The Erewan** White Sand Beach ☎ 039 510 668 ⓦ erewankohchang.com; map p.181. This newish, medium-sized hotel across the road from the beach wins praise for its friendly and efficient staff, rooftop pool, great design and buffet breakfast. B4600

**KC Grande Resort** White Sand Beach ☎ 039 552 111, ⓦ kckohchang.com; map p.181. The largest and priciest hotel on the beach is able to charge top dollar because it spreads over a huge area of the northern shorefront. Accommodation ranges from rows of a/c bungalows set in landscaped gardens fronting the beach to more expensive rooms, some with sea views, in the three-storey hotel block. Facilities are good and include a pool, a spa and a bar with live bands in the evening. Breakfast included. B4800

**Penny's Resort** Beyond the south end of White Sand Beach, down a lane behind the post office ☎ 039 551 122, ⓦ penny-thailand.com; map p.179. Welcoming, helpful, German-run place on what's sometimes called Pearl

Beach (Hat Khai Mook), though it's just a rocky extension of Hat Sai Khao. On a compact, flowery plot around a lovely little pool (and a kids' pool too), the well-maintained bungalows and hotel-style rooms all have a/c, hot water, TV, fridge and a few decorative touches; the smaller, cheaper ones are near the sea. B1400

★ **Saffron on the Sea** Beyond the south end of White Sand Beach, three doors north of Penny's ☎ 039 551 253, ⓦ facebook.com/saffronontheseakohchang; map p.179. In a lovely, lush garden behind a very good restaurant (see page 184) are seven attractive, homely rooms with a/c, hot water, TV and fridge; the cheaper rooms have no sea view. Management is friendly and there are free kayaks for guests' use. B1200

**Star Beach** White Sand Beach ☎ 089 574 9486 ⓦ starbeach-kohchang.com; map p.181. Basic, cheerily painted plywood huts cling limpet-like to the rock-face here, just above the sand on the quiet, northern stretch of the beach. Rooms are very simple (no wi-fi) but are all en suite (some with hot showers) and enjoy high-level sea views and breezes. B500

**White Sand Beach Resort** White Sand Beach ☎ 081 863 7737, ⓦ whitesandbeachkochang.com; map p.181. Spread across a long, attractive stretch of uncommercialized sand at the far north end of the beach, *White Sand* offers a big range of nicely spaced bungalows, many of them lapping up uninterrupted sea views. Interiors are fairly simple, but boast a/c, wooden floors, hot showers, TVs, fridges and a faintly contemporary style. If you're looking for a proper peaceful beach vibe and a little bit of affordable comfort, within a 10min walk of resort facilities, this is a good option. Arriving by songthaew, get off at the 7-Eleven beside *KC Grande* and phone for transport. Breakast included. **B1900**

## EATING AND DRINKING

**15 Palms** White Sand Beach ☎ 039 551 095, ⊛ 15palms.com; map p.181. One of the most popular of the row of restaurants that set their tables out on the sand, partly because of its nightly high-season fireshows and *katoey* shows on Tues & Sat. There's a barbecue every night (chicken kebab B295), plus Thai (seafood *tom yam* B155), Italian and Mexican à la carte, washed down with imported beers and lots of cocktails. Daily 8am–1am.

**Nong Bua Seafood** On the main road, White Sand Beach ☎ 039 551 595, ⊛ nongbuarestaurant.com; map p.181. Popular, bustling basic restaurant, serving noodle soups, fried noodles and fried rice with seafood (B70); other seafood dishes start at B150. Daily 7am–10pm.

**Oodie's Place** On the main road, White Sand Beach ⊛ facebook.com/oodies.place; map p.181. Ko Chang's most famous live-music venue, with live blues, rock, reggae and r'n'b played most nights, plus Thai food (from B80), pizzas (from B200) and French food (from B300). Daily 4pm–2am.

**Pen's** White Sand Beach; map p.181. Tiny beach restaurant in the northern bungalow cluster that serves exceptionally good home-style Thai food at fairly cheap prices (B80–150 for curries), as well as Western breakfasts. Daily 8.30am–9.30pm.

**Sabay Bar** White Sand Beach ☎ 081 864 2074, ⊛ facebook.com/Sabay-Bar-115498085538; map p.181. One of Ko Chang's longest-running institutions, where you can choose to sit in the chic a/c bar and watch the nightly live sets from the in-house cover band, or lounge on mats and cushions on the sand and listen in via the outdoor

## DIVING AND SNORKELLING IN THE KO CHANG ARCHIPELAGO

Because there's just one main tide a day in the inner Gulf, the **reefs** of the Ko Chang archipelago are much less colourful and varied than Andaman coast dive sites, and they can get very crowded, but they're rewarding enough to make a day-trip worthwhile. The main **dive and snorkel sites** are west of Ko Mak, in the national marine park around **Ko Rang** and its satellite islets. These range from beginners' reefs with lots of hard corals and anemones at depths of 4–6m, frequented by plenty of reef fish – including a resident ten-thousand-strong shoal of yellow fusiliers – and the occasional moray eel, to the more challenging 25m dive at the Pinnacles. There are also some technical wreck dives of Japanese boats from World War II and even some centuries-old Chinese trading ships. The coral around Ko Yuak, off Ko Chang's Hat Kai Bae, is mostly dead, though some operators still sell trips there.

### DIVE SHOPS ON KO CHANG

The biggest concentration of **dive shops** is on Ko Chang, though there are also some on Ko Mak and Ko Kood (see pages 193 and 197 respectively). All dive shops on Ko Chang will organize pick-ups from any beach.

Waves permitting, Ko Chang operators run trips year-round, though during the **monsoon season** (June–Sept), visibility can be poor. **Prices** for local dive trips, with two tanks, are about B2900, or from B950 for accompanying **snorkellers**. Dive courses cost about B14,500 for the four-day Open Water, and B4500 for the one-day Discover Scuba introduction.

**BB Divers** Shops at Lonely Beach, Khlong Kloi Beach and White Sand Beach, main office in Bang Bao ☎ 086 129 2305 or ☎ 039 558040, ⊛ bbdivers.com. Belgian-run, environmentally minded PADI Five-Star IDC centre and certified Reef Check Facility which uses fishing boats (with sun decks) rather than speedboats.

### SNORKELLING

From about November to May, several companies run dedicated **snorkelling trips** to reefs and islands around Ko Chang, Ko Wai and Ko Rang. Tickets are sold by tour agents on every beach and prices range from B600 to B1500, depending on the size of the boat (some take as many as a hundred people in high season) and the number of islands visited. In general the more islands "featured" (sailed past), the less time there is for snorkelling, though nearly all the actual snorkelling happens around **Ko Rang**.

speakers. You pay for the pleasure, however, as drinks are pricey. Also stages fire-juggling shows on the beach and full moon parties. Daily 6pm–2am.

**Saffron on the Sea** Beyond the south end of the beach, behind the post office three doors north of Penny's (see page 182) ☎ 039 551253; map p.179. On a pretty seafront deck, this restaurant is highly recommended for its Thai food, which doesn't stray too far from the usual suspects, such as deep-fried prawns with tamarind sauce (B350); also serves baguettes, wraps and pastas. Daily 8am–10pm.

## Laem Chaichet and Hat Khlong Phrao

Four kilometres south of Hat Sai Khao, the scenic, rocky cape at **LAEM CHAICHET** curves round into sweeping, casuarina-fringed **HAT KHLONG PHRAO**, one of Ko Chang's nicest beaches, not least because it has yet to see the clutter and claustrophobic development of its neighbours. Most of the restaurants, bars and shops are way off the beach, along the roadside, with the shorefront left mainly to a decent spread of accommodation. Laem Chaichet protects an inlet and tiny harbour and offers beautiful views south across the bay and inland to the densely forested mountains. To the south, Hat Khlong Phrao begins with a nice 1km-long run of beach that's interrupted by a wide khlong, whose estuary is the site of some characterful stilt homes and seafood restaurants. You can rent a kayak from almost anywhere along the beach to explore the estuary, and after dark you could paddle upriver to see the fireflies twinkling in the khlongside *lamphu* trees. Beyond the estuary, the long southern beach is partly shaded by casuarinas and backed in places by a huge coconut grove that screens the shore from the road; it's quite a hike to the roadside shops and restaurants from here though, at least 1km along mostly unlit roads.

Both Chaichet and Khlong Phrao have roadside tourist villages with **ATMs**, minimarkets, tour agents, dive centres, shops and restaurants. The **tourist police** have a post here, and from the southern end of Khlong Phrao it's only a few hundred metres south to the start of the Kai Bae tourist village amenities.

### Khlong Phlu Falls
2km east off the main road • B200

Upstream from Hat Khlong Phrao, the khlong that divides the beach in two tumbles into Ko Chang's most famous cascade, **Khlong Phlu Falls** (Nam Tok Khlong Phlu). Signs lead you inland to a car park and some hot-food stalls, where you pay your national park entry fee and walk the last five minutes to the 25m-high waterfall (best in the rainy season) that plunges into an invitingly clear pool defined by a ring of smooth rocks.

## ACCOMMODATION                                    LAEM CHAICHET AND HAT KHLONG PHRAO

**Baan Rim Nam** Hat Khlong Phrao ☎ 087 005 8575, ⓦ iamkohchang.com; map p.185. Peaceful, scenic and unusual, this converted fishing family's house is built on stilts over the wide, attractive khlong at the end of a walkway through the mangroves. Run by the British author of the best Ko Chang website (see page 180), it has just five comfortable a/c rooms with good hot-water bathrooms, plus decks for soaking up views of the khlongside village, but no restaurant. You can borrow kayaks and it's a couple of minutes' walk to the beach, or 20min to the main Khlong Phrao facilities. B1000

**Centara Tropicana** Hat Khlong Phrao ☎ 039 557122, ⓦ centarahotelsresorts.com/centara/ckc; map p.185. This well-designed resort features rooms in two-storey blocks and thatched bungalows, all surrounded by a profusion of tropical greenery. The spacious rooms are extremely comfortable. Facilities include a beachfront pool, kids' club and spa. B4700

**Emerald Cove Resort** Hat Khlong Phrao ☎ 039 552000, ⓦ emeraldcovekohchang.com; map p.185. Top-of-the-range hotel occupying a lovely, tranquil spot on the southern beach, complete with its own palm-shaded sandy terrace, spa and huge seafront swimming pool, with a palatial Jacuzzi. The rooms, in low-rise three-storey blocks set around the pool, tropical garden and lagoons, are in luxurious style, with wooden floors and balconies. B5000

**Koh Chang Paradise Resort** Laem Chaichet ☎ 039 551100–1, ⓦ kohchangparadise.com; map p.185. The biggest and most popular place to stay on the Chaichet end of the beach occupies a huge area between the road and the shore, so offers easy access to the beach as well as shops and restaurants. Its generously designed concrete bungalows have French windows and comfortable, hotel-style, a/c interiors. Some have private plunge pools and there's also a central swimming pool and a spa. B3820

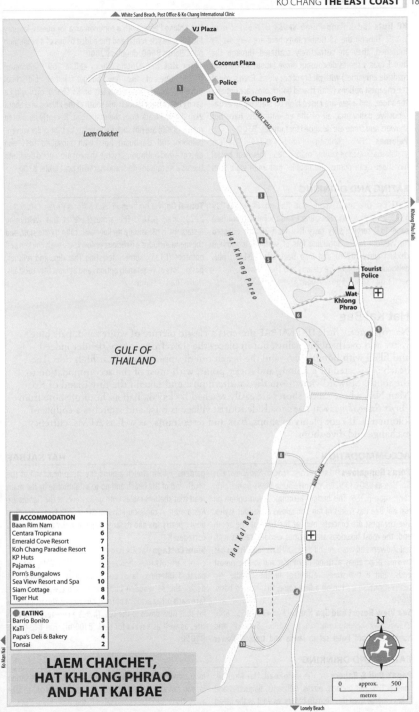

VJ Plaza

Coconut Plaza

Police

Ko Chang Gym

SUKAI ROAD

Laem Chaichet

2

Khlong Phu Falls

Hat Khlong Phrao

Tourist
Police

Wat
Khlong
Phrao

GULF OF
THAILAND

Hat Kai Bae

RURAL ROAD

Ko Man Nai

**ACCOMMODATION**

| Baan Rim Nam | 3 |
|---|---|
| Centara Tropicana | 6 |
| Emerald Cove Resort | 7 |
| Koh Chang Paradise Resort | 1 |
| KP Huts | 5 |
| Pajamas | 2 |
| Porn's Bungalows | 9 |
| Sea View Resort and Spa | 10 |
| Siam Cottage | 8 |
| Tiger Hut | 4 |

**EATING**

| Barrio Bonito | 3 |
|---|---|
| KaTi | 1 |
| Papa's Deli & Bakery | 4 |
| Tonsai | 2 |

**LAEM CHAICHET,
HAT KHLONG PHRAO
AND HAT KAI BAE**

N

0   approx.   500
metres

2

**KP Huts** Hat Khlong Phrao ☎084 077 5995; map p.185. Though the 35 timber huts here are very simply furnished, they are attractively scattered through the broad, grassy shoreside coconut grove (about 1.5km from roadside amenities) with plenty of sea views. Even some of the cheapest options (with shared bathrooms) are right on the shore, and a few are raised high on stilts for an extra-seductive panorama; all of the en-suite huts have hot showers and some are designed for families. **B500**

**Pajamas** Hat Khlong Phrao ☎039 510789, ⓦpajamaskohchang.com; map p.185. This neat hostel has super-clean dorms and doubles just 2min walk from Hat Khlong Phrao, with a common area for guests, laundry facilities, bicycle rental and the added bonus of a swimming pool. Dorms **B600**, doubles **B2800**

**Tiger Hut** Hat Khlong Phrao ☎084 109 9660; map p.185. One of the few budget-minded, old-school travellers' beach bungalows left on Ko Chang, occupying a sandy beachfront garden just south of the khlong and about 2km down a track from the main road. Recently renovated rooms (B900) are not such good value, but the older woven-bamboo and clapboard huts with mosquito nets and decent-sized bathrooms (some shared) are a good deal, and there's a restaurant deck and bar with pool table. **B300**

### EATING AND DRINKING

**KaTi** On the main road, Hat Khlong Phrao ☎039 557252; map p.185. Restaurant and cookery school (see page 182) serving very tasty Thai food, slightly adapted for Western tastes, including lots of seafood, *matsaman* chicken curry (B220) and *laap* beef salad (B140), plus delicious home-made ice creams and Thai desserts. Mon–Sat 11am–10pm, Sun 6–10pm.

**Tonsai** On the main road, Hat Khlong Phrao ☎089 895 7229; map p.185. The atmosphere at this welcoming restaurant is pleasingly mellow with calm, polite staff, and the menu includes a delicious yellow curry with chicken and potatoes (B135), some interesting Thai dips and relishes, pastas, lots of vegetarian options and at least fifty cocktails. Daily 10am–10pm.

## Hat Kai Bae

Narrow, pretty little **HAT KAI BAE** presents a classic picture of white sand, pale blue water and overhanging palms, but in places the shorefront is very slender indeed – and filled with bungalows – and the beach can disappear entirely at high tide. The beach is bisected by a khlong and rocky point, with most of the accommodation to the south. Seaward views from the southernmost end take in the tiny island of Ko Man Nai, whose sandy shores are easily reached by kayak, half an hour offshore from *Porn's Bungalows*. Kai Bae's roadside tourist village is busy and stretches a couple of kilometres. It's got plenty of shops, bars and restaurants, as well as ATMs, currency exchange and dive shops.

### ACCOMMODATION

**Porn's Bungalows** Off the access road to Sea View, Hat Kai Bae ☎080 613 9266, ⓦpornsbungalows-kohchang. com; map p.185. This budget accommodation option on Hat Kai Bae has scores of fan bungalows in various styles. The cheapest are concrete huts at the back at the south end; the most luxurious are spacious wooden cabins with hot showers and wraparound decks; all have fans. *Porn's* has two reception areas, at its northernmost and southernmost ends, and a two-storey restaurant in the middle. No reservations, so it's run on a first-come, first-served basis. **B600**

**Sea View Resort and Spa** Hat Kai Bae ☎039 552 888, ⓦseaviewkohchang.com; map p.185. Swanky and huge beachfront hotel set in lawns and tropical flower gardens, which stretch around the steep headland at the south end of the beach and up to a lighthouse by the main road that shelters tables with good views at the *Lighthouse Restaurant*. A cable car joins up the resort's two swimming pools, pretty spa and its large, light and airy a/c rooms and cottages. **B4600**

**Siam Cottage** Hat Kai Bae ☎089 153 6664, ⓦfacebook. com/siamcottagekohchang; map p.185. With cheerily painted interiors, fans, partly outdoor bathrooms and decks, the 36 wooden bungalows (some with a/c) here face each other across a narrow, but well-watered, flowery lot that runs down to the sea. There's a cute restaurant on site, as well as kayaks for rent (B100/hr). Fan **B650**, a/c **B1050**

### EATING AND DRINKING

**Papa's Deli & Bakery** On the main road, Hat Kai Bae; map p.185. Hot pretzels, pizzas, croissants, baguettes and cakes emerge from this German bakery, as well as the bread for some very tasty sandwiches (around B100). If you're sitting in, you can also tuck into pastas and good espressos; to take away, there are cheeses and salamis, too. Daily 8am–7pm.

★ **Barrio Bonito** On the main road, Hat Kai Bae ☎ 080 092 8208, ⓦ barriobonito.com; map p.185. Mexican-run bar-restaurant serving excellent Mexican food such as nachos with minced beef (B220), as well as some more unusual dishes, such as ceviche (B250) washed down with Corona and lots of tequila cocktails. It's a very congenial place, a popular meeting spot in the evening with Latin sounds all the way. Daily 2pm–10.30pm.

## Lonely Beach (Hat Tha Nam)

Hat Tha Nam – dubbed **LONELY BEACH** before it became Ko Chang's top place to party – is small and lively, with a shorefront that's occupied by increasingly expensive accommodation and a hinterland village, ten minutes' walk away, that's the most traveller-oriented on the island. It's at Lonely Beach, overlooking the rocks immediately south of the strand, and along the sandy sois that run inland to the main road, that most backpackers stay, in little bungalows and guesthouses squashed any old how beneath the remaining trees, with every other shop-shack offering tattoos or fruit smoothies. Despite the creeping concrete, creatively designed little wood and bamboo bar-restaurants abound, some of them offering chilled, low-key escapes from the loud dance music, all-night parties and buckets of vodka Red Bull that the beachfront places are notorious for.

Day and (especially) night, you should be extremely careful when swimming off Lonely Beach, particularly around *Siam Beach* at the northern end, as the steep shelf and dangerous current result in a sobering number of **drownings** every year, particularly during the monsoon season; do your swimming further south and don't go out at all when the waves are high. Also be very careful with your belongings – many a drunken night sees cameras, phones and wallets pilfered unnoticed.

Among the roadside shops you'll find an **ATM**, dive centres, tour agents and motorbike rental and repair.

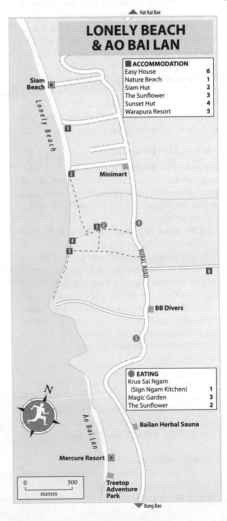

### LONELY BEACH & AO BAI LAN

| ■ ACCOMMODATION | |
|---|---|
| Easy House | 6 |
| Nature Beach | 1 |
| Siam Hut | 2 |
| The Sunflower | 3 |
| Sunset Hut | 4 |
| Warapura Resort | 5 |

| ● EATING | |
|---|---|
| Krua Sai Ngam | |
| (Sign Ngam Kitchen) | 1 |
| Magic Garden | 3 |
| The Sunflower | 2 |

## ACCOMMODATION
### LONELY BEACH

**Easy House** Inland, up a side road opposite Kachapura Resort, Lonely Beach ☎ 082 951 5663, ⓦ bit.ly/EasyHouse; map p.187. Laid-back place built around polished, dark-wood platforms. The old-style bungalows, decorated with murals and equipped with mosquito nets, fans and en-suite bathrooms, are quite crowded together, but quiet and cheap. **B500**

**Nature Beach** Central Lonely Beach ☎ 081 803 8933 ⓦ bit.ly/NatureBeach; map p.187.

2

Responsible for Lonely Beach's party reputation, this place's rooms, bar-restaurant (with built-in DJ station), swimming pool and the beach out front are all hugely popular. It occupies a prime location in the middle of the strand and is at the heart of the action (so if you prefer a quiet night's sleep, head elsewhere). Its recently renovated, air-conditioned bungalows range from attractive, polished-concrete en-suite abodes with verandas at the back by the road to bigger bungalows at the front with hot water and a partial sea view (B2000). B1200

**Siam Hut** Central Lonely Beach ☎ 086 609 7772, ⓦ siamhutkohchang.com; map p.187. The cheapest place to stay right on the beach, this classic traveller's rest has evening barbecues and movies, a dive school, a tattoo parlour, kayaks for rent and a 24hr kitchen. Accommodation consists of rows and rows of primitive, split-bamboo huts – eighty in total – all en suite (some with hot showers) and with little else but plank floors, mattresses and mozzie nets. As with many other budget lodgings on Ko Chang, there are no reservations, so it's first come, first served. Fan B480, a/c B560

**The Sunflower** Lonely Beach, inland on Soi Sunset ☎ 084 017 9960, ⓦ the-sunflower.com; map p.187. Run by a genial German and his Thai family, the two-dozen bungalows here are set under palm and banana trees 200m or so from the roadside village and equidistant from the

rocky coast at *Sunset Hut*, a 5min walk south of the sandy beach. Choose between bamboo or wooden fan bungalows with mosquito nets and open-roofed bathrooms, and concrete bungalows with a/c and hot showers; all have good thick mattresses and are kept very clean. The restaurant is good (see below). Fan B500, a/c B800

**Sunset Hut** Lonely Beach, 5min walk south beyond Siam Hut, on the rocks ☎ 088 549 9942; map p.187. The concrete en-suite fan bungalows here have hot showers, proper beds and big windows, though no wi-fi and some share bathrooms. There are also some big a/c bungalows, but all are tightly packed together in rows running parallel to the shore. The seafront deck-restaurant and bar holds occasional parties. Though you can only swim here at high tide, it's a short walk to the sandy beach and just 400m inland to roadside shops and restaurants. Fan B500, a/c B800

**Warapura Resort** Lonely Beach, 2min walk south beyond Sunset Hut, on the rocks ☎ 089 696 0966, ⓦ warapuraresort.com; map p.187. Welcoming place with a good dose of Bangkok chic in its twenty gleaming white, balconied rooms and villas, a few of which are on the seafront; all have large bathrooms with hot rain showers, a/c, minibars, TVs and DVD players. "Cozy" rooms are especially stylish, with dark-wood furniture and a large indoor sitting area (B2400). Good-sized, attractive pool and breakfast included. B1870

### EATING AND DRINKING

The most intense **partying** on Ko Chang happens down on the beach here, usually at *Nature Beach*, which kicks off most high-season nights with seafood barbecues, live music and fire-juggling shows; there's also a big beach party at *Siam Hut* on Friday nights.

**Krua Sai Ngam (Sign Ngam Kitchen)** On the main road, central Lonely Beach; map p.187. Popular, basic, authentic Isaan restaurant, which even does *som tam* with crab and *pla ra* (fermented fish sauce) – an acquired taste but very northeastern (on the menu as *som tam* e-sarn; B60). Also offers catfish and snakehead fish in various soups, curries and salads (try the *yam plaa duk foo*; B150), grilled chicken and simple dishes on rice (B60). No English sign, but look for the seafood displayed on ice at the front, directly opposite Soi Sunset. Daily noon–11.30pm.

**Magic Garden** On the main road, south of Lonely Beach ☎ 084 891 7637, ⓦ magicgardenresort.com; map p.187. This place serves excellent Thai and European dishes (mains around B100–B250), using homegrown vegetables wherever possible. There's also a well-stocked bar that stays open untill the early hours and features live music a couple of nights each week. It's very popular so reservations are recommended at peak eating times. Daily 8am–10pm.

**The Sunflower** Lonely Beach, inland on Soi Sunset ☎ 084 017 9960, ⓦ the-sunflower.com; map p.187. Friendly, laid-back guesthouse restaurant dishing up very generous set breakfasts (B200), authentically spicy Thai curries (from B80), a wide choice of pricier Western food and German beer. Flop on to the axe cushions and soak up the cool sounds or watch a movie. Daily 7am–10pm.

# Ao Bai Lan

A 15min walk along the road and over the hill from the southern end of Lonely Beach village will bring you to **AO BAI LAN**, which hasn't got much of a beach to speak of, but is the site of two of Ko Chang's most interesting attractions, the **Treetop Adventure Park** and the **Bailan Herbal Sauna**.

### Treetop Adventure Park

South end of Ao Bai Lan • Daily 9am–5pm • B1250/half-day, including roundtrip transfer • ☎ 084 310 7600, ⓦ treetopadventurepark.com

If you're happy with heights and like a physical challenge, make an afternoon of it at **Treetop Adventure Park**, an enjoyable and professionally managed jungle activity centre where you get to swing through the trees on a series of trapezes, flying foxes, aerial skateboards, rope ladders and webs. Everyone gets a full safety harness and gloves and starts off with a training session before tackling the two adventure courses (or the special kids' one), which take around two hours in all, though there's no limit to repeat attempts.

### Bailan Herbal Sauna

On the main road, Ao Bai Lan • Mon–Sat 3–9pm • Sauna B300, treatments from B100 • ☎ 084 464 4005, ⓦ herbalsaunabailan.com

**Bailan Herbal Sauna** is the perfect place to tease out any sore muscles. This charming, creatively designed US–Thai-run herbal steam sauna is an alternative little sanctuary of adobe buildings with glass-bottle windows, secluded within a patch of roadside forest. There's a sociable communal sauna, home-made DIY herbal treatments using fresh herbs from their own garden (kaffir lime for hair, white-mud for face and turmeric for skin), along with fresh juices and herbal teas.

## Bang Bao

Almost at the end of the west-coast road, the southern harbour village of **BANG BAO**, much of it built on stilts off a 1km-long central jetty, is the departure point for boat trips and transfers to the outer islands and is also a popular place to stay. Though it has no beach of its own, you're within a short motorbike ride of both little-developed Hat Khlong Kloi, 2km to the east, and Lonely Beach, 5km up the coast. It's possible to stay on the jetty itself and tuck into seafood at one of its famous restaurants, but you'll probably have to fight your way through vanloads of day-trippers, who clog the narrow path along the jetty as they linger over the trinket shops, clothes stalls and dive shops.

### ACCOMMODATION                                           BANG BAO

**Cliff Cottage** West side of Ao Bang Bao, next to Nirvana ☎ 080 823 5495, ⓦ cliff-cottage.com; map p.179. British-run resort with a nice deck restaurant on the west-facing cove, and kayaks and snorkels for rent. Choose between large, concrete rooms with air-con and hot water bathrooms, and "glamping" bell tents that aren't as glamorous as they sound but offer wide cliff-top views. Tents B650, rooms B850

★ **Nirvana Koh Chang** West side of Ao Bang Bao ☎ 039 510 611–3, ⓦ nirvanakohchang.com; map p.179. Secluded on a narrow neck of land across the bay to the west of the village, this boutique resort is a relaxed and lushly landscaped retreat with two swimming pools; there's no real beach but they run free boats over to Hat Khlong Kloi twice a day. Accommodation is in a wide range of chic, Balinese-accented rooms and villas, some with direct sea views, and there's an attractive restaurant too (see below). Good à la carte breakfast included. B3000

### EATING AND DRINKING

**Arabica Café** Opposite 7-Eleven, just before the start of Bang Bao jetty; map p.179. A leafy little café with cute fountains, serving up good espressos (B50), crepes (from 3pm), sandwiches and Western breakfasts. Daily 8am–9pm.

**Nirvana Koh Chang** West side of Ao Bang Bao ☎ 039 510611–3, ⓦ nirvanakohchang.com; map p.179. Even if you're not staying at *Nirvana Koh Chang*, you can come and eat at *Tantra* restaurant, next to the pool, or drink at the panoramic, sunset-facing *Sun Deck*, which is reached by a cliffside boardwalk. Creatively furnished with woodcarvings from the Indonesian archipelago, the restaurant serves a menu of contemporary Thai food such as panaeng curry. Most dishes will cost you between B150–B250. Sun Deck daily 4–7pm; Tantra daily 7–10pm.

**Ruan Thai** Bang Bao jetty ☎ 086 111 3435; map p.179. The best of several neighbouring restaurants, with a deck built on stilts off the west side of the jetty and fresh seafood awaiting its fate in tanks at the front. The fried rice with prawns is very good (B70), and there are plenty of fish, scallop and squid dishes too (B200–B400). Daily 8.30am–9pm.

## Hat Khlong Kloi

The nearest swimmable beach to Bang Bao is long, sandy **Hat Khlong Kloi**, 2km east of the village and not far short of the end of the tarmac. It's backed by a lagoon and a long stretch of beach-scrub, but has great views from its small beach cafés and deckchairs.

If you're coming by motorcycle, park up at the west end of the beach and walk, as the paved access road then takes a steep, tortuous route around the back of the beach.

**Klong Koi Cottage** 100m from the west end of Hat Khlong Kloi ☎039 558169, ⊛facebook.com/klongkloicottage. Friendly, popular spot situated on a nice stretch of beach, with a scattering of deckchairs and umbrellas and great views of the bay and the offshore islands. The rather scruffy compound has small, thatched, fan-cooled, en-suite bungalows at the back, concrete ones at the front. The simple bar-restaurant hosts a nightly beach barbecue throughout the high season. Fan $\underline{B800}$ a/c $\underline{B1500}$

# The east coast

The beaches along the mangrove-fringed **east coast** are less inviting than those in the west, but this side of Ko Chang is much less developed and makes for a fun day-trip; it's about 35km from Ao Khlong Son in the north to Salak Pet in the south.

## Than Mayom

South of the piers at Ao Saparot and Tha Dan Kao, the east-coast road runs through long swathes of rubber and palm plantations, with jungle-clad hills to the west and bronze-coloured beaches to the east, passing the national park office and bungalows at **Than Mayom**, where signs direct you inland to the short but lovely Than Mayom falls with two calm pools to swim in, a 45-minute uphill hike away.

## Salak Kok and Long Beach

Ao Salak Kok is a deep green bay hedged in with thick mangroves and wooden huts on stilts. To the south, it is at its most charming as the blue boats of the small fishing settlement of **SALAK KOK** bob into view. You can **rent kayaks** from the Salak Kok Kayak Station (B100/hr; run by the Koh Chang Discovery Club, a community tourism venture) to explore a marked route through the mangroves. From Salak Kok, the road continues to the tip of the southeastern headland where undeveloped **Hat Sai Yao**, or **LONG BEACH**, the prettiest white-sand beach on this coast, is good for swimming and has some coral close to shore. There are a few homestays and food stalls here for refuelling.

## Salak Pet

The little fishing port of **SALAK PET**, on the south coast, is served by daily songthaews all the way from Trat town (see page 174). There are some white-knuckle moments on the way here, as the road hugs the coast, rewarding you with incredibly clear views of the sea and coast. Still a fairly quiet spot, the village of Salak Pet has a simple temple but is best known for its excellent **seafood restaurant**, *Salakphet Resort* (see below). While you are able to rent kayaks here, the port town is a glimpse into life on Ko Chang without the tourists, and you'll often find only the fishermen here to keep you company.

★**Salakphet Resort** Salak Pet ☎081 429 9983, ⊛kohchangsalakphet.com; map p.179. The bayside dining deck here offers fine views and seafood so good that people travel all the way from Trat just for lunch; crab is a speciality – particularly stir-fried with black pepper, or with curry powder – but it's all fresh so the possibilities are infinite. Daily 8am–8pm.

**The Spa** Ao Salak Kok ☎083 115 6566, ⊛thespakohchang.com; map p.179. This spa is a beautifully designed, upmarket wellness and detox retreat offering a variety of courses, such as a 'Clean-Me-Out' Fasting Detox programme of ten days and nine nights that costs B26,500 (accommodation not included). The a/c accommodation is set in a lovely mature tropical garden that runs down to the mangrove-ringed bay of western Ao Salak Kok. Breakfast included. They also offer daily meditation and yoga classes (8–10am) for B450/person, and healthy meals in the restaurant. $\underline{B1630}$

**ISLAND HOPPING AROUND KOH CHANG**

Between November and April each year, several boat companies operate services from the mainland and from Ko Chang to the smaller islands to the southwest (Ko Wai, Ko Mak and Ko Kood). This makes it very tempting (and easy) to go on an island-hopping trip, taking in all three islands, together with Ko Chang. By contrast, from May to October this activity is not much fun due to rough seas, non-existent or erratic boat services and closed resorts and restaurants. You can see the boat schedules for each island at ⓦ kohchangferries.com. While such trips are all about spontaneity and making a plan as you go, it's advisable to book accommodation before arriving, as there are various piers on each island, each of which has access to a limited number of resorts.

# Ko Wai

The tiny island of **KO WAI** (just 4 square kilometres) is located about 6km south of Ko Chang and is a popular destination for boat day-trips as its bays provide some of the best spots for snorkelling in the entire archipelago. In fact, you don't even need a mask or snorkel – just stand waist-deep in the water and watch shoals of fish swim around you and the colourful corals. Watch your step though, as some corals are razor-sharp. There are just a few resorts here, and the place is wonderfully peaceful when the tour groups are not around, so it's definitely worth staying overnight. However, almost everywhere closes during the rainy season (May – October). If an island with gorgeous beaches, no villages, shops, roads or cars, and limited electricity is your idea of heaven, Ko Wai is for you. Regular boats, both slow and fast, stop at one of the piers on the island, depending where people are staying, and it's easy to move on to Ko Mak and Ko Kood from here too.

## ARRIVAL AND DEPARTURE                                                      KO WAI

The only access to Ko Wai is by ferry – from Laem Ngop on the mainland, from Bang Bao or Kai Bae piers on Ko Chang, or from Ko Mak/Ko Kood. Check ⓦ kohchangferries.com for detailed timetables. Remember that most resorts close in the rainy season, and ferry service is intermittent.

**VIA KO CHANG**

From Bang Bao pier on Ko Chang there are three boats a day; a slow, wooden boat (9am; 1hr; B300) and speedboats (9am and noon; 30min; B400). From Kai Bae pier, there's one daily speedboat (9am; 30min; B400).

**VIA LAEM NGOP**

Slow, wooden boats run three times a week between Laem Ngop and Ko Wai, stopping at the pier by Pakarang Resort (2hr 30min; B300). Speed boats are operated by Leelawadee and Seatales companies, run three times a day (40min; B450).

**VIA KO MAK OR KO KOOD**

Speedboats operated by Bang Bao Boat or Kai Bae Hut Speedboats depart from Ko Kood (1hr 30min; B700) and Ko Mak (30min; B400) to Ko Chang, stopping at Ko Wai en route.

## ACCOMMODATION

**Ko Wai Pakarang Resort** In the middle of the north coast ☎084 113 8946, ⓦfacebook.com/kohwaipakarang. The concrete bungalows here are not particularly attractive, but it's the only place on the north coast that stays open all year, has 24-hour electricity (from a noisy generator) and some a/c rooms. Fan B600, a/c B1500

**Ko Wai Paradise** On the west side of the north coast ☎061 424 1556, ⓦbit.ly/KoWaiParadise. All bungalows here share bathrooms and come in two sizes: big or small. All are equipped with fans, mattresses and mosquito nets, and electricity is only from 6pm–midnight. There's a good restaurant and the snorkelling in the bay in front is fantastic, although it's often crowded with day-trippers in the afternoon. Closed May–October. B200

# Ko Mak

Small, slow-paced, peaceful **KO MAK** (sometimes spelt "Maak") makes an idyllic, low-key alternative to Ko Chang, 20km to the northwest. Measuring just sixteen

**2**

square kilometres, it's home to little more than four hundred people, divided into five main clans, who work together to keep the island free of hostess bars, jet skis, banana boats and the like, collaborating instead on making the island eco-friendly. A few narrow concrete roads crisscross the island, which is dominated by coconut and rubber plantations; elsewhere a network of red-earth tracks cuts through the trees. Ko Mak is shaped like a star, with fine white-sand beaches along the northwest coast at **Ao Suan Yai** and the southwest coast at **Ao Kao**, where most of the island's (predominantly mid-range and upper-bracket) tourist accommodation is concentrated. The two main beaches are just about within walking distance of each other, and other parts of the island are also fairly easy to explore on foot, or by mountain bike, motorbike or kayak. The best way to discover the empty, undeveloped beaches hidden along the north and eastern coasts, such as Ao Laem Son in the northeast corner, where there are no resorts, just a couple of simple shacks serving food and drinks, is on foot. The **reefs** of Ko Rang are also less than an hour's boat ride away so snorkelling and diving trips are quite popular. There is as yet no major commercial development on the island and **no bank or ATM**, though a few places accept credit cards and bungalows on both beaches will change money. There's a small clinic off the Ao Nid road, though for anything serious a speedboat will whisk you back to the mainland.

During the **rainy season** (mid-May–late Oct), choppy seas mean that boat services to Ko Mak are much reduced. Most Ko Mak accommodation stays open – and offers tempting discounts – but the smaller places often don't bother to staff their restaurants. Islanders say that it can be very pleasant during this "green season", though you may be unlucky and hit a relentlessly wet few days.

## Ao Kao

Ko Mak's longest beach is **AO KAO** on the southwest coast, a pretty arc of sand overhung with stooping palm trees and backed in places by mangroves. The beach is

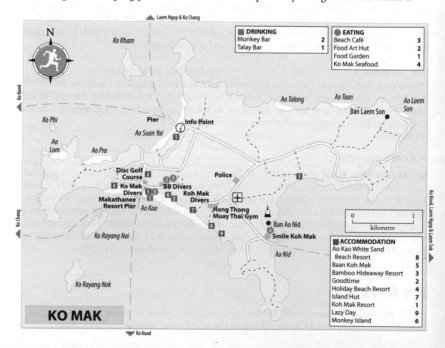

## ACTIVITIES ON KO MAK

The reefs of Ko Rang (see page 183), part of the Ko Chang National Marine Park, are less than an hour's boat ride west of Ko Mak and are the island's main **diving and snorkelling** destination; they're the main focus of Ko Chang dive and snorkel boats too, so you won't be alone. You can also join a **cookery class**, practice **muay thai** or play **disc golf**.

**BB Divers** On the road to Ao Kao just west of Food Art Hut ☎092 602 2260, ⓦbbdivers-koh-mak.com. Offers a Discover Scuba Diving course and one dive for B3000, two dives at Koh Rang for B3000 or snorkelling at Koh Rang for B1000; all include transfers.

**Disc Golf** Just south of Goodtime Resort; contact Pom at the Holiday Beach Resort for details ☎086 751 7668, ⓦfacebook.com/kohmakdiscgolf. Also known as 'frisbee golf', this relatively new sport is fun for all the family. Best in the late afternoon; a round of nine holes takes about an hour and costs B200.

**Hong Thong Muay Thai** On the road to Ao Kao just before the turning to Ao Nid ☎081 711 1428, ⓦfacebook.com/muaythaikohmak. A good chance to combine relaxing with a physical work-out. All

equipment provided and instruction by professional Thai boxing teachers. One session B400 (10am or 4.30pm), 10 classes B3000.

**Koh Mak Divers** On the Ao Kao road just east of the pier, and also further east on the same road, behind the Ao Kao White Sand Beach Resort ☎083 297 7724, ⓦkohmakdivers.com. British-run PADI centre that charges B2500 for two fun dives, B3500 for the beginners' one-day Discover Scuba Diving course and B790 for snorkellers, with transfers from your accommodation included.

**Smile Koh Mak** Next to Koh Mak Seafood restaurant at Ban Ao Nid ☎081 901 9972, ⓦsmilekohmak.com. 4hr cookery classes (10am–2pm; B1200, including a recipe book), with vegetarian options available.

---

divided towards its southern end by a low rocky outcrop that's straddled by *Ao Kao White Sand Beach Resort*, with *Lazy Day Resort* occupying the strand beyond, while the long western beach is shared by a dozen other sets of bungalows, most of them around the pier at the *Makathanee Resort*. The roadside inland from the main accommodation area is where you'll find most of the restaurants and bars: if you're walking from the southern end, by far the easiest access is via the beach, tides permitting.

## Ao Suan Yai and around

Long, curvy **AO SUAN YAI** is just as pretty a beach as Ao Kao; it only has a few resorts, but the sand is soft and white, the coconut palms lean seaward and the outlook is beautiful, with Ko Chang's hilly profile filling the horizon and Ko Kham and other islets in between. You'll need a bicycle or motorbike to access the variety of restaurants on the Ao Kao road.

### ARRIVAL AND DEPARTURE KO MAK

Check ⓦkohmak.com or ⓦkohchangferries.com for current routes and schedules for **boat services** from the mainland and the other islands. Boats arrive at one of Ko Mak's three **piers** – at *Koh Mak Resort* on Ao Suan Yai, at the *Makathanee Resort* on Ao Kao or at Ao Nid – and are usually met by a modest welcoming committee of accommodation staff offering free transport; similarly, if you book a room in advance, ask your resort for a free pick-up. When it comes to moving on, all hotels keep current boat schedules, can sell you a ticket and will transfer you to the pier. Slow boats to Laem Ngop cost B200 (8am; 3hr); speedboats B450 (several departures daily; 50min).

**VIA LAEM SOK**

A year-round catamaran service sails to Ao Nid on Ko Mak from Laem Sok pier, 30km south of Trat (☎090 506 0020, ⓦkohkoodcatamaran.com; daily; 50min; B400 including transfer to/from Trat bus station or downtown market). Some of the Laem Sok–Ko Kood high-season speedboats will call in at Ao Nid if they have enough customers (see page 199).

**VIA LAEM NGOP**

A year-round slow boat runs from the Krom Luang (Naval Monument) pier in Laem Ngop, some 20km southwest of Trat (3 weekly; 3hr; B300), to the Makathanee Resort pier on Ko Mak. From approximately October to May, Panan's speedboats also operate from this pier to *Ko Mak Resort* on Ao Suan Yai (2 daily; 45min–1hr; B450); the second of these is at 4pm, handy if you're arriving from Bangkok. A/c minibuses to Laem Ngop from Bangkok, for example, will sometimes only go as far as the Thammachat or Centrepoint Ko Chang piers, however – check exactly which piers are served when you buy your minibus ticket, or you may be able to pay the driver a little extra to go on to Krom Luang.

**VIA KO CHANG OR KO KOOD**
Boats run between Ko Chang, Ko Mak and Ko Kood in high season (see page 180).

## INFORMATION

**Tourist information** Most resorts can arrange boat and bus tickets, motorbike or kayak rental and provide general information about the island. There's also a travel agent at *Makathanee Resort* (☎ 081 870 6287), located by the pier on Ao Kao. For extra information, ⓦ kohmak.com is a useful, fairly comprehensive website about the island and its main attractions. At present there is no ATM on the island, so take cash with you.

## GETTING AROUND

The island has narrow, paved roads connecting most parts, as well as rough dirt paths, but hardly any traffic, and most visitors rent a mountain bike or motorbike.
**By taxi** ☎ 089 752 5292 or ☎ 089 833 4474. 'Taxi' on Ko Mak means a songthaew, a pick-up truck with a bench seat on each side. B50/person; B100/person after 10pm;

minimum charge per vehicle B100.
**By mountain bike or motorbike** These (respectively B150/day and B200–300/day) can be rented through accommodation or from *Ko Mak Resort*'s Info Point; otherwise, *Food Art Hut* on Ao Kao (see opposite) has a particularly wide choice of bicycles, including kids' bikes.

## ACCOMMODATION

### AO KAO
**Ao Kao White Sand Beach Resort** Ao Kao ☎ 083 152 6564, ⓦ aokaoresort.com; map p.192. This welcoming, efficiently managed and lively set of upmarket bungalows occupies an attractive garden fronting the prettiest part of the beach. Its 25 large, comfortable, attractive timber bungalows come with a/c, hot showers and most have direct sea views. There are four restaurants and bars and lots of activities, including swimming, spa treatments, massage, Thai boxing, tennis, beach volleyball, yoga, a kids' trampoline, free kayaks and motorbikes for rent. Breakfast included. B4490
★ **Baan Koh Mak** Near the pier on Ao Kao ☎ 089 895 7592, ⓦ baan-koh-mak.com; map p.192. Arrayed around a clipped lawn, the eighteen bungalows at this chic and welcoming resort are modern, bright and comfortable, cutely done out in futuristically angular white, green and polished concrete, with a/c, hot water, small bedrooms and decent-sized bathrooms. There's a very good restaurant here too. B1890
**Goodtime** Ao Kao ☎ 039 501000, ⓦ goodtime-resort. com; map p.192. Luxurious, tasteful, Thai-style rooms and villas, all with a/c, hot water, TV, fridge, DVD player and use of a pool. They're located on higher ground inland from Ao Kao's *Makathanee Resort*, around a 15min walk from the beach. Rooms B1880, villas B5100
**Holiday Beach Resort** Ao Kao ☎ 086 751 7668, ⓦ holidaykohmak.com; map p.192. Friendly, well-maintained place, facing a large, beachside lawn with deckchairs and tables. White clapboard is the architectural style of choice here, either in small cottages with verandas and hammocks in the second row, or in large, attractive

bungalows at the front. Kayaks, mountain bikes and motorbikes for rent. B1500
**Island Hut** Ao Kao ☎ 087 139 5537; map p.192. This little family-run place has the best-value and most idyllically sited accommodation on the beach, though not always the friendliest welcome. The two-dozen rough-hewn en-suite timber huts are more artfully designed than they might appear: most have cheery stripey doors and idiosyncratic driftwood artwork; all have fans, hanging space and their own deckchairs on decks or private sandy porches, but wi-fi in the restaurant area only. The cheapest share bathrooms, and there are a few a/c rooms with en-suite bathrooms too. Price depends on proximity to the narrow but pretty shore: the most expensive are at the water's edge and catch ocean breezes. Garden huts B250, beach huts B550, a/c B1200
**Lazy Day** Ao Kao ☎ 081 882 4002, ⓦ kohmaklazyday. com; map p.192. Civilized spot on a huge beachside lawn strewn with flowers and trees. As well as a/c, safes, hot showers and minibars (but no TVs, to preserve the quiet), the spacious, bright, mostly beachfront bungalows sport polished concrete floors, shining white walls and French windows out onto their balconies. Kayaks, bikes and motorbikes to rent. Breakfast included. B2700
**Monkey Island** Ao Kao ☎ 089 501 6030, ⓦ monkey islandkohmak.com; map p.192. There's a big range of bungalows here, all in timber and thatch, and a laid-back, hippyish vibe. Top-end "Gorilla" seafront villas are huge, with a/c, hot water and the possibility of connecting villas; the large a/c "Chimpanzee" bungalows are also good, while some of the small "Ape" and "Baboon" options share

bathrooms. There's also a kids' swimming pool, and a/c room rates include breakfast. Fan B400, a/c B1300

## AO SUAN YAI AND AROUND

**Bamboo Hideaway Resort** A couple of kilometres east of Ao Suan Yai, accessed via tracks through the rubber plantations ☎039 501085, ⓦbamboohideaway.com; map p.192. An idiosyncratic haven, built almost entirely from lengths of polished bamboo. Its comfortable a/c rooms all have mosquito nets on the beds, hammocks and hot showers, and are connected by a raised walkway. Although the south coast is just a couple of minutes' walk downhill, Ao

Suan Yai has the nearest decent beach. There's an attractive swimming pool on site, as well as a good restaurant. Breakfast included. Closed June–Sept. B1250

★ **Koh Mak Resort** Ao Suan Yai ☎089 600 9597, ⓦkohmakresort.com; map p.192. With no less than 1.5km of shoreline to play with, all of the bungalows here are beachfront (including the cheapest options, still with a/c and hot showers) and enjoy lovely panoramas from their verandas. There's a good-sized swimming pool as well as a kids' pool, a restaurant, a dessert bar, a shop and a helpful tour office. The resort also runs daily snorkelling trips to nearby Ko Kham. Breakfast included. B2800

## EATING AND DRINKING

### AO KAO

★ **Beach Café** At Baan Ko Mak, Ao Kao; map p.192. Coolly done out in black and white with some nice sofas, this restaurant serves exceptionally delicious Thai food, including good *tom kha* soups and a great *kaeng phanaeng* (both B92). Daily 8am–9.30pm.

**Food Art Hut** Opposite Monkey Island, Ao Kao; map p.192. Idiosyncratic all-rounder, offering ice cream, desserts, cakes and espressos, as well as Thai dishes and simple, passable Western food such as spaghetti bolognese (B140), breakfasts, pizzas and sandwiches. Daily 8am–3pm & 5–9pm.

**Food Garden** Opposite Monkey Island, Ao Kao; map p.192. This popular, cheap and enjoyable garden restaurant serves *phat thai*, various spicy salads and *matsaman* curries (B120), as well as seafood barbecues in the evening. Daily 10am–10pm.

**Monkey Bar** Monkey Island, Ao Kao; map p.192. Live music nightly, including jamming sessions, at this bar built

around the beachfront trees. A good place to meet young travellers, if you can hear yourself over the music. Daily 9pm–midnight.

**Talay Bar** On the beach in front of Beach Café at Baan Ko Mak, Ao Kao; map p.192. Tables on the sand – with a fire show at 8pm – and great margaritas (B150) plus a long list of other cocktails. Mellow music and evening barbecues. Open in high season only. Evenings till late.

### BAN AO NID

**Ko Mak Seafood** Just north of Ao Nid pier ☎089 833 4474; map p.192. Built out into the sea on stilts, with views of the bay, this restaurant is mostly true to its name, serving *phat thai* with fresh prawns (B80) and more complex dishes such as tasty squid with salted eggs (B200). (Don't get your hopes up about the advertised Ko Mak Museum next door, though – it's just a collection of old things in an old house.) Daily 10.30am–9pm.

# Ko Kood

The fourth-largest island in Thailand, forested **KO KOOD** (also spelt Ko Kut and Ko Kud) is still a wild and largely uncommercialized island. Though it's known for its sparkling white sand and exceptionally clear turquoise water, particularly along the west coast, Ko Kood is as much a nature-lover's destination as a beach-bum's. Swathes of its shoreline are fringed by scrub and mangrove rather than broad sandy beaches, and those parts of the island not still covered in virgin tropical rainforest are filled with palm groves and rubber plantations. There are just a few paved roads, and most of the 25km-long island is penetrated only by sandy tracks and, in places, by navigable khlongs. All of this makes Ko Kood a surprisingly pleasant place to explore on foot (or kayak), especially as the cool season brings refreshing breezes most days. The interior is also graced with some huge, ancient trees and several waterfalls, the most famous of which is Nam Tok Khlong Chao, inland from Ao Khlong Chao.

Because of its relative lack of roads, Ko Kood was once the exclusive province of package tourists, but things have become much easier for independent travellers, with a choice of scheduled boat services from the mainland, as well as from Ko Chang and Ko Mak, the emergence of some budget-minded guesthouses, and paved roads linking most beaches. The island is still pretty much a **one-season**

2

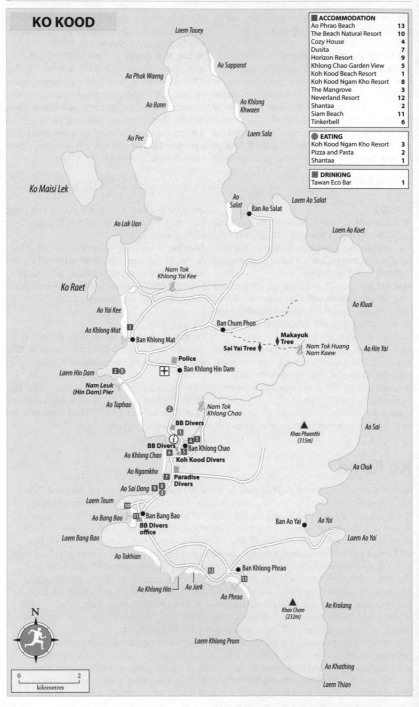

# KO KOOD

Laem Touey

Ao Sapparot

Ao Phak Waeng

Ao Bonn

Ao Khlong Khwaen

Ao Pee

Laem Sala

Ko Maisi Lek

Ao Salat

Ban Ao Salat

Laem Ao Salat

Ao Lak Uan

Laem Ao Koet

Ko Raet

Nam Tok Khlong Yai Kee

Ao Kluai

Ao Yai Kee

Ban Chum Phon

Makayuk Tree

Ao Klong Mat

Ban Khlong Mat

Sai Yai Tree

Nam Tok Huang Nam Kaew

Ao Hin Yai

Police

Laem Hin Dam

Ban Khlong Hin Dam

Nam Leuk (Hin Dam) Pier

Ao Taphao

Nam Tok Khlong Chao

Khao Phaenthi (315m)

Ao Sai

BB Divers

BB Divers

Ban Khlong Chao

Koh Kood Divers

Ao Khlong Chao

Ao Chuk

Ao Ngamkho

Paradise Divers

Ao Sai Dang

Laem Toum

Ban Bang Bao

Ao Bang Bao

BB Divers office

Ban Ao Yai

Ao Yai

Laem Bang Bao

Laem Ao Yai

Ao Takhian

Ban Khlong Phrao

Ao Khlong Hin

Ao Jark

Ao Phrao

Ao Kralang

Khao Chom (232m)

N

Laem Khlong Prom

Ao Khathing

Laem Thian

0    2
kilometres

## ACCOMMODATION

| | |
|---|---|
| Ao Phrao Beach | 13 |
| The Beach Natural Resort | 10 |
| Cozy House | 4 |
| Dusita | 7 |
| Horizon Resort | 9 |
| Khlong Chao Garden View | 5 |
| Koh Kood Beach Resort | 1 |
| Koh Kood Ngam Kho Resort | 8 |
| The Mangrove | 3 |
| Neverland Resort | 12 |
| Shantaa | 2 |
| Siam Beach | 11 |
| Tinkerbell | 6 |

## ● EATING

| | |
|---|---|
| Koh Kood Ngam Kho Resort | 3 |
| Pizza and Pasta | 2 |
| Shantaa | 1 |

## ■ DRINKING

| | |
|---|---|
| Tawan Eco Bar | 1 |

**DIVING AND SNORKELLING OFF KO KOOD**

Ko Kood's three **dive operators** charge around B3000 for two dives, with **snorkellers** paying B1000, and B14,500 for the four-day Open Water Diver course. You might prefer to opt for a local Ko Kood dive as the usual sites around Ko Rang (see page 183) are always packed with dive boats from Ko Chang and Ko Mak.

**BB Divers** On the main road at Ao Khlong Chao next to High Season Resort, and at Siam Beach Resort on Ao Bang Bao ☎ 082 220 6002, ⓦ bbdivers-koh-kood.com.
**Koh Kood Divers** On the main road at Ao Khlong Chao

near the junction with the road to Khlong Chao Falls ☎ 085 698 4122, ⓦ kohkooddivers.com.
**Paradise Divers** Opposite S-Resort on Ao Ngamkho ☎ 087 144 5945, ⓦ kohkood-paradisedivers.com.

destination, though, as rough seas mean that nearly all the boat services only operate from November through May. An increasing number of places are staying open year-round, however, and offer tempting discounts to those willing to chance the rains and the off-season quiet. There is some **malaria** on the island so be especially assiduous with repellent and nets if you are not taking prophylactics; there's a malaria-testing station in Ban Khlong Hin Dam.

Most of Ko Kood's fifteen hundred residents make their living from fishing and growing coconut palms and rubber trees. Many have Khmer blood in them, as the island population mushroomed at the turn of the twentieth century when Thais and Cambodians resident in nearby Cambodian territory fled French control.

The main settlements are **Ban Khlong Hin Dam**, just inland from the main Nam Leuk (Hin Dam) pier, **Ban Khlong Mat**, a natural harbour-inlet a few kilometres further north up the coast, the stilted fishing village of **Ban Ao Salat** across on the northeast coast and the fishing community of **Ban Ao Yai** on the southeast coast. On the southwest coast, several of the main beaches also have small villages. Of these, the obvious choices for budget travellers are **Ao Khlong Chao** and **Ao Ngamkho**, which both have a wide choice of accommodation and eating options and are within walking distance of each other; **Ao Bang Bao** also has several resorts and a beautiful beach but has no village and is more isolated. Seclusion is the thing on all the other west-coast beaches, most of which are the province of just one or two upmarket resorts.

## Ao Khlong Chao

About 5km south of the main Nam Leuk (Hin Dam) pier on the west coast, **AO KHLONG CHAO** (pronounced "Jao") is a fun place to stay, boasting both a wide, sandy beach and the pretty 2km-long mangrove-lined Khlong Chao, which runs down from the famous Khlong Chao Falls. Close by and upstream of the road-bridge that spans the khlong, just 300m from the palm-fringed beach, is a cluster of little guesthouses, some of them built partially on stilts over the river, which offer the cheapest accommodation on the island. The beachfront is occupied by high-end resorts.

## Nam Tok Khlong Chao (Khlong Chao Falls)

30min walk from Ao Khlong Chao, or kayak 20min upriver from the Khlong Chao bridge to the jetty near the falls, then walk for 10min; you can also drive to within 100m of the falls along a well-signed, paved road

The three-tiered **Nam Tok Khlong Chao** is a pretty if not exceptional waterfall that tumbles down into a large, refreshing pool that's perfect for a dip; it's quietest in the mornings, before the package groups arrive. The track continues beyond the falls through jungle for another few kilometres before terminating at a rubber plantation – if you walk the whole thing it's a pleasant and very quiet four-hour trip there and back, though watch out for snakes, especially cobras.

## Ao Ngamkho

South of Ao Khlong Chao, the road goes over a headland and dips down to the tiny village at **AO NGAMKHO** and its beach, actually a series of pretty, miniature bays either side of a khlong and between rocky points, with quite rewarding snorkelling and plenty of fish at its southern end.

## Ao Bang Bao

Beyond Ao Ngamkho, the road passes behind **AO BANG BAO**, with a side road leading a couple of kilometres down to the beach. This is one of Ko Kood's prettiest beaches, fronted by a longish sweep of bleach-white sand and deliciously clear turquoise water, plus the inevitable fringe of coconut palms, and embraced by a pair of protective promontories.

## Ao Jark

On the main southbound road at the Ao Bang Bao turn-off, the main road turns eastward, while a turning south passes through coconut and rubber plantations on the way to **Ao Khlong Hin**, a wild little bay that's dominated by a small coconut-processing centre and is not really great for swimming. A few minutes further along this road, which hugs the coast so close here it gets washed by the waves at high tide, remote and breathtakingly lovely little **AO JARK** sits at the mouth of a wide, serene khlong and feels secluded and private.

## Ao Phrao

The most southerly bay, **AO PHRAO**, is a long, stunning beach of white sand backed by densely planted palms and the slopes of Khao Chom; to get here, follow the main road eastwards from Ao Bang Bao. Behind Ao Phrao, the tiny fishing village of **Ban Khlong Phrao** occupies the mangrove-lined banks of Khlong Phrao (which extends another kilometre inland). There's a clinic here as well as a few small shops and hot-food stalls.

## Ban Ao Yai

A 5km road that's very steep in places connects Ban Khlong Phrao with **Ban Ao Yai**, the southeast coast's main, if rather lacklustre, fishing village, built entirely on stilts and jetties around the shoreline of a natural harbour. Its main visitors are the crews of anchored fishing boats from Thailand and Cambodia, who come here for drink, supplies, karaoke and the rest.

## Ban Khlong Hin Dam and around

The bays of northern Ko Kood, beyond Ao Khlong Chao, are even more thinly populated than the southwest coast, with just a few exclusive resorts hidden away. Inland is the island's administrative centre, **Ban Khlong Hin Dam**, 3.5km north of Ao Khlong Chao, site of a few shops, the hospital, police station, school and principal island temple. Ko Kood's main west-coast pier is a couple of kilometres to the west, at **Nam Leuk (Laem Hin Dam)**.

About 5km north of Ban Khlong Hin Dam, the small but appealing three-tiered waterfall **Nam Tok Khlong Yai Kee** is basically a miniature version of the famous Nam Tok Khlong Chao (see opposite) and rushes down into a good-sized pool that's ideal for swimming. It's accessible via a five-minute path that's very steep in places, but there are ropes at the crucial points.

# Ban Ao Salat and around

The road northeast from Ban Khlong Hin Dam ends after 9km at the tiny stilt village, fishing community and port of **Ban Ao Salat**. Several of the wooden houses strung out along the jetty-promenade serve food and this is a great place for a fresh-seafood lunch, especially crab.

East off this road, in the mature rainforest near Ban Chum Phon, are a couple of locally famous ancient trees, thought to be between 200 and 500 years old, known to islanders as *makayuk and sai yai*. They're both 35m or more in height and surrounded by sprawling buttress roots and drip with lianas and epiphytes. They are signposted on opposite sides of a paved road that leads through rubber trees and rainforest, from where a short walk along forest trails leads to the enormous boles. Further east, this road leads to Nam Tok Huang Nam Kaew, another beautiful waterfall surrounded by rainforest.

## ARRIVAL AND INFORMATION                                                    KO KOOD

### BY BOAT
All boat tickets to Ko Kood from the mainland should include transfers to the pier from Trat, though it's worth double-checking. Mainland and Ko Chang speedboats will drop off at and pick up from most of the west-coast accommodation. All Ko Kood hotels keep current timetables and sell tickets.

### FERRIES FROM THE MAINLAND
In all but the worst weather, Koh Kood Princess (☎ 082 878 9900, ⓦ kohkoodprincess.com) runs a year-round boat service to Ko Kood from the Trat mainland, departing from Laem Sok, about 30km south of Trat, occasionally calling at Ao Nid on Ko Mak, and terminating at Ao Salat on the island's northeast coast (daily at 12.30pm; about 1hr 30min; B350 including transfers on Ko Kood). There is also a service operated by the Ko Kut Express, which sails from Laem Sok to Nam Leuk pier on Ko Kood's west coast (☎ 084 524 4321, ⓦ kokutexpress.in.th; daily; 1hr 15min; B350). A third option, and the smoothest ride, is on the Boonsiri Catamaran (☎ 085 921 0111 ⓦ boonsiriferry.com), which runs twice a day (10.45am and 2.20pm; 1hr 15min; B500).

### SPEEDBOATS FROM THE MAINLAND
There are also several different companies offering high-season speedboat services between the Trat mainland and Ko Kood's western piers and beaches; these are faster and more expensive (up to 4 daily; about 1hr; B600) but can be wet and uncomfortable in all but the flattest seas. Schedules and mainland departure points vary, though most services depart from Laem Sok; ⓦ kohkoodferries.com is a useful resource.

### VIA KO CHANG AND KO MAK
Boats run between Ko Chang, Ko Mak and Ko Kood throughout high season (see page 180). Speedboats from Ko Chang to Ko Kood (9am, 9.30am and 12.30pm; 1hr 45min; B900) can be caught at the stop-off at Ao Nid on Ko Mak (10am; 45–60min; B400) if there are enough takers.
**Tourist information** There's a municipal tourist information office on Ao Khlong Chao, just north of the bridge on the west side of the road, though it's often unattended (daily 8.30am–6pm).

## GETTING AROUND

Exploring the southwest of the island on foot is both feasible and pleasant, and south of Ao Khlong Chao much of the route is shady. From Ao Khlong Chao to Ao Bang Bao takes about 40min; from Ao Bang Bao to Ao Jark is about 1hr, then another 20min to Ao Phrao.

**By songthaew** These can be chartered for around B1000/day.
**By motorbike** You can rent motorbikes through most guesthouses and resorts (from B250/day), but be warned that the mostly concrete west-coast road is narrow and steep, and badly rutted in places.

## ACCOMMODATION

### AO KHLONG CHAO
**Cozy House** On the south bank of the khlong, Ao Khlong Chao ☎ 089 094 3650, ⓦ kohkoodcozy.com; map p.196. This travellers' haunt, with bungalows spread around a big, grassy area beside the khlong, has upgraded its accommodation, but the basic fan bungalows are a good deal, and the a/c bungalows (B1200) are very spacious. Free kayak use and motorbike rental. Fan **B700**, a/c **B1000**

**Khlong Chao Garden View** 100m south of the bridge, at the junction of the main road and the road to the waterfall, Ao Khlong Chao ☎ 086 038 8420; map p.196. Away from the khlong, this friendly, laid-back place is situated on a lawn dotted with ornamental trees beside the road. You can choose between basic, fan-cooled huts with small bathrooms, and larger a/c bungalows with TVs. There's a good menu food of Thai dishes at the popular garden restaurant too – try the *kaeng phanaeng*. Fan B600, a/c B1000

★ **The Mangrove** On the south bank of the khlong, Ao Khlong Chao ☎089 936 2093, ⓦkohkood-mangrove. com; map p.196. The best of the khlongside options, with nice views of the water and sturdy wooden bungalows spaced around a well-tended lawn, dotted with pretty plants and trees. Interiors are modern and well furnished with TV and hot water. Free kayaks and motorbikes for rent. Includes breakfast. Fan B700, a/c B1500

**Tinkerbell** Ao Khlong Chao ☎081 813 0058, ⓦtinkerbell resort.com; map p.196. Stylishly designed and landscaped resort at the south end of the beach, which offers a difficult choice. For the same price (including breakfast), you can plump for either a bright, pastel-coloured villa with a/c, hot rain shower, fridge, TV, DVD player and large balcony right on the beach, or an equally attractive two-storey house in the second row, with a plunge pool and a separate large living room and toilet upstairs. There's a small swimming pool fed by an artificial waterfall. B9840

### AO NGAMKHO

**Dusita** Ao Ngamkho ☎081 420 4861, ⓦdusitakohkood. com; map p.196. Occupying the lion's share of Ao Ngamkho, this resort zealously guards its private pier and grounds with 'Do Not Trespass' signs, guaranteeing privacy to its guests. There are just 16 thoughtfully designed a/c wooden cabins, some with nice pebbledash outdoor bathrooms, that all enjoy beautiful sea views and some shade among the manicured gardens and towering palms. Standard rooms are a bit small but family rooms are bright and spacious. B3090

**Horizon Resort** Ao Ngamkho ☎088 457 1551, ⓦhorizon resortkohkood.com; map p.196. The large, modern, a/c, hot-water wooden chalets here, some with outdoor bathrooms, sit on a flower-strewn slope atop the little rocky point at the southern end of the bay, with polished floorboards, panoramic sea views and easy access to swimming and snorkelling among the coral off the point. B2700

**Koh Kood Ngam Kho Resort** Ao Ngamkho ☎084 653 4644; ⓦfacebook.com/kohkoodngamkhoresort.com; map p.196. Set in a lovely location at the south end of Ao Ngamkho, this family-run, budget resort is a great place to base yourself, if only for the fantastic food in the restaurant (see page 200). Rooms range from small, fan-cooled rustic cabins on stilts to spacious a/c concrete bungalows. Be prepared for a noisy reception from the family dogs. Fan B800, a/c B1500

### AO BANG BAO

**The Beach Natural Resort** Ao Bang Bao ☎084 717 0955, ⓦthebeachkohkood.com; map p.196. Though it doesn't actually sit on the nicest part of the beach, but behind a rocky area towards the northern end, this resort's diverse, thatched Balinese-style bungalows are tastefully furnished and have garden bathrooms; they're grouped

quite closely together so most only offer glimpses of the sea. All have hot showers and a/c. Facilities include massage service and rental of kayaks. Breakfast included. B4900

**Siam Beach** Ao Bang Bao ☎081 907 1940, ⓦsiambeach resortkohkood.com; map p.196. This resort occupies almost all of the best part of the beach, sprawling across an extensive area, and is popular with budget travellers, though some bungalows are cramped tightly together. Its big, no-frills huts and bungalows on the seafront nearly all enjoy uninterrupted bay views. Some of the newer a/c rooms are in a less idyllic spot close to a khlong and back from the shore a bit, but they're cheaper than the beachside a/c options and have hot showers. Breakfast included in high season rates. Fan B1400, a/c B2200

### AO JARK

**Neverland Resort** Ao Jark ☎081 762 6254, ⓦneverland resort.com; map p.196. This remote resort is set among the palms between the limpid blue sea and the calm green khlong. It offers comfortable, balconied, log-clad a/c bungalows, some with hot showers, in a pretty garden, as well as fully equipped two-person tents, kayaks and snorkels. Breakfast included. Tents B500, bungalows B2000

### AO PHRAO

**Ao Phrao Beach** Ao Phrao ☎081 429 7145, ⓦkokut. com; map p.196. Mainly but not exclusively package-oriented clusters of thatched and more expensive concrete a/c bungalows, all with hot showers and TVs; facilities include free kayaks and a karaoke room. Breakfast included. B2100

### AROUND BAN KHLONG HIN DDAM

**Koh Kood Beach Resort** Ao Khlong Mat, about 2km northwest of Ban Khlong Hin Dam ☎081 908 8966, ⓦkohkoodbeachresorts.com; map p.196. This resort is set in loads of space on a sweeping, grassy slope above a lovely pool and a nice stretch of sandy beach. Rooms are of two types, all with a/c, outdoor hot showers, minibars, TVs, DVD players and sea views from their generous decks: high-roofed, thatched Balinese-style bungalows and slightly more expensive "Thai Twin Houses", very suitable for families, in which two rooms are connected to one terrace with a Jacuzzi. Guests get free rental of snorkels and kayaks. Breakfast included. B3900

★ **Shantaa** North end of Ao Taphao, about 2km west of Ban Khlong Hin Dam ☎081 566 0607, ⓦshantaakohkood.com; map p.196. On a landscaped grassy rise, these beautifully designed villas have a/c and hot rain showers in attractive indoor-outdoor bathrooms. There are a couple of small beaches just a few steps away, and plenty of decks with sunloungers. There are no TVs in the rooms, in line with the owners' aspirations to make it an ecologically sound resort. The staff are extremely attentive and there's a great restaurant too. Breakfast included. B4900

## EATING AND DRINKING

★ **Koh Kood Ngam Kho Resort** Ao Ngamkho ☎084 653 4644; map p.196. The restaurant of this unassuming resort has an extensive menu of Thai and international cuisine, all of which is tasty, but note the early closing time. Try the seafood *tom yam* (B180), it's fantastic. A visit in the daytime brings the added benefit of gorgeous views across the bay. Daily 7am–8pm.

**Pizza and Pasta** South side of Ban Khlong Hin Dam ☎083 297 2860, ⓦpizzanpasta.info; map p.196. Genial Italian roadside restaurant serving a mean bolognese with home-made tagliatelle (B300), pizzas (B220), a few salads, pastries for breakfast and probably the best espresso on the island. Daily 9am–9pm.

**Shantaa** Resort Ao Taphao ☎081 566 0607; map p.196. Not only does this resort do a great job of making its guests supremely comfortable, its restaurant also serves up delicious dishes such as *mu cha muang* (slow-steamed pork with sour leaves; B280) and stir-fried seafood with crispy Thai herbs (B290). It's worth heading here to eat even if you're not staying at the resort. Daily 11am–4pm & 5.30pm–8.30pm.

**Tawan Eco Bar** Ao Khlong Chao, about 500m north of the bridge ☎ 098 337 4223, ⓦfacebook.com/ tawankohkood; map p.196. Small roadside bar in a wooden shack on stilts run by Jong, a friendly musician; live music every night. Daily 10am–1am.

## DIRECTORY

**Banks** There are a couple of ATMs on Ko Kood. One is at Ao Khlong Chao, next to BB Divers, and the other is immediately south of the hospital.

**Hospital** Ban Khlong Hin Dam (☎089 603 8685).

**Pharmacy** The shop across from the hospital in Ban Khlong Hin Dam has a small pharmacy section and sells antihistamine tablets for bites from sandflies (see page 63), which can be legion on Ko Kood.

**Police** Ban Khlong Hin Dam (☎087 958 1991).

# Southern Thailand: the Gulf coast

ANG THONG NATIONAL MARINE PARK

# Southern Thailand: the Gulf coast

Southern Thailand's gently undulating Gulf coast is famed above all for the Samui archipelago, three small, idyllic islands lying off the most prominent hump of the coastline. This is the country's most popular seaside venue for independent travellers, and a lazy stay in a beachfront bungalow is so seductive a prospect that most people overlook the attractions of the mainland, where the sheltered sandy beaches and warm clear water rival the top sunspots in most countries. Added to that you'll find scenery dominated by forested mountains that rise abruptly behind the coastal strip, and a sprinkling of fascinating historic sights.

The crumbling temples of ancient **Phetchaburi** are the first noteworthy sights you'll meet heading south out of Bangkok and fully justify a break in your journey. Beyond, the stretch of coast around **Cha-am** and **Hua Hin** is popular with weekending Thais escaping the capital and is crammed with condos, hotels and bars, not to mention a large population of foreign visitors. Far quieter and preferable are the beaches further south: the sophisticated little resort of **Pak Nam Pran**; golden-sand **Hat Phu Noi**, which is also the best base for exploring the karsts and caves of **Khao Sam Roi Yot National Park**; the welcoming town of **Prachuap Khiri Khan**, fronted by a lovely bay and flanked by an equally appealing beach; and laid-back, lightly developed **Ban Krud**.

Of the islands, **Ko Samui** is the most naturally beautiful, with its long white-sand beaches and arching fringes of palm trees. The island's beauty has not gone unnoticed by tourist developers of course, and its varied spread of accommodation these days draws as many package tourists and second-homers as backpackers. In recent years the next island out, **Ko Pha Ngan**, has drawn increasing numbers of independent travellers away from its neighbour: its accommodation is generally simpler and cheaper than Ko Samui's, and it offers a few stunning beaches with a more laid-back atmosphere. The island's southeastern headland, **Hat Rin**, has no fewer than three white-sand beaches to choose from, but now provides all the amenities the demanding backpacker could want, not to mention its notorious full moon parties. The furthest inhabited island of the archipelago, **Ko Tao**, has taken off as a **scuba-diving** centre, but despite a growing nightlife and restaurant scene, still has the feel of a small, rugged and isolated outcrop.

Tucked away beneath the islands, **Nakhon Si Thammarat**, the cultural capital of the south, is well worth a short detour from the main routes through the centre of the peninsula – it's a sophisticated city of grand old temples, delicious cuisine and distinctive handicrafts. With its small but significant Muslim population, and machine-gun dialect, Nakhon begins the transition into Thailand's deep south.

The Gulf coast has a slightly different **climate** from the Andaman coast and most of the rest of Thailand, being hit heavily by the northeast monsoon's rains, especially in November, when it's best to avoid this part of the country altogether. Most times during the rest of the year should see pleasant, if changeable, weather, with some effects of the southwest monsoon felt between May and October. Late December to April is the driest period, and is therefore the region's high season, which also includes July and August.

## ARRIVAL AND GETTING AROUND                        THE GULF COAST

The main arteries through this region are highways 4 (also known as the Phetkasem Highway, or usually Thanon Phetkasem when passing through towns) and 41, served by plentiful buses.

**By plane** The main airports in this region are on Ko Samui, at Chumphon, Surat Thani and Nakhon Si Thammarat, the last three providing, in combination with buses and boats, cheaper but slower competition for getting to the islands.

ROYAL PAVILION, THAM PHRAYA NAKHON CAVE COMPLEX

# Highlights

**❶ Phetchaburi** Charming historic town, boasting several fine old working temples, as well as delicious traditional desserts. See page 207

**❷ Pak Nam Pran** Chic, artfully designed boutique hotels on a long, sandy beach, a popular weekend escape for design-conscious Bangkokians. See page 219

**❸ Ang Thong National Marine Park** A dramatic, unspoilt group of over forty remote islands, accessible on boat trips from Samui, Ko Pha Ngan or Tao. See page 249

**❹ Full moon party at Hat Rin, Ko Pha Ngan** Party on, and on… See page 258

**❺ Ao Thong Nai Pan on Ko Pha Ngan** Beautiful, secluded bay with good accommodation. See page 260

**❻ A boat trip round Ko Tao** Satisfying exploration and great snorkelling, especially off the unique causeway beaches of Ko Nang Yuan. See page 263

**❼ Nakhon Si Thammarat** Historic holy sites, intriguing shadow puppets, great-value accommodation and excellent cuisine. See page 272

**❽ Krung Ching waterfall** Walk past giant ferns and screeching monkeys to reach this spectacular drop. See page 278

**HIGHLIGHTS ARE MARKED ON THE MAP ON PAGE 206**

# SOUTHERN THAILAND: THE GULF COAST

**HIGHLIGHTS**

1. Phetchaburi
2. Pak Nam Pran
3. Ang Thong National Marine Park
4. Full moon party at Hat Rin, Ko Pha Ngan
5. Ao Thong Nai Pan on Ko Pha Ngan
6. A boat trip round Ko Tao
7. Nakhon Si Thammarat
8. Krung Ching waterfall

BANGKOK
Ratchaburi
Samut Songkhram
Phetchaburi
Pattaya
KAENG KRACHAN NATIONAL PARK
Cha-am
Pala-u Falls
Hua Hin
Pranburi
Pak Nam Pran
Hat Phu Noi
KHAO SAM ROI YOT NATIONAL PARK
Kuiburi
Prachuap Khiri Khan
MYANMAR
Wang Duan
Ban Krud
GULF OF THAILAND
Bang Saphan Yai
Suan Luang
Thung Wua Laen
Chumphon
Hat Sai Ri
Ao Thung Makham
Ranong
Lang Suan
Ko Tao
ANDAMAN SEA
ANG THONG NATIONAL MARINE PARK
Ko Pha Ngan
Wat Suan Mokkh
Chaiya
Ko Samui
Don Sak
Khanom
Surat Thani
KHAO SOK NATIONAL PARK
Phunphin
Sichon
Krung Ching
Phang Nga
Khao Luang (1835m)
Nakhon Si Thammarat
Thung Song
Krabi
Ron Phibun
Phuket
Trang
Phatthalung

0    50
kilometres

N

**By train** The railway from Bangkok connects all the mainland towns, including a branch line to Nakhon; nearly all services depart from Hualamphong Station, but a few slow trains use Thonburi Station.

**By boat** Daily boats run to all three main islands from two jumping-off points: Surat Thani, 650km from Bangkok, is close to Ko Samui and is generally more convenient for Ko Pha Ngan too, but if you're heading from Bangkok to Pha Ngan you might want to consider Chumphon, which is certainly the main port for Ko Tao.

# Phetchaburi

Straddling the Phet River about 120km south of Bangkok, the provincial capital of **PHETCHABURI** (sometimes "Phetburi"; meaning "Diamond City") has been settled since at least the eleventh century, when the Khmers ruled the region. It was an important producer of salt, gathered from the nearby coastal salt pans, and rose to greater prominence in the seventeenth century as a trading post between the Andaman Sea ports and Ayutthaya. Despite periodic incursions from the Burmese, the town gained a reputation as a cultural centre – as the ornamentation of its older temples testifies – and after the new capital was established in Bangkok it became a favourite country retreat of Rama IV, who had a hilltop palace, **Phra Nakhon Khiri**, built here in the 1850s. Modern Phetchaburi is known for its limes and rose apples, but its main claim to fame is as one of Thailand's finest sweet-making centres, the essential ingredient for its assortment of *khanom* being the sugar extracted from the sweet-sapped palms that cover the province. This being very much a cottage industry, today's downtown Phetchaburi has lost relatively little of the ambience that so attracted Rama IV: the central riverside area is hemmed in by historic wats in varying states of disrepair, along with plenty of traditional wooden shophouses. The town's top three temples, described below, can be seen on a leisurely two-hour circular walk beginning from Chomrut Bridge, while Phetchaburi's other significant sight, the palace-museum at Phra Nakhon Khiri, is on a hill about 1km west of the bridge.

Despite the attractions of its old quarter, Phetchaburi gets few overnight visitors as most people see it on a day-trip from Bangkok, Hua Hin or Cha-am. The town sees more overnighters during the **Phra Nakhon Khiri Fair**, spread over at least a week usually in February, which features parades in historic costumes, cooking demonstrations and fireworks displays.

## Wat Yai Suwannaram
Thanon Phongsuriya, about 700m east of Chomrut Bridge

Of all Phetchaburi's temples, the most attractive is the still-functioning seventeenth-century **Wat Yai Suwannaram**. The temple's fine old teak **sala** has elaborately carved doors, bearing a gash reputedly inflicted by the Burmese in 1760 as they plundered their way towards Ayutthaya. Across from the *sala* and hidden behind high, whitewashed walls stands the windowless Ayutthaya-style bot. The bot compound overlooks a pond, in the middle of which stands a small but well-preserved scripture library, or **ho trai**: such structures were built on stilts over water to prevent ants and other insects destroying the precious documents. Enter the walled compound from the south and make a clockwise tour of the cloisters filled with Buddha statues before entering the bot itself via the eastern doorway (if the door is locked, one of the monks will get the key for you). The **bot** is supported by intricately patterned red and gold pillars and contains a remarkable, if rather faded, set of murals, depicting Indra, Brahma and other lower-ranking divinities ranged in five rows of ascending importance. Once you've admired the interior, walk to the back of the bot, passing behind the central cluster of Buddha images, to find another Buddha image seated against the back wall: climb the steps in front of this statue to get a close-up of the left foot, which for some reason was cast with six toes.

## Wat Kamphaeng Laeng

Thanon Phra Song, a 15min walk east and then south of Wat Yai

The five tumbledown prangs of **Wat Kamphaeng Laeng** mark out Phetchaburi as the likely southernmost outpost of the Khmer empire. Built probably in the thirteenth century to honour the Hindu deity Shiva and set out in a cruciform arrangement facing east, the laterite corncob-style prangs were later adapted for Buddhist use, as can be seen from the two that now house Buddha images. There has been some attempt to restore a few of the carvings and false balustraded windows, but these days worshippers congregate in the modern whitewashed wat behind these shrines, leaving the atmospheric and appealingly quaint collection of decaying prangs and casuarina topiary to chickens, stray dogs and the occasional tourist.

## Wat Mahathat

Thanon Damnoen Kasem

Heading west along Thanon Phra Song from Wat Kamphaeng Laeng, across the river you can see the prangs of Phetchaburi's most fully restored and important temple, **Wat Mahathat**, long before you reach them. Boasting the "Mahathat" title only since 1954 – when the requisite Buddha relics were donated by the king – it was probably founded in the fourteenth century, but suffered badly at the hands of the Burmese. The five landmark prangs at its heart are adorned with stucco figures of mythical creatures, though these are nothing compared with those on the roofs of the main viharn and the bot. Instead of tapering off into the usual serpentine *chofa*, the gables are studded with miniature *thep* and *deva* figures (angels and gods), which add an almost mischievous vitality to the place. In a similar vein, a couple of gold-embossed crocodiles snarl above the entrance to the bot, and a caricature carving of a bespectacled man rubs shoulders with mythical giants in a relief around the base of the gold Buddha, housed in a separate mondop nearby.

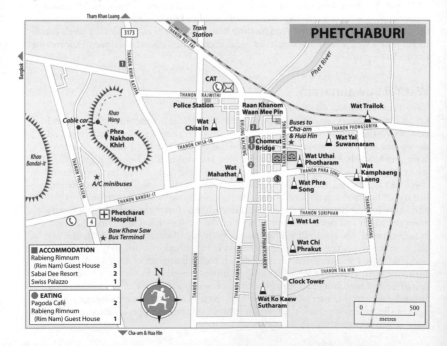

# Khao Wang

Dominating Phetchaburi's western outskirts stands Rama IV's palace, a stew of mid-nineteenth century Thai and European styles scattered over the crest of the hill known as **Khao Wang** ("Palace Hill"). During his day, the royal entourage would struggle its way up the steep brick path to the summit, but now there's a **cable car** (daily 8.30am–4.30pm; B200 including admission to the palace) which starts from the western flank of the hill off Highway 4; there's also a path up the eastern flank, starting near Thanon Rajwithi. If you do walk up the hill, be warned that hundreds of quite aggressive monkeys hang out at its base and on the path to the top.

Up top, the wooded hill is littered with wats, prangs, chedis, whitewashed gazebos and lots more, in an ill-assorted combination of architectural idioms – the prang-topped viharn, washed all over in burnt sienna, is particularly ungainly. Whenever the king came on an excursion here, he stayed in the airy summer house, **Phra Nakhon Khiri** (daily 8.30am–4pm; B150; visitors are asked to dress politely, covering knees and shoulders), with its Mediterranean-style shutters and verandas.

Now a museum, it houses a moderately interesting collection of ceramics, furniture and other artefacts given to the royal family by foreign friends. Besides being cool and breezy, Khao Wang also proved to be a good stargazing spot, so Rama IV, a keen astronomer (see page 224), had an open-sided, glass-domed observatory built close to his sleeping quarters.

## ARRIVAL AND DEPARTURE
PHETCHABURI

### BY TRAIN

Phetchaburi station is on the north side of the town centre. Destinations Bangkok (Hualamphong Station 11 daily; Thonburi Station 2 daily; 2hr 45min–3hr 45min); Chumphon (11 daily; 4hr–6hr 30min); Hua Hin (13 daily; 1hr); Nakhon Pathom (13 daily; 1hr 30min–2hr); Nakhon Si Thammarat (2 daily; 12–13hr); Prachuap Khiri Khan (10 daily; 2–3hr); Ratchaburi (13 daily; 40min–1hr); Surat Thani (10 daily; 6hr 45min–9hr); Trang (2 daily; 13hr).

### BY BUS

There's no longer a dedicated service between Bangkok and Phetchaburi, which is now served by through-buses on their way to or from Bangkok – all services between the capital and southern Thailand have to pass through the town on Highway 4.

**Through-buses** There's a small Baw Khaw Saw terminal on the east side of Highway 4 (Thanon Phetkasem), which is where southbound through-buses will set you down or pick you up. Northbound through-buses on their way to Bangkok stop on the opposite side of the highway: ask to get off at "Sii Yaek Phetcharat", the crossroads of Highway 4 and Thanon Bandai-It by Phetcharat Hospital – otherwise you might be put off at the Big C Department Store about 5km south of town. Songthaews and motorbike taxis run between Highway 4 and the town centre.

**From/to Cha-am and Hua Hin** Local, roughly half-hourly buses from and to Cha-am (1hr 20min) and Hua Hin (1hr 50min) use the small terminal in the town centre, less than a 10min walk from Chomrut Bridge.

### BY MINIBUS

Several companies, which all now congregate to the south of Khao Wang near Wat Tham Kaeo, offer licensed a/c minibuses to the Southern Bus Terminal in Bangkok, Ratchaburi, Nakhon Pathom, Kanchanaburi and Hua Hin.

## GETTING AROUND

**By samlor or songthaew** Shared songthaews circulate the town, but to see the major temples in a day and have energy left for Khao Wang, hire a samlor or a songthaew for a few hours, at about B100–200/hr, depending on distance.

**By bicycle or motorbike** You can rent bicycles (B100/day) and motorbikes (B100–250/day) from *Rabieng Rimnum Guest House* (see page 210), which is a popular way of exploring the area.

## INFORMATION AND TOURS

**Tourist information** There's no TAT office in town, but *Rabieng Rimnum Guest House* is a good source of local information. It can also book day-trips and multi-day visits to Kaeng Krachan National Park for hiking (two or three nights are good for trekking into the jungle), roughly from November to June or July.

## SWEET PHETCHABURI

Almost half the shops in Phetchaburi stock the town's famous **khanom** (sweet snacks), as do many of the souvenir stalls crowding the base of Khao Wang and vendors at the day market on Thanon Matayawong. The most well-known local speciality is *maw kaeng* (best sampled from Raan Khanom Waan Mae Pin on the west side of Thanon Matayawong, just north of Phongsuriya), a baked sweet egg custard made with mung beans and coconut and sometimes flavoured with lotus seeds, durian or taro. Other Phetchaburi classics to look out for include *khanom taan*, small, steamed, saffron-coloured cakes made with local palm sugar, coconut and rice flour, and wrapped in banana-leaf cases; and *thong yot*, orange balls of palm sugar and baked egg yolk.

## ACCOMMODATION

**Rabieng Rimnum (Rim Nam) Guest House** 1 Thanon Chisa-in, on the southwest corner of Chomrut Bridge ☎032 425707 or ☎089 919 7446; map p.208. Occupying a century-old house next to the Phet River and, less appealingly, a noisy main road, this popular, central guesthouse offers very simple rooms with shared, cold-water bathrooms, lots of local information and the best restaurant in town (see below). Excellent rates for singles (B150). **B240**

**Sabai Dee Resort** 65 Thanon Khlong Kacheng ☎086 344 4418; map p.208. Centrally placed and friendly budget option opposite *Rabieng Rimnum*, with a small garden running

down to the river. If you don't mind sharing a bathroom, go for one of the large, white fan rooms with polished wooden floors in the bright, airy, mostly wooden main building, which are more characterful than the small, en-suite, a/c rooms and bamboo bungalows in the garden. **B350**

**Swiss Palazzo** Thanon Khiri Rataya ☎032 400 250, ⊛swiss-palazzo.com; map p.208. Tastefully decorated in earth tones, this new boutique hotel has just four rooms, all with a/c, hot showers, TVs, espresso machines and balconies. Below is a café that makes its own pasta and ice cream. Continental breakfast included. **B1990**

## EATING

As well as for *khanom*, Phetchaburi is famous for savoury **khao chae**: originally a Mon dish designed to cool you down in the hot season, it consists of rice in chilled, flower-scented water served with delicate, fried side dishes, such as shredded Chinese radish and balls of shrimp paste, dried fish and palm sugar. It's available at the day market until sold out, usually around 3pm. There's a nice little **night market** on the small road parallel to and immediately west of Thanon Matayawong.

**Pagoda Café** Thanon Khlong Kacheng, opposite Wat Mahathat; map p.208. The cool industrial look of polished concrete and red bricks may be looking all-too-

familiar by now on your travels around Thailand, but the espresso coffees are very good, and they serve cakes and teas, too. Tues–Sun 9am–6pm.

**Rabieng Rimnum (Rim Nam) Guest House** 1 Thanon Chisa-in, on the southwest corner of Chomrut Bridge ☎032 425707 or ☎089 919 7446; map p.208. The town's best restaurant, an airy, wooden house with riverside tables, attached to the guesthouse of the same name. It offers a long and interesting menu of inexpensive Thai dishes, from banana-blossom salad (B80) to the tasty Phetchaburi speciality, sugar-palm fruit curry with prawns (B100) and is deservedly popular with local diners. Daily 8am–midnight.

# Cha-am and around

Forever in the shadow of its more famous neighbour, Hua Hin, 25km to the south, the resort of **CHA-AM** is nevertheless very popular with Thais on short breaks, and it sports one or two package-holiday high-rises and Western-style restaurants for Europeans, too. Mostly, though, it's weekending families and partying student groups from Bangkok who eat and drink at the rows of umbrella-shaded tables and deckchairs on the sand, or brave the sea on banana boats or rubber tyres, the women clad modestly in T-shirts and shorts rather than bikinis. The long, straight beach here is pleasantly shaded, though rather gritty and very narrow at high tide, and the water is perfectly swimmable, if not pristine. During the week the pace of life in Cha-am is slow, and it's easy to find a solitary spot under the thick canopy of casuarinas, particularly at the northerly end of the beach, but that's rarely possible at weekends, when prices shoot up and traffic thickens considerably.

Cha-am has a functional pocket of development around Thanon Phetkasem (Highway 4), close to the junction with Thanon Narathip, the main access road to the beach, 1km to the east. However, the 3km seaside promenade of Thanon Ruamchit is where you'll find most of the hotels, restaurants, a small tourist police station (corner of Thanon Narathip) and a few other tourist-oriented businesses; Thanon Ruamchit's sois are numbered according to whether they're north or south of Thanon Narathip.

## Phra Ratchaniwet Marukhathaiyawan

10km south of Cha-am, off the road to Hua Hin, Highway 4 • Daily except Wed 8.30am–4.30pm (ticket office closes 4pm) • B30 • Dress modestly (with shoulders and knees covered) as it's a former royal palace • Best accessed by private transport, but Cha-am–Hua Hin buses (roughly every 30min) stop within 2km of the palace at the sign for Rama VI Camp – just follow the road through the army compound

Set in beautiful grounds, the lustrous seaside palace of Rama VI, **Phra Ratchaniwet Marukhathaiyawan** (aka Mrigadayavan Palace), is rarely visited by foreigners, though it sees plenty of Thai visitors. Designed by an Italian architect, Ercole Manfredi, in a westernized Thai style, and completed in 1924, the entire, 400m-long complex of sixteen golden teak pavilions and connecting walkways is raised off the ground on over a thousand concrete columns, with a niche for water at the base of each to keep out ants. Commissioned by Rama VI, who'd been advised by his doctors to take the warm sea air for his rheumatoid arthritis, it's often referred to as "the palace of love and hope" as the king first visited with his pregnant queen, who later miscarried and was subsequently demoted to royal consort. After the king's death in 1925, the palace was abandoned to the corrosive sea air, until time-consuming restoration work began in the 1970s. During the current phase of works, scheduled to go on until 2024, the rooms upstairs are closed to visitors, but you can still wander the grounds and admire the architecture from below, a stylish composition of verandas and latticework painted in shades of cream and light blue. The king stayed in the central group of buildings, with the best sea view and a 50m-long elevated walkway to his private bathing pavilion, while the south wing contained the apartments of the royal consorts, with its own bathing pavilion connected by a walkway. You can look in on the spacious open hall on the ground floor of the north wing, hung with chandeliers and encircled by a first-floor balcony, which was once used as a meeting room and a theatre for the king to perform in his own plays. On the way back out towards Highway 4, towards the north end of the army camp, you can also explore a 300m boardwalk that's been laid over a mangrove swamp.

### ARRIVAL AND DEPARTURE CHA-AM

**By train** The station is a few blocks west of the main Phetkasem–Narathip junction.

Destinations Bangkok (Hualamphong Station 3 daily, Thonburi Station 2 daily; 3hr 30min–4hr 30min); Chumphon (3 daily; 5–7hr); Hua Hin (5 daily; 30min); Prachuap Khiri Khan (4 daily; 2hr).

**By bus** A handful of a/c minibus companies that run services to Bangkok's Southern Bus Terminal are based near the beach, including one on the south side of Thanon Narathip near the junction with Thanon Ruamchit that also serves Ratchaburi and Nakhon Pathom. However, these vehicles only depart when full, so for a wider choice of transport, you're better off heading to Highway 4, close to the junction with Thanon Narathip. Plenty of through-buses and the local, roughly half-hourly service between Hua Hin (35min) and Phetchaburi (1hr 20min) stop here, and there are several companies with desks on the pavement that operate a/c minibuses to Ratchaburi, Nakhon Pathom and Bangkok's Southern and Northern Bus Terminals and Don Muang Airport. Roong Reuang coaches from Hua Hin to Suvarnabhumi Airport or Pattaya will pick up passengers here, in front of the Government Savings Bank, just north of the crossroads.

### GETTING AROUND

**By bicycle or motorbike** Most people choose to get around Cha-am by bike. A number of shops along the beachfront rent motorbikes as well as bicycles, tandems and even three- and four-person bikes.

### INFORMATION

**Tourist information** The local TAT office (daily 8.30am–4.30pm; ☎032 471005–6, ✉tatphet@tat.or.th), which is located on Highway 4 (west side) about 1km south of Thanon Narathip, covers the whole of the Phetchaburi province, but can do little more than hand out a map of Cha-am, in Thai.

## ACCOMMODATION

There are no obvious backpacker-oriented places in Cha-am; instead you'll find mainly small, mid-range hotels and guesthouses, concentrated on Thanon Ruamchit and the adjoining sois (with a concentration of budget places on Soi 1 North), and upmarket, out-of-town resorts, many on the road down to Hua Hin (covered on page 216). Many Cha-am hotels put their prices up on Saturdays and over bank-holiday weekends.

**Golden Beach Cha-am Hotel** Just south of Soi Cha-am North 8 at 208/14 Thanon Ruamchit ☎032 472 850–3, ⓦgoldenbeachchaam.com. Good-value twenty-storey hotel with a full-height atrium, an attractive, free-form swimming pool and gym, set back from the promenade. The large, nicely appointed rooms have a/c, hot water, minibars and TVs, as well as balconies, all with sea views. B1700

**Nana North Beach** North of Soi Cha-am North 10 towards the canal ☎032 471 357, ⓦfacebook.com/nananorthbeach. Huge range of well-kept accommodation with a/c, hot water, TVs and fridges, including two-bedroom houses (B2500) and bright, pretty, tiled rooms either in the main building on the front or down the quieter side alley. B950

**Nirandorn 3** Just south of the Narathip junction on Thanon Ruamchit ☎032 470300. Clean, well-maintained hotel rooms and a few tightly packed, motel-style bungalows, decorated in crisp, modern whites and browns, with sofas, safes, a/c, TVs, fridges and hot water; all rooms in the hotel block are sea-facing, sporting balconies and deckchairs. There's also a small, attractive swimming pool. Rooms B700, bungalows B1000

**So Sofitel** 6km north of central Cha-am ☎032 709 555, ⓦso-sofitel-huahin.com. Sleek, designer hideaway featuring a triumphal, white-marble staircase up to the lobby and a huge reflective pool as its centrepiece. The accommodation blocks have a striking cubic look but are very comfortable, while contemporary Thai food is served at the hotel's *White Oven restaurant*. There are two swimming pools (an active pool for families and an adults-only chill-out pool) and a luxurious spa. B4700

## EATING AND DRINKING

The choice of **restaurants** in Cha-am is not a patch on the range you get in Hua Hin, but there should be enough Thai-style seafood to keep you satisfied, including at the dozens of deckchair-and-umbrella places on the beach.

**Didine** From the beachfront, take Soi Cha-am South 4, then turn left and right onto Soi Chao Lai ☎087 189 3864, ⓦdidine-chaam.com. One of the best places in Cha-am to get Western food, with a French chef and a long menu of tasty traditional favourites, such as beef *bourguignon* (B310), pizzas, pastas, salads and plenty of fish and seafood. Daily 5–10pm.

**Krua Medsai** North end of the beach, just after the canal ☎032 430 196. A very Thai institution, this huge, open-sided, thatched pavilion sits on the beach, with *luk*

*thung* on the sound system, views down to Hua Hin and nice breezes off the sea. People flock here for the very good seafood, simply grilled or in dishes along the likes of delicious stir-fried shrimp with acacia shoots (B250). Daily 10am–9.30pm.

**O-Zone** Thanon Ruamchit, north of Soi Cha-am North 7 ☎032 470 897. Popular bar-restaurant whose attractions include mellow live folk music in the early evening, followed from about 9pm by bands playing Thai and Western pop, and a menu that encompasses a handful of Western dishes such as pizza and steak, one-plate Thai dishes and more complex offerings along the likes of *miang kung sot* (fresh prawns with wild betel leaves; B180). Daily 5pm–midnight.

# Hua Hin

Thailand's oldest beach resort, **HUA HIN** used to be little more than an overgrown fishing village with one exceptionally grand hotel, but the arrival of mass tourism, high-rise hotels and farang-managed hostess bars has made a serious dent in its once idiosyncratic charm. With the far superior beaches of Ko Samui, Krabi and Ko Samet so close at hand, there's little to draw the dedicated sunseeker here. Hua Hin's most distinctive attractions are its distinctive squid-pier guesthouses and restaurants on Thanon Naretdamri, which are augmented by many other spots to enjoy fine seafood elsewhere in the resort, while at the other end of the scale the former *Railway Hotel* (now the *Centara Grand*) provides all the atmosphere you can afford. In addition, the town makes a convenient base for day-trips to Khao Sam Roi Yot National Park to the south and Pala-u Falls in Kaeng Krachan National Park to the west. Hua Hin also hosts the long-running annual Hua Hin International Jazz Festival, a free event on the beach featuring Thai and international musicians (ⓦhuahininterjazz.com).

### Brief history

The **royal family** were Hua Hin's main visitors at the start of the twentieth century, but the place became more widely popular in the 1920s, when the opening of the Bangkok–Malaysia rail line made short excursions to the beach much more viable. The Victorian-style *Railway Hotel* was opened in 1922, originally as a necessary overnight stop on the three-day journey to Malaysia. At the same time Rama VI commissioned the nine-hole Royal Hua Hin Golf Course (now 18 holes; ☎032 512475) to the west of the station, and in 1926 Rama VII had his own summer palace, Klai Klangwon ("Far from Worries"), erected at the northern end of the beach. It was here, ironically, that Rama VII was staying in 1932 when the coup was launched in Bangkok against the system of absolute monarchy. Before his death in 2016, Rama IX stayed here as often as he could, which put the local police and military on their best behaviour. As a result, both Thais and expats consider Hua Hin a comparatively safe, hassle-free place to live and do business – hence the number of farang-oriented real-estate agencies in the area.

## The central shorefront

The prettiest part of Hua Hin's 5km-long **beach** is the patch in front of and to the south of the *Centara Grand*, where the sand is at its softest and whitest. North of here the shore is crowded with tables and chairs belonging to a string of small restaurant shacks, beyond which the beach ends at a Chinese temple atop a flight of steps running down to Thanon Naretdamri. The coast to the north of the pagoda

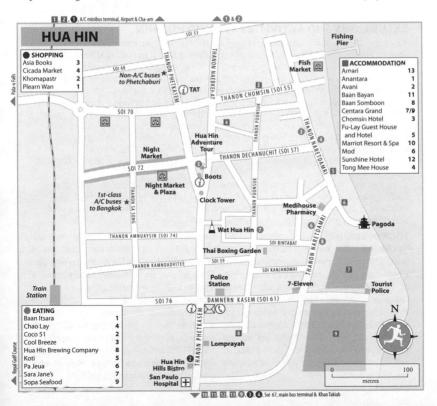

is dominated by the jetties and terraces of the squid-pier guesthouses and seafood restaurants, the hub of the original fishing village, which dates back to the early nineteenth century.

## South to Khao Takiab, Suan Son Pradiphat and Suan Ratchaphak

Green songthaews run to Khao Takiab every 20min or so from central Thanon Sa Song

South of the *Centara Grand*, hotels, holiday homes and high-rise condos overshadow nearly the whole run of beach down to the promontory known as Khao Takiab (Chopstick Hill), but during the week it's fairly quiet along here, with just a few widely spaced food stalls along the broad, squeakily soft beach. **Khao Takiab** itself is a wooded outcrop surmounted by a temple and home to a troupe of monkeys, about 6km south of the town centre; the road to the top is guarded by a tall, golden, standing Buddha and affords good coastal views. Beyond Khao Takiab stretches another quiet beach, **Suan Son Pradiphat**, which is backed by casuarina trees and maintained by the nearby army camp. If you've made it this far with your own transport, it's worth having a look at Suan Ratchaphak, on the west side of Highway 4, inland from the north end of Suan Son Pradiphat, for a glimpse into Thailand's obsession with royalty. Here, just after the military coup of 2014, colossal bronze statues of seven Thai kings, all in suitably militaristic poses, were erected, overlooking an enormous army parade ground-cum-car park. Dogged by allegations of corruption, the project cost an estimated B1 billion, funded from the public purse and private donations.

---

### EXCURSIONS AND ACTIVITIES AROUND HUA HIN

A popular day-trip from Hua Hin is 63km west to the fifteen-tiered **Pala-u Waterfall**, situated close to the Burmese border and within **Kaeng Krachan National Park** (B300; @nps.dnp.go.th). Though the falls themselves are hardly exceptional, the route there takes you through lush, hilly landscape and past innumerable pineapple plantations. There's no public transport to the falls, but every tour operator features them in its programme. To get there under your own steam, follow the signs from the west end of Thanon Chomsin along Highway 3218. Once inside the park you'll see hundreds of butterflies and may also catch sight of monitor lizards and six species of hornbill. A slippery and occasionally steep path follows the river through the fairly dense jungle up to the falls, passing the (numbered) tiers en route to the remote fifteenth level, though most people opt to stop at the third level, which has the first pool of any decent depth (full of fish but not that clear) and is a half-hour walk from the car park.

Hua Hin also offers excursions to Khao Sam Roi Yot National Park, Phetchaburi, Amphawa floating market and Kanchanaburi, not to mention the old summer palace of Phra Ratchaniwet Marukhathaiyawan just to the north (see page 211). In addition, a number of **activities** are available, such as cycling and kiteboarding.

#### TOUR OPERATORS

**Hua Hin Adventure Tour** 69/7 Thanon Naebkehat ☎032 530314, @huahinadventuretour.com. Offers a huge range of tours, including Pala-u Falls (from B1700/person), a boat trip in Kaeng Krachan National Park (from B2000), Khao Sam Roi Yot National Park (from B1700; including kayaking on Khao Daeng canal, from B2000), Phetchaburi (B1500), Amphawa Floating Market (B2000), sea cruises (B1800) and elephant watching in Kui Buri National Park (from B1900), as well as a selection of diving, snorkelling and traditional Thai cooking classes.

**Hua Hin Bike Tours** 15/120 Thanon Phetkasem ☎081 173 4469, @huahinbiketours.com. A variety of guided half-day (from B1450) and day rides (from B2950 including lunch), including transfers, as well as rental for B500/day and multi-day tours.

**Kiteboarding Asia** ☎081 591 4593, @kiteboardingasia.com. Kiteboarding courses and rental from three shops on the beach to the south of the *Centara Grand*, the first of which is between Soi 71 and Soi 73 (B4000 for a one-day course, B11,000 for three days; best conditions from Feb to mid-May); also offers stand-up paddleboarding courses and rental.

# Monsoon Valley Vineyard

45km west of Hua Hin ☎ 081 701 0222, ⓦ monsoonvalley.com • Shuttle service from Hua Hin Hills Bistro and Wine Cellar, next to Villa Market on Thanon Phetkasem (2 daily; B300 return)

This vineyard welcomes visitors to sample its wares (from B290 for a three-wine tasting set), among which the most successful is the Shiraz Rosé. Other activities include tours of the estate and vineyard by jeep, elephant or mountain bike; there's a restaurant with fine views from its terrace over the rows of vines to the broad, tranquil valley beyond.

## ARRIVAL AND DEPARTURE                                        HUA HIN

There are currently no scheduled services to Hua Hin Airport.

### BY TRAIN

All services between the south and Bangkok (mostly using Hualamphong, with a few stopping trains serving Thonburi station) stop at Hua Hin's photogenic 1920s station, a 10min walk west of the seafront.

Destinations Bangkok (Hualamphong 11 daily, Thonburi 2 daily; 3hr 30min–5hr); Padang Besar (for Malaysia; 1 daily; 13hr 40min); Chumphon (11 daily; 3hr 30min–5hr 20min); Nakhon Si Thammarat (2 daily; 12hr); Prachuap Khiri Khan (10 daily; 1hr 30min); Surat Thani (10 daily; 5hr 40min–8hr); Trang (2 daily; 12hr).

### BY BUS

**Baw Khaw Saw terminal** Most government and private buses (including some through services on their way from Bangkok to points south) use the main Baw Khaw Saw terminal, which is well to the south of the centre, between Thanon Phetkasem sois 96 and 98, though some services will drop you off at the central clocktower (Wat Hua Hin) on their way in.

Destinations Chiang Mai (3 daily; 12–13hr); Chumphon (roughly hourly in the morning, fewer in the afternoon; 3hr 30min–4hr 30min); Krabi (2 daily; 9–10hr); Phuket (via Ranong; 5 daily; 9–10hr); Surat Thani (2 daily; 7–8hr).

**From/to Bangkok's Southern Bus Terminal** A/c buses (roughly every 2hr 30min; 4hr) to Bangkok's Southern Bus Terminal, stopping at Cha-am and Phetchaburi, leave from beside the *Siri Phetkasem* hotel on Thanon Sa Song.

**From/to Bangkok's Suvarnabhumi Airport and Pattaya** Roong Reuang (ⓦ airporthuahinbus.com) operate coaches to and from Suvarnabhumi Airport (9 daily; 4hr) and Pattaya (1–2 daily; 5–6hr), from their base by the airport on the east side of Thanon Phetkasem, 6km north of the centre, which is linked to the clock tower by a non-stop shuttle van (B30).

**Non-a/c Phetchaburi buses, via Cha-am** Setting off from a spot north of TAT, located on Thanon Phetkasem, opposite the Esso petrol station (roughly every 30min; 1hr 50min).

**To the islands** Lomprayah, with an office situated on Thanon Phetkasem south of Thanon Damnern Kasem (☎ 032 533 739, ⓦ lomprayah.com), runs a twice-daily bus and catamaran service (daily at 8.30am & 11.30pm) to Ko Tao (B1050), Ko Pha Ngan (B1300) and Ko Samui (B1400), via Chumphon.

### BY MINIBUS

Several private, government-licensed companies based at a new terminal on Soi 51, just off Thanon Phetkasem, run a/c minibuses to and from many destinations in Bangkok, including the Southern and Northern Bus Terminals and Don Muang Airport, Kanchanaburi, Pranburi and Prachuap Khiri Khan.

### BY BOAT TO PATTAYA

Ferries operated by Royal Passenger Liner (☎ 087 905 2525) run once a day (2hr 30min; B1250) to the Bali Hai Pier in Pattaya from Soi Ao Hua Don 3, near Khao Takiab.

## GETTING AROUND

**By taxi** Hua Hin's taxi services include plentiful motorcycle taxis, samlors and pricy tuk-tuks.

**By songthaew** Shared songthaews of different colours operate several fixed routes in Hua Hin. Green ones run from the airport, located 6km north of town, via Thanon Sa Song to Khao Takiab in the south of town. White songthaews head down Thanon Phetkasem from the railway station all the way to Soi 112 and Wat Huay Mongkol (daytime service only). White ones with a red flash have two circular routes that both include a stretch on Thanon Phetkasem between Soi 94 and Soi 55 and Thanon Naebkehat, while the orange ones also run up Thanon Phetkasem from Soi 94, via Thanon Sa Song, terminating at the Makro hypermarket located far to the north of town.

**By car or motorbike** Car rental outlets include Avis, on the north side of town at 15/112 Thanon Phetkasem, near Soi 29, who will deliver and collect anywhere in Hua Hin or Cha-am (☎ 02 251 1131, ⓦ avisthailand.com). Among the transport touts who rent out mopeds for B200/day on Thanon Damnern Kasem, try Khun Dennapa (☎ 081 942 5615, ⓦ den-carrental.com), who hangs out on the pavement in front of the *Sirin Hotel*, near the 7-Eleven.

**3**

3

## INFORMATION

**Tourist information** The TAT office is on Thanon Phetkasem, just north of Thanon Chomsin (daily 8.30am–4.30pm; ☎032 513885). There's also a helpful municipal tourist information office (Mon–Fri 8.30am–4.30pm; ☎032 511047, ext 100) in the local government buildings on the corner of Thanon Damnern Kasem and Thanon Phetkasem, with a satellite office just up Phetkasem at the clocktower (Mon–Fri 8.30am–7pm, Sat & Sun 9am–5pm).

**Publications and websites** Among Hua Hin's many English-language publications and maps, the *Hua Hin Pocket Guide*, a free, monthly booklet that includes an outline of the town's songthaew routes, is worth keeping an eye out for.

## ACCOMMODATION

A night or two at the former *Railway Hotel* (now the *Centara Grand*) is reason in itself to visit Hua Hin, but there are plenty of other **places to stay**. The most unusual **guesthouses** are those built on the **squid piers** on Thanon Naretdamri, north of the pagoda, with rooms strung out along wooden jetties so you can hear, feel – and smell, especially at low tide – the sea beneath you, even if you can't afford a room with an actual sea view. Room rates at many places can drop significantly from Mondays to Thursdays, so don't be afraid to ask for a discount.

**Amari** 117/74 Thanon Takiab ☎032 616 600, ⊕amari. com; map p.213. About 3km south of the centre on the road to Khao Takiab (with a free shuttle service to town), the *Amari* is set around a beautiful, 40m garden pool fed by fountains. The spacious rooms are elegantly contemporary with big walk-in showers, and there's a delightful spa, Breeze, offering innovative treatments to suit your mood, as well as a gym and a fun kids' club. It's not on the strand itself but has a beach club with a pool and restaurant a 5min walk (or a shuttle ride) away. B3880

★ **Anantara** 5km north of central Hua Hin on Thanon Phetkasem ☎032 520250, ⊕anantara.com; map p.213. Set in effusive, beautifully designed tropical gardens, this is a lovely resort-style idyll, just out of town (with a regular shuttle service). Accommodation is in eight-room Thai-style pavilions, whose stylishly appointed rooms use plenty of red wood. The hotel has very good Italian, Thai and grill restaurants, two pools, a gorgeous spa, a cooking school, two tennis courts, a kids' club, free yoga classes and mountain bikes, and its own stretch of beach, with kayaks available. B6730

**Avani** About 8km north of central Hua Hin on Thanon Phetkasem ☎032 898 989, ⊕minorhotels.com/avani; map p.213. Chic luxury hotel on a long, narrow plot of landscaped gardens with no less than three expansive swimming pools. Diverse rooms, including pool villas (some with Jacuzzis on their balconies) are done out in cool blond woods with splashes of green and blue. There's an attractive contemporary spa, a kids' club and a fine Italian beachfront restaurant. B4470

★ **Baan Bayan** 119 Thanon Petchkasem ☎032 533540–4, ⊕baanbayan.com; map p.213. This very appealing boutique hotel has been sensitively renovated in keeping with the century-old Thai colonial-style villa at its heart, with polished teakwood floors, white clapboard walls, carved eaves and antique-style furniture. On the beachfront, there is a relaxing terrace café, together with separate kids' and adults' pools. Breakfast included. B3780

**Baan Somboon** 13/4 Soi Kaseam Sumphan, Thanon Damnern Kasem ☎032 511538, ⊕facebook.com/baansomboon; map p.213. Down a quiet but very central soi, this guesthouse divides between a lovely, old-fashioned house with polished teak floors, decorated with a melange of Thai antiques, woodcarvings and Western "old master" prints, and a small annexe. Spruce, homely rooms come with small, hot-water bathrooms, fridges, TVs, fans and a/c (B100 discount if you can manage without the a/c), and there's a small garden crammed with plants, songbirds and a fish tank. B800

★ **Centara Grand** 1 Thanon Damnern Kasem ☎032 512 021–38, ⊕centarahotelsresorts.com; map p.213. The original Thai "destination hotel", the main building is a classic of colonial-style architecture, boasting high ceilings, polished wood panelling, period furniture, wide sea-view balconies and a huge, landscaped garden full of topiary animals. Across the road, lush beachfront gardens shelter gorgeous, all-white clapboard villas, most with their own small marble pools, the rest with large outdoor Jacuzzis. With a total of four swimming pools, a lovely spa, tennis courts, a kids' club and a giant chessboard, you need never leave the grounds. You can even tuck into afternoon tea at *The Museum*, the original lobby, which now displays hotel memorabilia. B7040

**Chomsin Hotel** 130/4 Thanon Chomsin ☎032 515348 (bookable through ⊕booking.com); map p.213. Handsome, sand-coloured, small hotel with a pleasant welcome, offering smart, bright, compact rooms in neutral colours with a few decorative touches and plenty of amenities: a/c, hot showers, cable TV, fridges and safes. Some have balconies from which you can glimpse the sea over the rooftops. B1300

**Fu-Lay Guest House and Hotel** 110/1 Thanon Naretdamri, guesthouse ☎032 513145, ⊕fulayhuahin. net; hotel ☎032 513670, ⊕fulayhuahin.com; map p.213. *Fu-Lay* is in two halves, with guesthouse rooms strung along a jetty and a/c hotel accommodation, some with sea-view balconies, in a low-rise block across the street. The jetty guesthouse is the most stylish of its kind in Hua Hin, offering attractively appointed a/c rooms with nice hot-water bathrooms (B1050), plus some cheap en-suite

## SOI 67 GUESTHOUSES

About fifteen minutes' walk south down the beach from the *Centara Grand*, or 2km by road down Thanon Phetkasem, there's a little knot of accommodation on Soi 67. Here, facing each other across the short, narrow soi about 100m back from the beach, are a dozen little guesthouses, many Scandinavian–Thai run, which share a swimming pool; none comprises more than twenty rooms and most charge about B1000. They're very popular with older European couples, many of whom return for several months every winter, so booking is essential.

fan rooms (some with hot water) and a breezy seating area set right over the water, where you can enjoy breakfast. Fan B550, a/c B950

**Marriott Resort & Spa** 107/1 Thanon Phetkasem 032 904 666, marriott.com; map p.213. Water features are at the heart of this lively new 300-room hotel. Children will love all the waterpark-like slides and fountains at the kids' and teen pools (not to mention the kids' club); there's also an adult pool, as well as a huge loop pool for exploring the gardens. Stylish rooms include subtle Thai elements in their contemporary design, and there's an excellent beachfront restaurant, Big Fish. B6620

**Mod** 116 Thanon Naretdamri 032 512296, mod guesthouse.com; map p.213. A friendly and well-maintained little jetty guesthouse, where rooms are all shining white, with cable TV and small but attractive

bathrooms, and come with either fan and cold water or a/c and hot. There's a nice, breezy, covered sea-view terrace at the end. Fan B585, a/c B855

**Sunshine Hotel** Soi 67, off Thanon Phetkasem 032 515309, sunshine.guesthouse.beach@gmail.com; map p.213. Typical Soi 67 guesthouse, with friendly staff and a wide variety of clean, well-maintained a/c rooms, most with small balconies, and all with hot water, cable TV and fridge. B800

**Tong Mee House** 1 Soi Ruam Phow, Thanon Naebkehat 032 530725, tongmeehousehuahin.com; map p.213. In a modern, five-storey block on a quiet soi, this friendly guesthouse offers great value: six small but neat rooms with a/c, hot water, fridges, TVs and small balconies, and an attractive "penthouse" double with a large, shaded roof terrace (B1000). B600

### EATING AND DRINKING

Hua Hin is renowned for its **seafood**, and some of the best places to enjoy the local catch are the seafront and squid-pier restaurants along Thanon Naretdamri. Fish also features heavily at the large and lively **night market**, which sets up at sunset along Soi 72 (the western end of Thanon Dechanuchit). The biggest concentration of **bars** is in the network of sois between the *Hilton Hotel* and Wat Hua Hin, particularly along Soi Bintabat, Soi Kanjanomai and Thanon Poonsuk; most of these places are so-called "bar-beers", with lots of seating round the bar and hostesses dispensing beer and flirtation through the night.

**Baan Itsara** 7 Thanon Naebkehat, near Soi 10, north of Thanon Damrongrat (Phetkasem Soi 51) 032 530574; map p.213. Very good seafood in a traditional lime-green wooden house with simple tables on a seaside terrace. The speciality here is sweet basil sauce – which comes out something like pesto – served with, for example, the likes of crab claws (B250), but the grilled mackerel and the seafood *laap* with land-lotus leaves are also delicious. Daily 11am–10pm.

**Chao Lay** 15 Thanon Naretdamri; map p.213. Hua Hin's most famous jetty restaurant is deservedly popular, serving up high-quality seafood from live tanks out front via a big open kitchen, including rock lobster, blue crab, scallops, cottonfish, mixed seafood hot plates and specialities such as

the "prawn curry mousse" (*haw mok*). Most main dishes cost around B250–350. Daily 10am–10pm.

**Coco 51** Soi 51, off the east side of Thanon Naebkehat 032 515597, coco51.com; map p.213. Genteel, white-linen-tablecloth affair on a beachfront terrace, where the menu splits evenly between Western and Thai food, including a few southern specialities. The *chu chi* curry with king prawns and lychees (B390) and the chicken in pandanus leaves are especially good, and there's live music every night (Sunday is Latino night). Daily 11am–10.30pm.

**Cool Breeze** 62 Thanon Naretdamri 032 531062, coolbreezecafebar.com; map p.213. Either in the nice little garden at the back or amid the fresh, leafy decor inside an atmospheric old fisherman's house, you can tuck into some very tasty tapas (including plenty of vegetarian options) at this bar-café, which imports many of its ingredients from Spain. You can get a set of seven tapas for B995, and they also do baguettes, paella and other seafood and meat mains. Happy hour till 7pm includes 3-for-2 tapas and 2-for-1 sangria. Daily 11am until late.

**Hua Hin Brewing Company** Thanon Naretdamri; map p.213. Owned by the adjacent *Hilton*, this lively bar sports a nautical theme on its tiered streetside terraces and offers DJs, live bands, a pool table and TV sports. Daily 6pm–2am.

**Koti** Thanon Dechanuchit, corner of Thanon Phetkasem; map p.213. With pavement tables right on a prominent

3

corner opposite the night market, this very simple Thai-Chinese restaurant rustles up justifiably famous *hoy jor* (deep-fried crab sausage; B200), which goes nicely with its tasty fried rice with salted fish (B80). Expect to queue for a table in the evening. Daily noon–4pm & 6–10pm.

**Pa Jeua** Thanon Naretdamri, opposite the Hilton Hua Hin; map p.213. Famous roadside stall that sells Thailand's favourite dessert, delicious *khao niaw mamuang* (fresh mango with sticky rice and coconut milk), for B120. Daily 9.30am–2pm.

**Sara Jane's** 28/1 Thanon Poonsuk ☎032 532990; map p.213. This branch of an old Bangkok favourite provides an array of authentic northeastern Thai food, including *som tam* with raw salted crab (B95), delicious central Thai seafood dishes, as well as a selection of breakfasts, pizzas, pastas and other Western fare, all served to diners in a lovely big garden shaded by trees. Daily 9.30am–1pm & 5.30–11pm.

★ **Sopa Seafood** Soi Mooban Takiab (a right fork off the main Khao Takiab road), near Lunar Hut Resort and opposite Soi Ao Hua Don 9 ☎081 880 7112; map p.213. You won't regret the trek out to this excellent seafood restaurant, set on a wooden deck among banana trees, just inland from Khao Takiab. The *poo nim phat phong karii* (soft-shell crab fried in curry powder; B300) is exquisite and the *plaa meuk det diaw* (sun-dried squid; B200) is even better. Daily 9am–9pm (closed first Tues of the month).

## ENTERTAINMENT

**Thai Boxing Garden** Down a small soi off Thanon Poonsuk ☎032 515 269, ⍟thaiboxinghuahin.com. Generally speaking, Tuesdays and Saturdays are fight nights (certainly in high season, sometimes taking a break in the off-season) at the Thai Boxing Garden with programmes starting at 9pm (B600–800); it's owned by local *muay thai* champion Khun Chop, who also runs Thai boxing classes every day (B400/hr for a one-to-one session).

## SHOPPING

**Asia Books** Market Village shopping centre, Thanon Petchkasem near Soi 88/1 ☎098 494 1466; map p.213. Small branch of Thailand's main English-language bookstore chain. Mon–Thurs & Sun 10.30am–9pm, Fri & Sat 10.30am–10pm.

**Cicada Market** Suan Sri, Thanon Takiab (near the Hyatt Regency, about 4km south of the Centara Grand) ⍟cicadamarket.com; map p.213. Modelled on Chiang Mai's walking streets, this weekend market features jewellery, cute accessories, lots of T-shirts and other clothes, artists' stalls and, of course, plenty of food, plus regular performances of all kinds in the amphitheatre. Fri & Sat 4–11pm, Sun 4–10pm.

**Khomapastr** 218 Thanon Phetkasem ☎032 511250, ⍟khomapastrfabrics.com; map p.213. Famous outlet for *pha kiaw* (or *pha khomapastr*), brightly coloured, hand-printed cotton with lovely, swirling *kannok* patterns, usually with strong elements of gold – Khomapastr's founder, himself a prince, was inspired to start the business when rummaging through trunks of nineteenth-century royal clothing at Bangkok's National Museum in the 1940s. You can buy the cloth by the piece or metre to use in your own designs, or made up into skirts, shirts, cushion covers and bags. Mon–Sat 9am–7pm, Sun 9am–5pm.

**Plearn Wan** Thanon Phetkasem, between sois 38 and 40 ⍟plearnwan.com; map p.213. Curious exercise in nostalgia and commercialism – the name "Enjoy the Past" says it all – that's been a raging success with Thais from all over the country. It's essentially a shopping mall, but in the vintage style of Thai-Chinese wooden shophouses, selling retro everything: *luk krung* CDs, old-fashioned toys, traditional coffee and desserts, ukuleles… Mon–Thurs & Sun 9am–9pm, Fri & Sat 9am–10pm.

## DIRECTORY

**Banks and exchange** There are currency-exchange counters all over the resort, especially on Thanon Damnern Kasem and Thanon Naretdamri; most of the main bank branches with ATMs are on Thanon Phetkasem.

**Hospital** Bangkok Hospital, 888 Thanon Phetkasem, south of the centre near Soi 94 (☎032 616800, ⍟bangkokhospital.com/huahin).

**Immigration office** The place to go for extensions of tourist visas and tourist visa exemptions, and for re-entry permits at Bluport shopping centre, between sois 100 and 102, Thanon Petchkasem (Mon–Fri 10am–6pm).

**Meditation** English-medium courses in sitting and walking meditation, either weekly or week-long, with talks on Buddhism, at Wat Khao Santi, just off Soi 91, Thanon Phetkasem (free, donations welcome; ⍟meditation inhuahin.org).

**Pharmacy** Several in the resort, including the helpful and well-stocked Medihouse (daily 9.30am–11pm), opposite the *Hilton* on Thanon Naretdamri.

**Thai language** Classes and private lessons at TLC, 83/14 Wongchomsin Building, Thanon Phetkasem (near Soi 63/1; ☎032 533428, ⍟thailanguagecentre.org).

**Tourist police** For all emergencies, call the tourist police on the free, 24hr phoneline (☎1155), or contact them at their office opposite the *Centara Grand* at the beachfront end of Thanon Damnern Kasem.

# Pak Nam Pran

The stretch of coast between Hua Hin and Chumphon barely registers on most foreign tourists' radar, but many better-off Bangkokians have favourite beaches in this area, the nicest of which is sophisticated **PAK NAM PRAN** (aka Pranburi). Just 30km or so south of Hua Hin, Pak Nam Pran used to cater only for families who owned beach villas here, but in the past few years the shorefront homes have been joined by a growing number of enticing, if pricey, boutique hotels, and signs are there's more development to come. For now, facilities consist of just a few minimarkets, car-rental outlets and independent bars and restaurants, especially around the *Evason* hotel towards the northern end of the beach, plus the possibility of organizing day-trips to nearby Khao Sam Roi Yot National Park through hotel staff; there's also kiteboarding lessons and rental, as well as stand-up paddleboarding lessons, rental and tours, with Asian kiteboarding champion, Yoda (☎087 017 6428, ⓦfacebook.com/yodakiteschool), based at Preeburan Resort, about 2km south of the Evason.

As along much of the Gulf coast, the **beach** itself, also known as Hat Naresuan, is not exceptional (it has hardly any shade and is suffering from erosion in parts), but it is long, with fine sand, and nearly always empty, and you're quite likely to see dolphins playing within sight of the shore. The strand stretches south from Pak Nam Pran town at the mouth of the Pran River – which is known for its colourful fishing boats, specializing in squid – for around 7km to the headland at Khao Kalok ("Skull Mountain") and the tiny Thao Kosa Forest Park.

## ARRIVAL AND DEPARTURE

PAK NAM PRAN

Easiest access is via the town of **Pranburi**, which straddles Highway 4 some 23km south of Hua Hin. There's no public transport from Pranburi to Pak Nam Pran beach, 10km or so away, but hotels can arrange transfers and any Pranburi songthaew driver will taxi you there. Because of this and because the hotels and restaurants are well spread out along the beach, it's best to have your own transport. Pranburi's main crossroads (Highway 4 and Thanon Ratbamrung) is at Talat Chaikaew – if making your own way, the easiest route is to turn east off Highway 4 here and take minor road 3168 down to the sea, picking up the relevant sign for your hotel.

### FROM/TO PRANBURI

**By train** Pranburi's quaint old station is 4km east of the Highway 4 crossroads (Talat Chaikaew) towards the beach, off the north side of Route 3168.

Destinations Bangkok (Hualamphong 1 daily, Thonburi 2 daily; 5hr); Chumphon (2 daily; 4hr 30min); Prachuap Khiri Khan (3 daily; 1hr).

**By bus** As well as many through services to and from the south, Pranburi is served by a/c buses from Bangkok's Southern Bus Terminal and non-a/c buses from Thanon Sa Song in Hua Hin, which drop passengers close by the main Highway 4 crossroads at Talat Chaikaew.

Destinations Bangkok (every 30min; 3–4hr); Hua Hin (roughly every 30min; 30min).

**By minibus** A/c minibuses from Bangkok's Southern and Northern Bus Terminals generally stop at the Tesco Lotus supermarket on Highway 4 opposite Pranburi's City Hall, 2km north of Talat Chaikaew, but you could ask the driver to take you to your beach hotel for a little extra money.

## ACCOMMODATION

Pak Nam Pran's charming boutique **accommodation** is its biggest draw. With influences ranging from Greece to the South Pacific, from Morocco to Scandinavia, the style tends to be more arty than five-star, though you will certainly be comfortable. Some hotels aren't suitable for kids owing to their multiple levels and unfenced flights of steps. Breakfast is generally included in the price. During weekends in high season (Nov–May), prices rise and you'll need to book ahead. The following are spread over a 2km stretch of the beachfront road, starting about 4km south of Pak Nam Pran town.

**Aleenta** Central Pak Nam Pran beach ☎032 618333, ⓦaleenta.com. This stunningly designed, eco-friendly hotel,

divided between the Main Wing and the Frangipani Wing, 500m down the beach, offers a collection of gorgeous circular, thatched bungalows and very tasteful rooms, most with uninterrupted sea views, decks and plunge pools. The feel is modernist chic, with elegantly understated local furnishings and huge windows, and iPods and wi-fi capability rather than TVs. There are swimming pools in both wings and a spa, while the restaurant uses produce from its own organic farm. B5740

**The Beach House Bungalows** Northern Pak Nam Pran beach, set inland behind the Evason ☎090 141 7208, ⓦbeach-housepranburi.com. Popular with kiteboarders, this friendly English-run resort offers half a dozen smart, polished-concrete bungalows, with a/c, hot showers, smart TVs and fridges, plus a family apartment, around a communal plunge pool. **B800**

**Evason** Northern Pak Nam Pran beach ☎ 032 632111, ⓦ sixsenses.com/evason. The biggest and best-known hotel in Pak Nam Pran, but as accommodation is screened by graceful gardens, the feel is quite private. Rooms are cool and contemporary, with big balconies; for extra privacy, check into a super-luxe private-pool villa, a favourite choice of Thai film stars. Facilities include a huge pool, a spa, three restaurants, tennis courts and a kids' club. Breakfast included. **B5050**

★ **Huaplee Lazy Beach** Central Pak Nam Pran beach ☎ 032 630555, ⓦ huapleelazybeach.com. This exceptionally cute collection of six idiosyncratic white-cube beachfront rooms around a pretty lawn, as well as several nearby suites and villas, some with their own pools, is the brainchild of the architect-interior designer owners. It's a characterful place of whimsical, marine-themed interiors done out with white-painted wood floors, blue-and-white colour schemes and funky shell and driftwood decor. The rooms are airy and bright but all have a/c, fridges and TVs; some also have fantastic sea-view terraces. Breakfast included. **B3500**

### EATING

**Krua Jaew** On the edge of Pak Nam Pran town, about 2km north of the Evason ☎ 032 631 302. The best of several neighbouring seafront restaurants, offering an enormous, mid-priced menu of mostly fish and seafood dishes, including the local speciality, deep-fried sun-dried squid (*pla meuk det diaw*; B200), excellent crab curry and seafood curry soufflé (*haw mok thalay*, on the menu as "steamed seafood with spicy and coconut milk"). Unsigned in English, but it's the first restaurant you'll come to heading up the beach road into Pak

Nam Pran, on the left-hand side. Daily roughly 10am–9pm.

**Krua Sawatdikan Khao Kalok** On the south side of Khao Kalok's rocky outcrop at the far southern end of Pak Nam Pran beach ☎ 086 701 8597. This simple shorefront restaurant has an extensive menu of very good seafood dishes (mostly B90–150) and great views of Khao Sam Roi Yot from its beach tables under the casuarinas; mosquitoes are a problem here though, so take repellent. Daily 11am–8pm, sometimes later (especially at weekends).

# Khao Sam Roi Yot National Park

National park entry fee B200 • ☎ 032 821568, ⓦ nps.dnp.go.th

With a name that translates as "The Mountain with Three Hundred Peaks", **KHAO SAM ROI YOT NATIONAL PARK**, with its northern entrance 28km south of Pak Nam Pran beach or 63km from Hua Hin, encompasses a small but varied, mosquito-ridden coastal zone of just 98 square kilometres. The dramatic limestone crags after which it is named are the dominant feature, looming 600m above the Gulf waters and the forested interior, but perhaps more significant are the mud flats and freshwater marsh which attract and provide a breeding ground for thousands of migratory birds. **Bird-watching** at Thung Khao Sam Roi Yot swamp is a major draw, but the famously photogenic Phraya Nakhon Khiri cave is the focus of most day-trips, while a few decent trails and a couple of secluded beaches provide added interest.

**Orientation** in the park is fairly straightforward. One main inland road runs roughly north–south through it from the R3168 (the road from Pranburi's main junction to Pak Nam Pran), passing, in order: the 2km side road to **Hat Phu Noi**, a quiet, golden-sand beach that offers several resort alternatives to the park's accommodation and the chance to see dolphins in the cool season; the northern park checkpoint, 4km further on; the turn-offs for Ban Bang Pu (the jumping-off point for Tham Phraya Nakhon), Ban Khung Tanot (for Tham Sai) and Hat Sam Phraya (all to the east); then going over Khao Daeng canal, before looping westwards around the main massif, past the **park headquarters** (where park brochures and maps are available) and the southern checkpoint (14km from the northern checkpoint), to Highway 4 at kilometre-stone 286.5.

## Tham Phraya Nakhon

B400 return per boat from Wat Bang Pu

Khao Sam Roi Yot's most visited attraction is the **Tham Phraya Nakhon** cave system, hidden high up on a cliffside above **Hat Laem Sala**, an unremarkable sandy bay with a national park visitor centre that's inaccessible to vehicles. The usual way to get to Hat Laem Sala is by a five-minute boat ride from the knot of food stalls behind Wat Bang Pu on the edge of **Ban Bang Pu** fishing village (6km from the northern checkpoint). It's also possible to walk over the headland from behind Wat Bang Pu to Hat Laem Sala, along a signed, but at times steep, 500m trail. From Hat Laem Sala, another taxing though shaded trail runs up the hillside to Tham Phraya Nakhon in around thirty minutes.

The huge twin **caves** are filled with stalactites and stalagmites and wreathed in lianas and gnarly trees, but their most dramatic features are the partially collapsed roofs, which allow the sunlight to stream in and illuminate the interiors, in particular beaming down in the late morning on the famous royal pavilion, Phra Thi Nang Khua Kharunhad, which was built in the second cave in 1890 in honour of Rama V.

## Tham Sai

South of Tham Phraya Nakhon lies **Tham Sai**, a thoroughly dark and dank limestone cave, complete with stalactites, stalagmites and petrified waterfalls (electric lighting is switched on when there are enough visitors at weekends, but otherwise torches are available to rent). It's reached by a 20min trail from **Ban Khung Tanot** village (accessible by road, 8km on from the Ban Bang Pu turn-off).

## Khao Daeng and around

Canal cruise B600 for up to six people • ☎ 089 903 1619

The next turning off the main road will take you down to **Hat Sam Phraya**, a quiet, kilometre-long beach with a national park visitor centre, while a little further on the road crosses mangrove-fringed **Khao Daeng canal**. From beside Wat Khao Daeng, on the west side of the main road here, you can charter a boat for a one-hour cruise that's best in the early morning or the late afternoon.

A couple of kilometres on, you can scramble up **Khao Daeng** itself, a 157m-high outcrop that offers good summit views over the coast, via a thirty-minute trail that begins near the park headquarters. The park's 45-minute **Mangrove Forest Nature Trail** also begins close to the headquarters leading through the swampy domiciles of monitor lizards and egrets, with the chance of encountering long-tailed (crab-eating) macaques.

## Thung Khao Sam Roi Yot

Accessed not from the main park road, but by turning east off Highway 4, 200m north of kilometre-stone 276, and continuing for 9km

The park hosts up to three hundred species of **birds** and between September and November the mud flats are thick with migratory flocks from Siberia, China and northern Europe. To the west of Khao Sam Roi Yot lies Thailand's largest freshwater marsh, **Thung Khao Sam Roi Yot** (aka Beung Bua), near the village of Rong Jai (Rong Che). With open-sided shelters over the water, this is an excellent place for observing waders and songbirds, and is one of only two places in the country where the **purple heron** breeds.

### ARRIVAL AND GETTING AROUND

### KHAO SAM ROI YOT

Like most of Thailand's national parks, Khao Sam Roi Yot is hard to explore without your own **transport**, and its sights are spread too far apart to walk between.

**By bicycle, motorbike or car** All three are available at *Dolphin Bay Resort* (see page 222) while motorbikes

can be rented in Hua Hin (which also has car rental) or Prachuap Khiri Khan.

**With a tour** The park can be visited on a one-day tour from Hua Hin, including cycling tours (see page 214), Pak Nam Pran or *Dolphin Bay Resort*.

**3**

### ACCOMMODATION AND EATING

Given the limitations of the park accommodation, many people prefer to stay a few kilometres to the north at the long, pleasingly shaded beach of Hat Phu Noi.

#### IN THE PARK

**National Park accommodation** ☎ 032 821 568, Ⓦ nps.dnp.go.th. Bungalows (for 5–6 people, with hot showers; from B1200) are available at the headquarters and should be booked ahead. At Hat Laem Sala, there are tents to rent (B180–230 per tent) and a restaurant, but the national park bungalows are currently unavailable. Hat Sam Phraya, a beach between Khao Daeng canal and Ban Khung Tanot, also has tents to rent and a restaurant. Camping is possible at Thung Khao Sam Roi Yot if you bring your own tent.

#### HAT PHU NOI

**Brassiere Cozy Beach** Bottom end of Hat Phu Noi ☎ 032 630555, Ⓦ brassierebeach.com. Under the same architect owners as *Huaplee* at Pak Nam Pran (see p.523), *Brassiere Cozy Beach* gets its name from the two conical Nom Sao ("Breast") islands offshore and the mainland spirit house where fishermen leave bras for good luck, and contains rooms with playful monikers like "La Perla". That may sound a bit naff to some, but the hotel itself is the height of quirky chic, airy and light-filled, with a mostly white-and-blue colour scheme. Some rooms have their own small Jacuzzi and pool or an outdoor bathroom, and canoes and bicycles are available, as well as sailing and stand-up paddleboarding. Breakfast included; prices go up a little at weekends. B2500

**Dolphin Bay** Northern end of the beach ☎ 032 825190, Ⓦ dolphinbayresort.com. Eco-conscious, family-focused resort just across the quiet road from the beach, offering comfortable a/c rooms, bungalows and family suites with fridges, hot water and TVs, large children's and adults' pools set in an attractive, palm-fringed lawn, plus a kids' playground. Pick-ups from Pranburi (B350) and Hua Hin (B700) can be arranged and there's plenty of things to do once you're here: transport to Tham Phraya Nakhon (B500) and Thung Khao Sam Roi Yot (B700), half-day tours to see wild elephants at Kuiburi National Park (from B950/person), boat trips to Tham Phraya Nakhon and local islands, plus kayak, catamaran and stand-up paddleboard rental. B1490

# Prachuap Khiri Khan and around

Despite lacking any must-see attractions, the tiny, unfrequented provincial capital of **PRACHUAP KHIRI KHAN**, 67km south of Pranburi, makes a pleasant place to break any journey up or down the coast. Apart from pineapples – the province is the biggest producer in Thailand, with truckloads for sale all along Highway 4 – its greatest asset is its setting: a huge, palm-fringed, half-moon bay, dotted with colourful fishing boats and tipped by a rocky outcrop at the north end and by a small group of jungly islands to the south – the waterfront promenade in the town centre is great for a seafood lunch with a view. There's a lovely **beach** in the next bay to the south, Ao Manao, and generally Prachuap is a fine spot to settle into small-town Thai life.

The town is contained in a small grid of streets that runs just 250m east to west, between the sea and the train station – with Highway 4 about 2km west of the station – and around 1km north to south, from the Khao Chong Krajok hill at the northern end to the Wing 5 air-force base in the south. **Orientation** couldn't be simpler. The major central road across from the station to the pier is Thanon Kongkiat, while Highway 326, the main east–west access road to Highway 4, cuts across the north end of town, and there are four main north–south roads: Thanon Phitak Chat near the station, Thanon Salacheep, Thanon Susuek and the seafront road, Thanon Chai Thalay, which to the north of the pier becomes a **walking street** on Friday and Saturday evenings, selling food, clothes and handicrafts.

## Khao Chong Krajok

The monkey-infested hill of **Khao Chong Krajok** is Prachuap's main sight: if you climb the 417 steps from Thanon Salacheep to the golden-spired chedi at the summit you get a great perspective on the scalloped coast below and west to the mountainous Burmese border, just 12km away.

## Ao Manao

Inside Wing 5 air-force base (you usually need to sign in at the base checkpoint and may need to show your passport) • Head south down Thanon Salacheep (or down the promenade and turn right) to reach the checkpoint and continue for 2km through the base to the beach • Tuk-tuk to the beach around B80

At the far southern end of town, the long, clean, sandy beach at **Ao Manao** is the best place in the area for swimming and sunbathing, sheltered between pristine, tree-covered headlands. On weekdays you're likely to have the sand almost to yourself, but it's a very popular spot with Thai families on weekends when the stalls at the beachfront food centre do a roaring trade in the locally famous *som tam puu* (spicy papaya salad with fresh crab), which you can eat at the deckchairs and tables under the thick canopy of pine trees on the beach. You can walk to the north end of the bay to the base of an outcrop known as Khao Lommuak, where a memorial commemorates the skirmish that took place here between Thai and Japanese forces in World War II.

## King Mongkut Memorial Park of Science and Technology

12km south of town, on the beach at Wa Ko (Waghor) • Daily 9am–4pm, fish-feeding at 11am & 2pm (subject to change) • Aquarium B30 • ☎ 032 661103, ⓦ waghor.go.th • To get there, turn east off Highway 4 at kilometre-stone 335, or go through Ao Manao air-force base, bearing left along the coast all the way

The main feature of the **King Mongkut Memorial Park of Science and Technology** (also signed as Phra Chomklao Science Park) is the extensive and well-stocked **Waghor Aquarium**. Highlights include an underwater tunnel, touch pools and fish-feeding, and there are display boards and labels for most of the fish in English. It's nothing like as slick as Sea Life Ocean World in Bangkok, but then again it's less than a thirtieth of the price. About 500m south along the beach road, the park also contains an astronomy museum that's decidedly low-tech but with enough labels in English to maintain interest.

The park is thought to mark the spot where **Rama IV** came to observe a solar eclipse on August 18, 1868. Having predicted the eclipse's exact course, King Mongkut decided to publicize science among his subjects by mounting a large expedition, aiming specifically to quash their centuries-old fear that the sun was periodically swallowed by the dragon Rahoo, and more generally to rattle traditional notions of astrology and cosmology. To this end, he invited scientists all the way from France and the British governor of Singapore, and himself turned up with fifty elephants and all his court, including the astrologers – who, as the leader of the French expedition noted, "could hardly be blamed if they did not display much enthusiasm for the whole project". Unfortunately, both the king and his 15-year-old son contracted malaria at Waghor; Mongkut passed away in Bangkok on October 1, but Chulalongkorn survived to become Thailand's most venerated king, Rama V.

---

**ARRIVAL AND DEPARTURE**                                    **PRACHUAP KHIRI KHAN**

**BY TRAIN**

Most services on the Southern Line from Bangkok stop at the train station, which is just on the west side of the centre, at the western end of Thanon Kongkiat.

**Destinations** Bangkok (8 daily to Hualamphong, 2 to Thonburi; 5–7hr); Chumphon (9 daily; 2hr–3hr 30min); Nakhon Si Thammarat (2 daily; 10hr 30min); Surat Thani (8 daily; 4hr 30min–6hr); Trang (1 daily; 11hr).

**BY BUS OR MINIBUS**

Prachuap's bus terminal is out on Highway 4, north of

Highway 326, the main access road to town. The number of long-distance bus services to and from the town centre is dwindling fast, with many people either heading out to the terminal to catch a through-bus (for points south, best in the morning or around midnight), or taking an a/c minibus from the centre.

**Buses from/to Bangkok** Pudtan Tour, on Thanon Phitak Chat just south of Thanon Kongkiat, runs a "first-class" a/c service to Bangkok's Southern Terminal (1 daily; 4hr 30min–5hr), which stops at Pranburi, the Hua Hin bypass (Highway 37) and Phetchaburi.

**A/c minibuses** Several companies in the town centre offer a/c minibuses to Bangkok, including one located near the start of Highway 326, just west of the Provincial Hall and the tourist office, which serves the Southern and Northern Bus Terminals, as well as Hua Hin. Just around the corner, just a short way down Thanon Phitak Chat, you'll find more a/c minibuses that head to Bangkok's Southern Bus Terminal. On Thanon Tessaban Bamrung (the road immediately north of Thanon Kongkiat), situated between Phitak Chat and Salacheep roads, you'll find services going to Chumphon, which will stop on Highway 4 near Ban Krut.

## INFORMATION AND GETTING AROUND

**Tourist information** There's a small but helpful municipal tourist information office (Mon–Fri 8.30am–4.30pm; ☎032 611491), where town maps are available, at the far northern end of town in a compound of provincial offices; it's on the ground floor at the north end of a large modern building that faces the beachfront road across a car park.
**Motorbike rental** Motorbikes (B200–250/day) can be rented from *Sun Beach Guesthouse.*

## ACCOMMODATION

**Faa Chom Khleun** Ao Manao ☎032 661088–9, ⓦaomanao.com. If you don't mind cosying up to the Thai military, this spruce air-force hotel on the Wing 5 base puts you right on the beach. All rooms have sea-view balconies, a/c, hot water, TV and fridge, and there's a large swimming pool. Breakfast included. B1240

**Hadthong Hotel** 21 Thanon Susuek, but also with an entrance just south of the pier on the beachfront road ☎032 601050, ⓦhadthong.com. Well-run, typical Thai provincial hotel, with comfortable rooms, many sporting balconies and peerless sea views, all with fridges, a/c, hot water and TVs – plus a 15m swimming pool overlooking the beach and snooker club. The cheapest rooms have mountain views, but it's only B100 more for a sea view. Breakfast included. B1100

**House 73** 73 Thanon Susuek, about 400m south of Thanon Kongkiat ☎086 046 3923, ⓦhomestay prachuap.blogspot.com. Striking modernist guesthouse with great views of the bay from its roof terrace and four a/c rooms which have been hand-painted in bold colours by the owners, taking inspiration from their favourite songs. B800

★ **Sun Beach Guesthouse** 160 Thanon Chai Thalay, 1km or so down the promenade from the pier ☎032 604770, ⓦsunbeachguesthouse.com. Run by a welcoming and helpful Thai–German couple, this palatial guesthouse is done out like a Mediterranean villa, with Corinthian columns and smart tiling everywhere. The bright, comfortable, mostly sky-blue rooms come with a/c, hot water, fridges, TVs and balconies, with prices varying according to the quality of the sea view. There's a seductive pool and whirlpool. B800

**Thur Hostel** 58 Thanon Chai Thalay, just south of Hadthong Hotel ☎096 047 5622, ⓦfacebook.com/thurhostelprachuap. Newly opened, all-a/c hostel in an attractive white clapboard building with a sociable bar and pool table. Smart dorms have bunk beds and hot showers, while the private rooms range from twins with shared hot showers to en-suite doubles with large balconies overlooking the bay. There's a shared kitchen and bicycles for rent. Dorms B380, doubles B600

## EATING AND DRINKING

Prachuap's famously good seafood is most cheaply sampled at the daytime food stalls at Ao Manao and at the town's lively and varied main **night market**, which sets up shop in the empty lot around the junction of Thanon Kongkiat and Thanon Phitak Chat.

**Ma-prow** 48 Thanon Chai Thalay, just south of Hadthong Hotel ☎092 667 2332. Mellow, rustic, airy restaurant overlooking the bay across the road (main courses around B150–200), which serves tasty squid with salted eggs and deep-fried spring rolls of crabmeat wrapped in tofu skin (*hoy jor*), as well as Western dishes including fish and chips. Daily 9am–9pm (last orders).

★ **Ploen Samut** South of the pier at 44 Thanon Chai Thalay, alongside the Hadthong Hotel ☎032 611115. The town's best restaurant opens out onto a pleasant, spacious courtyard facing the sea, and serves dishes along the likes of pan-fried oysters, tasty crab claws and excellent *kaeng pa pla say* (silver whiting fish in country curry; B120) on its seafood-dominated menu. Daily 9.30am–10pm.

**Rap Lom** About 1km north of the centre, beyond Khao Chong Krajok and the adjacent bridge. Another locals' favourite for seafood, including a very good version of the regional speciality, *plaa meuk det diaw* (sun-dried squid; B170), but also offering some wild-boar dishes. On the landward side of the beach road, with views of the sea. Daily 10am–9pm.

**Rome Seafood (MC Club House)** Thanon Chai Thalay, just south of Thur Hostel. Excellent spot for a waterside drink and maybe a bite to eat, hung with motorcycle memorabilia and home to some of the friendliest bikers you're ever likely to meet. Daily 5/6pm until late.

# Ban Krud

Graced with a tranquil, 5km sweep of white sand, pale-blue sea and swaying casuarinas, **BAN KRUD**, 70km south of Prachuap, supports a dozen or so fairly upmarket bungalow outfits and seafood restaurants along the central stretch of its shorefront road. About 1km inland from the main T-junction at the beach, the small, traditional village, which includes several ATMs, clusters around the train station. At the beach's northern end are a colourful fishing village that hosts a lively market on Thursday afternoons and a panoramic headland, **Khao Thongchai**, which is dominated by the 14m-high Phra Phut Kitti Sirichai Buddha image and its sparkling modern temple, **Wat Thang Sai**. Crowned with nine golden chedis, the temple displays an impressive fusion of traditional and contemporary features, including a series of charming modern stained-glass windows depicting Buddhist stories; reach it via a 1.5km-long road that spirals up from the beachfront road. Other than a visit to the temple and possibly a snorkelling trip to Ko Thalu (from B400/person through, for example, *Bayview*), the main pastime in Ban Krud is sitting under the trees and enjoying a long seafood lunch or dinner.

**3**

## ARRIVAL AND DEPARTURE                                   BAN KRUD

**By train** Half a dozen train services on the Southern Line from Bangkok stop at Ban Krud's tiny train station, where you should be able to easily find a motorbike taxi (with sidecar).

Destinations Bangkok (6 daily from Hualamphong, 1 from Thonburi; 5hr–7hr 30min); Chumphon (7 daily; 2hr); Nakhon Si Thammarat (1 daily; 9hr); Surat Thani (6 daily; 4hr–5hr 30min); Trang (1 daily; 10hr).

**By bus** Most southbound buses drop passengers on Highway 4, from where motorbike-and-sidecar taxis cover the 8km down to the beach; just one Bangkok–Bang Saphan a/c bus a day stops at Ban Krud itself.

## ACCOMMODATION

**Bayview** North of the headland, 4km from Sala Thai on Hat Tangsai ☎ 032 695 566–7, ⓦ bayviewbeachresort. com. Very welcoming, relaxed and shady spot on a long, quiet stretch of beach, with a swimming pool, a kids' pool and a lovely area for deckchairs under the beachside casuarinas. All the well-spaced, diverse bungalows boast a/c, fridges, TVs and hot water, and there's an excellent restaurant, free bicycles, and kayaks, motorbikes and cars to rent. Prices rise a little at weekends. Breakfast included. **B1600**

**Sala Thai** About 1km north of the central beachfront T-junction ☎ 032 695181, ⓦ salathaibeachresort.com. Friendly resort where a wide variety of smart concrete bungalows and log cabins, all with a/c, hot water, fridge and TV, are arranged around a spacious, pretty garden with lots of shady trees, just across the road from the beach; it also has a popular burger bar. Bikes and motorbikes are available for rent. Prices rise a little at weekends. Breakfast included. **B1000**

# Chumphon

South Thailand officially starts at **CHUMPHON**, where the main highway splits into west- and east-coast branches, and inevitably the provincial capital saddles itself with the title "gateway to the south". Most tourists take this tag literally and use the town as nothing more than a transport interchange between the Bangkok train and boats to **Ko Tao, Pha Ngan and Samui**, so the town is well equipped to serve these passers-through, offering clued-up travel agents and efficient transport links. In truth, there's little call for exploring the fairly average beaches, islands and reefs around town when the varied and attractive strands of Ko Tao are just a short hop away.

## ARRIVAL AND DEPARTURE                                   CHUMPHON

**BY PLANE**
Nok Air flies to Chumphon from Bangkok's Don Muang Airport (2 daily; 1hr). It's possible to buy a combination ticket all the way from Bangkok through to Ko Tao with

Nok, who also lay on a/c minibuses to Chumphon town for B200/person. At the time of writing, Air Asia were about to start a once-daily flight from Don Muang to Chumphon.

## BY TRAIN

Chumphon train station is on the northwest edge of town, less than a 10min walk from most guesthouses and hotels. Destinations Bangkok (10 daily to Hualamphong, 1 to Thonburi; 6hr 30min–9hr 30min); Padang Besar (for Malaysia; 1 daily; 9hr 30min); Nakhon Si Thammarat (2 daily; 7hr); Surat Thani (10 daily; 2hr 5min–4hr); Trang (2 daily; 7hr).

## BY BUS OR MINIBUS

The government bus station is inconveniently located 11km west of town on Highway 41 (B150 on a motorbike taxi), though long-distance services will sometimes drop in town. There's a wide choice of destinations served by the bus station, but most that you're likely to be interested in are served by private, government-licensed a/c bus and minibus services based in town, departing from various locations. These include Suwanathee and Chokeanan Tour (w chokeanantour.com) buses to Bangkok, and Rungkit buses to Phuket, via Ranong and Khao Lak. Agents such as *Suda* and *Fame* (see page 228) can also fix you up with tourist a/c minibus tickets to Krabi, Ko Lanta and Khao Sok. Destinations Bangkok (roughly hourly; 7–9hr); Hua Hin (roughly hourly; 3hr 30min–4hr 30min); Khao Lak (8 daily; 5–7hr); Nakhon Si Thammarat (8 daily; 5hr); Phuket (8 daily; 7–10hr); Prachuap Khiri Khan (every 45min; 3hr); Ranong (roughly hourly; 2hr 30min–3hr); Surat Thani (roughly hourly; 2hr 30min–4hr 30min).

## BY BOAT

There are several different boat services from Chumphon to Ko Tao, Pha Ngan and Samui, tickets for all of which are sold by travel agents and guesthouses in town. Of these, the Songserm Express and the night boats are the most likely to be cancelled if the weather is very bad.

**Lomprayah Catamaran** Office at the train station ☎ 081 956 5644, w lomprayah.com. Daily 7am and 1.30pm from Ao Thung Makham Noi, 27km south of Chumphon, with a bus between pier and station costing B100 extra; 1hr 45min to Ko Tao (B600); around 3hr 45min to Ko Pha Ngan (B1000); around 4hr to Maenam, Ko Samui (B1100).

**Songserm** Office at the pier ☎ 077 506205, w songserm. com. Daily 7am from Pak Nam, about 20km south of Chumphon, with transport to the pier from town included (pick-ups available from guesthouses and the station); 2hr 45min to Ko Tao (B500); around 5hr to Ko Pha Ngan (B800); around 6hr 15min to Na Thon, Ko Samui (B900).

**Night boats to Ko Tao** Cargo boats and car ferries of varying levels of comfort chug between Chumphon and Ko Tao overnight, taking about 6hr, some including transport to the pier from town in the ticket price, some not. Every night, except in the heaviest weather, at least one of these tubs will be running, though departure times may be affected by tides and storms; one of the more comfortable boats is the Porntaweesin (Tues, Thurs,

3

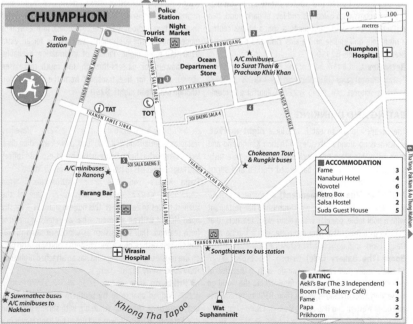

CHUMPHON

- Airport
- Police Station
- Tourist Police
- Night Market
- Train Station
- THANON KROMLUANG
- THANON KRAWIN MUANG
- Ocean Department Store
- A/C minibuses to Surat Thani & Prachuap Khiri Khan
- Chumphon Hospital
- THANON SALA DAENG
- SOI SALA DAENG 6
- TAT
- TOT
- SOI DAENG SALA 4
- THANON TAWEE SINKA
- THANON SUKSUMER
- A/C minibuses to Ranong
- SOI SALA DAENG 3
- Farang Bar
- THANON PRACHA UTHIT
- Chokeanan Tour & Rungkit buses
- THANON SALA DAENG
- THANON THA TAPAO
- Virasin Hospital
- THANON PARAMIN MANKA
- Songthaews to bus station
- Suwanathee buses
- A/C minibuses to Nakhon
- Khlong Tha Tapao
- Wat Suphannimit
- Highway 4, Bus station & Airport
- Tha Yang, Pak Nam & Ao Thung Makham

**ACCOMMODATION**
| | |
|---|---|
| Fame | 3 |
| Nanaburi Hotel | 4 |
| Novotel | 6 |
| Retro Box | 1 |
| Salsa Hostel | 2 |
| Suda Guest House | 5 |

**EATING**
| | |
|---|---|
| Aeki's Bar (The 3 Independent) | 1 |
| Boom (The Bakery Café) | 4 |
| Fame | 3 |
| Papa | 2 |
| Prikhorm | 5 |

Sat and Sun 11pm, from Tha Yang, about 15km south of Chumphon; ☎092 978 8302), charging B450, including transport from town and bunk beds, blankets and pillows in an a/c room.

## INFORMATION AND TOURS

**TAT office** Down a short soi at 111 Thanon Tawee Sinka (daily 8.30am–4.30pm; ☎077 501831, ✉tatchumphon@tat.or.th).

**Suda Guest House** Thanon Sala Daeng Soi 3 (aka Soi Bangkok Bank), 30m off Thanon Tha Tapao ☎080 144 2079 or ☎077 504366. The best source of local information and fixer in town, offering a personal, unbiased service, is Suda at her eponymous guesthouse. As well as tickets to Ko Tao, Suda offers a selection of discounted dive packages; bus and minibus tickets; twice-daily visa runs via Ranong to Myanmar (from B650; best in the morning); motorbike rental (B200–300/day); packages to Ko Chang (Ranong) and Ko Phayam; and local snorkelling and night-fishing trips.

## ACCOMMODATION

**Fame** 188/20–21 Thanon Sala Daeng ☎077 571077, ⓦchumphon-kohtao.com; map p.227. Above the restaurant and tour agency of the same name, this place has basic but good-sized and very clean rooms, with fans and hot water in either shared or en-suite bathrooms; the cheapest have mattresses on the floor. B150

**Nanaburi Hotel** 335/9 Thanon Pracha Uthit ☎077 503888, ⓦnanaburihotel.com; map p.227. Spread across two buildings in a quiet area set back from the main roads, the large rooms here have a pleasant, simple decor of wood and white paint and are equipped with a/c, hot showers, cable TV and fridges. B900

**Novotel** 15km southeast near Pak Nam ☎077 529529, ⓦnovotel-chumphon.com; map p.227. This low-rise luxury hotel on Paradornpab beach, done out in an unobtrusive Thai contemporary style, features spacious rooms with balconies and lots of dark wood, two restaurants, two swimming pools, a spa, a fitness centre, a nine-hole golf course and a kids' club and playground. Breakfast included. B2350

**Retro Box** About 1km east of the train station, just off Thanon Kromluang Chumphon on Soi 3 ☎077 510333, ⓦretroboxhotel.com; map p.227. Colourful a/c rooms with hot showers, TVs and fridges in salvaged shipping containers stacked up around an inviting swimming pool. The cheapest rooms only have enough space for bunk beds, while more expensive rooms have balconies, some of which give direct access to the pool. Light breakfast included. B690

**Salsa Hostel** Thanon Kromluang ☎077 505005, ⓦsalsahostel.com; map p.227. Welcoming hostel offering shining white, six- and seven-bed a/c dorms with modern bunk beds – with nice touches like individual reading lights – as well as a kitchen and rooftop terrace. Buffet breakfast included. Dorms B300

★ **Suda Guest House** Thanon Sala Daeng Soi 3 (aka Soi Bangkok Bank), 30m off Thanon Tha Tapao ☎080 144 2079 or ☎077 504366; map p.227. Chumphon's most welcoming homestay, offering clean, well-maintained rooms, some en suite but most with shared hot-water showers (two bedrooms to one bathroom), in the owner's modern house; the a/c can be switched on for an extra B100–150/room/night. Plenty of information available, B30 showers for passers-through and much more (see above). Phone for free transport from the train station (though not late at night). B250

## EATING AND DRINKING

The cheapest place to eat is the local **night market**, which sets up along both sides of Thanon Kromluang and is an enjoyable place to munch your way through a tasty selection of fried noodles, barbecued chicken and sticky, coconut-laced sweets.

**Aeki's Bar (The 3 Independent)** Opposite the train station; map p.227. Rustic, wood-furnished bar-restaurant with a pool table, popular with young expat teachers, that doubles as a muay thai gym complete with a boxing ring. Daily 10am–midnight (kitchen closes at 10pm).

**Boom (The Bakery Café)** Thanon Tha Tapao ☎077 511523; map p.227. A bakery-cafe with a handful of pavement tables that are perfect for watching the world go by, serving a mix of good espressos (from B35), tasty brownies and other Western and Thai cakes. Mon–Sat 8am–7pm.

**Fame** 188/20–21 Thanon Sala Daeng ☎077 571077, ⓦchumphon-kohtao.com; map p.227. Travellers' restaurant specializing in Italian food, as well as Indian dhal, lots of sandwiches using home-baked bread, espresso coffees and huge breakfasts (B100–150). Daily 5am–9.30pm.

**Papa** Across from the train station on Thanon Kromluang ☎077 504504; map p.227. One of the liveliest places to eat dinner, this huge restaurant – mostly open-air, but with an a/c room – has an extensive menu of fresh seafood, Thai salads such as wingbean salad (B140) and Chinese dishes, plus a few Western standards. Also puts on live music every evening, and has an attached nightclub, *Papa 2000*. Daily 11am–3am.

★ **Prikhorm** Thanon Tha Tapao ☎077 570707; map p.227. A good chance to try southern Thai food such as tasty *nam phrik kung siap* (chilli dip with shrimp paste and dried prawns; B100), prawns and green bai liang leaves in a coconut curry and spicy *kaeng som*, which (thankfully) can be spiced to order. The main restaurant is a comfortable, a/c spot decked out in shades of green and entered from the car park at the back, but they also have a simple street-side canteen, serving curry on rice from B40. Daily 11am–9pm (last orders).

# Chaiya

About 140km south of Chumphon, **CHAIYA** is thought to have been the capital of southern Thailand under the Srivijayan civilization, which fanned out from Sumatra between the eighth and thirteenth centuries. Today there's little to mark the passing of Srivijaya, but this small, sleepy town has gained new fame as the site of **Wat Suan Mokkh**, a progressively minded temple whose meditation retreats account for the bulk of Chaiya's foreign visitors (most Thais only stop to buy the famous local salted eggs). Unless you're interested in one of the retreats, the town is best visited on a day-trip, either as a break in the journey south, or as an excursion from Surat Thani.

**3**

## Wat Phra Boromathat

Western side of town, on the access road from Highway 41

The main sight in Chaiya is **Wat Phra Boromathat**, where the ninth-century chedi – one of very few surviving examples of Srivijayan architecture – is said to contain relics of the Buddha himself. Hidden away behind the viharn in a pretty, red-tiled cloister, the chedi looks like an oversized wedding cake surrounded by an ornamental moat. Its unusual square tiers are spiked with smaller chedis and decorated with gilt, in a style similar to the temples of central Java.

## National Museum

On the eastern side of the temple • Wed–Sun 9am–4pm • B100

The **National Museum** is a bit of a disappointment. Although the Srivijaya period produced some of Thailand's finest sculpture, much of it discovered at Chaiya, the best pieces have been carted off to the National Museum in Bangkok. Replicas have been left in their stead, which are shown alongside fragments of some original statues, two intricately worked 2000-year-old bronze drums, found at Chaiya and Ko Samui, and various examples of Thai handicrafts. The best remaining pieces are a calm and elegant sixth- to seventh-century stone image of the Buddha meditating from Wat Phra Boromathat, and an equally serene head of a Buddha image, Ayutthayan-style in pink sandstone, from Wat Kaeo.

## Wat Kaeo

On the south side of town

Heading towards the centre of Chaiya from Wat Phra Boromathat, you can reach this imposing ninth- or tenth-century brick chedi by taking the first paved road on the right, which brings you first to the restored base of the chedi at Wat Long, and then after 1km to **Wat Kaeo**, enclosed by a thick ring of trees. Here you can poke around the murky antechambers of the chedi, three of which house images of the Buddha subduing Mara.

## Wat Suan Mokkh

6km south of Chaiya on Highway 41 • Ⓦ suanmokkh.org • All buses between Surat Thani and Chumphon stop near the wat

The forest temple of **Wat Suan Mokkh** (Garden of Liberation) was founded by the abbot of Wat Phra Boromathat, **Buddhadasa Bhikkhu**, southern Thailand's most revered monk until his death in 1993 at the age of 87. His radical, back-to-basics philosophy, encompassing Christian, Zen and Taoist influences, lives on and continues to draw

## MEDITATION RETREATS AT SUAN MOKKH

**Meditation retreats** are led by Western and Thai teachers over the first ten days of every month at the International Dharma Heritage (Ⓦ suanmokkh-idh.org), a purpose-built compound 1km from the main temple at Wat Suan Mokkh. Large numbers of foreign travellers, both novices and experienced meditators, turn up for the retreats, which are intended as a challenging exercise in mental development – it's not an opportunity to relax and live at low cost for a few days. Conditions imitate the rigorous lifestyle of a *bhikkhu* (monk) as far as possible, each day beginning before dawn with meditation according to the Anapanasati method, which aims to achieve mindfulness by focusing on the breathing process. Although talks are given on Dharma (the doctrines of the Buddha – as interpreted by Buddhadasa Bhikkhu) and meditation technique, most of each day is spent practising Anapanasati in solitude. To aid concentration, participants maintain a rule of silence, broken only by daily chanting sessions, although supervisors are sometimes available for individual interviews if there are any questions or problems. Men and women are segregated into separate dormitory blocks and, like monks, are expected to help out with chores.

### PRACTICALITIES

Turn up at Wat Suan Mokkh as early as possible (by 3pm at the latest) on the last day of the month to register (you can stay in Suan Mokkh the night before registration for free). The busiest period for the retreats is December–April, especially February and March. The fee is B2000 per person, which includes two vegetarian meals a day and accommodation in simple cells. Participants are required to hand in their mobile phones and tablets and are not allowed to leave the premises during the retreat – bring any supplies you think you might need (though there is a small, basic shop on site).

Thais from all over the country to the temple, as well as hundreds of foreigners. It's not necessary to sign up for one of the wat's **retreats** to enjoy the temple – you can simply drop by for a stroll through the wooded grounds.

The unusual layout of the wat is centred on the Golden Hill: scrambling up between trees and monks' huts, past the cremation site of Buddhadasa Bhikkhu, you'll reach a hushed clearing on top of the hill, which is the temple's holiest meeting place, a simple open-air platform decorated with images of the Buddha and the Wheel of Law. At the base of the hill, the outer walls of the Spiritual Theatre are lined with bas-reliefs, replicas of originals in India, which depict scenes from the life of the Buddha. Inside, every centimetre is covered with colourful didactic painting, executed by resident monks and visitors in a jumble of realistic and surrealistic styles.

### ARRIVAL AND DEPARTURE                                                      CHAIYA

**By train** The town lies on the main Southern Rail Line, served by trains (mostly overnight) from and to Bangkok's Hualamphong Station (8 daily; 8–11hr).

**By bus** Chaiya is 3km east of Highway 41, the main road down this section of the Gulf coast: buses running between Chumphon and Surat Thani will drop off (or pick up) on the highway, from where you can catch a motorbike taxi or blue songthaew into town.

**By a/c minibus** From Surat Thani's Talat Kaset II bus station, hourly a/c minibuses take 45min to reach Chaiya town centre.

# Surat Thani

Uninspiring **SURAT THANI** ("City of the Good People"), 60km south of Chaiya, is generally worth visiting only as a jumping-off point for the Samui archipelago. Strung along the south bank of the Tapi River, with a busy port for rubber and coconuts near the river mouth, the town is experiencing rapid economic growth and paralyzing traffic jams. It might be worth a stay, however, when the Chak Phra Festival (see page 232) is on, or as a base for seeing the nearby historic town of Chaiya.

## ARRIVAL AND DEPARTURE

### SURAT THANI

Be aware that there have been reports of thefts from bags left in the luggage compartments of long-distance buses from Surat (keep your valuables with you); and of overcharging and **scams** by unregistered agents and touts selling tickets for minibus and bus services out of Surat, especially involving any kind of combination ticket, including those heading for Khao Sok National Park, Phuket, Krabi and Malaysia. To avoid the latter, either go direct to the relevant a/c minibus office at Talat Kaset II bus station (local offices are generally on the west side of the station, long-distance ones on the east side, and they all have to be authorized by the provincial office), or buy a bus ticket direct from the station.

### BY PLANE

Arriving by air from Bangkok (currently Air Asia 7 daily, Nok Air 4 daily and Lion Air 4 daily from Don Muang, and Thai Smile 2 daily from Suvarnabhumi; 1hr 15min), Chiang Mai (Air Asia 2 daily; 2hr) or Kuala Lumpur (Malaysia, Air Asia 1 daily; 1hr 30min), you can take a B100 shuttle bus through Phantip (see below) for the 27km journey south from the airport into Surat Thani, while combination tickets through Lomprayah, for example, cost from B450 to Ko Samui, from B500 to Ko Pha Ngan and B950–1000 to Ko Tao. Avis (☎ 02 251 1131–2, ⓦ avisthailand.com) and Budget (☎ 077 441166, ⓦ budget.co.th) have outlets at the airport for car rental. Nok Air and Air Asia offer convenient flight-bus-boat through-tickets from Bangkok to Ko Samui and Ko

Pha Ngan via Surat airport; Air Asia offer similar tickets to Ko Tao (though it's possible that these will stop when their Bangkok–Chumphon flights start). If you're flying out of Surat, you can most easily catch the airport shuttle bus from town at the Phantip office.

### BY TRAIN

Arriving by train means arriving at Phunphin, 13km to the west, from where non-a/c buses run into Surat Thani, via the Baw Khaw Saw bus terminal, during daylight hours (in theory, every 15min, but more irregular than that). It's also possible to buy through-tickets to Ko Samui, Ko Pha Ngan and Ko Tao from a branch of Phantip Travel (see below) opposite the train station, including a connecting bus to the relevant pier. Buses heading out of Surat to Phang Nga and Phuket make a stop at Phunphin train station. You can book train tickets in Surat at Phantip travel agency, in front of Talat Kaset I at 293/6–8 Thanon Taladmai (☎ 077 272230, ⓦ phantiptravel.com).
Destinations Bangkok (10 daily; 9–12hr); Padang Besar (for Malaysia; 1 daily; 7hr); Nakhon Si Thammarat (2 daily; 4hr 30min); Trang (2 daily; 4hr 30min).

### BY BUS

Buses use three different terminals, two of which are on Thanon Taladmai in the centre of town: Talat Kaset I on the north side of the road (Phunphin, non-a/c Nakhon Si Thammarat and other local buses); and opposite at Talat Kaset

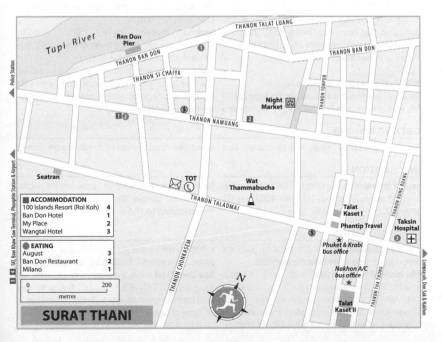

## THE CHAK PHRA FESTIVAL

At the start of the eleventh lunar month (usually in October) the people of Surat Thani celebrate the end of Buddhist Lent with the **Chak Phra Festival** (Pulling the Buddha), which symbolizes the Buddha's return to earth after a monsoon season spent preaching to his mother in heaven. On the Tapi River, tugboats pull the town's principal Buddha image on a raft decorated with huge nagas, while on land sleigh-like floats bearing Buddha images and colourful flags and parasols are hauled across the countryside and through the streets. As the monks have been confined to their monasteries for three months, the end of Lent is also the time to give them generous offerings in the *kathin* ceremony, of which Surat Thani has its own version, called Thot Pha Pa, when the offerings are hung on tree branches planted in front of the houses before dawn. Longboat races, between teams from all over the south, are also held during the festival.

II (most long-distance buses, including a/c services to Nakhon Si Thammarat; those for Phuket and Krabi have an office on the south side of Thanon Taladmai, opposite Phantip Travel). The Baw Khaw Saw terminal, 2km southwest of the centre on the road towards Phunphin, handles mostly Bangkok services. In addition, Phantip Travel runs many of its own a/c buses and minibuses to popular tourist destinations.

Destinations Bangkok (Southern Terminal; 20 daily; 9–12hr); Chumphon (roughly hourly; 3hr 30min–4hr 30min); Khao Lak (7 daily; 4hr); Khao Sok (7 daily; 2hr 30min); Krabi (every 30min; 3hr); Nakhon Si Thammarat (hourly; 2hr 30min–3hr); Phang Nga (6 daily; 3hr 30min); Phuket (every 40min; 5hr); Phunphin (irregular; 40min).

### BY MINIBUS

A/c minibuses (to Chaiya, Chumphon, Ranong, Ratchabrapa Dam, Khao Sok, Phang Nga, Phuket, Krabi, Trang and Nakhon Si Thammarat) congregate around Talat Kaset II bus station, on the south side of Thanon Taladmai.

### BOAT OPERATORS IN SURAT

Details of boat services to Ko Samui, Ko Pha Ngan and Ko Tao, most of which leave from Don Sak pier, located 68km east of Surat, are given in the account of each island – see pages 233, 252 and 263, respectively. Phunphin and the bus stations are teeming with touts, with transport waiting to escort you to their employer's boat service to the islands – they're generally reliable, but make sure you don't get talked onto the wrong boat. If you manage to avoid getting hustled, you can buy tickets direct from the various boat operators or from Phantip travel agency (see page 231).

**Lomprayah** Tapi Pier, 5km northeast of the centre near the mouth of the Tapi River ☎081 893 3663, ⓦlomprayah.com. Catamarans to Samui and Pha Ngan from Tapi Pier, and a passenger ferry to Samui and Pha Ngan from Don Sak, with their own connecting buses from Phunphin train station and the airport and connections on to Ko Tao via Ko Pha Ngan.

**Seatran** Thanon Taladmai ☎077 950559, ⓦseatranferry.com. Vehicle ferries to Samui (with their own connecting buses), from Don Sak.

**Night boats** The night boats to Samui, Pha Ngan and Tao, which are barely glorified cargo boats, line up during the day at Ban Don Pier in the centre of Surat; it's just a question of turning up and buying a ticket.

### GETTING AROUND

**By share-songthaew** Small share-songthaews buzz around town, charging around B20/person for a short journey.

### INFORMATION

**Tourist information** TAT's office is at the western end of town at 5 Thanon Taladmai (daily 8.30am–4.30pm; ☎077 288817–9, ⓔtatsurat@tat.or.th).

**Tourist police** On the southern bypass near the junction with Thanon Srivichai, the westward continuation of Thanon Taladmai (☎1155 or ☎077 421281).

### ACCOMMODATION

A lot of **accommodation** in Surat Thani is noisy, grotty and overpriced, but there are a few notable exceptions.

**100 Islands Resort (Roi Koh)** On the southern bypass near the tourist police and opposite Tesco Lotus ☎077 201 150–8, ⓦ100islandsresort.com; map p.231. Though out of the centre, this place offers attractive, comfortable rooms with a/c, hot water, TVs and minibars, a small spa and a decent-sized, free-form pool set in a lush garden with a waterfall. Breakfast included. B900

**Ban Don Hotel** Above a restaurant at 268/2 Thanon Namuang ☎077 272167; map p.231. Most of the very clean rooms here, with en-suite bathrooms, TV and fans or a/c (some of the latter have hot showers), are set back from the noise of the main road. Fan B250, a/c B400

**My Place** 247/5 Thanon Namuang ☎077 272288, ⓦmyplacesurat.com; map p.231. A welcoming, modern Thai–Chinese hotel and café in the town centre with some bright splashes of colour and attractive floral motifs; the cheapest rooms have shared cold showers. Fan B199, a/c B490

**Wangtai Hotel** 1 Thanon Taladmai, on the western side of the centre by the TAT office ☎077 283020–5, ⓦwangtaisurat.com; map p.231. Surat Thani's best upmarket option, and surprisingly good value, with over two hundred large, smart, recently refurbished rooms around a good-sized swimming pool, as well as fitness and massage rooms. Breakfast included. B1150

### EATING

Besides the restaurants listed below, there's a large **night market** between Thanon Namuang and Thanon Ban Don, which displays an eye-catching range of dishes; a smaller offshoot by Ban Don pier offers less choice but is handy if you're taking a night boat.

**August** Thanon Taladmai; map p.231. Colourful café, decorated with cartoon murals, serving tuna sandwiches (B90), all-day breakfasts, espresso coffees and smoothies. Daily 7am–7pm.

**Ban Don Restaurant** 268/2 Thanon Namuang; map p.231. Basic, bustling restaurant with plain, marble-topped tables, which serves large portions of tasty, inexpensive Thai and Chinese food – mostly noodle and rice dishes (around B50), but also green curry and *tom yam*. Daily 6am–4/5pm.

**Milano** Opposite the night-boat piers on Thanon Ban Don ☎077 285633; map p.231. This place has an authentic oven turning out very tasty and reasonably priced pizzas (from B200), though its home-made pasta is not so successful. Also serves other Western main courses, Mexican dishes, sandwiches and espresso coffees. Daily 11am–10pm.

# Ko Samui

Over a million visitors a year, ranging from globetrotting backpackers to suitcase-toting fortnighters, come to southern Thailand just for the beautiful beaches of **KO SAMUI**, 80km from Surat. At 15km across and down, Samui is generally large enough to cope with this diversity – except during the rush at Christmas and New Year – and the paradisal sands and clear blue seas have to a surprising extent kept their good looks, enhanced by a thick fringe of palm trees that gives a harvest of more than two million coconuts each month. However, development behind the beaches – which has brought the islanders far greater prosperity than the crop could ever provide – speeds along in a messy, haphazard fashion with little concern for the environment. At least there's a local bylaw limiting new construction to the height of a coconut palm (usually about three storeys), though this has not deterred either the luxury hotel groups or the real-estate developers who have recently been throwing up estates of second homes for Thais and foreigners.

For most visitors, the days are spent indulging in a few watersports or just lying on the beach waiting for the next drinks-seller, hair-braider or masseur to come along. For something more active, you should not miss the almost supernatural beauty of the **Ang Thong National Marine Park** (see page 249), which comprises many of the eighty islands in the Samui archipelago. Otherwise, a day-trip by rented car or motorbike on the 50km round-island road will throw up plenty more fine beaches.

The island's most appealing strand, **Chaweng**, has seen the heaviest, most crowded development and is now the most expensive place to stay, though it does offer by far the best amenities and nightlife, ranging from tawdry bar-beers to cool beach clubs. Its slightly smaller neighbour, **Lamai**, lags a little behind in terms of looks and top-end development, but retains pockets of backpacker bungalow resorts. The other favourite for backpackers is **Maenam**, which, though less attractive again, is markedly quiet, with plenty of room to breathe between the beach and the round-island road. Adjacent **Bophut** is similar in appearance, but generally more sophisticated, with a cluster of boutique resorts, fine restaurants and a distinct Mediterranean feel in its congenial beachfront village, now dubbed "Fisherman's Village". **Choeng Mon**, set apart in Samui's northeast corner, offers something different again: the small, part-sandy, part-rocky bay is tranquil and pretty, the seafront between the handful of upmarket hotels is comparatively under-developed, and Chaweng's nightlife is within easy striking distance.

No particular **season** is best for coming to Ko Samui (see also page 56). The northeast monsoon blows heaviest in November, but can bring rain at any time between October and January, and sometimes causes high waves and strong currents, especially on the east coast. January is often breezy, March and April are very hot, and between May and October the southwest monsoon blows onto Samui's west coast and causes some rain.

At the lower end of Samui's **accommodation** scale, there are very few rooms left for under B500, while at the most upmarket places you can pay well over B5000 for the highest international standards. The prices listed are based on high-season rates, but out of season (roughly May, June, Oct & Nov) dramatic reductions are possible.

## ARRIVAL AND DEPARTURE                                    KO SAMUI

### BY PLANE
Flights to Samui Airport, in the northeastern tip of the island, are among the most expensive in Thailand, so you might want to consider flying from Bangkok to Surat Thani (see page 230) or Nakhon Si Thammarat (see page 272), nearby on the mainland; Nok Air and Air Asia offer good-value through-tickets via either of these airports, including flight, bus and boat to Samui.

**Routes** You can get to Ko Samui direct from Suvarnabhumi

Airport with Bangkok Airways, which also operates flights from Chiang Mai, Krabi, Pattaya and Phuket. There are also direct flights from Malaysia, Singapore, Hong Kong and mainland China.

**Airport facilities** As well as bars and restaurants, the terminals have currency-exchange facilities and ATMs, a post office and several car rental outlets, including Avis (☏ 02 251 1131–2, ⊛ avisthailand.com) who will deliver and collect around the island.

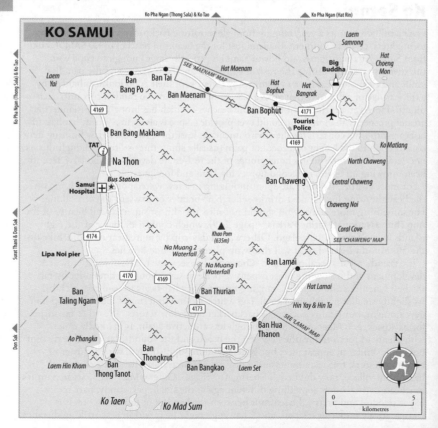

KO SAMUI

## KO SAMUI ACTIVITIES

Samui has over a dozen scuba-diving companies, offering trips for divers and snorkellers and courses throughout the year, and there's a recompression chamber at Bangrak (☎077 427427, ⓦsssnetwork.com). Most trips for experienced divers, however, head for the waters around Ko Tao (see page 263); a day's outing costs around B4000–5500, but of course if you can make your own way to Ko Tao, you'll save money. Also on offer are plenty of spas, as well as meditation retreats, island tours, ziplines, kiteboarding and cooking and circus classes.

### DIVE OPERATORS

**Easy Divers** Head office opposite Sandsea Resort, Lamai ☎077 231190, ⓦeasydivers-thailand.com. PADI Five-Star dive centre, with branches on Chaweng and Bangrak.

**Planet Scuba** Next to the Seatran pier on Bangrak ☎077 413050, ⓦplanetscuba.net.

### SPAS

**Banyan Tree** Lamai ☎077 915 333, ⓦbanyantree. com. The beautiful spa at this luxury resort is home to Southeast Asia's only hydrotherapy spa, The Rainforest, in which you walk through around ten stations of hot, cold and massaging showers, jets, waterfalls and pools, as well as a sauna, steam room and ice fountain. Lasting an hour, it costs B1750 and can be combined with all manner of indulgent massage and beauty treatments.

**Eranda** Far north end of Chaweng ☎077 300323, ⓦerandaspa.com. Set on a waterfall- and flower-splashed hillside with a plunge pool, offering plenty of style (2hr Thai massage B2300).

**Peace Tropical Spa** On Route 4169 near the centre of Bophut beach ☎077 430199, ⓦpeacetropicalspa. com. Many types of massage, including a 2hr Thai massage for B1800, as well as body and facial treatments.

**The Spa Resort** Lamai ☎099 406 4503, ⓦthespa resorts.com. Everything from Thai massage (B450/ hr) for non-guests, to multi-day residential fasting and detox programmes. Also on offer are yoga and tea ceremonies, as well as in-house accommodation, either on the beach or in the hills above Lamai.

**Tamarind Springs** Lamai ☎085 926 4626, ⓦtamarindsprings.com. Set in a beautiful, secluded coconut grove just off the main road. A 90-minute session in its herbal steam caves, set between boulders by waterfall-fed plunge pools, plus a 2hr 30min Thai massage, for example, costs B5500; it also offers villas, a spa café and yoga holidays.

### OTHER ACTIVITIES

**Canopy Adventures** ☎077 300340, ⓦcanopy adventuresthailand.com. A series of ziplines between treehouses and past waterfalls in the hills 4km above Maenam (2–3hr; B2200, including transfers).

**The Hub** Elysia Resort, east of the village T-junction in Bophut ☎077 430 317, ⓦelysiasamui.com. Classes in various types of yoga (B400/person), as well as meditation sessions, according to a schedule posted on their website.

**Kiteboarding Asia** ☎083 643 1627, ⓦkite boardingasia.com. Instruction in kiteboarding (B4000 for one day), either from the beach south of Ban Hua Thanon or from Nathon, depending on the time of year, as well as rentals and stand-up paddleboarding.

**Mr Ung's Magical Safari Tours** ☎077 230114, ⓦungsafari.com. Day-trips that traverse the rough tracks of the mountainous interior to some spectacular viewpoints, as well as taking in Hin Yay Hin Ta, the Big Buddha and waterfall-swimming (from B1500 for a full day, including transfers and lunch).

**Samui Circus Studio** Coral Cove, south of Chaweng ☎087 881 0866, ⓦsamuicircus.com. Group and private circus classes, including juggling and clown skills, for adults and kids, from B300/person.

**Samui Institute of Thai Culinary Arts (SITCA)** Soi Colibri, opposite Centara Grand Resort in Chaweng ☎077 413172, ⓦsitca.com. This highly recommended outfit runs 2hr 30min cookery classes in the morning and afternoon (B1850), plus six- and twelve-day courses and fruit-carving classes. Closed Sun.

**Wat Suan Mokkh meditation retreats** ⓦdipab havan.weebly.com. Wat Suan Mokkh (see page 229) offers retreats from the 3rd to the 10th and the 20th to the 27th of each month at Dipabhavan, a hermitage in the hills above Lamai (full details on the website); pick-ups are laid on from *Utopia Resort*, north of the central crossroads in Lamai.

3

---

**Minibus transfers** A/c minibuses meet incoming flights (and connect with departures, bookable through your accommodation), charging B120 to Na Thon for example. Destinations Bangkok (25 daily; 1hr–1hr 30min); Chiang Mai (1 daily; 2hr); Krabi (1 daily; 55min); Pattaya (U-Tapao; 1 daily; 1hr); Phuket (6 daily; 50min).

### BY BOAT AND BUS

The most obvious route for getting to Ko Samui by boat (45min–1hr 30min) is from Surat Thani, with most boats departing from the port of Don Sak, 68km east of town; catching a boat from Chumphon is generally more expensive and leaves you a long time on the often-choppy sea. There are also boats from Ko Samui to Ko Pha Ngan (see page 253) and to Ko Tao (see page 265); all offer the same service in the return direction. If your boat company or travel agent offers a drop-off at (or pick-up from) your hotel on Samui, take it: it'll be a lot cheaper than taking a taxi.

**FROM SURAT THANI**

**Don Sak to Na Thon** From Don Sak, hourly Seatran vehicle ferries (☎077 950 559, ⊕seatranferry.com) and a once-daily Lomprayah passenger ferry (on Samui ☎077 950028 or ☎077 950 700–4, ⊕lomprayah.com) run to the island capital, Na Thon, all with their own connecting buses from Surat.

**Don Sak to Lipa Noi** Raja vehicle ferries run hourly between Don Sak and Lipa Noi, 8km south of Na Thon (☎02 276 8211–2, ⊕rajaferryport.com), some of which have their own connecting buses from Surat. From Lipa Noi, you can catch an a/c minibus direct to the beaches (B200 to Chaweng, for example).

**Surat Thani to Na Thon** Lomprayah runs a catamaran to Na Thon from Tapi Pier (three daily), 5km northeast of central Surat near the mouth of the Tapi River. The night boat leaves Ban Don pier in Surat Thani itself for Na Thon at 11pm Mon–Sat, as long as it has enough cargo and passengers to make it worthwhile; tickets are sold at the pier on the day of departure.

**Fares and journey times** Ferries from Don Sak take about 1hr 30min to reach Samui, while the connecting Surat–Don Sak buses take 1hr–1hr 30min. The Lomprayah catamaran from Tapi Pier gets to Na Thon in 2hr. Seatran charges B230 from downtown Surat to Samui including connecting bus, while Phantip charges B280 from Phunphin train station (see page 206). For transport from Surat Thani Airport, see page 230. Lomprayah's catamarans from Tapi Pier cost B600. The night boat takes 6hr and costs B400.

**LLONG-DISTANCE SERVICES**

Ko Samui's government bus terminal (Baw Khaw Saw) is 2km south of Na Thon, just west off Route 4169 towards Samui Hospital (☎077 426354–5). It handles bus-and-boat services (via Don Sak and Lipa Noi), for example from Bangkok (8–11 daily; 12–13hr; mostly overnight, some from the Southern Bus Terminal, some from Mo Chit, some stopping at both), which cost from B508 on a basic a/c bus to B790 on a VIP bus – these are far preferable to the cheap deals offered by dodgy travel agents on Thanon Khao San, as the vehicles used on the latter services are often substandard and many thefts have been reported. The Baw Khaw Saw also sells through-tickets to Nakhon Si Thammarat, which combine the ferry to Don Sak either with a bus or an a/c minibus. Lomprayah also offers through-tickets from Bangkok, costing from B1400 (14hr 30min), including a VIP bus from its office on Thanon Ram Bhuttri in Banglamphu (☎02 629 2569–70), via Hua Hin, and a catamaran from Chumphon via Ko Tao and Ko Pha Ngan.

## GETTING AROUND

**BY SONGTHAEW**
Songthaews, which congregate at the car park near the southerly pier in Na Thon, cover a variety of set routes during the daytime, either heading off clockwise or anticlockwise on Route 4169, to serve all the beaches in the area; destinations are marked in English and typical fares are around B80 to Maenam and B100 to Chaweng. In the evening, they tend to operate more like taxis and you'll have to negotiate a fare to get them to take you exactly where you want to go.

**BY TAXI**
Ko Samui sports dozens of a/c taxis. Although they all have meters, you'd be wasting your breath trying to persuade any driver to use his; instead, the quoted flat fares will take your breath away: B500 from Na Thon to Maenam, B1200 to Chaweng.

**BY MOTORBIKE OR CAR**
You can rent a motorbike for around B200 in Na Thon and on the main beaches. Dozens are killed on Samui's roads each year, so proceed with great caution, and be sure to wear a helmet – apart from any other consideration you can be landed with an on-the-spot B500 fine by police for not wearing one. In addition, thieves have been snatching bags from the front baskets of moving motorbikes on Samui, so try to keep yours on your person – or potentially think about upgrading to a four-wheel drive (from around B800/day) or a car (available through companies such as Avis – see page 277).

## INFORMATION

**Tourist information** The TAT office (daily 8.30am–noon & 1–4.30pm; ☎077 420504, ⊕tatsamui@tat.or.th) is tucked away on an unnamed side road in Na Thon (north of the pier and inland from the post office). Here, and at many other places around Samui, you can pick up Siam Map Company's detailed map of the island.

**Immigration office** Soi 1, Maenam (Mon–Fri 8.30am–4.30pm; ☎077 421069).

**Tourist police** The tourist police are on the Route 4169 ring road between Bophut and Chaweng, north of Big C supermarket on the same side of the road (☎1155 or ☎077 430017–8).

# Na Thon

The island capital, **NA THON**, at the top of the long western coast, is a frenetic small town which most travellers use only as a service station before hitting the sand: although all the main beaches now have currency-exchange facilities, ATMs, supermarkets, travel agents and clinics, and most of them have post offices, the tightest concentration of amenities is here. The town's layout is simple: the three piers come to land at the promenade, Thanon Chonvithi, which is paralleled first by narrow Thanon Ang Thong, then by Thanon Tawecratpakdee, aka Route 4169, the round-island road; the main cross-street is Thanon Na Amphoe, by the central pier. If you're driving yourself, note that there's a one-way system in the centre of town: south on Taweeratpakdee, north on Chonvithi.

## ACCOMMODATION AND EATING
NA THON

Several stalls and small cafés purvey inexpensive Thai food around the market on Thanon Taweeratpakdee and on Thanon Chonvithi (including a lively night market by the piers).

**Nathon Residence** Thanon Taweeratpakdee next to Thanachart Bank ☎077 236081, bookable through ⓦexpedia.com. If you really need a place to stay in Na Thon, this is your best bet. A friendly, well-run establishment with plain but spotless tiled rooms with a/c, cable TV, fridges and en-suite, hot-water bathrooms – ask for a quiet room at the back. **B650**

★**The Road Less Travelled** West side of Thanon Taweeratpakdee, just north of Thanon Na Amphoe. This is Samui's café of the moment, which is as sophisticated as anything that Bangkok might have to offer, and fetchingly done out with recycled wood and birdcage lampshades. It serves excellent espresso (and cold-brewed) coffees, using Arabica beans from northern Thailand, signature mixed juices, cocktails and all kinds of brunches Including burritos (B220), as well as home-made chocolates, croissants and cakes. Tues–Sun 9.30/10am–6pm, until 8pm Fri & Sat.

## DIRECTORY

**Hospital** The state hospital (☎077 421230–2) is 3km south of town off Route 4169.

**Post office** Towards the northern end of the promenade, just north of the central pier (Mon–Fri 8.30am–4.30pm,

Sat & Sun 9am–noon), with poste restante and packing services. International telephones upstairs (Mon–Fri 8.30am–4.30pm).

# Maenam

**MAENAM**, 13km from Na Thon in the middle of the north coast, is Samui's most popular beach for budget travellers. Its exposed 4km-long bay is not the island's prettiest, being more of a broad dent in the coastline, and the sloping, yellow-sand beach is relatively narrow and slightly coarse by Samui's high standards. But Maenam features many of the cheapest bungalows on the island, unspoilt views of Ko Pha Ngan, and good swimming. Despite the recent opening of some upmarket developments on the shoreline and a golf course in the hills behind, this is still the quietest and most laid-back of the major beaches. Though now heavily built up with multi-storey concrete shophouses (including several banks) and rows of small bars, the main road is set back far from the sea, connected to the beachside bungalows by an intricate maze of minor roads through the trees. At the midpoint of the bay, **Ban Maenam** is centred on a low-key road down to the fishing pier, which is flanked by cafés, bars, restaurants, travel agents and small boutiques. On Thursday evenings this becomes a pleasant **walking street** (modelled on those in Chiang Mai), with performances of traditional music and dance. On offer are lots of cheap clothes and some souvenirs, everything from bras to ukeleles, but what's most tempting is the panoply of food, both savoury and sweet, that locals cook up to sell.

## ACCOMMODATION
MAENAM

★**Four Seasons Resort** About 5km west of Maenam near Laem Yai ☎077 243000, ⓦfourseasons.com; map p.238. The top hotel in the Maenam area, this ultra-luxury

spot has its own small beach and enjoys lovely views of Ko Pha Ngan and the setting sun. Each of the large, beautiful villas, designed for indoor-outdoor living in a subtle, modern but natural style, using brown and marine colours, has its own infinity-edge swimming pool; the resort lays on a wide range of other activities, from spa treatments to *muay thai* and tennis. B33,500

**The Hammock** Just east of the village ☎077 423815–6, ⓦhammocksamui.com; map p.238. Stylish, flashpacker resort with a small swimming pool surrounded by red beanbags and swings. Featuring beige- and white-painted concrete and lots of dark wood, the rooms offer a/c, small hot-water bathrooms, minibars, TVs and DVD players; though crammed together in one- and two-storey rows on a small plot, they all have a small balcony or patio. Breakfast included. B2145

**Harry's** At the far western end, near Wat Na Phra Larn ☎077 447097, ⓦharrys-samui.com; map p.238. Popular, well-run place, set back about 200m from the beach amid a secluded and shady tropical garden. The public areas feature strong elements of traditional Thai architecture, less so in the bungalows, which are nevertheless clean and spacious, with a/c, hot water, TV, fridge and safe. There's also a decent-sized, free-form swimming pool and Jacuzzi. B1200

**Lolita** On the east side of Santiburi Resort ☎077 425134, ⓦlolitakohsamui.com; map p.238. Quiet, friendly and efficiently run resort in a beautiful, grassy garden on a long stretch of beach. A wide variety of large, wood and concrete bungalows, all with hot showers, cluster around a kitsch, circular bar-restaurant adorned with pink Corinthian columns, and come with fans (at the back), or with a/c and fridges on the beach. Fan B800, a/c B1700

**Maenam Resort** 500m west of the village, just beyond Santiburi Resort ☎077 247286–7, ⓦmaenamresort. com; map p.238. A welcoming, tranquil resort (no TVs) in tidy, shady grounds, with an especially long stretch of beach. The large bungalows, with verandas, hot water, fridges and a/c, offer good-value comfort. B1930

**Moonhut** On the east side of the village ☎077 425 247, ⓦmoonhutsamui.com; map p.238. Welcoming English-run place on a large, sandy, shady plot, with a lively restaurant and beach bar, and colourful, substantial and very clean bungalows; all have verandas, mosquito screens, wall fans and en-suite bathrooms, and some have hot water and a/c. Kayaking, waterskiing and stand-up paddleboarding available. Fan B650, a/c B1300

**New Lapaz Villa** Down a 1km access road, east of the village centre but just west of the post office ☎077 425 296, ⓦnewlapaz.com; map p.238. Enjoying plenty of shade, the lush, spacious grounds here shelter a small swimming pool and fifty recently renovated bungalows on stilts, with verandas, a/c, TVs, fridges and hot showers, many in bright pastel colours. Their "Superior Seaview" rooms offer good value for a beachfront pad (B1800). Breakfast included. B1400

**Treehouse Silent Beach** At the eastern end of the bay ☎062 240 4305, ⓦtree-house.org; map p.238. This long-running place has been recently reborn as a new-school hippy resort, combining the tagline "Follow the Flowers" with super-fast wi-fi. The colourful bungalows are quite close together, but feature hot showers and hammocks on their verandas; the shaggy thatched roofs of the beachfront bungalows (B800) are especially appealing. The cheapest offerings are bamboo huts with shared bathrooms. Fan B350, a/c B1100

### EATING AND DRINKING

**Angela's Bakery** Almost opposite the police station on the main through-road, east of the pier ☎077 961952, ⓦfacebook.com/angelasbakerycafe; map p.238. American-style, a/c diner with comfortable booths, offering great breakfasts and a wide choice of sandwiches (chicken and avocado B150), salads, soups and Western main courses, as well as home-made cakes and apple pie. Daily 8am–3pm.

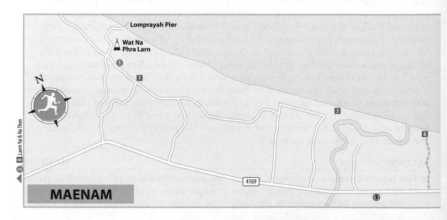

**Haad Bang Po** About 5km west of Maenam, at the far west end of Ban Bang Po; map p.238. The last of a string of locally popular seafood restaurants, this rough-hewn, sand-between-your-toes affair enjoys pretty views of Ko Pha Ngan. You'll need to go off-menu and practise your Thai a little to get the best out of it, but the superb khai jiaw haw mok thalay, (seafood coconut-milk curry omelette served with shrimp paste chilli dip and vegetables; B150), fully justifies the effort. Other available southern Thai favourites that are not on the English-language menu include kaeng som (fiery yellow curry), kaeng liang (peppery soup) and seasonal het loop, a kind of sea cucumber. Daily 10am–10pm.

**Ko Seng** On the road parallel to and just east of the pier road ☎ 077 425365; map p.238. This locally famous seafood restaurant, simply decorated apart from the chunky wooden tables and chairs, has featured on national TV. Buy your fish and seafood according to weight, splash out on the crab and king prawn specialities, or plump for noodles (B120) or dishes such as fish and fish roe curry with tamarind paste (*kaeng som plaa*; B350), which can be spiced to order. Daily 10am–9pm.

**Sunshine Gourmet** At the west end of the bay, signposted on a lane that runs east from Wat Na Phra Larn; map p.238. Popular, clean and friendly food and drink spot that does a bit of everything, from cappuccinos and breakfasts, through sandwiches, to Thai and international, especially German, main courses. Daily 8am–10pm.

## Bophut

The next bay east is **BOPHUT**, which has a similar look to Maenam but shows a marked difference in atmosphere and facilities, with a noticeable Mediterranean influence. The quiet, 2km-long beach attracts a mix of young and old travellers, as well as families, and **Ban Bophut**, now tagged "**Fisherman's Village**", at the east end of the bay, is well geared to meet their needs, with a sprinkling of boutique hotels and banks, ATMs, scuba-diving outlets, travel agents and minimarts. While through traffic sticks to Route 4171 towards the airport and Route 4169 to Chaweng, which is now lined with hypermarkets and multiplex cinemas, development of the village has been reasonably sensitive, preserving many of its old wooden shophouses on the two narrow, largely car-free streets that meet at a T-junction next to the small pier.

At night, in sharp contrast to Chaweng's frenetic beach road, it's a fine place for a promenade, with a concentration of good upmarket restaurants and low-key farang-run bars, particularly to the west of the T-junction; on Friday evenings, the village hosts a **walking street**, very similar to Maenam's Thursday affair (see page 237). The nicest part of the beach itself is at the west end of the bay, towards *Zazen* resort, but again the sand is slightly coarse by Samui's standards. With several branches along the beach, including in front of *Free House Bungalows*, Orange Wave offers all manner of watersports, including jet skis and stand-up paddleboards (☎ 080 525 0650, ⓦ orangewave-watersports.com).

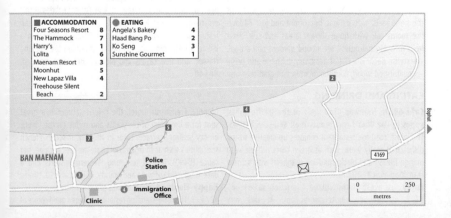

| ■ ACCOMMODATION | | ● EATING | |
|---|---|---|---|
| Four Seasons Resort | 8 | Angela's Bakery | 4 |
| The Hammock | 7 | Haad Bang Po | 2 |
| Harry's | 1 | Ko Seng | 3 |
| Lolita | 6 | Sunshine Gourmet | 1 |
| Maenam Resort | 3 | | |
| Moonhut | 5 | | |
| New Lapaz Villa | 4 | | |
| Treehouse Silent Beach | 2 | | |

BAN MAENAM

Police Station

Immigration Office

Clinic

4169

Bophut

0     250
metres

## ACCOMMODATION

BOPHUT

Most establishments here are spaced out at regular intervals along the length of the beach, though a handful of small, stylish, good-value boutique hotels cluster together in Ban Bophut itself.

★ **Anantara** West of the village on the main road ☎077 428300, ⓦanantara.com. Luxury hotel with attentive service in the style of an opulent oriental palace. The balconied rooms are arrayed round lush gardens and ponds that are lit at night with flaming torches, and there's an attractive infinity-edge swimming pool on the beachfront and a central bar and restaurant, specializing in contemporary Australian cuisine. A very attractive spa, a kids' club and a huge range of activities, from yoga and cocktail mixing classes to tennis and watersports, round out the picture. Breakfast included. B8010

**Cactus** Access from the highway, west Bophut ☎077 245565, ⓦcactus-bungalow.com. Ochre cottages with attractive bed platforms, large French windows and stylish, earth-tone bathrooms stand in two shady rows, running down to the inviting beachfront restaurant with a wood-fired pizza oven. Choose either fan and cold shower or a/c and hot shower. Fan B800, a/c B1350

**Cocooning** East of the village T-junction, opposite The Waterfront ☎085 781 4107, ⓦcocooninghotel.com. Small, good-value hotel set back from the beach, with compact but well-equipped rooms (a/c, hot shower, fridge, safe, DVD player) in a bright and breezy contemporary style; the English owner is a mine of local information. B1300

★ **Free House** West of the village ☎077 427517. On a quiet plot that's shaded by a thick canopy of trees, running back from the popular beachfront bar-restaurant, the tasteful en-suite bungalows here are well designed and maintained, with plenty of natural light. Made either of white-painted concrete or slatted dark wood, they feature mosquito nets, hammocks, hot showers and verandas. Fan B700, a/c B1500

**Hansar** At the west end of the village ☎077 245511, ⓦhansarsamui.com. You'll be surprised how spacious this hotel feels, with its long beachfront and just 74 low-rise rooms (all with huge shower areas and sea views from their big balconies), set around gardens and a pool. The stylish decor is a riot of geometry in brown and beige – unvarnished wood, bamboo, marble and granite – and

there's a spa, gym and luxury restaurant, H Bistro, with ingredients flown in from around the world. Breakfast included. B7300

**Juzz'a Pizza** East of the village T-junction ☎077 332512–3. Above a good restaurant (see page 241), four small but smart rooms, well equipped with comfy beds, a/c, hot showers, fridges, cable TV and DVD players. Two rooms have no view, while the other two have beachside terraces with great views. B1200

**The Lodge** Towards the western end of the village ☎077 425337, ⓦlodgesamui.com. Small, three-storey, beachfront hotel with immaculately clean and tastefully decorated modern rooms, all with balconies looking over the water, and boasting a/c, ceiling fan, minibar, satellite TV, plus marble bathrooms with tubs to soak in. There's a seafront bar downstairs where you can get breakfast. Now also offers a few simple rooms with a/c, fridge and hot showers in an annexe (B550). B2680

**Us Hostel** Off Route 4169 at the east end of Bophut ☎095 427 1525, ⓦfacebook.com/ushostelsamui. Friendly, new hostel with smart bunks in a/c recycled shipping containers, hot showers, an attractive pool and wooden chill-out decks scattered with beanbags. Dorms B380, doubles B1000

**The Waterfront** East of the village T-junction ☎077 427165, ⓦthewaterfrontbophut.com. English-run boutique hotel, sociable and family-friendly, with a small swimming pool in a grassy garden. All of the tastefully decorated rooms and bungalows have a/c, hot water, minibars, safes, cable TV, DVD players and views of the sea. Minimum stay 2 nights. Free airport pick-ups and drop-offs; breakfast included in the price. B3120

**Zazen** At the far west end of the beach ☎077 425085, ⓦsamuizazen.com. Stylish bungalows and villas clustered round a cute pool and kids' pool, furnished with Thai and other Asian objets d'art, as well as satellite TV, DVD player, minibar and daybed; all sport a tropical-style open-air bathroom with rain shower. Other facilities at this eco-friendly resort include a spa, a Thai-Mediterranean restaurant that hosts Thai dancing (Thurs & Sun) and a Western restaurant offering classic afternoon tea, cooking classes, and free kayaks and bicycles. Breakfast included. B6540

## EATING AND DRINKING

**Café 69** On Highway 4169 west of the traffic lights, opposite The Wharf community mall ☎081 978 1945. This plush roadside restaurant conjures up creative fusion dishes that really work, such as green curry *roti* pie with mango (B229) and black squid-ink spaghetti with salmon laap. Mon–Sat 1–10pm.

**Enjoy** Just west of the village T-junction ☎081 485 7112, ⓦenjoybeach-hotel-samui.com. At this very

friendly, French-run hotel, the café-restaurant is a great spot for a breakfast of croissants and coffee on the lovely, breezy seafront terrace. Later in the day, it serves French specialities such as tournedos of charolais beef with pepper sauce (B490), lots of tempting Western desserts and a decent selection of wine and brandy. Daily 8am–10.30pm.

**Happy Elephant** West of the village T-junction ☎077 427 222. This long-standing restaurant offers a good choice of mostly Thai food, including a few less mainstream dishes such as pork *nam tok* (B260) and lots of seafood, which is displayed out front and priced by weight. Service is friendly and there's an attractive beachside terrace. Daily 11am–10pm.

**Juzz'a Pizza** East of the village T-junction ☎077 332 512–3. Friendly, small, elegant restaurant with a beachside terrace, serving authentic pizzas (from B260), with vegetarian and seafood options, as well as pastas, sandwiches and Thai and Western main courses. Tues–Sun noon–10pm.

**Ninja Crepes** Far east end of the bay, on the road towards Bangrak. In a beachfront location with nice tables on a terrace by the sea, this is a popular option for cheap, decent-quality Western and Thai meals along with breakfasts and sweet and savoury crepes. Main dishes around B80. Daily 9am–8pm.

**Ristorante alla Baia** Just west of the village T-junction, next to Enjoy ☎077 332647. Run by an Italian who is passionate about his food and has come up with a well-designed menu of standard but authentic dishes, such as *scaloppine al vino bianco* (pork or chicken fillets in white wine; B370), using meat imported from Argentina. Also on offer are pizzas, pasta and seafood, with the catch of the day displayed outside. With white tablecloths and plants, lots of wrought iron and a terrace on the beach, you could almost be sitting by the Adriatic. Daily noon–10.30pm.

**The Shack Grill** West of the village T-junction ☎087 264 6994, ⓦtheshackgrillsamui.com. Small, pricey spot run by an ebullient New Yorker, and focused on the large, open grill at the front of the restaurant: here all manner of local seafood and imported meats priced by weight, such as Wagyu beef tenderloin (B1800/200g) and New Zealand lamb, are cooked to your liking. Delicious apple pie and decent house wine. Daily 5.30–11pm.

## Bangrak

Beyond the sharp headland with its sweep of coral reefs lies **BANGRAK**, sometimes called **Big Buddha Beach** after the colossus that gazes sternly down on the sun worshippers from its island in the bay. The beach is no great shakes, especially during the northeast monsoon, when the sea retreats and leaves a slippery mud flat, but Bangrak still manages to attract the watersports crowd, and every Sunday locals and expats descend for the Sunday Sessions at Secret Garden Beach Resort on the main beach road (☎077 332661, ⓦsecretgardensamui.com), with barbecues, drinks and live music from around 7pm. Generally, however, it's hard to recommend staying on Bangrak, as the resorts are squeezed together in a narrow, noisy strip between busy Route 4171 and the shore, next to the busy inter-island piers and underneath the airport flight path.

Built in 1972, the **Big Buddha** (*Phra Yai*) is certainly big and works hard at being a tourist attraction, but is no beauty. A short causeway at the eastern end of the bay leads across to a messy clump of souvenir shops and food stalls in front of the temple, catering to day-tripping Thais as well as foreigners. Ceremonial dragon-steps then bring you up to the covered terrace around the Big Buddha, from where there's a fine view of the sweeping north coast. Look out for the B10 rice-dispensing machine, which allows you symbolically to give alms to the monks at any time of the day.

## Choeng Mon

After Bangrak comes the high-kicking boot of Samui's **northeastern cape**, with its small, rocky coves overlooking Ko Pha Ngan and connected by narrow lanes. Songthaews run along Route 4171 to the largest and most beautiful bay, **Choeng Mon**, whose white sandy beach is lined with casuarina trees that provide shade for the bungalows and upmarket resorts. Choeng Mon is now popular enough to support small supermarkets, travel agents, a post office and a bank, but on the whole it remains relatively laid-back.

| **ACCOMMODATION** | **CHOENG MON** |
|---|---|

**Imperial Boat House Beach Resort** Central Choeng Mon ☎077 425041–52, ⓦmelia.com. Named after the two-storey rice barges that have been converted into suites in the grounds, the *Boat House* also offers good-value luxury rooms with balconies in more prosaic modern buildings, often filled by package tours. As well as a beachside boat-shaped pool, there's a garden pool with attached kids' pool, a spa, kayaks and table tennis. **B4030**

**Island View** Tucked in on the east side of the Boat House Hotel ☎ 083 221 2450, ⓦ islandviewsamui.com. Smart, good-value rooms and chalets with a/c, hot water, TV and fridge, in a lively compound that crams in a supermarket and a beachfront bar-restaurant that specializes in southern Thai food, as well as a massage *sala* and jet-skis on the beach. B1350

**Ô Soleil** West of the Boat House Hotel ☎ 077 425232, ⓦ osoleilbungalow.com. Lovely, orderly, Belgian-run place in a tranquil, pretty garden dotted with ponds. Among the well-built, clean bungalows, the cheapest are fan-cooled, with cold showers, at the back, while the elegant beachside restaurant has a nice shaded deck area and serves six hundred cocktails. Fan B600, a/c B1100

**Sea Dance Resort** Just south of Choeng Mon on Hanuman Bay ☎ 077 426621, ⓦ seadanceresort.com (bookable through ⓦ secret-retreats.com). You'll get a warm welcome at this relaxing resort, which has a cute little spa and a free-form outdoor pool on the tranquil, part-sandy, part-rocky bay. The villas, many of which have their own plunge pools on lawns surrounded by hedges, are luxurious, with touches of rustic chic in their thatched canopies and bamboo furniture. Breakfast included. B5400

★ **Tongsai Bay** North side of Choeng Mon ☎ 077 245480, ⓦ tongsaibay.co.th. Easy-going, environmentally aware establishment with excellent service. The luxurious rooms, red-tiled cottages and palatial villas (some with their own pool) command beautiful views over the huge, picturesque grounds, the private beach and two swimming pools. In addition they nearly all sport second bathtubs on their secluded open-air terraces, and some also have outdoor, four-poster beds with mosquito nets if you want to sleep under the stars. There's also an array of very fine restaurants and a delightful spa. Breakfast included. B10,500

# Chaweng

For looks alone, none of the other beaches can match **CHAWENG**, with its broad, gently sloping strip of white sand sandwiched between the limpid blue sea and a line of palm trees. Such beauty has not escaped attention of course, which means, on the plus side, that Chaweng can provide just about anything the active beach bum demands, from thumping nightlife to ubiquitous and diverse watersports. The negative angle is that the new developments are ever more cramped and expensive, while building work behind the palm trees and repairs to the over-commercialized main beach road are always in progress.

## North Chaweng

The 6km bay is framed between the small island of Ko Matlang at the north end and the 300m-high headland above Coral Cove in the south. From **Ko Matlang**, where the waters provide some decent snorkelling, an often exposed coral reef slices southwest across to the mainland, marking out a shallow lagoon and **North Chaweng**. This S-shaped part of the beach is comparatively peaceful, though it has some ugly pockets of development; at low tide it becomes a wide, inviting playground, and from October to January the reef shelters it from the northeast winds.

## Central Chaweng and Chaweng Noi

South of the reef, the idyllic shoreline of **Central Chaweng** stretches for 2km in a dead-straight line, the ugly, traffic-clogged and seemingly endless strip of amenities on the parallel main drag largely concealed behind the tree line and the resorts. Around a low promontory is **Chaweng Noi**, a little curving beach in a rocky bay, which is comparatively quiet in its northern part, away from the road. Well inland of Central Chaweng, the round-island road, Route 4169, passes through the original village of **Ban Chaweng**.

## Coral Cove

South of Chaweng, the road climbs past **Coral Cove**, a tiny, isolated beach of coarse sand hemmed in by high rocks, with some good coral for snorkelling. It's well worth making the trip to *Vikasa Resort*'s restaurant, at the tip of the headland dividing Chaweng from Lamai, for a jaw-dropping view over Chaweng and Choeng Mon to the peaks of Ko Pha Ngan.

## ACCOMMODATION

## CHAWENG

Over fifty **bungalow resorts** and **hotels** at Chaweng are squeezed into thin strips running back from the beachfront at right angles. The cheapest digs here, however, are set back from the beach and are generally little more than functional.

### NORTH CHAWENG

**Amari** North Chaweng ☎077 300 306–9, ⓦamari. com; map p.243. Congenial, eco-friendly luxury hotel that's unpretentious and good value. Cheery and spacious contemporary accommodation, stretching back across the road from the beach, includes family-friendly duplexes, and there are two elegant restaurants, including *Prego* (see page 245), a full-service spa, a gym, a kids' club and two free-form swimming pools with kids' pools. **B5085**

**Anantara Lawana** North Chaweng ☎077 960333, ⓦanantara.com; map p.243. The design of this recently renovated luxury hotel was inspired by Chinese merchants' houses in Thailand in the last century, which gives a pleasing retro feel to the spacious rooms, most of which have indoor-outdoor bathrooms. Much of the accommodation is in two-storey houses, in which the ground-floor room has a plunge pool and the first-floor room a terrace; other villas either have their own pools or share semi-private ones. There's also a main, semi-circular pool, of course, down by the beach, as well as an excellent spa, a good concierge service and fine restaurants, including *Tree Tops*, where you eat in romantic, open-sided treehouses. Breakfast included. **B8630**

**3**

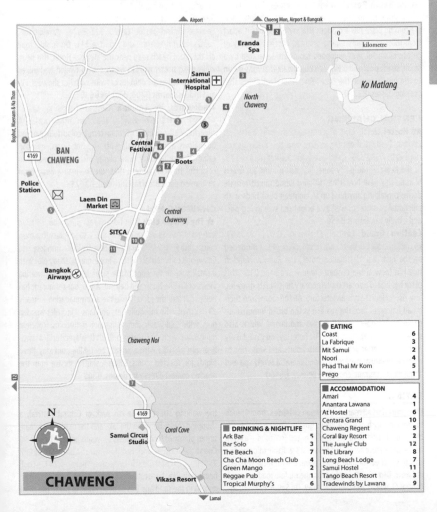

| ● EATING | |
|---|---|
| Coast | 6 |
| La Fabrique | 3 |
| Mit Samui | 2 |
| Noori | 4 |
| Phad Thai Mr Kom | 5 |
| Prego | 1 |

| ■ ACCOMMODATION | |
|---|---|
| Amari | 4 |
| Anantara Lawana | 1 |
| At Hostel | 6 |
| Centara Grand | 10 |
| Chaweng Regent | 5 |
| Coral Bay Resort | 2 |
| The Jungle Club | 12 |
| The Library | 8 |
| Long Beach Lodge | 7 |
| Samui Hostel | 11 |
| Tango Beach Resort | 3 |
| Tradewinds by Lawana | 9 |

| ■ DRINKING & NIGHTLIFE | |
|---|---|
| Ark Bar | 5 |
| Bar Solo | 3 |
| The Beach | 7 |
| Cha Cha Moon Beach Club | 4 |
| Green Mango | 2 |
| Reggae Pub | 1 |
| Tropical Murphy's | 6 |

CHAWENG

**3**

**Chaweng Regent** At the bottom end of North Chaweng ☎ 077 300 500, ⓦ chawengregent.com; map p.243. Reliable, well-run, luxury place offering elegant bungalows and low-rise rooms with private terraces and all mod cons, around lotus ponds, two large pools with kids' pools, a fitness centre and spa. B5500

★ **Coral Bay Resort** At the far north end of North Chaweng ☎ 077 234 555, ⓦ coralbay.net; map p.243. A charming, eco-friendly vision of how Chaweng might have developed – if only there'd been more space. In quiet, ten-acre gardens with over 500 species of plants, the huge, thatched villas have been thoughtfully and tastefully designed with local woods, bamboo and coconut; all have extensive verandas and waterfall showers. There's an attractive free-form pool and a good beachside bar-restaurant. Breakfast included. B6850

**Tango Beach Resort** North Chaweng ☎ 077 300451, ⓦ tangobeachsamui.com; map p.243. This helpful and welcoming place has a modern Thai style that sets it apart from most of Samui's farang-oriented hotels: a variety of cutesy, colourful, well-equipped rooms are separated by a small, shady pool and a wooden boardwalk that runs down to the beach, where the *Lazy Wave* restaurant offers Thai cooking classes. B2200

## CENTRAL CHAWENG

**At Hostel** North end of Central Chaweng, between Central Festival shopping centre and the main beach road ☎ 077 332 555, ⓦ athostelsamui.com; map p.243. In the heart of the party zone, just down from Soi Green Mango, this new hostel has shining-white mixed/female dorms containing anything up to eighteen bunk beds with individual curtains, as well as a bright red swimming pool and a lively bar. Dorms B450

**Centara Grand** Central Chaweng ☎ 077 230500, ⓦ centarahotelsresorts.com; map p.243. Modelled on the first Thai "destination hotel", the *Railway Hotel* in Hua Hin (now also a *Centara Grand* – see page 216), this place has added a smart contemporary finish to its graceful, low-rise, colonial-style architecture. All the rooms and their broad balconies face the sea across the broad immaculate gardens of hedgerows, palm trees and lawns, which also shelter a huge, free-form pool. The hotel lays on varied daily programmes of activities for both adults and kids, not to mention plenty of watersports, and there's a lovely spa and a fine bar-restaurant, *Coast* (see below). B8360

**The Library** Central Chaweng ☎ 077 422767–8, ⓦ thelibrarysamui.com; map p.243. High-concept design hotel, based around a shining white library of books, DVDs and CDs. The idea is continued in the rooms, which all feature iMacs and Blu-ray players, and have a sleek, cubic theme; they're divided into suites (downstairs) and studios with balconies (upstairs). There's a blood-red swimming pool, a fitness centre, a beachfront terrace restaurant, *The Page*, and a roadside cocktail bar-restaurant, The Drink Gallery. B13,200

**Long Beach Lodge** Towards the north end of Central Chaweng ☎ 077 422162, ⓦ longbeachsamui.com; map p.243. An unusually spacious, sandy compound for this part of the beach, with plenty of shade. All the orderly, clean bungalows and rooms are a decent size and have hot water, fridge, TV and a/c. Service is friendly, and breakfast is included in the price. B1500

**Samui Hostel** South end of Chaweng, beyond the Centara Grand Hotel ☎ 085 922 9426, ⓦ facebook.com/samuihostelthailand; map p.243. On a side road off the main beach road near the Mercure Hotel, this neat, welcoming hostel has fan or a/c six- to twelve-bed mixed dorms, as well as a/c doubles or twins with hot showers, TVs and fridges. Dorms B200, doubles B600

**Tradewinds by Lawana** Central Chaweng ☎ 077 414294, ⓦ tradewindsbylawana.com; map p.243. A cheerful, well-run place of characterful, colourfully painted bungalows and rooms (all with a/c, hot water, minibar, cable TV and balcony), with plenty of room to breathe in colourful tropical gardens that run down to a beachfront swimming pool. Breakfast included. B3625

## CHAWENG NOI

★ **The Jungle Club** 2km up a steep, partly paved road behind Chaweng Noi ☎ 081 891 8263, ⓦ jungleclubsamui.com; map p.243. Breezy, French–Thai antidote to Chaweng's commercial clutter: a huge, grassy, shady plot with a small pool on the edge of the slope to catch the towering views of Ko Pha Ngan and beyond. A chic bar-restaurant has been built into the rocks, while the accommodation – nearly all thatched, with mosquito nets and fans – includes wooden huts with cold-water indoor-outdoor bathrooms, concrete bungalows with hot water and DVD players and a two-bedroom a/c villa with a private pool. Minimum stay three nights for selected rooms. Offers a shuttle service from the beach – contact directly for details. B800

## EATING

Chaweng offers all manner of foreign **cuisines**, from French to Russian, much of it of dubious quality. Among all this, it's quite hard to find good, reasonably priced Thai food – as well as the places recommended below, it's worth exploring the cheap and cheerful food stalls, popular with local workers, at **Laem Din night market**, on the middle road between Central Chaweng and Highway 4169. On Saturday evenings, the walking street in the car park of Central Festival, a shopping centre between the lake and the main beach road, serves plenty of food, as well as souvenirs and clothes.

**Coast** Centara Grand Hotel, Central Chaweng ☎ 077 230500, ⓦ coast-beach-club.com; map p.243. Cool, beachclub-like bar-restaurant with swing chairs, sunken booths in the sand and lots of beachfront to make the most of the sea views. The focus of the well-designed menu is on excellent seafood and grills, but you'll also find pizzas (B420), tapas, and meat and cheese platters. A DJ and fire-jugglers entertain over the Monday evening beach barbecue. Daily noon–11pm.

**La Fabrique** Route 4169, Ban Chaweng; map p.243. Branch of Lamai's excellent French café-patisserie, handily placed by the traffic lights at Chaweng's main junction. Daily (except Wed) 8.30am–5pm.

**Mit Samui** Ban Chaweng road ☏ 089 727 2034, ⓦ mitsamui-restaurant.com; map p.243. Very popular with both locals and tourists, this large, bustling, simple restaurant specializes in pick-your-own seafood (priced by weight), but also serves tasty stir-fried squid with salted egg (B200), satay and fresh fruit juices. Daily 11am–midnight.

**Noori** Opposite Chaweng Buri Resort towards the north end of Central Chaweng, just up from McDonald's ☏ 077 300757, ⓦ nooriindiasamui.com; map p.243. Superior Indian food (around B200/dish) in relatively basic surroundings, including all the old favourites such as chicken tikka masala, as well as over twenty types of bread, plenty of seafood and vegetarian options and Indian desserts. Also offers Indian cooking classes. Daily 11am–11.30pm.

**Phad Thai Mr Kom** Route 4169, Ban Chaweng; map p.243. You'll get an energetic welcome at this basic little restaurant, where you can tuck into tasty *phat thai* with your choice of extras (from B60). It's in Buffalo Market, an open-air food mall (also serving *som tam*, rice porridge, Japanese and pasta) that's popular with Thais. Mon–Sat 11.30am–11pm.

★**Prego** Amari Palm Reef Hotel, North Chaweng ☏ 077 300317, ⓦ prego-samui.com; map p.243. Excellent, chic restaurant that would stand on its own two feet in Milan, the head chef's home town. The varied menu of contemporary rustic Italian dishes includes good *antipasti*, pizzas from a proper wood-fired oven, handmade pastas and top-notch risottos, with many ingredients flown in from Italy, and there's a very good selection of wines. Booking advised in high season. Daily noon–midnight.

## DRINKING AND NIGHTLIFE

Avoiding the raucous hostess bars and English-themed pubs on the main through road, the best place to **drink** is on the beach: at night dozens of resorts and dedicated bars lay out candlelit tables on the sand, especially towards the north end of Central Chaweng and on North Chaweng.

**Ark Bar** North end of Central Chaweng ⓦ ark-bar.com; map p.243. Hosts very popular beach parties on Wed & Fri, with international and Thai house DJs, a swim-up pool bar and fire shows. Daily 2pm–2am.

**Bar Solo** North end of Central Chaweng, on the main road just north of Green Mango ⓦ facebook.com/solobarsamui; map p.243. One of the bars of the moment, whose black-and-white industrial look is matched by tech house on the sound system, with international DJs like Goldie occasionally flying in. Diversions include a pool table, and there's a great streetside patio out the front for people-watching. Daily 6pm–2am.

★**The Beach** Chaweng Noi, south of the Sheraton (not to be confused with The Beach Bar at the Impiana Resort just to the south) ⓦ facebook.com/thebeachbarsamui; map p.243. Big, chic, new, indoor-outdoor beach bar with plenty of room along the sand for beanbags and mats to kick back on. Expect the best of Thai and international techno and house DJs, including the likes of Nakadia, who get to work on a top-quality sound system. Daily 10am–1am.

**Cha Cha Moon Beach Club** North end of Central Chaweng, next to Ark Bar ⓦ facebook.com/chachamoonbeachclub; map p.243. Stylish beach bar with daybeds on the sand and Thai and international DJs spinning house and techno, especially for the weekly climax of full, black and half-moon parties. Daily roughly 3pm–2am.

**Green Mango** North end of Central Chaweng ⓦ facebook.com/thegreenmangoclub; map p.243. Long-standing dance venue, in a huge shed that combines an industrial look with that of a tropical greenhouse. Now with its own alley, Soi Green Mango, lined with other vibrant bars and clubs. Daily roughly 9pm–2am.

**Reggae Pub** Inland from Central Chaweng across the lake ☏ 077 422331–3; map p.243. Chaweng's oldest nightclub is a venerable Samui institution – with a memorabilia shop to prove it. It does time now as an unpretentious, good-time, party venue, with some nice lakeside tables, pool tables, big-screen sports and live bands every night. Daily 7pm–2am.

**Tropical Murphy's** Opposite McDonald's in Central Chaweng ☏ 077 413614, ⓦ tropicalmurphys.com; map p.243. One theme pub that is worth singling out: with draught Guinness, Kilkenny and Hoegaarden, a huge range of big-screen sports, pool tables and decent food, *Murphy's* has turned itself into a popular landmark and meeting place. Daily 9am–1am.

## DIRECTORY

**Airlines** Bangkok Airways, south end of Ban Chaweng on Route 4169 ☏ 077 601300.

**Hospital** The private Samui International Hospital (☏ 077 300394–5, ⓦ sih.co.th) provides 24hr ambulance and emergency services, a dental clinic and travel inoculations.

**Pharmacy** Boots has several branches in Central Chaweng, including one just up the road from *Tropical Murphy's* pub (☏ 077 413724; daily 10am–11pm).

# Lamai

**LAMAI** is like a second city to Chaweng's capital, not quite as developed and much less frenetic, while lacking the latter's wide range of chic hotels, restaurants and nightclubs. Development is concentrated into a farang toytown of tawdry open-air hostess bars and Western restaurants that has grown up behind the centre of the beach, interspersed with supermarkets, clinics, banks, ATMs and travel agents; on Sunday evenings, the area to the east of the market hosts a **walking street** similar to the one in Maenam on Thursday. Running roughly north to south for 4km, the white, palm-fringed beach itself is still a picture, and generally quieter than Chaweng, with far less in the way of watersports – it's quite easy to get away from it all by staying at the peaceful extremities of the bay, where the backpackers' resorts are preferable to Chaweng's functional

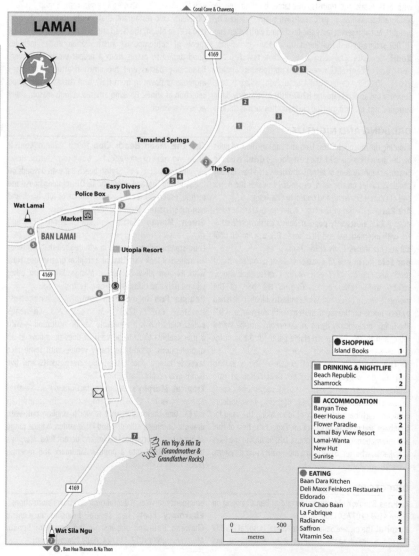

**LAMAI**

Coral Cove & Chaweng

4169

Tamarind Springs

The Spa

Easy Divers

Police Box

Wat Lamai

Market

**BAN LAMAI**

Utopia Resort

4169

Hin Yay & Hin Ta
(Grandmother &
Grandfather Rocks)

Wat Sila Ngu

Ban Hua Thanon & Na Thon

| ● SHOPPING | |
| --- | --- |
| Island Books | 1 |

| ■ DRINKING & NIGHTLIFE | |
| --- | --- |
| Beach Republic | 1 |
| Shamrock | 2 |

| ■ ACCOMMODATION | |
| --- | --- |
| Banyan Tree | 1 |
| Beer House | 5 |
| Flower Paradise | 2 |
| Lamai Bay View Resort | 3 |
| Lamai-Wanta | 6 |
| New Hut | 4 |
| Sunrise | 7 |

| ● EATING | |
| --- | --- |
| Baan Dara Kitchen | 4 |
| Deli Maxx Feinkost Restaurant | 3 |
| Eldorado | 6 |
| Krua Chao Baan | 7 |
| La Fabrique | 5 |
| Radiance | 2 |
| Saffron | 1 |
| Vitamin Sea | 8 |

0          500
metres

guesthouses. At the northern end, the spur of land that hooks eastward into the sea is perhaps the prettiest spot and is beginning to attract some upmarket development: it has more rocks than sand, but the shallow sea behind the coral reef is protected from the high seas of November, December and January.

The original village of **Ban Lamai**, set well back on Route 4169, remains surprisingly aloof, and its wat contains a small museum of ceramics, agricultural tools and other everyday objects. Most visitors get more of a buzz from **Hin Yay** (Grandmother Rock) and **Hin Ta** (Grandfather Rock), small rock formations on the bay's southern promontory, which never fail to raise a giggle with their resemblance to the male and female sexual organs.

## ACCOMMODATION LAMAI

Lamai's **accommodation** is generally less cramped and slightly better value than Chaweng's, though it presents far fewer choices at the top end of the market. Budget accommodation is concentrated around the beach's northern and southern ends. Lamai supports two famous spa resorts, *Tamarind Springs* and *The Spa Resort* (see page 235).

**Banyan Tree** On the bay's northern headland ☎077 915333, ⊛banyantree.com; map p.246. Occupying a steep-sided, landscaped valley, with towering views of Chaweng from the lobby bar, *Banyan Tree* provides the height of luxury in its beautiful, stilted pool villas: lofty living rooms, walk-in wardrobes, possibly the biggest big-head showers in Thailand and landscaped pools. Electric buggies will ferry you down to the spa, the main swimming pool, kids' pool and private cove with a good stretch of beach, where plenty of watersports are on offer. B25,520

**Beer House** In the central section of the northern part of the beach ☎077 256591, ⊛beerhousebungalow. com; map p.246. Appealing bungalows with fans, hot showers, verandas and hammocks in a lush, shaded compound – try to bag one of the four on the beachfront, which are only B50 extra. Double B600

**Flower Paradise** On the bay's northern headland ☎077 270675, ⊛samuiroestiland.com; map p.246. A short walk from the beach, a friendly, well-run German–Swiss place in a small but beautiful garden. All the attractive bungalows of varying sizes have verandas and hot water, and there's a good restaurant, *Röstiland* (closed Sun), specializing in the eponymous hash browns. Fan B400, a/c B800

**Lamai Bay View Resort** On the bay's northern headland ☎077 458778–9, ⊛bayviewsamui.com; map p.246.

Neat, stylish bungalows with verandas, minibars and hot-water bathrooms in an extensive, flower-bedecked, grassy compound; the poshest come with a/c and cable TV. Offers a friendly, German–Thai welcome, kayaking and great sunset views of the beach from the attractive restaurant. Fan B1650, a/c B1750

**Lamai-Wanta** East of the central crossroads ☎077 424550, ⊛lamaiwanta.com; map p.246. Welcoming, well-placed hotel with a seductive beachfront swimming pool and a good restaurant. Set around trim lawns, the seventy large, bright rooms and villas are decorated in white and dark wood in a restrained Thai style, with terracotta floor tiles and a few splashes of colour; all have a/c, TVs, minibars, safes and hot water. Discounts for longer stays. B2800

**New Hut** Beer House's eastern neighbour on the northern part of the beach ☎077 230437, ⊛newhut bungalow.com; map p.246. These bungalows are tightly packed and luridly coloured but they're right on the beach and there's a good restaurant attached. The cheapest are rustic A-frames with nothing more than a mattress, fan and mosquito net, sharing cold-water bathrooms, while the more expensive en suites come with a/c. Fan B400, a/c B600

**Sunrise** On the Hin Yay Hin Ta access road ☎077 424433, ⊛sunrisebungalow.com; map p.246. Welcoming and clued-up establishment on the far southern end of the beach, with a decent restaurant, a gym and snorkels to rent. In a quiet, shady garden amid coconut palms, choose between clean fan rooms with cold or hot showers and larger a/c bungalows with hot water, cable TV and fridge. Fan B600, a/c B1600

## EATING AND DRINKING

Besides the **restaurants** recommended below, there's a **market** of cheap takeaway food stalls and simple restaurants inland just off Highway 4169 (east of Tesco Lotus supermarket) that's popular with locals for lunch and dinner (closes around 8 or 9pm). Apart from a few bar-restaurants on the beach near *Lamai-Wanta*, Lamai's **nightlife** is all within spitting distance of the central crossroads.

**Baan Dara Kitchen** Highway 4169, Ban Lamai; map p.246. A locals' favourite right beside the entrance to Wat

Lamai, this simple but attractive restaurant serves cheap and very tasty noodle soup with pork (B70), dim sum, *phat thai*, green curry and espressos made with organic coffeebeans. Daily 8am–6pm.

**Beach Republic** On the bay's northern headland ☎077 458100, ⊛beachrepublic.com; map p.246. Although it features accommodation and a spa, this chic beach club is best known for its restaurant and bar, arrayed around two pools and a Jacuzzi, with plenty of loungers and day-

**3**

beds and fine views of the bay. Among sandwiches, global tapas, pasta and pizza, the very good beer-battered fish and chips (B420) on the daytime menu stand out. Weekly events include two DJ sets on weekend afternoons, "Soulful Saturdays" and "Sunday Sessions" with a special Sunday brunch. Restaurant daily 7–10.30am & 11am–10.30pm.

**Deli Maxx Feinkost Restaurant** North of the central crossroads, near Highway 4169 ☎077 419010; map p.246. At this popular little bar-restaurant, you can tuck into a wide selection of Western, mostly German, food, including plenty of sausages, wiener schnitzel (B240) and good steaks and pizzas, and wash it all down with German beer. Tues–Sun 6pm–2am.

**Eldorado** Just west of the central crossroads ☎094 409 0614, ⓦfacebook.com/eldorado.lamai; map p.246. Highly recommended friendly, good-value Swedish restaurant, serving a few Thai and Swedish favourites including meatballs, salads, steaks, pizzas and other international main courses. All-you-can-eat barbecue on Wednesday (B290). Mon–Sat 3pm–midnight.

**Krua Chao Baan** Highway 4169, about 1km south of Hin Yay Hin Ta ☎077 418589; map p.246. With a cute little garden and scenic seafront terraces between the road and the sea, this well-regarded restaurant concentrates on seafood (mostly sold by weight) and serves a few southern Thai dishes such as *kaeng som kung* ("sour prawn curry"; B150). Daily 10am–10pm.

★ **La Fabrique** Route 4169, just south of the temple in Lamai village; map p.246. Authentic French patisserie-café, a civilized retreat from the busy road. Breakfast sets, superb custard cakes, sweet and savoury crepes, quiches (B85), omelettes, pizzas, salads and sandwiches. Daily 6.30am–8pm.

**Radiance** The Spa Resort, at the far north end of the beach; map p.246. Excellent, casual beachside restaurant, serving a huge range of vegetarian Thai and international (including Mexican) dishes, plus raw and vegan food, as well as plenty of meat and marine offerings. The veggie "ginger nuts" stir-fry (B140) and *som tam* with spicy Thai sausage (B125) are excellent. A long menu of "longevity drinks" – juices, smoothies and shakes – includes a delicious lime juice with honey. Daily 6am–10.30pm (last orders).

**Saffron** Banyan Tree Resort (see page 247); map p.246. Feast your eyes on the views over the restaurant's private inlet – the rest of Samui might as well not be there – and on the artistic presentations of its imaginative Thai haute cuisine. The foundation is central Thai cooking, with seafood featuring heavily, but there's a nod to regional flavours: the northeastern *nam tok* with Australian tenderloin is excellent (B520), while the northern curry noodle soup, *khao soi*, here comes with salmon and its roe (B790). Daily 6–11pm.

**Shamrock** North of the central crossroads ⓦthesamuishamrock.com; map p.246. Popular, friendly Irish bar with lots of TV sports, which also hosts lively cover bands every evening and serves Guinness, Magner's cider and Kilkenny bitter (all on draught). Daily 9am–2.30am.

★ **Vitamin Sea** On Highway 4169 in Ban Hua Thanon, 50m north of the dogleg in the road and about 2km south of Hin Yay Hin Ta ⓦthesamuishamrock.com; map p.246. Genial, Belgian-run bar-restaurant on a lovely, breezy terrace right over the beach, artfully done out in white, aquamarine and recycled wood. The *coq au vin* is very tasty (B320), but the real stars are the chips it comes with, thick cut and double-fried. Mon–Sat 11am–11pm (kitchen closes 9.30pm).

## SHOPPING

**Island Books** On Highway 4169, opposite Beer House bungalows ☎061 193 2132, ⓦisland-books-samui.com; map p.246. Samui's best secondhand bookshop for buying, selling, renting or trading, with its stock of tens of thousands of books mostly detailed on the website. Daily 9am–7pm.

# The south and west coasts

Lacking the long, attractive beaches of the more famous resorts, the **south and west coasts** have much less to offer in the way of accommodation, though there are one or two interesting spots that are worth heading for on a round-island tour. If you happen to be here in November, the west coast's flat, unexceptional beaches might make a calm alternative when the northeast winds buffet the other side of the island.

## Ko Taen and Ko Mad Sum

The two small islands of **Ko Taen** and **Ko Mad Sum**, a short way off the south coast, offer some of Samui's best snorkelling, especially around Ko Taen. TK Tour in Ban Thongkrut (☎077 334052–3, ⓦtktoursamui.com) goes to both islands on a four- to five-hour boat trip, costing B1300 per person (B1500 with kayaking, or with a quick look at Ko Si Ko Ha, the heavily guarded islands to the west where sea gypsies gather swifts' nests for bird's-nest soup – see page 370), including pick-up from your accommodation, snorkelling equipment and lunch. Island Hoppers World (☎081 361 5605, ⓦislandhoppersworld.com) offers snorkelling day-trips to Ko Taen (B1490, including pick-up from your accommodation, all equipment and lunch), as well as overnight trips, staying in bungalows on the island. Both TK and Island Hoppers World also offer sunset snorkelling trips to Ko Taen and trips to the mainland coast near Khanom to see pink dolphins.

### Na Muang Falls
About 5km inland of **Ban Hua Thanon**, near **Ban Thurian**, the **Na Muang Falls** make a popular outing as they're not far off the round-island road (each of the two main falls has its own signposted kilometre-long paved access road off Route 4169). The lower fall splashes and sprays down a 20m wall of rock into a large pool, while Na Muang 2, upstream, is a more spectacular, shaded cascade. However, don't expect to appreciate the sparkling scenery in tranquillity, as the falls are now on most package tour itineraries, surrounded by water slides, zip lines and elephant camps.

3

# Ang Thong National Marine Park
Closed Nov & most of Dec • Park entry fee B300 • Park headquarters ☎077 280222 or ☎077 286025, ⓦ nps.dnp.go.th (look for "Mu Ko Ang Thong" – mu ko means "archipelago")

Even if you don't get your buns off the beach for the rest of your stay on Samui or Pha Ngan, it's worth taking at least a day out to visit the beautiful **Ang Thong National Marine Park**, a lush, dense group of 42 small islands strewn like dragons' teeth over the deep-blue Gulf of Thailand, 30km or so west of Samui. Once a haven for pirate junks, then a Royal Thai Navy training base, the islands and their white-sand beaches and virgin rainforest are now preserved under the aegis of the National Parks Department. Erosion of the soft limestone has dug caves and chiselled out fantastic shapes that are variously said to resemble seals, a rhinoceros, a Buddha image and even the temple complex at Angkor.

The surrounding waters are home to dolphins, wary of humans because local fishermen catch them for their meat, and *pla thu* (short-bodied mackerel), part of the national staple diet, which gather in huge numbers between February and April to spawn around the islands. On land, long-tailed macaques, leopard cats, wild pigs, sea otters, squirrels, monitor lizards and pythons are found, as well as dusky langurs, which, because they have no natural enemies here, are unusually friendly and easy to spot. Around forty bird species have had confirmed sightings, including the white-rumped shama, noted for its singing, the brahminy kite, black baza, little heron, Eurasian woodcock, several species of pigeon, kingfisher and wagtail, as well as common and hill mynah; in addition, island caves shelter swiftlets, whose homes are stolen for bird's-nest soup (see page 370).

### Ko Wua Talab
The largest landmass in the group is **Ko Wua Talab** (Sleeping Cow Island), where the park headquarters shelter in a hollow behind the small beach. From there, you can climb to the island's peak to gawp at the panorama, which is especially fine at sunrise and sunset: in the distance, Ko Samui, Ko Pha Ngan and the mainland; nearer at hand, the jagged edges of the surrounding archipelago; and below the peak, a secret cove on the western side and an almost sheer drop to the clear blue sea to the east. It's a fairly tricky 500m trail, with some scrambling including a patch of sharp rocks at the summit (allow about 2hr return at a comfortable pace with a break at the top; bring walking sandals or shoes). Another climb from the beach (allow about 1hr return) leads to **Tham Buabok**, a cave set high in the cliff-face. Some of the stalactites and stalagmites are said to resemble lotuses, hence the cave's appellation, "Waving Lotus". If you're visiting in September, look out

for the white, violet-dotted petals of **Ang Thong lady's slipper orchids** among the rocks and cliffs, an endemic species found only on the archipelago.

## Ko Mae Ko

The park's name, Ang Thong ("Golden Bowl"), comes from a landlocked saltwater lake, 250m in diameter, on **Ko Mae Ko** to the north of Ko Wua Talab, which was the inspiration for the setting of the bestselling novel and film, *The Beach*. Steep steps (allow 30min return) lead from the beach to the rim of the cliff wall that encircles the lake, affording another stunning view of the archipelago and of the shallow, blue-green water below, which is connected to the sea by an impassable natural underground tunnel.

### ARRIVAL AND DEPARTURE                    ANG THONG

There are no scheduled boats to Ang Thong, only organized **day-trips**, which can be booked through your accommodation or a travel agent. If you do want to stay, you can go over on a boat-trip ticket, through Highway for example – it's valid for a return on a later day.

### FROM KO SAMUI

**Blue Stars** ☎ 077 300615 or ☎ 077 413884, ⊛ bluestars. info. If you want to make the most of the park's beautiful scenery of strange rock formations and hidden caves, take a dedicated kayaking trip with Blue Stars. For a one-day trip, taking in the lake at Ko Mae Ko, snorkelling at Ko Thai Plao in the northern part of the park and kayaking at both islands, it charges B2500 (in a group of two people), including pick-up from your accommodation and boat from Na Thon over to the park, buffet lunch and snorkelling gear.

**Highway** ☎ 077 421290 or ☎ 081 843 1533, ⊛ highsea tour.com. The main operator, whose big boats leave Na Thon every day at 8.30am, returning at 4.30–5pm. In between, there's a 150min stop to explore Ko Wua Talab (just enough time to climb to the viewpoint and have a quick swim – or possibly visit the cave – so don't dally), lunch on the boat, some cruising through the archipelago, a visit to the viewpoint over the lake on Ko Mae Ko and some snorkelling time. Tickets cost B1100/person (B1650 with kayaking), including pick-up.

**The Dive Academy** ☎ 092 464 3264, ⊛ thedive academysamui.com. This highly recommended dive school on Bophut offers small-group snorkelling day-trips to Ang Thong in a speedboat (B4000, including pick-up from your accommodation, snorkelling with good masks and fins, optional kayaking, lunch and national park entrance fee), with a high ratio of experienced guides to customers, taking in Ko Mae Ko but not Ko Wua Talab.

### FROM KO PHA NGAN

Similar day-trips to those from Samui are available on Pha Ngan, and they include transfers from the main beaches, lunch and snorkelling. If you want to do a dedicated kayaking trip with Blue Stars (see above), the first Lomprayah catamaran from Thong Sala will get you over to Nathon pier on Samui just in time for their boat departure. **Orion** ☎ 081 894 5076, ⊛ phanganboattrips.com. Recommended, well-organized day-trips in a wooden cruiser, costing B2000, or B2200 with kayaking (including national park entrance fee, light breakfast, a good buffet lunch, snacks, fruit and soft drinks), taking in Ko Mae Ko and Ko Wua Talab.

### FROM KO TAO

**Island Travel** (see page 268). Weekly, small-group day-trips in a speedboat, costing B3600 for snorkellers, B5100 for divers (including pick-up from your accommodation, national park entrance fee, all equipment, lunch, snacks, fruit and soft drinks), taking in Ko Mae Ko.

### GETTING AROUND

**Boat and kayak rental** For getting around the archipelago from Ko Wua Talab, it's possible to charter a motorboat or rent a kayak from marine park staff at headquarters, who also rent out snorkelling gear; the archipelago's waters are heavily sedimented from the Tapi River and are too shallow for really good coral, but the best of it is just off Ko Thai Plao, located in the north of the park.

### ACCOMMODATION AND EATING

**National park bungalows** At park headquarters on Ko Wua Talab ☎ 077 280222 or ☎ 077 286025, ⊛ nps. dnp.go.th. Simple two- to eight-berth bungalows and a restaurant, in a sheltered glade behind the main beach. **B500**

**Camping** At park headquarters on Ko Wua Talab and on Ko Samsao. If you're keen to camp out in the park, two-person tents can be rented for around B250 a night from park headquarters.

# Ko Pha Ngan

In recent years, backpackers have tended to move over to Ko Samui's fun-loving little sibling, **KO PHA NGAN**, 20km to the north, which still has a comparatively simple atmosphere, mostly because the poor road system is an impediment to the developers. With a dense jungle covering its inland mountains and rugged granite outcrops along the coast, Pha Ngan lacks the huge, gently sweeping beaches for which Samui is famous, but it does have plenty of coral to explore and some beautiful, sheltered bays. If you're seeking total isolation, trek out to **Hat Khuat** (**Bottle Beach**) on the north coast or the half-dozen pristine beaches on the east coast; **Thong Nai Pan**, at the top of the east coast, is not quite as remote, and offers a wide range of amenities and accommodation; while on the long neck of land at the southeast corner, **Hat Rin**, a pilgrimage site for ravers, is a thoroughly commercialized backpackers' resort in a gorgeous setting.

Much of Pha Ngan's development has plonked itself on the south and west sides along the only coastal roads on the island, which fan out from **Thong Sala**, the capital. The long, straight south coast is lined with bungalows, especially around **Ban Tai** and **Ban Khai**, to take the overspill from nearby Hat Rin, but it's hard to recommend staying here, as the beaches are mediocre by Thai standards, and the coral reef that hugs the length of the shoreline gets in the way of swimming. The west coast, however, offers several handsome sandy bays with great sunset views, notably **Hat Yao** and **Hat Salad**.

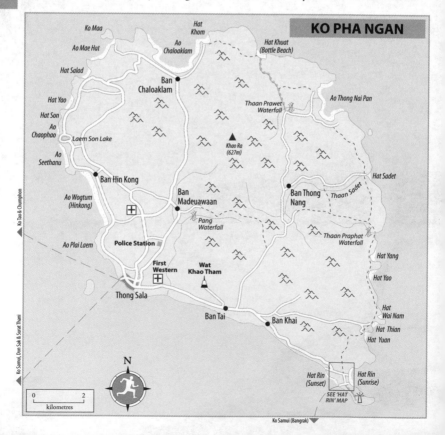

## KO PHA NGAN ACTIVITIES

The most popular activities on Ko Pha Ngan are trips to Ang Thong National Marine Park (see page 249) and **snorkelling trips**, typically encompassing Hat Salad, Mae Hat, Hat Khom and Bottle Beach, and sometimes Thong Nai Pan and Thaan Sadet, which can be arranged at most travel agents and bungalow resorts around the island (around B900/person, including simple lunch and snorkelling equipment, sometimes with the option of kayaking too). The island isn't a great base for **scuba diving**: getting to the best sites around Ko Tao involves time-consuming and expensive voyages, and there aren't as many dive companies here as on Ko Samui or Ko Tao. Other **activities** include learning to cook Thai food, bicycle tours, yoga, wakeboarding and kiteboarding. Many of Pha Ngan's activities are available through the booking site ⓦbackpackersthailandtravel.com.

**Agama Yoga** North of Thong Sala, with several bases around Ao Seethanu ☎089 233 0217, ⓦagamayoga.com. Yoga drop-in classes and retreats.

**Kiteboarding Asia** Lime and Soda Resort, just east of Thong Sala ☎080 600 0573, ⓦkiteboardingasia. com. Kiteboarding classes and rental; the action moves to Ao Chaloaklam during the northeast monsoon (roughly Nov to mid-Jan).

**Eco Nature Tour** ☎062 421 4244, ⓦfacebook.com/ phanganisland2017. A well-received programme of half- and one-day tours that might take in snorkelling, zip lining, Thai boxing, archery, Pang Waterfall and boating to Bottle Beach; free pick-ups from most parts of the island.

**Jungle Gym** Hat Rin ☎077 375115, ⓦjunglegym andecolodge.com. Gym offering Thai boxing classes and yoga.

**Lotus Diving** Dive resort on Ao Chaloaklam ☎077 374142, ⓦlotusdiving.com. SSI centre, which offers frequent courses and trips to Ang Thong National Marine Park, Southwest Pinnacle and Sail Rock (see page 249), halfway between Pha Ngan and Tao.

**My Wok and Me** Ao Chaloaklam ☎087 893 3804, ⓦfacebook.com/pages/My-Wok-and-Me/146999 882047571. Highly recommended cooking classes, including a trip to the local food market; vegetarian menu available.

**Phangan Bicycle Tours** Thong Sala ☎064 053 4112, ⓦphanganbicycletours.com. Danish-run half-day sightseeing tours on well-maintained bikes, either in the morning or early evening, including a family option with kids' seats, trailers and bikes available.

**Siam Healing Centre** Thong Sala ☎089 965 8752, ⓦsiamhealing.com. Have a Thai massage, learn how to massage or drop in for a yoga class.

**Wake Up** Ao Chaloaklam ☎087 283 6755, ⓦwakeup wakeboarding.com. Wakeboarding in the sheltered bay here (best Feb–Nov).

3

Pha Ngan's **bungalows** all now have running water and electricity, and plenty of places offer air conditioning, though there is only a handful of real luxury hotels. The three hundred-plus resorts generally have more space to spread out than on Ko Samui, and the cost of living is lower. The **prices** given on the following pages are standard for most of the year (though on Hat Rin they vary with the phases of the moon), but in slack periods you'll be offered discounts (possible, roughly, in May, June, Oct & Nov), and at the very busiest times (especially Dec & Jan) Pha Ngan's bungalow owners are canny enough to raise the stakes. **Nightlife** is concentrated at Hat Rin, climaxing every month in a wild **full moon party** on the beach; several smaller outdoor parties have now got in on the act, all at Ban Tai on the south coast: the **Half Moon Festival** (twice monthly, about a week before and after the full moon; ⓦhalfmoonfestival.com) and the monthly **Black Moon Culture** (ⓦblackmoon-culture.com) have now been joined by the Waterfall Party (two days before and two days after each full moon; ⓦfacebook. com/waterfallparty) and Jungle Experience (one day before each full moon; ⓦjungle-experience.com). Meanwhile, 5 Senses Thailand (ⓦfacebook.com/5sensesfest) held its first twelve-day festival in early February 2018, featuring dozens of international house and techno DJs at diverse locations across the island, day and night.

## ARRIVAL AND DEPARTURE                                    KO PHA NGAN

The most obvious way of getting to Ko Pha Ngan is on a boat from the **Surat Thani** area, but there are also boats from Chumphon (see page 226). Nok Air and Air Asia offer combination flight-bus-boat tickets from Bangkok's Don Muang Airport via Surat Thani and Nakhon Si Thammarat airports.

**FROM SURAT THANI OR DON SAK**

**Surat Thani to Thong Sala** Boat services fluctuate according to demand, but the longest-established is the night boat from Ban Don pier in Surat Thani to Thong Sala, which leaves at 11pm Mon–Sat (☎ 077 284928 or ☎ 081 326 8973; 7hr; B400); in the opposite direction, the night boat departs from Thong Sala at 10pm. Tickets are available from the pier on the day of departure, but note that sometimes these boats don't depart if they haven't got enough takers to make it worth their while, especially in the rainy season. In addition, there are three Lomprayah catamaran services a day from Tapi Pier, 5km northeast of central Surat (2hr 30min; B700; on Pha Ngan ☎ 077 423761–2, ⊛ lomprayah.com).

**Don Sak to Thong Sala** There are one Lomprayah passenger ferry and six Raja vehicle ferries a day (on Pha Ngan ☎ 077 377452–3, ⊛ rajaferryport.com) from Don Sak, 68km east of Surat Thani, most of which have connecting buses to the pier from Surat, with a total journey time of around 4hr (from B350).

**FROM BANGKOK**

**Bus packages** From Bangkok bus packages similar to those for getting to Ko Samui are available, notably government buses from the Southern Terminal (first-class a/c 2 daily B585; VIP 1 daily B910; 13hr–15hr 30min). Leaving Pha Ngan, you can catch these buses from the Raja Ferry pier in Thong Sala (☎ 077 238507 or ☎ 077 238762). Lomprayah also offers through-tickets from Bangkok, costing B1300 (2 daily; 12hr), including a VIP bus from its office on Thanon

Ram Bhuttri in Banglamphu (☎ 02 629 2569–70), via Hua Hin, and a catamaran from Chumphon via Ko Tao.

**FROM KO SAMUI**

**To Thong Sala** Three Lomprayah catamarans a day do the 30min trip from Na Thon on Ko Samui to Thong Sala (B300; at Na Thon ☎ 077 950028, on Ko Pha Ngan ☎ 077 423761–2). Three Seatran Discovery boats a day (B300; at Bangrak ☎ 077 954171, on Pha Ngan ☎ 077 953056; ⊛ seatrandiscovery. com) and three Lomprayah boats a day (B250; at Bangrak ☎ 077 953084), both from the east end of Bangrak, and two Lomprayah catamarans from Maenam (B300; at Maenam ☎ 077 950700–4) call in at Thong Sala after 30min.

**To Hat Rin and the east coast** From the centre of Bangrak, the *Haad Rin Queen* crosses four times a day to Hat Rin in under an hour. Times have remained constant over the years, with extra services operated around the full moon: from Bangrak 10.30am, 1pm, 4pm & 6.30pm, from Hat Rin 9.30am, 11.40am, 2.30pm & 5.30pm (B200; on Samui ☎ 077 484668, on Pha Ngan ☎ 077 375113; ⊛ haadrinqueen.com). If there are enough takers and the weather's good enough – generally reliable between roughly Jan and Oct – one small boat a day crosses from the pier in Ban Maenam at noon to Hat Rin, before sailing up Ko Pha Ngan's east coast, via Hat Thian and Hat Sadet, to Thong Nai Pan; tickets to Hat Sadet, for example, cost B350.

**FROM KO TAO**

There are boats from Ko Tao to Ko Pha Ngan (see page 253); all offer the same service in the return direction.

## INFORMATION

**Tourist information** There's no TAT office on Ko Pha Ngan, but a free, widely available booklet, *Phangan Info*, provides regularly updated information about the island, along with useful maps, and it also has a complementary website (⊛ phangan.info) and an app, on which you can book accommodation.

# Thong Sala

Like the capital of Samui, **THONG SALA** is a port of entrance and little more, where the incoming ferries, especially around noon, are met by touts sent to escort travellers to bungalows elsewhere on the island. Seatran and Lomprayah share a pier, while a short way to the north, the Raja Ferry pier gives onto the town's dusty main street, which is flanked by banks, supermarkets, travel agents, a day market and a night market. Branching off south is the old main street, which on Saturday evenings becomes a "Walking Street" weekly market, selling clothes, crafts and food. Songthaews, jeeps and air-conditioned minibuses to the rest of the island congregate by the pier heads.

## GETTING AROUND                                                                 THONG SALA

**By motorbike or jeep** Many people get around by motorbike or 4WD. Motorbikes (B150–200/day) and jeeps

(B800–1000/day) can be rented from many places on the main road to the piers.

## ACCOMMODATION AND EATING

**Charu Bay Villas** On the beach about 2km east of the Thong Sala piers on the road to Ban Tai ☎ 084 242

2299, ⊛ charubayvillas.com. Luxurious studios and villas, featuring lots of polished concrete in a colourful, contemporary style, with self-catering facilities and a shared swimming pool among many thoughtful amenities. Minimum stay two nights. B2000

**Nira's Home Bakery** South along the waterfront from the main street, opposite the Seatran pier ☎077 377 524 or ☎086 595 0636. Very pleasant café offering "quick meals to catch the boat": all-day breakfasts, espressos, shakes, baked goods such as quiche lorraine and deli sandwiches. Daily 7am–7pm; closed on the 10th of every month.

**Goodtime Beach Backpackers** About 2km east of the Thong Sala piers on the road to Ban Tai ☎077 377 165, ⓦgoodtimethailand.com. If you really need to stay near Thong Sala, make a beeline for this new hostel on the beach, which offers an outdoor swimming pool and a wide selection of dorm rooms (some of them right on the beachfront), private rooms, bungalows and even a treehouse, all with hot showers. Dorms B275, doubles B800

## DIRECTORY

**Cinema** Moonlight Cinema, on the east side of town at the start of the Ban Chaloaklam road (B150; ☎093 638 5051, ⓦfacebook.com/moonlightphangan), shows films every evening (except Monday) in a lovely garden setting, accompanied by popcorn, seasonal smoothies and vegan, gluten-free food.

**Hospitals** The island's basic main hospital (☎077 377034) is located 3km north of town, on the inland road towards Mae Hat. This has recently been joined by several small private hospitals, including First Western on the Ban Tai

road on the east side of town, which lies about 1km from the post office (☎077 377474, ⓦfirstwesternhospital. healthcare). There's also an island-wide 24hr emergency rescue service, staffed entirely by volunteers (☎077 377500).

**Police** The main station is 2km up the Ban Chaloaklam road (☎077 377501 or ☎077 377114), and there's a tourist police office at the main pier in Thong Sala (☎1155).

**Post office** About 500m southeast of the piers on the old main street (Mon–Fri 8.30am–4.30pm, Sat 9am–noon).

# Pang (Phaeng) Waterfall

Than Sadet–Ko Pha Ngan National Park, 4km northeast of Thong Sala off the road to Chaloaklam • Free admission • Take a Chaloaklam-bound songthaew as far as Ban Madeuawaan, from where it's a 1km signposted walk east

From most places on the island, it's fairly easy to get to the grandiosely termed Than Sadet–Ko Pha Ngan National Park, which contains **Pang (Phaeng) Waterfall**, Pha Ngan's biggest drop. The park headquarters are northeast of Thong Sala off the main road to Chaloaklam. From here, the main fall – bouncing down in stages over the hard, grey stone – is a steep 250m walk up a forest path. The trail then continues for 300m to a stunning viewpoint overlooking the south and west of the island.

# Hat Rin

**HAT RIN** is firmly established as the major party venue in Southeast Asia, especially in the peak seasons of August, December and January, but it's most famous for its year-round **full moon parties** – something like *Apocalypse Now* without the war. Hat Rin's compact geography is ideally suited to an intense party town: it occupies the flat neck of Pha Ngan's southeast headland, which is so narrow that the resort comprises two back-to-back beaches, joined by transverse roads at the north and south ends.

The eastern beach, usually referred to as **Sunrise**, or Hat Rin Nok (Outer Hat Rin), is what originally drew visitors here, a classic curve of fine white sand between two rocky slopes; there's still some coral off the southern slope to explore, though the water is far from limpid these days. This beach is the centre of Hat Rin's action, with a solid line of bars, restaurants and bungalows tucked under the palm trees.

**Sunset** beach, or Hat Rin Nai (Inner Hat Rin), which for much of the year is littered with flotsam, looks ordinary by comparison but has plenty of quieter accommodation. Bandon International Hospital, a large private hospital on Ko Samui, runs a clinic here, on the southern transverse near the pier (☎077 375471). Unfortunately, development between the beaches does no justice to the setting: it's ugly, cramped and chaotic, with new low-rise concrete shophouses thrown up at any old angle. Businesses here are concentrated around **Chicken Corner** (where the southern transverse road meets the road along the back of Sunrise), named after the legendary, Israeli-style chicken schnitzel sandwiches at Mama's round-the-clock café; they include supermarkets, plenty of ATMs and bank currency-exchange booths, as well as outlets for more outré services such as bikini waxing and Playstation rental. Half-hearted attempts to tart up the large body of water in the middle of the headland with a few park benches and lights have been undermined by all-too-accurate signposts pointing to "Hat Rin Swamp".

## ARRIVAL AND DEPARTURE                                                        HAT RIN

**By songthaew or minibus** Songthaews and a/c minibuses run between Thong Sala and Hat Rin (B100 during the day, more at night); in Hat Rin, you can find them or their touts at the pier, Chicken Corner or near the police box.

**By boat** The easiest approach to Hat Rin, if you're coming from Ko Samui, or even Surat Thani, is on the boat from Bangrak on Samui's north coast (see page 254): four boats a day cross to the pier on Sunset beach in under an hour.

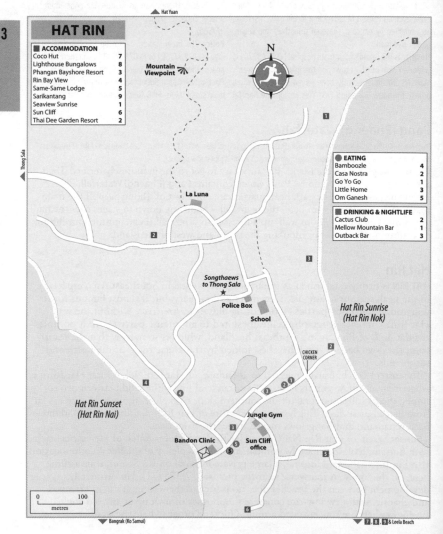

## GETTING AROUND

**By jeep or motorbike** Plenty of places on Hat Rin rent motorbikes (around B250 for 24hr) and a few have jeeps (about B1000/day). There have been lots of reports, however, of travellers being charged exorbitant amounts if they bring the vehicle back with even the most minor damage – at the very least, check the vehicle over very carefully before renting and ask if you can leave cash instead of your passport as a deposit. *Sun Cliff* (see below), which has an office just off the southern transverse, is a reliable place for motorbikes, and won't try this scam. The section of road between Hat Rin and Ban Khai is paved but winding and precipitous – take care if you're driving yourself.

## ACCOMMODATION

Staying on **Sunrise** is often expensive and noisy, though you should have more luck towards the north end of the beach. On **Sunset**, the twenty or more resorts are squeezed together in orderly rows, and are especially quiet and inexpensive between April and June and in October. Many visitors choose to stay on the **headland** to the south of the main beaches, especially at white-sand, palm-fringed **Leela Beach** on the west side of the promontory, which is a twenty-minute walk along a well-signposted route from Chicken Corner. At any of the places out here your bungalow is likely to have more peace and space and better views, leaving you a torchlit walk to the night-time action.

**Coco Hut** Leela Beach ☎077 375 368–9, ⓦcocohut. com; map p.256. On a clean, quiet stretch of beach, this lively, efficiently run place is smart and attractive, with some traditional southern Thai elements in the architecture. On offer is a wide variety of upscale accommodation, from wooden bungalows with a/c, hot showers, minibars, TVs and DVDs, to beachfront villas with plunge pools, as well as two pools and an adobe-style spa. Free pick-up from Hat Rin. Breakfast included. B4460

**Lighthouse Bungalows** On the far southwestern tip of the headland ☎098 014 4930, ⓦfacebook.com/lighthouse.bungalows; map p.256. At this friendly haven about 30min walk from Chicken Corner, wooden and concrete en-suite bungalows, sturdily built to withstand the wind on a boulder-strewn slope and backed by trail-filled jungle, are priced according to size and comfort; all have good-sized balconies with hammocks. The restaurant food is varied and tasty, and they host regular DJ parties. Currently reached by a wooden walkway over the rocky shoreline, though they may be forced by the authorities to replace this with a track over the hills. Fan B600, a/c B1800

**Phangan Bayshore Resort** In the middle of Sunrise ☎077 375 224, ⓦphanganbayshore.com; map p.256. Hat Rin's first upmarket resort, a well-ordered, slightly institutional place, boasting 80m of beachfront that's party central at full moon time. There's a large, shamrock-shaped pool and a wide variety of close-knit bungalows and rooms with a/c, hot water, TV, safety box and minibar, on a green lawn shaded with palms. Around the full moon, as well as a minimum stay of five nights, there's a big hike in prices. B2600

**Rin Bay View** Near the pier on Sunset ☎077 375188; map p.256. A good-value, friendly option in a tightly squeezed central location, occupying a narrow strip of land running down to a small, beachfront, infinity-edge pool, ornamented with flowers and trees. The a/c rooms with hot showers, TVs, fridges, safety boxes and balconies are a decent size and generally well maintained and clean. B1000

**Same-Same Lodge** Above the south end of Sunrise at the start of the road to Leela Beach ☎077 375 200, ⓦsame-same.com; map p.256. Sociable Danish-run spot set above a popular, often raucous, bar-restaurant that hosts lively full moon warm-up parties. The clean, colourful and decent-sized rooms come with fan and cold showers or a/c and hot water; there are also tightly packed a/c dorms. Free safety boxes. Dorms B500, fan doubles B550, a/c doubles B850

**Sarikantang** Leela Beach ☎077 375 055–6, ⓦsarikantang.com; map p.256. Boutique resort with two swimming pools (one with a kids' pool), a beachside spa and a good measure of style. Accommodation ranges from bungalows with a/c, TVs, minibars, verandas, hammocks and hot-water bathrooms to villas with DVD players, iPod docks, separate living rooms and outdoor Jacuzzis. Free kayaks, cooking classes and kids' activities; free pick-ups from Sunset pier and shuttles to downtown Hat Rin. Breakfast included. B2500

**Seaview Sunrise** Northern end of Sunrise ☎077 375160, ⓦseaviewsunrise.com; map p.256. On a big plot of shady, flower-strewn land at the quieter end of the beach, this clean, friendly, orderly old-timer with a good restaurant offers over forty bungalows and rooms. The bungalows on the beachfront are all fan-cooled with hot showers. Further back are a/c versions, as well as the cheapest rooms with cold showers. Kayaks for rent. Comparatively small price rise at full moon. Minimum stay 2 nights (5 at full moon). Fan B500, a/c B900

**Sun Cliff** High up on the tree-lined slope above the south end of Sunset ☎077 375134 or ☎077 375463, ⓔrsvnsuncliff@hotmail.com; map p.256. Friendly, spacious place with excellent views of the south coast and Ko Samui, especially from its heart-shaped swimming pool by the restaurant. Among a wide range of bungalows that are a bit rough around the edges, you'll find some quirky architectural features such as rock-built bathrooms and fountains; some even have huge decks for partying. A/c rooms all have hot showers, fridges and TVs. The

3

## FULL MOON PARTIES: A SURVIVOR'S GUIDE

Even if you're not the type to coat yourself in day-glo and dance till dawn, a **full moon party** at Hat Rin is certainly a sight to see, and the atmosphere created by thousands of folk mashing it up on a beautiful, moon-bathed beach, lit up by fireworks and fire-jugglers, is quite a buzz. If you're planning to get in on the action, first of all you'll need to check exactly when the party is: when the full moon coincides with an important **Buddhist festival**, the party is moved one night away to avoid a clash; check out Ⓦfullmoon.phangan.info for details. There's also a big party at Hat Rin on Christmas Day, and a massive one on New Year's Eve. Party-goers not staying on Hat Rin are charged an admission fee of B100. On the nights around the full moon, foam, pool and all sorts of other parties are organized.

On full moon night, *Paradise*, at the very southern end of Sunrise, styles itself as the main party **venue**, sometimes bringing in big-name international DJs. However, the mayhem spreads along most of Sunrise, fuelled by hastily erected drinks stalls and around a dozen major **sound systems**. Next morning, as the beach party winds down, *Back Yard* hosts the afterparty, with the best of the previous night's DJs; it's up the hill behind the south end of Sunrise off the path to Leela Beach.

**Drug**-related horror stories are common currency in Hat Rin, and some of them are even true: dodgy MDMA, *ya baa* (Burmese-manufactured methamphetamines), Ice (crystal meth), magic mushrooms and all manner of other concoctions put several farangs a month into hospital for psychiatric treatment. The local authorities have started clamping down on the trade in earnest, setting up a permanent police box at Hat Rin (with a temporary tourist police office nearby for the full moon), instigating regular roadblocks and bungalow and personal searches, paying dealers, bungalow and restaurant owners to inform on travellers to whom they've sold drugs, and drafting in scores of police (both uniformed and plain-clothes) on full moon nights. It doesn't seem to have dampened the fun, only made travellers a lot more circumspect. Not only that but the "bucket" sellers on Sunrise Beach replace brand-name spirits with dodgy, illegal, home-brewed alcohol, which often contain harmful substances that will give you more of a hangover than you bargained for.

Other **tips** for surviving the full moon are mostly common sense: leave your valuables in your resort's safe – it's a bad night for bungalow break-ins – and don't take a bag out with you; keep an eye on your drink to make sure it's not spiked; watch out for broken bottles and anchors on the beach; and do not go swimming while under the influence – there have been several deaths by drowning at previous full moon parties. There have also been several reports of sexual assaults on women – don't walk or take a taxi home alone – of muggings and of unprovoked, late-night gang attacks in Hat Rin, especially around full moon night.

### ACCOMMODATION AND TRANSPORT

Hat Rin now has around five thousand **rooms** – some of them hastily converted dorms that open at party time, charging B600–1000 per person – but on full moon nights up to thirty thousand revellers may turn up. Unless you're prepared to forget about sleep altogether, you should book well in advance (booking sites such as Ⓦbackpackersthailandtravel.com offer multi-day full moon, half moon and New Year's Eve packages) or arrive several days early to bag a room, as resort owners specify a minimum stay of three–five nights (in some places up to ten nights, especially over the Christmas and New Year's Eve parties). Alternatively, you can take the Had Rin Queen over from Bangrak on Ko Samui and back in the morning (see page 241), or hitch up with one of the many **party boats** (about B1000 return per person) organized through guesthouses and restaurants on Ko Samui, especially at Bangrak and Bophut, which leave in the evening and return in the early hours until around dawn, though they're sometimes dangerously overcrowded. There's also transport by boat or car from all the other beaches on Pha Ngan; at nearby Ban Tai, there are also dorms to take the overflow.

cheapest options are the rooms situated out on the road by the front office. Fan B400, a/c B600

**Thai Dee Garden Resort** Northern transverse ☎ 098 701 8898; map p.256. Pleasant staff and a range of smart concrete and white clapboard bungalows, on a broad, grassy slope strewn with trees and plants and set back from the road. Choose either fan and cold water or a/c and hot. A likely spot to have rooms free at full moon, although, as well as a minimum stay of five nights, there's a big hike in prices. Fan B400, a/c B650

## EATING

**Bamboozle** Off the southern transverse, near Sunset pier ☎085 471 4211; map p.256. Among a wide variety of tasty Mexican food here, the chicken fajitas with all the trimmings (B250) are especially good. Also offers pizzas and a short menu of tapas. Sprawl on an axe cushion in the tree-shaded courtyard, play a bit of pool or swing in a hammock. Daily roughly 4pm–after midnight.

**Casa Nostra** On the southern transverse ☎094 881 0421; map p.256. Tiny Italian café-restaurant which prepares great pastas – try the spaghetti bolognese (B220) or go for one of the day's specials – pizzas, espresso coffee, salads and plenty of vegetarian dishes, washed down with Italian wines and spirits. 3/4–11pm, closed most Sundays.

**Go Yo Go** On the southern transverse; map p.256. Chichi Italian-run gelateria, serving delicious frozen yoghurt, crêpes and waffles, plus a good selection of cocktails. An espresso and a slice of their *torta della nonna* (cashew and vanilla tart; B160) makes a great breakfast. Daily 10.30am–2am.

**Little Home** On the southern transverse; map p.256. This well-organized, basic restaurant is your best bet for cheap Thai food in Hat Rin, serving staples such as *phat thai* (B70), chicken and cashew nuts and green, red and yellow curries, plus Western breakfasts and home-made yoghurt. Daily 10.30am–10.30pm.

**Om Ganesh** On the southern transverse near the pier ☎086 063 2903; map p.256. Relaxing Indian restaurant with a good thalis (from B160), biryanis, plenty of veggie dishes and breads, Indian breakfasts and cheerful service. Free deliveries. Daily 10am–11.30pm.

## NIGHTLIFE

**Cactus Club** South end of Sunrise; map p.256. Centrally placed open-air dance hall that pumps out mostly radio-friendly dance music onto low-slung candlelit tables and mats on the beach. Evenings till late.

**Mellow Mountain Bar** North end of Sunrise; map p.256. Made for chilling, this trippy hangout occupies a great position up in the rocks, with floor cushions, hammocks and peerless views of the beach. Closed by the authorities for supposed "encroachment" issues at the time of writing, but likely to have reopened with a bang by the time you read this. Evenings till late.

**Outback Bar** On the southern transverse; map p.256. Lively meeting place with a "no trance" music policy, free pool tables, big-screen sports, a selection of bottled ciders and well-received English breakfasts, cottage pies and the like. Daily 11am–late.

# Hat Yuan, Hat Thian and Hat Sadet

North of Hat Rin, there are no roads along the rocky, exposed east coast, which stretches as far as **Ao Thong Nai Pan**, the only substantial centre of development. First up are the adjoining small, sandy bays of **HAT YUAN** and **HAT THIAN**, which have established a reputation as a quieter alternative to Hat Rin. A rough track has recently been bulldozed from Ban Khai, and the bays now sport about a dozen bungalow outfits between them.

Steep, remote **HAT SADET**, about 8km as the crow flies from Hat Rin, has a handful of bungalow operations, sited here because of their proximity to **Thaan Sadet**, a boulder-strewn brook that runs out into the sea. The spot was popularized by various kings of Thailand – Rama V visited no fewer than fourteen times – who came here to walk, swim and vandalize the huge boulders by carving their initials on them; the river water is now considered sacred and is transported to Bangkok for important royal ceremonies. A paved road carves through the woods above and parallel to Thaan Sadet to connect with the road from Thong Sala to Ao Thong Nai Pan.

If you're feeling intrepid, you could try hiking along this stretch of coast, which in theory is paralleled by a steep, 15km trail, though it's reported to be overgrown in many places. With decent navigational skills, the leg between Hat Rin, starting from near *La Luna Bungalows*, and Hat Yuan should certainly be manageable (about 2hr), aided by green dot and white arrow markers.

## ARRIVAL AND DEPARTURE     HAT YUAN, HAT THIAN, HAT SADET

**By boat** A daily, seasonal boat runs via the east coast beaches from Hat Rin to Thong Nai Pan, having started its voyage across at Maenam on Ko Samui (see page 237). Otherwise there are ample longtails at Hat Rin that will take you up the coast – around B150/person to Hat Yuan, for example.

## ACCOMMODATION

### HAT YUAN

**Barcelona ☎** 077 375113, **⊕** barcelonakpg.com. Good, relaxing budget choice, with great views and decent accommodation, mostly in colourful, stilted bungalows running up the steep hillside from the beach, equipped with fans, mosquito nets, balconies and hot showers. **B700**

**Pariya ☎** 081 737 3883, **⊕** pariyahaadyuan.com. The most luxurious resort in the vicinity of Hat Rin comprises forty spacious octagonal villas, some with their own private Jacuzzi pool, and half-a-dozen much smaller rooms, all with lots of polished concrete, rain showers, bathtubs and large verandas, set on a steep slope running down to the beach. There's a free-form pool and kids' pool and a spa. Breakfast included. **B3125**

### HAT THIAN

★ **The Sanctuary ☎** 081 271 3614, **⊕** thesanctuary thailand.com. This magical fairyland, connected by a labyrinth of paths, offers a huge range of basic and luxury en-suite bungalows, as well as dorm accommodation (B350), built into the lush promontory. It also hosts all-inclusive yoga and detox courses, and has a spa that does massage, facials and beauty treatments. The beautiful timber restaurant serves up good vegetarian meals, seafood and home-made bread and cakes. The cheaper accommodation is not bookable in advance, but you can phone up on the morning of your planned arrival and they'll hold a spot for you until later in the afternoon. **B950**

### HAT SADET

**Mai Pen Rai ☎** 093 959 8073, **⊕** thansadet.com. The main operation on Hat Sadet, with its own reggae bar, this welcoming spot has a huge variety of attractive bungalows with airy bathrooms, fans and hammocks (some with big upstairs terraces), either on the beach at the stream mouth or scattered around the rocks for good views. A jeep taxi leaves Thong Sala for the resort every day at 1pm (B200/ person). **B580**

# Ao Thong Nai Pan

**AO THONG NAI PAN** is a beautiful, semicircular bay backed by steep, green hills, which looks as if it's been bitten out of the island's northeast corner by a gap-toothed giant, leaving a tall hump of land (occupied by *Panviman Resort*) dividing the bay into two parts: **Thong Nai Pan Noi** to the north, **Thong Nai Pan Yai** to the south. With lovely, fine, white sand, the longer, more indented Thong Nai Pan Yai has marginally the better beach, but both halves of the bay are sheltered and deep enough for swimming. A paved road winds its way for 13km over the steep mountains from Ban Tai on the south coast to Thong Nai Pan, but once you get here you'll find most of the basic amenities you'll need: travel agents, dive outfits, ATMs, supermarkets and clinics.

## ARRIVAL AND DEPARTURE          AO THONG NAI PAN

**By jeep** Jeeps connect with incoming and outgoing boats at Thong Sala every day (B300/person).

**By boat** One seasonal boat a day runs via the east coast beaches from Hat Rin to Thong Nai Pan, having started its voyage across at Maenam on Ko Samui (see page 237).

## ACCOMMODATION AND EATING

★ **Anantara Rasananda** Thong Nai Pan Noi ☎ 077 956 660, **⊕** anantara.com. Congenial and chic luxury hideaway, with speedboat transfers from Samui. Accommodation is in sixty spacious, contemporary villas and suites, all with their own plunge pool, most with indoor-outdoor bathrooms. There's also a main, infinity-edge swimming pool, which forms the central hub of the resort, along with a sociable bar, a beach bistro and a Japanese teppanyaki restaurant. The very good spa stretches up the hillside behind, with a steam room built into the rocks. Other activities include kayaking, cooking and yoga classes. **B12,810**

**Baan Panburi Village** Southern end of Thong Nai Pan Yai ☎ 077 445075. Two rows of well-designed bungalows with verandas and deckchairs run down a slope dotted with wicker hammocks, either side of a small, artificial waterfall. Choose between old-style, thatched, wood-and-bamboo huts with mosquito nets, fans and cold showers, and large, wooden, a/c affairs with hot water and tiled floors. Fan **B600**, a/c **B1400**

**Longtail Beach Resort** At the far southern end of Thong Nai Pan Yai ☎ 077 445018, **⊕** longtailbeachresort.com. In four quiet, leafy rows on either side of two long strips of lawn that run down to the attractive beachfront restaurant, spa and small swimming pool, these diverse, mostly wooden, partly thatched bungalows are well designed and maintained; all have verandas, hammocks and hot showers, and for most of them, you can choose whether to pay extra for a/c or not. Fan **B850**, a/c **B1000**

**Sand in My Shoes** Northern end of Thong Nai Pan Noi ☎087 429 4949, ⓦfacebook.com/sandinmyshoeskohphangan. One of the destinations of the moment, this chic bar-restaurant-pizzeria on the beach has added a handful of stylish and luxurious guest rooms, kitted out with platform beds, balconies and geometric objets d'art – with more bedrooms planned. Good breakfast included. B5040

★ **Siam House** About 100m from the beach towards the main road, behind Dreamland Resort, Thong Nai Pan Yai ⓦfacebook.com/dolphinbrandcafe. Run by the former proprietors of *Dolphin Resort*, this mellow café-bar is situated in a lovely, open-sided, two-storey house with a garden and lotus pond (and now boasts a beach bar annexe nearby). It serves great coffee and breakfasts, as well as light salads and other Western lunches (mains cost from around B100). Easygoing barbecues are held on Tues and Fri evenings. Daily 8.30am–2pm, plus Tues & Fri 6.30–11pm.

# The north coast

The largest indent on the **north coast**, Ao Chaloaklam, has long been a famous R&R spot for fishermen from all over the Gulf of Thailand, with sometimes as many as a hundred trawlers littering the broad and sheltered bay. As a tourist destination, it has little to recommend it – save that its village, **Ban Chaloaklam**, can easily be reached from Thong Sala, 10km away, by songthaew (B150) along a paved road – but the small, quiet beaches to the east, Hat Khom and Hat Khuat, have much more to offer.

## Hat Khom

Dramatically tucked in under Ao Chaloaklam's eastern headland is the tiny cove of **HAT KHOM**. Linked to the outside world by a partly paved road, it offers an attractive strip of white sand backed by shady trees, good coral close to the beach for snorkelling and plenty of seclusion.

## Hat Khuat (Bottle Beach)

If the sea is not too rough, longtail boats run several times a day for most of the year from Ban Chaloaklam (east of the fishing pier; B100/person or about B600/boat) to isolated **HAT KHUAT (BOTTLE BEACH)**, the best of the beaches on the north coast, sitting between steep, jungle-clad hills in a perfect cup of a bay that's good for swimming. You could also walk there along a testing trail from Hat Khom in around ninety minutes.

**ACCOMMODATION AND EATING**                    **THE NORTH COAST**

**Caffè della Moca (Cucina Italiana)** Ban Chaloaklam ☎086 470 4253. Run by a friendly, enthusiastic native of Rimini, this simple, authentic Italian restaurant towards the west end of the village offers tables on the sand and great pizzas (around B200), home-made gnocchi, lasagne and tiramisu. 5pm–late; closed Wed.

**Haad Khuad Resort** Hat Khuat ☎077 445153–4, ⓦhaadkhuadresort.com. Well-organized spot in the middle of the bay, offering deluxe rooms in a two-storey hotel block with view-filled French windows, a/c, hot water, TV, minibars and breakfast included. Also has a choice of wooden or concrete fan bungalows and rooms with cold showers on the beachfront and in the garden. Kayaks available. Daily transfers from Thong Sala (B400/person). Fan B500, a/c B1500

**Smile Resort** Western end of Hat Khuat ☎085 429 4995. Set on a rocky slope strewn with flowers and trees on the western side of the beach, with fun owners and a sociable bar-restaurant area. The attractive, bamboo-clad, en-suite bungalows come with wall fans and mosquito nets. B520

# The west coast

Pha Ngan's **west coast** has attracted about the same amount of development as the forgettable south coast, but the landscape here is more attractive and varied, broken up into a series of long sandy inlets with good sunset views over the islands of the Ang Thong National Marine Park to the west. Most of the bays, however, are sheltered by reefs which can keep the sea too shallow for a decent swim, especially between May and October.

## Ao Chaophao and Hat Yao

Just north of the small, pretty bay of **AO CHAOPHAO** lies the west coast's main beach, **HAT YAO**, a long, gently curved strip of fine sand. It's gradually and justifiably becoming busier and more popular, with several stand-alone bars, diving outfits, a 7-Eleven supermarket, a pharmacy, ATMs and jeep and bike rental, as well as a nonstop line of bungalows.

## Hat Salad

To the north of Hat Yao, **HAT SALAD** is another pretty bay, sheltered and sandy, with good snorkelling off the northern tip. On the access road behind the beach is a rather untidy service village of shops, travel agents, and bike and jeep rental outlets. Take your pick from a dozen or so bungalow outfits.

## Ao Mae Hat

On the island's northwest corner, **AO MAE HAT** is good for swimming and snorkelling among the coral that lines the sandy causeway to the tiny islet of Ko Maa. The broad, coarse-sand bay supports several bungalow resorts.

### ARRIVAL AND GETTING AROUND | THE WEST COAST

**By motorbike or jeep** There's a paved coastal road up as far as Hat Salad, where it loops inland to meet the main inland road from Thong Sala via the hospital to Ao Mae Hat.

**By songthaew** Songthaews from Thong Sala serve all of the beaches on the west coast, charging B200–300/person to go as far as Ao Mae Hat, for example.

### ACCOMMODATION

#### AO SEETHANU

**Loy Fa** ☎ 077 377 319, ⓦ loyfanaturalresort.com. Well-run, friendly, flower-strewn place that commands good views from its perch on the steep southern cape of otherwise nondescript Ao Seethanu. There's good snorkelling and swimming from its private beach below, as well as two saltwater pools. Smart bungalows are scattered around the hilltop and the slope down on the beach, and come with large verandas, a/c, hot water, minibar, TV and DVD player. Breakfast and transfers from Thong Sala included. B2450

#### AO CHAOPHAO

★ **Seaflower** ☎ 077 349 090, ⓦ seaflowerbungalows. com. Quiet, congenial spot, set in a lush, shady garden, with good veggie and non-veggie food and nice touches like an annual sandcastle-building competition. Bright, en-suite, a/c bungalows with their own hot-water bathrooms vary in price according to their size, age and distance from the beach. Even cheaper rooms have marble-tiled floors and bathrooms and big balcony seating areas. Free pick-ups from Thong Sala with 24hr notice. Minimum stay two nights. B1200

#### HAT YAO

**Long Bay Resort** ☎ 077 349 057–9, ⓦ longbay-resort. com. Hat Yao's nicest upmarket spot boasts a long stretch of beach and spacious gardens towards the north end of the bay. Choose between small but smart bungalows ("Garden Huts") and a range of large cottages, all with verandas, a/c

and hot water. There's an attractive, free-form swimming pool with kids' pool and kayaks and snorkels to rent. Transfer from Thong Sala and breakfast included. B1800

**Shiralea** ☎ 077 349 217, ⓦ shiralea.com. On a broad, grassy bank beneath coconut trees set back from the north end of the beach, the spacious, very attractive thatched bungalows here all come with hot water and verandas with hammocks, and there's a seductive pool with a pool bar, smart a/c dormitories, a games room and a sociable atmosphere. Dorms B270, fan doubles B640, a/c B1180

#### HAT SALAD

★ **Salad Hut** ☎ 077 349246, ⓦ saladhut.com. Among the dozen or so bungalow outfits here, this congenial, family-friendly and well-run old-timer stands out. Behind a small, infinity-edge swimming pool, in a shady, colourful garden, are stylish bungalows done out in dark woods, red and white, with day beds with axe cushions and hammocks on their large verandas, as well as larger villas and family rooms. All come with hot water, minibar and TV, and a cooked breakfast at the chic bar-restaurant is included. Library, pool table and snorkel and kayak rental. Fan B2200, a/c B2500

#### AO MAE HAT

**Wang Sai Resort** Ao Mae Hat ☎ 077 374238, ⓦ wangsairesort.com. Popular, friendly spot by a shady creek at the south end of the bay. On a huge plot of land, most of the en-suite bungalows are set back from the beach, including the cheapest options, with fans and cold showers, which are set on a slope with great sunset views. The best and most expensive are across the creek on the

beach, all with a/c, fridge and hot water, some with TV. On-site dive school and kayaks and snorkels for rent. Fan B1200, a/c B1600

# Ko Tao

KO TAO (Turtle Island) is so named because its outline resembles a turtle nose-diving towards Ko Pha Ngan, 40km to the south. The rugged shell of the turtle, to the east, is crenellated with secluded coves, where one or two bungalows hide among the rocks and there's good snorkelling. On the western side, the turtle's underbelly is a long curve of classic beach, **Hat Sai Ree**, facing **Ko Nang Yuan**, a beautiful Y-shaped group of islands offshore, also known as Ko Hang Tao (Turtle's Tail Island). The 21 square kilometres of granite in between are topped by dense forest on the higher slopes and dotted with huge boulders that look as if they await some Easter Island sculptor. It's fun to spend a couple of days exploring the network of rough trails, after which you'll probably know all 2200 of the island's inhabitants. Ko Tao is now best known as a venue for **scuba-diving courses**, with a wide variety of dive sites in close proximity.

The island is the last and most remote of the archipelago that continues the line of Surat Thani's mountains into the sea. It served as a jail for political prisoners from 1933 to 1947, then was settled by a family from Ko Pha Ngan. Now, there are around 150 sets of **bungalows** for visitors, just about enough to cope during the peak seasons of December to March, July and August, concentrated along the west and south sides; they include a rapidly growing number of upscale resorts with such luxuries as air conditioning, hot water and swimming pools. There's a limited government supply of electricity, so some of it still comes from private generators on the remotest beaches, usually evenings only.

If you're just arriving and want to stay on one of the less accessible beaches, it might be a good idea to go with one of the touts who meet the ferries at **Mae Hat**, the island's main village, with pick-up or boat on hand, since at least you'll know their bungalows aren't full; otherwise call ahead, as even the remotest bungalows now have landlines or mobile phones and most owners come to market once a day (pick-ups are either free or B50–150/person). Some resorts with attached scuba-diving operations have been known to refuse guests who don't sign up for diving trips or courses; on the other hand, most of the dive companies now have their own lodgings, available free or at a discounted price to divers. With a year-round customer base of divers – and resident dive instructors – a growing number of sophisticated Western **restaurants** and **bars** are springing up all the time, notably in Mae Hat and on Hat Sai Ree. For nightlife, your best bet is to watch out for posters advertising weekly and monthly parties around the island, which keep the crowds rotating; women should be careful getting back to their

---

### ECO TAO

With so many divers and other visitors coming to this tiny island, the pressures on the environment, both above and below the waterline, are immense. Coral nurseries have been started around Ko Tao, as well as more than half a dozen artificial reefs, which allow divers to practise their skills without damaging coral. You might want to ask your dive operator if they get involved in regular beach and dive-site clean-ups and coral monitoring programmes, but much of what visitors can do to help is common sense: avoiding littering, recycling where possible and turning down plastic bags when you're shopping. The island suffers from a scarcity of water, with occasional droughts during the hot season after a poor rainy season, so conserve water whenever possible. In the sea, the main rule is not to touch the coral, which may mean avoiding snorkelling when the water is low from April to September – if in doubt, ask locally for advice, be careful and go out at high tide. Don't take away dead shells, and don't buy coral or shell jewellery.

bungalow late at night and should avoid walking home alone. The biggest event to hit the island in many years was the eco-friendly Tao Festival, held over a long weekend in March 2017 ⊛ taofestival.live) that featured DJs such as Gilles Peterson, Kevin Yost and Santiago Salazar, rappers Arrested Development and visual artists like Alex Face; the second instalment is scheduled for August 2018.

The **weather** is much the same as on Pha Ngan and Samui (see page 56), but being that bit further off the mainland, Ko Tao feels the effect of the southwest monsoon more: June to October can have strong winds and rain, with a lot of debris blown onto the windward coasts.

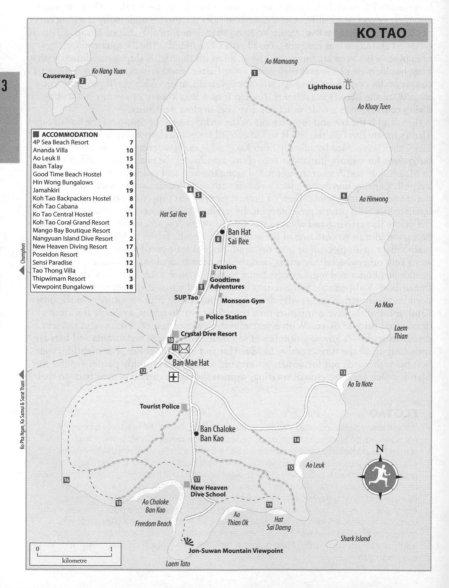

## KO TAO

**3**

Chumphon

Ko Pha Ngan, Ko Samui & Surat Thani

Causeways **2**

Ko Nang Yuan

Ao Mamuang

**1**

Lighthouse

Ao Kluay Tuen

**3**

**4** **5**

Hat Sai Ree **7**

● Ban Hat
Sai Ree
**8**

Evasion

Goodtime
Adventures **9**

SUP Tao

Monsoon Gym

■ Police Station

Crystal Dive Resort
**10**
**11** ✉
■ Ban Mae Hat
**12**
✚

**6** Ao Hinwong

Ao Mao

Laem
Thian

**13** Ao Ta Note

Tourist Police ■

● Ban Chaloke
Ban Kao

**14**

**15** Ao Leuk

**16**

**18**

**17**
New Heaven
Dive School

Ao Chaloke
Ban Kao

Freedom Beach

Ao
Thian Ok

**19**

Hat
Sai Daeng

Shark Island

Jon-Suwan Mountain Viewpoint

Laem Tato

N

| ■ ACCOMMODATION | |
|---|---|
| 4P Sea Beach Resort | 7 |
| Ananda Villa | 10 |
| Ao Leuk II | 15 |
| Baan Talay | 14 |
| Good Time Beach Hostel | 9 |
| Hin Wong Bungalows | 6 |
| Jamahkiri | 19 |
| Koh Tao Backpackers Hostel | 8 |
| Koh Tao Cabana | 4 |
| Ko Tao Central Hostel | 11 |
| Koh Tao Coral Grand Resort | 5 |
| Mango Bay Boutique Resort | 1 |
| Nangyuan Island Dive Resort | 2 |
| New Heaven Diving Resort | 17 |
| Poseidon Resort | 13 |
| Sensi Paradise | 12 |
| Tao Thong Villa | 16 |
| Thipwimarn Resort | 3 |
| Viewpoint Bungalows | 18 |

0 ──────── 1
kilometre

## BOAT TOURS AND SNORKELLING ON KO TAO

Some dive companies will take along **snorkellers**, usually on their afternoon trips, when they visit the shallower sites, but your best bet for snorkelling is probably a round-island **boat tour**. Available through your bungalow or at Island Travel (see page 268) in Mae Hat for example (from B600/person for a day-trip, including lunch, equipment and pick-ups and drop-offs, or around B2000 to hire your own longtail boat for the day), these take in snorkelling at Ao Thian Ok (aka Shark Bay), Ao Leuk, Ao Hinwong, Ao Mamuang and the beautiful Japanese Gardens off Ko Nang Yuan, but you'll have to pay the B100 entrance fee if you set foot on the island to climb up to the viewpoint.

## ARRIVAL AND DEPARTURE                                                        KO TAO

All boats to Ko Tao dock at Mae Hat. Boat services and prices may fluctuate according to demand, and in high season extra boats may appear. Voyages to and from Ko Tao may occasionally be affected by the weather at any time between June and January.

### FROM CHUMPHON AND BANGKOK

The main jumping-off point for boats to Ko Tao is Chumphon (see page 226), which is connected to Bangkok by train and bus. The two main Chumphon–Ko Tao boat companies both offer through-tickets from Bangkok; with Lomprayah (on Ko Tao ☏ 077 456176, ⓦ lomprayah.com), for example, this costs B1100, including a VIP bus from its office on Thanon Ram Bhuttri (☏ 02 629 2569–70), via Hua Hin. It's better to buy a Bangkok–Tao through-ticket direct from the boat company's website or office in the capital rather than from a travel agency, otherwise you're unlikely to get your money back if the boat turns out to be full, which is possible in high season, or is cancelled because of very bad weather. Both Nok Air and Air Asia offer flight-bus-boat combination tickets to Ko Tao from Bangkok's Don Muang Airport.

### FROM KO PHA NGAN AND KO SAMUI

Two main companies operate daily scheduled boats between Thong Sala on Ko Pha Ngan and Ko Tao: Lomprayah (3 daily; around 1hr 15min; B500–600) and Seatran (on Ko Tao ☏ 077 953057, ⓦ seatrandiscovery.com; 3 daily; around 1hr 30min; B450). Lomprayah offer services either from Maenam (2 daily) or Na Thon (1 daily) on Ko Samui, while all the Seatran boats originate at Bangrak (total journey time to Ko Tao on all services about 1hr 45min–2hr 30min; B600–700).

### FROM SURAT THANI

**With Lomprayah** If you're coming from Surat Thani, you could for example take Lomprayah's catamaran service from Tapi Pier, about 5km northeast of Surat town centre (2 daily; total journey time from Surat about 4–5hr; B800–900).
**With the night boat** There are night boats from Ban Don pier in Surat Thani town, departing at 10pm (in theory, 1–2 daily, though they don't always run; 8hr; B500); in the opposite direction, this leaves Ko Tao at 9pm; book at the piers.

## GETTING AROUND

You can **get around** easily enough on foot, but there are roads of sorts now to most of the resorts, though some are still very rough, steep tracks, suitable for 4WD only.
**By pick-up taxi** Pick-ups (starting from B100/person to Chaloke Ban Kao, for example, depending on how many people are going; rates are higher at night, or for a 4WD to somewhere more remote) are available in Mae Hat.
**By motorbike** As on Ko Phangan, there have been lots of reports of travellers being charged exorbitant amounts if they bring their rented motorbike back with even the most minor damage – avoid the outfits immediately in front of

the main pier in Mae Hat, and rent from your bungalow or someone reliable like Island Travel (Koh Tao Scooters, ⓦ kohtaoscooters.com), who offer environmentally friendly bikes from B200/day (insurance and drop-offs/pick-ups around the island available; leave your passport or a deposit). If you can, resist the temptation to rent a quad bike, or ATV – not only do they have a disproportionate number of accidents, but they're also very polluting.
**By mountain bike** Mountain bikes can be rented for B150/day from Evasion on Hat Sai Ree (see page 269).

## INFORMATION

There isn't a TAT office on Ko Tao, but the regularly updated and widely available free booklet, *Koh Tao Info*, is a useful source of information, along with its associated website, ⓦ kohtao-online.com. This is now in competition with ⓦ kohtaocompleteguide.com, though its hard-copy format is more difficult to find.

**3**

## DIVING OFF KO TAO

Some of the best **dive sites** in Thailand are found off Ko Tao, which is blessed with outstandingly clear (visibility is up to 35m), safe and relatively deep water, studded with underwater pinnacles close in to shore, as well as sheltered bays for beginners to practice. On top of that, there's a kaleidoscopic array of coral species and other marine life – you may be lucky enough to encounter whale sharks, barracudas, leatherback turtles and pilot whales – and a couple of popular wreck-diving sites. Diving is possible at any time of year, with sheltered sites on one or other side of the island in any **season** – the changeover from southwest to northeast monsoon in November is the worst time, while **visibility** is best from April to July, in September (usually best of all) and October. Dive courses on Ko Tao are particularly heavily subscribed in the days after the full moon party on Ko Pha Ngan, when it would be worth booking in advance. Ko Tao supports several evacuation centres, clinics that specialize in diving medicine, while the nearest recompression chamber is on Ko Samui, ninety minutes away by speedboat (see page 233).

### DIVE COMPANIES, COURSES AND TRIPS

Ko Tao has about fifty **dive companies**, making this the largest dive-training centre in the world. Most of the companies are staffed by Westerners and based at Mae Hat, Hat Sai Ree or Ao Chaloke Ban Kao. You'll generally be offered discounted or free accommodation while you're diving but ask exactly how long it's for (three or four nights for an Openwater course), where it is and what it's like. **Operators** on Ko Tao include Crystal (☎077 456106, ⓦcrystaldive.com), a large, lively, sociable PADI Five-Star Career Development Centre based on the north side of Mae Hat just beyond Ananda Villa, with two swimming pools, three big boats and a speedboat, offering courses in small groups in dozens of languages, plus a wide choice of good accommodation in three resorts on the north side of Mae Hat. At the other end of the scale are schools that are small, personal and laid-back (though with no compromising on safety) such as New Heaven in the centre of Ao Chaloke Ban Kao (☎077 457045, ⓦnewheavendiveschool.com), which takes a maximum of four people per course or dive trip. Both of these companies have a strong commitment to marine conservation (also check out the website of Crystal's marine conservation partner, ⓦecokohtao.com, which features internships and gap-year programmes) and run reef conservation and research programmes for qualified divers among many other activities. You'll find further advice on choosing a dive company in Basics (see page 51).

By far the most popular **course**, PADI's four-day "Openwater" for beginners, costs around B9800 in high season with a reputable dive centre. One-day introductions to diving are also available for B2000, as is the full menu of PADI courses, up to "Instructor". For **qualified divers**, one dive typically costs B1000, a ten-dive package B7000, with ten- to fifteen-percent discounts if you bring your own gear. Crystal (see above) offers wreck diving, nitrox and underwater photography courses.

## Mae Hat and around

**MAE HAT**, a small, lively village and port in a pleasant, beachfront setting, boasts the lion's share of the island's amenities. A paved high street heads straight up the hill from the main pier, paralleled by another paved road just to the north heading up the hill from the Seatran pier and another to the south heading inland from the Songserm pier, with a narrower front street running at right angles, parallel to the seafront. Three of the ferry companies each have their own pier, Lomprayah and Songserm to the south of the main one, Seatran to the north.

### ACCOMMODATION                                    MAE HAT AND AROUND

**Ananda Villa** North end of the village, on the beach ☎077 456478, ⓦanandavilla.com; map p.264. Cute, well-designed and maintained a/c rooms set in a two-storey block, sporting French windows that give onto balconies with wooden balustrades. Inside, silks and other decorative touches set off the dark wood furniture; facilities include large, hot-water bathrooms, DVD players and fridges. Also has a handful of a/c wooden bungalows

dotted throughout the garden (B1200) and fan rooms in a beachside single-storey block that are tiny but boast hot showers. Fan B600, a/c B1800

**Ko Tao Central Hostel** On the Seatran road in Ban Mae Hat ☎077 456925, ⓦkohtaohostel.com; map p.264. English-run hostel – look out for the London Underground logo – encompassing the Island Travel agency (located where reception is) and *The Reef Sports*

## MAIN DIVE SITES

**Ko Nang Yuan** Surrounded by a variety of sites, with assorted hard and soft corals and an abundance of fish: the Nang Yuan Pinnacle (aka Red Rock), a granite pinnacle with boulder swim-throughs, morays and reef sharks; Green Rock, a maze of boulder swim-throughs, caves and canyons, featuring stingrays and occasional reef sharks; Twins, two rock formations covered in corals and sponges, with a colourful coral garden as a backdrop; and the Japanese Gardens, on the east side of the sand causeway, which get their name from the hundreds of hard and soft coral formations here and are good for beginners and popular among snorkellers.

**White Rock (Hin Khao)** Between Hat Sai Ree and Ko Nang Yuan, where sarcophyton leather coral turns the granite boulders white when seen from the surface; also wire, antipatharian and colourful soft corals, and gorgonian sea fans. Plenty of fish, including titan triggerfish, butterfly fish, angelfish, clown fish and morays.

**Shark Island** Large granite boulders with acropora, wire and bushy antipatharian corals, sea whips, gorgonian sea fans and barrel sponges. Reef fish include angelfish, triggerfish and barracuda; leopard and reef sharks may be found as well as occasional whale sharks.

**Hinwong Pinnacle** At Ao Hinwong; generally for experienced divers, often with strong currents. Similar scenery to White Rock, over a larger area, with beautiful soft coral at 30m depth. A wide range of fish, including blue-spotted fantail stingrays, sweetlips pufferfish and boxfish, as well as hawksbill turtles.

**Chumphon** or **Northwest Pinnacle** A granite pinnacle for experienced divers, starting 14m underwater and dropping off to over 36m, its top covered in anemones; surrounded by several smaller formations and offering the possibility of exceptional visibility. Barrel sponges, tree and antipatharian corals at deeper levels; a wide variety of fish, in large numbers, attract local fishermen; barracudas, batfish, whale sharks (seasonal) and huge groupers.

**Southwest Pinnacle** One of the top sites in terms of visibility, scenery and marine life for experienced divers. A huge pyramid-like pinnacle rising to 6m below the surface, its upper part covered in anemones, with smaller pinnacles around; at lower levels, granite boulders, barrel sponges, sea whips, bushy antipatharian and tree corals. Big groupers, snappers and barracudas; occasionally, large rays, leopard and sand sharks, swordfish, finback whales and whale sharks.

**Sail Rock (Hin Bai)** Midway between Ko Tao and Ko Pha Ngan, emerging from the sand at a depth of 40m and rising 15m above the sea's surface. Visibility of up to 30m, and an amazing 10m underwater chimney (vertical swim-through). Antipatharian corals, both bushes and whips, and carpets of anemones. Large groupers, snappers and fusiliers, blue-ringed angelfish, batfish, kingfish, juvenile clown sweetlips and barracuda; the most likely spot in the area for sighting whale sharks year round.

*Bar and Restaurant.* Expect smart, partitioned dorm beds with a/c and hot showers. There are also discounts available for guests at many outlets around the island. Dorms **B340**

**Sensi Paradise** On the lower slopes of the headland just south of the village ☎077 456244, ⓦsensi paradiseresort.com; map p.264. Charming resort in flower-covered grounds, offering a pretty beachside restaurant, an attractive free-form pool and some of the best upmarket accommodation on the island: well-designed Thai-style cottages, family houses and villas made of polished red wood with minibars and a/c, most with hot showers and some with large terraces and open-air bathrooms. Transfer from the pier and breakfast included. **B3300**

**Tao Thong Villa** Cape Jeda Gang ☎077 456078; map p.264. A clutch of sturdy, en-suite bungalows dotted around the rocky outcrop of Cape Jeda Gang and the slope behind, with a breezy restaurant set above the tiny, grassy isthmus with two small beaches in between. Expect plenty of shady seclusion, great views and good snorkelling and swimming spots. About 1hr walk south of Mae Hat, or get there by pick-up or boat taxi. Fan **B500**, a/c **B1600**

## EATING AND DRINKING

**Cappuccino** 100m from the pier, up the high street on the left ☎077 456 870. French-run café and bakery that does a mean *pain au chocolat*, plus gourmet sandwiches on home-made bread, burgers and panini. Daily 7am–6pm.

**The Factory** About 1km up the Ao Leuk road ☎098 718 6712, ⓦfacebook.com/thefactorykohtao. Trek out to this cool, industrial-looking café during the day for their great all-day vegetarian and vegan brunches such as

**3**

eggs benedict (B160), healthy drinks and espresso coffees. Come back after dark for one of their club nights, including a "Sunday Service" of underground tech house, featuring international DJs. Tues–Sun 8am–5pm.

★ **Kakureya** Up a small hill on the southeast side of the village, off the south side of the road that heads inland from the Songserm pier ☎087 936 2160, ⓦfacebook. com/kakureyatao. Small, authentic Japanese restaurant with nice sunset views, serving some of the best food on the island: appetizer tasting sets, salmon and tuna sashimi and lots of other fish dishes, home-smoked ham and noodles. Asahi beer on draught and a good choice of sake. Usually closed part of June and Nov – check Facebook. Daily 4–10pm.

**Moov** On the southeast side of the village, on the south side of the road that heads inland from the Songserm pier ☎063 083 5537, ⓦfacebook.com/moovinn. Chilled-out, artsy bar with a lovely big garden, providing alternative nightlife events, which can mean anything from Latin parties and drum and bass DJs to movie nights. Also has a hostel if you really want to get lost in Tao's alternative scene. Daily 8.30am–late.

★ **Whitening** 200m south of the main pier down the front street ☎077 456199. Congenial, mellow and chic bar-restaurant with a great outdoor deck and relaxing beach tables and beanbags overlooking the bay, all in crisp white tones. It dishes up some very tasty Thai food, such as green curries (B140), and more creative, pricier Western food, as well as lunchtime sandwiches, evening seafood barbecues and a selection of good cocktails. Daily 11am–midnight.

## DIRECTORY

**Banks** Thanachart (Siam City Bank), up the high street on the left, with an ATM.

**Health** Mae Hat shelters a small government hospital (halfway up the high street, turn right; ☎077 456490), plus several private clinics and pharmacies. Ko Tao now has a 24hr volunteer emergency response team, equipped with pick-ups and speedboats (☎087 979 0191, ☎077 456031 or ☎1669).

**Police** The tourist police (☎1155 or ☎077 430 018) are based a short way out on the Ao Chaloke Ban Kao road, about 1km from the main pier, while the main police station is a 5min walk north of Mat Hat, on the narrow road towards Hat Sai Ree (☎077 456 631 or ☎077 456 098).

**Post office** At the top of the Seatran road (parallel to and north of the high street), near the start of the main paved road to Ban Hat Sai Ree (Mon–Fri 9am–noon & 1–5pm, Sat 9am–noon).

**Travel agent** Reliable, English-run Island Travel on the Seatran road (parallel to and north of the high street; ☎077 456769, ⓦislandtravelkohtao.com) offers all kinds of transport tickets, tours and activities on the island and visa services, as well as renting out good motorbikes and having a useful website.

# Hat Sai Ree

To the north of Mae Hat, beyond a small promontory, you'll find **Hat Sai Ree**, Ko Tao's only long beach. The strip of white sand stretches for 2km in a gentle curve, backed by a smattering of coconut palms and scores of bungalow resorts. Around the northerly end of the beach spreads **BAN HAT SAI REE**, a burgeoning village of supermarkets, clinics, pharmacies, travel agents, currency-exchange booths, ATMs, restaurants and bars. A narrow, mostly paved track runs along the back of the beach between Mae Hat and Ban Hat Sai Ree, paralleled by the main road further inland.

## ACCOMMODATION

HAT SAI REE

★ **4P Sea Beach Resort** North end of Ban Hat Sai Ree ☎077 456116; map p.264. This popular old-timer (formerly Blue Wind) offers a variety of well-kept, en-suite rooms and bungalows scattered about a shady compound, most of which have been recently reconstructed in an appealing southern Thai style, with clapboard walls and nice balcony furniture, some with four-poster beds and mosquito nets. Fan B700, a/c B1800

**Good Time Beach Hostel** South end of Hat Sai Ree ☎061 461 0933, ⓦgoodtimethailand.com; map p.264. Sociable hostel run by the island's adventure specialists, who offer weekly booze cruises too. Smart, well-equipped private rooms and six- to ten-person dorms, some with balconies on the beach, have a/c and hot showers. Dorms B500, doubles B1600

**Koh Tao Backpackers Hostel** Ban Hat Sai Ree, inland from Silver Sands Resort ☎088 447 7921, ⓦkohtaobackpackers.com; map p.264. Functional, four- and eight-bed dorms with a/c and hot showers in a small, concrete building set back from the beach. Free use of the adjacent pool of affiliated dive company Davy Jones' Locker, which has its own bar-restaurant. Dorm B300

**Koh Tao Cabana** Far north end of beach ☎089 698 2266, ⓦkohtaocabana.com; map p.264. Welcoming, eco-friendly, rustic-chic luxury resort and spa, with a long beach frontage backed by elegant day beds and a waterfall-

## HAT SAI REE ACTIVITIES

Goodtime Adventures, towards the southern end of the beach (☎087 275 3604, ⓦgtadventures.com), offer **rock-climbing** and **abseiling**, as well as beginner and advanced flying trapeze lessons. Just north of here, Evasion (☎062 665 2860, ⓦevasionkohtao.com) do bouldering, guided hiking trips, wakeboarding and kitesurfing lessons and rental. SUP Tao (☎093 348 7661) at Maya Beach Club further towards the southern end of the beach offer stand-up paddleboarding, while drop-in **yoga** classes are held at 4P Sea Beach Resort towards the north end of the beach (1–2 daily; ☎084 440 6755, ⓦshambhalayogakohtao. com). Monsoon Gym, on the main road behind the south end of Hat Sai Ree (☎086 271 2212, ⓦmonsoongym.com), is a well-equipped gym and muay thai fight camp (with dorm beds available for committed pugilists).

fed swimming pool. Most of the a/c accommodation is in thatched rooms with open-air bathrooms, including round, adobe-style villas up the slope behind the beach and stilted cottages on the headland, some with fantastic views and some with private pools. Breakfast included. B5000

**Koh Tao Coral Grand Resort** North of Ban Hat Sai Ree ☎077 456431, ⓦkohtaocoral.com; map p.264. Welcoming luxury beachfront development with a dive school, where the sandstone-pink octagonal cottages with polished coconut-wood floors and large, attractive bathrooms gather – some a little tightly – around a pretty,

Y-shaped pool; all have balconies, hot water, TV and a/c. Round-trip pier transfers and breakfast included. B2500

**Thipwimarn Resort** North of Hat Sai Ree, opposite Ko Nang Yuan ☎077 456409, ⓦthipwimarnresort.com; map p.264. Stylish, eco-friendly, upscale spot with a spa, which tumbles down a steep slope, past an elevated, infinity-edge swimming pool, to its own small beach. Dotted around the hillside, smart, thatched, whitewashed villas, most with hot water, enjoy a fair measure of seclusion, satellite TV, DVD players, minibars and fine sunset views. Breakfast included. Fan B2000, a/c B2200

### EATING AND DRINKING

**Choppers** On the main transverse road down to the beach ☎077 456641, ⓦchoppers-kohtao.com. Popular, well-run, full-service Aussie bar, with good food, plenty of imported bottled and draught beers, live bands on weekday nights and no fewer than seventeen screens for TV sports (with schedules posted on its website). Plenty of offers on drink, including happy hours 4–7pm. Daily 9am–late.

**Fizz Beach Lounge** On the beach at Silver Sands Resort ☎095 069 0350, ⓦfacebook.com/fizz.beachlounge. Chic beach lounge, where you can sink into the trademark green beanbags, sip great cocktails and bask in glorious sunsets. The DJ roster includes Soul Heaven on Saturdays and regular appearances by international names, and the Thai and Western food's good, too. Daily noon–1am (sometimes opening at 4pm in low season).

★ **The Gallery** On the east side of central Ban Hat Sai Ree, 50m down the Ao Hin Wong/Ao Mao road

on the right ☎077 456547, ⓦthegallerykohtao. com. This classy restaurant, with an attached wine and cocktail lounge and a photographic gallery, serves carefully sourced wines and excellent food from inherited family recipes (main courses start at B170), including its signature dish, seafood and chicken curry soufflé served in a young coconut (haw mok), superb prawn cakes and Thai desserts. Worth making a reservation in high season. Daily noon–11pm.

**Lotus Bar** On the beach near New Heaven Café. Raucous, very popular late-night haunt for drinking and dancing, with fire and tightrope shows. Evenings until very late.

**New Heaven Café** On the beach road on the south side of the village centre. Stylish, mostly organic spot offering great home-baked breads and cakes, as well as all-day Western breakfasts (around B100), sandwiches, salads, ice cream, espressos and juices. Daily 7.30am–5.30pm.

# Ko Nang Yuan

One kilometre off the northwest of Ko Tao, **KO NANG YUAN**, a close-knit group of three tiny islands, provides the most spectacular beach scenery in these parts, thanks to the causeway of fine white sand that joins up the islands. You can climb up to the mountain viewpoint on the northernmost island, and swim off the east side of the causeway to snorkel over the Japanese Gardens, which feature hundreds of hard and soft coral formations. However, there's little chance of having the place to yourself, as the island swarms with day-trippers and their boats: try to get there in the early morning, if you can.

## ARRIVAL AND DEPARTURE

**By boat** Boats from the Lomprayah pier in Mae Hat, just south of the main pier, run back and forth (departing 10.30am, returning at 1.30pm & 4.30pm; B200 return), and there are other, irregular services from Hat Sai Ree; Ko Nang

### KO NANG YUAN

Yuan features on all round-island boat trips, too. Note that rules to protect the environment here include banning all visitors from bringing cans, plastic bottles and fins with them, and day-trippers are charged B100 to land on the island.

## ACCOMMODATION AND EATING

**Nangyuan Island Dive Resort** ☎086 312 7128, ⓦnangyuan.com; map p.264. The decor at this resort is not much to write home about, but it certainly makes the most of its beautiful location – which you'll be able to enjoy in some peace after the day-trippers have

gone– spreading its a/c bungalows, all with en-suite hot showers, TVs and fridges, over all three islands. There's also a restaurant, a coffee shop and an on-site dive shop. Transfers from and to Mae Hat and breakfast included. **B2500**

# The north and east coasts

**Ao Mamuang** (Mango Bay), the lone bay on the **north coast**, is a beautiful, tree-clad bowl, whose shallow reef is a popular stop on snorkelling day-trips and on beginners' dive trips, though there's little in the way of a beach. The attractive bar-restaurant of *Mango Bay Boutique Resort* spreads its large deck over the rocks here.

The sheltered inlets of the **east coast**, most of them containing one or two sets of bungalows, can be reached by boat, pick-up or 4WD. The most northerly habitation here is at **Ao Hinwong**, a deeply recessed, limpid bay strewn with large boulders and great coral reefs, which has a particularly remote, almost desolate, air.

In the middle of the coast, the dramatic tiered promontory of Laem Thian shelters on its south side a tiny beach and a colourful reef, which stretches down towards the east coast's most developed bay, **Ao Ta Note**, with half a dozen resorts and a mostly paved road from Mae Hat. Ta Note's horseshoe inlet is sprinkled with boulders and plenty of coarse sand, with excellent snorkelling just north of the bay's mouth.

The last bay carved out of the turtle's shell, **Ao Leuk**, has a well-recessed beach and water that's deep enough for good swimming and snorkelling, featuring hard and soft coral gardens. Snorkels are available to rent at the beachfront bar.

## ACCOMMODATION

### THE NORTH AND EAST COASTS

### AO MAMUANG
**Mango Bay Boutique Resort** ☎02 107 1409, ⓦmangobayboutiqueresort.com; map p.264. At this remote resort, the well-appointed, thatched bungalows on stilts are scattered across a rocky slope; all come with hot water, a/c, minibars, TVs and balconies and some have huge verandas. Snorkels and kayaks available for rent. Transfers from Mae Hat and breakfast included. **B2780**

### AO HINWONG
**Hin Wong Bungalows** ☎077 456006 or ☎081 229 4810; map p.264. The oldest of this bay's small handful of resorts is welcoming and quiet, providing good en-suite accommodation on a steep, grassy slope above the rocks, in wooden huts with mosquito nets, hammocks, large, cold-water bathrooms and great views. It has a beach bar and restaurant and rents out kayaks and snorkels. Discounts for longer stays. **B600**

### AO TA NOTE
**Poseidon Resort** ☎077 456734, ⓦposeidontao. atspace.com; map p.264. At this friendly, mellow resort, the basic fan bungalows with en-suite cold showers, balconies and hammocks are set back a little from the sands on the flower-strewn, rocky slopes. The beachfront restaurant has a nice big deck and there are kayaks and snorkels for rent. **B800**

### AO LEUK
**Ao Leuk II** ☎077 456779, ⓦaowleuk2.net; map p.264. Large bungalows and family rooms, with big balconies, panoramic windows, fans and hot showers, on the bay's southern cape. If there happens to be no room here, don't worry – the same friendly family own two other resorts in the bay (including some cheaper, cold-shower bungalows), its taxis and the beachfront bar. Breakfast included. **B1600**

★ **Baan Talay** ☎077 457045, ⓦbaantalaykohtao.com; map p.264. Sustainable, secluded retreat owned by New Heaven Dive School (see page 266), with great views from its hillside location that slopes down to the north side of the bay. A clutch of stylish bungalows on stilts sport big verandas, mosquito nets on the beds and hot showers; the cheaper hardwood "huts" have shaggy thatched roofs and indoor-outdoor bathrooms. Yoga courses and kayaks for rent. Free transfers from Mae Hat pier. Fan B1200, a/c B2500

## The south coast

The southeast corner of the island sticks out in a long, thin mole of land, which points towards Shark Island, a colourful diving and snorkelling site just offshore; the headland shelters the sandy beach of **Hat Sai Daeng** on one side if the wind's coming from the northeast, or the rocky cove on the other side if it's blowing from the southwest. Beyond quiet, sandy **Ao Thian Ok**, the next bay along on the south coast, the deep indent of **Ao Chaloke Ban Kao** is protected from the worst of both monsoons, and consequently has seen a fair amount of development, with several dive resorts taking advantage of the large, sheltered, shallow bay, which sometimes gets muddy at low tide. Behind the beach are clinics, ATMs, supermarkets, bike rental shops, bars and restaurants. At New Heaven dive school (see page 266), drop-in **yoga** classes are held once or twice a day (not Mondays) on a veranda overlooking the bay.

On the east side of Ao Chaloke Ban Kao, carved out of the Laem Tato headland, the idyllic white sand of **Freedom Beach** is a secluded palm-lined spot with a beach bar; it's reached by walking through *Taatoh Freedom Beach Bungalows*. A fifteen-minute walk above the bungalows, the last stretch up a steep hillside, will bring you to **Jon-Suwan Mountain Viewpoint**, which affords fantastic views, especially at sunset, over the neighbouring bays of Chaloke Ban Kao and Thian Ok and across to Ko Pha Ngan and Ko Samui.

**ACCOMMODATION AND EATING** **THE SOUTH COAST**

### HAT SAI DAENG AND AO THIAN OK
**Jamahkiri** ☎077 456 400, ⓦjamahkiri.com; map p.264. The remote, rocky coastline between Sai Daeng and Thian Ok provides the spectacular location for this luxurious resort. There's a panoramic bar-restaurant, a full-service spa, a dive centre and a lovely swimming pool, as well as opulent, secluded rooms and bungalows, in a chic mix of Thai and Western design, with great sea views. Free transfers from Mae Hat and free boat transfers to sandy Ao Thian Ok. Breakfast included. B6110

### AO CHALOKE BAN KAO
**New Heaven Diving Resort** On the main road near the centre of the beach, attached to New Heaven Dive School (see page 266) ☎077 457 045, ⓦnewheavendiveschool.com; map p.264. Friendly, eco-conscious resort offering stylish, balconied private rooms, some with a/c and hot water, and a/c dorms with well-equipped, curtained-off bunk beds, as well as a small swimming pool overlooking the bay. There's also a lovely little café-restaurant by the pool, Koppee, serving everything from espresso coffees to Thai main courses. Dorms B350, fan doubles B800, a/c doubles B1800
**Viewpoint Bungalows** ☎091 823 3444, ⓦviewpoint resortkohtao.com; map p.264. Run by a friendly bunch, these distinctive bungalows sprawl along the western side of the bay and around the leafy headland beyond, with a seafront free-form pool and great sunset views; architect-designed in chic Balinese style, they boast indoor-outdoor bathrooms, lovely polished hardwood floors, mosquito nets and attractive verandas. There are also half a dozen tasty villas with their own infinity-edge pools (from B10,000). Breakfast included. B3050

# Nakhon Si Thammarat

**NAKHON SI THAMMARAT**, the south's second-largest town, occupies a blind spot in the eyes of most tourists, whose focus is fixed on Ko Samui, 100km to the north. Nakhon's neglect is unfortunate, for it's an absorbing place: the south's major pilgrimage site and home to a huge army base, it's relaxed, self-confident and sophisticated, well known for its excellent cuisine and traditional **handicrafts**. The stores on Thanon Thachang are especially good for local niilloware (*kruang tom*), household items and jewellery,

---

### FESTIVALS IN NAKHON

Known as *muang phra*, the "city of monks", Nakhon is still the religious capital of the south, and the main centre for **festivals**. The most important of these are the **Tamboon Deuan Sip**, held during the waning of the moon in the tenth lunar month (either Sept or Oct), and the **Hae Pha Kheun That**, which is held several times a year, but most importantly on Makha Puja, the full moon of the third lunar month, usually February, and on Visakha Puja, the full moon of the sixth lunar month, usually May (see page 47). The purpose of Tamboon Deuan Sip is to pay homage to dead relatives and friends; it is believed that during this fifteen-day period all *pret* – ancestors who have been damned to hell – are allowed out to visit the world, and so their relatives perform a merit-making ceremony in the temples, presenting offerings from the first harvest to ease their suffering. A huge ten-day fair takes place at Thung Talaat park on the north side of town at this time, as well as processions, shadow plays and other theatrical performances. The Hae Pha Khun That also attracts people from all over the south, to pay homage to the relics of the Buddha at Wat Mahathat. The centrepiece of this ceremony is the Pha Phra Bot, a strip of yellow cloth many hundreds of metres long, which is carried in a spectacular procession around the chedi. Meanwhile, Nakhon is still a centre of Brahminism, which plays an important part in Thai royal ceremonials. During Songkhran (the Thai New Year in April), Buddhism and Brahminism both have their moment in the sun: the Phra Buddha Sihing image is paraded through the streets and blessed with lustral water; and at the Hindu shrine of Phra Isuan on Thanon Ratchadamnoen, the Giant Swing ceremony has recently been revived – two Brahmins swing up to grab a bag of gold coins from a tree, in honour of Shiva (in Thai, Phra Isuan) and Vishnu (in Thai, Phra Narai).

---

elegantly patterned in gold or silver, often on black, and *yan lipao*, sturdy basketware made from intricately woven fern stems of different colours. Nakhon is also the best place in the country to see how Thai **shadow plays** work, at Suchart Subsin's workshop, and the main jumping-off point for towering **Khao Luang National Park** and its beautiful waterfall, **Krung Ching** (see page 278).

**Orientation** in Nakhon is simple, though the layout of the town is puzzling at first sight: it runs in a straight line for 7km from north to south and is rarely more than a few hundred metres wide; originally this was a long sand dune dotted with fresh-water wells and flanked by low, marshy ground. The modern centre for businesses and shops sits at the north end around the landmark **Tha Wang intersection**, where Thanon Neramit meets Thanon Ratchadamnoen. To the south, centred on the elegant, traditional mosque on Thanon Karom, lies the old Muslim quarter; south again is the start of the old city walls, of which few remains can be seen, and the historic centre, with the town's main places of interest now set in a leafy residential area.

## Brief history

Nakhon Si Thammarat seems to have been part of the shadowy early kingdom of Tambralinga, and was well placed for trade with China and southern India (via an overland route from the port of Trang, on the Andaman Sea) from at least the early centuries AD. The first local event that can be dated with any reliability occurred in 1001 AD, when Tambralinga asserted its independence from the regional powers of Srivijaya and Angkor by sending its own tribute mission to China. From the twelfth century, Nakhon had significant contacts with Sri Lanka, including a major rebuilding of the prestigious Buddha-relic chedi at Wat Mahathat in the Lankan style; in the following century, Sri Lankan monks from Nakhon are said to have helped spread the Theravada form of Buddhism to Sukhothai, the major new Thai city-state to the north.

By the sixteenth century, Nakhon Si Thammarat had come under the control of Ayutthaya, which sent out governors to rule this rich and important region, in place of native princes. In the same century, trading links began with the Portuguese, who were followed by the Dutch, the English and the French; Nakhon – which was generally known to the Westerners by its Malay name, Ligor, to Thais as Lakhon – could offer local pepper, tin and hides. After the Burmese destruction of Ayutthaya and its treasures in 1767, the town played an important part in the cultural rebirth of the nation, sending its copy of the Tripitaka (the Buddhist scriptures) to King Taksin's new capital at Thonburi to be transcribed, as all the kingdom's copies had been lost.

## Wat Mahathat

Main entrance faces Thanon Ratchadamnoen, about 2km south of the modern centre

Missing out **Wat Mahathat** would be like going to Rome and not visiting St Peter's, for the Buddha relics in the vast chedi make this the south's most important shrine. In the courtyard inside the temple cloisters, row upon row of smaller chedis, spiked like bayonets, surround the main chedi, the 60m-tall **Phra Boromathat**. This huge, stubby Sri Lankan bell supports a slender, ringed spire, which is in turn topped by a shiny pinnacle said to be covered in 600kg of gold. According to the chronicles, tooth relics of the Buddha were brought here from Sri Lanka over two thousand years ago by an Indian prince and princess and enshrined in a chedi. It's undergone plenty of face-lifts since then: two earlier Srivijayan versions, models of which stand outside the entrance to the cloisters, are encased in the present twelfth-century chedi. The most recent restoration work, funded by donations from all over Thailand, rescued it from collapse, although it still seems to be leaning dangerously to the southeast. Worshippers head for the north side's vast enclosed stairway, framed by lions and giants, which they liberally decorate with gold leaf to add to the shrine's radiance and gain some merit. At the base of the stairway, look out for two delicate gilded reliefs showing the "Great Retirement", as the Buddha leaves his palace and family on horseback to become an ascetic; and for the two magnificent, Ayutthaya-period doors depicting Vishnu and Brahma.

## Viharn Phra Kien Museum

Extends north from the chedi • Hours irregular, but usually daily 8.30am–4pm • Free

An Aladdin's cave of bric-a-brac, the **Viharn Phra Kien Museum** is said to house fifty thousand artefacts donated by worshippers, ranging from ships made out of seashells to gold and silver models of the Bodhi Tree. At the entrance to the museum, you'll pass the Phra Puay, an image of the Buddha giving a gesture of reassurance. Women pray to

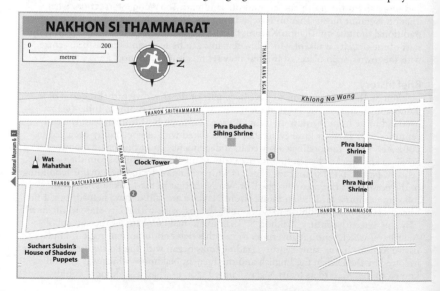

the image when they want to have children, and the lucky ones return to give thanks and leave photos of their chubby progeny.

### Viharn Luang

Outside the cloister to the south

Raised on elegant slanting columns, the eighteenth-century **Viharn Luang** (actually a bot, surrounded by eight *sema* stones) is a beautiful example of Ayutthayan architecture. Beyond the pediment, with its gilded figure of Vishnu on his traditional elephant mount Erawan, you'll find that the interior is austere at ground level, but the red coffered ceiling shines with carved and gilded stars and lotus blooms. In the spacious grounds around the viharn, cheerful, inexpensive stalls peddle local handicrafts such as shadow puppets, bronzeware and basketware.

## The National Museum

Thanon Ratchadamnoen, a 10min walk south from Wat Mahathat • Wed–Sun 9am–noon & 1–4pm • B150

The **National Museum** houses a small but diverse collection, mostly of artefacts from southern Thailand. In the prehistory room **downstairs**, look out for the two impressive ceremonial bronze kettledrums dating from the fifth century BC; they were beaten in rainmaking rituals and one of them is topped with chunky frogs (the local frogs are said to be the biggest in Thailand and a prized delicacy). Also on the ground floor are some interesting Hindu finds, including several stone lingams from the seventh to ninth centuries AD and later bronze statues of Ganesh, the elephant-headed god of wisdom and the arts. Look out especially for a vivacious, well-preserved bronze of Shiva here, dancing within a ring of fire on the body of a dwarf demon, who holds a cobra symbolizing stupidity. Among the collections of ceramics **upstairs**, you can't miss the seat panel from Rama V's barge, a dazzling example of the nielloware for which Nakhon is famous – the delicate animals and landscapes have been etched onto a layer of gold which covers the silver base, and then picked out by inlaying a black alloy into the background. The nearby exhibition on local wisdom includes interesting displays on Buddhist ordinations and weddings, and on *manohra*, the southern Thai dramatic dance form.

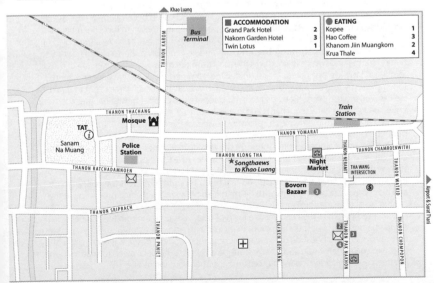

## Suchart Subsin's House of Shadow Puppets

Ban Nang Thalung Suchart Subsin, 110/18 Soi 3, Thanon Si Thammasok, a 10min walk east of Wat Mahathat • Daily 8am–5pm • Free •
☎ 075 346394

The best possible introduction to *nang thalung*, southern Thailand's **shadow puppet theatre** (see below), is to head for the atmospheric compound of the late Suchart Subsin, a designated National Artist who was one of the south's leading exponents of *nang thalung* until his death in 2015. His sons and former apprentices have now succeeded him as puppeteers and have kept their workshop open to the public. There's a small museum of puppets from Thailand, Indonesia and Cambodia dating back as far as the eighteenth century, and, especially if you phone in advance, they'll usually be able to show you a few scenes from a shadow play in the small theatre (by donation, about B50/person). You can also see the intricate process of making the leather puppets and can buy the finished products as souvenirs: puppets sold here are of much better quality and design than those usually found on southern Thailand's souvenir stalls.

## The Phra Buddha Sihing shrine

In the provincial administration complex on Thanon Ratchadamnoen • Mon–Fri 8.30am–4.30pm • Free

Magically created in Sri Lanka in the second century, the **Phra Buddha Sihing** statue was, according to legend, sent by ship to the king of Sukhothai in the thirteenth century, but the vessel sank and the image miraculously floated on a plank to Nakhon. Two other images, one in the National Museum in Bangkok, one in Wat Phra Singh in Chiang Mai, claim to be the authentic Phra Buddha Sihing, but none of the three

---

### SHADOW PUPPETS

Found throughout southern Asia, **shadow puppets** are one of the oldest forms of theatre, featuring in Buddhist literature as early as 400 BC. The art form seems to have come from India, via Java, to Thailand, where it's called *nang*, meaning "hide": the puppets are made from the skins of water buffalo or cows, which are softened in water, then pounded until almost transparent, before being carved and painted to represent the characters of the play. The puppets are then manipulated on bamboo rods in front of a bright light, to project their image onto a large white screen, while the story is narrated to the audience.

The grander version of the art, **nang yai** – "big hide", so called because the figures are life-size – deals only with the *Ramayana* story (see page 446). It's known to have been part of the entertainment at official ceremonies in the Ayutthayan period, but has now almost died out. The more populist version, **nang thalung** – *thalung* is probably a shortening of the town name, Phatthalung (which is just down the road from Nakhon), where this version of the art form is said to have originated – is also in decline now: performances are generally limited to temple festivals, marriages, funerals and ordinations, lasting usually from 9pm to dawn. As well as working the 60cm-high *nang thalung* puppets, the puppet master narrates the story, impersonates the characters, chants and cracks jokes to the accompaniment of flutes, fiddles and percussion instruments. Not surprisingly, in view of this virtuoso semi-improvised display, puppet masters are esteemed as possessed geniuses by their public.

At big festivals, companies often perform the *Ramayana*, sometimes in competition with each other; at smaller events they put on more down-to-earth stories, with stock characters such as the jokers Yor Thong, an angry man with a pot belly and a sword, and Kaew Kop, a man with a frog's head. Yogi, a wizard and teacher, is thought to protect the puppet master and his company from evil spirits with his magic, so he is always the first puppet on at the beginning of every performance.

In an attempt to halt their decline as a form of popular entertainment, the puppet companies are now incorporating modern instruments and characters in modern dress into their shows, and are boosting the love element in their stories. They're fighting a battle they can't win against television and cinemas, although at least the debt owed to shadow puppets has been acknowledged – *nang* has become the Thai word for "movie".

is in the Sri Lankan style, and all three may have originated as replacements for a lost original. Although similar to the other two in size and shape, the image in Nakhon, dated between the thirteenth and sixteenth centuries, has a style unique to this area, distinguished by the heavily pleated flap of its robe over the left shoulder, a beaky nose and harsh features, which sit uneasily on the short, corpulent body. The statue's plumpness has given the style the name *khanom tom*, after a kind of coconut and rice pudding. The much-revered image is sheltered by a delicate, golden five-tiered parasol, and housed in an attractive, 100-year-old, Ayutthaya-style shrine.

## ARRIVAL AND DEPARTURE
## NAKHON SI THAMMARAT

### BY PLANE
The airport (☎075 369540–2), served daily by Nok Air, Lion Air and Air Asia from Bangkok's Don Muang Airport (12 daily; 1hr 10min), is about 20km northwest of the city off the Surat Thani road. From here, taxis charge around B250 to take you into Nakhon (B1500 to Don Sak, for ferries to Ko Samui and Ko Pha Ngan) while big hotels such as the *Twin Lotus* offer airport shuttle buses; an airport bus to town is being considered – check with the TAT office. Nok Air and Air Asia offer flight-and-boat through-tickets to Ko Samui, Ko Pha Ngan and Ko Tao, and Seatran (☎077 950559, ⓦseatranferry.com) have a counter at the airport offering bus-and-boat through-tickets to the three islands.

### BY TRAIN
The train station is very central and sits at the end of a branch off the main southern line from Bangkok (2 daily; 15hr 30min–16hr 30min).

### BY BUS AND A/C MINIBUS
All buses and a/c minibuses now use the terminal on the west side of the centre.

Destinations Bangkok (Southern Terminal; 20 daily; 13hr); Chumphon (8 daily; 5hr); Don Sak (for ferries to Ko Samui and Ko Pha Ngan; a/c minibuses when full; 2hr); Krabi (hourly; 3–4hr); Phuket (hourly; 5–6hr); Surat Thani (every 30min; 2–3hr); Trang (hourly; 2hr).

## GETTING AROUND AND INFORMATION

**By share-songthaew** Small blue share-songthaews ply up and down Thanon Ratchadamnoen for B10 a ride.

**By taxi** Metered taxis can be booked by phone (☎077 357 888) and hang out at the bus station and airport. Be aware though, that from these locations you may well have a hard job persuading them to switch their meters on. Motorbike taxis also buzz around town.

**By rented car** Avis, based at the airport (☎02 251 1131–2, ⓦavisthailand.com), will deliver and collect vehicles anywhere in Nakhon Si Thammarat.

**Tourist information** TAT has an office housed in a restored 1920s government officers' club that's on Sanam Na Muang (daily 8.30am–4.30pm; ☎075 346 515–6, ⓔtatnksri@tat.or.th).

## ACCOMMODATION

Nakhon has no guesthouses or traveller-oriented accommodation, but the best of its hotels offer very good value in all price ranges.

**Grand Park Hotel** 1204/79 Thanon Pak Nakhon ☎075 317 666–75, ⓦgrandparknakhon.com; map p.274. If you're looking for an upmarket option in the centre of town, this place, set back a little from the busy road, is worth considering – it's large, smart and bright, with a/c, hot water, TV and minibar in every room, and cheery and attentive staff. B700

★ **Nakorn Garden Hotel** 1/4 Thanon Pak Nakhon ☎075 313 333; map p.274. A rustic but comfortable

haven in two three-storey, red-brick buildings overlooking a big tree-shaded courtyard. The large, attractive rooms are looking a bit tired now but come with a/c, hot water, cable TV and minibar. B445

**Twin Lotus** About 3km southeast of the centre at 97/8 Thanon Patanakarn Kukwang ☎075 323 777, ⓦtwinlotushotel.net; map p.274. Gets pride of place in Nakhon – though not for its location; sports Thai and Chinese restaurants, a beer garden, a small spa, a large, attractive outdoor swimming pool, a sauna and a fitness centre. Breakfast and round-trip airport transfers included with Superior rooms (B1500). B800

## EATING AND DRINKING

Nakhon is a great place for inexpensive food, not least at the busy, colourful **night market** on Thanon Chamroenwithi.

**Kopee** Thanon Nang Ngam ☎089 4319 999; map p.274. This faithful and attractive re-creation of an old Chinese-style, southern Thai coffee shop, with marble-

topped tables, quaint wooden shutters and ceiling fans, is famous nationwide for its southern dishes such as *khua kling* (a dry curry of minced pork, served on rice; B40), *khao mok* kai (a kind of chicken biryani) and sweet and savoury *roti* pancakes, all washed down with steaming mugs of traditional, cloth-filtered coffee (*kopi*). Daily 6.30am–11pm.

**Hao Coffee** In the Bovorn Bazaar, Thanon Ratchadamnoen; map p.274. Popular place in a quiet courtyard, modelled on an old Chinese-style coffee shop and packed full of ageing lamps, clocks and other antiques. Offers a wide selection of inexpensive Thai dishes, a few Western breakfasts, teas, juices and espresso coffees (from B35), including delicious iced cappuccinos. Daily 7am–4pm.

**Khanom Jiin Muangkorn** 23 Thanon Panyom, near Wat Mahathat ☎075 342 615; map p.274. Justly famous, inexpensive indoor-outdoor restaurant dishing up one of the local specialities, *khanom jiin*, rice noodles

topped with hot, sweet or fishy sauce served with *pak ruam*, a platter of crispy raw vegetables. Daily 8am–3.30pm.

★ **Krua Thale** Thanon Pak Nakhon, opposite the Nakorn Garden Hotel; map p.274. The town's best restaurant, renowned among locals for its excellent, varied and inexpensive seafood. Plain and very clean, with an open kitchen and the day's catch displayed out front, and relaxing patio tables and an a/c room at the back. Recommended dishes include a very good *yam plaa duk foo*, shredded and deep-fried catfish with a mango salad dip (B120), whole baked fish and king prawns (priced by weight and delicious with tamarind sauce), and *hoy maleang poo op mordin*, large green mussels in a delicious herb soup containing lemon grass, basil and mint. Daily 4–10pm (last orders 9pm).

# Khao Luang National Park

Headquarters to the south of the summit near Karom Waterfall • National park admission fee B200 • ☎ 075 300 494, ⓦ nps.dnp.go.th

Rising to the west of Nakhon Si Thammarat and temptingly visible from all over town is 1835m-high **Khao Luang**, southern Thailand's highest mountain. A huge **national park** encompasses Khao Luang's jagged green peaks, beautiful streams with numerous waterfalls, tropical rainforest and fruit orchards. The mountain is also the source of the Tapi River, one of the peninsula's main waterways, which flows into the Gulf of Thailand at Surat Thani. **Fauna** here include macaques, musk deer, civets and binturongs, as well as more difficult-to-see Malayan tapirs, serows, tigers, panthers and clouded leopards, plus over two hundred bird species. There's an astonishing diversity of **flora** too, notably rhododendrons and begonias, dense mosses, ferns and lichens, plus more than three hundred species of both ground-growing and epiphytic orchids, some of which are unique to the park.

The best **time to visit** is after the rainy season, from January onwards, when there should still be a decent flow in the waterfalls, but the trails will be dry and the leeches not so bad. However, the park's most distinguishing feature for visitors is probably its difficulty of **access**: main roads run around the 570-square-kilometre park with spurs into some of the waterfalls, but there are no roads across the park and very sparse public transport along the spur roads. The Ban Khiriwong Visitor Service Centre (☎075 533113 or ☎075 533 370) can arrange **treks** to the peak roughly between January and July, beginning at Ban Khiriwong, a village famous for its organic orchards and crafts on the southeast side of the park, and including two nights camping on the mountain, meals and guides, as well as homestays in the village. Otherwise only **Krung Ching Waterfall**, one of Thailand's most spectacular, really justifies the hassle of getting to the park.

## Krung Ching Waterfall

A trip to **Krung Ching**, a nine-tier waterfall on the north side of the park, makes for a highly satisfying day out with a **nature trail** taking you through dense, steamy jungle to the most beautiful, third, tier. Starting at the Krung Ching park office, which lies 13km south of Ban Huai Phan, this shady, mostly paved, 4km trail is very steep in parts, so you should allow four hours at least there and back. On the way you'll pass giant ferns, including a variety known as *maha sadam*, the largest fern in the world, gnarled banyan trees, forests of mangosteen and beautiful, thick stands of bamboo. You're bound to see colourful birds and insects, but you may well only hear macaques and other mammals. At the end, a long, stepped descent brings you to a perfectly positioned wooden platform with fantastic views of the 40m fall, which used to appear on the back of thousand-baht notes; here you can see how, shrouded in thick spray, it earns its Thai name, Fon Saen Ha, meaning "hundreds of thousands of rainfalls".

## ARRIVAL AND DEPARTURE                                                                    KHAO LUANG

**By songthaew** Irregular songthaews on the main roads located around Khao Luang National Park and to Ban Khiriwong congregate on Thanon Klong Tha in Nakhon. None of them is scheduled to go to Krung Ching – you'd have to catch one to the T-junction (*saam yaek*) at Ban Na Leng in the Nopphitam district (about 1hr), then change to another songthaew for the last 25km or so to get to the falls.

**By car** Rental cars are available from Avis (see page 215). The easiest way to get to Krung Ching from Nakhon with your own transport is to head north on Highway 401 towards Surat Thani, turning west at Tha Sala on to Highway 4140, then north again at Ban Na Leng in Nopphitam district on to Highway 4186, before heading south from Ban Huai Phan on Highway 4188, the spur road to the Krung Ching park office, a total journey of about 70km.

## ACCOMMODATION AND EATING

**National park accommodation** ☎ 075 460463, ⊛ dnp.go.th. Two- to twenty-person bungalows, most with hot water and fridges, are available at the Krung Ching park office. There's also a campsite. Bungalows __B600__

**National park canteen** There's a basic canteen situated near the Krung Ching park head office for travellers after a light meal during their visit. However, note that food needs to be ordered in advance.

3

# Southern Thailand: the Andaman coast

KHAO TAPU (JAMES BOND ISLAND), AO PHANG BAY

# Southern Thailand: the Andaman coast

As Highway 4 switches from the east flank of the Thailand peninsula to the Andaman coast it enters a markedly different country: nourished by rain nearly all the year round, the vegetation down here is lushly tropical, with forests reaching up to 80m in height, and massive rubber, palm-oil and coconut plantations replacing the rice and sugar-cane fields of central Thailand. Sheer limestone crags spike every horizon and the translucent Andaman Sea laps the most dazzlingly beautiful islands in the country, not to mention its finest coral reefs. This is of course the same sea whose terrifyingly powerful tsunami waves battered the coastline in December 2004, killing thousands and changing countless lives and communities forever. The legacies of that horrific day are widespread (see page 307), but all the affected holiday resorts have been rebuilt, with the tourist dollar now arguably more crucial to the region's well-being than ever before.

The **cultural mix** along the Andaman coast is also different from central Thailand. Many southern Thais are Muslim, with a heritage that connects them to Malaysia and beyond. This is also the traditional province of nomadic *chao ley*, or sea gypsies, many of whom have now settled but still work as boat captains and fishermen. The commercial fishing industry, on the other hand, is mostly staffed by immigrants – legal and not – from neighbouring Myanmar, just a few kilometres away along the northern Andaman coast.

The attractions of the northern Andaman coast are often ignored in the race down to the high-profile honeypots around Phuket and Krabi, but there are many quiet gems up here, beginning with the low-key little sister islands of **Ko Chang Noi** (quite different from its larger, more famous east-coast namesake) and the fast-developing **Ko Phayam**, where the hammocks and paraffin lamps still offer an old-style travellers' vibe that's harder to find further south. Snorkellers and divers are drawn in their hundreds to the reefs of the remote National Park island chains of **Ko Surin** and **Ko Similan**, with many choosing to base themselves at the mainland beach resort of **Khao Lak**, though homestay programmes around **Khuraburi** offer an interesting alternative. Inland, it's all about the jungle – with twenty-first-century amenities – at the enjoyable **Khao Sok National Park**, where accommodation is on rafts on the lake and in treehouses beneath the limestone crags.

**Phuket**, Thailand's largest island, is the region's major resort destination for families, package tourists and novice divers; its dining, shopping and entertainment facilities are second to none, but the high-rises and hectic consumerism dilute the Thai-ness of the

---

## THE KRA ISTHMUS

Thailand's Andaman coast begins at **Kraburi**, where, at kilometre-stone 545 (the distance from Bangkok), a signpost welcomes you to the **Kra Isthmus**, the narrowest part of peninsular Thailand. Just 44km separates the Gulf of Thailand from the Andaman Sea's Chan River estuary, and Burmese border, here. Though a seemingly obvious short cut for shipping traffic between the Indian Ocean and the South China Sea, avoiding the 1500km detour via the Strait of Malacca, the much-discussed **Kra Canal** project has yet to be realized, despite being on the table for over three hundred years.

SINO-PORTUGUESE ARCHITECTURE IN PHUKET TOWN

# Highlights

**❶ Island idylls** Tranquillity rules on the uncommercial islands of Ko Phayam, Ko Yao Noi and Ko Jum. See pages 293, 340 and 374

**❷ Khao Sok National Park** Sleep in a jungle treehouse or on a lake amid spectacular karst scenery, and wake to the sound of hooting gibbons. See page 301

**❸ Ko Similan** Remote island chain offering the finest snorkelling and diving, and easily accessible on day-trips and live-aboards. See page 312

**❹ Sea-canoeing in Ao Phang Nga** The perfect way to explore the limestone karsts and

hidden lagoons of this spectacular bay. See page 347

**❺ Phuket Town** Handsome Sino-Portuguese architecture and some of the most interesting sleeping, eating and drinking options on the island. See page 317

**❻ Rock-climbing** Even novices can get a bird's-eye view of the Railay peninsula's fabulous coastal scenery. See page 362

**❼ Ko Lanta Yai** The "island of long beaches", with an atmospheric old town, offers an appealing choice of relaxing mid-range facilitles. See page 378

**HIGHLIGHTS ARE MARKED ON THE MAP ON PAGE 284**

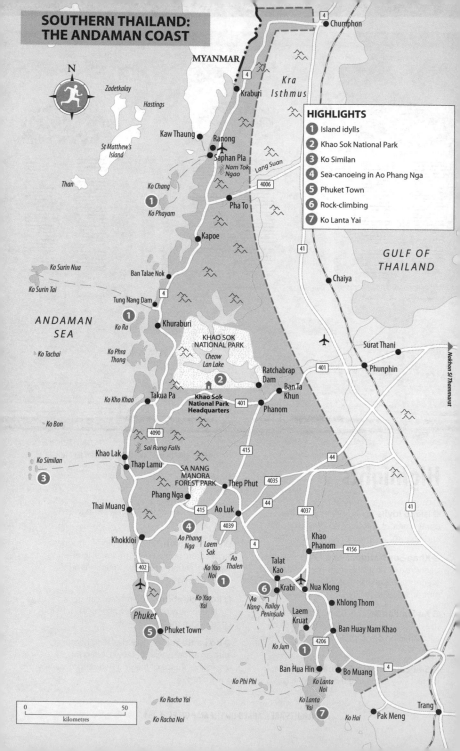

experience. There's Thai life in spades across on the quiet rural island of **Ko Yao Noi**, scenically located within the spectacular bay of **Ao Phang Nga**, whose scattered karst islets are one of the country's top natural wonders, best appreciated from a sea-canoe. The Andaman coast's second hub is **Krabi** province, rightly famous for its turquoise seas and dramatic islands. Flashiest of these is the flawed but still handsome **Ko Phi Phi**, with its great diving, gorgeous beaches and high-octane nightlife. Mainland and mainstream **Ao Nang** can't really compete, but is at least close to the majestic cliffs and superb rock-climbing of the **Railay** peninsula at **Laem Phra Nang**. Offshore again, there's horizon-gazing aplenty at mellow **Ko Jum** and the choice of half a dozen luxuriously long beaches, and plentiful resort facilities, at **Ko Lanta Yai**.

Unlike the Gulf coast, the Andaman coast is hit by the **southwest monsoon**, which usually generally lasts from the end of May until at least the middle of October. During this period, heavy rain and high seas render some of the outer islands inaccessible, but conditions aren't usually severe enough to ruin a holiday on the other islands, or on the mainland, and you'll get tempting discounts on accommodation. Some bungalows at the smaller resorts shut down entirely during low season (highlighted in the text), but most beaches keep at least one place open, and some dive shops lead expeditions year-round.

### ARRIVAL AND DEPARTURE                                THE ANDAMAN COAST

There is no rail line down the Andaman coast, but many travellers take the **train** from Bangkok to the Gulf coast's transport hub Surat Thani and then nip across by bus. There are also plenty of direct **buses** that travel south from the capital overnight. The fastest option is to arrive by **plane**: both Phuket and Krabi have international airports, and there's a domestic airport at Trang, not far from Ko Lanta in the deep south.

**4**

# Ranong

Despite being the soggiest town in the country, with over 5000mm of rain a year, **RANONG** has a pleasing buzz about it, fuelled by its mix of Burmese, Thai, Chinese and Malay inhabitants. It's a prosperous town, the lucrative nineteenth-century tin-mining concessions now replaced by a thriving fishing industry centred on the port of Saphan Pla, 5km southwest of town, and its scores of fishing boats and fish-processing factories staffed mainly by notoriously poorly treated Burmese workers. As with most border areas, there's also said to be a flourishing illegal trade in amphetamines, guns and labour, not to mention the inevitable tensions over international fishing rights, which sometimes end in shoot-outs, though the closest encounter you're likely to have will be in the pages of the *Bangkok Post*. Thai tourists have been coming here for years, to savour the health-giving properties of the local spring water, but foreign travellers have only quite recently discovered it as a useful departure point for the alluring nearby little islands of **Ko Chang Noi** and **Ko Phayam**. The other reason to stop off in Ranong is to make a visa run to the Burmese town of **Kaw Thaung,** but double check with local travel agents (or come equipped with a 60-day Thai tourist visa), as immigration attitudes toward visa runs keep changing, and you may have trouble re-entering Thailand.

A stroll along Ranong's main road, **Thanon Ruangrat**, brings its history and geography to mind. The handsome, if faded, shopfront architecture bears many of the hallmarks of nineteenth-century Sino-Portuguese design (see page 318), with its arched "five-foot" walkways shading pedestrians, pastel paintwork and shuttered windows. Chinese goods fill many of the shops – this is a good place to stock up on cheap clothes too – and many signs are written in the town's three main languages: Thai, Chinese and curly Burmese script.

## First Governor's House

West off Thanon Ruangrat on the northern edge of town • Daily 9am–4.30pm • Free

Ranong's history is closely associated with its most famous son, Khaw Soo Cheang, a poor Hokkien Chinese emigrant turned tin baron who became the first governor of

Ranong province in 1854; he is still so esteemed that politicians continue to pay public homage at his grave, and his descendants bear the respected aristocratic surname "na Ranong" ("of Ranong"). Little now remains of Khaw Soo Cheang's house, but in its grounds stands a Khaw clan house and small museum, the **First Governor's House** (Nai Khai Ranong), containing interesting photos of the governor.

## The geothermal springs

Raksawarin Park, about 3km east of the Thanon Ruangrat market • **Raksawarin Hot Springs** daily 7am–9pm • free; Tinidee pools B40, or B60 including transfer from Tinidee Hotel (see page 288) • **Siam Hot Spa Ranong** daily noon–9pm • treatments from B200 ☎ 077 813551–4, ⊚ siamhotsparanong.com • Accessible on red songthaew #2 from the market or by motorbike taxi

It can be fun to follow the crowds of domestic tourists who flock to Ranong's famously pure **geothermal springs** for its stress-relieving and supposed medicinal properties. The springs are the focus of forested Raksawarin Park, which is set in a narrow, lush river valley, surrounded by restaurants and souvenir shops. At the park's Raksawarin Hot Springs, you can bathe or paddle in either the open-access, public mineral spa pools or the better-appointed and deeper, Jacuzzi-type spa pools, which are run by the *Tinidee Hotel*. Alternatively, you may opt to relax on the heated floor of the elephant-adorned pavilion behind the pools or take a leisurely soak at the indoor Siam Hot Spa Ranong across the road, which offers public and private Jacuzzi pools, private bathrooms and inexpensive massage and steam treatments.

### ACCOMMODATION
| | |
|---|---|
| The B | 1 |
| Kiwi Orchid Guesthouse | 5 |
| Luang Poj | 2 |
| Sino Mansion | 3 |
| Tinidee Hotel | 4 |

### EATING
| | |
|---|---|
| 209 Kafe | 1 |
| Pon's Place | 2 |

RANONG

## ARRIVAL AND DEPARTURE

**By plane** Budget airline Nok Air (ⓦnokair.com) flies from Bangkok's Don Mueang airport (2 daily; 1hr 30min) to Ranong airport, 20km south of town on Highway 4. *Pon's Place* (ⓣ081 597 4549, ⓦponplace-ranong.com) has a tours booth at the airport and can also arrange a transfer into town or the Saphan Pla pier for B200–300/person. You can also wait on the highway outside of the terminal for a songthaew (B25) into town.

**By bus or minibus** Most Andaman-coast buses travelling between Bangkok or Chumphon and Khuraburi, Takua Pa or Phuket stop briefly at Ranong's bus station on Highway 4 (Thanon Phetkasem), 1km southeast of the central market. If coming from Khao Sok or Surat Thani, you'll usually need to change buses at Takua Pa, though there is also an a/c minibus service from and to Surat Thani (hourly 6am–5pm; 3hr). There are direct buses operated by Rungkit from Chumphon (4 daily; 2–3hr), as well as faster a/c minibuses (hourly 6am–5pm; 2hr; B150), so from Bangkok it's often more comfortable to take a night train to Chumphon and then change on to a bus or minibus. Alternatively, Chokeanan and New Mittour run VIP buses from opposite Wat Bowoniwes and the Siam Commercial

Bank in Banglamphu, via the Southern Bus Terminal, to Chumphon's Thanon Tha Muang. Rungkit buses to Chumphon and Phuket and the a/c minibuses operate out of Ranong Bus Station.

Destinations: Bangkok (7 daily; 9hr); Chumphon (hourly 7am–5pm; 2–3hr); Hat Yay (3 daily; 7hr); Hua Hin (3 daily; 5hr 30min); Khao Lak (5 daily; 3hr 45min); Khuraburi (4 daily; 2hr); Krabi (2 daily; 5hr); Phang Nga (4 daily; 4hr); Phuket (via Khao Lak; 4 daily; 5–7hr); Surat Thani (10 daily; 4hr); Takua Pa (4 daily; 3hr).

**By boat to the islands via Saphan Pla** Boats to Ko Chang Noi (see page 289) and Ko Phayam (see page 293) leave from Ranong's port at Saphan Pla, 5km southwest of the town centre and served by songthaews (see below) or by share-taxi from *Pon's Place* (B50). Songthaews drop passengers on the main road through Saphan Pla, from where it's a 500m walk south to the Islands Pier, while share-taxis take you to the pier itself, and also wait around for passengers when boats return from the islands.

Destinations: Ko Chang Noi (3 longtail boats daily; 1hr–1hr 30min; 200B); Ko Phayam (up to 10 speedboats daily; 45min; 350B).

## GETTING AROUND AND INFORMATION

**By songthaew** Songthaews shuttle across and around Ranong, starting from the Thanon Ruangrat market, close to the town-centre hotels. Many have their destinations written in English on the side, and most charge around B15 per ride. Several songthaews pass Ranong bus station, including the #2 (red), which runs to the Thanon Ruangrat hotels and day market, and the #6 (blue), which starts at the day market and heads on to the port area at Saphan Pla, 5km to the southwest (for boats to Ko Chang Noi, Ko Phayam and Kaw Thaung); red #3 songthaew runs direct from the market on Thanon Ruangrat to the Saphan Pla port area.

**Car and bike rental** *Pon's Place*, 129 Thanon Ruangrat (daily 7.30am–9pm; ⓣ081 597 4549, ⓦponplace-ranong.

com), rents bicycles (80B/day), motorbikes (200B/day manual and 250B/day automatic) and cars (1200B/day).

**Tourist information** The best source of tourist information in town is the ever helpful Pon at *Pon's Place* restaurant and tour agency, 129 Thanon Ruangrat (daily 7.30am–9pm; ⓣ081 597 4549, ⓦponplace-ranong.com; also a booth at Ranong airport), where you can also organize a visa run to Myanmar and back (1300b), arrange tours of the local area, book accommodation on Ko Chang Noi and Ko Phayam, and buy air, bus and minibus tickets, as well as train tickets from Chumphon or Surat Thani. There's a branch of Smiling Seahorse Diving (see page 286) along Thanon Ruangrat (ⓣ086 0110614; ⓦthesmilingseahorse.com).

## ACCOMMODATION

**The B** 295/2 Thanon Ruangrat ⓣ077 823111, ⓦfacebook.com/thebranong; map p.286. Ranong's classiest boutique hotel offers immaculate, spacious en-suite rooms with industrial chic design and rainwater showers. Rooms are set over three floors that alternate between bright-coloured door frames and darker, shabby-chic furnishings. Breakfast and free bicycle rental is included, and the annexed bistro is a great place to check out some local live bands. B̲1̲2̲0̲0̲

**Kiwi Orchid Guesthouse** 96/19–20 Moo 1, off Thanon Phetkasem ⓣ081 6910404, ⓔkiwiorchid@hotmail. com; map p.286. A run-down place right next to the bus terminal, but the fan rooms are surprisingly quiet and comfortable, and the affable owner always ready to give

useful advice on what to do in the area and how to get around. Shared bathrooms are a little grimy, but the hostel makes a handy transit to plan your next move with other budget travellers over a beer in the restaurant, which serves good vegetarian dishes (from B80). B̲3̲0̲0̲

**Luang Poj** 225 Thanon Ruangrat ⓣ077 833377, ⓔluangpoj@gmail.com; map p.286. Appealing conversion of a Sino-Portuguese shophouse with polished wooden floors, which styles itself as a "boutique hostel" despite no dorms. Modern bedrooms come with attractive murals: heavy sleepers who like to be in the thick of the action will like the two fan rooms with wooden shutters facing the street; others may prefer to opt for the same priced, windowless a/c options. Hot showers are shared and there's a restaurant too. B̲6̲0̲0̲

4

## INTO MYANMAR: KAWTHAUNG (KO SONG)

The southernmost tip of Myanmar – known as **Kawthaung** in Burmese, Ko Song in Thai, and Victoria Point when it was a British colony – lies just a few kilometres west of Ranong across the gaping Chan River estuary and is easily reached by longtail boat from Saphan Pla fishing port just outside Ranong town centre when the crossing is open (daily 8am–6pm). Kawthuang can be used as an entry point for travelling in Myanmar (you'll need to arrange an eVisa at least three days in advance; see ⓦevisa.moip.gov.mm), though its position in the far south doesn't make it the most convenient option; most people, however, choose to use this crossing for a visa run. Note that immigration regulations are subject to change and have become stricter recently, so it is advisable to check the present situation before you make the journey (see page 29).

You can either try the visa run independently, as described below, or you can make use of one of the all-inclusive **"visa run" services** advertised all over town, including at *Pon's Place* (B1300 including visa; see page 288). Most visa-run operators use the Saphan Pla route, but they can also book you on the faster, more luxurious **Andaman Club boat** (6 daily 7am–4pm, later boats available for those staying overnight; 20min each way; B1500 including visa), which departs from the Andaman Club pier 5km north of Ranong's town centre and travels to and from the swanky *Andaman Club* hotel (ⓦandamanclub.com), casino and duty-free complex, located on a tiny island in Burmese waters just south of Kawthaung.

**Boats to Kawthaung** leave from the so-called Burmese Pier (go through the PTT petrol station on the main road) in the port of Saphan Pla, 5km southwest of town and served by songthaews from Ranong market (B15) – the blue #6 goes via the bus station but the red #3 is more direct. Thai exit formalities are done at the pier (daily 8am–6pm), after which longtail boats take you to Kawthaung (B300–400 return per boat, or B50 one-way on shared boat – pay at the end; 30min each way) and **Burmese immigration**. Don't get off the boat at the mid-way checkpoint hut. Here you pay US$10 (or B500) for a pass that should entitle you to stay in Kawthaung for a week but forbids travel further than 8km inland. Note that Myanmar time is thirty minutes behind Thailand time, and that to get back into Thailand you'll have to be at the immigration office in Saphan Pla before it closes at 6pm. Thai money is perfectly acceptable in Kawthaung.

There's nothing much to do in **Kawthaung** itself, but it has quite a different vibe to Thai towns. As you arrive at the quay, the market, immigration office and tiny town centre lie before you, while over to your right, about twenty minutes' walk away, you can't miss the hilltop **Pyi Taw Aye Pagoda**, surmounted by a huge reclining Buddha and a ring of smaller ones. Once you've explored the covered market behind the quay and picked your way through the piles of tin trunks and sacks of rice that crowd the surrounding streets, all that remains is to take a coffee break in one of the quayside pastry shops.

★**Sino Mansion** 28/8 Thanon Ruangrat ☎077 985 988, ⓦfacebook.com/baansino; map p.286. Set 50m back from the road behind a small market, this beautifully refurbished, white-tinted mansion is an atmospheric throwback to Ranong's Sino-Portuguese legacy. Peranakan-style floor tiles and Neoclassical columns make for a good introduction to two floors of immaculate en suite rooms; there's also an inviting lounge and restaurant. Breakfast costs B100 extra. **B890**

**Tinidee Hotel** 41/144 Thanon Tha Muang ☎077 835240, ⓦtinideeranong.com; map p.286. The top digs in town are at this welcoming, good-value high-rise hotel, just a 10min walk from the market, which fully lives up to its name ("It's good here"). The large, bright a/c rooms are tastefully furnished and all come with minibars, TVs and bathtubs fed by the local mineral water; there's also a spa and an attractive swimming pool and Jacuzzi. **B1560**

## EATING

Ranong's ethnic diversity ensures a tasty range of eating options, and a stroll up Thanon Ruangrat takes you past Muslim food stalls and Chinese pastry shops as well as a small but typically Thai night market. A bigger night market convenes at dusk just east of the CAT phone office off Thanon Phoem.

**209 Kafe** 209 Thanon Ruangrat ☎089 2125205, ⓦbit. ly/2AWsmm4; map p.286. Housed in a former barbershop,

this narrow yet cosy café and sweet shop uses its original fittings to great choreographic effect. It bristles with young locals and expatriates, who come here for the fresh fruit smoothies (B40), ice creams (from B45) and home-made cakes (B80). Wed–Mon 10am–7pm, closed Tues.

**Pon's Place** 129 Thanon Ruangrat ☎081 597 4549; map p.286. This nice little restaurant, which is decorated with orchids, is the obvious place for farang-style breakfast

(French toast B55) with traditional Thai coffee, free wi-fi and as much local information as you care to gather. It also offers sandwiches and standard Thai dishes, including plenty of seafood and some veggie options. Daily 7.30am–9pm.

# Ko Chang Noi

Not to be confused with the much larger Ko Chang off Thailand's east coast (see page 178), Ranong's **KO CHANG NOI** is a forested little island about 5km offshore, whose car-free, ATM-free, ultra laid-back, roll-your-own vibe more than compensates for the less-than-perfect beaches. The pace of life here is very slow, encouraging long stays, and for the relatively small number of tourists who make it to the island the emphasis is strongly on kicking back and chilling out – bring your own hammock and you'll fit right in. Those in search of livelier scenes head across the water to sister-island Ko Phayam (see page 293). Most islanders make their living from fishing and from the rubber, palm and cashew nut plantations that dominate the flatter patches of the interior. The beaches are connected by tracks through the trees and there are only sporadic, self-generated supplies of electricity for a few hours each evening.

The best of Ko Chang Noi's beaches are on the west coast, and of these the longest, nicest and most popular is **Ao Yai**. The tiny bays to the north and south mostly hold just one set of bungalows each and are good for getting away from it all, though access to Ao Yai is easy enough if you don't mind the hike. About halfway between the west and east coasts, a crossroads bisects Ko Chang Noi's only **village**, a tiny settlement that is home to most of the islanders and holds just a few shops, restaurants and a clinic.

Nearly all the bungalows on Ko Chang Noi **close** down from about late April or early May until mid-to-late October, when the island is subjected to very heavy rain, the beaches fill with flotsam, paths become dangerously slippery and food supplies dwindle with no ice available to keep things fresh. Many bungalow staff relocate to the mainland for this period, so you should phone ahead to check first if you're thinking of heading out here.

## Ao Yai (Long Beach) and Ao Daddaeng

Effectively divided in two by a *khlong* (canal) and the stumps of a long wooden pier, **Ao Yai**, or **Long Beach**, enjoys a fine view of the brooding silhouette of Myanmar's St Matthew's Island, which dominates the western horizon. The 800m-long stretch of Ao Yai that runs north from the *khlong* is the most attractive on the island, nice and wide even at high tide, and especially good for kids. South of the *khlong*, the beach is very narrow at high tide, but when the water goes out you have to walk a longish distance to find any depth. Further south still, around a rocky headland, tiny secluded gold-sand **Ao Daddaeng** (Tadang) is sandwiched between massive boulders and holds just a few bungalows: reach it via a five-minute footpath from behind Tadang Bay Bungalows.

Most longtail boats from Ranong will moor directly in front of your resort of choice on Ao Yay. Alternatively, a narrow concrete road connects central Ao Yai with the mangrove-filled little harbour on the east coast, stretching for a distance of around 3km that can be walked in under an hour. The western end of the road begins beside the island's only temple, **Wat Pah Ko Chang**, whose bot and monks' quarters are partially hidden among the trees beside the beach, with a sign that asks tourists to dress modestly when in the area and not to swim or sunbathe in front of it.

## Northern Ko Chang Noi

**North of Ao Yai**, the crenellated coast reveals a series of tiny bays occupied by just one set of bungalows apiece. The gritty gold-sand beaches are secluded and feel quite remote, accessible only via a track through forest and rubber plantations. Even if you don't want to base yourself up here, you can do an enjoyable **loop** around the northern

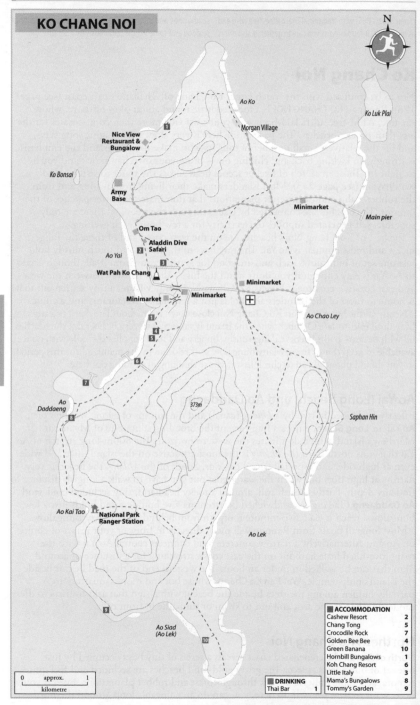

**KO CHANG NOI**

N

*Ao Ko*

*Ko Luk Plai*

Morgan Village

Nice View
Restaurant &
Bungalow

*Ko Bonsai*

Army
Base

Minimarket

*Main pier*

Om Tao

Aladdin Dive
Safari

*Ao Yai*

Wat Pah Ko Chang

Minimarket

Minimarket

Minimarket

*Ao Chao Ley*

4

373m

*Ao
Daddaeng*

*Saphan Hin*

*Ao Kai Tao*

National Park
Ranger Station

*Ao Lek*

*Ao Siad
(Ao Lek)*

0  approx.  1
kilometre

**ACCOMMODATION**
| | |
|---|---|
| Cashew Resort | 2 |
| Chang Tong | 5 |
| Crocodile Rock | 7 |
| Golden Bee Bee | 4 |
| Green Banana | 10 |
| Hornbill Bungalows | 1 |
| Koh Chang Resort | 6 |
| Little Italy | 3 |
| Mama's Bungalows | 8 |
| Tommy's Garden | 9 |

**DRINKING**
| | |
|---|---|
| Thai Bar | 1 |

## ACTIVITIES ON KO CHANG NOI

Going for walks (and not minding getting lost) is the most popular activity on this large, traffic-free island, but several resorts, including *Koh Chang Resort*, run **fishing, snorkelling and camping trips** to Ko Kham, which is famed for its beautiful beaches and reefs, and to Ko Phayam. For **divers**, Ko Chang Noi is particularly well placed for the sites in the Mergui Archipelago across the border in Myanmar, while the top local dive sites in Thailand are Ko Surin, Ko Bon, Ko Tachai, Ko Similan and Richelieu Rock.

**Aladdin Dive Safari** Cashew Resort, Ao Yai, and at the Islands Pier in Saphan Pla ☎ 087 278 6908, ⓦ aladdindivesafari.com. This German–Dutch-run dive shop teaches PADI diving courses and runs a huge selection of live-aboards that take in all the local dive sites (from B14,900 for three days excluding equipment and national park fees).

**Om Tao** North of Cashew Resort, Ao Yai ☎ 085 470 9312, ⓦ omtao.net. Morning yoga classes and t'ai chi in season.

bays in well under three hours from Ao Yai. Alternatively, you could make use of the Ranong boats, which charge about B50 for any hop up or down the west coast.

Following **the track** inland from just north of Om Tao, a 10min walk north brings you to the top of the first of several hills and the barbed-wire perimeters of a military camp, established here to monitor activity along the (maritime) Thai–Myanmar border. A further 10min walk will bring you to the aptly named *Nice View* restaurant and bungalows: perched atop an outcrop with glorious panoramas over the unfolding little bays and islets beyond, this is a perfect spot to break for lunch or a drink. It's another twenty minutes to *Sea Eagle* (you need to go via the beach at *Hornbill* before returning inland), the last of the northern bay bungalows, beyond which a 10min walk up and over the next hill takes you to the edge of the northeast-facing Morgan fishing village, an unprepossessing place complete with incongruous Christian church. This is **Ao Ko**, which is linked by road to the east coast's rainy-season pier, and also to Ao Yai.

## Southern Ko Chang Noi

**Ao Siad**, at the southern end of the island, is even more isolated than the north coast and makes a good focus for a day-walk, or a source of extra secluded accommodation options. It's sometimes known as **Ao Lek**, though the real **Ao Lek** is the mangrove-lined bay fifteen minutes' walk to the northeast, on the other coast. From Ao Daddaeng, a clear path takes you south, in about an hour, to **Ao Kai Tao**, a pretty beach and site of the national park ranger station. From here, the route then follows an indistinct path across the saddle between two hills and along a creek bed to reach east-coast Ao Lek (this takes another hour), after which it's fifteen minutes south to Ao Siad. Retracing your steps to Ao Lek to start with, it's then about 5km (2hr) to the crossroads in the village.

### ARRIVAL AND INFORMATION                                          KO CHANG NOI

*Cashew Resort* (see page 292) can arrange bus tickets.

**BY BOAT**

**To/from Ranong** From early November through to late April, there are two guaranteed daily boat departures to Ko Chang Noi from Saphan Pla's Islands Pier (9.30am & 2pm; 1hr 30min; B200), which stop at most resorts along the west coast. Note that these boat services are sometimes cancelled in the rainy season. Ask your resort or at *Pon's Place* in Ranong (see page 288) for the latest travel schedules.

**To/from Ko Phayam** The only option is to hop onto one of the speedboats that travel from Ranong to Ko Phayam, which stop at Ko Chang Noi's east coast pier on demand. Ask your resort to call ahead and book you a seat, which will cost between B270 and B350. If arriving from Ko Phayam, you should be able to arrange a pick-up from the pier through your resort; otherwise, it's B100 on a motorcycle taxi or a simple 3km walk to Ao Yai. A charter between the two islands costs about B2000 per boat.

**Tourist information** For general information on the island see ⓦ kohchang-ranong.com.

## ACCOMMODATION AND EATING

Most of the bungalows on Ko Chang Noi are simple, old-school wooden-plank or woven bamboo constructions with mosquito nets on the beds; you shouldn't necessarily expect flush toilets (buckets and dippers are provided), curtains or a door on your bathroom. Though the bungalow resorts nearly all have their own generators (which usually only operate between 6 and 10pm, together with wi-fi), some stick to candles and paraffin lamps in the bungalows so it's best to bring a torch; very few bungalows have fans. There are no stand-alone restaurants, and as the distances between resorts are long and there's no easy transport, most visitors dine at their own resort's restaurant.

### AO YAI (LONG BEACH)

**Cashew Resort** ☎ 081 4584530 or ☎ 081 485 6002, ✉ cashew_resort@hotmail.com; map p.290. The longest-running accommodation on the island, and also the largest, *Cashew* feels like a tiny village, with its forty en-suite bungalows spread among the cashew trees along 700m of prime beachfront, and returnees personalizing their bungalows like mini homes. All the wood or brick bungalows enjoy both a sea view and some privacy, and some have big glass windows. The resort offers the most facilities on the island, including foreign exchange, Visa and MasterCard capability, transport bookings, massage and books to borrow. Its restaurant bakes bread and serves Thai and a few German dishes. **B500**

**Chang Tong** ☎ 089 875 3353, ✉ aoy_changthong@hotmail.com; map p.290. The cheapest wood and bamboo bungalows at this friendly spot are very basic, though they're all en suite and are well spaced beneath the shoreside trees; pay a bit more for newer, better appointed ones on the beachfront. **B350**

**★ Crocodile Rock** ☎ 081 370 1434 or ☎ 087 040 8087, ⓦ facebook.com/CrocodileRockBungalows; map p.290. In a shady, secluded, elevated position at the start of Ao Yai's southern headland, with great views of the whole bay, on which the friendly owners have capitalized, with attractive decks at the restaurant and picture windows in some of the bathrooms. Bungalows have a touch more style than the Ko Chang Noi average, though only the larger ones and the restaurant have electricity at night. The restaurant bakes its own bread, cookies and banana muffins, and serves fresh juices and espresso coffee. Computer-based internet access. **B400**

**Golden Bee Bee** On the middle section of Ao Yai, just after the bridge over the khlong ☎ 085 795 3955, ⓦ bit.ly/GoldenBeeBungalow; map p.290. Simple family-run collection of wooden en-suite bungalows, set between the forest and the sea. The restaurant serves good portions of the usual Thai curries and fish dishes. Those on a small budget may also camp out on the beach (B50 per pitch). Wi-fi only available in the restaurant and in the evenings. **B300**

**Koh Chang Resort** ☎ 081 896 1839, ⓦ kohchangandaman.net; map p.290. Occupying a fabulous spot high on the rocks right over the water, the best of the en-suite wooden bungalows here have fine sea views from their balconies; the cheaper bamboo ones are set further back beside the path. Interiors are very rudimentary but the decks are huge, and there's also a large, more luxurious family bungalow, and two concrete bungalows with fans (between B1500/2000). You can swim below the rocks at low tide, or the more reliable beach is just a couple of minutes' scramble to south or north. They offer fishing boat tours, and there's the very chilled, fairy-lit *Air Bar*. They have wi-fi and electricity, which run from 8am to midnight. **B200**

**Little Italy** ☎ 084 851 2760, ✉ daniel060863@yahoo. it; map p.290. This tiny Italian–Thai-run outfit has just three attractive bungalows set in a shady, secluded garden of paperbark trees 100m inland from *Cashew Resort*. The two double-storey bungalows have exceptionally clean, smartly tiled papaya-coloured bathrooms downstairs and Thai-style bamboo-walled sleeping quarters upstairs, with varnished wood floors and big decks. The garden restaurant serves deliciously authentic pastas. **B350**

### AO DADDAENG

**★ Mama's Bungalows** 5min walk south over the headland from Ao Yai, on Ao Daddaeng ☎ 087 276 7784, ⓦ bit.ly/MamasBungalows; map p.290. The fourteen attractive, well-maintained wooden and bamboo bungalows at this congenial spot have colourfully decorated bathrooms and come in several sizes, some of them with big decks. They're built in a pretty flower garden staggered up the hillside; several are on the beach and the uppermost ones overlook the bay from the edge of a rubber plantation. The restaurant serves espresso coffee and generous portions of carefully prepared food, including tasty *tzatziki* and many German specialities. Very popular, so book ahead. No wi-fi. **B250**

### NORTHERN BAYS

**Hornbill Bungalows** North around two headlands from Ao Yai, about a 35min walk ☎ 089 590 6008, ✉ 66_hornbill@hotmail.com; map p.290. Set among the trees fronting their own little gold-sand bay, the unobtrusive en-suite bungalows here are constructed to different designs, some of them extremely comfortable, and all enjoy sea views. The food here has a good reputation and the owner is very welcoming. It lives up to its name, as majestic black-and-white hornbills are a common sight. Internet access, kayaks and boat trips on offer. **B350**

### SOUTHERN BAYS

**Green Banana** On the southern end of Ao Siad ☎ 081 728 5147; map p.290. A pirate-themed, ultra-basic complex of driftwood bamboo and thatch pavilions and bungalows run by Thai Rastafarians in a secluded corner of Ao Siad. Rooms consist of mattresses on the floor and mosquito nets, with simple shared toilets. Located right on an attractive, long stretch of beach. No internet connection. **B300**

**Tommy's Garden** On the western corner of Ao Siad ☎ 093 710 8966, ⓦ facebook.com/Tommys

gardenbungalow; map p.290. Perched on a forested slope overlooking the secluded bay at the western end of Ao Siad, these rustic hillside bungalows are as basic as they can be (including squat toilets), but enjoy beautiful sunset views over a secluded bay with decent swimming. For a bit more (B450), the beach front bungalows are no less spartan but more spacious. **B300**

## DRINKING

**Thai Bar** In the middle section of Ao Yai, between the bridge over the khlong and Golden Bee ☎ 093 151 2833; map p.290. A local attempt to make Ao Yai a little less sleepy, Thai Bar attracts a crowd thanks to its jolly driftwood

and bamboo bar set right on the beach and shaded by low trees. Come for beers and cocktails (B80), occasional free fish barbecues, table football and live music. Daily 3pm until late.

# Ko Phayam

Like it or not, in recent years the diminutive kangaroo-shaped island of **KO PHAYAM** has not only surfaced on the tourist radar, but it's also become a hit with Thai tourists, who now come in droves to enjoy its first Maldives-style (and price) five-star resort, *Blue Sky*. Things are set to change even more drastically: at the time of writing, unlimited electric supply cables from the mainland were about to be connected, meaning that a breath of modernity threatens to overturn the island's chilled and low-key reputation. Regardless, Ko Phayam still offers fine white-sand beaches and coral reefs, and is home to around five hundred people, most of whom either make their living from prawn, squid and crab fishing, or from growing cashew nuts, *sator* beans, coconut palms and rubber trees.

Most islanders live in Ko Phayam's only **village**, tucked behind the pier on the northeast coast, which connects to other corners of the island via a network of concrete roads and a few rutted tracks. The bays either side of the village have a couple of nice places to stay, but the main beaches and accommodation centres can be found on the west coast, at **Ao Yai** and **Ao Kao Kwai**. A motorbike taxi service covers all routes, but no journey is very long as the island measures just 10km by 5km at its widest point.

Ko Phayam has a much livelier, younger and more developed feel than neighbouring Ko Chang Noi (see page 289), underlined by a low-key beach-bar scene – all hand-painted signs and driftwood sculptures – and the presence of a significant number of foreigners who choose to spend six or more months here every year. Some expats even take up the **rainy-season** challenge, staying on through the downpours and rough seas that lash the island from June to October, but a number of bungalows close down during this time and staff take refuge in Ranong. It's important to mention that, even though they are currently lined with rows of bungalows and small resorts, both Ao Yai and Ao Kao Kwai have been reclaimed by the Thai government as forest reserves. At present, nobody really knows what this means for the future of tourism on Ko Phayam. For the moment, the place is definitely thriving – for better or for worse.

## The village and around

The tiny cluster of homes and shops that constitute Ko Phayam's only **village** is connected to the pier via a strip lined with tourist facilities and boat ticket stalls. There are a few little general stores here, plus several restaurants and a **clinic**. A little way north up the shoreline stands the island **temple**, with its circular *viharn* resting on a huge concrete lotus flower at the end of its own pier.

## Ao Yai

Ko Phayam's main beach is the 3km-long **AO YAI** on the southwest coast, a wide and handsome sweep of powdery white sand backed by an unbroken line of casuarina trees, which curves quite deeply at its northern and southern ends into rocky outcrops that offer some snorkelling possibilities. The shore is pounded by decent waves that are fun for boogie-boarding and pretty safe; the sunsets are quite spectacular too. For the moment Ao Yai's bungalow operations are mostly widely spaced along the shoreline, and much of the forest behind the beach is still intact. You're more than likely to see – and hear – some of the resident black-and-white hornbills at dawn and dusk, along with many white-bellied sea eagles, and sightings of crab-eating macaques are also common.

## Ao Kao Kwai and around

The northwest coast is scalloped into **AO KAO KWAI**, a name that's pronounced locally as **Ao Kao Fai** and translates as **Buffalo Horn Bay**; from the cliffside midway along the bay you can see how the two halves of the beach curve out into buffalo-like horns. The southern half of Ao Kao Kwai is subject to both very low and very high tides, which makes it unreliable

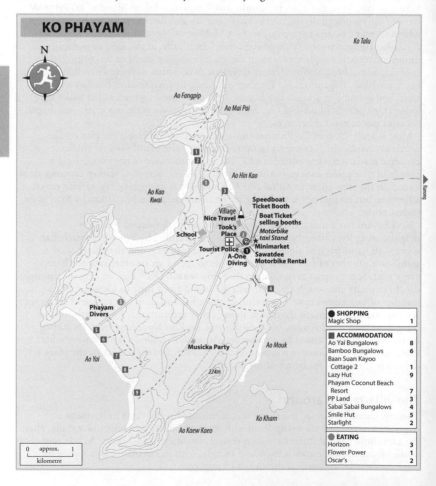

## ACTIVITIES ON KO PHAYAM

Most bungalows can arrange **fishing** and **snorkelling** day-trips, while *Oscar's* in the village takes people **wakeboarding** in the bay. The **dive companies** teach PADI courses and run live-aboards to Ko Surin, Richelieu Rock, Ko Tachai, Ko Bon and Ko Similan (from about B16,000 for three days, plus B600 per day for equipment rental).

**A-One Diving** In the village ☎ 081 891 5510, ⓦ a-one-diving.com. Also does live-aboards to Burma Banks and the Mergui archipelago just across the Burmese border.

**Phayam Divers** Phayam Lodge, Ao Yai ☎ 095 665 3915, ⓦ phayamlodge.com. One-day trips to Ko Surin or Richelieu Rock for B4900 (plus equipment rental and national park fee).

for swimming, but the northern stretch is exceptionally pretty, secluded between outcrops with decent swimming at any tide, and none of the big waves that characterize Ao Yai. It is also the best spot on the island to see the famed glowing-pink sunsets.

From the northern end of Ao Kao Kwai, a 30min walk brings you to the pretty little sandy beach at **Ao Fangpip** (also spelt Ao Kwang Pib), which is the best spot on the island for snorkelling. There's also some snorkellable reef at **Ao Hin Kao** on the northeast coast.

### ARRIVAL AND DEPARTURE
KO PHAYAM

**Took's Place**, north of the pier-head in the village (☎ 093 713 8380), sells bus, train, airline and boat tickets, including direct transfers to Ko Pha Ngan (see page 254), Ko Samui (see page 233) and Ko Tao (see page 263). Nearby **Oscar's** (☎ 084 842 5070; see below) also sells transport tickets and charters speedboats to other islands. Most bungalows sell boat tickets, and some sell bus tickets, too.

#### BY BOAT
Motorbikes meet incoming boats at the main pier on the northwest coast.

**To/from Ranong** From November to May there are two daily slow boats to Ko Phayam from the Taikak pier, about

2km south of Saphan Pla (see page 285), and 5km south of Ranong town centre (10am & 3pm, returning from the island at 11.30am & 1.30pm; 2hr; B200). There are also two express boats (9am & 1pm; 1hr 30m; B250), as well as up to ten speedboat services a day (45min; B350). During the rainy season, services are reduced; *Pon's Place* in Ranong (see page 288) keeps the latest timetables.

**To/from Ko Chang Noi** The only way of travelling between Ko Phayam and Ko Chang Noi is by taking one of the speed boats to Ranong (B350 – the full price of a one-way ticket), which will stop on demand at Ko Chang Noi's east coast pier (see page 291 for arrival details). A charter between the two islands costs about B2000 per boat.

### GETTING AROUND

Many travellers heading into the village from one of the beaches opt to walk at least one way: from Ao Yai's *Smile Hut* it's an enjoyable 7km stroll along the narrow concrete road that cuts through the cashew plantations. It takes less than an hour to walk from southern Ao Kao Kwai to the village.

**Motorbike taxis** Motorbike taxis can be booked directly at the pier; a ride between the village and the beaches

costs about B100 depending on distance (note that there are no cars on the island).

**Motorbike rental** You can rent your own motorbike for about B250 through resorts on the beaches and outlets in the village next to the pier, such as the recommended Sawatdee Motorbike Rental (☎ 083 187 7887, ✉ supachai338@hotmail.com).

**Bike rental** Ask at your resort or in the village.

### INFORMATION

**Took's Place** ☎ 093 713 8380, daily 8.30am–7pm, and **Starlight** ☎ 098 013 5301, daily 8.30am–6pm. Both information centres are located in the village, change money and offer Visa cash advances (charging 4 percent), as there are no ATMs on the island. They can also arrange

boat hire and fishing tours, book onward flights, bus and train tickets.

**Oscar's Bar** In the village ☎ 084 842 5070. A good source of island information and tickets; also changes money at good rates.

### ACCOMMODATION

Most bungalows only provide electricity from around 6 to 11pm and the cheapest rooms often don't have a fan. Unless

otherwise stated, all bungalows open year-round, and offer worthwhile discounts in low season.

## THE VILLAGE AREA

Most people choose to stay at the west-coast beach centres, but there are a couple of nice little hideaways within easy reach of the village and its facilities.

**PP Land** ☎081 678 4310, ⓦppland-heavenbeach. com; map p.294. Fronting a small beach about a 10min walk north from the village, this Belgian–Thai place, with an organic garden, is a cut above most places to stay on the island. Its tasteful, green-painted shaggy thatched bungalows line the beach and boast pretty furnishings, polished wood floors inside and out, nice bathrooms, and big comfy decks. They don't accept children under 15 so as to maintain the quiet atmosphere – children are more than welcome at their sister property *Heaven Beach Arts Resort*, in Ao Kao Kwai. There's an attractive swimming pool, plus 24-hour electricity. B900

**Sabai Sabai Bungalows** 5min walk south of the pier ☎087 895 4653, ⓦsabai-bungalows.com; map p.294. Once a feel-good backpacker dig, *Sabai Sabai* still dominates the secluded little beach, but has upgraded facilities and prices to keep up with the island's development. The sea-breeze-catching wooden bungalows, some with 24hr electricity, come in en-suite (B800) and shared bathroom varieties. There's also a gracious lounge with wi-fi, sunset yoga sessions (B200), and occasional movie-nights. B500

## AO YAI

**Ao Yai Bungalows** ☎083 389 8688 or ☎084 061 3283, ⓦaowyaibungalows.com; map p.294. Established by a French–Thai couple, this was the first set of bungalows on the island and remains one of the most popular, although prices have gone up considerably. The 26 good-quality en-suite bungalows are dotted around an extensive garden of flowers, fruit trees and palms and come in various styles: the cheapest wooden or thatched bamboo affairs come with mosquito nets but no fans, while the most expensive are built with concrete and have hot showers. Snorkels and kayaks available to rent. B800

**Bamboo Bungalows** Southern end of Ao Yai ☎077 820012, ⓦbamboo-bungalows.com; map p.294. Ao Yai's liveliest accommodation is Israeli–Thai managed and very traveller-savvy, offering snorkels, kayaks, surf- and boogie-boards, currency exchange and an internet connection. Its en-suite bungalows are set under the trees in a well-tended flower garden and range from luxuriously large chalets with pretty furnishings to shell-studded concrete bungalows and a choice of bamboo and wood huts with mosquito nets, all with fan. Electricity is 24hr in high season, but with more limited in low season. B550

★ **Lazy Hut** Southern end of Ao Yai ☎093 668 7619, ⓦfacebook.com/lazyhutthailandkohphayam; map p.294. The most attractive bungalows on Ao Yai are sheltered by a row of tall trees and fronted by inviting sunbeds that spill onto the beachfront. Completely built from dark bamboo, the bungalows feature plush beds with mosquito nets, large en-suite bathrooms and breezy verandas. Wi-fi is available at the restaurant, which serves Thai and international cuisines. B500

**Phayam Coconut Beach Resort** Central Ao Yai ☎089 920 8145; map p.294. Occupying a great spot in the centre of the bay and run by a Ko Phayam family, the 27 good-value bungalows here are of a high standard, each set in its own tiny garden. Accommodation ranges from small bamboo en-suite huts through larger wood or bamboo versions to big concrete or clapboard air-conditioned bungalows at the top end (up to B2500). Closed during the worst of the rainy season. B500

**Smile Hut** Northern side of Ao Yai ☎081 515 0856, ⓦsmilehutthai.com; map p.294. Like *Bamboo*, this is a very popular choice with travellers. The split-bamboo and wooden huts with mosquito nets are simple but en suite and are spread among the shorefront trees, with the slightly cheaper versions set one row behind. Wi-fi is available only in the evening, and they have kayaks. B500

## AO KAO KWAI

**Baan Suan Kayoo Cottage 2** Northern end of Ao Kao Kwai ☎063 970 8794, ⓦbit.ly/BaanSuanKayoo; map p.294. This cluster of simple en-suite bungalows on stilts is a good budget option, set on a shady forest slope and next to a small stream. It's a 1min walk from the northernmost end of the beach, where there's a restaurant with wi-fi and strategically positioned loungers. B300

★ **Starlight** Northern end of Ao Kao Kwai ☎081 978 5301, ⓦfacebook.com/starlightresortkophayam; map p.294. Dominating a stretch of beach with arguably the best sunset views in Ao Kao Kwai, the American-run *Starlight* offers a series of attractive beachfront bungalows (B1500) and cheaper, smaller rooms in a concrete block set further back from the sea. There's a good-sized beach-facing swimming pool, and a restaurant that, besides the obvious Western breakfast sets and Thai mains, is the only sushi bar on the island. B800

## EATING

## THE VILLAGE

**Oscar's** Just north of the pier ☎084 842 5070; map p.294. Offers breakfasts, including home-baked bread, Thai standards such as *tom yam kung* (B90), pizzas, Indian curries, shepherd's pie (B190) and other English favourites, but is most famous for its partially open-air bar, which is a fun, relaxed focal point of the expat social scene. Daily 7am–late.

## AO YAI

**Horizon** Just inland on the Ao Yai road; map p.294.

Congenial outdoor restaurant for very tasty Thai food, all of it offered vegetarian, with the option of adding meat: a toothsome *matsaman* curry with carrot, pumpkin and potatoes costs B70; add chicken for B20. Also does a few Western main courses, sandwiches, breakfasts, Thai desserts, plus teas, juices and lassis. Nov–May daily 7/8am–8/9pm; June–Oct daily 7/8am–sunset (closed when it rains).

### AO KAO KWAI
★ **Flower Power** On the northern end of Ao Kao Kwai road ☎ 096 430 4260, ⓦ facebook.com/ flowerpowerphayam; map p.294. Besides a clutch of good-value bungalows, this Italian-run jungle resort has a spacious restaurant serving authentic Italian and Burmese food. It's one of the few vegan-friendly eateries on the island, and the menu heavily relies on their own organic produce, including tomatoes, courgettes and basil. Try the delicious thin-crust pizzas (from B170), pastas (from B100) and large-sized bruschettas (from B70). Wash them all down with the house's home-made *limoncello*, whisky and chocolate creams. Open all year round. Daily 8am–9pm.

### DRINKING

There's not a massive scene Ko Phayam, although several laid-back little beach-bars, including the long-running *Rasta Baby* on Ao Yai and the *Hippie Bar* on Ao Kao Kwai, put on fire shows and occasional parties. On Saturdays, the *Musicka Parties* bring people together in a forest clearing more or less halfway along the paved path to Ao Yai.

### SHOPPING

### THE VILLAGE
**Magic Shop** Just opposite Took's Place on the village main road ☎ 081 678 4310; map p.294. A good selection of locally produced soap bars, skincare products, jewellery and beads, plus a bakery that sells the famed local nuts. Daily 7am–6pm.

**4**

# Khuraburi and around

The small town of **KHURABURI**, 110km south of Ranong on Highway 4, is the main departure point for the magnificent national park island chain of Ko Surin. Much closer to Khuraburi are the islands of **Ko Ra** and **Ko Phra Thong**, which offer empty beaches and decent snorkelling and bird-watching, or there's the chance to participate in typical village life at **homestays** in mainland coastal communities.

Khuraburi's commercial heart is a 500m strip of shops and businesses either side of Highway 4. Most travellers use the town just as a staging post en route to or from the Surin islands: the main pier for boats to the islands is just 7.5km away, and Khuraburi's tour agents sell boat tickets and offer transport to the pier. Though lacking in famous attractions, the local area is nonetheless scenic, both offshore and inland: with an afternoon or more to spare, you could either rent a motorbike, mountain bike or kayak to explore it independently, or charter a motorbike taxi or longtail boat.

## Ko Ra

Hilly, forested **Ko Ra** (measuring about 10km north to south and 3km across) sits just off Khuraburi pier's mangrove-lined estuary and is graced with intact rainforest full of towering trees, hornbills and wild, empty beaches. The island is home to some two dozen *chao ley* people (see page 300), but at the time of writing, there was no accommodation available, and visiting was only possible by chartering boats for day-trips (about B1500).

## Ko Phra Thong

Immediately to the south of Ko Ra, just 1km or so off the Khuraburi coast, **Ko Phra Thong** (Golden Buddha Island) also has some lovely beaches, the nicest of which, on the west coast, is 10km long and blessed with fine gold sand. This is the site of the *Horizon Beach Bungalows* and of the British-run Blue Guru Dive Centre (☎ 080 144

## ANDAMAN DISCOVERIES HOMESTAY PROGRAMME

Khuraburi is the headquarters of the community-based tourism initiative Andaman Discoveries (☏087 917 7165, ⊛andamandiscoveries.com), which runs a recommended **day-trip and homestay programme** in several local villages, as well as interesting trips to Ko Surin (see page 299). It was established after the tsunami to help the area's many devastated fishing communities get back on their feet and has since developed a range of stimulating one- to seven-day packages (from B1600 per person per day) featuring all sorts of village jobs and activities, from soap-making and batik design to cashew nut-farming and roof-thatching. The office is just east off the highway (south of the bus station), up the soi beside the police box, across from the post office.

0551, ⊛blue-guru.org). The resort offers kayaking, trekking and yoga, while Blue Guru runs all manner of snorkelling tours, PADI courses, dive trips and live-aboards to Ko Tachai, Ko Surin, Richelieu Rock and into Myanmar. Blue Guru's owners also organize longtail tours of the island's mangroves and maintain a website to promote the island, ⊛kohphrathong.com, which includes information about homestays and budget bungalows.

### ARRIVAL AND DEPARTURE
### KHURABURI AND AROUND

#### KHURABURI
**By bus** Services between Phuket and Ranong and Phuket and Chumpon stop at the bus station, which is located just off the east side of Highway 4 in the centre of town. Note that some of the long-distance through buses only stop on the highway.
Destinations: Chumpon (5 daily; 3hr 20min); Khao Lak (10 daily; 1hr 45min); Phuket (10 daily via Khao Lak; 3hr 30min); Ranong (10 daily; 3hr); Takua Pa (10 daily; 1hr).

#### KO RA
**By boat** A longtail transfer from the pier at Khuraburi costs B1000 (on demamd; 20min).

#### KO PHRA THONG
**By boat** A longtail transfer to your resort from the pier at Khuraburi (the only way to get to Ko Phra Thong) costs B1800 (90min) and B1700 (90min; must be pre-booked) with Blue Guru Dive Centre.

### GETTING AROUND

#### KHURABURI
**Bike and motorbike rental** Tom & Am Tour, which has their office on the west side of the main road in the town centre and maintains a desk located in the bus station in high season (☏086 272 0588, ✉tom_am01@hotmail.com, ⊛bit.ly/2Dd7SHc), rents a mix of bicycles, motorbikes and cars. *Boon Piya Resort* (see below) also rents motorbikes.

### ACCOMMODATION

#### KHURABURI
**Boon Piya Resort** 100m north of the bus station, on the same side of the main road ☏076 491 969. Well-appointed, if rather tightly packed, motel-style concrete bungalows dotted around a tree-strewn courtyard, situated just back off the road. All have a/c and powerful hot showers; they're the usual choice of sales reps and NGOs. B650
**Tararin Resort** On the south bank of the river towards the northern end of town, about 200m north of the bus station ☏061 183 8101. This rustic-style place located next to the river is home to a string of fifteen en-suite bungalows, the best of which are perched on stilts and sit in the river, opening onto small private balconies. The row of shabbier concrete rooms across the courtyard is certainly less attractive, but they are still pretty good value for the price. Fan B300, a/c B350

#### KO PHRA THONG
**Golden Buddha Beach Resort** ☏081 892 2208, ⊛goldenbuddharesort.com. Tasteful complex of 25 individually decorated wooden Thai-style homes of varying price, sleeping two to six, with a spa and clubhouse. It feels like you have the island and beach to yourself here, and this tranquillity is why most choose Ko Phra Thong over other islands. Prices are for two (including breakfast) and drop significantly in low season (late Oct–mid-Dec). Closed May–Oct. B2700

**EATING AND DRINKING**

**KHURABURI**

The morning market (daily from 5am) just across from *Boon Piya* is the place to stock up on food for the Surin islands.

**Kosak Seafood** Along Highway 4 in the central part of town, across the road from Tararin Resort ☎081 079 9442. Buzzy, very popular place to tuck into excellent seafood dishes along the likes of *pla nueng manaw* (steamed fish served with spicy lime sauce, B300) or simpler Thai staples such as fried noodles and rice (B60). Daily 10.30am–10pm.

# Ko Surin

Mu Ko Surin National Park, about 60km offshore • Nov–April • B500 entry fee, B300 child, valid for 5 days • ⓦ dnp.go.th

Unusually shallow reefs, a palette of awesomely clear turquoise waters and dazzling white sands, and dense forests of lofty dipterocarps combine to make the islands of **Ko Surin** one of the most popular destinations in south Thailand. However, Ko Surin's most famous feature, its spectacular and diverse coral lying in fields just below the surface at the perfect depth for snorkelling, was severely bleached by a sudden rise in sea temperature in early 2010. Four of the most popular reefs are still closed to visitors, though half a dozen other sites that were less severely affected by the bleaching remain open; the national park is still a good spot for snorkellers, with plenty of fish to see, but it will take many years for the reefs to recover.

Ko Surin is very much an outdoors experience, with the bulk of accommodation in national park tents, no commerce on the islands at all, and twice-daily snorkelling the main activity. Several tour operators run snorkelling day-trips from Khuraburi, and there are diving trips too, most of which also take in nearby Richelieu Rock, considered to be Thailand's top dive site (see page 335), but independent travel is also recommended. Because the islands are so far out at sea, Ko Surin is closed to visitors from roughly May to October, when monsoon weather renders the 60km trip a potentially suicidal undertaking.

## Surin Nua and Surin Tai

The most easily explored of the reefs are those off the two main islands in the group, Ko Surin Nua (north) and Ko Surin Tai (south), which are separated only by a narrow channel. **Surin Nua**, slightly the larger at about 5km across, holds the national park headquarters, visitor centre and park accommodation.

Across the channel, **Surin Tai** is the long-established home of a community of **Moken** *chao ley* (see page 300), who are no longer allowed to fish in national park waters but make their living mostly as longtail boatmen for snorkellers staying on Surin Nua. Their recent history has been an unhappy one: not only were their settlements destroyed in the 2004 tsunami, but the aid and outside intervention that followed has changed the community forever, amalgamating two villages, building new homes too close together and introducing various modern-day vices; on top of that, tourist numbers are down since the coral bleaching in 2010. In **Ao Bon** village is a visitor centre built by Bangkok's Chulalongkorn University with English display boards, where you can hire a Moken guide to lead you on a nature trail around the village; don't go just in your swimwear, but take a sarong for modesty's sake. You can also make a positive contribution by buying one of the woven pandanus-leaf souvenirs or wooden model boats the villagers make; donations of toothpaste and clothes would also be appreciated. One of the Moken traditions that does persist is the new year celebration that's held every April, during Songkhran, when *chao ley* from nearby islands (including those in Burmese waters) congregate here and, among other rites, release several hundred turtles into the sea, a symbol of longevity.

## THE CHAO LEY: MOKEN AND URAK LAWOY

Sometimes called sea gypsies, the **chao ley** or *chao nam* ("people of the sea" or "water people") have been living off the seas around the west coast of the Malay peninsula for hundreds of years. Some still pursue a traditional nomadic existence, living in self-contained houseboats known as **kabang**, but many have now made permanent homes in Andaman coast settlements in Thailand, Myanmar and Malaysia. Dark-skinned and sometimes with an auburn tinge to their hair, the *chao ley* of the Andaman Sea are thought to number around five thousand, divided into five groups, with distinct lifestyles and dialects.

Of the different groups, the **Urak Lawoy**, who have settled on the islands of Ko Lanta, Ko Jum, Ko Phi Phi, Phuket and Ko Lipe, are the most integrated into Thai society. They came north to Thailand from Malaysia around two hundred years ago (having possibly migrated from the Nicobar Islands in the Indian Ocean some two centuries prior) and are known as *Thai Mai*, or "New Thai". Thailand's Urak Lawoy have been recognized as Thai citizens since the 1960s, when the late Queen Mother granted them five family names, thereby enabling them to possess ID cards and go to school. Many work on coconut plantations or as fishermen, while others continue in the more traditional *chao ley* **occupations** of hunting for pearls and seashells on the ocean floor, attaching stones to their waists to dive to depths of 60m with only an air-hose connecting them to the surface; sometimes they fish in this way too, taking down enormous nets into which they herd the fish as they walk along the sea bed. Their agility and courage make them good bird's-nesters as well (see page 370).

The **Moken** of Thailand's Ko Surin islands and Myanmar's Mergui archipelago probably came originally from Myanmar and are the most traditional of the *chao ley* communities. Some still lead remote, itinerant lives, and most are unregistered as Thai citizens, owning no land or property, but dependent on fresh water and beaches to collect shells and sea slugs to sell to Thai traders. They have extensive knowledge of the plants that grow in the remaining jungles on Thailand's west-coast islands, using eighty different species for food alone, and thirty for medicinal purposes.

The *chao ley* are **animists**, with a strong connection both to the natural spirits of island and sea and to their own ancestral spirits. On some beaches they set up totem poles as a contact point between the spirits, their ancestors and their shaman. The sea gypsies have a rich **musical heritage** too. The Moken do not use any instruments as such, making do with found objects for percussion; the Urak Lawoy, on the other hand, due to their closer proximity to the Thai and Malay cultures, are excellent violin- and drum-players. During community entertainments, such as the Urak Lawoy's twice-yearly full moon **festivals** on Ko Lanta (see page 380), the male musicians form a semicircle around the old women, who dance and sing about the sea, the jungle and their families.

**Building a new boat** is the ultimate expression of what it is to be a *chao ley*, and tradition holds that every newly married couple has a *kabang* built for them. But the complex art of constructing a seaworthy home from a single tree trunk, and the way of life it represents, is disappearing. In Thailand, where **assimilation** is actively promoted by the government, the truly nomadic flotillas have become increasingly marginalized, and the number of undeveloped islands they can visit unhindered gets smaller year by year. The 2004 tsunami further threatened their cultural integrity: when the waves destroyed the Moken's boats and homes on Ko Surin, they were obliged to take refuge on the mainland, where some were encouraged by missionaries to convert from their animist religion. Though the Moken have since returned to the Surin islands, inappropriate donations and the merging of two villages have exacerbated family rivalries and caused divisions that may prove lethal to their traditional way of life.

## ARRIVAL AND GETTING AROUND

**By boat** There are no public boats to Ko Surin, but if you want to stay on the islands, it's perfectly possible to come over on one of the tour boats from Khuraburi and return on another day.

**By longtail** Once on the islands, there's an efficient system of boat hire: Moken longtails depart twice a day from the national park campsites to the different reefs and Ao Bon village and charge around B150/person for half-day (snorkel sets cost an extra B80/day). If you want a little more flexibility, you can also charter your own longtail boat (maximum fifteen people) for the price of B1500/B3000 per half-day/day.

## TOURS

Most visitors either do **snorkelling day-trips** to the islands from Khuraburi or opt for **dive trips** or live-aboards out of Ko Phra Thong, Khao Lak, Phuket, Ranong, Ko Chang Noi or Ko Phayam. During the season, speedboat snorkelling trips to Ko Surin depart most days from Khuraburi pier, 7.5km northwest of Khuraburi town; big, slow, wooden boats (2–3hr; B1300 return) only run at weekends and on national holidays for large groups of Thai tourists.

**Andaman Discoveries** Khuraburi (see page 297) @ andamandiscoveries.com. Four-day trips, with two nights on Ko Surin, focusing on learning about Moken life, including guided forest, village and snorkelling tours and cooking classes (B14,000).

**Blue Guru Dive Centre** Ko Phra Thong (see page 297) @ surinislands.com. Upmarket day-trips on a dive cruiser or speedboat, including "gourmet lunch", for snorkelling (from B3300 including national park fee); transfers from Khuraburi hotels included. Also offers multi-day live-aboard trips to Surin from Khao Lak (4D/4N from B22500 plus B1800 for national park fees).

**Boon Piya Resort** Khuraburi (see page 297). Sells boat tickets and packages, including discounts on national park bungalows on weekdays.

**Tom & Am Tour** Office on the west side of the main road in Khuraburi town centre, but they also maintain a desk in the bus station in high season ☎ 086 272 0588, ✉ tom_am01@yahoo.co.th. Speedboats to Ko Surin (1hr 15min–2hr), departing the pier at 8.30am, leaving the islands at about 2pm; B1650 return including transfers. They also rent tents (B50–100/day), bedding sets (B20/day), snorkel sets (B50/day) and fins (B50/day) for Ko Surin (all cheaper than national park prices).

## ACCOMMODATION

All island accommodation is on Surin Nua and is provided by the national park. Both campsites have bathrooms, lockers (B100/day) and dining rooms where meals are served at fixed times three times a day (B100–250); many people take their own supplies from Khuraburi instead. Bungalows need to be booked in advance either through the national parks websites (@ dnp.go.th or @ thaiforestbooking.com) or at the Khuraburi pier office (☎ 076 472145–6), but tents should be available on spec except during public holidays and long weekends.

**Ao Chong Khad** On the beach here, near the park headquarters and pier, you have the choice between en-suite national park bungalows (for two people) and either renting a national park tent or pitching your own (available for rent in Khuraburi); bedding sets cost B60/day. No wi-fi. Camping pitches B80, tents B300, bungalows B2000

**Ao Mai Ngam** Home to the nicer campsite, with tents (B300–450/day) and pitches (B80/day) but no bungalows, and reached via a 2km trail from headquarters or by longtail. No wi-fi. Pitches B80, tents B300

# Khao Sok National Park

☎ 077 395139, @ khaosok.com • B300, B150 for children up to 14 years old, payable at the checkpoint at headquarters and valid for 24hr; you'll have to pay again at Cheow Lan Lake if you arrive more than 24hr later

Most of the Andaman coast's highlights are, unsurprisingly, along the shoreline, but the stunning jungle-clad karsts of **KHAO SOK NATIONAL PARK** are well worth heading inland for. Located about halfway between the southern peninsula's two coasts and easily accessible from Khao Lak, Phuket and Surat Thani, the park has become a popular stop on the travellers' route, offering a number of easy trails, a bit of amateur spelunking and some scenic rafthouse accommodation on Cheow Lan Lake. Much of the park, which protects the watershed of the Sok River and rises to a peak of nearly 1000m, is carpeted in impenetrable rainforest, home to gaurs, leopard cats and tigers among others – and up to 155 species of bird. The limestone crags that dominate almost every vista both on and away from the lake are breathtaking, never more so than in the early morning: waking up to the sound of hooting gibbons and the sight of thick white mist curling around the karst formations is an experience not quickly forgotten.

The park has two centres: the **tourist village** that has grown up around the park headquarters and trailheads, which offers all essential services, including an **ATM** at Morning Mist Minimarket and currency exchange at Khao Sok Track & Trail; and the dam, 65km further east, at the head of **Cheow Lan Lake**. Most visitors stay in the tourist village and organize their lake trips from there, but it's also feasible to do one or more nights at the lake first. Take plenty of water when hiking as Khao Sok is notoriously humid.

## GUIDED TREKS AND TOURS OF KHAO SOK

### PARK TREKS AND NIGHT SAFARIS

The vast majority of visitors choose to join a **guided trek** at some point during their stay in the park. Though the trails are waymarked and easy to navigate alone, the guided experience alerts you to details you'd certainly miss on your own – the claw marks left by a sun-bear scaling a tree in search of honey, for example, or the medicinal plants used for malarial fevers and stomach upsets – and is both fun and inexpensive; prices are fixed but exclude the national park entrance fee.

The usual **day trek** (B700–900) goes to Ton Kloi waterfall, and from about December to March there's also a special route (B700) that takes in the blooming of the world's second-biggest flower, the **rafflesia kerrii meier**, a rather unprepossessing brown, cabbage-like plant whose enormous russet-coloured petals unfurl to a diameter of up to 80cm; it's also known as "stinking corpse lily" because it gives off a smell like rotting flesh.

After-dinner **night safaris** along the main park trails (B700, excluding park entrance fee, for 2–4hr) are also popular, not least because they're good for spotting civets, mouse deer and slow lorises and, if you're exceptionally lucky, elephants and clouded leopards as well – more likely on darker nights away from the full moon.

You get to stay out in the jungle on the **overnight camping trips** (about B2500), usually around Tan Sawan falls.

Reputable and long-serving **guides** include those booked through *Bamboo House*, *Nung House* and *Khao Sok Rainforest Resort* and at Khao Sok Track & Trail (☎081 958 0629, ⓦkhaosoktrackandtrail.com).

Any guesthouse can also arrange a two-hour visit to the **elephant sanctuary** (B1200) and fix you up with equipment and transfers for **tubing** and **canoeing** trips along the Sok River (from B350/800).

### CHEOW LAN LAKE TOURS

Most Khao Sok guesthouses can organize tours to Cheow Lan Lake, but all rely on the floating lake house accommodation managed by Khao Sok Smiley (☎089 871 5744, ⓦkhaosoksmiley. com), which also has headquarters (and tree houses, see below) in the tourist village. It makes sense to just arrange your tour directly with them. Charges are B1500 for a day-trip to the lake and around B2500 for two-day, one-night trips; the fee include four meals, trekking and a morning boat cruise, but excludes park entry fees. It's also possible to simply turn up at the dam and hire a boat for a day-trip for around B2000.

## The trails

Seven of the park's nine attractions (waterfalls, pools, gorges and viewpoints) branch off the clearly signed main **trail** that runs west of the park headquarters and visitor centre, along the Sok River. The first 3.5km constitute the **interpretative trail** described in *Waterfalls and Gibbon Calls* (see page 304), an unexceptional ninety-minute one-way trail along a road-like track. Most people continue to **Ton Kloi waterfall**, 7km from headquarters (allow 3hr each way), which flows year-round and tumbles into a pool that's good for swimming. En route, signs point to **Bang Liap Nam waterfall** (4.5km from HQ), which is a straightforward hike; and **Tan Sawan waterfall** (6km from HQ), which involves wading along a river bed for the final kilometre and should not be attempted during the rainy season. The trail to the rather spectacular eleven-tiered **Sip-et Chan waterfall** (4km from HQ), which follows the course of the Bang Laen River northwards, is no longer much used and can be quite indistinct. There's a fair bit of climbing, plus half a dozen river crossings, so allow three hours each way.

## Cheow Lan Lake

65km from national park headquarters

Dubbed Thailand's Guilin because of its photogenic karst islands, forested inlets and mist-clad mountains encircling jade-coloured waters similar to those sprouting around

China's world-famous village, the vast 28km-long **Cheow Lan Lake** (also known as **Ratchabrapa Dam** reservoir) is Khao Sok's most famous feature and the most popular destination for guided tours. It was created in 1987 when the Khlong Saeng River was dammed to power a new hydroelectricity plant, and its forested shores and hundred-plus islands now harbour abundant bird life, as well as some primates, most easily spotted in the very early morning. Tours generally combine a trip on the lake with a wade through the nearby flooded cave system and a night on a floating rafthouse. The lake can only be explored by longtail boat tour, arranged either from Khao Sok or from Ratchabrapa Dam.

For many people, the highlight of their lake excursion is the adventurous three-hour trek to and through the 800m-long horseshoe-shaped **Nam Talu cave**, a five-minute

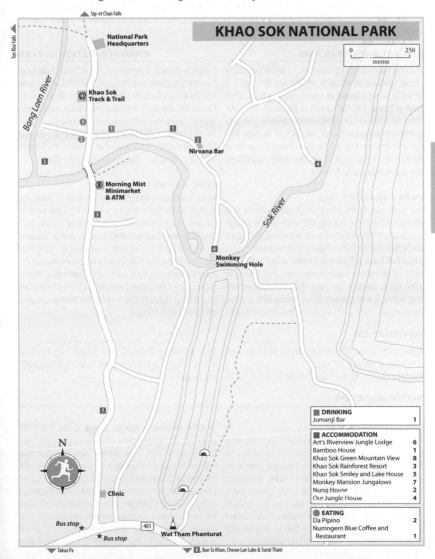

KHAO SOK NATIONAL PARK

0        250
metres

4

**DRINKING**
Jumanji Bar                              1

**ACCOMMODATION**
Art's Riverview Jungle Lodge             6
Bamboo House                             1
Khao Sok Green Mountain View             8
Khao Sok Rainforest Resort               3
Khao Sok Smiley and Lake House           5
Monkey Mansion Jungalows                 7
Nung House                               2
Our Jungle House                         4

**EATING**
Da Pipino                                2
Numngern Blue Coffee and
Restaurant                               1

boat ride from the national park rafthouses, or about an hour's boat ride from the dam. The **trek** is not for everyone, however, as the cave section entails an hour-long wade through the river that hollowed out this tunnel: it's slippery underfoot and pitch black and there will be at least one 20m section where you have to swim. When the river level is high there will be longer swims. Never attempt the cave without an authorized park guide and heed any closure signs posted because of high water levels and strong currents; in October 2007 a flash flood caused nine fatalities here and the park authorities are now stricter. Wear sandals with decent grip and request (or take) your own torch.

Part of the appeal of a night spent in a rafthouse on Cheow Lan Lake is the **dawn safari** the following morning, when you've a good chance of seeing langurs, macaques and gibbons on the lakeshore; some tours include this safari option, or you can usually borrow a kayak from your accommodation and paddle around the shore yourself.

## ARRIVAL AND DEPARTURE
## KHAO SOK NATIONAL PARK

Khao Sok National Park headquarters, its tourist village and Cheow Lan Lake are all north off Highway 401, which is served by frequent **buses**: all services between the junction town of **Takua Pa**, 40km south of Khuraburi, and Surat Thani come this way, including some Surat Thani services to and from Khao Lak and Phuket. Coming from Bangkok, Hua Hin or Chumphon, take a Surat Thani-bound bus as far as the Highway 401 junction, about 20km before Surat Thani, and change onto one for Takua Pa.

Nang (2hr 30min), Ranong (4hr), Surat Thani's Talat Kaset II via the train station at Phunphin (1hr 45min), Ko Chang Noi (4hr 45min), Ko Lanta (4hr), Ko Phayam (4hr 30min), Ko Samui (3hr), Pha Nga (3hr), Trang (4hr 30min), Hat Yay (8hr) and even across the southern border into Malaysia.

**Bus destinations:** Bangkok (via Surat Thani, Hua Hin and Petchaburi; daily; 11hr); Khao Lak (9 daily; 1hr 30min); Surat Thani (hourly; 1–2hr); Takua Pa (9 daily; 50min).

## CHEOW LAN LAKE

Access to the lake is via the town of Ban Ta Khun, 50km east of Khao Sok on Route 401, from where it's 12km north to the dam. Many travellers book their tour of the lake from their Khao Sok accommodation, in which case all transport is included, but if coming from Surat Thani or Phang Nga, you could do the lake first. There's a regular minibus service from Talat Kaset II in Surat Thani, via Phunphin train station, to Cheow Lan Lake (about every 2hr; 1hr), or you could take a Surat Thani–Takua Pa bus, alight at Ban Ta Khun and get a motorbike taxi to the dam.

## PARK HEADQUARTERS

The access road to the tourist village and trailheads is at kilometre-stone 109 on Highway 401, where guesthouse staff meet bus passengers and offer free lifts to their accommodation, the furthest of which is about 3km from the main road.

**Khao Sok Track & Trail** in the tourist village (📞 081 958 0629, 🌐 khaosoktrackandtrail.com) sells bus (including a VIP bus to Bangkok, via Surat Thani), boat, plane and train tickets, as well as tickets for a/c minibuses to multiple destinations including Chiang Mai (12hr), Krabi (2hr), Ao

## INFORMATION

**Map** The checkpoint office at headquarters supplies a small sketch map of the park and trails.
**Guidebooks** The best introduction to Khao Sok is the

great guidebook *Waterfalls and Gibbon Calls* by Thom Henley, which is available at some Khao Sok minimarkets and bungalows.

## ACCOMMODATION

### PARK HEADQUARTERS

The bulk of the budget accommodation is scenically sited beneath the karsts near the park headquarters, but despite the edge-of-the rainforest location, it can get noisy of an evening, with the sound systems at some backpacker bars pitched against the chattering of the cicadas. Every guesthouse offers its own park and lake trips, so it is worth talking to the park guides before booking a trip. Around here, "treehouses" means bungalows built on very tall stilts among the trees, rather than actually in the trees.

★ **Art's Riverview Jungle Lodge** 📞 081 489 8489 or 📞 090 167 6818, 🌐 artsriverviewlodge.com; map p.303. Popular place nicely located away from the main fray next to a good swimming hole, surrounded by jungle. The cheaper bungalows are spacious, tastefully designed wooden affairs, with shutters and a deck, while the deluxe versions (B2500) are bigger still and attractively furnished, some with red-brick outdoor bathrooms and waterfall-style showers. All rooms have fans and mosquito nets, wi-fi is available at the lobby area, and breakfast is included. They offer free pick-ups from the highway junction (advance booking required). B1000

**Bamboo House** ☎081 787 7484, ✉bamboohouse. khaosok@gmail.com; map p.303. Set in a grassy orchard, this was one of the first guesthouses in the park and is run by welcoming members of the park warden's family. The simple, stilted, en-suite wooden huts with mosquito nets here are the cheapest in this part of the park and there are also pebble-dashed concrete versions, a couple of treehouse-style bungalows and large, wooden affairs with hot showers and balconies on stilts right over the river (B800). B300

**Khao Sok Green Mountain View** 1500m north up a mostly paved road from Highway 401, just east of the km 106 marker ☎087 263 2481, ⊛khaosok-greenmountainview. com; map p.303. This is a great budget option if you want a remote location, situated as it is in a very quiet spot far from almost everyone else. The seven good-quality bamboo and wood bungalows of varying sizes are all en suite and have some nice touches, with pretty open-roofed bathrooms, fans, mosquito nets, decks and hammocks. They sit on the edge of a rubber plantation on the other side of the karsts from the main accommodation area. There's free transport to the park village or you can walk to *Our Jungle House* across the river in 15min and on to the park headquarters in another 25. B300

**Khao Sok Rainforest Resort** ☎064 224 9654, ⊛khaosokrainforest.com; map p.303. This welcoming place has some spectacularly sited mountain view bungalows that are set high on a jungle slope and affording unsurpassed karst views, plus a/c treehouses (B2500) and a/c riverside bungalows (B2000). Interiors are decent enough though lacking style, and wi-fi is only available at the restaurant, where breakfast (included in rate) is served. B1500

**Khao Sok Smiley and Lake House** ☎089 871 5744, ⊛khaosoksmiley.com; map p.303. Set beyond a not-so-attractive restaurant and lounge, these two rows of concrete bungalows (B500) and wooden treehouses have fairly basic toilets and facilities, but are overall good value – especially the latter, with their spacious verandas backed by lush vegetation. They are also the main tour operator for Cheow Lan lake (see page 302), where they manage prettier floating raft houses. B300

★ **Monkey Mansion Jungalows** ⊛facebook.com/ khaosokjungalows; map p.303. This Thai–German-run, tree-covered wooden house is a perfect spot for both backpackers and families. There's a welcoming veranda with a vegan-friendly restaurant that's perfect for chilling out and offers luggage storage and book-exchange facilities. The different types of en-suite bungalows – some bamboo-walled, others made of wood and concrete – all have mosquito nets and are set around an attractive stone and wood garden next to a pond filled with carp. When available, the family rooms can also function as dorms (B200) for walk-in guests. B450

**Nung House** ☎077 380 723 and 086 283 31037, ⊛nunghouse.com; map p.303. Friendly place run by the park warden's son and his family, with eighteen very good huts set around an attractive grassy garden full of rambutan trees. Choose between simple but sturdy bamboo and wood constructions with en-suite facilities, brick and concrete bungalows, and treehouses. The *Nirvana Bar* (next door) is a good spot to meet other travellers and have a few drinks. B300

**Our Jungle House** ☎081 417 0546, ⊛khaosok accommodation.com; map p.303. Peaceful, upmarket riverside option, a 20min walk from park headquarters, secluded in lush rainforest where you might spot hornbills and several species of monkey. Choose between airy, well-designed, wood and bamboo bungalows and treehouses (B2900); all have fans and mosquito nets and most are on the river bank, which has a small beach. B950

## CHEOW LAN LAKE

On overnight tours to the lake (see page 302), accommodation is either in tents in the jungle or at rafthouses on the lake. There are both private and national park rafthouses moored at various scenic spots around the lake shore, mostly around an hour's boat ride from the dam. All rafthouse huts are rudimentary bamboo structures with nets and mattresses, offering fabulous lake views from your pillow. If you've arranged your own boat transport, you can stay at any of the lake's rafthouses for B600 per person, including meals. Accommodation packages that include boat transfers from the dam and a cave tour cost around B2500 with *Khao Sok Smiley and Lake House* (☎089 871 5744, ⊛khaosoksmiley.com). *Jungle Yoga* runs yoga, meditation and massage retreats at the remote *Praiwan* rafthouses from December to April (⊛jungleyoga.com).

## EATING

There are just a couple of places that might tempt you away from your guesthouse restaurant in the tourist village here.

### PARK HEADQUARTERS

**Da Pipino** map p.303. Homely, rustic, not to say scruffy, Italian restaurant, strewn with lovely plants in a scenic spot by the river. The menu runs to seafood antipasti, decent fettuccine bolognese (B195), a few Italian main courses and a wide range of tasty handmade pizzas. Daily noon–10pm.

**Numngern Blue Coffee and Restaurant** Towards the end of the village road, close to park headquarters ☎083 391 3391; map p.303. Simple yet cosy little restaurant serving excellent brews and a good menu of hearty, mostly vegetarian Thai cuisine. Standout dishes include *ma khu yao kraug gang* (curry sauce with eggplant and tofu, B90) and *pad med ma muang* (stir-fried cashew nut with mushrooms, tofu and onion, B90). Daily 8am–9pm.

## DRINKING

**PARK HEADQUARTERS**

**Jumanji Bar** Next to Nung House; map p.303. Pure reggae-style, bamboo bar that earns a few extra points thanks to its nice location in a quiet spot, with low driftwood tables surrounded by trees. Most cocktails, including mojitos and Singapore slings, cost B150. Daily 8am–9pm.

# Khao Lak

Handily located just an hour north of Phuket International Airport, and some 30km south of Takua Pa, **KHAO LAK** has established itself as a thriving, mid-market beach resort with plentiful opportunities for diving and snorkelling, easy access to the supreme national park reefs of Ko Similan and a style that is determinedly unseedy. It lacks sophistication and is mostly a bit pricey for backpackers – aside from a handful of very well-run hostels – but is ideal for families and extremely popular with European tourists. High season here runs from November to April, when the weather and the swimming are at their best and the Similan Islands are open to the public; during the rest of the year, Khao Lak quietens down a lot – and becomes much cheaper too.

The area usually referred to as Khao Lak is in fact a string of beaches west off Highway 4. **Khao Lak** proper is the southernmost and least developed, 5km from the most commercial part of the resort, **Nang Thong** (aka Bang La On), which throngs with shops, restaurants, dive centres and countless places to stay, both on the beachfront and inland from Highway 4. North again about 3km (5min by taxi or a 45min walk up the beach) is lower-key, slightly more youthful **Bang Niang**, a lovely long stretch of golden sand that's backed by a developing tourist village whose network of sois is away from the highway and feels more enticing than its neighbour. Removed from all this commerce, **Laem Pakarang**, 12km further up the coast, a headland and popular sunset-watching spot that gives onto 11km Hat Pakweeb (Hat Bang Sak), is where you find the area's best accommodation.

There is, thankfully, little obvious evidence these days of the area's devastating experience during the December 2004 **tsunami**, when the undersea earthquake off Sumatra sent a series of murderous waves on to Khao Lak's shores (and the rest of the Andaman coast), vaporizing almost every shorefront home and hotel here and killing thousands. Nang Thong quickly became the centre of a huge reconstruction effort, with thousands of volunteers arriving to help, and rebuilding was mostly completed within a couple of years, though for many survivors recovery will probably take a lifetime.

## Police Boat Memorial

Bang Niang

Inland from the highway – and accessible from it across a field and a bridge – a **beached police boat** has become a memorial to the extraordinary power of the tsunami waves. It was propelled up here, 2km inland, while patrolling the waters in front of *La Flora* resort, where Princess Ubolrat and her children, one of whom perished in the disaster, were staying. To the right there's an overpriced (daily 9am–9pm; B300) **Tsunami Memorial Museum**, which essentially offers a room with pictures and data remembering the devastating effects the catastrophe had on the region.

## Ban Nam Khem Memorial

13km north of Laem Pakarang up Highway 4, then left for a signposted 3km

The main local tsunami memorial is on the beach at **Ban Nam Khem**, the worst-hit village in Thailand, where half of the four thousand inhabitants died in the waves, as described in Erich Krauss's *Wave of Destruction* (see page 437). Built by the Thai army, it's an evocative installation: you walk down a path between a curling,

## AFTER THE TSUNAMI

The **Boxing Day tsunami** hit Thailand's Andaman coast just after 9.30am on December 26, 2004. The first place to suffer significant damage was Phuket, and the next two hours saw village after resort get battered or decimated by the towering waves thundering in from the Sumatra fault line, 1000km away. The entire coastline from Ranong to Satun was affected, but not all of it with the same intensity: the worst-hit province was Phang Nga, where 4200 people were recorded dead or missing, many of them in the resort of Khao Lak; over 2000 suffered a similar fate on Ko Phi Phi; and more than 900 died on the beaches of Phuket, especially on Patong and Kamala. There were 8212 fatalities in all, a third of them holidaymakers. Another 6000 people were made homeless and some 150,000 lost their jobs, mostly in the tourism and fishing industries. By the end of that day, nearly a quarter of a million people in a dozen countries around the Indian Ocean had lost their lives in the worst natural disaster in recorded history.

Many homes, shops and hotels were quite swiftly rebuilt, but the emotional and social **legacy** of the tsunami endures and most residents along the Andaman coast have a story of terror and bereavement to tell. It's no surprise that many survivors are now afraid of the sea: fearing ghosts, some longtail boatmen won't motor solo past where villages once stood, and hundreds of hotel staff have since sought new jobs in the northern city of Chiang Mai, as far from the sea as they could go.

Immediately after the tsunami, many were surprised when then prime minister Thaksin Shinawatra declined offers of **aid** from foreign governments. But help poured in instead from the Thai government and from royal foundations and local and foreign NGOs and individuals. Of the many **projects** established to help support and rebuild affected communities, the majority have now completed their task; others have evolved into longer-term NGO ventures, including an English-teaching programme in Khao Lak (see page 65), and the community-based tourism company Andaman Discoveries in Khuraburi (see page 298).

Generosity and altruism were not the only responses to the disaster, however. Almost every tsunami-affected community talks of **dishonourable practice** and **corruption**, experiences which have caused bitterness and rifts. Many allegations concern donated money and goods being held back by the local leaders charged with distributing them, and in some cases big business interests muscled in on land deemed "ownerless" because the paperwork had been lost to the waves. Most small businesses had no insurance, and government **compensation** was inconsistently awarded and invariably lacking. In a country where most family enterprises scrape by season to season, it's sobering to contemplate the number of tsunami victims who simply picked up and started over.

Determined not to be caught unawares again, in the unlikely event of Thailand being struck by a second tsunami, the government has created a **tsunami early-warning system** that relays public announcements from towers all the way down the Andaman coast. They have also mapped out evacuation routes, flagged by innumerable "Tsunami Hazard Zone" signs in all the big resorts. For their part, Phuket authorities have remodelled stretches of Ao Patong's beachfront as a building-free zone, creating a park that doubles as a tsunami **memorial**. Krabi officials now require all new buildings to be constructed at least 30m inland from a high-tide boundary, and they even forbid the use of sunloungers below that point. In Khao Lak, a beached police boat (see page 306) has become an eloquent memorial: it rests where it was hurtled by the wave, 2km inland, on the other side of the highway.

4m-high, concrete "wave" and a grassy bank, representing the land, on which plaques commemorate individual victims. Through a window in the concrete wave, a fishing boat looms over you – this "miracle boat" was swept inland but stopped just short of devastating a house and its occupants.

While you're out here, it's worth popping in on the Saori weaving factory and shop (Mon–Sat), on the left about 1km further up Highway 4 from the Ban Nam Khem turn-off, towards the northern end of Ban Bang Muang village. It's a regeneration and occupational therapy project, where you can watch the women weaving and buy some lovely scarves.

## DIVING AND SNORKELLING AROUND KHAO LAK

Khao Lak is the closest and most convenient departure point for **diving and snorkelling trips** to the awesome national park islands of **Ko Similan** (see page 312), which can be reached in three to four hours on a live-aboard or other large boat or in two hours in a much less comfortable speedboat. The islands are currently only open from approximately October to May and all divers have to pay a one-off national park fee of B400 plus a B200-a-day diving fee, usually on top of dive-trip prices. **Local Khao Lak dives** are generally possible year-round, especially the highly rated **wreck** of a tin-mining boat near Bang Sak, which is especially rich in marine life such as ghost pipefish, moray eels, scorpion fish, nudibranchs and yellow-tail barracuda. All Khao Lak dive shops also teach PADI **dive courses**, with the last two days of the Open Water course often done on location in the Similans; for advice on choosing a dive shop see "Basics" (see page 51).

**Big Blue Diving** Along Bang Niang's main tourist road ☎ 076 485544, ⓦ bigbluedivingkhaolak.com. Established PADI Centre that specializes in 4D/4N live-aboard trips to the Similans, on a big dive boat (from B31,500) and day-trips to several dive sites, including Richelieu Rock (from B4,800). Their PADI courses cost B16,200.

**Sea Dragon Dive Center** Nang Thong ☎ 076 485420, ⓦ seadragondivecenter.com. Highly recommended PADI Five-Star Instructor Development Centre which has three live-aboard boats – including budget and deluxe options – running frequent three-day trips to the Similans and Ko Bon (from B10,900 including equipment), and four-day trips to the Similans, Surin islands, Ko Bon, Ko Tachai and Richelieu Rock (from B19,600). No national park fees are included here. Snorkellers get about one-third off. Also offers local wreck and other dives (starting from B2000, not including equipment, for a two-tank dive) and PADI dive courses: the four-day Open Water is B10,500, or B15,000 with one day-trip diving the Similans.

**Wicked Diving** Along Bang Niang's main tourist road ☎ 076 468868, ⓦ wickeddiving.com/wd-locations/khao-lak/. A reliable company offering six-day live-aboard diving trips to the Similans and Richelieu Rock (US$995, includes fees), discover scuba, Open Water courses and fun dives.

## ARRIVAL AND DEPARTURE                                                    KHAO LAK

**By plane** Khao Lak is just 70km north of Phuket airport (1hr; B1700–2200 by taxi).

**By bus and minibus** All buses running from Phuket to Takua Pa and Ranong (and vice versa) pass through Khao Lak and can drop you anywhere along Highway 4; coming from Krabi or Phang Nga, you'll generally need to change buses in Khokkloi, from Khao Sok, in Takua Pa. On departure, you can flag down most buses on the main road, but the Bangkok services use a bus station at the far north end of Bang Niang. There are also a/c tourist minibuses that run at least daily to Surat Thani (via Khokkloi, not Khao Sok; 4hr), Krabi/Ao Nang (3hr/3hr

30min) and Trang (change in Krabi; 5hr 30min). Bus and a/c minibus tickets can be booked through a number of travel agents, including Khao Lak Land Discovery in Nang Thong (☎076 485411, ⓦkhaolaklanddiscovery.com), who also offer transfers to and from Phuket Airport (B600/person or B1500/minibus).

Destinations: Bangkok (3 daily; 12hr); Phuket (20 daily; 2hr 30min); Ranong (8 daily; 2hr 30min–3hr); Takua Pa (18 daily; 30min).

**By boat** Boats to the Similans depart from the pier at Thap Lamu, which is 6km south of Nang Thong, then 5km west off Highway 4.

## GETTING AROUND

**By songthaew** A few public songthaews shuttle between Nang Thong and Bang Niang (where they have a base in front of the market), mostly by day, charging B20–50, but largely they act as private taxis instead and charge more than B100.
**Motorbike and car rental** Many hotels rent motorbikes, and rental cars are available through tour operators.

## ACCOMMODATION

### LAEM PAKARANG

★ **Memories Bar & Bungalows** About 10km north of Khao Lak and 2km inland off Highway 4, at the end of a dirt-road marked by a surfboard ☎ 08 97292251, ⓦ memoriesbar-khaolak.com; map p.309. Even though it attracts well-heeled customers from nearby resorts, this established surf-school turned hip beach restaurant is a perfect, under the radar, traveller hangout. Set on 300 metres of pristine beach right before the cape's headland, it's blessed by Khao Lak's best waves and sunset views. Accommodation is in a cluster of simple, yet well-manned and clean, thatched-bamboo bungalows with floor

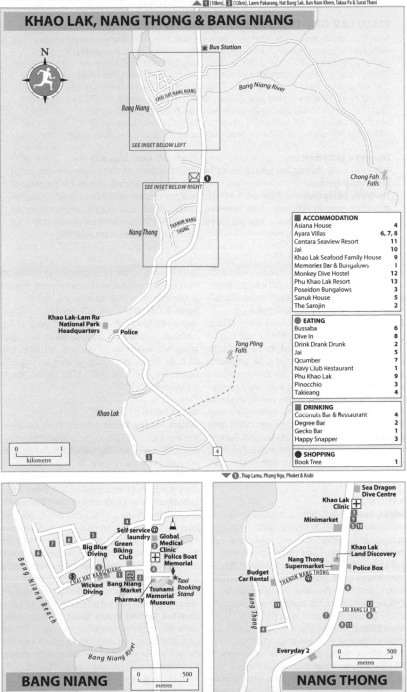

▲ **1** (10km), **2** (12km), Laem Pakarang, Hat Bang Sak, Ban Nam Khem, Takua Pa & Surat Thani

# KHAO LAK, NANG THONG & BANG NIANG

N

★ Bus Station

Bang Niang River

CHAI HAT BANG NIANG

Bang Niang

Chong Fah Falls

SEE INSET BELOW LEFT

SEE INSET BELOW RIGHT

Nang Thong

THANON NANG THONG

Khao Lak-Lam Ru
National Park
Headquarters

Police

Tong Pling
Falls

Khao Lak

| ACCOMMODATION | |
|---|---|
| Asiana House | 4 |
| Ayara Villas | 6, 7, 8 |
| Centara Seaview Resort | 11 |
| Jai | 10 |
| Khao Lak Seafood Family House | 9 |
| Memories Bar & Bungalows | 1 |
| Monkey Dive Hostel | 12 |
| Phu Khao Lak Resort | 13 |
| Poseidon Bungalows | 3 |
| Sanuk House | 5 |
| The Sarojin | 2 |

| ● EATING | |
|---|---|
| Bussaba | 6 |
| Dive In | 8 |
| Drink Drank Drunk | 2 |
| Jai | 5 |
| Qcumber | 7 |
| Navy Club Restaurant | 1 |
| Phu Khao Lak | 9 |
| Pinocchio | 3 |
| Takieang | 4 |

| DRINKING | |
|---|---|
| Coconuts Bar & Restaurant | 4 |
| Degree Bar | 2 |
| Gecko Bar | 1 |
| Happy Snapper | 3 |

| ● SHOPPING | |
|---|---|
| Book Tree | 1 |

▼ **1**, Thap Lamu, Phang Nga, Phuket & Krabi

4

0        1
kilometre

4

---

**BANG NIANG**

Bang Niang Beach

Self service @
laundry

Big Blue
Diving

Green
Biking
Club

Global
Medical
Clinic

Police Boat
Memorial

CHAI HAT BANG NIANG

Wicked
Diving

Bang Niang
Market

Tsunami
Memorial
Museum

Pharmacy

★ Taxi
Booking
Stand

Bang Niang River

0        500
metres

---

**NANG THONG**

Sea Dragon
Dive Centre

Khao Lak
Clinic

Minimarket

Khao Lak
Land Discovery

Nang Thong
Supermarket

Police Box

THANON NANG THONG

Budget
Car Rental

Nang Thong

SOI BANG LA ON

Everyday 2

0        500
metres

## KHAO LAK DAY-TRIPS AND OTHER ACTIVITIES

Aside from diving and snorkelling trips (see page 308), there are several other attractions within day-tripping distance of Khao Lak, including a number of local **waterfalls**. Of these, Sai Rung (Rainbow Falls), about 16km north of Nang Thong in Bang Sak, is the most satisfying. Others include Tong Pling, across from the *Merlin* resort in Khao Lak; Nam Tok Lumphi, about 20km south of Khao Lak; and Chong Fah Falls, located less than 5km east of Bang Niang, but subject to a B200 entry fee because it's part of Khao Lak–Lam Ru National Park (⊛dnp.go.th). The national park's headquarters is on the headland between Nang Thong and Khao Lak beaches, and about 1km south of it, you can easily walk down to a quiet, pretty sandy cove – look for a sign saying "small sandy beach" on the west side of the main road, opposite a layby.

**Everyday 2 Restaurant** South end of Nang Thong ☎085 299 0410. Morning Thai cooking courses for B1200, including pick-ups.
**The Green Biking Club** Bang Niang ☎076 443211, ⊛facebook.com/greenbikingclub. Runs interesting guided mountain-bike trips around rural and coastal Khao Lak (from B2400 for half a day).

**Khao Lak Land Discovery** Nang Thong ☎076 485411, ⊛khaolaklanddiscovery.com. One of the best and most reputable, though not the cheapest, local tour operators, whose day-trips include dolphin-spotting sunset cruises (B2500), elephant-riding and bathing (B1900) and trekking and canoeing in Khao Sok National Park and Cheow Lan Lake (B750).

mattresses and mosquito nets, set right on the seafront. The shared toilets are very clean, and the staff make you feel like you are part of the family. There's no wi-fi and food is a little on the costly side, at around B250 for a meal. **B500**
**The Sarojin** 12km north of Khao Lak ☎076 427905, ⊛thesarojin.com; map p.309. With a staff-to-guest ratio of two to one and a style and attitude that exudes understated, unpretentious class, this is the top place to stay around Khao Lak. The 56 sleek, tastefully simple rooms are discreetly sited around the wide beachfront garden and stunning square turquoise swimming pool. It's an obvious honeymoon choice, with a policy of no under-10s, a range of excursions designed for two, and private candlelit tables for dinner on the beach or at a nearby waterfall. There are complimentary non-motorized watersports and mountain bikes, and a spa. All-day breakfast with sparkling wine included. Special promotions often available. **B12,000**

### BANG NIANG
**Asiana House** Tucked along a backroad connecting the highway to the beachside ☎081 577 1921, ✉asianahouse@hotmail.co.th; map p.309. These eight delightful en-suite rooms and mini-apartments come in pastel hues, with wooden floors and bed-stands. They are within easy walking distance of the beach and most of Bang Niang's facilities, yet offer a more secluded atmosphere as they are housed in concrete bungalows at the back of a private Thai home. Breakfast included. **B1500**
**Ayara Villas** ☎076 486478–9, ⊛ayara-villas.com; map p.309. An attractive upper-mid-range option, spread over three different compounds with two swimming pools. At the top end are beachfront villas right on the sand; many others are terraced bungalows just a few metres from the sea, and the rest are in a three-storey building, with ground-

floor rooms enjoying direct pool access. The a/c interiors are nicely furnished with dark wood in contemporary style and all have kitchenettes. Breakfast included. **B5000**
**Sanuk House** ☎083 390 3229, ⊛sanukresort.com; map p.309. Dinky little Swiss-managed group of five comfortable and spacious brick bungalows in a walled garden with a heart-shaped whirlpool, just 100m from the beach. Popular with German-speaking and long-term tourists. Bungalows come with a/c, hot showers, fridges and kitchenettes. **B1600**

### NANG THONG
**Centara Seaview Resort** On Nang Thong's southern beachfront ☎076 429800, ⊛centarahotelsresorts.com; map p.309. A good choice for families or those looking for peace and a bit of luxury. Rooms are located in two-storey beachfront wing set around a swimming pool facing the sea, or in a large building beyond the access road. There is ample parking space and wi-fi in all rooms. Continental breakfast is included in the rate and is served around the pool. **B5,500**
**Jai** ☎076 485390, ✉jai_bungalow@hotmail.com; map p.309. A busy, family-run place that offers some of the cheapest accommodation in Khao Lak. The good-quality, decent-sized, en-suite concrete bungalows are set around a lawn dotted with trees behind the popular restaurant, quite close to the highway and about 600m from the beach; a/c options have hot showers and fridges. Fan **B450**, a/c **B650**
**Khao Lak Seafood Family House** Soi Noen Thong ☎076 485318, ⊛khaolakseafood.com; map p.309. The large, good-quality bungalows here are set well back from the road in a garden behind the eponymous restaurant. The fan ones are especially good value for Khao Lak: roomy and nicely designed with good, hot-water bathrooms; a/c rooms in a couple of two-storey blocks are also available.

It's a family business and very popular with returning guests and long stayers. Fan B600, a/c B1200

★ **Monkey Dive Hostel** At the southern end of Nhang Thong's main highway ☎ 082 424 9257 and 081 956 5654, ⓦ monkeydivekhaolak.com; map p.309. Possibly the best backpacker option in Khao Lak, this new, industrial chic hostel has a huge, comfortable common area with TV and beanbags that is a great place to socialise. The immaculate dorms have charging stations, LED lights and free lockers (bring your own padlock though). There's also a series of smart private rooms with futon-styled beds (B500) on wooden mezzanines, each with interesting trivia on a different sea creature etched on the pastel-coloured walls. The weekly barbecues (held on Saturdays) are cheap (B35 per skewer) and a great way to meet new people. B350

**Phu Khao Lak Resort** ☎ 076 485141; map p.309. There is a luxurious amount of space at this well-run place, where the thirty large, spotlessly clean bungalows sit prettily amid a grassy park-style coconut plantation. Fan rooms have

tiled floors and most have hot-water bathrooms; a/c ones have picture windows and quite stylish interiors. There's a swimming pool and a good restaurant. About 500m walk from the beach. Fan B800, a/c B1800

### KHAO LAK

**Poseidon Bungalows** 7km south of central Nang Thong ☎ 087 895 9204, ⓦ similantour.com; map p.309. Surrounded by rubber plantations and set above a sandy shore of wave-smoothed rocks just north of the Thai navy's private beach, this Swedish–Thai-run guesthouse is both a quiet place to hang out for a few days and a long-established organizer of snorkelling expeditions to the Similan islands (see page 312). All fifteen bungalows are en suite and fan cooled, with generous amounts of space, hot showers and balconies, some enjoying sea views. There's also motorbike rental available. Get off the bus at the *Poseidon* sign between kilometre-stones 53 and 54, then phone for a pick-up or walk 1km. B950

## EATING

### BANG NIANG

**Drink Drank Drunk** Right across the road from Bang Niang Market's entrance ☎ 076 671466, ⓦ facebook. com/khaolakdrinkdrankdrunk; map p.309. Almost hidden between two hotels, this Italian–Thai-run open-air wine restaurant (B120 per glass) dishes up good seafood platters and brick-oven baked pizzas (from B240), as well as some interesting fusion dishes, such as the calzone *phat thai* (B290). Daily 12pm–10pm.

**Pinocchio** ☎ 076 443079; map p.309. Home-made pasta, decent pizza made in a wood-fired oven (around B300), a few Italian meat main courses and lots of seafood, topped off with tiramisu and other home-made desserts. Look for the white picket fence and fairy lights. Daily 1–11pm.

**Takieang** map p.309. Wooden roadside restaurant that's gone slightly upmarket, offering authentic Thai food, including good *tom yum kung* (B150), banana-flower salad (B120) and exceptional seafood hotplates (B270). Daily noon–10pm.

### NANG THONG

**Bussaba** map p.309. Welcoming bistro with a long menu of Thai food, including seafood and fish priced by weight and some slightly more unusual dishes such as shrimp green curry with *roti* bread (B189). Also does sandwiches and good espressos. Daily 1.30–11pm.

★ **Dive In** Khao Lak Banana resort, Soi Bang La On; map p.309. Owner and chef Sunny cooks up a storm here and is a favourite with expats, locals and returning tourists. Highlights include a deliciously aromatic *matsaman* curry (B90) and *khanom jiin* Phuket-style noodles with fish and red curry. The Western menu runs to home-made cakes and bread, breakfasts and espressos. Free wi-fi. Daily 6.30am–11pm.

**Jai** map p.309. This lofty, open-sided, roadside restaurant is deservedly popular for its hearty, often fiery curries in good-sized portions (B120), including *kaeng phanaeng* and *matsaman*, seafood and *tom yam kung*. Also does a few Thai desserts and Western breakfasts. Daily 8.30am–10pm.

**Phu Khao Lak** ⓦ phukhaolak.com; map p.309. Well-known and good-value restaurant attached to the bungalows of the same name serving exceptionally good Thai food from a picture menu that stretches to over a hundred dishes. Everything from red, yellow and green curries (B140–170) to seafood platters. Daily 7am–10pm.

**Qcumber** Along the southern end of Nhang Thong's main highway ☎ 063 994 2211, ⓦ facebook.com/qcumbersaladbar; map p.309. This little café has a hip vibe with plenty of paintings on the walls, naked light-bulbs and an eclectic menu that ranges from healthy (and pricey) Thai mains such as *pat thai* with tofu and bean sprouts (B149), to Western-style salad and vegetarian mains (from B90). They also offer Thai cooking classes (9am–12pm Tue, Thurs & Sat; B1500/person).11am–9pm, closed Wed.

### THAP LAMU

**Navy Club Restaurant** On the right by the pier, 11km southwest of Nang Thong ☎ 081 648 8656; map p.309. It's worth the trip out here for some authentic Thai food and the freshest seafood, at prices lower than in Khao Lak itself. Specialities include soft-shell crab, white snapper, pomfret (B35/100g), king prawns and squid, and there are dozens of Thai salads (B80). The restaurant is unprepossessing, but you could phone ahead to book a table on the terrace overlooking the harbour. Daily 10am–10pm.

4

## DRINKING

### BANG NIANG

**Degree Bar** At the entrance of Khao Niau Road; map p.309. With its wooden tables, water-buffalo skulls and folksy, Thai-country vibe, this welcoming and local bar-restaurant is a fun – and cheap – place to listen to live bands, from 10pm, playing Thai and Western pop. Daily 9pm–2am.

**Gecko Bar** ☎ 081 41544167, ⓦ bit.ly/GeckoBarKhaolak; map p.309. This small and cosy snooker bar, festooned with global football memorabilia and beer banners is popular among the foreign instructors who work at the local dive centres. Beers (B80) and spirits (B100) come cheap and the friendly owners love to challenge their guests to a game of table football. Daily 7pm–2am.

### NANG THONG

**Coconuts Bar and Restaurant** On Nang Thong's beach southern headland, next to Suwan Resort ☎ 061 401 5637

or 061 401 5636, ⓦ facebook.com/coconutsnangthong; map p.309. This feel-good beachside bistro is casual enough to hang out in with friends whilst tucking your toes in the sand, but also sees a steady flow of higher-end resort clientele. Pricewise, however, there's something for everyone, from fish and chips and spaghetti (both B160), to grilled seafood mixed platters (B900). Happy hour is actually five hours – from 3 to 8pm every day – and beers cost B160 during this time. Daily 7am–10pm.

**Happy Snapper** ⓦ facebook.com/HappySnapperBar; map p.309. Khao Lak's most famous dive-staff hangout is a chilled and pleasant spot to spend an evening, with a folksy lounge ambience and a drinks menu of over one hundred cocktails. There's a live band every night, from around 10.30pm, except on Sundays, when there is a chill-out DJ. Expect the occasional open-mic session too. Daily 8.30pm–1am.

## SHOPPING

Nang Thong offers plenty of shopping, mainly for clothes, souvenirs and handicrafts, with countless tailors and opticians too. Bang Niang has a popular street market in the soi, parallel to the main bar and accommodation strip (Mon, Wed, Thurs and Sat; 10am–10pm)

**Book Tree** Far north end of Nang Thong; map p.309. Sells plenty of new and second-hand books plus magazines, newspapers and art cards, and also serves good coffee. Daily 9am–9pm.

# Ko Similan

Mu Ko Similan National Park • B400, valid for 5 days if staying within the national park • Closed May to Oct

Rated as one of the world's best spots for both above-water and underwater beauty, the eleven islands at the heart of the **Mu Ko Similan National Park** are among the most exciting **diving** destinations in Thailand. Massive granite boulders set magnificently against turquoise waters give the islands their distinctive character, but it's the 30m visibility that draws the divers. The 5000-year-old reefs are said to be the oldest in Thailand, so there's an enormous diversity of species, and the underwater scenery is nothing short of overwhelming: the reefs teem with coral fish, and you'll also see turtles, manta rays, moray eels, jacks, reef sharks, sea snakes, red grouper and quite possibly white-tip sharks, barracuda, giant lobster and enormous tuna.

The **islands** lie 64km off the mainland and include the eponymous Ko Similan chain of nine islands as well as two more northerly islands, Ko Bon and Ko Tachai, which are both favoured haunts of manta rays and whale sharks and are halfway between the Similan chain and the islands of Ko Surin. The Similans are numbered north–south from nine to one and are often referred to by number: Ko Ba Ngu (9), Ko Similan (8), Ko Payoo (7), Ko Hin Posar (aka Ko Hok; 6), Ko Ha (5), Ko Miang (4), Ko Pahyan (3), Ko Pahyang (2) and Ko Hu Yong (1). The national park headquarters and accommodation is on Ko Miang and there's also a campsite and restaurant on Ko Similan. Ko Similan is the largest island in the chain, blessed with a beautiful, fine white-sand bay and impressive boulders and traversed by two nature trails; Ko Miang has two pretty beaches, twenty minutes' walk apart, and three nature trails; Ko Hu Yong has an exceptionally long white-sand bay but access is restricted by the Thai navy as **turtles** lay their eggs there from November to February.

Such beauty has not gone unnoticed and the islands are extremely popular with day-trippers from Phuket and Khao Lak, as well as with divers and snorkellers on longer live-aboard trips. This has caused inevitable congestion and environmental problems and the Similan reefs have been damaged in places by anchors and by the local practice of using dynamite in fishing. National parks authorities have responded by banning fishermen and enforcing strict regulations for tourist boats, including **closing the islands** during the monsoon season, from May to October.

## ARRIVAL AND GETTING AROUND
KO SIMILAN

Independent travellers wanting to stay on the island for a few days can usually use the snorkelling tour boats for transfers (about B900 one-way). There are also plenty of live-aboard diving or snorkelling trips to the islands, the best and cheapest of which run out of Khao Lak (see page 308). **Snorkelling tours** Most travel agents in Khao Lak, Phuket and Phang Nga sell snorkelling packages to Ko Similan, usually as day-trips featuring at least four island stops (from B3500 including national park fees); two-day, one-night (B5800 staying in tents), and three-day, two-night (B7200) packages, staying on Ko Miang, are also available. The majority of these trips carry quite large groups and use fast boats that depart from Thap Lamu pier, about

11km southwest of Khao Lak's Nang Thong, 90km north of Phuket town, at about 8.30am and get to the islands in under two hours. They depart the islands at around 3pm. Companies offering this service, all of which offer pick-ups in Khao Lak and Phuket, include Seastar (076 485595, seastarandaman.net) and Green Andaman Travel (076 485598, greenandamantravel.net), both of which have offices at the Thap Lamu pier; and Khao Lak Land Discovery in Nang Thong (076 485411, khaolaklanddiscovery.com). **Getting around** If travelling independently, you'll need to use Ko Similan longtail boats to travel between the islands and to explore different reefs: prices are fixed and cost around B200 per person one-way.

## ACCOMMODATION AND EATING

Limited accommodation is available on **Ko Miang**, mainly in the shape of national park rooms and bungalows (fan B1000, a/c B2000) and tents (B450), and there's a campsite on **Ko Similan** too; both islands also have a restaurant. Accommodation should be booked ahead, either at the national parks office 500m east of Thap Lamu pier (076 453272) or online (dnp.go.th or thaiforestbooking.com), as facilities can often get crowded with tour groups, especially on weekends and during holidays.

# Phuket

Thailand's largest island and a province in its own right, **PHUKET** (pronounced "Poo-ket") has been a prosperous region since the nineteenth century, when Chinese merchants got in on its tin-mining and sea-borne trade, before turning to the rubber industry. It remains the wealthiest province in Thailand, with the highest per-capita income, but what mints the money nowadays is **tourism**: with an annual influx of visitors that tops five million, Phuket ranks second in popularity only to Pattaya, and the package-tour traffic – particularly from Russia – has wrought its usual transformations. Thoughtless tourist developments have scarred much of the island, and the trend is upmarket, with few budget possibilities (expect to shell out up to twice what you'd pay on the mainland for accommodation and food, and sometimes more than double for transport, which is a particular headache on Phuket). However, many of the beaches are still strikingly handsome, resort facilities are second to none, and the offshore snorkelling and diving are exceptional. Away from the tourist hubs, many inland neighbourhoods are clustered round the local mosque – 35 percent of Phuketians are **Muslim**, and there are said to be more mosques on the island than Buddhist temples; though the atmosphere is generally as easy-going as elsewhere in Thailand, it's especially important to dress with some modesty outside the main resorts, and not to sunbathe topless on any of the beaches.

Phuket's capital, Muang Phuket, or **Phuket town**, is on the southeast coast, 42km south of the Sarasin Bridge causeway to the mainland. Though it's the most culturally stimulating place on Phuket, most visitors pass straight through the town on their way to the **west coast**, where three resorts corner the bulk of the trade: high-rise **Ao Patong**, the most developed and expensive, with an increasingly seedy nightlife; the slightly nicer, if unexceptional, **Ao Karon**; and adjacent **Ao Kata**, the smallest of the trio.

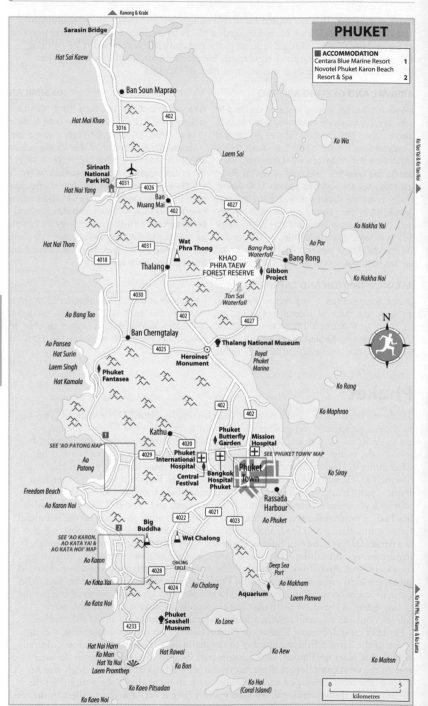

Ranong & Krabi

**PHUKET**

**ACCOMMODATION**
| | |
|---|---|
| Centara Blue Marine Resort | 1 |
| Novotel Phuket Karon Beach Resort & Spa | 2 |

Sarasin Bridge

Hat Sai Kaew

Ban Soun Maprao

Hat Mai Khao

3016
402

Laem Sai

Ko Wa

Sirinath National Park HQ
4031
4026

Hat Nai Yang

Ban Muang Mai
402
4027

Hat Nai Thon
4031
4018

Wat Phra Thong

Bang Pae Waterfall

KHAO PHRA TAEW FOREST RESERVE

Bang Rong

Ao Por

Ko Nakha Yai

Thalang

Gibbon Project

Ko Nakha Noi

4030

Ton Sai Waterfall

Ao Bang Tao

402

4027

Ban Cherngtalay
4025

Ao Pansea
Hat Surin
Laem Singh
Hat Kamala

Heroines' Monument

Thalang National Museum

Royal Phuket Marina

Ko Rang

Phuket Fantasea

Ko Maphrao

Kathu

4020

402

402

Phuket Butterfly Garden

Mission Hospital

SEE 'PHUKET TOWN' MAP

SEE 'AO PATONG MAP'

4029

Phuket International Hospital

Central Festival

Bangkok Hospital Phuket

Phuket Town

Ko Siray

Ao Patong

Freedom Beach

Ao Karon Noi

Rassada Harbour

Ao Phuket

4022
4021
4023

Big Buddha

SEE 'AO KARON, AO KATA YAI & AO KATA NOI' MAP

Wat Chalong

Deep Sea Port

Ao Karon

CHALONG CIRCLE
4028

Ao Kata Yai

4024

Ao Chalong

Aquarium

Ao Makham

Laem Panwa

Ao Kata Noi

Phuket Seashell Museum

Ko Lone

4233

Hat Nai Harn
Ko Man
Hat Ya Nui
Laem Promthep

Hat Rawai

Ko Bon

Ko Aew

Ko Maiton

Ko Kaeo Pitsadan

Ko Hai (Coral Island)

Ko Kaeo Noi

N

Ko Yao Yai & Ko Yao Noi

Ko Phi Phi, Ao Nang & Ko Lanta

0          5
kilometres

If you're after a more peaceful spot, aim for the 17km-long national park beach of **Hat Mai Khao**, its more developed neighbour **Hat Nai Yang**, or one of the smaller alternatives at **Hat Nai Thon** or **Hat Kamala**. Most of the other west-coast beaches are dominated by just a few upmarket hotels, specifically **Hat Nai Harn**, **Ao Pansea** and **Ao Bang Tao**; the southern and eastern beaches are better for seafood than swimming.

As with the rest of the Andaman coast, the sea around Phuket is at its least inviting during the **monsoon**, from June to October, when the west-coast beaches in particular become quite rough and windswept. At any time of year, beware the strong **undertow** and heed any red warning flags; there are dozens of fatalities in the water each year, but there is currently no official lifeguard service on the island. Some stretches of Phuket's coast were very badly damaged by the December 2004 **tsunami** (see page 307), which caused significant loss of life and destroyed a lot of property. Reconstruction was swift, however, and a first-time visitor to the island is now unlikely to notice any major post-tsunami effect.

## ARRIVAL AND DEPARTURE                                        PHUKET

### BY PLANE

**Phuket International Airport** (☎076 327230–79) is near the northern tip of the island, between Hat Mai Khao and Hat Nai Yang, 32km northwest of Phuket town. It has ATMs, currency exchange, a post office, a Bangkok Hospital clinic, a hotel booking and travel agency counters plus a left-luggage service (daily 6am–10pm; B80 per item per day). There are scores of international flights into Phuket, including several direct services from Australia. Between them, Thai Airways, Air Asia, Bangkok Airways, Orient Thai, Thai Lion Air and Nok Air run around thirty domestic flights a day between Bangkok and Phuket, while Bangkok Airways and Air Asia fly from Chiang Mai, Air Asia flies from Udon Thani and Bangkok Airways connects Phuket with Pattaya and Ko Samui.

**Onward transport** The orange airport bus (☎080 4655666, ✆airportbusphuket.com; B100; 1hr 20min) runs every 90min to/from the bus station in Phuket town, via Thalang, with an inconvenient 2hr 30min wait after the 4pm bus from the airport and after the 8am bus from the bus station; as it doesn't serve the beaches, you'll need to change on to the songthaews in town to reach those. Travel agents in and outside the arrivals hall run a/c minibuses that seat ten but is it up to passengers to rustle up other people if they wish to share the costs to Phuket town (B1100), Rassada Harbour pier (B1400), Patong (B1400) and Kata (B1600). Outside the arrivals hall at the south end of the building, you'll find booths for set-rate taxis to Phuket town (B450), Patong (B650) and Kata (B750), which includes a B100 airport charge. On departure from the beaches, most people use taxis organized by their hotel – about B500 for the hour's ride from Patong or Karon. If you're landing at the airport and want to catch a bus north, you can save going into Phuket town by getting a taxi or the airport bus to Ban Muang Mai, about 6km southeast of the airport on Highway 402, where you can pick up your northbound bus.

Destinations: Bangkok (30 daily; 1hr 20min); Chiang Mai (3 daily; 2hr); Ko Samui (2–5 daily; 50min); Pattaya/U-Tapao (daily; 1hr 35min); Udon Thani (1 daily; 2hr).

### BY BUS AND MINIBUS

A pink songthaew from bay 12 of Bus Station 2 shuttles to/from Bus Station 1 (B10; every 30min until 7pm; 30min).

**Bus Station 1** The "old" Baw Khaw Saw bus station, Bus Station 1, is off the eastern end of Thanon Phang Nga in Phuket town. It's a 10min walk or a short tuk-tuk ride to the town's central hotel area. On the west side of the bus station, licensed private companies offer a/c minibuses to Krabi, Ko Lanta, Surat Thani, Nakhon Si Thammarat, Trang and Hat Yai. Songthaews to the beaches depart from here and continue to the market area, so are another option for getting to the Old Town.

Destinations: Khao Lak (20 daily; 2hr 30min); Khao Sok (4 daily; 3–4hr); Takua Pa (20 daily; 2hr 30min–3hr); Phang Nga (at least hourly; 2hr 30min).

**Bus Station 2** The "new" Phuket Bus Station 2, 4km north of Phuket town, is now the main station for long-distance destinations, and also has minibuses. Most a/c buses from Bangkok's Southern Bus Terminal to Phuket make the journey overnight, departing from mid-afternoon onwards. There's no train service to Phuket, but you could book an overnight sleeper train to Surat Thani, about 290km east of Phuket, and take one of the regular buses from there to Phuket Bus Station 2 (about 5hr).

Destinations: Bangkok (21 daily; 12hr); Chiang Mai (1 daily; 18hr); Chumphon (4 daily; 5hr); Hat Yai (43 daily; 6hr); Khuraburi (hourly; 3hr); Ko Lanta (8 daily; 6hr); Ko Samui (daily; 6hr); Krabi town (11 daily; 4hr); Nakhon Si Thammarat (17 daily; 6hr); Phang Nga Town (54 daily; 1hr); Ranong (3 daily; 4hr); Satun (8 daily; 6hr); Surat Thani (17 daily; 4hr); Trang (17 daily; 5hr30min).

### BY BOAT

If you're coming to/from Phuket from Ko Lanta or Ao Nang in Krabi province, the quickest and most scenic option is to take the boat. Most hotels can arrange trips that include minivan transfers to the harbour. Infrequent songthaews run between Phuket town's Thanon Ranong market and the pier at Bang

## PHUKET DAY-TRIPS AND OTHER ACTIVITIES

Bookings for most of the following **Phuket day-trips and activities** can be made through any tour agent and should include return transport from your hotel (though not for the cooking classes). In addition to the trips listed below, diving is also available (see page 334). Other **sights** worth checking out, especially for kids, include the Phuket Butterfly Garden and Insect World in Phuket town (see page 320), the Aquarium on Laem Panwa (see page 338), the Shell Museum in Rawai (see page 337), the Big Buddha near Chalong (see page 338) and the Gibbon Rehabilitation Project near Thalang (see page 340). Avoid any tour that features Ko Siray (Ko Sireh), the island across the narrow channel from Phuket town, which merely encourages tour-bus passengers to gawp at Phuket's largest and longest-established indigenous *chao ley* community (see page 300).

**Bicycle touring** Full- and half-day guided mountain-bike rides into Phuket's rural hinterlands and to Ko Yao Noi, as well as multi-day rides around Phang Nga Bay, with Action Holidays Phuket (📞076 263575, ⊚biketoursthailand. com; full day with transfers from B3200).

**Kiteboarding** One- (B4000) and three-day courses (B11,000) at Hat Nai Yang and Ao Chalong (depending on the season) are offered by Kiteboarding Asia (📞081 591 4594, ⊚kitephuket.com).

**Mini-golf** If you just need a little time off from the beach or to entertain kids, head for the eighteen-hole Dino Park mini-golf (daily 10am–midnight; B240; ⊚dinopark. com), next to *Marina Phuket Resort* on the headland between Ao Karon and Ao Kata, which is part of a pseudo-prehistoric theme park comprising a dinosaur restaurant and an erupting "volcano" (evenings only).

**Sea-canoeing** There are dozens of companies offering canoeing and kayaking in Phuket, but the two with the best reputations are John Gray's Sea Canoe (📞076 254505–7, ⊚johngray-seacanoe.com), who offer afternoon and evening trips around the spectacular limestone karsts of Ao Phang Nga (B3950, including transfers), as well as the option of multi-day and self-paddle trips; and Paddle Asia (📞076 241519, ⊚paddleasia.com), who run day-trips to Ao Phang Nga (B4300, including transfers) and multi-day trips, which can also take in Khao Sok National Park and include other adventure activities.

**Surfing** The rainy season (roughly May–Oct) is the best time for surfing off Phuket's west coast; courses (B1500 for a 90min private lesson) and board rental are available from Phuket Surf on Ao Kata Yai (📞087 889 7308, ⊚phuketsurf.com).

**Thai cookery courses** Most famously, every Sat and Sun morning at *The Boathouse* hotel on Ao Kata Yai (B2200; 📞076 330015, ⊚boathouse-phuket.com); but also at the *Holiday Inn Phuket*, 86/11 Thanon Thavee Wong, Patong (Wed, Sat & Sun 10am; B2575; 📞076 340608, ⊚phuket.holiday-inn.com); and the *Blue Elephant Restaurant*, 96 Thanon Krabi, Phuket town (B2800 for a half-day class; daily 8.30am & 1.30pm; 📞076 354355, ⊚blueelephantcookingschool.com/phuket).

Rong, via the Heroines' Monument (about 1hr; B50). A taxi to Bang Rong from town or the main beaches costs about B500, from Phuket airport B450, or about B260 if you can cajole the driver into turning his meter on; the taxi service at Bang Rong pier charges B500 to the airport, B800 to Patong.

**To/from Ko Phi Phi** During peak season, up to three ferries a day, plus a speedboat or two, head to and from Ko Phi Phi, docking at Rassada Harbour on Phuket's east coast; during low season, there's at least one ferry a day in both directions.

**To/from Ko Yao Noi** Boats from Ko Yao Noi and the high-season speedboat service from Ao Nang via Ko Yao Noi terminate at Bang Rong on Phuket's northeast coast.

**To/from Ko Lanta** Travellers from Sala Dan on Ko Lanta (Nov–May only) may have to change boats at Ao Nang or Ko Phi Phi to get to Phuket's Rassada Harbour.

**To/from Ao Nang** Ferries go to Rassada Harbour; speedboats from Ao Nang via Ko Yao Noi terminate at Bang Rong.

**Onward transport from Rassada Harbour** Shared a/c minibuses meet the ferries at Rassada Harbour and charge B50 per person for transfers to Phuket town hotels, B150 to Patong and B200 to the airport; taxis charge B500–600 per car to the major west-coast beaches or the airport (leave plenty of extra time if you have a flight to catch as boats are notoriously tardy).

**Onward transport from Bang Rong** Infrequent songthaews shuttle between Bang Rong and Phuket town (about 1hr; B40), while taxis charge B500–800 to the airport or the west-coast beaches.

Destinations: Ao Nang (Nov–May 2 daily; 2hr); Ko Lanta Yai (Nov–May several daily; 4hr 30min); Ko Phi Phi Don (several daily; 2hr); Ko Yao Noi (roughly hourly; 40min–1hr 10min).

## GETTING AROUND

Getting around the island is a nightmare: on the one hand, tuk-tuks and taxis know that they have a captive audience and charge through the nose; on the other, Phuket has often steep and winding roads, with quite a few hairpin bends – if you do decide to drive yourself, stay alert. There is a system of public songthaews (supplemented by buses) radiating out from Phuket town, but to get from one beach to another by this method you nearly always have to go back into town. For transport within resorts, the cheapest option is to make use of the public songthaews where possible, or to hail a motorbike taxi where available (B30–100).

**By songthaew** Songthaews run regularly throughout the day (when they have a full complement of passengers) from Thanon Ranong at the market in the centre of Phuket town to the coast and beaches and cost B25–45.

**By tuk-tuk or taxi** Tuk-tuks and taxis do travel directly between major beaches, but are notoriously overpriced (there are almost no metered taxis on the island), charging at least B150 from Kata to Karon or B300 between Patong and Karon

and often doubling their prices after dark – they have been known to ask for B1000 to go from Patong to Karon at night. Phuket TAT (see page 320) issues a list of price guidelines but you'll have to bargain hard to get near the quoted prices.

**Motorbike rental** Many tourists rent their own motorbike or moped, which are widely available (from B300/day), but be warned that there is a very sobering average of ten thousand motorbike injuries a year on Phuket, and about a hundred fatalities; it makes sense to obey the compulsory helmet law, which is anyway strictly enforced in most areas of Phuket, with flouters subject to a B500 fine.

**Car rental** At the airport, there are offices of Avis (☎ 02 251 1131/2, ⓦ avisthailand.com) and Budget (☎ 1 800 283 438, ⓦ budget.co.th), who also have a branch on Patong (see page 328); both charge from around B1200/day.

## INFORMATION

**On the web** There's a wide-ranging website about Phuket, ⓦ phuket.com, which is great for discounted accommodation.
**Guidebooks** For a detailed historical and cultural guide to the island, it's hard to better Oliver Hargreave's impressive

*Exploring Phuket & Phi Phi* (Within Books).
**Tourist office** Phuket's TAT office is in Phuket Town (see page 320) and has a small number of displays with photos on the history of Phuket Town but little else.

## DIRECTORY

**Dentists** At Phuket International Hospital and Bangkok Hospital Phuket (see below).

**Hospitals** Phuket International Hospital (☎ 076 249400, emergencies ☎ 076 210935, ⓦ phuketinternationalhospital. com), north of Central Festival shopping centre on Highway 402, just west of Phuket town, is considered to have Phuket's best hospital facilities, including an emergency department and an ambulance service. Reputable alternatives include Bangkok Hospital Phuket, on the northwestern edge of Phuket town just off Thanon Yaowarat at 2/1 Thanon Hongyok Uthis (☎ 076 254425, ⓦ phukethospital. com), and the Mission Hospital (aka Phuket Adventist

Hospital), on the northern outskirts at 4/1 Thanon Thepkasatri (☎ 076 237220–6, emergencies ☎ 076 237227, ⓦ missionhospitalphuket.com).

**Immigration office** At the southern end of Thanon Phuket, in the suburb of Saphan Hin, Phuket town (☎ 076 221905, ⓦ phuketimmigration.go.th; Mon–Fri 8.30am–noon & 1–4.30pm), plus an information centre in Patong.

**Tourist police** For all emergencies, contact the tourist police, either on the free, 24hr phone line (☎ 1155), at their main office at 327 Thanon Yaowarat in Phuket town (☎ 076 223891, ⓦ phukettouristpolice.go.th), or at their branch in Patong (see page 331).

# Phuket Town

Though it has plenty of hotels and restaurants, **PHUKET TOWN** (Muang Phuket) stands distinct from the tailor-made tourist settlements along the beaches as a place of tangible history and culture. Most visitors hang about just long enough to jump on a beach-bound songthaew, but you may find yourself returning for a welcome dose of real life; there's plenty to engage you in a stroll through the small but atmospherically restored heart of the Old Town, along with many idiosyncratic cafés and art shops, several notable restaurants and some good handicraft shops. The town works well as an overnight transit point between the islands and the bus stations or airport, but is also worth considering as a base for exploring the island, with more interesting and affordable accommodation, eating and drinking options than the beaches, but linked to them by regular songthaews.

## The Old Town

Between Thanon Dibuk and Thanon Rat Sada ⓦ lestariheritage.net/phuket
Phuket town's most interesting features are clustered together in the **Old Town** conservation zone, a grid of streets between Thanon Dibuk and Thanon Rat Sada whose colonial-

## PHUKET TOWN SINO-PORTUGUESE ARCHITECTURE

As Chinese immigrant merchants got rich on tin-mining profits they started building homes, the vast majority of which are eminently practical terraced **shophouses** at the heart of the merchant district. Phuket's Old Town retains south Thailand's finest examples, some of which are open to the public, but there are also intact, if less well-conserved, shophouse neighbourhoods in many other southern cities, including Ranong and Takua Pa.

Shophouse design followed a standard prototype favoured by the mixed-race Chinese–Malay ("Baba-Nyonya") and Straits Chinese immigrants from Penang, Melaka and other parts of the Malay Peninsula. It's a style now widely dubbed **Sino-Portuguese** because Melakan architecture of the time was itself strongly influenced by the territory's Portuguese former colonists, though it also incorporates traits from Dutch and Anglo-Indian colonial architecture. Although some features have evolved with changing fashions the basic look is still recognizably mid-nineteenth century.

Because streetside space was at a premium, shophouses were always long and thin, with narrow frontages, recessed entrances and connecting porches that linked up all the way down the block to make shady, arched colonnades known as **five-foot walkways**, ideal to protect pedestrians and shoppers from the tropical sun and rain. The front room was (and often still is) the business premises, leaving the rest of the two- or three-storey building for living. A light well behind the front room encouraged natural ventilation and sometimes fed a small courtyard garden at its base, and the household shrine would always occupy a prominent and auspicious position. Outside, the hallmark features that make the neighbourhoods so striking today include pastel-painted **louvred windows** that might be arched or rectangular and perhaps topped by a pretty glass fantail, lacquered and inlaid wooden doors, fancy gold-leaf fretwork, detailed **stucco mouldings** and perhaps Neoclassical pilasters.

style **Sino-Portuguese shophouses** (see below) date back to the nineteenth century, the former homes of emigrant Chinese merchants from Penang, Singapore and Melaka. Indeed, modern-day residents have put a lot of effort into restoring these handsome old neighbourhoods, and with plenty of mural art, budget traveller accommodation and hip streetside cafés, the Old Town truly resembles the two aforementioned Unesco-protected Malaysian towns. The Phuket Old Town Foundation helps to publish the excellent free **Phuket Town Treasure Map**, available all over the Old Town, and also stages the **Old Town Festival** just before Chinese New Year (sometime between Jan & March).

Some of the Old Town's most elegant buildings line the western arm of **Thanon Thalang**, where a dozen signboards – including at *Thalang Guest House* at no. 37 (see page 321) and outside the *China Inn Café* at no. 20 (see page 321) – highlight the special features worth an upward or sideways glance: pastel-coloured doors and shutters, elaborate stucco mouldings, ornate wooden doors, and the distinctively arched "five-foot walkways" that link them. Further east along Thanon Thalang there's more of an Islamic emphasis, with many old-style shops selling fabric and dressmaking accessories, including lots of good-value sarongs from Malaysia and Indonesia. The road's former red-light alley, **Soi Romanee**, has also been given a major multicoloured face-lift and these days buzzes come sundown with arty accommodation options, little bars and red lanterns, while on nearby **Thanon Dibuk** the doors and window shutters of *Dibuk Restaurant* at no. 69 display intricate wooden and gold-leaf fretwork. You'll find other renovated Sino-Portuguese buildings on **Thanon Yaowarat**, and on **Thanon Ranong** (where the Thai Airways office occupies a fine old mansion), **Thanon Phang Nga** (especially the *On On Hotel*) and **Thanon Damrong**, whose town hall, just east of the Provincial Court, stood in for Phnom Penh's US embassy in the film *The Killing Fields*.

### Peranakan Museum Phuket Town

Corner of Phang Nga Road and Phuket Road • Tue–Sun 9am–4.30pm • Free • ⓦ peranakan-phuket-museum.business.site/

Phuket Town's latest museum celebrates the islands' links to Peranakan Chinese culture. The experience is quite modest, and there aren't many explanations beyond a short video on the second floor. The collection of textiles and original furniture is pretty impressive though, and the helpful staff are more than happy to show visitors around.

## Phuket Thaihua Museum

28 Thanon Krabi • Daily 9am–5pm • B200 + B200 for cameras • ⓦ phuket.com/attractions/phuket-thai-hua-museum.htm

The **Phuket Thaihua Museum** is housed in a 1930s Neoclassical former school – complete with grand columns, stucco decoration, shuttered windows and central light well. Some of the old school desks are still *in situ*, but the focus of the museum's excellent displays, videos and historic photos is on the role and traditions of Phuket's main immigrant groups, namely the Chinese and mixed-race Baba-Nyonya (Malay–Chinese) communities who arrived to work in the island's burgeoning tin-mining industry.

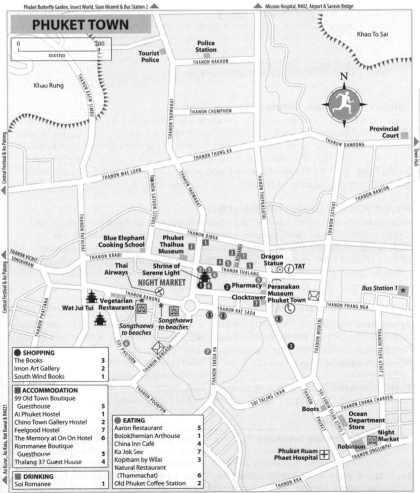

PHUKET TOWN

4

## NGAN KIN JEH: THE VEGETARIAN FESTIVAL

For nine days, usually in October or November, at the start of the ninth lunar month (see Ⓦ phuketvegetarian.com for exact dates), the celebrations for **Ngan Kin Jeh** – the Vegetarian Festival – set the streets of Phuket town buzzing with processions, theatre shows and food stalls, culminating in the unnerving spectacle of men and women parading about with steel rods pierced through their cheeks and tongues. The festival marks the beginning of **Taoist Lent**, a month-long period of purification observed by devout Chinese all over the world, but celebrated most ostentatiously in Phuket, by devotees of the island's five Chinese temples. After six days' abstention from meat (hence the festival's name), alcohol and sex, the white-clad worshippers flock to their local temple, where drum rhythms help induce a trance state in which they become possessed by spirits. As proof of their new-found transcendence of the physical world they skewer themselves with any available sharp instrument – fishing rods and car wing-mirrors have done service in the past – before walking over red-hot coals or up ladders of swords as further testament to their otherworldliness. In the meantime, there's singing and dancing and almost continuous firework displays, with the grandest festivities held at Wat Jui Tui on Thanon Ranong in Phuket town.

The ceremony dates back to the mid-nineteenth century, when a travelling Chinese opera company turned up on the island to entertain emigrant Chinese working in the tin mines. They had been there almost a year when suddenly the whole troupe – together with a number of the miners – came down with a life-endangering fever. Realizing that they'd neglected their gods, the actors performed elaborate rites and kept to a vegetarian diet, and most were soon cured. The festival has been held ever since, though the self-mortification rites are a later modification, possibly of Hindu origin.

### San Jao Saeng Tham (Shrine of Serene Light)

Accessed via a soi through the narrow archway next to South Wind Books on Thanon Phang Nga • Daily 8.30am–noon & 1.30–5.30pm

The spiritual heritage of Phuket's Chinese immigrants is kept very much alive by their descendants, notably in the extraordinary spectacle of the annual Vegetarian Festival (see box above). They also maintain many shrines around town, including **San Jao Saeng Tham**, the tiny **Shrine of Serene Light**, whose roof is decorated with intensely coloured ceramic figurines of dragons, carp and sages in bright blues, greens and reds.

### Phuket Butterfly Garden and Insect World

2km beyond the northern end of Thanon Yaowarat at 71/6 Soi Paneang in Ban Sam Kong • Daily 9am–5pm • B300 • ☎ 076 210861, Ⓦ phuket.com/attractions/phuket-butterfly-garden.htm • A tuk-tuk from the town centre should cost around B200 return

Kids usually enjoy the **Phuket Butterfly Garden and Insect World**, whose thousands of butterflies of some twenty indigenous species flit around the prettily landscaped grounds; there's also a silk museum documenting the amazingly industrious short life of the silkworm, plus scorpions, tarantulas and other notorious creepy-crawlies.

### ARRIVAL AND INFORMATION

PHUKET TOWN

**By songthaew** Songthaews (supplemented by buses) run regularly throughout the day from the market on Thanon Ranong in the town centre to all the main beaches and cost B25–45. Return songthaews can finish as early as 4pm so check before you go.

**Tourist information** The TAT office is at 63 Thanon Thalang (daily 8.30am–4.30pm; ☎ 076 212213, ✉ tatphket@tat.or.th), and has a small number of displays with photos on the history of Phuket Town and unique souvenirs but little else.

**Travel agent** The travel desk in the lobby of *The Memory at On On Hotel* on Thanon Phang Nga (☎ 076 216161), is a helpful agent, good for all kinds of transport bookings, including cheap boat tickets, as well as activities and day-trips.

### ACCOMMODATION

★ **99 Old Town Boutique Guesthouse** 99 Thanon Talang ☎ 081 797 4311, Ⓦ 99oldtownguesthouse. com; map p.319. Atmospheric renovation of an original Sino-Portuguese shophouse, which retains original blinds, shutters and wooden partitions, set along lantern-lit corridors paved with crimson and golden tiles. The rooms, all with hanging LED screens and industrial chic en-suite bathrooms, may be a bit small, but the curtained bed-frames and dark-wooden flooring really help preserve the building's heritage. <u>B890</u>

**Ai Phuket Hostel** 88 88 Thanon Yaowarat ☎076 212881, ⊛aiphukethostel.com; map p.319. Funky and friendly hostel that looks better beyond the reception and tour desk, where dark-wood floorboards lead to two storeys of rooms and a cosy garden. The dorms have no windows but are spotless and come with plush mattress and lockers. The few grey-hued, luminous and attractive doubles are a step up in price but better value. There is free wi-fi and a coin-operated laundry machine for guests. Dorms B250, doubles B900

**Chino Town Gallery Hostel** Thanon Yaowarat ☎086 941 8783, ⊛chinotownphuket.com; map p.319. A very good budget option with a spacious dark wooden floored a/c dorm filled with single beds, each with individual reading lights and electric sockets, and a few compact yet surprisingly smart rooms (some en-suite) with Peranakan Chinese motifs on the floor tiles. Dorms B200, doubles B590

**Feelgood Hostel** 92 Thanon Phang Nga ☎095 4273846, ⊛feelgoodhostel.com; map p.319. As the name suggests, this hostel has a friendly atmosphere, tempting travellers to stay longer than planned. The spotless dorms have two rows of bunkbeds with privacy curtains and are set in a spacious wooden-floored loft. Potted plants spruce up the industrial chic shared bathrooms. There's free wi-fi and coffee too; even a simple breakfast is included in the price. Couples can stay in the one en-suite private room (B800). B280

**The Memory at On On Hotel** 19 Thanon Phang Nga ☎076 363700, ⊛thememoryhotel.com; map p.319. This stunningly renovated, colonial-style 1920s building may no longer cater to budget travellers, but it's still a very atmospheric option to enjoy the Old Town's lovely heritage charms. The double rooms all have a/c as well as en-suite bathrooms, plus there's a tour agent on site. B1600

**Rommanee Boutique Guesthouse** 15 Soi Rommanee ☎089 7289871, ⊛therommanee.com/rommaneeboutique/; map p.319. Artistic flourishes abound in the seven rooms, which feel more luxurious than their price tag may suggest. Rustic mirrors, designer furniture, high ceilings and plush bedding make for a comfortable stay in this renovated 80-year-old building. All come with en suite, a/c and a simple breakfast. The café downstairs has international brews (from B55), home-made pastries, and is a relaxed spot to mingle with other travellers. B1200

**Thalang 37 Guest House** 37 Thanon Thalang ☎076 214225, ⊛facebook.com/thalangguesthouse37; map p.319. Housed in a 1940s, Sino-Portuguese, wood-floored shophouse in one of the Old Town's most attractive streets, this place is fairly simple but full of character, traveller-friendly and good value. The twelve fan and a/c rooms are large and en suite – the best of them are up on the rooftop, affording unusual panoramic views. It's very popular, so it's best to book ahead; rates include a simple breakfast. Fan B400, a/c B500

## EATING

Phuket town has the largest concentration of good Thai food on the island, well worth making the trip here for. Unlike Thais in most other parts of the country, Phuketians like to breakfast on noodles rather than rice; spindly white *khanom jiin* noodles, made with rice-flour and ladled over with one of several different fiery, soupy curry sauces, are a local speciality and served at some of the restaurants listed below. You can try snacks such as fresh hot tofu and sticky rice at the night market, which starts by the beach songthaews on Thanon Ranong. Over half a dozen simple Thai vegetarian restaurants display tasty look-and-pick mock-meat curries and cold veg dishes with rice for B30–60 on Thanon Ranong and Soi Puthorn, west of Wat Jui Tui. They are open from the early morning till nearly midnight.

**Aaron Restaurant** Thanon Talang ☎098 016 6562; map p.319. This hole-in-the-wall coffee shop dishes up delicious Malay-style *rotis*, pulled and baked to perfection on a metal table right before your eyes. They also have beef soup and authentic *khaoyam pattani* (a tossed rice salad with fresh vegetables, typical of south Thailand). A meal will set you back about B100. Daily 6.30am–5pm.

**Bo(ok)hemian Arthouse** 61 Thanon Thalang ☎096 524223; map p.319. Artsy little bookstore and hangout for cappuccinos (B60), free wi-fi, DVD rental and occasional film screenings. Mon–Fri 9am–7pm, Sat & Sun 9am–8.30pm.

**China Inn Café** 20 Thanon Thalang ☎081 979 8258, ⊛facebook.com/chinainnphuket; map p.319. This beautifully renovated heritage house and courtyard garden would be reason enough to stop by for a meal, but the menu is also enticing, proffering Thai dishes such as *phat thai* (B210) and spicy salads like the inspired pomelo, coconut and prawn (B290), as well as a few Western, mostly Italian, dishes. Streetside, the gallery shop displays Asian antiques, textiles and lacquerware. Tues–Sun 10.30am–6.30pm, closed Mondays.

**Ka Jok See** 26 Thanon Takuapa ☎076 217903; map p.319. A Phuket institution, housed in a charmingly restored traditional shophouse (unsigned), this place serves fabulous Thai food on a pricey set menu (B2000) and fosters a fun, sociable atmosphere – after meals, tables are literally set against the walls by the staff, who attempt to coax everyone into dancing. Mains are sophisticated and beautifully presented – their *goong sarong*, individual shrimps bound in a crisp-noodle wrap, is famous island-wide. Reservations are essential. Daily 7.30pm–late.

**Kopitiam by Wilai** 14 & 18 Thanon Thalang ☎83 6069776; map p.319. Eating at the dark-wood tables while surrounded by vintage Chinese scrolls and typewriters can transport you into the rustic world of old Phuket Town. The extensive Thai menu includes Phuket-style grilled pork

4

with Chinese herbs (B125), and even Peranakan Chinese *hokkien mee* and *bak kut the* (B130); be sure to try the delicious passionfruit juice (B50). Mon–Sat 11am–10pm.

★ **Natural Restaurant (Thammachat)** 62/5 Soi Putorn ☎076 224287, ⓦnaturalrestaurantphuket.com; map p.319. There are plenty of reasons to linger over a casual dinner at this rambling, hugely popular restaurant, not least the two hundred different choices on the menu, and the affordable prices (main dishes around B150). Highlights include fried sea bass with chilli paste,

fried chicken with Muslim herbs, soft-shelled crab with garlic and pepper, and spicy Phuket bean salad. Daily 10.30am–11.30pm.

**Old Phuket Coffee Station** 72/1 Thanon Yaowarat ☎099 475 6846; map p.319. Hip bistro in an old mansion, all furnished in Old World style, including an impressive wall of vintage radios and assorted memorabilia that fills up every corner. The coffee (B60) is good and they also serve staple Thai fried-rice and noodle dishes (from B130). Daily 9am–8pm.

## DRINKING

**Soi Romanee** map p.319. This artfully restored, plant-strewn soi connecting Dibuk and Thalang roads shows off its handsome pastel paintwork and stuccoed Old Town facades with half a dozen little café-bars whose seating spills out on to the pavement for ultimate architectural appreciation. Try *Glasnost* for live music, particularly jazz, and its bohemian atmosphere. Most places serve classic Thai dishes and beers and get going 6–10pm, staying open slightly later Nov–April.

## ENTERTAINMENT

**Siam Niramit Phuket** North of town off Thanon Chalerm Prakiat ☎076 335000, ⓦsiamniramit.com. An offshoot of the Siam Niramit Bangkok extravaganza, this 70min show presents a tourist-oriented rendering of traditional Thai theatre, in a high-tech spectacular of fantastic costumes and huge chorus numbers, enlivened by acrobatics and flashy special effects. Tickets from B1500. Mon & Wed–Sun 8.30pm.

## SHOPPING

The two most fruitful shopping roads for local handicrafts and antiques are Thanon Yaowarat and Thanon Rat Sada, while the cluster of shops on eastern Thanon Thalang keep a phenomenal range of well-priced sarongs, mostly of Burmese, Malaysian and Indonesian designs. *Art and Culture South*, a useful, free, quarterly booklet that's available at TAT and other outlets, details some of the best shops and galleries in the town and around. For retro enamelware and gifts, visit the shop attached to the *Rommanee Classic* hotel.

**The Books** Thanon Phuket; map p.319. Decent selection of new English-language books and magazines, with a coffee corner and internet access. Daily 10am–9pm.

**Imon Art Gallery** Thanon Phang Nga ☎086 961 8968, ⓦbit.ly/2Bvmgth; map p.319. An impressive collection of woodcut prints and arty postcards by local artist Monthian. Daily 9am–7.30pm.

**South Wind Books** Thanon Phang Nga, ☎089 724 2136; map p.319. Big, sprawling range of secondhand books. Mon–Sat 9am–5pm, Sun 10am–3pm.

# Hat Mai Khao

Phuket's longest and quietest beach, the 17km **HAT MAI KHAO**, unfurls along the island's upper northwest coast, beginning some 3km south of the Sarasin Bridge causeway and ending just north of the airport (34km from Phuket town). It's a beautiful piece of casuarina- and palm-shaded coastline, minimally developed and protected in part as **Sirinath National Park** because of the few giant marine turtles that lay their eggs here between October and February.

## ARRIVAL AND DEPARTURE                                    HAT MAI KHAO

It's possible to get to Hat Mai Khao on foot via the adjacent beaches; otherwise, the beach is easily reachable by using your own transport or via a taxi, which is usually the most practical way.

## ACCOMMODATION

Accommodation on Hat Mai Khao is predominantly five-star: an enclave of half a dozen luxury hotels is elegantly spaced behind the sloping shoreline towards the north end of the beach, accessed by an all-but-private road that is not served by any public transport. Most of the resorts have a swimming pool as the undertow here can be fierce and unpredictable.

★ **Anantara Phuket Villas** ☎076 336100–9, ⓦphuket.anantara.com. Set amid stylishly landscaped grounds and lagoons, all the secluded villas here have their own plunge pool, outdoor bath and garden *sala*, while the luxurious interiors feature antique furniture, lots of dark wood, dressing rooms and espresso machines. There's an impressive selection of free activities, including sailing and yoga, a kids' club, a beautiful spa and excellent seafood at the stylish restaurant, *Sea Fire Salt*. Rates are sometimes reduced by more than half in low season; check the website for regular promotions. B15,500

**Mai Khao Beach Bungalows** Next door to the Holiday Inn 081 895 1233, maikhaobeach.wordpress. com. Six simple en-suite bungalows sit in spacious, grassy grounds just behind the shore beneath coconut palms hung with hammocks. There's a restaurant and motorbike rental here too, but not much else. Easiest access to *Mai Khao*

*Beach Bungalows* is by bus to or from Phuket town: ask to be dropped at Thachatchai police box, 4km away on Highway 402, from where you can phone the bungalows for a pick-up. Closed Augest, sometimes longer, during the rainy season; you have to pay more for hot water. Fan B1000, a/c B1500

**Sala Phuket** 076 338888, salahospitality.com/ phuket. The sharp, Sino-modern architecture of the villa compounds here – all done out in cool creams and silver, with colour-coordinated planting and the occasional lacquered screen – attract mainly couples, especially honeymooners, who enjoy the style and privacy, especially of the pool villas. There's an enticing open-air seafront lounging area here too, with deliciously squishy sofas, plus a rooftop terrace, a spa and three swimming pools. Breakfast included. B10,000

# Hat Nai Yang

The long, curved sweep of **HAT NAI YANG**, 5km south of Hat Mai Khao and 30km north of Phuket town, is partly under the protection of Sirinath National Park and has only fairly low-key development. In the plentiful shade cast by the feathery casuarinas and cajeput trees that run most of the length of the bay stand more than a dozen small seafood restaurants, and a small, low-rise tourist village of travel agents, a few accommodation options, ATMs, a massage pavilion, internet and dive shops. The beach is clean and good for swimming at the southern end, and there's a reasonable, shallow **reef** about 1km offshore (10min by longtail boat) from the Sirinath National Park headquarters, which is a fifteen-minute walk north of the tourist village (if you're driving yourself to Hat Nai Yang, when the main access road hits the beach, turn left for the tourist village, right for the national park).

## ARRIVAL AND DEPARTURE                                    HAT NAI YANG

**By taxi** Hat Nai Yang is just 2km south of the airport, about B200 by taxi.

**By songthaew** An infrequent songthaew service (B40; 1hr 45min) runs between Phuket town and Hat Nai Yang.

## ACCOMMODATION

**Discovery Beach Resort** 081 6939359, discovery-phuket@hotmail.com. Set inside a beachfront mansion that doesn't look too attractive from the roadside, the spacious en-suite rooms here have wooden floors, a/c, TV and most importantly, are right on the beach, behind a line of trees. The family rooms for four people (B2200) are great value for this area. B1500

**The Slate** 076 327006, theslatephuket. com. Luxurious rooms and villas look onto attractively

landscaped plantation-style gardens that run down to the southern end of the beachfront road; facilities include a meandering lagoon-like saltwater swimming pool, a dive shop, an inventively programmed activities centre, a spa and a kids' club. Interiors are designed to evoke Phuket's tin-mining history, with metallic colour schemes, polished cement floors and a penchant for industrial art, but the look is softened by very comfortable furniture, generous balconies and plenty of greenery. B10,000

## EATING

The tourist village in Nai Yang is locally famous for its small shorefront restaurants that serve mostly barbecued seafood (and the odd wood-fired pizza), on mats under the trees and at tables on the sand, which are candlelit and exceptionally tranquil at night.

**The Beach Restaurant** On the northern end of the beach 088 7612310, kio.thebeach@gmail.com. One of several little beach bars in the tourist village, that

besides being a cool, relaxed place for a drink in its low-slung track-side chairs on the beach, has a good selection of Thai rice and noodle curries (from B170). Happy hour(s) between 3–5pm & 10–11pm. Daily noon–1am.

**Black Ginger** The Slate 076 327006, facebook. com/BlackGingerRestaurant. For a really top-notch romantic dinner, you can't beat the intimate, black-painted, award-winning *sala* here, accessible only by boat.

Highlights from the classy menu (from B300) include the Phuket lobster with red coconut curry, fresh Vietnamese-style rice flour pancakes stuffed with shrimps, coriander and other herbs, and local *kaeng leuang* (yellow curry with fish fillet; B900). Reservations advisable as can get quite busy. Daily 6.30–11pm.

## Hat Nai Thon

The next bay south down the coast from Hat Nai Yang is the small but perfectly formed 500m-long gold-sand **HAT NAI THON**, backed by pristine viridian hills and with good snorkelling at reefs a short longtail ride offshore. Shops, hotels and restaurants line the inland side of its narrow little shorefront road, but there's still a low-key, village-like atmosphere here. 1km up the hill, along road 4018 is the turn off to **BANANA BEACH**, a secluded cove accessible only by foot, that sees few visitors despite its stunning location at the bottom of a viridian slope.

### ARRIVAL AND DEPARTURE                                    HAT NAI THON

Most visitors to Hat Nai Thon tend to rent their own transport as songthaews don't make the detour from the highway and taxis are very thin on the ground around these parts.

### ACCOMMODATION

**Andaman White Beach Resort** About 2km south of Hat Nai Thon over the southern headland ☎076 316300, ⓦandamanwhitebeach.com. Occupying secluded cliff-side land that runs down to a gorgeous little private bay of white sand and turquoise water (sometimes known as Hat Nai Thon Noia), this resort offers luxurious rooms and villas with unsurpassed views, including some designed for families, plus a 40m swimming pool and a lovely spa. B7200

**Naithonburi Beach Resort** ☎076 318700, ⓦnaithonburi.com. Huge resort, with over two hundred posh a/c rooms in a U-shaped complex enclosing an enormous pool, some of them with direct pool access, though it doesn't dominate the bay. B2800

### EATING

**Tycoon Ting** Across the road from the northern end of the beach ☎076 602286. High-class, industrial-chic glass and concrete restaurant with a *sala* filled with white furniture, and a menu of reasonably priced dishes. It's a perfect option for wine and cocktails, or Western-Thai fusion plates, including fried minced pork with fish cake (B200), pastas (from B220) and stir-fried chicken with cashew nut (B190). Daily 11am–11pm.

## Ao Bang Tao

Re-landscaped from a former tin-mining concession to encompass lagoons, parkland and Phuket's best eighteen-hole golf course, **AO BANG TAO** is dominated by the vast, upscale *Laguna Phuket*, a gated "integrated resort" of seven luxury hotels on an impressive 8km shorefront. It's a world away from the thrust and hustle of Patong and a popular choice for families, with no need to leave the *Laguna* village, though beware of the undertow off the coast here, which confines many guests to the hotel pools. There's free transport between the seven hotels, which between them offer a huge range of leisure and sports facilities, as well as a shopping centre.

### ARRIVAL AND ACCOMMODATION                              AO BANG TAO

Half-hourly **songthaews** (B25; 1hr 15min) cover the 24km from Phuket town to Ao Bang Tao during the day, or there are resort shuttle **buses** and on-site **car** rental.
**Laguna Phuket** ☎076 362300, ⓦlagunaphuket.com. The main website sometimes has discounted rates at *Laguna*'s seven hotels, while the family-oriented *Best Western Allamanda Laguna* (☎076 324050, ⓦallamandaphuket.com), comprising 150 apartment-style suites with kitchenette and separate living area, has the cheapest rates in the complex. Haunt of high society and sports stars, the exclusive *Banyan Tree Phuket* (☎076 372400, ⓦbanyantree.com/en/thailand/phuket) offers lavish villas in private gardens, many with private pools, and the gloriously indulgent, award-winning, Banyan Tree spa. Best Western B6000, Banyan Tree B21,930

## Hat Surin and Ao Pansea

South around Laem Son headland from Ao Bang Tao, handsome little **HAT SURIN** is a favourite weekend getaway for sophisticated Phuketians and a big draw for expats, who inhabit the ever-expanding forest of condo developments inland from the small, pretty beach. The shorefront gets very crowded, however, packed with sunloungers and beach restaurants, so it can be hard to appreciate the setting.

Eating and shopping facilities cater to the upmarket clientele, and beachfront dining and drinking is the favoured pastime here. Things are much quieter on Hat Surin's northern bay, **AO PANSEA**, which is divided from the main beach by a rocky promontory.

### ARRIVAL AND DEPARTURE                                    HAT SURIN AND AO PANSEA

**By songthaew** Songthaews travel the 24km route between Phuket town and Hat Surin, departing approximately every half-hour during the day and costing around B35.

### ACCOMMODATION

**Benyada Lodge** 103 Thanon Hat Surin ☎076 271261, ✆benyadalodge-phuket.com. Located just across the small park from the beach, this thirty-room lodge with high standards of service is well maintained in a crisp, bright contemporary style, with the addition of a rooftop swimming pool and bar-restaurant. The spacious a/c rooms all have hot showers, TV and fridge. Breakfast included. B2800

### EATING

**Taste** ☎087 886 6401, ✆tastebargrill.com. This sophisticated seafront restaurant is known for its great seafood, such as steamed red snapper fillet with a lemon and butter sauce (B490), but also serves international mains, from Italian gorgonzola-garnished flatbreads (B225) to Mexican tostadas (B345). Tues–Sun 3.30pm–midnight.

**Twin Brothers** ☎089 7231874, ✆bit.ly/TwinBrothersSurinBeach. The eponymous local twins pair a spectacular location under the palm trees on the sand with down-to-earth prices for their menu of Thai seafood dishes (white snapper B100/100g) and Western food. Daily 8am–10pm.

## Hat Kamala and Laem Singh

With its cheerfully painted houses and absence of high-rises, the small, village-like tourist development at **HAT KAMALA** is low-key and mid-market, sandwiched between the beach and the predominantly Muslim town of Ban Kamala, about 300m west of the main Patong–Surin road, 6km north of Patong and 26km northwest of Phuket town. Accommodation, shops, restaurants and other tourist services are mostly clustered either side of shoreside Thanon Rim Had (also spelt Rim Hat) which, despite its limited choice, is a much pleasanter place to browse than the big resorts. The beach gets prettier and quieter the further north you go, away from Thanon Rim Had, with restaurant shacks renting sunloungers along most of its course. A stretch of this area is backed by the Muslim cemetery, so it's particularly important to respect local sensibilities and avoid going topless.

Kamala was very badly hit by the 2004 **tsunami**, which tragically killed many residents and completely wiped out the beachfront school, the temple and countless homes and businesses. Though extensive rebuilding has extinguished most of the physical scars, a copper sculpture in the park opposite *Print Kamala* bears witness to the devastation, and a volunteer English-teaching programme at the school, Phuket Has Been Good to Us (see page 65), aims to continue rebuilding some of the young lives affected.

About 1km northeast of Hat Kamala, a couple of steep paths lead west off the main Patong–Surin road down to **Laem Singh** cape, a pretty little sandy cove whose picturesque combination of turquoise water and smooth granite boulders makes it one of Phuket's finest. It's good for swimming and very secluded, plus there's a decent patch of shade throughout the day.

## ARRIVAL AND DEPARTURE

**By songthaew** The cheapest way to get to Hat Kamala is by songthaew from Phuket town (departs approximately every half-hour during the day, 1hr 15min; B40).

## ACCOMMODATION

Hat Kamala is popular with long-stay tourists, and several hotels offer rooms with kitchenettes; there's also a preponderance of small-scale places.

**Baan Kamala Fantasea Hostel** On the soi parallel to the beachside road, ☎076 279053, ⓦbaankamalaphuket.com. It would be a mistake to dismiss this guesthouse for its tacky nautical theme, which is visible from the street. But get past the boat-shaped reception desk and bar, through charming pastel-coloured corridors dotted with potted plants and both the dorms and doubles will prove to be some of the best value in the area. Dorms have plush beds and sparkling clean common bathrooms, while the more expensive private rooms (some with little balconies and all en suite) are much better equipped than you might think for the price. Dorms B450, doubles B2000

**Benjamin Resort** 83 Thanon Rim Had, opposite the school at the southerly end of the beachfront road ☎084 1906848, ⓔbenjaminresort@hotmail.com. Set right on the beach and about the cheapest deal in Kamala, this block of 37 a/c rooms has seen better days but couldn't be closer to the sea. Although views are obstructed from all but the most expensive rooms (B800), the spacious interiors are almost identical and all have a balcony, fridge, TV and hot water. There's no wi-fi and breakfast is an additional B99. B500

## HAT KAMALA AND LAEM SINGH

**Kamala Dreams** 74/1 Thanon Rim Had, ☎076 279131, ⓦkamalabeach.net. Epitomising all the best things about Kamala, this is a really nice, small hotel set right on the shore, in the middle of the tourist village and above its annexed seafood restaurant. Its eighteen rooms are large and furnished in contemporary style, and all have a/c, TVs, a kitchenette and a large balcony overlooking the pool and the sea. B2300

★**Layalina** 75 Thanon Kamala ☎076 385944, ⓦlayalinahotel.com. This gem of a mid-range hotel has breezy wooden partitions and a beachfront café. A central staircase gives way to two floors of large rooms that use their wooden fittings to great effect. The en-suite bathrooms have Jacuzzi-style bathtubs, and the large windows on the ground floor give access to a small yet pretty sea-facing swimming pool. There's also a private sunbathing deck on the rooftop; breakfast is included. B4000

**Swissotel Resort Phuket Kamala** North of Kamala beach, on the way to Hat Surin ☎ 076 303000, ⓦswissotel.com/phuket. Attractive mini apartment-style rooms in several concrete blocks shaded by tall palm trees, all set around the resort's centrepiece: an attractive, huge swimming pool with its own water slide and wooden bridges connecting the different wings. The poolside bar plays techno tunes well into the night. Continental buffet breakfast included. B4275

## EATING, DRINKING AND ENTERTAINMENT

Most people eat and drink on the beach, especially at the restaurant shacks and bars that pretty much line the shore all the way north from opposite *Print Kamala*; seafood is the big seller here, and you can bury your feet in the sand.

**Le Café Lafayette** On the soi parallel to the beachside road ☎099 4017017, ⓦfacebook.com/lafayettefrenchbakery. Cosy industrial-style building that opens onto an inner courtyard filled with potted plants, offering a quiet break from the hustle and bustle of the beachfront. Coffees (from B70) are strong, the fresh-fruit smoothies (B130) refreshing, whilst the eclectic cakes (such as delicious Mango Charlotte, B120) attract plenty of expats and European tourists looking to step back into their comfort zones. Daily 7.30am–7.30pm.

**Duck Spicy** Thanon Kamala near corner with Thanon Rim Had. Spicy really means spicy here, so be careful what you ask for from the extensive, authentic Thai menu. The place itself is not fancy, but it makes a welcome dose of reality to eat dishes such as duck and mint salad (B120) with the locals, away from the resorts. Daily 8am–10pm.

# Ao Patong

The busiest and most popular of all Phuket's beaches, **AO PATONG** – 5km south of Ao Kamala and 15km west of Phuket town – is vastly overdeveloped and hard to recommend. A congestion of high-rise hotels, tour agents and souvenir shops disfigures the beachfront road, tireless and tiresome touts are everywhere, and hostess bars and strip joints dominate the nightlife, attracting an increasing number of single Western men to the most active scene between Bangkok and Hat Yai. On the plus side, the broad, 3km-long beach offers good sand and plenty of shade beneath the parasols and there are hundreds of shops and bars plus a surprising number of good restaurants to keep you busy after dark.

## ARRIVAL AND GETTING AROUND

**By songthaew** Songthaews from Phuket town (approx every 15min, 6am–6pm; 30min; B30) approach Patong from the northeast, driving south along one-way Thanon Raja Uthit Song Roi Phi (Thanon Raja Uthit 200 Phi) then circling back north along beachfront Thanon Thavee Wong (also one-way) via the *Patong Merlin*, where they wait to pick up passengers for the return trip.

**Vehicle rental** National car rental (☎ 076 340608, ⓦ nationalcarthailand.com) has a desk inside the *Holiday Inn*, the local Budget agent is at the nearby *Patong Merlin*

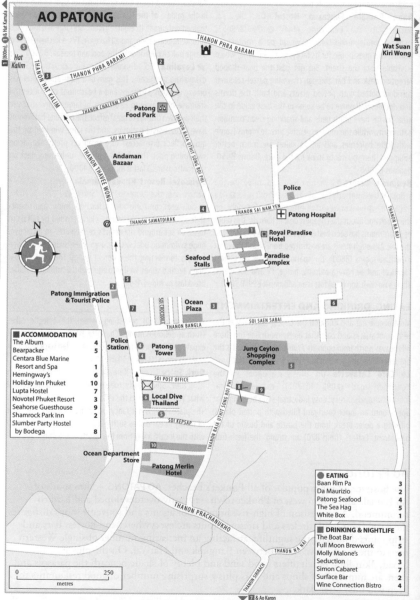

**AO PATONG**

ACCOMMODATION
| The Album | 4 |
| Bearpacker | 5 |
| Centara Blue Marine Resort and Spa | 1 |
| Hemingway's | 6 |
| Holiday Inn Phuket | 10 |
| Lupta Hostel | 7 |
| Novotel Phuket Resort | 3 |
| Seahorse Guesthouse | 9 |
| Shamrock Park Inn | 2 |
| Slumber Party Hostel by Bodega | 8 |

EATING
| Baan Rim Pa | 3 |
| Da Maurizio | 2 |
| Patong Seafood | 4 |
| The Sea Hag | 5 |
| White Box | 1 |

DRINKING & NIGHTLIFE
| The Boat Bar | 1 |
| Full Moon Brewwork | 5 |
| Molly Malone's | 6 |
| Seduction | 3 |
| Simon Cabaret | 7 |
| Surface Bar | 2 |
| Wine Connection Bistro | 4 |

(☎076 292389, ⓦbudget.co.th); beware of renting jeeps and motorbikes from transport touts on Thanon Thavee Wong as scams abound.

**Tours and activities** Most of the tour agents have offices on the southern stretch of Thanon Thavee Wong, offering a number of day-trips and activities (see box, page 316); this is also where you'll find many of the dive operators (see box, page 334).

## ACCOMMODATION

Regardless of its seediness, Patong offers something for every budget. Overall, upper-end hotels are reasonable value.

**The Album** 29 Thanon Sawatdirak ☎076 297023, ⓦthealbumhotel.com; map p.328. Tiny urban-chic boutique inn, where the 22 carefully designed a/c rooms all have a flatscreen TV, DVD player and a petite balcony. There's a small Jacuzzi pool on the fourth-floor roof terrace; rates include continental breakfast and high tea. Discounts of up to fifty percent are available online. B6000

**Bearpacker** 140 Thanon Thavee Wong ☎076 685118, ⓔbearpackerhostel@gmail.com; map p.328. Four-storey backpacker hostel, decorated with blue-and-white cartoonish bears and packed to the gills. Featuring sparkling clean a/c dorms with plush bedding, reading lights and individual lockers (bring your own padlock, or pay B50). Also has a rooftop restaurant with a tiny Jacuzzi pool. Free coffee and tea is served from 8 to 10am. B500

★ **Centara Blue Marine Resort and Spa** 290/1 Prabaramee Road ☎076 370400, ⓦcentarahotels resorts.com/centara/cmp/; map p.328. Just north of Ao Patong, this hillside Thai chain hotel retains all the quiet and calm the beach is missing. Most rooms are in concrete blocks facing the bay. There's an Olympic-size swimming pool, and the inclusive continental breakfast is above average. Free shuttle service to Patong Beach several times a day. B4452

**Hemingway's** 179/95–8 Soi Saen Sabai ☎076 540895, ⓦpatonghemingways.com; map p.328. Smart, modern, a/c rooms done out in dark wood, black and red, with small, hot-water bathrooms, TVs and fridges. Wicker chairs and old-fashioned ceiling fans downstairs are all that conjure up the ghost of Ernest Hemingway, but the big plus-point of this place is the small rooftop pool, Jacuzzi and bar with views of the surrounding hills. Breakfast is B200 extra. B1800

**Holiday Inn Phuket** 52 Thanon Thavee Wong ☎076 370200, ⓦphuket.holidayinnresorts.com; map p.328. Well-run, innovative, upmarket chain hotel that offers smart, contemporary rooms just across the road from the beach, and fosters an informal, unpretentious atmosphere. The poshest Busakorn villa rooms have their own interconnected pools and there are several restaurants and an interesting programme of daily activities. The hotel makes a big effort to be family-friendly, with special suites for children, an all-day kids' club and a teens' club and two children's pools. Also offers wheelchair-accessible rooms. Breakfast included. B4788

**Lupta Hostel** 138 Thanon Thavee Wong, across the road from Rip Curl's shop ☎076 602462, ⓦluptahostel.com; map p.328. Attractive apartment that has been converted into a chic hostel with a common area filled with beanbags, four- and eight-person dorms with plush bedding, privacy curtains, and one room for three people (B1200). The shared toilets are squeaky clean and there's a washing machine for guests' use. Free wi-fi and flow of hot drinks provided. B450

**Novotel Phuket Resort** Thanon Phra Barami/Thanon Hat Kalim ☎076 342777, ⓦnovotelphuket.com; map p.328. Luxurious and relaxing chain hotel built on the hillside above Kalim Bay, the quieter, northern end of the resort, a 10min walk or a free shuttle ride to Patong's main beach and shops, but very close to some of the best restaurants. Occupying sloping landscaped tropical gardens and offering exceptional high-level sea views, it's especially popular with families as it offers heaps of activities plus a multi-level swimming pool. Large discounts online. B5270

**Seahorse Guesthouse** 189/7 Rat U Thit 200 Pee Road ☎091 826 1817, ⓦseahorsephuket.com; map p.328. Sociable hostel tucked away in a quiet soi, yet not far from Thanon Bangla's action and the beach. Dorms and shared bathrooms are functional and clean, there's motorbike rental (B350/day); a simple toast and coffee breakfast is B50 extra. The few private doubles have en-suite toilets and small balconies. Dorms B250, doubles B1000

**Shamrock Park Inn** Above The Deli supermarket, 31 Thanon Raja Uthit Song Roi Phi ☎076 340991; map p.328. Friendly, good-value three-storey hotel at the northern end of the resort with large, pleasant, well-maintained and cheerily painted a/c rooms, all with TVs, fridges and safety boxes. Ask for a room on the north side of the building: they're cooler, have balconies and are away from the noise of the adjacent Irish bar. B800

**Slumber Party Hostel by Bodega** 189/3 Rat U Thit 200 Pee Road ☎076 602 191, ⓦslumberpartyhostels.com/locations/phuket/; map p.328. With a hall that looks like the entrance of a fraternity house and a name that says it all, this is the perfect place for the young party crowd. Beside pub crawls and plenty of social activities, the dorm rooms, each with its own en-suite bathroom, are sparkling clean and equipped with everything today's backpacker has come to expect. Dorms B500

## EATING

Much of the food on Patong is dire, but in among the disastrous little cafés advertising everything from

Hungarian to Swedish "home cooking" you'll find a few genuinely reputable, long-running, upmarket favourites;

**4**

reservations are recommended at all the places listed here. For well-priced Thai fast food, there are the regional speciality stalls at the *Food Haven* food centre in Jung Ceylon, the *Patong Food Park* night market that sets up around 5pm towards the northern end of Thanon Raja Uthit Song Roi Phi, and the row of seafood stall-restaurants further south, opposite the *Royal Paradise Hotel* complex.

★ **Baan Rim Pa** Across from the Novotel on Thanon Hat Kalim ✆ 076 340789, 🌐 baanrimpa.com; map p.328. One of Phuket's most famous fine-dining restaurants, this elegant spot is beautifully set in a clifftop teak building overlooking the bay, with tables also on its sea-view terrace. Known for its classic "Royal Thai" cuisine (from about B350), including banana blossom salad, creamy duck curry and fried tiger prawns with tamarind sauce, as well as for its wine cellar. Live jazz every night in the *Piano Bar*. Daily noon–midnight.

**Da Maurizio** Across from the Novotel on Thanon Hat Kalim ✆ 076 344079, 🌐 baanrimpa.com/italian-restaurant; map p.328. Superior Italian restaurant in a stunning location set over the rocks beside the sea. Serves authentic antipasti and home-made pasta such as pappardelle with scallops and crab in a spicy tomato sauce, Phuket lobsters and other great seafood, and a good wine list. Main dishes from B450. Daily noon–midnight.

**Patong Seafood** 98/2 Thanon Thavee Wong ✆ 081 691 5298; map p.328. Established Thai restaurant on the main beach strip, decked out in wood and specialising in seafood and Western staples. The prices are pretty good for the location: Thai noodles start at B150, pastas at B220, and seafood goes by the kilo. Daily 11am–midnight.

★ **The Sea Hag** Down Soi Dr Wattana (Soi Permpong 3), on the southern side of Patong Beach ✆ 076 341111, 🌐 seahag-patong.com; map p.328. The same chef has been cooking great seafood here for two decades and this is where expat hoteliers come for a good Patong feed. Fish and seafood cooked any number of Thai-style ways for B200–400. Daily noon–4pm & 6pm–midnight.

**White Box** Thanon Hat Kalim, 1.5km north of the Novotel ✆ 076 346271, 🌐 whitebox.co.th; map p.328. This chic, sophisticated waterside restaurant and bar, strikingly designed as a modernist cube with panoramic picture windows, is a magnet for visiting celebs and style-conscious expats. The very expensive menu (mains from B520) mixes Thai and Mediterranean flavours – think sea-bass fillet with truffles, grilled hazelnut and vegetables (B850), or red curry with roasted duck – and the rooftop sofas are ideal for a relaxing pre- or post-dinner drink. Daily 11am–11.30pm.

## DRINKING AND ENTERTAINMENT

After dark, everyone heads to pedestrianised Thanon Bangla for their own taste of Patong's notorious **nightlife** and the road teems with a cross section of Phuket tourists, from elderly couples and young parents with strollers, to glammed-up girlfriends and groups of lads. One of the big draws is Thanon Bangla's Soi Crocodile, better known as Soi Katoey, where barely clad transgender women dance and pout on podiums at the mouth of the soi and charge for photos with tourists. But the real action happens further down the many bar-filled sois shooting off Thanon Bangla, where open-air bar-beers and neon-lit go-go clubs packed with strippers and goggle-eyed punters pulsate through the night. The pick-up trade pervades most bars in Patong, and though many of these joints are welcoming enough to couples and female tourists, there are a few alternatives, listed below, for anyone not in that kind of mood. The **gay** entertainment district is concentrated around the Paradise Complex, a network of small sois and dozens of bar-beers in front of *Royal Paradise Hotel* on Thanon Raja Uthit Song Roi Phi: see 🌐 gaypatong.com for events listings, including dates for the annual Gay Pride festival, which has recently been held in late April. If you're looking for something else to do with yourself (or your kids) in the evening, check out the *katoey* (transgender) Simon Cabaret or head to the Jung Ceylon shopping centre, which has the seven-screen SF Cinema City.

**The Boat Bar** Soi 5, Paradise Complex, off Thanon Raja Uthit Song Roi Phi 🌐 boatbar.com; map p.328. Long-

running, very popular gay bar and disco, with two cabaret shows nightly, at around midnight and 1.30am. Daily 9pm–late.

**Full Moon Brewwork** Port Zone (next to the replica junk), Jung Ceylon shopping centre, Thanon Raja Uthit Song Roi Phi ✆ 076 366 753, 🌐 fullmoonbrewwork. com; map p.328. The best of this microbrewery's offerings is their dark ale, a decent bitter that might appease homesick Brits, and there's good food, too, including *tom yam kung* (B180) and bangers and mash. Live music upstairs (Mon, Wed & Fri–Sat 7.30–10pm). Daily 11am–midnight.

**Molly Malone's** 94/1 Thanon Thavee Wong ✆ 076 292771; map p.328. Genial Thai–Irish pub chain next to *McDonald's* that serves draught Guinness and Kilkenny, shows international sports TV, stages live bands playing pub rock from 9.30pm and has pool tables, a small beer garden and no overt hostess presence. Daily 10am–2am.

**Seduction** Soi Happy, off Thanon Bangla 🌐 seduction disco.com; map p.328. A favourite dance venue for partying couples and others not looking for freelance company, this four-storey bar and club has fairly classy lounge areas, hi-tech lighting and Euro dance, and occasionally brings in big-name international DJs. Free until midnight, B300–500 thereafter. Touts outside give useful discount vouchers but avoid the short-lived, diluted-drinks package on the door. Daily 10pm–4am.

**Simon Cabaret** 8 Thanon Sirirach, south end of Patong ✆ 076 3420 114–6, 🌐 phuket-simoncabaret.com; map p.328. Famously flamboyant extravaganza starring a troupe of *katoey*. It's all very Hollywood – a little bit risqué but not at all sleazy – and popular with tour groups and families. Daily 6pm, 7.45pm & 9.30pm.

**Surface Bar** Top floor, La Flora Resort Patong, 39 Thanon Thavee Wong ☎ 076 344 241 ⓦ laflorapatong. com/surface_bar.html; map p.328. The perfect place for a sophisticated sundowner, enjoyed from the comfort of enormous sofas on the hotel's wide rooftop terrace. Expansive ocean views and a sea breeze as well. Daily 5pm–midnight.

**Wine Connection Bistro** First floor of Banana Walk shopping mall, 124/11 Thanon Thavee Wong ☎ 076 510 622, ⓦ wineconnection.co.th; map p.328. Imported international wines, from New Zealand to Italy and South Africa (from B500 per glass), served on a pleasant terrace with a sea view, right in the centre of Patong, yet without any hint of seediness. Daily 10am–12pm.

## DIRECTORY

**Immigration** The tiny Patong branch (information only) of Phuket's immigration office is next to *Surface Bar* on Thanon Thavee Wong (☎ 076 340 477; Mon–Fri 10am–noon & 1–3pm).

**Post office** Thanon Thavee Wong (daily 9am–7pm).

**Shopping** Though you can't move for shops in downtown Patong, by far the best, and least hectic, place to browse is Jung Ceylon on Thanon Raja Uthit Song Roi Phi (daily 11am–10pm; ⓦ jungceylon.com), an enormous shopping centre, whose refreshingly tasteful and spacious design includes fountains and plaza seating plus countless shops and restaurants. There are branches of Robinsons Department Store and, on the ground floor at the front end, Boots the Chemist and Asia Books (for English-language books, magazines and newspapers), plus the That's Siam Thai handicrafts emporium in the basement.

**Tourist police** In front of the immigration office on Thanon Thavee Wong (☎ 076 340244 or ☎ 1155).

# Ao Karon

**AO KARON**, Phuket's second resort, after Patong, is very much a middle-of-the-road destination. Far less lively, or congested, than Patong, but more commercial and less individual than the smaller beaches, it's the domain of affordable guesthouses and package-tour hotels and appeals chiefly to mid-budget tourists, many of them from Scandinavia and Russia. The 2.5km-long **beach** is graced with squeaky soft golden sand and is completely free of developments, though there's very little natural shade; an embankment screens most of the southern half of the beach from the road running alongside, but north of the *Hilton* the road is more often in view and parts of the shore back on to lagoons and wasteland. Karon's main **shopping and eating areas**, with all the usual resort facilities, are grouped around the *Centara Karon Resort* on the northern curve of Thanon Patak; along and around Thanon Luang Pho Chuain, location of the Karon Plaza enclave of accommodation, restaurants and bars; and along Thanon Taina (sometimes referred to as Kata Centre).

The **undertow** off Ao Karon is treacherously strong during the monsoon season from June to October, so you should heed the warning signs and flags and ask for local advice – fatalities are not uncommon. The tiny bay just north of Ao Karon – known as **Karon Noi** or Relax Bay – is almost exclusively patronized by guests of the *Le Meridien* hotel, but non-guests are quite welcome to swim and sunbathe here.

## ARRIVAL AND DEPARTURE ___ AO KARON

**By songthaew** Ao Karon is 5km south of Patong and 20km southwest of Phuket town. Most songthaews from Phuket town (approx every 20min; 30min; B40) arrive in Karon via Thanon Patak, hitting the beach at the northern end of Ao Karon and then driving south along beachfront Thanon Karon, continuing over the headland as far as *Kata Beach Resort* on Ao Kata Yai. To catch a songthaew back into town, just stand on the other side of the road and flag one down. Transport touts throughout the resort rent motorbikes and jeeps.

## ACCOMMODATION

★ **Casa Brazil** 9 Soi 1, Thanon Luang Pho Chuain ☎ 076 396317, ⓦ phukethomestay.com; map p.332. Appealingly arty little hotel, designed in Santa Fe style, with adobe-look walls, earth-toned paintwork, and funky decor and furnishings. The 21 rooms are comfortable, with hot showers, fridges and TVs, and nearly all have a/c. Choose rooms at the back for a rare green and peaceful view of Karon's hilly backdrop, best enjoyed from the French windows and private balconies. Rates include breakfast. Fan B1200, a/c B1400

**Centara Grand Beach Resort** 683 Thanon Patak ☎076 201234, ⓦcentarahotelsresorts.com/centaragrand/cpbr/; map p.332. Huge, low-rise, beachfront luxury hotel, which very loosely echoes Phuket's Sino-Portuguese architecture, all in different shades of pink. It's particularly good for children, with two kids' clubs, a kids' pool, a free-form main pool and a "Lazy River", an artificial river that runs under bridges and under tunnels for exploration on inner tubes. There's an adults-only pool too, and grown-ups can also enjoy kayaking, windsurfing, tennis, the spa and a long menu of other activities. Large discounts on their website. B̲1̲0̲,̲5̲0̲0̲

**Le Meridien** Ao Karon Noi (also known as Relax Bay), north of Ao Karon ☎076 370100, ⓦlemeridien.com; map p.332. This huge hotel complex has the tiny bay all to itself and boasts an amazing breadth of facilities: ten restaurants and bars, two lagoon-style swimming pools (with islands), a spa, squash and tennis courts, free non-motorized watersports and private woods. A good choice for kids, with babysitting and a kids' club. Breakfast included. B̲8̲5̲0̲0̲

**Lucky Guest House** 110/44–45 Thanon Taina, Kata Centre ☎076 330572, ⓔluckyguesthousekata@hotmail.com; map p.332. Good-value place offering unusually large, bright en-suite rooms in a low-rise block (the best have balconies) and some rather plain but very clean semi-detached bungalows on land further back; set back a bit down a small soi, this guesthouse has a refreshing sense of space that's at a premium on this road packed with shops, bars and restaurants. Fan B̲6̲0̲0̲, a/c B̲9̲0̲0̲

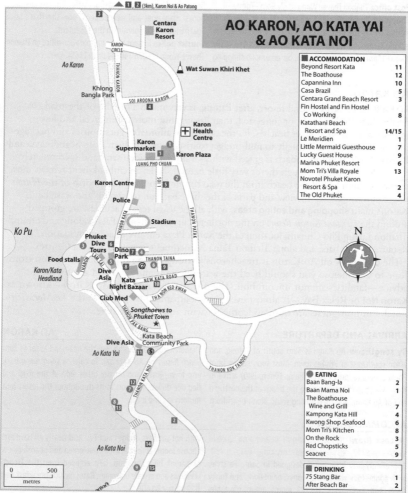

**AO KARON, AO KATA YAI & AO KATA NOI**

■ **ACCOMMODATION**

| | |
|---|---|
| Beyond Resort Kata | 11 |
| The Boathouse | 12 |
| Capannina Inn | 10 |
| Casa Brazil | 5 |
| Centara Grand Beach Resort | 3 |
| Fin Hostel and Fin Hostel Co Working | 8 |
| Katathani Beach Resort and Spa | 14/15 |
| Le Meridien | 1 |
| Little Mermaid Guesthouse | 7 |
| Lucky Guest House | 9 |
| Marina Phuket Resort | 6 |
| Mom Tri's Villa Royale | 13 |
| Novotel Phuket Karon Resort & Spa | 2 |
| The Old Phuket | 4 |

● **EATING**

| | |
|---|---|
| Baan Bang-la | 2 |
| Baan Mama Noi | 1 |
| The Boathouse Wine and Grill | 7 |
| Kampong Kata Hill | 4 |
| Kwong Shop Seafood | 6 |
| Mom Tri's Kitchen | 8 |
| On the Rock | 3 |
| Red Chopsticks | 5 |
| Seacret | 9 |

■ **DRINKING**

| | |
|---|---|
| 75 Stang Bar | 1 |
| After Beach Bar | 2 |

**Marina Phuket Resort** 47 Thanon Karon, far southern end of Ao Karon, on the Karon/Kata headland ☎076 330625, ⓦmarinaphuket.com; map p.332. Enjoying both a very central location, backing on to the beach, just steps from restaurants and shops, and a luxuriously spacious and secluded tropical garden in a former coconut plantation, this is a good upper-end choice. Garden View cottages are old-fashioned and plain, but Jungle View versions are very appealing – and there's a pool and the prettily located *On the Rock* restaurant. Breakfast included; book through their website for free dinner and airport transfer. B7290

**Novotel Phuket Karon Resort & Spa** 568 Patak Road ☎076 358 666, ⓦnovotelphuketkaron.com; map p.332. One of the latest offerings from the chain is set 1.5km north of the beach but makes up for the distance with a central free-form swimming pool. Around it, there are several blocks of excellent and modern rooms, including some with private plunge pools. There's a spa centre and a Western–Thai fusion restaurant. A continental buffet breakfast is included. B4380

**The Old Phuket** Soi Aroona Karon, 192/36 Thanon Karon ☎076 396353–6, ⓦtheoldphuket.com; map p.332. The Sino wing at this attractive, peacefully secluded, heritage-conscious hotel is designed to evoke Sino-Portuguese shophouse architecture. Its rooms are both pretty and modern, with coloured glass window panels and East Indies-style wooden doors. Furnishings in the more expensive Serene Wing are much more contemporary and minimalist, and many of its rooms have direct access to the lagoon-like swimming pool. B7000

## EATING

Karon's choice of restaurants is underwhelming, lacking either the big-name restaurants of Patong or Kata, or the authenticity of Phuket town. Though go-go bars haven't arrived yet, clusters of outdoor bar-beers with hostess service are popping up at a depressing rate.

**Baan Bang-la** 6 Soi Patak, off Thanon Patak ☎81 968 5878; map p.332. The seafood here has a good reputation and there are also pasta dishes and pizzas – made in a brick oven by an Italian *pizzaiolo* – on the menu too. Dining is mostly alfresco in Thai *salas* set around a pretty little garden. Mains B180–300. Daily 6pm–late.

**Baan Mama Noi** Karon Plaza, next door but one to Pineapple Guesthouse on a lane off Thanon Patak ☎ 091 889 2381; map p.332. Expats, dive staff and Italian tourists fill this place at lunch and dinnertime, savouring the home-from-home taste of the excellent, mid-priced, Italian food, such as spaghetti bolognese (B150). Daily 9.30am–10pm.

**Kwong Shop Seafood** 114 Thanon Taina, ☎076 3285201; map p.332. Unassuming but very popular, friendly family-run institution sporting gingham tablecloths that's famous for its well-priced fresh fish (all B40/100g) and seafood cooked to order. Daily 8am–midnight.

**On the Rock** In the grounds of Marina Phuket Resort, Kata/Karon headland ☎076 330625, ⓦmarinaphuket. com/restaurants; map p.332. Occupying a fine spot above the rocks at the southern end of Ao Karon, this open-air restaurant serves especially good baskets of grilled and deep-fried seafood, such as lobster gratin (B1500), baked mussels and mixed seafood satay. It's especially romantic at night. Main dishes cost from around B350. Daily 12am–12pm.

## DRINKING

**75 Stang Bar** Karon Plaza, up a lane off Thanon Luang Pho Chuain, near Thanon Patak ☎085 471 5759, ⓦfacebook.com/75StangReggaeBar; map p.332. Amongst the sports bars and rooms for rent in Karon Plaza, there are a couple of art bars run by locals, including this invitingly bohemian outdoor place. It's a charming mess of driftwood and found objects, where the only things that seem to have been bought new are the red, gold and green stools, which match the reggae bands on stage on most nights. Drinks are cheap. Daily 1pm–2am.

# Ao Kata Yai and Ao Kata Noi

Broad, curving **AO KATA YAI** (Big Kata Bay) is only a few minutes' drive around the headland from Karon (17km from Phuket town), but both prettier and safer for swimming, thanks to the protective rocky promontories at either end. It's also a good distance from the main road. The northern stretch of Kata Yai is overlooked by the unobtrusive buildings of the *Club Med* resort, and the southern by *Kata Beach Resort*: in between, the soft sand is busy with sunloungers and the occasional drink and fruit stall. The rest of the accommodation, and the bulk of the tourist village, with its restaurants, bars, tour operators and many shops, fans out eastwards from the walled *Club Med* compound, up to the main road, Thanon Patak.

Beyond the southern headland, **AO KATA NOI**'s (Little Kata Bay) smaller white-sand bay feels secluded, being at the end of a no-through road, but is very popular and filled with loungers and parasols. Kata Noi has its own low-key but rather charmless cluster of businesses, including an ATM and minimarket, though it's dominated by the various sections of the enormous *Katathani* hotel; public access to the beach is down to the right just beyond the hotel's Thani wing.

## ARRIVAL AND DEPARTURE                                          AO KATA YAI AND AO KATA NOI

**By songthaew** Most songthaews from Phuket go first to Karon, then drive south past *Club Med* and terminate beside *Kata Beach Resort* on the headland between Kata Yai and Kata

Noi (B30; returning songthaews depart approx every 20min 5am–4.30pm). To get to Kata Noi, continue walking over the hill (around 20min), or take a tuk-tuk for about B200.

## ACCOMMODATION

**Beyond Resort Kata** Thanon Kata, Kata Yai ☎076 330530–4, ⓦkatagroup.com/kata-beach/home/; map p.332. Recently re-branded, this huge 275-room, four-storey hotel occupies a great spot right on Kata Yai's white-sand beach. It has a seafront restaurant, two outdoor swimming pools, a lovely palm-shaded seaside garden, a spa and a dive shop. Some of the attractive, balconied, wooden-floored rooms have direct access to the pool, whilst some have sea views. Continental breakfast included. B5500

**The Boathouse** 182 Thanon Kok Tanode, Kata Yai ☎076 330015–7, ⓦboathouse-phuket.com; map p.332. Exclusive contemporary beachfront boutique hotel, with 38 elegant seafront rooms, classy service and a top-notch restaurant. There's a pool, a spa and weekend cooking classes. Advance booking essential. B12,600

**Capannina Inn** The Beach Centre, "New Kata Road", Kata Yai ☎076 284450, ⓦphuket-capannina-inn.com; map p.332. Smart, modern, large bedrooms and well-equipped bathrooms, with a/c, cable TV, hot water, fridges

---

## DIVING AND SNORKELLING OFF PHUKET

The reefs and islands within sailing distance of Phuket rate among the most spectacular in the world, and **diving and snorkelling** trips are both good value and hugely popular. Many trips operate year-round, though some of the more remote islands and reefs become too dangerous to reach during part or all of the monsoon season, roughly June to October.

### DIVE SHOPS AND TRIPS

All the dive **shops** listed below are established and accredited PADI Five-Star Instructor or Career Development Centres; they teach courses, organize dive trips and rent equipment. Advice on choosing a dive shop and other general diving information can be found in "Basics" (see page 51). Expect to pay around B4000 for a one-day introductory **diving course**, and B16,000 for the four-day Open Water course, including equipment. **Day-trips** to the closest of the dive sites listed below, including at least two dives, cost around B4900, while multi-day **live-aboard** cruises to the more distant top-rated reefs of Ko Similan and Ko Surin, Hin Daeng and Hin Muang, and the Mergui archipelago can cost as much as B33,000 for four days, including sixteen dives and full board but excluding equipment and national park fees.

There are **recompression chambers** at Phuket International Hospital in Phuket town (see page 317), and at Vachira Hospital, Soi Wachira, Thanon Yaowarat, Phuket town (☎076 211114, ⓦvachiraphuket.go.th).

**Dive Asia** 23/6 Thanon Karon, Kata/Karon headland, Ao Karon, and 1/21 Patbang Rd, Ao Kata ☎081 894 8588, ⓦdiveasia.com.
**Local Dive Thailand** The diving centre's small office is

located close to *McDonald's*, Ao Patong T062 2262354, ⓦlocaldivethailand.com.
**Phuket Dive Tours** Laem Sai Road, Ao Kata ☎087 0225356, ⓦphuketdivetours.com.

### SNORKELLING TRIPS

The most popular snorkelling destination from Phuket is **Ko Phi Phi** (see page 365). All travel agents sell mass-market day-trips there, on huge ferries with capacities of a hundred plus; prices average B3800 and include snorkelling stops at Phi Phi Leh and Phi Phi Don, snorkel rental and a seafood lunch. Smaller speedboat trips to Ko Phi Phi are usually worth the extra money to avoid the big groups; those run by Offspray Leisure (B3500; ☎076 281375, ⓦoffsprayleisure.com) get good reviews, and they also run speedboat snorkel trips to **Ko Racha Yai** (B3500). Day-trip packages to the remote but beautiful **Ko Similan** islands start from B6900 (see page 312). Many and espresso machines. Guests have the use of an attractive, shared, garden pool in front. It's set in a newer development of shops and hotels, a 5min walk from the beach –there's a free tuk-tuk to the beach and the restaurant. Continental breakfast included. B1800

★ **Fin Hostel** and **Fin Hostel Co Working** 100/20 Kata Night Plaza, Kata Yai ☎ 088 753 1162, ⓦ finhostel phuket.com; map p.332. Facing each other on a busy corner of Kata Yai's village area, these two surfer-friendly hostels have squeaky clean a/c dorm rooms featuring reading lights and charging stations. Toilets are luxurious for the category and look swanky with their bare walls, naked light bulbs and potted plants. Fin also has some en-suite doubles, a kitchen for guest use and a rooftop swimming pool. *Fin Co Working* has capsule pods for couples at a bargain B450 and two halls dotted with computer stations on the ground floor that – as the name suggests – serve as working space for digital nomads. They are free for guests, but they can be also rented for B100/hour. Dorms B400, doubles B2000

**Katathani Beach Resort and Spa** 14 Thanon Kata Noi, Kata Noi ☎ 076 318 350, ⓦ katathani.com; map p.332.

The various wings and offshoots of the enormous and luxurious *Katathani* now occupy almost the entire shoreline of small, secluded Kata Noi. The beachfront all-suite Thani wing has the prime position, with the narrow lawn dropping seamlessly onto the white sand; all rooms here have seaview balconies. Across the effectively private, no-through road, the cheaper, garden-view Bhuri wing has a distinctively contemporary, pastel-coloured look and its rooms too are very deluxe. There's daily shuttle service to town and to Patong. The hotel has six restaurants, six swimming pools and a spa, plus an arm-long menu of activities and a kids' club. Breakfast included. B14,000

**Little Mermaid Guesthouse** 126 Thaina Road, Kata Yai ☎ 076 330873, ⓦ facebook.com/littlemermaid guesthouserestaurant; map p.332. Spacious en-suite rooms above a popular Thai bar. Most of the rooms have certainly seen better days but are still kept very clean and are good value for the price, considering there's wi-fi, a/c and hot water. Paying a bit extra will get you a window with courtyard view (B840). B790

**Mom Tri's Villa Royale** 12 Thanon Kata Noi, Kata Noi ☎ 076 333569, ⓦ villaroyalephuket.com; map p.332.

of the dive companies listed welcome snorkellers on board their day-trips, and sometimes on the live-aboards (from two days/one night B15,000) too, for a discount of about thirty percent.

4

## ANDAMAN COAST DIVE AND SNORKEL SITES

**Anemone Reef** About 22km east of Phuket. Submerged reef of soft coral and sea anemones starting about 5m deep. Lots of fish, including leopard sharks, tuna and barracuda. Usually combined with a dive at nearby Shark Point. Unsuitable for snorkellers.

**Burma Banks** About 250km northwest of Phuket; only accessible on live-aboards. A series of submerged "banks", well away from any landmass and very close to the Burmese border. Only worth the trip for its sharks. Visibility up to 25m.

**Hin Daeng** and **Hin Muang** 56km southwest of Ko Lanta. Hin Daeng is an exceptional reef wall, named after the red soft corals that cover the rocks, with visibility up to 30m. One hundred metres away, Hin Muang also drops to 50m and is good for stingrays, manta rays, whale sharks and silvertip sharks. Visibility up to 50m. Because of the depth and the current, both places are considered too risky for novice divers who have logged fewer than twenty dives. Unsuitable for snorkellers.

**King Cruiser** Near Shark Point, between Phuket and Ko Phi Phi. Dubbed the *Thai Tanic*, this became a wreck dive in May 1997, when a tourist ferry sank on its way to Ko Phi Phi. Visibility up to 20m, but hopeless for snorkellers because of the depth, and collapsed sections make it dangerous for any but the most experienced divers.

**Ko Phi Phi** 48km east of Phuket's Ao Chalong (see page 365). Visibility up to 30m. The most popular

destination for Phuket divers and snorkellers. Spectacular drop-offs; good chance of seeing whale sharks.

**Ko Racha Noi** and **Ko Racha Yai** About 33km and 28km south of Phuket's Ao Chalong respectively. Visibility up to 40m. Racha Yai (aka Raya Yai) is good for beginners and for snorkellers; at the more challenging Racha Noi there's a good chance of seeing manta rays, eagle rays and whale sharks.

**Ko Rok Nok** and **Ko Rok Nai** 100km southeast of Phuket, south of Ko Lanta (see page 383). Visibility up to 18m. Shallow reefs that are excellent for snorkelling.

**Ko Similan** 96km northwest of Phuket; easiest access from Khao Lak (see page 306). One of the world's top diving spots. Visibility up to 30m. Leopard sharks, whale sharks and manta rays, plus caves and gorges.

**Ko Surin** 174km northwest of Phuket; easiest access from Khuraburi (see page 297). Shallow reefs of soft and hard corals that are good for snorkelling.

**Richelieu Rock** Just east of Ko Surin, close to Burmese waters. A sunken pinnacle that's famous for its whale sharks. Considered by many to be Thailand's top dive spot.

**Shark Point (Hin Mu Sang)** 24km east of Phuket's Laem Panwa. Protected as a marine sanctuary. Visibility up to 10m. Notable for soft corals, sea fans and leopard sharks. Often combined with the *King Cruiser* dive and/or Anemone Reef; unrewarding for snorkellers.

Luxurious suites, richly decorated with fine textiles and teak, a renowned restaurant (see below), an excellent spa and two saltwater and one freshwater pools, all set in landscaped tropical gardens with fine views above Kata Noi. **B18,100**

## EATING

**The Boathouse Wine and Grill** Thanon Kok Tanode, Kata Yai ☎076 330015–7, ⓦboathouse-phuket.com; map p.332. One of the best-known restaurants on Phuket – not least for its famously extensive, award-winning wine list – where the skills of the French chef are best sampled on four-course Thai or French tasting menus (just over B1800, or B3300 with paired wines). The beachside terrace and dining room, decorated with nautical touches and attached to the boutique hotel of the same name, enjoy fine sunset views, and there are cooking classes here every weekend (see page 301). Reservations recommended. Daily 11am–11pm.

**Kampong Kata Hill** 12 Patak Road, on the slope right above the Little Mermaid ☎076 330 103, ⓦfacebook.com/kampongkatahill; map p.332. Atmospheric Thai and seafood restaurant decked out like a timeless Asian temple, with all the quirky statues, potted tropical plants, teakwood and faux architecture. It is touristy, but it pulls off the concept pretty well. There are Western-style starters and salads, but the king prawns and lobster platters steal the show. A meal for two will set you back around B1500. Daily 4pm–11pm.

**Mom Tri's Kitchen** Mom Tri's Villa Royale, 12 Thanon Kata Noi, Kata Noi ☎076 333569, ⓦmomtriphuket.

com; map p.332. Highly regarded luxury restaurant, offering Thai and European fine dining, in dishes such as veal parmigiana and jumbo prawns in red curry. Mains from B590. Reservations recommended. Daily 6.30am–11.30pm.

**Red Chopsticks** Next to the Marina Hotel ☎ 098 015 0519; map p.332. The Kata outlet of this Thai franchise, a part of the *Marina Hotel*, features a well-choreographed dining room, the ceiling of which is covered with thatched lamps, nets and other northern Thai memorabilia. The usual local staples, such as fried chicken with cashew nuts and fried red curry, come in big portions here and start at B199. Daily 10am–10pm.

★ **Seacret** Katathani Beach Resort and Spa, 14 Thanon Kata Noi, Kata Noi ☎076 330124–6, ⓦkatathani.com; map p.332. Excellent Phuket and southern Thai cuisine, such as the classic dried-shrimp relish, *nam prik kung siap*, *pla thawt khamin* (deep-fried fish with turmeric and pineapple relish; B290) and *muu hong* (stewed pork belly with cinnamon). All this and an attractive, open-air setting by the swimming pool, with the best tables on a deck under fairy-lit trees by the beach. Daily 11am–5pm & 6–10.30pm.

## DRINKING

**After Beach Bar** 44 Thanon Kata, up the hill past Andaman Cannacia Resort ☎ 089 594 7475, ⓦbit.ly/2q8cZGi; map p.332. Long-running, rustic reggae-style bar set on top of a hill. The wooden deck offers great views over Kata's coast; highly recommended for a romantic sundowner (from B100). Daily 12pm–9pm.

# Hat Nai Harn

The favourite beach of the many expats who live in nearby Rawai, **HAT NAI HARN**, 18km southwest of Phuket town, is an exceptionally beautiful curved bay of white sand backed by a stand of casuarinas and plenty of food stalls but only minimal development. It does get crowded with Russian tourists, parasols and loungers, however, and during the monsoon the waves here are huge.

## ARRIVAL AND DEPARTURE HAT NAI HARN

**By songthaew** Songthaews departing from Phuket town (approximately every 30min; 45min; around B40) head to Nai Harn, via Rawai, with the last one returning in the afternoon – at an early 4pm.

## ACCOMMODATION

**All Seasons Naiharn Phuket** ☎076 289327, ⓦallseasons-naiharn-phuket.com. Run by the French Accor group, this well-sited hotel offers contemporary-styled rooms with ocean or garden view, five restaurants and bars, a spa, a kids' club and a decent-sized swimming pool. It's located just over the narrow road from the shore, next door to *Royal Phuket Yacht Club* (under lengthy renovations). **B2950**

## EATING

**Rock Salt** ☎076 380200, ⓔrocksalt@thenaiharn.com. An expensive restaurant that forms part of *The Naiharn Resort*, set in a stunning location over the northern end of the beach. The oyster and *fruit de mer* plates don't come cheap (from B1750), but they definitely make an impression. They also rustle up tasty pasta dishes (from

B450) and tandoori chicken and *naan* bread (B550). Daily 12.30pm–10pm.

★ **Trattoria del Buongustaio** ☎087 467 2554, ⓦtrattoriabuongustaio.ilmiosito.net. This Italian-run restaurant offers gorgeous views of the bay from a lovely balcony above the rocks on the northern headland and is reachable via the paved road through *The Naiharn Resort*. The full menu covers a wide choice of starters and meat and especially seafood main courses, plus risottos and pastas such as delicious seafood ravioli with sage and butter (B370). Daily noon–12.30am; the kitchen closes at 11pm, while the downstairs lounge bar closes at 2am.

# Hat Ya Nui and Laem Promthep

Follow the coastal road 2km south around the lumpy headland from Hat Nai Harn and you reach the tiny roadside beach of **Hat Ya Nui**, which gets a surprising number of visitors despite being so small and right next to the admittedly quiet road. There are coral reefs very close to shore, though the currents are strong, and kayaks and sunloungers for rent.

The rugged, wind-blasted headland of **Laem Promthep**, 1km beyond Hat Ya Nui, marks Phuket's southernmost tip, jutting dramatically into the Andaman Sea. The cape is one of the island's top beauty spots, and at sunset busloads of tour groups get shipped in to admire the spectacle; Thais pay their respects at the Hindu shrine here, offering elephant figurines to honour the enshrined four-headed god Brahma and his elephant mount, Erawan. Escape the crowds by following the trail along the ridge and down to the rocks just above the water.

### ARRIVAL            HAT YA NUI AND LAEM PROMTHEP

Songthaews to and from Nai Harn pass through Rawai, so to explore both places, you could catch a songthaew from Phuket town to Nai Harn (approx every 30min; 45min; B40), then walk up and around the promontory in a couple of hours, to pick up another songthaew back to town from Rawai (see below).

### ACCOMMODATION

**Nai Ya Beach Bungalow** 99 Moo 6 Tumbon Rawai, a few hundred metres along Soi Naya off Road 4233 ☎076 288676, ⓦnaiyabeachbungalow.com. Two hundred metres uphill from Ya Nui beach towards the cape, this friendly and pleasant place is home to a clutch of attractive, sturdy, thatched-roofed bamboo bungalows with fans, en-suite cold showers and verandas. They're set in a flowery garden that's nicely shaded by cashew nut trees and bougainvillaea and enjoys high-level sea views. Closed May–Oct. B990

### EATING AND DRINKING

**Yanui Restaurant** ☎087 2808937, ✉nuk-yanui@ hotmail.com. Casual bamboo and driftwood eatery under an umbrella of tree branches that stretches right across from the beach. They serve juicy pastas (from B160) and fish (B350), and it's a chilled spot for a fruit smoothie or a sundowner (from B150). Daily 8am–9pm.

# Hat Rawai

Phuket's southernmost beach, **HAT RAWAI**, was the first to be exploited for tourist purposes, but, half a century on, the hoteliers have moved to the far more appealing sands of Kata and Karon, leaving Rawai to its former inhabitants, the Urak Lawoy chao ley (see page 300), and to an expanding expat population. Most visitors are here for the many alfresco seafood restaurants along Thanon Viset's beachside promenade.

## Phuket Seashell Museum

1500m north of the beach on Highway 4024 • Daily 8am–5.30pm • B200

Aside from its seafront restaurants, Rawai's chief attraction is the **Phuket Seashell Museum**, which displays some two thousand species of shell, including 380-million-year-old fossils, giant clams and a 140-carat gold pearl.

### ARRIVAL               HAT RAWAI

**By songthaew** Songthaews departing from Phuket town pass through Hat Rawai (approximately every half-hour, 35min; costing around B30) on their way to and from Nai Harn.

## ACCOMMODATION

**Sandy House** 62 Moo 6 Viset Road, tucked at the upper end of a soi parallel to the beach; turn left about one hundred metres down the alley straight opposite from Nikita ☎ 085 8880821, ✉ peachmaker_yib@hotmail.com. Sparkling clean en-suite rooms with a/c and mini balconies with chairs and tables, set in a Thai home shaded by a lush garden. There's free wi-fi, motorbike rental and free bicycles for guests; breakfast costs B100 extra. Prices are slashed in low season, making it popular with long-term visitors. B950

## EATING

**Nikita's** Towards the northern end of the promenade ☎ 076 288703, ⊛ nikitas-phuket.com. A standout among the many expat-favoured bar-restaurants in the area, not least for the horizon-gazing potential from its peaceful tables on the sand (candlelit at night). Pizzas from a wood-fired oven (from B240) feature on its Thai and Western menu, alongside well-priced cocktails, wines by the glass and espresso coffees. Daily 10am–2am at the latest, kitchen closes 11pm.

**Salaloy** Opposite Nikita's, towards the northern end of the promenade ☎ 076 613740. The best and most famous of Rawai's restaurants, this is an excellent spot for relaxing dinners. Highlights from the menu include *pla thawt khamin* (fried fish with turmeric) and omelette topped with baby oysters (B110); it also has some lovely outdoor tables right on the shorefront under the casuarinas. Daily 10am–9.30pm.

# Ao Chalong, Laem Panwa and around

North of Rawai, the sizeable offshore island of Ko Lone protects the broad sweep of **AO CHALONG**, where many a Chinese fortune was made from the huge quantities of tin mined in the bay. These days, Ao Chalong is the main departure point for dive excursions and snorkelling and fishing trips, which mostly leave from Chalong Pier, east of the bottle-neck roundabout known as Chalong Circle, or Chalong Ha Yaek.

## Wat Chalong

8km southwest of Phuket town, on Thanon Chao Fa Nok, aka Route 4022 • Phuket–Karon songthaews pass the entrance

For islanders, Chalong is important as the site of **Wat Chalong**, Phuket's loveliest and most famous temple, which enshrines the statue of revered monk Luang Pho Saem, who helped resolve a violent rebellion by migrant Chinese tin miners in 1876. Elsewhere in the temple compound, the Phra Mahathat chedi is believed to contain a relic of the Buddha.

## Big Buddha of Phuket

Access is via the very steep and winding 6km Soi Jao Fa 51, signed west off Thanon Chao Fa Nok (Route 422), 2km south of Wat Chalong, or 1km north of Chalong Circle • ⊛ mingmongkolphuket.com

With your own transport, a visit to Wat Chalong combines well with a pilgrimage to the modern-day **Big Buddha of Phuket** (officially Phra Phuttha Mingmongkol Eaknakakeeree), a towering 45m statue atop the aptly named Khao Nakkerd hill, which dominates many island vistas, including from Kata Yai to the southwest, and is easily spotted from aeroplane windows. Made of concrete but faced with glistening white-marble tiles, the eastward-looking Buddha boasts enormous proportions: sitting on a lotus flower that's nearly 25m across with individual hair curls measuring almost 1m each. Views from the base of the statue extend east over Ao Chalong to hilly Ko Lone beyond, while western panoramas take in Kata Noi; it's a popular sunset-viewing spot.

## Phuket Aquarium

Laem Panwa, 10km south of Phuket town • Daily 8.30am–4.30pm, feeding show Sat & Sun 11am • B180 • ⊛ phuketaquarium.org • Songthaews leave from the market in Phuket town (B30), the last one returning at about 3.30pm

Ao Chalong tapers off eastwards into **Laem Panwa**, at the tip of which you'll find the **Phuket Aquarium**. Run by the island's Marine Biological Centre, it's not a bad primer for what you might see on a reef and has walk-through tunnels, a sea-turtle pool and a shark-feeding show.

**ARRIVAL**                                           **AO CHALONG**

**By songthaew** Songthaews to Ao Chalong departing from Phuket town charge around B30.

**ACCOMMODATION**

**Shanti Lodge** Soi Bangrae, 1500m south down Thanon Chao Fa Nok from Wat Chalong; the Phuket–Karon songthaew can drop you close by ☎076 280233, ⓦshantilodge.com. Though there's no special reason to stay on this part of the island, you might make an exception for this place. It's set in a relaxing garden and is home to a saltwater swimming pool, book exchange and vegetarian restaurant. There are fan and a/c double rooms, with or without private hot-water bathrooms – some of which are wheelchair-accessible – and a few family rooms. Discounts are offered for long stays. Fan B750, a/c B850

**EATING**

**Kan Eang @ Pier** Ao Chalong ☎076 381212, ⓦkaneang-pier.com. Classy, long-running restaurant, which is handily, and scenically, sited on a 200m frontage at the mouth of Chalong Pier. The big draw here is the seafood, the best of it barbecued old-style on burning coconut husks (from B1200/kg); deep-fried seaweed with shrimps and chilli sauce is also good, and the *haw mok* (fish curry steamed in a banana leaf) is exceptional. Sister restaurant *Kan Eang Seafood*, north up the beach (☎076 381323, ⓦphuket-seafood.com), enjoys a similarly good reputation and offers free pick-ups. Daily 10.30am–11pm.

# Thalang and around

There's not a great deal for tourists in the northeast of Phuket island around the district town of **THALANG**, but you're quite likely to pass the landmark **Heroines' Monument**, which stands in the centre of the Tha Rua junction, 12km north of Phuket town on Highway 402. The monument commemorates the repulse of the Burmese army by the widow of the governor of Phuket and her sister in 1785; together they rallied the island's womenfolk who, legend has it, frightened the Burmese away by cutting their hair short and rolling up banana leaves to look like musket barrels – a victory that's celebrated every March 13 to 15 with a monks' ordination ceremony and processions.

### Peranakan Phuket Museum

On Route 402, in the Garden Mall complex opposite Home Pro · Daily 9am–6pm · B300 · ☎076 313556 · ⓦperanakanphuketmuseum.com

Opened in 2017, the **Peranakan Phuket Museum** is dedicated to Phuket's Peranakan heritage. The upstairs exhibit features outfits, furniture and original Peranakan homeware, the stories of which are all explained by knowledgeable English-speaking guides. Downstairs, in a huge hall choreographed like an old Sino-Portuguese town, the experience is much more commercial: visitors can dress up in traditional Peranakan clothes and have their pictures taken in a studio, buy jewellery, or sample Peranakan-style coffee and dishes at the *Yaya Kitchen* restaurant and *Pinana Café* (both Daily 9am–6pm).

### Thalang National Museum

On Route 4027, 200m east of the Heroines' Monument · Wed–Sun 9am–4pm · B30 · All mainland-bound traffic and all songthaews between Phuket and Hat Surin and Hat Nai Yang pass the monument

As the only official introduction to Phuket's rich and intriguing history, **Thalang National Museum** doesn't really match up to the task, but taken in conjunction with the privately funded Thaihua Museum in Phuket town (see page 319), the picture starts to flesh out. Displays include some interesting exhibits on the local tin and rubber industries, accounts of some of the more colourful folkloric traditions and photos of the masochistic feats of the Vegetarian Festival (see page 320).

### Wat Phra Thong

Just beyond the crossroads in Thalang town, 8km north of the Heroines' Monument

**Wat Phra Thong** is one of Phuket's most revered temples on account of the power of the Buddha statue it enshrines. The solid gold image is half-buried and no one dares dig it up for fear of a curse that has struck down excavators in the past. After the wat was built around the statue, the image was encased in plaster to deter would-be robbers.

## Khao Phra Taew Forest Reserve

Visitor centre 3km east of the crossroads in Thalang town • B200

Several paths cross the small hilly enclave of **Khao Phra Taew Forest Reserve**, leading you through the forest habitat of macaques and wild boar, but the most popular features of the park are the Gibbon Rehabilitation Project and the Ton Sai and Bang Pae waterfalls, which combine well as a day-trip or on a tour (see page 316). You can get drinks and snacks at the food stall next to the Rehabilitation Centre, and the route to the waterfalls is signed from here.

### The Gibbon Rehabilitation Project

10km northeast of the Heroines' Monument, off Route 4027 • Daily 9am–3.30pm • ⓦ gibbonproject.org • Songthaews from Phuket town, more frequent in the morning, will take you most of the way: ask to be dropped off at Bang Pae (a 40min drive from town) and then follow the signed track for about 1km to get to the project centre

Phuket's forests used to resound with the whooping calls of indigenous white-handed lar gibbons (see page 434), but they make such charismatic pets that they were poached to extinction on the island by the mid-1980s. The lar is now an endangered species, and in 1992 it became illegal in Thailand to keep them as pets, to sell them or to kill them. Despite this, you'll come across a depressing number of pet gibbons on Phuket, kept in chains by bar and hotel owners as entertainment for their customers. The **Gibbon Rehabilitation Centre** aims to reverse this by rescuing pet gibbons and then re-socializing and re-educating them for the wild before finally releasing them back into the forests. It is not unusual for gibbons to be severely traumatized by their experience as pets: not only will they have been taken forcibly from their mothers, but they may also have been abused by their owners.

Visitors are welcome at the project, which is centred in the forests of Khao Phra Taew Forest Reserve, protected as a "non-hunting area", close to Bang Pae waterfall, but because the whole point of the rehab project is to minimize the gibbons' contact with humans, you can only admire the creatures from afar. There's a small exhibition here on the aims of the project, and the well-informed volunteer guides will fill you in on the details of each case and on the idiosyncratic habits of the lar gibbon. The website has details on how you can become a **project volunteer**, adopt a gibbon, or make a donation.

## Bang Pae and Ton Sai waterfalls

If you follow the track along the river from the Gibbon Project, you'll soon arrive at **Bang Pae Falls**, a popular picnic and bathing spot, ten to fifteen minutes' walk away. Continue on the track south for another 2.8km (about 1hr 30min on foot) and you should reach **Ton Sai Falls**: though not a difficult climb, the route is unsigned and indistinct, is steep in places and rough underfoot. There are plenty of opportunities for cool dips in the river en route. Once at Ton Sai you can either walk back down to the access road to the Khao Phra Taew Forest Reserve visitor centre and try to hitch a ride back home, or return the way you came.

# Ko Yao Noi

Located in an idyllic spot in Phang Nga bay, almost equidistant from Phuket, Phang Nga and Krabi, the island of **KO YAO NOI** enjoys magnificent maritime views from almost every angle and makes a refreshingly tranquil getaway. Measuring about 12km at its longest point, it's home to some four thousand islanders, the vast majority of them Muslim, who earn their living from rubber and coconut plantations, fishing and shrimp-farming. Tourism is increasing as visitors keep trickling from nearby Andaman

Coast hotspots, lured by Ko Yao Noi's famed rural ambience and lack of commercial pressures. In reality, several high-end resorts have popped up along the coastline and the beaches lack the wow factor of more sparkling nearby sands. Nonetheless, there's decent swimming off the east coast at high tide, and at low tide too in a few places, and plenty of potential for kayaking, rock-climbing and other activities.

Most tourists stay on the east side, which has the bulk of the accommodation, at **Hat Tha Khao**, **Hat Khlong Jaak** (**Long Beach**), **Hat Pasai** and **Laem Sai**. Exploring the interior is a particular pleasure, either via the barely trafficked round-island road as it runs through tiny villages and the island's diminutive town, **Ban Tha Khai**, or via the trails that crisscross the forested interior, where you've a good chance of encountering monkeys as well as cobras and even pythons, not to mention plenty of birds, including majestic oriental pied hornbills.

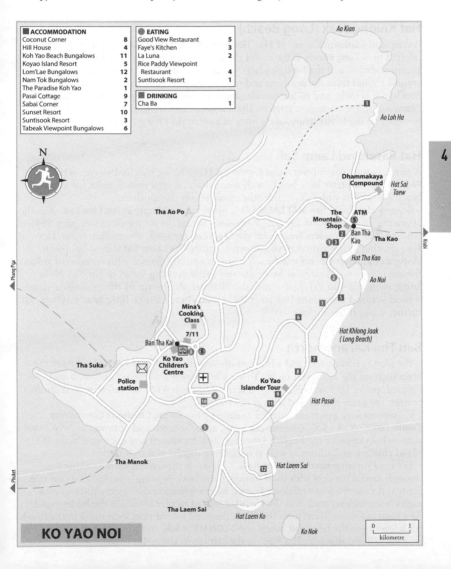

**■ ACCOMMODATION**
| | |
|---|---|
| Coconut Corner | 8 |
| Hill House | 4 |
| Koh Yao Beach Bungalows | 11 |
| Koyao Island Resort | 5 |
| Lom'Lae Bungalows | 12 |
| Nam Tok Bungalows | 2 |
| The Paradise Koh Yao | 1 |
| Pasai Cottage | 9 |
| Sabai Corner | 7 |
| Sunset Resort | 10 |
| Suntisook Resort | 3 |
| Tabeak Viewpoint Bungalows | 6 |

**● EATING**
| | |
|---|---|
| Good View Restaurant | 5 |
| Faye's Kitchen | 3 |
| La Luna | 2 |
| Rice Paddy Viewpoint Restaurant | 4 |
| Suntisook Resort | 1 |

**■ DRINKING**
| | |
|---|---|
| Cha Ba | 1 |

**KO YAO NOI**

## Hat Tha Kao and Hat Sai Taew

The most northerly of the main eastern beaches is **HAT THA KAO**, site of a small village, **BAN THA KAO**, with a couple of shops and restaurants, an ATM, the pier for boats to and from Krabi and a cluster of accommodation. It's not an attractive beach itself, barely swimmable, but is the closest point to Ko Yao's nicest beach, so-called **Temple Beach** or **Hat Sai Taew**, 2km away, whose pretty, gold-sand shore is great for swimming at any tide. However, it's backed by private land that belongs to the Dhammakaya Foundation, a populist Buddhist sect, and is unsigned and a bit tricky to find. From Tha Kao pier, head inland and take the first right behind the shops, walk alongside the khlong and its sheltered marina, over the bridge, then via the faint trail over the hill to the beach. Alternatively, you can kayak there from the pier.

## Hat Khlong Jaak (Long Beach)

A couple of kilometres south of Hat Tha Kao, **HAT KHLONG JAAK**, more commonly referred to as **Long Beach**, is the site of the longest-running and best-known tourist accommodation and the liveliest places to eat and drink. The beach is indeed long, around 1500m from the northern end to *Sabai Corner* on the southern headland. Much of it is rocky and all but unswimmable at low tide, except in front of *Koyao Island Resort*, the smoothest stretch. The seaward views are glorious from every angle, however, taking in the many lovely islets of eastern Ao Phang Nga.

## Hat Pasai and Laem Sai

A minute's walk south from *Sabai Corner* on Hat Khlong Jaak and you're on **HAT PASAI**, a rather pretty little beach, with some shade, several resorts and a few simple beach restaurants with tables under the casuarinas at the south end.

Beyond Hat Pasai, tiny **HAT LAEM SAI** is often known simply as **Hat Lom'Lae**, after the appealing Thai–Canadian *Lom'Lae Bungalows*, which sits on the shore (see page 344).

A few hundred metres west from the *Lom'Lae* turn-off, about 3km from Tha Kai, another side-road takes you down towards **Tha Laem Sai** (Laem Sai pier), along a coast that has no real beach but is scenically dotted with houses on stilts, fishing platforms, dozens of longtails and some inviting views of Ko Yao Noi's larger twin, Ko Yao Yai, just across the channel. At the tip of the peninsula stands a good seafood restaurant (see page 345), and there's a nice little beach 300m east further around the rocks.

## Ban Tha Kai and north

The island's commercial and administrative centre is **BAN THA KAI**, inland from the main piers on the southwest coast. This is where you'll find the post office, banks, hospital, police station, obligatory 7-Eleven shop with ATM, as well as several internet centres, the main market and several *roti* stalls.

Visitors are very much encouraged to drop by the **Ko Yao Children's Community Centre** (☎087 929 4320, ⌨koyao-ccc.com), at the western end of town, an NGO that aims to help improve the English-language, arts, handicraft and computer skills of island children and adults, as well as organizing regular beach clean-ups.

The road running **north from Tha Kai**'s 7-Eleven is particularly scenic, taking you through several hamlets with their mosques and latex-pressing mangles, and past rice fields and their resident buffaloes, framed by mangroves in the middle distance, sea eagles hovering overhead, and the rounded hills of nearby islands in the background. At a junction about 3km from Tha Khai, the northbound road soon turns into a rough track leading to the beautiful beach at **AO LOH HA**, while veering right will take you over the hill and down to Tha Kao on the east coast, about 4km away.

## KO YAO NOI ACTIVITIES

### KAYAKING AND SNORKELLING

Kayaking around the coast is a very enjoyable pastime, and the dozens of tiny islands visible from eastern shorelines make enticing destinations for experienced paddlers; kayaks can be rented through Ko Yao Noi hotels for about B400 per day. Try **Pasai Kayak** (☎08640164713; limited English spoken), located on the north side of Pasai Beach. Just about every hotel and travel agent sells kayaking and snorkelling trips to Ko Hong and other islands in Ao Phang Nga.

### DIVING

**Koh Yao Diver** Lom'Lae Resort, Laem Sai ☎089 92 72871 or 089 868 8642, ⓦkohyaodiver.com. Diving trips and courses on the island are the speciality of Koh Yao Diver, where two local dives are B4000 or two dives at the reefs around Ko Phi Phi in a longtail boat cost B7200. Alternatively, the Open Water diving course costs B16,700.

### ROCK-CLIMBING

Ko Yao Noi is fast becoming a respected destination for **rock-climbers**, who appreciate the fresh sites and uncrowded routes compared to the hectic scene at nearby Ton Sai and Railay. There are over 150 bolted routes on the island, from beginner level to advanced (5 to 8A), established by the American and Thai climbers who run The Mountain Shop in Ban Tha Kao. Many routes are over water and accessible only by boat, or at the least via a hike off the dirt track to *Paradise* hotel.

**The Mountain Shop** In a house, set 50m along the road to the right of Ban Tha Kao's main jetty junction ⓔthemountainshopadventures@gmail. com, ⓦfacebook.com/mountainshopadventures. For beginners, prices start from B2500 for a half-day's course, with multi-day courses also available; there are guides and rental gear for experienced climbers.

**Mina's Cooking Classes** 500m from Ban Tha Kai's roundabout ☎087 887 3161, ⓦminas-cooking-classes.com. Three-hour cooking classes in chef Mina's beautiful Thai wooden home, with two time slots: either 10.30am or 3.30pm. Costs B1800/person for up to six people, or B2500 for individual one-to-one culinary lessons.

**Ulmer's Nature Lodge** Hat Tha Kao ☎087 3879475, ⓦthailand retreats.com. Daily drop-in yoga classes (B600), plus diverse workshops and retreats (4D/3N from B5,600).

### OTHER CLASSES AND ACTIVITIES

**Lam Sai Hotel** ⓦphuket-krabi-muaythai.com. B600 for a two-hour Thai boxing class; B10,000 for a week.

## ARRIVAL AND DEPARTURE

KO YAO NOI

There are three mainland departure points for **boats** to Ko Yao Noi – from Phuket, Krabi's Ao Thalen, and Phang Nga – plus services from Ao Nang. On Ko Yao Noi, shared songthaew **taxis** meet all arriving boats and charge up to B100 per person (depending on distance) for transfers to accommodation, or B150 if chartered for a single traveller. In high season, private speedboats depart to Railay, Ko Jum, Ko Lanta, Ko Kradan, Ko Mook, Trang's Haad Yao pier, Ko Bulon Lae and Ko Lipe. They all leave at 9am, doing multiple stops at different islands/piers. Book tickets a day in advance at **The Pier Restaurant** (☎089 728 0740) on the main junction in front of Ban Tha Khao's jetty.

**To/from Phi Phi** From November to April there's a daily direct speedboat service from Ko Yao Noi's Manor Pier to Phi Phi's Tonsai, leaving at 9.00 am (50min; B1500). It returns from Ko Phi Phi at 3.00pm. You must book ahead with *Sun Smile Tours* (☎ 099 479 1410 or 093 698 1911, ⓦfivestartravelandtours. com/product-category/sun-smile-tours).

**To/from Phuket** The most common route is from Bang Rong on Phuket's northeast coast to Tha Manok on Ko Yao Noi's southwest coast, which is covered by four longtail boats (1hr 10min; B150) and at least seven speedboats a day (40min; B200), with the last service at around 5pm. Returning to Bang Rong, boats depart Tha Manok every hour or so until 5.40pm.

**To/from Ao Thalen** Most of the Krabi province boats leave from Ao Thalen, 33km northwest of Krabi town, and arrive at the Tha Kao pier on Ko Yao Noi's northeast coast. There are about ten services a day, via longtail boat (1hr; B150) or speedboat (30min; B200), the last leaving at 4pm from Ko Yao Noi, and between 4.30 and 5pm from Thalen. In Thalen, an infrequent songthaew service to Krabi Town runs until 2.30pm. A taxi will cost around B700. You can also drive yourself and park cars and motorbikes (B100/50 per night) overnight.

**To/from Ao Nang** In high season, speedboat services connect Ao Nang's Hat Nopparat Thara with Ko Yao Noi once a day (45min; B650, including pick-ups in the Krabi area). They leave Tha Manok pier at 3.30pm and Noppharattara pier in Ao Nang at 11am.

**To/from Phang Nga** The most scenic journey to Ko Yao Noi is the daily (Mon–Sat) boat service from Phang Nga, which takes you through the heart of Ao Phang Nga, passing close by the stilt-house island of Ko Panyi (see page 346). It departs the Phang Nga bay pier at Tha Dan, 9km south of Phang Nga town, at 1pm and returns from Tha Suka on Ko Yao Noi at 7.30am (90min; B200); songthaews connect Phang Nga town with the pier.

## GETTING AROUND AND INFORMATION

**Getting around** Songthaew taxis are easily arranged and many hotels can organize motorbike (B200–350/day) and bicycle (B150) rental. Several shops at Ban Tha Khao's pier also offer motorbike rental.

**Tourist information** ⓦkohyaotravel.com and ⓦkoyaonoi. com have good information on ferry time tables, resorts and available tours. There are ATMs in front of the Mountain Shop in Ban Tha Khao and at the 7-Eleven in Ban Tha Kai.

## ACCOMMODATION

### HAT THA KAO

**Nam Tok Bungalows** ☎087 292 1102; map p.341. Set back from the beach around a khlong, a 5min walk south from the Tha Kao ferry pier, this ultra laid-back set of bungalows is one of the cheapest places to stay on the island. The budget options are comfortable bamboo and wood huts, with cute bathrooms and hammocks on the deck, encircling a small garden full of flowers and a fish pond; the more luxurious ones have hot water. They sometimes organize camping trips to Ko Pak Bia (from B2400 per boat). Fan B550, a/c B1700

**Hill House** 10min walk south from the Tha Kao ferry pier ☎089 875 5486; map p.341. Set back from the beach around a khlong, this handful of attractive terraced wooden bungalows offer good views over the bay. All rooms have en-suite bathrooms, fridges, deckchairs and hammocks you'll hardly want to leave. B1100

★ **Suntisook Resort** ☎089 781 6456, ⓦkohyaotravel. com/suntisook; map p.341. Genial, well-organized place where the bungalows are nicely spaced around a garden and come with TVs, fridges and good, hot-water bathrooms. They're all a bit different but each has a deck and a hammock and some have a/c and three beds. Motorbikes, mountain bikes and kayaks for rent. a/c B1800

### HAT KHLONG JAAK (LONG BEACH)

**Koyao Island Resort** ☎076 597474, ⓦkoyao.com; map p.341. This lovely, stylish resort occupies the best part of the beach and comprises just eighteen chic, thatched, mostly fan-cooled cottage compounds, all of them with separate living areas, huge bathrooms with open-air showers, and sliding doors that give access to the spacious garden and its fine bay views. There's a swimming pool and spa, and if you book directly on their website, free use of mountain bikes and kayaks. Breakfast included. B12,000

★ **Sabai Corner** ☎081 892 1827, ⓦsabaicorner bungalows.com; map p.341. Occupying Long Beach's rocky southern headland, this long-established, laid-back little Italian–Thai outfit has eleven thoughtfully designed wooden bungalows, all with fans, nets and rustic bathrooms, plus decks and hammocks. They're dotted along a rise between the road and the beach, under cashew and jackfruit trees. There's a

good restaurant, serving home-made bread and yoghurt, plus Italian and Thai food, and kayak hire on site. B1000

**Tabeak Viewpoint Bungalows** ☎089 590 4182, ⓦkohyaotravel.com/hotel.htm; map p.341. Two hundred metres inland, on a cross-island track, this Japanese–Thai place has large, well-outfitted, fan-cooled wood and bamboo bungalows, all with hot showers, polished wood floors and French windows and balconies that give commanding views of the islands. The Thai owner is a community policeman and enthusiastic fisherman, and an excellent source of island information. B800

### HAT PASAI

**Coconut Corner** ☎076 454221, ⓦbit.ly/CoconutCorner; map p.341. Offering some of the cheapest and most traveller-friendly accommodation on the island, in simple en-suite bungalows set around a small garden just across the road from the northern end of Hat Pasai beach. It's just a few minutes' walk from *Pyramid Bar* on Long Beach and has bicycle and motorbike rental. B600

**Koh Yao Beach Bungalows** ☎076 454213, ⓦkohyao beach.com; map p.341. Clean, well-kept bungalows around a pretty, well-tended lawn, across the main road from the south end of the beach. The fan bungalows are thatched, with mosquito nets, cold-water bathrooms and TVs; a/c options are big and smart with hot showers. Fan B800, a/c B1500

**Pasai Cottage** ☎089 240 8326, ⓦpasaicottage. blogspot.com; map p.341. The ten bamboo cottages here, just across from Pasai's beach but set back from the road, have unexpectedly tasteful interiors, folding glass doors and prettily tiled bathrooms. B1200

### LAEM SAI

★ **Lom'Lae Bungalows** ☎076 597486, ⓦlomlae.com; map p.341. Beautiful, secluded haven, backed by rice fields and rubber plantations and enjoying stunning bay views from its palm-fringed beach and grassy garden. The attractive, airy, wooden, fan-cooled bungalows are thatched and widely spaced, and have sliding doors, fridges and kitchenettes, as well as hammocks to make the most of the views. Some

have additional upstairs loft beds, and there are two-bedroom family houses as well. Kayaks, two bikes or a motorbike is included in the price and there's a dive shop. **B3500**
**Sunset Resort** Along the uphill road leading to rice paddy ☎082 331 6581, ⓦlamsaivillagehotel.com; map p.341. A few bungalows set high on the hill that dominates the southern side of the island. Some rooms are simpler than others, but all are en suite and have cosy verandas. There's a restaurant with sunset views. Fan **B500**, a/c **B1200**

### EATING AND DRINKING

There's a lively nightmarket on Ban Thai Kao's pier, perfect for cheap barbecued fish, rice flour pancakes and mingling with the locals.

### HAT THA KAO
**Suntisook Resort** map p.341. Charming restaurant serving a long menu of Thai food, including fish (according to market price) and a good, generous chicken *matsaman* curry, as well as spaghetti, mashed potato and Western breakfasts. Daily 7.30am–9pm.

### HAT KHLONG JAAK (LONG BEACH)
★ **Cha Ba** ☎ 087 266 1404, ⓦfacebook.com/chabacafe; map p.341. Thai–Swiss run organic vegetarian café that doubles up as a wine shop and secondhand bookstore. It serves vegan-friendly food, including zesty paninis (from B140), vegan burgers (B200) and pastas (from B180). The restaurant is a joyful open-air affair, full of driftwood and recycled boat parts that have been turned into tables, whilst the wine bar has its own intimate terrace, where the island's residents come to chatter at night. Daily 9am–5pm.
**La Luna** ☎084 629 1550, ⓦlalunakohyao.com; map p.341. Congenial, Italian-owned bar-restaurant in a garden setting with hammocks. On offer are home-made pastas, including very tasty tagliatelle with cream and prosciutto (B230), proper pizzas (around B250), Italian desserts and lots of cocktails. Call for free delivery to your resort. Daily 2pm–late, although the kitchen closes at 9.30/10pm.

### AO LOH HA
**The Paradise Koh Yao** ☎076 584450, ⓦparadise-kohyao.com; map p.341. Sitting right on a lovely but isolated strand of beach, these large, deluxe, thatched rooms and villas all have air conditioning, along with plenty of outdoor space and semi-outdoor bathrooms, some with private Jacuzzis. There's a huge outdoor swimming pool, a little spa, kayaks and yoga classes. Breakfast included. **B7,600**

### LAEM SAI
**Good View Restaurant** On the main road between Tha Manok and Hat Laem Ko ☎089 290 5407, ⓦbit.ly/GoodView; map p.341. Named after its attractive palm-fringed beach location, set before a quiet bay that is perfect for sundowners (from B120) and romantic dinners (try the barbecue prawns, B250), this seafood restaurant's outdoor terrace is a popular spot to spending an evening. Daily 11am–12pm.
**Rice Paddy Viewpoint Restaurant** On top of a hill overlooking Tha Manok and Tha Laem Sai ☎076 410 233, ⓦricepaddy.website; map p.341. Lovable organic café and ice cream parlour with wooden tables spilling on a cliff-top and unmatched views over the island's southern beaches. They serve a range of international cuisines, from hummus (B120) to overpriced Thai mains like chicken *pat thai* (B180). But the views and friendly atmosphere, especially at sunset, just about make up for the price hike. Booking is recommended in high season. Tues–Sun 1pm–late, Mon 4pm–late, closed Mon between April and October.

### BAN THA KAI
**Faye's Kitchen** At the village's roundabout ☎084 645 8963 ⓦfacebook.com/fayeskohyao; map p.341. This welcoming vegan-friendly, foreign-owned restaurant has a warm wooden décor and dishes up hearty pastas (from B180), burgers and sandwiches (from B260) and Thai food. They serve a good selection of cocktails (from B190) and beers (B110). Daily 9am–10pm.

# Ao Phang Nga

National Park admission B300 • ⓦdnp.go.th

Protected from the ravages of the Andaman Sea by Phuket, **AO PHANG NGA** has a seascape both bizarre and beautiful. Covering some four hundred square kilometres of coast between Phuket and Krabi, the mangrove-edged bay is spiked with limestone karst formations up to 300m in height, jungle-clad and craggily profiled. This is Thailand's own version of Vietnam's world-famous Ha Long Bay, reminiscent too of Guilin's scenery in China, and much of it is now preserved as **national park**. The bay is thought to have been formed about twelve thousand years ago when a dramatic rise in sea level flooded the summits of mountain ranges, which over millions of years had been eroded by an acidic mixture of atmospheric carbon dioxide and rainwater. Some

### THE HONGS

**Hongs** are the *pièce de résistance* of Ao Phang Nga: invisible to any passing vessel, these secret tidal lagoons are enclosed within the core of seemingly impenetrable limestone outcrops, accessible via murky tunnels that can only be navigated at certain tides in kayaks small enough to slip beneath and between low-lying rocky overhangs. Like the karsts themselves, the *hongs* have taken millions of years to form, with the softer limestone hollowed out from above by the wind and the rain, and from the side by the pounding waves. Eventually, when the two hollows met, the heart of the karst was able to fill with water via the wave-eroded passageway at sea level, creating a lagoon. The world inside these roofless hollows is an extraordinary one, protected from the open bay by a ring of cliff faces hung with vertiginous prehistoric-looking gardens of upside-down cycads, twisted bonsai palms and tangled ferns. And as the tide withdraws, the *hong's* resident creatures emerge to forage on the muddy floor, among them fiddler crabs, mudskippers, dusky langurs and crab-eating macaques, with white-bellied sea eagles often hovering overhead.

of these karst islands have been further eroded in such a way that they are now hollow, hiding secret lagoons or *hongs* that can only be accessed at certain tides and only by kayak. The main *hong* islands are in the **western** and **eastern** bay areas – to the west or east of Ko Yao Noi, which sits roughly midway between Phuket and Krabi. But the most famous scenery is in the **central bay** area, which boasts the biggest concentration of karst islands, and the weirdest rock formations.

## The central bay

On tours of the **central bay**, the standard itinerary follows a circular or figure-of-eight route, passing extraordinary karst silhouettes that change character with the shifting light – in the eerie glow of an early morning mist it can be a breathtaking experience. Some of the formations have nicknames suggested by their weird outlines – like **Khao Machu (Marju)**, which translates as "Pekinese Rock". Others have titles derived from other attributes – **Tham Nak** (or Nark, meaning Naga Cave) gets its name from the serpentine stalagmites inside; **Ko Thalu** (Pierced Cave) has a tunnel through it; and a close inspection of **Khao Kien** (Painting Rock) reveals a cliff wall decorated with paintings of elephants, monkeys, fish, crabs and hunting weapons, believed to be between three thousand and five thousand years old.

Ao Phang Nga's most celebrated features, however, earned their tag from a movie: the cleft **Khao Ping Gan** (Leaning Rock) and its tapered outcrop **Khao Tapu** (Nail Rock) are better known as **James Bond Island**, having starred as Scaramanga's hideaway in *The Man with the Golden Gun*. Every boat stops off here so tourists can pose in front of the iconic rock – whose narrowing base is a good example of how wave action is shaping the bay – and the island crawls with seashell and trinket vendors.

The central bay's other major attraction is **Ko Panyi**, a Muslim village built almost entirely on stilts around the rock that supports the mosque. Nearly all boat tours stop here for lunch, so you're best off avoiding the pricey seafood restaurants around the jetty, and heading instead towards the islanders' food stalls near the mosque. You can enjoy a more tranquil Ko Panyi experience by joining one of the overnight tours from Phang Nga town (see page 348), which include an evening meal and guesthouse accommodation on the island – and the chance to watch the sun set and rise over the bay; you can also rent a kayak from the jetty and go exploring yourself.

At some point on your central-bay tour you should pass several small brick **kilns** on the edge of a mangrove swamp, which were once used for producing charcoal from mangrove wood. You'll also be ferried beneath **Tham Lod**, a photogenic archway roofed with stalactites that opens onto spectacular limestone and mangrove vistas.

## The western bay: Ko Panak and Ko Hong

The main attraction of **the western bay** is **Ko Panak**, whose limestone cliffs hide secret tunnels to no fewer than five different **hongs** within its hollowed heart. These are probably Ao Phang Nga's most spectacular hidden worlds, the pitch-black tunnel approaches infested by bats and the bright, roofless *hongs* an entire other world, draped in hanging gardens of lianas and miniature screw pines and busy with cicadas and the occasional family of crab-eating macaques. Western-bay tours also usually take in nearby **Ko Hong** (different from the Ko Hong in the eastern bay), whose exterior walls are coated with red, yellow and orange encrusting sponges, oyster shells and chitons (560-million-year-old slipper-shaped shells), which all make good camouflage for the scuttling red, blue and black crabs. Ko Hong's interior passageways light up with bioluminescent plankton in the dark and lead to a series of cave-lagoons.

## The eastern bay: Ko Hong, Ao Thalen and Ao Luk

The principal *hong* island in the **eastern bay**, known both as **Ko Hong** and **Ko Lao Bileh**, lies about midway between Krabi's Hat Klong Muang beach and the southeast coast of Ko Yao Noi. The island is fringed by white-sand beaches and exceptionally clear aquamarine waters that make it a popular snorkelling destination. The island's actual *hong* lacks the drama of Ao Phang Nga's best *hongs* because it's not fully enclosed or accessed via dark tunnels as at Ko Panak, but it is pretty, full of starfish, and tidal, so can only be explored at certain times.

The eastern bay's other big attractions are the mangrove-fringed inlets along the mainland coast between Krabi and Phang Nga, particularly around **Ao Luk** and **Ao Thalen** (sometimes Ao Talin or Talane), though the latter can get very crowded with tour groups. Trips around here take you through complex networks of channels that weave through the mangrove swamps, between fissures in the limestone cliffs, beneath karst outcrops and into the occasional cave. Many of these passageways are *hongs*, isolated havens that might be up to 2km long, all but cut off from the main bay and accessible only at certain tides. The **Ban Bor Tor** (or Ban Bho Tho) area of Ao Luk bay is especially known for **Tham Lod**, a long tunnel hung with stalactites whose entrance is obscured by vines, and for nearby **Tham Phi Hua Toe**, whose walls display around a hundred prehistoric cave paintings, as well as some interestingly twisted stalactite formations.

---

**TOURS OF THE BAY**                                               **AO PHANG NGA**

**By sea canoe** The most rewarding, and generally the most expensive, option for exploring Ao Phang Nga is to join a sea-canoeing trip (either guided or self-paddle), which enables you both to explore inside the *hongs* and to see at close quarters the extraordinary ecosystems around and inside the karst islands. Most sea-canoeing tours use large support boats carrying groups of up to thirty people. They can be arranged from any resort in Phuket, or through the specialist operators John Gray's Sea Canoe and Paddle Asia (see page 316); at Khao Lak, for example through Khao Lak Land Discovery (see page 310); at all Krabi beaches and islands and in Krabi town (see page 349), and on Ko Yao Noi (see page 340). The itinerary is usually determined by your departure point, with Phuket trips focusing on the western bay and Krabi tours concentrating on the eastern half.

**By tour boat** Most tours of the central bay are either in large tour boats booked out of Phuket or Krabi, which generally feature snorkelling and beach stops rather than kayaking, or in inexpensive, small-group longtail boats that depart from Phang Nga town (see page 348), as well as from Phuket and Ko Yao Noi. All the main areas of the bay are extremely popular so don't expect a solitary experience.

# Phang Nga town

Friendly, if unexciting, little **PHANG NGA TOWN**, beautifully located under looming limestone cliffs edged with palm groves midway between Phuket and Krabi, serves mainly as a point from which to organize budget longtail trips around the spectacular karst islands of Ao Phang Nga (see page 348). But there are also several caves and waterfalls nearby, accessible on cheap tours run by Phang Nga tour operators.

## ARRIVAL AND INFORMATION

**By bus** Phang Nga has good bus connections, but its bus station is inconveniently located around 7km south of town, along Highway 415. Some guesthouses can help with pick-ups and drop-offs, if contacted in advance, or a taxi into town will cost around B120. If you're heading to Khao Sok National Park headquarters (see page 301), it's usually fastest to take a Surat Thani bus and change in Phanom. Some of the services to Bangkok's Southern Bus Terminal continue to Mo Chit station on the north side of the city. Destinations: Bangkok (5 daily; 13hr); Ko Samui (daily; 6hr); Krabi (hourly; 1hr 30min–2hr); Phuket (at least

### PHANG NGA TOWN

hourly; 1hr 30min–2hr 30min); Ranong (5 daily; 3hr); Satun (3 daily; 8hr); Surat Thani (every 2hr; 4hr); Takua Pa (hourly; 1hr); Trang (every 1hr; 6hr).
**By boat** The pier for boats around Ao Phang Nga, and to Ko Yao Noi (daily; 90min), is at Tha Dan, 9km south of town and served by songthaews that pass on Thanon Phetkasem (B25).
**Tourist information** The TAT information office for Phang Nga is inconveniently located 2km south of the town on Highway 4 (daily 8.30am–4.30pm; ☎076 411586). You will find the tour desk at *Thaweesuk Hotel* (see below) more helpful.

## ACCOMMODATION

Phang Nga's best hotels are all clustered in the northeastern end of Thanon Phetkasem (Highway 4).
**Baan Phang Nga** 100/2 Thanon Phetkasem (on the left-hand side) ☎076 413276 and 095 9456546, ⓦfacebook.com/BaanPhangnga. Friendly guesthouse and bakery above a café that was being renovated at the time of writing. The a/c rooms have TVs, small, hot-water bathrooms and kitsch contemporary décor. There's a simple local art gallery and souvenir shop on the ground floor. **B650**
★**Thaweesuk Hotel** 77 Thanon Phetkasem (near Krung Thai Bank) ☎ 076 412100 or 094 316 6053,

ⓦthaweesukhotel.com. Recently renovated and catering to budget travellers, this is an exquisite old-style mansion built by a Penang architect. The spacious reception and lounge has a small café that's good to relax in with a book, and the *Sayan Tour* desk for unbiased local information. Up a wooden staircase are well-maintained and very clean and bright fan rooms, a couple of huge a/c options (B800) and a rooftop terrace. Breakfast, which is prepared with fresh fruit from the manager's garden, is B80 extra. **B500**
**The Sleep** 144 Thanon Phetkasem (in front of a small mosque and Ibank) ☎076 411828, ⓦthe-sleep-phang-

---

## TOURS FROM PHANG NGA TOWN

### AO PHANG NGA

The most popular budget tours of Ao Phang Nga (see page 345) are the **longtail boat trips** run by local tour operators who offer almost identical itineraries. The recommended Sayan Tour (☎076 430348, ⓦsayantour.com) operates from the lobby of *Thaweesuk Hotel* (see above). They offer half-day tours of the bay (daily at about 8.30am & 2pm; 3–4hr) costing B950 per person (including national park fee; minimum four people), as well as full-day trips, which cost B1250, including lunch and national park fee. Take the 8.30am tour to avoid seeing the bay at its most crowded. All tours include a chance to swim in the bay, and most offer the option of an hour's canoeing around Ko Thalu as well, for an extra B500.

All tour operators also offer the chance to **stay** overnight at their own guesthouse on **Ko Panyi**. This can be tacked onto the half- or full-day tour for an extra B500; dinner, accommodation and breakfast are included in the price.

### LOCAL SIGHTS AROUND PHANG NGA TOWN

You can arrange trips (B600) to **Tham Phung Chang**, or **Elephant Belly Cave**, a natural 1200m-long tunnel through the massive 800m-high wooded cliff that towers over the Provincial Hall, about 4km west of the town centre. With a bit of imagination, the cliff's outline resembles a kneeling elephant, and the hollow interior is, of course, its belly. You can travel through the elephant's belly to the other side of the cliff and back on a two-hour excursion that involves wading, rafting and canoeing along the freshwater stream, Khlong Tham, that has eroded the channel. There are also tours (from B500) that take in several other local caves, plus **Sa Nang Manora Forest Park**, which has hiking trails through thick, impressive rainforest and several waterfalls with swimmable pools, 9km north of the town centre.

A 2km walk west from the *Thaweesuk Hotel* brings yyou to the quirky garden of **Wat Tham Ta Pan**, which is filled with macabre life-sized statues depicting the Naraka, the Buddhist hell. Enter through the open-mouthed, neon-lit guardian stone dragon.

## MANGROVE TOURS

A boat trip through the eerily scenic **mangrove**-lined channels of the Krabi estuary is a fun way to gain a different perspective on the area. As well as a close-up view of the weird creatures that inhabit the swamps, you'll get to visit a riverside cave or two. **Tours** are best organized directly with the longtail boatmen who hang around Krabi's two piers and the surrounding streets (B300–500/boat/hr) but can also be arranged through most tour agents.

The estuary's most famous features are the twin limestone outcrops known as **Khao Kanab Nam**, which rise a hundred metres above the water from opposite sides of the Krabi River near the *Maritime Park and Spa Resort* and are so distinctive that they've become the symbol of Krabi. One of the twin karsts hides caves, which can be explored – many skeletons have been found here over the centuries, thought to be those of immigrants who got stranded by a flood before reaching the mainland. You can also choose to visit the Muslim island of Ko Klang (see page 350).

nga-th.book.direct. A brand-new boutique hostel that is fronted by an open front porch filled with wooden tables, and a few floors of good value en-suite rooms, all with air conditioning, plush beds and contemporary décor. Breakfast is not included in the price, but coffee is free for guests. **B600**

### EATING

**Duang** Thanon Phetkasem, a couple of doors away from Baan Phang Nga Guesthouse (a tiny sticker shows the name in English). Locals rate this simple but friendly restaurant as the best in town; it's been going thirty years and serves a good squid salad (*yam plu meuk*; B200), as well as rice and noodle dishes for about B80. Daily 10.30am–10pm.
**Kafeh** Thanon Phetkasem (no English sign). For a great local Thai breakfast, head left down Phetkasem about 200m from *Thaweesuk Hotel* to find this hugely popular dessert place on the left-hand side. Fill your tray with an assortment of delicious Thai *khanom* – banana-leaf parcels of sticky rice laced with sweet coconut milk and stuffed with banana, mango or other delights – at about B10 apiece, then order from the selection of hot and cold coffees and watch Thai breakfast TV with everyone else. Daily 6am–6pm.

# Krabi town

The estuarine town of **KRABI** is both provincial capital and major hub for onward travel to some of the region's most popular islands and beaches, including Ko Phi Phi, Ko Lanta, Ao Nang, Klong Muang and Laem Phra Nang (Railay). So efficient are the transport links that you don't really need to stop here, but it also makes an appealing base, strung out along the west bank of the Krabi estuary, with mangrove-lined shorelines to the east, craggy limestone outcrops on every horizon, and plenty of guesthouses. The beaches of **Ao Nang** (see page 356) and **Railay** (see page 361) are both within 45 minutes of town, and other nearby attractions include the **mangrove swamps** and villagey **Ko Klang** peninsula across the estuary, the dramatically sited Tiger Cave Temple at **Wat Tham Seua** and **Khao Phanom Bencha National Park**. A number of organized **day-trips in the Krabi area**, including snorkelling and kayaking excursions, are available (see page 359).

Krabi town has no unmissable sights but is small enough for a pleasant stroll around its main landmarks by day and excellent street food markets by night. Its chief attraction is its setting, and a good way to appreciate this is to follow the paved **riverside walkway** down to the fishing port, about 800m south of Tha Chao Fa; several hotels capitalise on the views here, across to mangrove-ringed Ko Klang, and towards the southern end the walkway borders the municipal Thara Park.

Inland, in the centre of town, you can't fail to notice the bizarre sculptures of hulking **anthropoid apes** clutching two sets of traffic lights apiece at the Thanon Maharat/Soi 10 crossroads. They are meant to represent Krabi's most famous ancestors, the tailless *Siamopithecus oceanus*, whose forty-million-year-old remains were found in a lignite mine in the south of the province and are believed by scientists to be among the earliest examples worldwide of the ape-to-human evolutionary process.

## Wat Kaew Korawaram

West off Thanon Maharat • Free

It's hard to miss the striking white walls of the minimalist modern bot at the town-centre temple, **Wat Kaew Korawaram** (Grovaram), approached via a grand naga staircase. The interior murals depict traditional scenes, including *Jataka* episodes from the lives of the Buddha, but are spiced up with some modern twists – including warring hairy foreigners on either side of the door.

## Ko Klang

Across the river from Krabi town • Frequent shared longtails from Tha Chao Fa (B20; 10min) and Tha Thara Park (B20; 3min; bicycles carried); longtail charter also possible (B60–100)

Most of Krabi's longtail boatmen come from **Ko Klang**, the mangrove-encircled peninsula just across the channel from Tha Chao Fa and Tha Thara Park. On a two-hour mangrove tour, you can choose to stop off on the peninsula for a visit, or you can

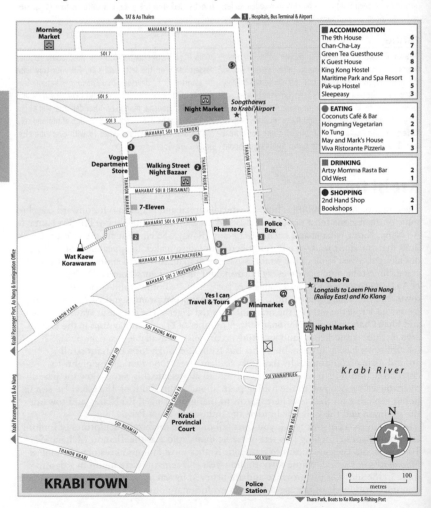

| ■ ACCOMMODATION | |
| --- | --- |
| The 9th House | 6 |
| Chan-Cha-Lay | 7 |
| Green Tea Guesthouse | 4 |
| K Guest House | 8 |
| King Kong Hostel | 2 |
| Maritime Park and Spa Resort | 1 |
| Pak-up Hostel | 5 |
| Sleepeasy | 3 |

| ● EATING | |
| --- | --- |
| Coconuts Café & Bar | 4 |
| Hongming Vegetarian | 2 |
| Ko Tung | 5 |
| May and Mark's House | 1 |
| Viva Ristorante Pizzeria | 3 |

| ■ DRINKING | |
| --- | --- |
| Artsy Momma Rasta Bar | 2 |
| Old West | 1 |

| ● SHOPPING | |
| --- | --- |
| 2nd Hand Shop | 2 |
| Bookshops | 1 |

**KRABI TOWN**

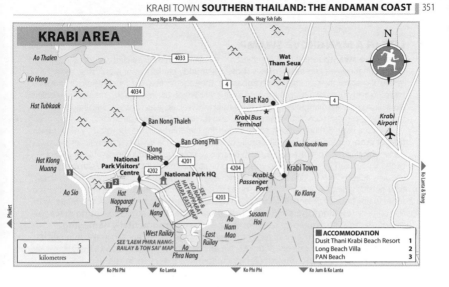

go there yourself, on one of the public longtail **boats** that shuttle across from Krabi town throughout the day. You can also stay in Ban Ko Klang as part of a **homestay** programme, which can be booked locally through Krabi Friendly Tour or in advance as part of a package with Tell Tale Travel (ⓦ telltaletravel.co.uk).

The predominantly Muslim peninsula is home to three small **villages** housing a total of around four thousand people, most of whom earn their living from tourism and fishing. Seafood restaurants have sprung up at the pier and can give free mini tours of their fish farms. The island is no great beauty but therein lies its charm, offering the chance to experience a little of typical southern Thai life, which is a highlight of staying in Krabi Town. You can swim off Ko Klang's long, wild southwestern **beach**, from where you also get an excellent view of the distinctive profiles of all the famous local **islands** – Laem Phra Nang (30min boat ride away), Ko Poda (45min), Bamboo Island, Ko Phi Phi (2hr) and Ko Jum; any Ko Klang boatman will take you to the beach for the same price as from Krabi town. Wandering around the village on foot is equally fascinating.

## Wat Tham Seua

10km northeast of Krabi town, about 2km north of Highway 4 • Minibuses (100B) leave Krabi Town for the temple every two hours from 7am to 5pm, collecting passengers at most guesthouses. Return trips to Krabi Town depart from the temple between 10am and 7.30pm.

Spectacularly situated amid limestone cliffs within a tropical forest, **Wat Tham Seua** (Tiger Cave Temple) is a famous meditation temple of caves, wooded trails and panoramic viewpoints. As it's a working monastery, visitors are required to wear respectable dress (no shorts or sleeveless tops for men or women).

Wat Tham Seua's abbot is a renowned teacher of Vipassana meditation, and some of his educational tools are displayed in the main **bot**, on the left under the cliff overhang, in the main temple compound. Though these close-up photos of human entrails and internal organs may seem shockingly unorthodox, they are there as reminders of the impermanence of the body, a fundamental tenet of Buddhist philosophy; the human skulls and skeletons dotted around the rest of the compound serve the same purpose. Beyond the bot, follow the path past the nuns' quarters to reach the pair of steep **staircases** that scale the 600m-high cliffside. The first staircase is long (1272 steps) and very steep, and takes about an hour to climb, but the vista from the summit is quite spectacular, affording fabulous views over the limestone outcrops and out to the

## LIFE IN A MANGROVE SWAMP

**Mangrove swamps** are at their creepiest at low tide, when their aerial roots are fully exposed to form gnarled and knotted archways above the muddy banks. Not only are these roots essential parts of the tree's breathing apparatus, they also reclaim land for future mangroves, trapping and accumulating water-borne debris into which the metre-long mangrove seedlings can fall. In this way, mangrove swamps also fulfil a vital ecological function: stabilizing shifting mud and protecting coastlines from erosion and the impact of tropical storms.

Mangrove swamp mud harbours some interesting creatures too, like the instantly recognizable **fiddler crab**, named after the male's single outsized reddish claw, which it brandishes for communication and defence purposes; the claw is so powerful it could open a can of baked beans. If you keep your eyes peeled you should be able to make out a few **mudskippers**. These specially adapted fish can absorb atmospheric oxygen through their skins as long as they keep their outsides damp, which is why they spend so much time slithering around in the sludge; they move in tiny hops by flicking their tails, aided by their extra-strong pectoral fins. You might well also come across **kingfishers** and white-bellied **sea eagles**, or even a **crab-eating macaque**.

Though the Krabi mangroves have not escaped the **environmentally damaging** attentions of invasive industry, or the cutting down of the bigger trees to make commercial charcoal, around fifteen percent of the Andaman coastline is still fringed with mangrove forest, the healthiest concentration of this rich, complex ecosystem in Thailand.

islands beyond. Watch out for the monkeys: they are high skilled at stealing food and valuables, so try to avoid carrying unnecessary items and any plastic bags. There's a large seated Buddha image and chedi at the top, and a few monks' cells hidden among the trees. The second staircase, next to the large statue of the Chinese Goddess of Mercy, Kuan Im, takes you on a less arduous route down into a deep dell encircled by high limestone walls. Here the monks have built themselves self-sufficient meditation cells (*kuti*) in and around the rocky crannies, linked by paths through the lush ravine: if you continue along the main path you'll eventually find yourself back where you began, at the foot of the staircase. The valley is home to squirrels and monkeys as well as a pair of remarkable trees with overground **buttress roots** over 10m high.

## ARRIVAL AND DEPARTURE
KRABI TOWN

You can buy bus, a/c minibus, boat, train and air tickets, including combination bus and train tickets, to Bangkok via Surat Thani and through-tickets to Ko Samui and Ko Pha Ngan, from clued-up, helpful Krabi Friendly Tour & Travel, 9/3 Thanon Chao Fa (☎075 612558).

### BY PLANE
Krabi airport (☎075 636541–2, ⌨krabiairport.org) is just off Highway 4, 18km east of Krabi town, 35km from Ao Nang. It's served by many international flights and by domestic flights from Bangkok with Thai Airways, Bangkok Airways, Nok Air, Thai Lion Air and Air Asia, from Chiang Mai with Air Asia and from Ko Samui with Bangkok Airways. An airport shuttle bus (hourly; B150 per person) runs to Krabi town, stopping at Krabi Provincial Court, or there are fixed-price taxis at B350 per car to Krabi town and port. Frequent songthaews (20min; B40) from the airport depart on the main road 400m from the terminal and drop passengers anywhere along Thanon Utrakit; but to the airport drop you off at departures, leaving from north Thanon Utrakit in Krabi

Town. Car rental is also available.
Destinations: Bangkok (up to 15 daily; 1hr 20min); Chiang Mai (2 daily; 2hr); Ko Samui (1 daily; 50min).

### BY BUS
Numerous long-distance buses run to Krabi's bus terminal, which is 5km north of the town centre in the suburb of Talat Kao, beside Highway 4. Frequent red songthaews (B20) shuttle between the town centre (where they do a little circuit to pick up passengers, starting from the 7-Eleven on Thanon Maharat or *Pak-up Hostel* on Thanon Utrakit) and the bus station. Between 6am and 6.30pm, white songthaews to Ao Nang depart from Krabi bus terminal roughly every 15 minutes.
**To/from Bangkok** A/c and VIP buses between Bangkok's Southern Bus Terminal and Krabi depart mainly in the late afternoon or evening, arriving at the other end in the early morning. Think twice before taking a private bus direct from Thanon Khao San.
**By a/c minibus** Private a/c minibus services (all roughly hourly) run from Krabi to Surat Thani, Nakhon

THAI MASSAGE ON THE BEACH, KO LANTA

OIL MASSAGE   350$
FOOT MASSAGE  300$
PAINTING NAIL  250$
BRAID HAIR
ALL PRICE FOR 1 HOUR

Si Thammarat, Trang and Ko Lanta. Aimed specifically at tourists, in competition with the boats, the Lanta service will pick up from hotels in Krabi and charges B250–350, depending on which beach you want to be dropped off at on Ko Lanta Yai. From the Talat Kao bus terminal, you can also catch an a/c minibus that originates on Lanta to Phuket airport/town (roughly every 2hr; 2–3hr; B400/350 bookable through Krabi hotels and travel agents).

**Bus destinations:** Bangkok (12 daily; 12hr); Hat Yai (hourly from 7am to 5pm; 4–5hr); Khao Sok (every 2 hours from 7.30am to 4pm; 4–5hr); Ko Lanta (hourly from 7am to 5pm; 2–3hr); Nakhon Si Thammarat (at least hourly; 3hr); Phang Nga (every 30min; 2hr); Phuket Town Bus Station 2 (at least hourly; 3hr); Ranong (2 daily; 5hr); Satun (4 daily; 5hr); Surat Thani (hourly from 7.30am to 4.30pm; 2hr); Takua Pa (4 daily; 3hr 30min–4hr 30min); Trang (hourly until 5pm; 2–3hr); Satun (4 daily; 4hr).

### BY TRAIN AND BUS

A more comfortable alternative to taking a bus from Bangkok is to catch an overnight train from the capital to Surat Thani or Trang, and then change on to one of the frequent a/c buses or minibuses to Krabi (hourly; 2hr).

### BY BOAT

Ferries to Ko Phi Phi, Ko Lanta and Ko Jum leave from Krabi Passenger Port (sometimes referred to as Tha Khlong Jilad; ☎075 620052), a couple of kilometres southwest of Krabi town centre. Ferry tickets bought from tour operators in town should include a free transfer to Krabi Passenger Port, but there are also red songthaews that do a circuit of the town

centre before heading out to the port. Songthaews from Krabi town connect with most boats, leaving about an hour before from the morning market on Maharat Soi 7, passing the 7-Eleven on Thanon Maharat and Talat Kao bus terminal.

**Ko Jum** Boats leave year-round from the Laem Kruat pier, about 40km south of Krabi Town. Catch the yellow and blue songthaew (B100) from the Siam Bank, near the piers and the 7-Eleven.

**Ko Phi Phi** Ferries to Ko Phi Phi from Krabi Passenger Port depart four times daily in high season and at least twice daily in low season (2hr; B350–400).

**Ko Lanta Yai** Going by a/c minibus to Ko Lanta is more popular these days, but there's still one ferry a day from Krabi Passenger Port, via Ko Jum (B350; 2hr), in peak season (roughly mid-Nov to mid-April 11.30am; 2hr 30min; B400).

**Ko Phi Phi** Ferries to Ko Phi Phi from Krabi depart three times daily (five times on weekends; 2hr; B480).

**Ko Yao Noi** In addition to boats from Ao Nang, there are services from the pier at Ao Thalen, 33km northwest of Krabi town to Ko Yao Noi (see page 340).

**Laem Phra Nang (East Railay)** Longtail boats for East Railay on Laem Phra Nang (45min; B1500/boat or B150/person if there are 8–10 passengers) leave on demand from the town-centre pier at Tha Chao Fa on Thanon Kong Ka.

**Ko Yao Noi** As well as boats from Ao Nang, there are services from the pier at Ao Thalen, 33km northwest of Krabi town, to Ko Yao Noi.

**Destinations:** Ko Jum (roughly mid-Nov to mid-April daily; 1hr 30min–2hr); Ko Lanta Yai (roughly mid-Nov to mid-April daily; 2hr 30min); Ko Phi Phi Don (2–4 daily; 2hr); Ko Yao Noi (from Ao Thalen; 6–7 daily; 1hr).

### GETTING AROUND

**By songthaew** Most of the public songthaew services to local beaches, towns and attractions circulate around town before heading out, making stops outside the 7-Eleven just south of the Soi 8 intersection on Thanon Maharat and along Thanon Utrakit; most run at least twice an hour from dawn till noon, and then less frequently until dusk. For getting around town, the most useful are probably the red songthaews that run between Tesco Lotus, out on Highway 4 beyond the Wat Tham Seua turn-off, and Krabi Passenger

Port. White songthaews start at Talat Kao bus terminal and do a spin around town before heading out to Ao Nang (B50 daytime, B60 after 6pm).

**By car or motorbike** Budget (☎075 636171, ⓦbudget.co.th) and Avis (☎089 969 8676, ⓦavisthailand.com) have desks at the airport. Most accommodation offer rental motorbikes.

**By bicycle** *Pak-up Hostel* (see page 355) rents mountain bikes for B150/day.

### INFORMATION AND TOURS

**Tourist information** Krabi's unhelpful TAT office (daily 8.30am–4.30pm; ☎075 612812, ⓔtatkrabi@tat.or.th) is inconveniently located 2km north of the centre on Thanon Maharat.

**Books** If you're spending some time in this region, it's worth buying a copy of *Krabi: Caught in the Spell – A Guide*

to Thailand's Enchanted Province, expat environmentalist Thom Henley's lively and opinionated book about Krabi people, islands and traditions (see page 438).

**Tour agents** Yes I can Travel & Tour on Thanon Chao Fa (☎098 194 4532, ⓔsweet_rose001@hotmail.com) has many day-trip options (see page 359) and sells bus, flight and train tickets.

### ACCOMMODATION

★ **The 9th House** 9/9 Thanon Chao Fa ☎075 656485, ⓦfacebook.com/the9house9; map p.350. Eight spacious

en-suite rooms with wall windows and small balconies set on the upper storeys of a well-kept Thai home. It's smack in the middle of the action, yet retains a homely, secluded vibe that appeals to both couples and families. B1300

★ **Chan-Cha-Lay** 55 Thanon Utrakit ☎ 075 620952; map p.350. With its stylish blue-and-white theme throughout, funky bathrooms, white-painted wooden furniture and blue shutters, this is the most charming and arty place to stay in Krabi. The en suites in the garden come with fan or a/c and are by far the nicest option, further from the street; quieter rooms in the main building share bathrooms and some don't have windows. Fan B500, a/c B800

**Green Tea Guesthouse** 4 Issara Road ☎ 075 630 609; map p.350. A veritable cheapie run by a friendly Thai family on the first floor of a traditional corner house. It has twins and doubles with basic shared bathrooms, with attractive wooden floors and walls that are a throwback to a bygone era of budget travel in Thailand. B200

**K Guest House** 15–25 Thanon Chao Fa ☎ 075 623166, ✉ kguesthouse@yahoo.com; map p.350. Deservedly popular and well run, in a peaceful but central spot, this long, timber-clad row house has bedrooms with wooden floors, panelled walls, streetside balconies and hot showers – ask for a more attractive upstairs room. Also offers some cheaper shabby rooms with windows onto the hall and shared bathroom downstairs and at the back. Fan B400, a/c B600

**King Kong Hostel** 44 Maharaj Road right opposite Wat Kaew's entrance ☎ 075 623 199; map p.350. Sparkling new central hostel with a hair salon in the lobby and clean

and comfortable dorms, immaculate shared toilets and a few rooms that are perhaps a bit too cramped for the price. Dorms B300, doubles B650

**Maritime Park and Spa Resort** 2km north of town off Thanon Utrakit ☎ 075 620028–35, ⊛ maritimeparkandspa.com; map p.350. Beautifully located upper-end hotel, set beside the limestone karsts and mangroves of the Krabi River. Rooms are a little old-fashioned but large and comfortable and have fine views over the extensive landscaped grounds and lake. There's a big pool and a spa, and shuttles into Krabi town and Ao Nang. Good-value packages sometimes available on their website. Breakfast included. B2600

**Pak-up Hostel** 87 Thanon Utrakit ☎ 075 611955, ⊛ pakuphostel; map p.350. Colourful, modern hostel in a short tower block on probably Krabi's busiest corner, with smart ten-bed a/c dorms and two private doubles. This is the place backpackers come to be sociable, with lots of common areas, beer pong tournaments, a rooftop bar and an adjacent garden bar. Dorms B360, doubles B1500

**Sleepeasy** 248 Thanon Utrakit ☎ 089 2870163, ⊛ sleepeasykrabi.com; map p.350. This central Thai–British run guesthouse offers dorms, doubles, triples and family rooms, all with shared and very clean bathrooms, in three storeys, topped by a sociable rooftop bar with views over the river. There's free tea, coffee, and fresh fruit for guests. Double B700

## EATING

Krabi offers plenty of traveller-oriented restaurants but there's also inexpensive local-style dining at the night markets on riverside Thanon Kong Ka and on Maharat Soi 10. The Walking Street night bazaar on Soi 8 (Fri, Sat & Sun 5–10pm) also brims with excellent food stalls, as well as an entertainment stage and trinket and craft stalls.

**Coconuts Café and Bar** Thanon Chao Fa ☎ 094 6978 999, ⊛ bit.ly/CoconutsCafe; map p.350. This welcoming bistro serves fresh coffee (from B50), healthy smoothies and breakfast sets – try the bargain granola, yogurt and muesli bowls (B80). It packs quite a crowd of travellers who come here to indulge in some European comforts, such as hot dogs made with original English Cumberland sausages (B60) and fast wi-fi. Daily 7am–4pm & 6pm–10pm.

**Hongming Vegetarian** 83 Thanon Pruksa Uthit ☎ 075 621 273; map p.350. A relaxed local spot to get a mix of Thai greens in one dish, even if you aren't vegetarian. The bain-maries are loaded with soy-meat and veg dishes such as matsaman curry and aubergine tofu bake. Two choices on rice is a thrifty B35. Mon–Sat 7am–5pm.

★ **Ko Tung** 66 Thanon Maharat, about 2km north of town centre towards the bus station ☎ 075 656 822; map p.350. Though it looks nothing much, this little Thai restaurant is always packed with locals savouring the excellent, good-value, southern-style seafood. Special highlights include the sweet mussels (hawy wan), baked crab, and mushroom, long bean and shrimp yam salads. Most dishes B80–100. Mon–Sat 11am–10pm.

**May and Mark's House** Soi 2, Thanon Maharat ☎ 075 612 562, ⊛ facebook.com/MayAndMarkHouse; map p.350. Early hours, home-baked bread (like real sourdough), fresh coffee (B50) and full-English fry-ups make this a popular spot for breakfast. Also does tacos, sandwiches, cheese and tuna melts (B180), pizzas (B200) and Thai, German and vegetarian food. Daily 7am–9pm.

**Viva Ristorante Pizzeria** 29 Thanon Pruksa Uthit ☎ 089 220 4796; map p.350. Genuine Italian-owned joint serving home-made pastas and ravioli (from B160), thin crispy pizzas (from B200), and some imported beers from Belgium and Germany. Daily 11am–11pm.

## DRINKING

**Artsy Momma Rasta Bar** Thanon Chao Fa ☎ 061 806 6652; map p.350. This hole-in-the-wall, driftwood and bamboo reggae-style bar draws a decent crowd thanks to

occasional live music and its cheap drinks: beers are B80 and cocktails start at B120. Daily 2pm–1am.

**Old West** Thanon Utrakit ☎ 089 195 8575, ⊛ bit.ly/

4

OldWestBar; map p.350. All bare wood and Wild West photos, with racks of imported spirits behind the long bar. The top-notch sound system churns out wall-to-wall rock music and there are a couple of pool tables. Daily 4pm–4am.

## SHOPPING

**2nd Hand Shop** Thanon Pruksa Uthit ☎ 075 815343; map p.350. Everything from books to bikes to furniture at pre-loved prices. Daily 10am–9pm.

**Bookshops** Pakarang on Thanon Utrakit; map p.350. Buys and sells secondhand books, as well as selling handicrafts and espresso coffees. Daily 8am–9pm.

## DIRECTORY

**Hospitals** Krabi Hospital is about 1km north of the town centre at 325 Thanon Utrakit (☎ 075 611202) and also has dental facilities, but the better hospital is considered to be the private Muslim hospital, Jariyatham Ruam Phet Hospital (☎ 075 611223), which is about 3km north of town at 514 Thanon Utrakit and has English-speaking staff.

**Immigration office** In the compound of government offices on the way to Krabi Passenger Port (Mon–Fri 8.30am–4.30pm; ☎ 075 611097).
**Police** For all emergencies, call the tourist police on the free, 24hr phone line ☎ 1155, or contact the local branch of the tourist police in Ao Nang on ☎ 075 637208.

# Ao Nang

**AO NANG** (sometimes confusingly signed as Ao Phra Nang), 22km west of Krabi town, is a busy, continually expanding, rather faceless mainland resort that mainly caters for mid-budget and package-holiday tourists. Although it lacks the fine beaches of the nearby Railay peninsula (an easy 10min boat ride away), it is less claustrophobic, and has a much greater choice of restaurants and bars, masses of shopping (mostly beachwear, DVDs and souvenirs), plus a wealth of dive shops, day-tripping and snorkelling possibilities and other typical resort facilities. Adjacent **Hat Nopparat Thara**, part of which comes under the protection of a national marine park, is prettier, and divided into two separate beaches by a khlong. The uncrowded, 2km-long **eastern beach** is effectively linked to Ao Nang by a conurbation of accommodation and shops, but the **western beach**, sometimes known as **Hat Ton Son**, across the khlong, is an altogether quieter and more beautiful little enclave, accessible only via longtail or a circuitous back road. Fifteen kilometres' drive west of Ao Nang, **Hat Klong Muang** is no great shakes as a beach but does have some attractive four- and five-star accommodation.

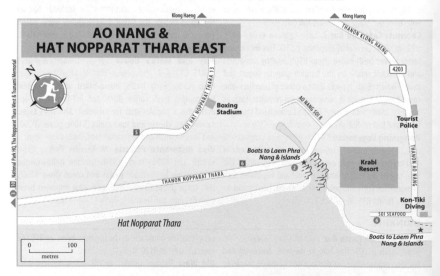

## DIVING FROM AO NANG

Ao Nang is Krabi's main centre for **dive shops**, with a dozen or more outlets, the most reputable of which include Kon-Tiki (☎075 637826, ⓦkontiki-thailand.com) and Poseidon (☎075 637263, ⓦposeidon-diving.com); they have a price agreement for PADI courses, but Poseidon is cheaper for dive trips. Diving with Ao Nang operators is possible year-round, with some dive staff claiming that off-season diving is more rewarding, not least because the sites are much less crowded.

Most one-day **dive trips** head for the area round Ko Phi Phi (from B2700 including two tanks; B1700 for snorkellers with Poseidon) and often include dives at Shark Point and the "King Cruiser" wreck dive (see page 335); the Ko Ha island group, near Ko Lanta, is also popular but more expensive (see page 383).

Two dives in the Ao Nang area – at Ko Poda and Ko Yawasam – cost B2800–3200 (B11500 for snorkellers with Poseidon). PADI dive courses cost B4900 for the introductory Discover Scuba day, or B14,900 for the Open Water.

The nearest recompression chambers are on Phuket (see page 317); check to see that your dive operator is insured to use one of them. General information on diving in Thailand can be found in Basics (see page 51).

# Central Ao Nang and Ao Phai Plong

**Ao Nang**'s central beach is unexceptional and busy with longtail traffic, though it's backed by a pleasantly landscaped promenade. The nicer stretch is east beyond *Ao Nang Villa Resort*, accessed by the pavement that takes you all the way along the shore to the appropriately named *Last Café*, a very pleasant spot for a shady drink. Follow the wooden walkway from beyond *The Last Café* and scale the steps up and over the headland to reach, in about ten minutes, the beach at diminutive **Ao Phai Plong**, which is the sole province of the luxurious *Centara Grand* hotel.

# Hat Nopparat Thara east

Immediately west of Ao Nang, beyond the headland occupied by *Krabi Resort* but reached by simply following the road (on foot or in one of the frequent Krabi-bound songthaews), **Hat Nopparat Thara east** is long and pretty, with the road running along

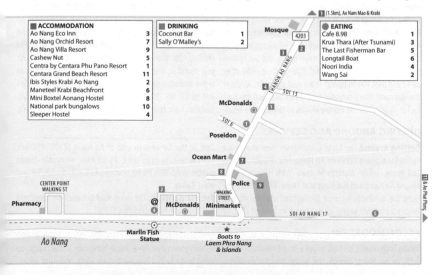

a landscaped promenade behind it. Its eastern hinterland is developing fast with hotels and restaurants, but the other end, close to the T-junction with Route 4202, is the site of the Hat Nopparat Thara–Mu Ko Phi Phi **national park headquarters** and accommodation. Here too is the **tsunami memorial**, *Hold Me Close* by Louise Bourgeois (2005), a roofless, wood-slatted corncob structure in disrepair enclosing two pairs of hands, joined, prayer like and pleading, extending from a lumpy sea.

At low tide it's almost impossible to swim on this beach, but the sands come alive with thousands of starfish and hermit crabs, and the view out towards the islands is glorious; you can walk to the nearest outcrop at low water.

The **national park visitor centre** is at the end of the beach, beside the khlong and its sheltered marina and jetty, Tha Nopparat Thara, which is the departure point for Ao Nang ferry services to Phuket, Phi Phi and Ko Lanta, as well as for longtails to the western beach. The visitor centre's car park is famous for its **seafood restaurants**, and Krabi residents also like to picnic under the shorefront casuarina trees here.

## Hat Nopparat Thara west

**Hat Nopparat Thara west** has a quite different atmosphere from its eastern counterpart: just a handful of small bungalow hotels and a few private residences share its long swathe of peaceful casuarina- and palm-shaded shoreline, making it a great place to escape the crowds and commerce of other Krabi beaches. The views of the karst islands are magnificent, though swimming here is also tide-dependent. Without your own transport you can only get here by longtail across the narrow but deep khlong beside the national park visitor's centre, but with a car or bike you can arrive via the very quiet back road that snakes through the mangroves from the Klong Muang road to the edge of the bungalow properties.

### ARRIVAL AND DEPARTURE — AO NANG

Ao Nang has no proper transport terminals of its own so most long-distance journeys entail going **via Krabi town** (see page 349), though tour services on every corner of Ao Nang can arrange direct a/c minivans to the same destinations with convenient hotel transfers, such as to Phuket town (B300). Taxis from Krabi to Ao Nang charge about B500. From the **airport** a shuttle bus runs to Ao Nang for B200, while taxis charge B600–900 to Ao Nang and Klong Muang.

**By songthaew** The cheapest onward connection from Krabi to Ao Nang is by white songthaew, which run regularly throughout the day from Krabi town centre and bus station (generally every 10min; 45min; B50 daytime, B60 after dark) and pass Hat Nopparat Thara east en route. Alight at the Nopparat Thara national park T-Junction and car park for longtails across the narrow khlong to the western beach

(B100) or, with your own transport, follow the Klong Muang road until signs direct you off it. There's also a songthaew service from Krabi town to Hat Klong Muang.

**By boat** In addition to the ferries listed below, longtails to Laem Phra Nang (see page 361) and boats to Ko Yao Noi (see page 340) are also available; the latter include a daily, high-season Green Planet speedboat (book through any tour agent) that continues to Bang Rong in Phuket (B1200 from Ao Nang). There are once-daily ferry services from Tha Nopparat Thara west, near the national park visitors' centre, to Ko Phi Phi Don (2hr 30min; B450) and to Phuket (3hr; B700), both year-round in theory although they sometimes don't run in the monsoon season; and to Ko Lanta (2hr 30min; B550) and Ko Yao Noi (3hr; B650) from roughly November to May. Transfers from Ao Nang hotels are included in the ticket price.

### GETTING AROUND AND SERVICES

**Getting around** The Krabi songthaews (see above) are useful for nipping between Ao Nang, Hat Nopparat Thara and town, while motorcycle taxis with sidecars buzz around Ao Nang and Hat Nopparat Thara. Motorbikes and jeeps are available for rent throughout the resort; and there are rentable kayaks on the beach in front of *The Last*

*Café* at the far eastern end of Ao Nang (B100–150/hr), from where, in calm seas, it's an easy, enjoyable 15min paddle to Ao Phai Plong or about 45min to Ao Ton Sai and West Railay.

**Tourist police** On the main road between Ao Nang and Hat Nopparat Thara (☎ 075 637208).

### ACCOMMODATION

During high season, it's hard to get a double room for under B600 in Ao Nang, though the many backpacker dorms

remain good value. For a simple bungalow on the beach you need to go to Hat Nopparat Thara west. Mid- and upper-

## ACTIVITIES AROUND KRABI, AO NANG AND LAEM PHRA NANG

Any tour agent in Krabi town, Ao Nang, Klong Muang or Railay can set you up on these **snorkelling day-trips** and other **activities**; prices usually include transport from your accommodation. Diving (see page 357) and rock-climbing (see page 362) are also available.

### SNORKELLING DAY-TRIPS

By far the most popular organized outings from Krabi, Ao Nang and Laem Phra Nang are the **snorkelling trips** to nearby islands. The main **islands** in question are Ko Poda, Ko Tub and Chicken Island, all of them less than half an hour's longtail ride from Ao Nang or Railay. There are various permutations, offered by numerous companies, including the number of islands you visit (usually three, four or five) and whether you go in a longtail boat, a larger wooden boat or speedboat; prices start as low as B450 for a longtail trip to three islands, including packed lunch and snorkel set. In all cases you should be prepared to share the experience with dozens, even hundreds, of others, because pretty much everyone congregates at the same spots. It's a lot more fun than it sounds though – so long as you're not expecting a solitary experience.

It's also possible to organize your own boat trip with the **longtail boatmen** on Ao Nang waterfront, leaving earlier to beat some of the crowds. Their prices are fixed, but don't include park entry fees, snorkelling equipment or lunch: for the return trip to either Ko Poda, Ko Tub or Chicken Island (8am–4pm), they charge B300 per person, minimum six people; for Ko Hong (see page 347) it's B2800 per boat per full day, for Bamboo Island, near Ko Phi Phi (see page 365), B3800 per boat per full day. Krabi town is quite a bit further away so its boatmen charge B1800–2300 for the three main islands.

From some angles, one of the pinnacles on **Chicken Island** does indeed look like the scrawny neck and beaky head of a chicken. There's decent snorkelling off its coast, with a fair range of reef fish and quite a lot of giant clams, though most of the reef is either bleached or dead. Its dazzlingly white-sand northeastern shore, which has a food stall, toilets and kayak rental, is connected to the islets of **Ko Tup** by a sandbank, which is walkable at low tide – quite a striking sight as you arrive to see other visitors seemingly walking on water. Nearby **Ko Poda**, which sits directly in front of the Ao Nang beachfront, is encircled by lovely white-sand beaches and clear turquoise water. There's a restaurant here and plenty of shade under the casuarina trees, so this is the typical lunch stop; sandwich-selling boats dock here too. Though you might get three hundred people lunching on the shore here at any one time, it's big enough to cope. Some itineraries also feature **Ao Phra Nang** and its cave, on the Laem Phra Nang (Railay) peninsula (see page 361), and this is the one to avoid unless you enjoy scrambling for your metre of sand on this overrun little bay.

### OTHER ACTIVITIES

**Cycle rides** Half- and full-day cycle rides into the untamed Krabi countryside, or to Ko Klang, Khao Phanom Bencha falls or Khlong Tom's Emerald Pool, with Krabi Eco Cycle, based about 2km inland from the Hat Nopparat Thara National Park visitors' centre on Route 4202 (from B1500; 081 607 4162, www.krabiecocycle.com).

**Sea canoeing** Guided and self-paddle trips take place around the spectacular karst islands and secret lagoons of Ao Phang Nga, usually focusing on Ao Luk, Ao Thalen and Ko Hong in the eastern bay. Dozens of companies offer these trips, including Sea Kayak Krabi, Soi 2, Thanon Maharat, Krabi town (075 630270, seakayak-krabi.com), who offer a multitude of day and multi-day trips, charging B1500 for a full-day trip to Ao Thalen, for example.

**Thai cookery lessons** Ya's Thai Cookery School, about 4km inland of Ao Nang off Route 4203, runs four different morning and afternoon courses (Mon–Sat 9am–1pm & 2–6pm; from B1200 including transport; 081 979 0677, yacookeryschool.com).

---

end accommodation is plentiful throughout and of a high standard; you can usually get decent discounts through online booking agents. Prices across the board drop by up to fifty percent during the rainy season (May–Oct).

### AO PHAI PLONG

**Centara Grand Beach Resort** Ao Phai Plong, east end of Ao Nang 075 637789, centarahotelsresorts.

com; map p.356. Ao Nang's top hotel has the secluded sandy bay of Ao Phai Plong all to itself and is connected by longtail boat to the shops and restaurants of Ao Nang or free speedboat shuttle to Hat Nopparat Thara east. Designed to sit almost seamlessly against the forested crags behind, there's a lovely green feel here and seaward vistas are also beautiful. Nearly all rooms in the four-storey hotel buildings and detached villas have sea views. Interiors are modern

**4**

and generous with sun-balconies and shaded outdoor daybeds. There's a big pool, a diving and watersports centre, kids' club, gym and spa. **B7000**

## CENTRAL AO NANG

**Ao Nang Eco Inn** Moo 5 Thanon Ao Nang ☎075 695184, ⓦaonang-ecoinn.com; map p.356. Compact and functional boutique guesthouse with better rooms than the price suggests. Each comes with en-suite bathrooms, some with bathtubs, balconies and writing desks. A light breakfast is included. **B1300**

**Ao Nang Orchid Resort** 141 Thanon Ao Nang ☎075 638426–8, ⓦaonangorchid-resort.com; map p.356. This medium-sized but well-appointed hotel is good value for Ao Nang. Choose from rooms in the hotel wing, where the nicest overlook the pool and karst mountains beyond (rather than those with "city" views), or go for stand-alone villas with direct access to the lagoon pool. Interiors are chic and attractive, and the rooms and bungalows all have decks. **B3300**

**Ao Nang Villa Resort** 113 Thanon Ao Nang ☎075 637 271–4, ⓦaonangvilla.com; map p.356. A very popular hotel and spa whose grounds run down to the beachfront walkway. The upscale, a/c rooms are contained within several low-rise wings, a few of them enjoying a sea view, but most overlooking the garden or the bigger of the resort's two pools. Breakfast included. **B5200**

**Centra by Centara Phu Pano Resort** Off a side road 1.5km north of Ao Nang ☎ 075 607 888, ⓦcentara hotelsresorts.com/centra/cpp; map p.356. Set in a quiet location facing Ao Nang's limestone peaks, this new hotel has comfortable en-suite rooms and mini-apartments for families that come with bunk beds. There's a picturesque swimming pool next to the restaurant; continental breakfast costs an additional B400. **B2550**

**Ibis Styles Krabi Ao Nang** 725 Moo 2, Thanon Ao Nang, opposite a mosque ☎026 592888, ⓦibis.com; map p.356. Being further away from the beach has its benefits with the karst cliffs and wild trees shielding the pool and kids' playground here, offering an oasis of good-value rooms. Rooms are comfortable and a/c, with TV and large safes. The beach is just a 20min walk away past the Ao Nang shops and good street food, or there's a shuttle bus. Breakfast included. **B2500**

**Mini Boxtel Aonang Hostel** Off Thanon Ao Nang ☎086 9046613, ⓦminiboxtel.com; map p.356. Tucked in a corner off the main road, this female-only a/c dorm has twelve cosy individual pods with plush beds, duvets, power sockets and privacy curtains. Mixed groups can rent the whole space, and the downstairs café, *Lion & Shark*, serves a great breakfast (included). **B550**

★ **Sleeper Hostel** 350 Thanon Ao Nang ☎075 695531, ⓦsleeperhostel.com; map p.356. This dorm-only hostel is loved by travellers for its several storeys of mixed and female dorms. The shared toilets have naked lightbulbs,

potted plants and red privacy curtains. The front desk can organize cheap bus-and-boat tickets to most Thai islands, and there's a list of fun daily activities that include pub crawls (B450), sunset kayaking (B490) and rock climbing (B900). **B300**

## HAT NOPPARAT THARA EAST

**Cashew Nut** Soi Hat Nopparat Thara 13 ☎081 081 8095, ⓦcashewnutbungalows.com; map p.356. Good, sturdy en-suite brick and concrete bungalows with fan or a/c and hot showers ranged around a peaceful garden full of cashew trees, just 5min walk from Hat Nopparat Thara east. Family-run, welcoming and peaceful. Fan **B600**, a/c **B800**

**Maneetel Krabi Beachfront** 225 Moo 3 Noppharattara Beach ☎ 06 534 86225, ⓦfacebook.com/Maneetel KrabiBeachfront; map p.356. Sleek boutique hotel that marries industrial touches, including bare rough walls and naked bulbs, together with Arabic motifs in the bed stands and room furnishings. There's also an outdoor pool and breakfast included. **B2200**

**National park bungalows** Beside the national park headquarters on Thanon Nopparat Thara east ☎075 637 200, ⓦdnp.go.th; map p.356. Fan-cooled, en-suite bungalows, 2km from Ao Nang's main facilities but just across the road from a nice stretch of beach and a 5min walk from the seafood restaurants near the visitors' centre. **B1000**

## HAT NOPPARAT THARA WEST

**Long Beach Villa** 600m west from the khlong ☎087 465 6680, ⓦlongbeachvilla.com; map p.351. Set round a grassy, tree-strewn lawn next to a secluded beach, the main offerings at this place are attractive wood-and-bamboo bungalows with fans, mosquito nets and en-suite bathrooms; it also has large, concrete eight-person family bungalows with two bathrooms and four bunk beds, with fan (B4500). Electricity at night only and wi-fi only in restaurant. Informal cooking classes, snorkelling trips and reasonably priced pick-ups. **B2500**

**PAN Beach** At the westernmost end of the beach, about 700m walk from the khlong ☎089 866 4373, ⓦpanbeachkrabi.com; map p.351. Sturdy, simply furnished wooden bungalows in two sizes and styles (non a/c is B800), each with screened windows, fans and bathrooms, set just back from the shore around a lawn. Also has motorbikes and cars for rent, and organizes local boat trips. Electricity at night only. Free pick-ups in the morning from Ao Nang. **B1200**

## HAT KLONG MUANG

**Dusit Thani Krabi Beach Resort** ☎075 628000, ⓦdusit.com/dusitthani/krabibeachresort; map p.351. The top-notch *Dusit Thani* was built among the mangroves and alongside a khlong; the result is refreshingly green and cool – and full of birdsong. The sandy shore – the nicest in Klong Muang – just a few steps away, accessible via a series of wooden walkways. Rooms are large, sleek and very comfortable; there are two beachfront pools, a spa and a variety of restaurants to choose from. Breakfast is included. **B11,050**

## EATING

At weekends, locals flock to the **seafood restaurants** in the national park visitors' centre car park on Hat Nopparat Thara, or buy fried chicken from nearby stalls and picnic on mats under the shorefront trees.

### CENTRAL AO NANG

**Café 8.98** 143/7–8 Moo 2 ☎075 656 980, ⓦcafe898. com; map p.356. Smart Western-style all-day café that attracts a good crowd thanks to its hearty breakfast and brunch sets (from B180), pastries and waffles (from B55), and strong Arabica roasted coffee beans. Daily 7am–11pm.

**The Last Fisherman Bar** Soi Ao Nang 17 ⓦfacebook. com/thelastfisherman; map p.356. On the sand at the far east end of the beach, serving simple Thai food and a huge range of sandwiches for lunch, but most famous for its evening barbecues (from B500), which come with baked potatoes, corn-on-the-cob, salads and desserts. Daily 11.30am–4.30pm & 6pm–midnight.

**Longtail Boat** ☎075 638093, ⓦfacebook. com/longtailboatrestaurant; map p.356. A mix of Thai and Italian dishes, including lasagne, pastas, plenty of fish and seafood, which is displayed on ice and in tanks at the entrance. A meal will set you back around B600. Daily 2.30–11pm.

**Noori India** 245/5 Moo 2 Ao Nang Beach, opposite Sally O Malley's ☎081 396 0283, ⓦnooriindiakrabi.com; map p.356. This Indian restaurant, located on Ao Nang's main strip, is a good choice for vegetarian food such as *paneer pakora* plates (B180) and *baigan bartha* (sauteed eggplant with tomatoes and onions; B150), and also serves meat – try the yummy lamb sheek kebab (B350). Daily 11am–11pm.

### HAT NOPPARAT THARA EAST

**Krua Thara (After Tsunami)** National park visitors' centre car park ☎091 825 9252; map p.356. Hugely popular with locals, expats and visiting Thais for its reasonably priced fresh seafood (mostly sold by weight), but also serves northeastern salads, rice and noodle dishes (around B80) and excellent espresso coffees. Daily 11am–10pm.

★ **Wang Sai** Beside the bridge at the eastern end of Thanon Nopparat Thara ☎075 638128; map p.356. Good sunset views from its beachfront tables, an enormous range of seafood and lots of southern Thai specialities. The hearty *haw mok thalay* (on the menu as "steam seafood curry sauce"; B200) is excellent, stuffed with all kinds of fish and seafood, or you can get seafood fried rice for just B80. Daily 10.30am–10pm.

## DRINKING

The bar scene is mainly focused around **Center Point Walking Street**, a U-shaped passageway behind the beachfront shops that's packed with rock, reggae and all-sorts bars, including Krabi's first pole-dancing club.

**Coconut Bar** Along Thanon Ao Nang, about 200m from the beach ☎095 418 7095, ⓦbit.ly/ CoconutBarThailand; map p.356. A step up in the reggae-bar category, this venue has welcoming wooden interiors, a proper stage for live bands, fire shows, and B100 Happy hour on all cocktails between 5.30 and 8pm. Daily 12pm–late.

**Sally O'Malley's** Up a small soi off the promenade ⓦbit.ly/SallyOmalleys; map p.356. Friendly, Irish-themed pub with a long bar, regular live bands and a pool table. Kilkenny bitter, Guinness and cider are all on draught. Daily 11am–1/2am.

# Laem Phra Nang: Railay and Ton Sai

Seen from the close quarters of a longtail boat, the combination of sheer limestone cliffs, pure white sand and emerald waters around the **LAEM PHRA NANG** peninsula is spectacular – and would be even more so without the hundreds of other admirers gathered on its four beaches. The peninsula (often known simply as **Railay**) is effectively a tiny island, embraced by impenetrable limestone massifs that make road access impossible – but do offer excellent, world-famous **rock-climbing**; transport is by boat only, from Krabi town or, most commonly, from nearby Ao Nang. It has four beaches within ten minutes' walk of each other: **Ao Phra Nang** (walkable via East Railay) graces the southwestern edge, and is flanked by **East and West Railay**, just 500m apart; **Ao Ton Sai** is beyond West Railay, on the other side of a rocky promontory. Almost every patch of buildable land fronting East and West Railay has been taken over by bungalow resorts, and development is creeping up the cliffsides and into the forest behind. But at

---

### ROCK-CLIMBING AND KAYAKING ON LAEM PHRA NANG

Ton Sai and Railay are Thailand's biggest **rock-climbing** centres, attracting thousands of experienced and novice climbers every year to the peninsula's seven hundred bolted routes, which range in difficulty from 5a to 8c (see ⓦrailay.com for a full rundown). Of the many climbing **schools** that rent out equipment and lead guided climbs, the most established include King Climbers on Walking Street on West Railay (ⓣ075 662096, ⓦrailay.com/railay/climbing/climbing_king_climbers.shtml) and Basecamp Tonsai on Ton Sai (ⓣ081 149 9745, ⓦbasecamptonsai.com). A typical half-day introduction costs B1800, a full day B2800, while B6000 will get you a three-day course, learning all rope skills; equipment can be rented for about B2400 per day for two people from Railay Rock Climbing Shop (ⓣ081 7972517) on West Railay's Walking Street. If you don't need instruction, the locally published and regularly updated guidebooks, Basecamp Tonsai's *Rock Climbing in Thailand and Laos* and King Climbers' Thailand *Route Guide Book*, will give you all the route information you need. Unaided over-water climbing on cliffs and outcrops out at sea, known as **deep-water soloing**, with no ropes, bolts or partner, is also becoming a big thing around here and can be arranged through most climbing schools for about B1000.

**Kayaking** around this area is also very rewarding – you can get to Ao Nang in less than an hour; kayaks cost B200 per hour to rent, for example on the beach in front of *Flame Tree* restaurant on West Railay. **Freebird** (ⓣ 061 953 9913, ⓦgofreebird.com) rents paddle boards (B250/hour) and organizes floating yoga classes (B600 minimum four people) and two-hour long guided night tours of the bay at 6pm (B1700/person).

---

least high-rises don't feature, and much of the construction is hidden among trees or set amid prettily landscaped gardens. Accommodation is at a premium and not cheap, so the scene on West and East Railay, and Ao Phra Nang, is predominantly holidaymakers on short breaks rather than backpackers. The opposite is true on adjacent Ao Ton Sai, Krabi's main travellers' hub and the heart of the rock-climbing scene.

## West Railay

The loveliest and most popular beach on the cape is **WEST RAILAY**, with its gorgeous white sand, crystal-clear water and impressive karst scenery at every turn. The best of the peninsula's bungalow hotels front this shoreline, and longtail boats from Ao Nang pull in here too, so it gets crowded.

## East Railay

Follow any of the paved tracks inland, through the resort developments, and within a few minutes you reach **EAST RAILAY** on the other coast, lined with mangrove swamps and a muddy shore that make it unsuitable for swimming; boats from Krabi town dock here. There's more variety in accommodation choices and prices here, although its mostly an uncomfortable mix of uninspired, low-grade developments and unsubtle bars with names like *Skunk* and *Stone*. Depressingly, much of East Railay's hinterland is despoiled by trash and building rubble, but inland it's another story, with a majestic amphitheatre of forested karst turrets just ten minutes' walk away, on the back route to Ao Ton Sai.

## Ao Phra Nang

Head to the far south end of East Railay's shoreline to pick up the path to the diminutive, cliff-bound beach at **AO PHRA NANG** (also called **Hat Tham Phra Nang**). Though exceptionally pretty, the bay can be hard to appreciate beneath the trinket sellers and crowds of day-trippers who are deposited here in their hundreds, by boats that pollute the coastal waters. Better to visit before 10am or after 4pm if you can.

The walkway from East Railay winds between the super-lux *Rayavadee* hotel and the lip of a massive karst before emerging at the beach beside **Tham Phra Nang**, or **Princess**

**Cave**. The beach and cave, and indeed the peninsula, are named for this princess (*phra nang* means "revered lady"): according to legend, a boat carrying an Indian princess sank in a storm here and the royal spirit took up residence in the cave. Local fisherfolk believe she controls the fertility of the sea and, to encourage large catches, leave red-tipped wooden phalluses as offerings to her at the cave entrance. Buried deep inside the same cliff is **Sa Phra Nang (Princess Lagoon)**, which is accessible only via a steep 45-minute descent that starts halfway along the walkway. You'll need proper shoes for it, as slippery descents and sharp rocks make it hard in flip-flops or bare feet. After an initial ten-minute clamber, negotiated with the help of ropes, the path forks: go left for a panoramic view over East and West Railay, or right for the lagoon. (For the strong-armed, there's the third option of hauling yourself up ropes to the top of the cliff for a bird's-eye view.) Taking the right-hand fork, you'll pass through the tropical dell dubbed "big tree valley" before eventually descending to the murky lagoon.

## Ao Ton Sai

The beach at **AO TON SAI**, north across the oyster rocks from West Railay, is not the prettiest, prone to murk and littered with rocks that make it impossible to swim at low tide. But its orange-and-ochre-striped cliffs are magnificently scenic, dripping with curlicues and turrets

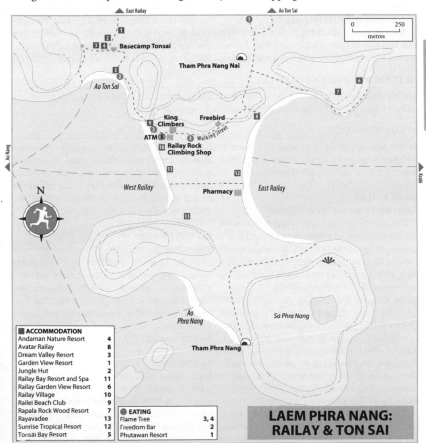

ACCOMMODATION

| | |
|---|---|
| Andaman Nature Resort | 4 |
| Avatar Railay | 8 |
| Dream Valley Resort | 3 |
| Garden View Resort | 1 |
| Jungle Hut | 2 |
| Railay Bay Resort and Spa | 11 |
| Railay Garden View Resort | 6 |
| Railay Village | 10 |
| Railei Beach Club | 9 |
| Rapala Rock Wood Resort | 7 |
| Rayavadee | 13 |
| Sunrise Tropical Resort | 12 |
| Tonsai Bay Resort | 5 |

EATING

| | |
|---|---|
| Flame Tree | 3, 4 |
| Freedom Bar | 2 |
| Phutawan Resort | 1 |

**LAEM PHRA NANG: RAILAY & TON SAI**

that tower over a central tree-filled bowl and host scores of challenging rock climbs. Most of the accommodation here is aimed at climbers and travellers, and is well hidden several hundred metres back from the shore, scattered within the remains of a forest and along the shady path that, beyond *Sai Tong*, takes you to East Railay in about twenty minutes. The vibe here is green and comradely, with climbers doing their thing during the day and partying at the several chilled bars after dark. At low tide, you can easily scramble up the hill path next to *Railay Beach Club* on West Railay, or you can pick your way over the razor-sharp rocks. At high tide you'll either need to swim or get a longtail.

## ARRIVAL AND DEPARTURE                                   LAEM PHRA NANG

Laem Phra Nang is only accessible by **boat**.

**To/from Krabi town** Longtail boats to Laem Phra Nang depart from the Krabi riverfront (45min; B200/person, minimum eight people, or around B18000 when chartered), leaving throughout the day as soon as they fill up. Depending on the tide, all Krabi boats land on or off East Railay, so you may have to wade; they do run during the rainy season, but the waves make it a nerve-wracking experience, so you're advised to go via Ao Nang instead. Coming back, contact a travel agent or your guesthouse on Laem Phra Nang about the half a dozen timed departures a day.

**To/from Ao Nang and beyond** Ao Nang is much closer than Krabi town to Laem Phra Nang, and shared longtails run from the beachfront here to West Railay, Ao Phra Nang

and Ao Ton Sai when full (10min; B100 until 6pm, B150 after dark; minimum eight people; return tickets are open, allowing return from any of the three beaches). There are several longtail boat stations with ticket booths, including one at the Hat Nopparat Thara national park visitor centre, all charging the same price; the one at the eastern end of the beachfront road is the most popular, so you'll probably have the shortest wait for the boat to fill up here. Expect to get your legs wet wading out to the songthaew on both beaches. During high season there should also be daily ferries from Ao Nang via West Railay to Ko Phi Phi (9.45am; 2hr 30min; B450), Ko Lanta (10.30am; 2hr; B600), and Phuket (3.15pm year-round, plus a 10.30am speedboat in high season; 2hr; B650); if not, you'll need to travel via Ao Nang.

## GETTING AROUND AND SERVICES

**Getting around** Shared longtail boats between Ao Ton Sai and West Railay cost B50 per person (minimum four people).

**ATM** Several in the resort, including nearly opposite *Flame Tree* restaurant.

## ACCOMMODATION

Because demand is so high, from November to March it's often hard to get a room on spec on West or East Railay, though you should have more luck on Ao Ton Sai.

### WEST RAILAY

**Railay Bay Resort and Spa** ☎ 075 819 401–3, ⊛ krabi-railaybay.com; map p.363. There's a huge range of rooms and bungalows here, in a shady coconut grove that runs down to both East and West Railay, plus two swimming pools and a spa. The pick of the bunch are the very large beachfront suites, which have marble bathrooms with Jacuzzi tubs and great sea views from their verandas. B4800

**Railay Village** ☎ 075 819412–3, ⊛ railayvillagekrabi. com; map p.363. Occupying very pretty gardens in between the two beaches, with nowhere more than 300m from the West Railay shore, the style here is elegant tropical, in whitewashed Jacuzzi villas (B7500) and pool-access hotel rooms, all roofed in low-impact wooden tiles, with wooden floors and Thai furnishings completing the look. There are two pools and a spa. Breakfast included. B6000

**Railei Beach Club** ☎ 086 685 9359, ⊛ raileibeachclub. com; map p.363. Unusual compound of charming, mostly fan-cooled private houses, built of wood in idiosyncratic Thai style and rented out by their owners. One- to four-bed

houses are available, all well-spaced, and there are a couple of cheaper private rooms; most have kitchen. The compound is only minimally screened from the beach, so seafront houses get good views but may lack privacy and bear the brunt of the noisy longtail traffic. Minimum stays of three nights, rising to seven from mid-Dec to mid-Jan. B2900

### AO PHRA NANG

**Rayavadee** ☎ 075 620440, ⊛ rayavadee.com; map p.363. The supremely elegant two-storey spiral-shaped pavilions here, some set in enclosed gardens, some with whirlpools, are set in a beautifully landscaped, eco-friendly compound with lotus ponds that borders all three beaches. Facilities include a pool with a kids' pool, a spa, a squash court and tennis courts, a gym and two restaurants. Breakfast is included. B17,550

### EAST RAILAY

**Avatar Railay** ☎ 075 818 333, ⊛ avatarrailay.com; map p.363. A collection of modern and spacious rooms and villas set right below the karsts and in two concrete blocks, separated by a long, attractive swimming pool. The pool villas have direct access to the water from their balconies, and there's a restaurant and a cocktail bar. Breakfast is included. B2500

★ **Railay Garden View Resort** ☎ 085 888 5143, ⓦ railaygardenview.com; map p.363. This place really stands out for its simple rustic-chic style, great high-level views over the mangroves and sea beyond, and green surrounds in a garden of jackfruit, banana and papaya trees. The fan-cooled bungalows, built from good-quality split bamboo, are widely spaced and on stilts, with colour-washed cold-water bathrooms, wooden-floored bedrooms and decks, and plenty of triangular cushions for lounging. The drawback is that it's up a steep stairway beyond the far north end of East Railay, accessed via a short walkway beyond *The Last Bar*, about 15min walk from West Railay. Breakfast included. B1450

**Rapala Rock Wood Resort** ☎ 083 703 5006, ⓦ facebook.com/RAPALARailay; map p.363. Climb a steep flight of stairs to reach the thirty rough-hewn, fan-cooled timber and brick huts here, which are among the cheapest on Railay, set around a scruffy, breezy garden high above the beach, with some enjoying dramatic karst views from verandas. There's also a communal deck among the treetops, and a friendly restaurant that serves Indian food and bakes its own tasty biscuits. Walk-ins only and no wi-fi. B500

★ **Sunrise Tropical Resort** ☎ 075 819418–20, ⓦ sunrisetropical.com; map p.363. The most stylish of the affordable hotels on the cape offers just forty rooms, most in elegantly designed a/c bungalows, and some in a couple of two-storey buildings, all with Thai furnishings and generously spacious living areas, set around a landscaped tropical garden with a pool and spa. Doubles B4500, villas B5800

### AO TON SAI

**Andaman Nature Resort** ☎ 081 979 6050, ⓦ bit.ly/ AndamanNature; map p.363. Wooden bungalows fan out in the jungle behind the large stilted restaurant of this long-standing and good value budget option. Rooms are basic, with mosquito nets and en-suite bathrooms, and the friendly staff try hard to make guests feel like family. B400

**Dream Valley Resort** ☎ 075 819810–2, ⓦ dream valleykrabi.com; map p.363. The ninety bungalows here are ranged discreetly among the trees, running far back towards the cliff-face, offering a range of good-quality accommodation in various categories, from wooden bungalows with fans, mosquito screens and bathrooms through to a/c villas with hot showers, the best of which are the premier accommodation on Ao Ton Sai. Breakfast included. B2500

**Garden View Resort** ☎ 085 793 7449; map p.363. Set among Ao Ton Sai's bars, the simple yet spacious en-suite rooms here are all set in a concrete block, which is removed from the main road. Rooms have small porches facing a well-kept hillside garden, making it easy to relax and forget about the crowds. B500

**Jungle Hut** ☎ 062 118 5289, ⓦ facebook.com/ Junglehut.Tonsai; map p.363. Rustic en-suite wooden bungalows with fan and mosquito nets catering to backpackers. Located next to the popular Chill Out Bar, which plays dance music well into the night. B500

**Tonsai Bay Resort** ☎ 075 695599, ⓦ tonsaibaykrabi. com; map p.363. With its large, widely spaced and plain but comfortable bungalows and rooms, this is one of the top places to stay on Ao Ton Sai. The detached and semi-detached bungalows (B2700) boast huge glass windows and big decks from which to soak up the pretty location in a grove of trees set back from the shore, and all have a/c, hot shower, satellite TV, fridge and safety box. Breakfast included. B2600

## EATING AND DRINKING

There's no shortage of traveller-style bars on Laem Phra Nang, especially at the north end of East Railay and on the beach at Ton Sai, with their fire-juggling, driftwood furniture, chillums and occasional parties.

### WEST RAILAY

**Flame Tree** On the seafront ☎ 088 819 9221, ⓦ bit. ly/Flametree; map p.363. This sprawling, laid-back, semi-outdoor place has a more varied menu than most of the restaurants on Laem Phra Nang, including cashew nut salad (B175), some southern Thai dishes, mushroom sauce steak (B395), pasta, sandwiches, a variety of breakfasts and espresso coffees. Daily 6.30am–10.30pm.

### EAST RAILAY

**Phutawan Resort** map p.363. Quietly located in the middle of the spectacular cliff-lined basin on the track to Ton Sai, a 10min walk from both East and West Railay, the restaurant here offers fine views and good food, mostly seafood and Thai curries, and largely in the reasonable B120–150 range. Daily 7.30am–10pm.

### AO TON SAI

**Freedom Bar** ⓦ facebook.com/freedombar.tonsai; map p.363. The unmissable beachfront location makes *Freedom Bar* a popular spot to enjoy a cocktail or two (from B150) or a beer (from B70). Daily 10am–12pm.

# Ko Phi Phi Don

About 40km south of Krabi, the island of **KO PHI PHI DON** looks breathtakingly handsome as you approach from the sea, its classic arcs of pure white sand framed by dramatic cliffs and lapped by water that's a mouthwatering shade of turquoise. A

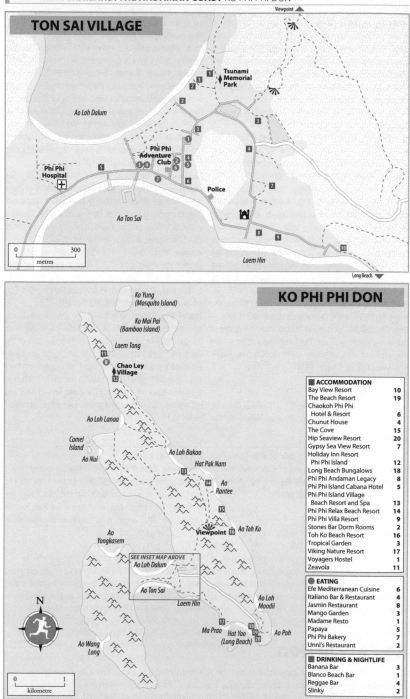

## TON SAI VILLAGE

Viewpoint

Tsunami Memorial Park

Ao Loh Dalum

Phi Phi Adventure Club

Phi Phi Hospital

Police

Ao Ton Sai

Laem Hin

Long Beach

0 — 300
metres

**4**

## KO PHI PHI DON

Ko Yung (Mosquito Island)

Ko Mai Pai (Bamboo Island)

Laem Tong

Chao Ley Village

Ao Loh Lanaa

Camel Island

Ao Nui

Ao Loh Bakao

Hat Pak Nam

Ao Rantee

Ao Yongkasem

Viewpoint

Ao Toh Ko

SEE INSET MAP ABOVE
Ao Loh Dalum

Ao Ton Sai

Laem Hin

Ao Loh Moodii

Ma Prao

Hat Yao (Long Beach)

Ao Poh

Ao Wang Long

N

0 — 1
kilometre

Ko Phi Phi Leh

| ■ ACCOMMODATION | |
|---|---|
| Bay View Resort | 10 |
| The Beach Resort | 19 |
| Chaokoh Phi Phi Hotel & Resort | 6 |
| Chunut House | 4 |
| The Cove | 15 |
| Hip Seaview Resort | 20 |
| Gypsy Sea View Resort | 7 |
| Holiday Inn Resort Phi Phi Island | 12 |
| Long Beach Bungalows | 18 |
| Phi Phi Andaman Legacy | 8 |
| Phi Phi Island Cabana Hotel | 5 |
| Phi Phi Island Village Beach Resort and Spa | 13 |
| Phi Phi Relax Beach Resort | 14 |
| Phi Phi Villa Resort | 9 |
| Stones Bar Dorm Rooms | 2 |
| Toh Ko Beach Resort | 16 |
| Tropical Garden | 3 |
| Viking Nature Resort | 17 |
| Voyagers Hostel | 1 |
| Zeavola | 11 |

| ● EATING | |
|---|---|
| Efe Mediterranean Cuisine | 6 |
| Italiano Bar & Restaurant | 4 |
| Jasmin Restaurant | 8 |
| Mango Garden | 3 |
| Madame Resto | 1 |
| Papaya | 5 |
| Phi Phi Bakery | 7 |
| Unni's Restaurant | 2 |

| ■ DRINKING & NIGHTLIFE | |
|---|---|
| Banana Bar | 3 |
| Blanco Beach Bar | 1 |
| Reggae Bar | 4 |
| Slinky | 2 |

flat sandy isthmus connects the hilly east and west halves of the island, scalloped into the much-photographed symmetrical double bays of Ao Ton Sai and Ao Loh Dalum. The vast majority of the tourist accommodation is squashed in here, as is the island's wild nightlife, with just a few alternatives scattered along eastern coasts. Phi Phi's few indigenous islanders mostly live in the northeast.

Such beauty, however, belies the island's turbulent recent history. By the early 1990s, Phi Phi's reputation as a tropical idyll was bringing unfeasibly huge crowds of backpackers to its shores, and the problem worsened after uninhabited little sister island **Ko Phi Phi Leh** – under national marine park protection on account of its lucrative bird's-nest business – gained worldwide attention as the location for the movie *The Beach* in 1999, adding day-trippers, package tourists and big hotels to the mix on Phi Phi Don. Then, in December 2004, the **tsunami** struck (see page 307). As a 5m-high wave crashed in from the north, over the sunbathers on Ao Loh Dalum, a 3m-high wave from the south hurtled in across the ferry dock and tourist village at Ao Ton Sai. The waves met in the middle, obliterating seventy percent of all buildings on the sandy flats and killing two thousand. The rest of the island was barely affected.

Volunteers and donations poured in to help the island back on its feet, and though the rebuild was dogged by much political wrangling, the Phi Phi of today thrives much as it ever did, firmly re-established as the destination to be ticked off on almost any itinerary in southern Thailand. Unfortunately, few of the pre-tsunami **problems** have been properly resolved – in part because tsunami survivors were desperate to make a new start as fast as they could. The island is now once again floundering under unregulated, unsightly and unsustainable development, with inadequate rubbish disposal and a plague of overpriced accommodation, at its most acute around the Ton Sai–Loh Dalum hub. There's always more building work going on, while thousands of visitors from all corners of the world fight for space in the narrow maze of pedestrianized alleys in Ton Sai village, sometimes generating an unusually aggressive atmosphere for Thailand. The noise pollution from the untrammelled outdoor bars and clubs is an additional turn-off for some – though it is a fun place to party, and there are enough more remote escapes for a peaceful stay too.

All boats dock in **Ao Ton Sai**, from where it's a short walk to the main accommodation centres – in **Ton Sai village**, at **Laem Hin**, the next little stretch of sand to the east, and on **Ao Loh Dalum**, the still attractive, deeply curved bay across the isthmus. **Hat Yao**, another fine beach just a short boat ride away, is also very popular. To escape the crowds you need to aim for one of the smaller bays further north: **Ao Toh Ko**, **Ao Rantee** and **Hat Pak Nam** are all good for moderately priced breakaways, while **Ao Loh Bakao** and **Laem Tong** are pricier and more luxurious.

## Ton Sai village, Ao Loh Dalum and Laem Hin

**Ton Sai village** is a hectic warren of a place, both strangely old-fashioned with its alley traffic of bicycles and pushcarts, its fresh market tucked away in the middle and its squalid shanty town and stinky sewers hidden along the edges, and bang up to date, the narrow lanes bursting with state-of-the-art dive companies, shops advertising DVD players for rent and trendy boutiques.

West of the pier, **Ao Ton Sai** beach is an attractive little retreat under the limestone karsts, though it gets busy for a couple of hours around lunchtime and you're not far from the longtail moorings. Most people simply head for **Ao Loh Dalum** instead, less than 300m north across the narrow isthmus, which looks astonishingly pretty at high tide, with its glorious curve of powder-white sand beautifully set off by pale blue water; it's a different story at low water, however, as the tide goes out for many kilometres. There's a tiny Tsunami Memorial Park of carefully tended shrubs, epitaphs and photos at the eastern end, a bit further up from *Stones Bar*.

East along the coast from the Ton Sai pier, about ten minutes' walk along the main alley, is the promontory known as **Laem Hin**, beyond which lies a small beach and bungalows that enjoy a little more space. Inland, there are island homes and a mosque.

### The viewpoint

B30

The **viewpoint** that overlooks eastern Ao Loh Dalum affords a magnificent panorama over the twin bays and every evening a stream of people make the steep fifteen-minute climb up the steps for sunset shots; early morning is also photogenic, and the shop at the "Topview" summit, set within a pretty tropical garden, serves coffee as well as cold drinks. There are good, free views just metres before the viewpoint entrance and from the restaurant patio halfway up. From the viewpoint, you can descend the rocky and at times almost sheer paths to the trio of little east-coast bays at Ao Toh Ko, Ao Rantee (Lanti) and Hat Pak Nam, each of which takes about thirty minutes.

## Hat Yao (Long Beach)

With its fine white sand and large reefs packed with polychromatic marine life just 20m offshore, **HAT YAO** (Long Beach) is considered the best of Phi Phi's main beaches, but it's lined with hotels so gets very busy. UK-run Long Beach Divers (⋓longbeachdivers.com) here runs all the same **dive** trips and courses as shops in the village and offers discounted stays at *Long Beach Bungalows* (see page 372) for dive students.

Longtail **boats** do the ten-minute shuttle between Hat Yao and Ao Ton Sai (B100/ person, or B150 after dark), but at low tide it's also possible to **walk** between the two in half an hour, via the coast in front of *Bay View Resort* on Laem Hin and then via *Viking*. The island's single **road** follows an inland route to *The Beach Resort* from *The Rock* junction in the village, passing the post-tsunami housing project and Water Hill reservoir en route; it's a hot, hilly and unshaded forty-minute walk.

## Ao Toh Ko, Hat Rantee and Hat Pak Nam

Travellers wanting to escape the crowds around Ton Sai and Hat Yao without spending a fortune head for the trio of little bays midway along the east coast: **AO TOH KO** and adjacent **AO RANTEE** (Lanti) and **HAT PAK NAM**. You can reach the bays inland, via steep forest trails that run from the Viewpoint above Ao Loh Dalum (see page 367) in half an hour, while you can walk from Ao Toh Ko to Ao Rantee in five minutes at low tide. Rantee is probably the pick of the three, a palm- and casuarina-fringed white-sand bay, with great snorkelling at the reef right off the beach.

## Ao Loh Bakao and Laem Tong

Far removed from the hustle of Ao Ton Sai and its environs, the beautiful, secluded northern beaches at Ao Loh Bakao and Laem Tong are the domain of just a few upscale resorts. *Phi Phi Island Village Beach Resort and Spa* (see page 372) has the gorgeous 800m-long white-sand beach and turquoise waters of **AO LOH BAKAO** all to itself. If you tire of these white sands, and the hotel's four restaurants, there's a cluster of reasonably priced local restaurants behind the resort, and you can walk to the long, semi-circular beach at **Ao Loh Lanaa**, across on the west coast, in ten minutes, or to Laem Tong in half an hour.

Almost right at Phi Phi's northernmost tip, **LAEM TONG** is busier and more commercial than Loh Bakao, with several upmarket resorts and stand-alone restaurants along its white-sand shores, and views across to nearby Bamboo and Mosquito islands. The beach is home to a group of Urak Lawoy *chao ley* "sea gypsies" (see page 300), whose village is next to the *Holiday Inn*; all longtail boat tours and transfers are run by Laem Tong's *chao ley* cooperative.

## PHI PHI ACTIVITIES

### SNORKELLING

There's some great **snorkelling** around Phi Phi's shallow fringing reefs, most rewardingly at strikingly beautiful **Ko Mai Pai (Bamboo Island)**, off Phi Phi Don's northeast coast, where much of the reef lies close to the surface, and at nearby **Ko Yung (Mosquito Island)**, with its spectacular, steep-sided drop. Phi Phi Don has its own worthwhile reefs too, including at west-coast **Ao Yongkasem**, within kayaking distance of Loh Dalum, but **Ao Maya** on Phi Phi Leh is more famous, and a lot more crowded (see page 370).

Outings are easily arranged as part of an **organized tour** (B500–800 including equipment) or by **hiring your own longtail** boatman (B1500/3000 per boat per half/full day), the latter far preferable to the largest tour boats, whose groups of forty-plus trippers inundate the reefs. **Overnight camping trips** to Ao Maya are a neat way of avoiding the crowds, offering late-afternoon snorkelling, and possibly kayaking, rounded off with a beach barbecue.

### DIVING

Offering visibility touching 30m, a great diversity of healthy hard and soft corals, and potential encounters with white-tip sharks, moray eels and stingrays, the diving around Ko Phi Phi is the best in the area and the usual destination of dive boats from Ao Nang and Phuket. Highlights include the gorgonian sea fans, barracudas, manta rays and even whale sharks at **Ko Bidah Nok** and **Ko Bidah Nai**, the mass of leopard sharks at **Hin Bidah**, and the *King Cruiser* **wreck** (see page 335).

There are at least twenty dive shops on Phi Phi, the majority of them in Ton Sai. Note that it's considered risky for a novice diver with fewer than twenty dives to dive at Hin Daeng and Hin Muang (see page 335), due to the depth and the current; reputable dive shops will only take Advanced Divers there. There are also small dive centres on Hat Yao, Ao Loh Bakao and Laem Tong.

Prices for **day-trips** including two tanks, equipment and lunch start at B2500, while the four-day PADI Open Water **course** costs B13,800. Check that your dive operator is insured to use one of the recompression chambers on Phuket (see page 317).

### ROCK-CLIMBING

The main **rock-climbing** area is just to the west of Ao Ton Sai, and includes the Ton Sai Tower and the Drinking Wall, with thirty routes from grades 5 to 7a. A newer attraction is **deep-water soloing**, unaided climbing on cliffs and outcrops over the sea.

#### OPERATORS

**Maya Bay Tours** East of Ao Ton Sai pier, Ko Phi Phi Don, on the fourth north–south alley ⓦ mayabay tours.com. Overnight camping on Phi Phi Leh for B3500.
**Phi Phi Adventure Club** East of Ao Ton Sai pier, Ko Phi Phi Don, on the fourth north–south alley ⓣ 081 895 1334, ⓦ diving-in-thailand.net. Responsible, small-group dive trips, courses and snorkelling trips ("with sharks guaranteed"; 3hr; B1100).
**Phi Phi Scuba Diving Centre** East of the pier, on the fourth north–south alley ⓦ ppscuba.com. The largest scuba-diving operator on the island, with an array of options available for divers.
**Spidermonkey** Next to Princess Divers on the route to the east end of Loh Dalum ⓣ 087 881 2450, ⓦ spidermonkeyphiphi.com/climbing.  Climbing instruction (from B1200 for half a day), guide service and equipment rental. Also runs snorkelling (on Phi Phi Leh) and climbing day-trips (B2000).
**Viking Divers** East of the pier, on the fourth north–south alley ⓦ vikingdiversthailand.com. Phi Phi Diving Association member.

# Ko Phi Phi Leh

B400

More rugged than its twin, Ko Phi Phi Don, and a quarter the size, **KO PHI PHI LEH** is the number one day-tripping destination from Phi Phi Don, twenty minutes north, and a feature of snorkelling tours out of Phuket and Ao Nang (the national park admission fee is only levied if you set foot on the island, but not if you only snorkel offshore). It is very scenic indeed, and world famous, following its starring role in the film *The Beach*, so expect huge crowds, a plethora of discarded polystyrene lunch boxes, and a fair bit of damage to the reefs from the carelessly dropped anchors of tourist and

4

fishing boats. The best way to appreciate the island is probably on one of the overnight camping and snorkelling trips from Phi Phi Don (see page 369).

Most idyllic of all the island's bays, and the most famous backdrop of the film *The Beach*, is **Ao Maya** (or Maya Bay) on the southwest coast, where the water is still and very clear. However, be prepared to share it with the hundreds of tourists that visit daily during high season. At the time of writing, Ao Maya was closed to boat access between June and September 2018 to prevent further damage to its corals, but it isn't clear whether these measures will be repeated or whether a cap on daily visitors will be introduced in the future.

**Ao Phi Leh**, an almost completely enclosed east-coast lagoon of breathtakingly turquoise water, is also beautiful. Nearby, the **Viking Cave** gets its misleading name from the scratchy wall paintings of Chinese junks inside, but more interesting than this 400-year-old graffiti is the **bird's-nesting** that goes on here (see page 370): rickety bamboo scaffolding extends hundreds of metres up to the roof of the cave, where intrepid *chao ley* harvesters spend the day scraping the unfeasibly valuable nests made by tiny sea swifts off the rockface, for export to specialist Chinese restaurants all over the world.

## ARRIVAL AND DEPARTURE                                    KO PHI PHI DON

Tour agents in Phuket, Ao Nang, Krabi town and Ko Lanta all organize snorkelling day-trips to Phi Phi Don and Phi Phi Leh. Touts and bungalow staff always meet the ferries at the pier in Ton Sai; if you've pre-booked accommodation your luggage will usually be transported in a handcart. There is a waste management fee of B20 in cash on arrival; and a left-luggage booth (B50/piece).

**To/from Phuket** Large, crowded ferries leave from Rassada Harbour (see page 316) in Phuket to Ko Phi Phi Don three times daily (11am, 13.30pm & 3pm; 2hr; B400). Andaman Wave Master (w andamanwaveferry. com; 8.30am, 12.30pm & 1.30pm; 2hr) has three daily departures in high season, calling in at Ao Ton Sai (B750), and continuing up the west coast to Laem Tong (B800 single), where the resorts send out longtail boats to pick up guests from the ship. A daily speedboat also runs from Rassada to Phi Phi (which continues to Ko Lanta), but it costs B1500 for the 50min journey.

**To/from Krabi** From Krabi Passenger Port, there are boats to Phi Phi daily year-round, with at least four a day in high season (2hr; B400). You can also reach Phi Phi by once-daily ferries from Ao Nang, via West Railay (2hr 30min; B450), which are year-round in theory though they sometimes don't run in the monsoon season.

**To/from Ko Lanta Yai** From Ban Sala Dan on Ko Lanta Yai, there are two daily departures to Ko Phi Phi in high season (8am & 1pm; 1hr 30min; B450).

**To/from Ko Jum** In high season a daily ferry runs to Ko Jum (2pm; 2hr; B600). Private charters can be arranged for B2000–2500 at the pier or through travel agents in Ton Sai village.

## BIRD'S-NESTING

Prized for its aphrodisiac and energizing qualities, **bird's-nest soup** is such a delicacy in Taiwan, Singapore and Hong Kong that ludicrous sums of money change hands for a dish whose basic ingredients are tiny twigs glued together with bird's spit. Collecting these nests is a lucrative but life-endangering business: sea swifts (known as edible-nest swiftlets) build their nests in rock crevices hundreds of metres above sea level, often on sheer cliff-faces or in cavernous hollowed-out karst. **Nest-building** begins in January and the harvesting season usually lasts from February to May, during which time the female swiftlet builds three nests on the same spot, none of them more than 12cm across, by secreting an unbroken thread of saliva, which she winds round as if making a coil pot. **Gatherers** will only steal the first two nests made by each bird, allowing the bird to build a final nest and raise her chicks in peace. Gathering the nests demands faultless agility and balance, skills that seem to come naturally to the *chao ley* (see page 300), whose six-man teams bring about four hundred nests down the perilous bamboo scaffolds each day, weighing about 4kg in total. At a market rate of up to $2000 per kilo, so much money is at stake that a government franchise must be granted before any collecting commences, and armed guards often protect the sites at night. The *chao ley* seek spiritual protection from the dangers of the job by making offerings to the spirits of the cliff or cave at the beginning of the season; in the Viking Cave, they place buffalo flesh, horns and tails at the foot of one of the stalagmites.

## GETTING AROUND

It's possible to **walk** along the paths across the steep and at times rugged interior. There are only a few short motorbike tracks and one road, from the back of Ton Sai village to *The Beach Resort* on Long Beach, which takes around forty minutes on foot.

**By boat** From Ao Ton Sai, east of the main pier, you can catch a longtail to any of the other beaches, which range in price from B100 per person (minimum two people) to Hat Yao, to B1000 per boat to Laem Tong; prices often double after dark. The Andaman Wave Master ferry (see above) and a smaller shuttle boat each run twice a day between Ton Sai and the east-coast bays as far as Laem Tong (both B200). You could also get about by kayak (B700 per day from in front of *Slinky Bar* on Ao Loh Dalum), which is the perfect way to explore the limestone cliffs and secluded bays, without the roar of an accompanying longtail or cruise ship.

## ACCOMMODATION

As demand for accommodation frequently outstrips supply on Phi Phi, if you haven't made a reservation, it's worth using the agents' booking service at the pier head, where pictures and – genuine – room prices for hotels in all categories are posted for easy browsing; staff then call ahead to secure your room, and might even carry your bag there. Be warned though that rooms are very expensive on Phi Phi, and often poorly maintained. We've quoted rates for high season, which runs from November to April, but most places slap on a thirty- to fifty-percent surcharge during Christmas and New Year and, conversely, will discount up to fifty percent in quiet periods between May and October.

### TON SAI VILLAGE AND AO LOH DALUM

Ton Sai hotels are the least good value on the island and almost none, however expensive, is out of earshot of the thumping all-night beats cranked up by the various bars and clubs; bring some heavy-duty earplugs if you're not planning to party every night.

★**Chaokoh Phi Phi Hotel & Resort** 350m walk to the right of Tonsai pier ⓦchaokohphiphihotel.com; map p.366. Despite being walking distance from Tonsai pier, this collection of spacious en-suite deluxe rooms complements its quiet location by blending futuristic design with simple carved wooden panels and beams. Some suites have sea-facing balconies and bathtubs, while there's a small swimming pool set in a private garden. Breakfast is included and served at the beach-facing restaurant. B4000

**Chunut House** Turn right at The Rock and walk for about 5min back towards Laem Hin ☎075 601227, ⓦchunuthouse.com; map p.366. Very welcoming, relaxing place in a leafy, sloping garden, in a relatively quiet location. Big, stylish, thatched cottages come with a/c, flatscreen TVs, minibars and spacious, attractive, hot-water bathrooms. Breakfast included. B2600

**Phi Phi Island Cabana Hotel** West of the pier on Ton Sai ☎075 601 170–7, ⓦphiphi-cabana.com; map p.366. The views from the contemporary a/c rooms at this large, imposing hotel are breathtakingly lovely. Most look out across the scoop of Ao Loh Dalum and its framing cliffs, and ground-floor ones have direct access to the sand. There's a huge infinity pool and a spa, and two restaurants; the Beach Terrace is ideal for a romantic evening. On the negative side, the hotel lacks atmosphere, and some rooms are affected by late-night club noise. B5000

**Stones Bar Dorm Rooms** A 5min walk down the right side of Ao Loh Dalum, past Slinky's and Chillout Bar ☎094 803 1539, ⓦstonesbardorm.weebly.com; map p.366. Sociable dorm-only hostel with a popular beachfront bar. There are over thirty a/c bunk beds split over two floors, with three en-suite bathrooms per room and secure access via key card. It's not the quietest choice for sleeping, but guests come here to enjoy the party vibe and the superb beach location. B500

**Tropical Garden** Beyond the turn-off for the path to the viewpoint ☎081 729 1436, ⓦthailandphiphi.com; map p.366. Here you'll find a wide variety of rooms and good-sized rough-timber bungalows, which are mostly built on stilts up the side of an outcrop. The better ones have a breezy veranda (though not much of a view) and there's a refreshing amount of greenery around, plus a small pool, despite being surrounded by other accommodation. Fan B900, a/c B1700

**Voyagers Hostel** Opposite the tsunami shelter, ⓦbit.ly/VoyagersHomestay; map p.366. Revered by travellers for its central yet quiet location, and the enthusiasm and care bestowed upon all guests by the manager, Yui. The two a/c dorm rooms and shared bathrooms are clean, yet cramped with bunk beds; overall, you'll get a good night's sleep here. B500

### LAEM HIN

**Bay View Resort** ☎075 601127, ⓦphiphibayview.com; map p.366. The draw at the seventy large, a/c bungalows here is their prime location: they're set high on the cliffside at the far eastern end of Laem Hin beach, strung out along the ridge almost as far as Hat Yao. All have massive windows and decks to enjoy the great views and there's a pool here too. Be prepared for lots of steps though. Breakfast included. B3900

**Gypsy Sea View Resort** About 150m down the track between the mosque and Phi Phi Andaman Legacy ☎075 601044, ⓦgypsyseaview.com; map p.366. The forty spacious and colourful en-suite rooms here all have a/c, LED TVs and face a good-sized swimming pool, flanked by sunbeds. It's just minutes from the action, yet has an air of seclusion. Breakfast is included. B3000

4

**Phi Phi Andaman Legacy** ☎ 075 601106, ⊛ ppandaman legacy.com; map p.366. Set in a secluded enclosure just a few metres back from the beach, the rather old-fashioned bungalows here are arranged in a square around a large lawn and small central swimming pool, while the 36 more modern rooms occupy a three-storey hotel building at the back. All rooms are a/c and come with TVs, hot water, fridges and safety boxes. Breakfast included. B2500

**Phi Phi Villa Resort** ☎ 075 601100, ⊛ phiphivillaresort. com; map p.366. The best of the many options at this outfit are the huge a/c family cottages occupying the front section of the prettily landscaped garden, near the pool. Also available are smaller bungalows and stylish newer rooms in an annexe set back from the beach, all with a/c, hot water, fridge and TV. Breakfast included. B3200

### LONG BEACH (HAT YAO)

**The Beach Resort** ☎ 075 819206, ⊛ phiphithebeach. com; map p.366. One of the poshest options on Hat Yao, this place has a throng of large, stilted timber-clad chalets up the hillside, with the tallest, most deluxe ones enjoying commanding views of Phi Phi Leh. Interiors are fairly upscale, with a/c and wooden flooring and wall panels. There's also a small beachfront pool, a restaurant and a dive centre. B6300

**Hip Seaview Resort** ☎ 095 851 4000, ⊛ facebook.com/ HIPseaview; map p.366. Dominating the azure waters off Shark Point, this resort is a good choice away from the hustle and bustle, but still just a short boat ride (B100), or a 30min walk, from the main jetty and next to two of Phi Phi's best beaches. The a/c rooms have sleek minimal designs and en-suite bathrooms, with cosy outdoor porches boasting lounge sofas. A good breakfast selection is included. B3500

**Long Beach Bungalows** ☎ 086 470 8984, ✉ longbeach@gmail.com; map p.366. The first choice of most budget travellers, this relatively cheap, well-located and long-running option has dozens of tightly packed huts for rent, ranging from simple, clean bamboo huts with fans, mosquito nets and cold-water bathrooms, to smart beachfront cottages with hot water. Wi-fi is patchy. B1500

**Viking Nature Resort** ☎ 075 819399, ⊛ viking natureresort.com; map p.366. Tucked away on and above two private little coves just west of Hat Yao, with easy access via a rocky path, this is a very stylish take on classic Thai beach-bungalow architecture. It's nearly all wood and bamboo here, with no a/c, but interiors are styled with Asian boho-chic artefacts. The most glamorous accommodation is in the enormous, high-level, one- to four-bedroom "Makmai" tree houses, with their massive living-room decks overlooking the bay. There's a stylish lounge and dining area on the beach; kayaks and snorkels are available. B2000

### AO TOH KO

**Toh Ko Beach Resort** ☎ 081 537 0528, ⊛ tohko beachresort.com; map p.366. Only accessible by longtail boat or jungle trek, this is the place to stay if you want to get away from Tonsai's parties and modern comforts. The accommodation, which is in en-suite, thatched bamboo huts or a/c concrete bungalows (some right on the sand), is quite basic. The common area, with mats right on the beach, is very charming though. They organize two free boat transfers daily; the other option is an expensive charter from the main port after sunset. Wi-fi only works in the common room and electricity is only switched on after 6pm. Fan B2000, a/c B2500

### HAT RANTEE

**The Cove** ☎ 087 474 7770, ⊛ thecovephiphi.com; map p.366. Choose between the very good value en-suite garden, ocean or cliff-view bamboo-decked villas and bungalows, all facing Rantee Bay and easy swimming distance from a good snorkelling spot. All rooms are spacious, with hot rain showers, private balconies and sun beds. There's also a sea-facing restaurant; breakfast is included. B3000

### HAT PAK NAM

**Phi Phi Relax Beach Resort** ☎ 094 756536, ⊛ phiphirelaxresort.com; map p.366. Rustic but comfortable and very welcoming accommodation, in 51 attractive, en-suite wood and bamboo bungalows, set in rows in among the beachfront trees. Kayaks available and there's pick-ups from the pier twice a day (B150 per person). Advanced online bookings get worthwhile discounts. B1900

### AO LOH BAKAO

**Phi Phi Island Village Beach Resort and Spa** ☎ 075 628999, ⊛ phiphiislandvillage.com; map p.366. This plush, a/c resort on a lovely beach is a popular honeymoon spot, and a great location for anyone looking for a quiet, comfortable break. The thatched, split-bamboo bungalows and pool villas are mostly designed in traditional Thai style and furnished with character and elegance. There's a large pool and a spa in the prettily landscaped tropical gardens, as well as a dive centre. B14,000

### LAEM TONG

**Holiday Inn Resort Phi Phi Island** ☎ 075 627300, ⊛ phiphiisland.holidayinnresorts.com; map p.366. The *Holiday Inn* enjoys nearly a kilometre of beachfront at the southern end of the bay, but its 120 deluxe a/c bungalows and spacious, balconied, sea-view rooms are nicely hidden by the shoreline trees and sit in graceful gardens of tidy lawns and flowering shrubs. There's a popular sunset bar at the top of the ridge, two swimming pools, a dive centre, a massage pavilion and tennis courts, plus cooking classes, free kayaks and snorkelling equipment are available. B10,000

**Zeavola** ⓣ075 627000, ⓦzeavola.com; map p.366. High-end resort made up of beautiful Asian teakwood suites and villas with glass walls, all set in hibiscus-lined gardens just minutes from the beach. The plush king-sized beds, bamboo blinds that open on private verandas with loungers, and indoor or outdoor showers with aromatic bath products are a great set up to get away from it all. Breakfast included. **B12,000**

## EATING

Ton Sai has the widest selection of cuisines on the island, but there are good beachfront restaurants, aside from the resorts on Laem Tong.

### TON SAI VILLAGE

**Efe Mediterranean Cuisine** East of the pier, off the fourth north–south alley, on the main route north ⓣ095 150 4434, ⓦfacebook.com/eferestaurant; map p.366. A favourite Turkish and Mediterranean spot, specialisoing in grilled kebabs, hummus and lamb kofte, burgers and pizzas, served in a cosy, small *sala* with an intimate outdoor patio (mains from B170–700). Tues–Sun 12pm–10pm.

**Italiano Bar & Restaurant** On the main alley running east from the pier ⓣ075 601 065, ⓦitaliano restaurantphiphi.com; map p.366. Italian, Western and Thai food, all served in an attractive wooden-decked sala topped by a bamboo and thatch-roofed umbrella. The brick oven bakes excellent crispy pizzas (from B200), which pair well with the imported cold cuts and other authentic Italian mains. Daily 11am–11pm.

**Mango Garden** On the main alley running east from the pier ⓣ095 250 3954, ⓦfacebook.com/themangogarden; map p.366. Vegan-friendly, breakfast and dessert bistro for serious aficionados of the sticky fruit. Try the mango or banana-topped waffles (B140). Serves delicious smoothies (from B90) and hearty breakfast toast sets (B110). Daily 7am–10pm.

**Madame Resto** East of the pier, off the fourth north–south alley, on the main route heading towards the beach; map p.366. Deservedly popular for its curries – *phanaeng*, *matsaman*, green and red – mostly B80. Also offers thin-crust pizzas and a decent vegetarian selection, as well as Western breakfasts and espresso coffees. Daily 8am–11pm.

**Papaya** East of the pier, just off the fourth north–south alley ⓣ087 280 1719; map p.366. One of the best of several village-style kitchens whose authentic and reasonably cheap Thai standards, including noodle soups, *phat thai*, fried rice dishes and fiery curries (B150), make it very popular with locals and dive staff. Infact it's so popular that a sister restaurant, *Papaya 2*, opened one block away. Daily 9am–10pm.

**Phi Phi Bakery** On the main alley running east from the pier ⓣ075 601 017, ⓦfacebook.com/phiphibakery; map p.366. This place, and *Patcharee Bakery*, square up to each other across the narrow alley, vying for the breakfast trade. Croissants – plain, chocolate (B30), almond or savoury – are the thing here, washed down with espresso coffees. There are also pastas and pizzas, and vegetarian-friendly meals. Daily 7am–5pm.

**Unni's Restaurant** East of the pier, off the fourth north–south alley, on the main route north ⓣ091 837 5931, ⓦfacebook.com/unnis.phiphi; map p.366. Beloved bistro, popular for its home-made breakfast bagels, Greek salads, pastas, burritos, nachos, and indulgent cocktails – think Baileys, cream, chocolate and espresso. Mains from B140. Daily 8am–11pm.

### LAEM TONG

**Jasmin Restaurant** On the beach ⓣ086 277 0959; map p.366. Run by a *chao ley* family, this simple beachfront restaurant impresses with larger-than-life portions of fiery Thai food, best enjoyed with an ice-cold beer, whilst tucking your toes in the sand. Part of the earnings goes to support the local school. Daily 8am–11pm.

4

## NIGHTLIFE AND ENTERTAINMENT

### TON SAI VILLAGE AND AO LOH DALUM

Concentrated on the beach at Loh Dalum, Ton Sai nightlife is young and drunken, involving endless buckets of SangSom Thai rum and Red Bull, dance music played until dawn, and fire-juggling shows on the beach. Most of the bars offer a pretty similar formula, so it's often the one-off events and happy hours that make the difference.

**Banana Bar** East of the pier, off the fourth north–south alley, on the main route heading towards the beach ⓣ087 330 6540, ⓦfacebook.com/BananaBarPhiPhi; map p.366. Tonsai's only rooftop bar is spread on multiple levels and removed from the beach's techno cannonade. Start the evening with tasty Tex-Mex food (from B250) and a free movie (daily at 7pm). Later, the bar turns into the usual dance floor, but with neon paint, UV lights and a wider range of music, it beats the competition. Daily 11am–1am.

**Blanco Beach Bar** On the beach at the east end of Loh Dalum ⓦblancobeachbarkohphiphi.com; map p.366. Part of a hostel of the same name, it's not for everyone, but it is where most of the under-35 action is. Their boat parties (B2000, including entry fee to Maya Bay and free flow of drinks; ⓣblancoboatparty.com) are a fun and inexpensive way to get around Phi Phi's main sights, although you may not remember it the next day. Daily, open roughly 10am–3am.

**Reggae Bar** East of the pier, off the fourth north–south alley, on the main route heading towards The Rock; map p.366. A Phi Phi institution in the heart of the village that's been running for years in various incarnations. These days it arranges regular amateur *muay thai* bouts in its boxing ring at around 9pm – "beat up your friend and win free buckets" – and has pool tables and a bar around the sides. There's even reggae karaoke. Daily roughly 10am–1am.

**Slinky** Towards the east end of Loh Dalum, where the left fork just before The Rock hits the beach; map p.366. The messy, throbbing heart of Phi Phi nightlife, with a booming sound system, fire shows, and buckets and buckets of booze. Daily 6pm–late.

## DIRECTORY

**ATMs and exchange** Plenty of ATMs in Ton Sai village; one is next to the Siam Commercial Bank exchange counter (daily 9am–8.30pm), on the main alley running east of the pier.
**Hospital** Phi Phi Hospital (☎075 622151 or ☎081 270 4481) is situated at the western end of Ao Ton Sai.

**Police** As well as a police station (☎075 611177) located on the main alley running east of the Ao Ton Sai pier, out towards Laem Hin, there's a tourist policeman on Phi Phi (☎1155).

# Ko Jum

Situated halfway between Krabi and Ko Lanta Yai, **KO JUM** (whose northern half is known as **Ko Pu**) is the sort of laid-back spot that people come to for a couple of days, then can't bring themselves to leave. Though there's plenty of accommodation on the island, there's nothing more than a handful of beach bars for evening entertainment, and little to do during the day except try out the half-dozen west-coast beaches. The beaches may not be pristine and are in some places unswimmably rocky at low tide, but they're mostly long and wild, and all but empty of people. Nights are also low-key: it's paraffin lamps and starlight after about 11pm (or earlier) at those places that are off the main grid, and many don't even provide fans as island breezes are sufficiently cooling.

The island is home to around three thousand people, the majority of them Muslim, though there are also communities of *chao ley* sea gypsies on Ko Jum (see page 300), as well as Buddhists. The main village is **Ban Ko Jum**, on the island's southeastern tip, comprising a few local shops and small restaurants, one of the island's three piers for boats to and from Laem Kruat on the mainland, and a beachfront school. It's about 1km from the village to the southern end of the island's most popular beach, the appropriately named **Long Beach**. Long Beach is connected to **Golden Pearl Beach**, which sits just south of **Ban Ting Rai**, the middle-island village that's about halfway down the west coast and about 1km north of **Mutu Pier**, with the most boats to Laem Kruat. North of Ban Ting Rai, a trio of smaller, increasingly remote beaches at **Ao Si**, **Ao Ting Rai**, and **Ao Luboa** completes the picture. The island's third village, **Ban Ko Pu**, occupies the northeastern tip, about 5km beyond Ban Ting Rai, and has another Laem Kruat ferry pier. Many islanders refer to the north of the island, from Ban Ting Rai upwards, as Ko Pu, and define only the south as Ko Jum. Much of the north is made inaccessible by the breastbone of forested hills, whose highest peak (422m) is Khao Ko Pu.

Very high winds and heavy seas mean that Ko Jum becomes an acquired taste from May through October, so nearly all accommodation and restaurants **close** for that period: the few exceptions are highlighted in the text.

## Long Beach and Golden Pearl Beach

**LONG BEACH** (sometimes known as **Andaman Beach**) is the main backpackers' beach and is indeed long – at around 2.5km – with large chunks of the shoreline still uncultivated, backed by trees and wilderness, and well beyond sight of the island road. From *New Bungalow* towards the southern end it's a twenty-minute walk into Ban Ko Jum village.

At its northern end, Long Beach segues into **GOLDEN PEARL BEACH**, which is about a 15min walk north up the beach from *Bo Daeng*, 5km by road from Ban Ko Jum and

1km south of Ban Ting Rai. Like Long Beach, it also has only a few bungalow outfits along its curving shoreline, though these are close by the island road.

## Ao Si

Around the rocky headland from Golden Pearl Beach, accessible in ten minutes at low tide or quite a bit further by road, long and beautifully uncluttered **AO SI** is good for swimming. There are a few places to stay, and a big troupe of monkeys makes its home here too. A ten-minute walk through the rubber trees from the uppermost of *Ao Si*'s bungalows brings you to Magic Beach, just south of Ao Ting Rai.

## Ban Ting Rai, Khao Ko Pu and Ao Ting Rai

The road begins to climb as soon as you leave Golden Pearl Beach, taking you up through the ribbon-like village of **Ban Ting Rai**, pretty with bougainvillaea and wooden houses, and the location of a few small restaurants and noodle shops. At 422m, **Khao Ko Pu**, which rises in the distance, is the island's highest mountain and home to macaques that sometimes come down to forage on the rocks around the northern beaches; guided treks up the eastern flank to the summit take about an hour and

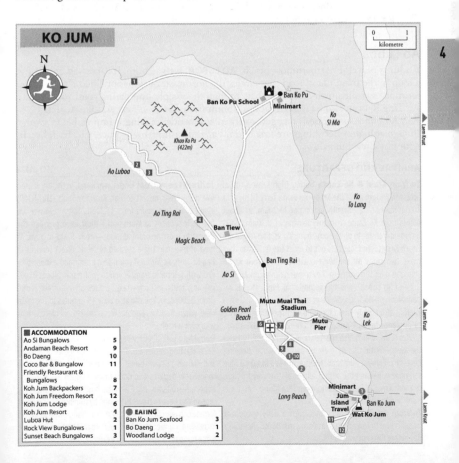

**KO JUM**

N

0   1
kilometre

4

Rock View Bungalows   1
Ban Ko Pu School
Minimart
Ban Ko Pu

Ko Si Ma

Laem Kruat

*Khao Ko Pu (422m)*

*Ao Luboa*   2
3

Ko To Lang

*Ao Ting Rai*   4
**Ban Tiew**

*Magic Beach*   5

**Ban Ting Rai**

*Ao Si*

Mutu Muai Thai Stadium

Laem Kruat

*Golden Pearl Beach*   6   7
Mutu Pier

Ko Lek

9   8
1  10
2

Minimart
1
Jum Island Travel   Ban Ko Jum
*Long Beach*
11   Wat Ko Jum
12

Laem Kruat

**ACCOMMODATION**

| | |
|---|---|
| Ao Si Bungalows | 5 |
| Andaman Beach Resort | 9 |
| Bo Daeng | 10 |
| Coco Bar & Bungalow | 11 |
| Friendly Restaurant & Bungalows | 8 |
| Koh Jum Backpackers | 7 |
| Koh Jum Freedom Resort | 12 |
| Koh Jum Lodge | 6 |
| Koh Jum Resort | 4 |
| Luboa Hut | 2 |
| Rock View Bungalows | 1 |
| Sunset Beach Bungalows | 3 |

**EATING**

| | |
|---|---|
| Ban Ko Jum Seafood | 3 |
| Bo Daeng | 1 |
| Woodland Lodge | 2 |

## ACTIVITIES ON KO JUM

Most bungalows can organize **day-trips**, as will tour agencies in Ban Ko Jum, for example to Ko Phi Phi, Bamboo Island and Mosquito Island (about B3500–4000/boat), or around Ko Jum (B2500/boat). Many offer guided hikes up **Khao Ko Pu** (about B1000, including lunch). Ko Jum Divers, at *Ko Jum Beach Villas* at the north end of Long Beach (☎082 273 7603, ⊛kohjum-divers.com), run daily **dive** trips to Ko Phi Phi (B3900 for two dives), with snorkellers welcome (B1900), and diving courses on offer (fun dive B4600; Open Water B14,200).Koh Jum Explorer (T086 477 7731 or 088 267 0966) organizes 3-hour long kayaking, kayak-fishing and biking trips at 9am and 2pm (B800/person).

Baan Tiew (T095 429 1717 Wbantiew.com) offers batik-painting and three different cooking classes (B1500/person, minimum 2 people).

reward you with fine 360-degree panoramas encompassing the entire island, the mainland and the outer islands.

The little bay of **AO TING RAI**, sometimes known as **Hat Kidon**, has some nice places to stay and good snorkelling off its shore, with a reef to explore and plenty of fish. At low tide it's too rocky for swimming; you'll need either to pick your way over the rocks, rent a kayak, or walk south 500m along the coastal road, to get to the little sandy crescent known as **Magic Beach**, which is swimmable at any tide. You can walk to Ao Ting Rai from Ao Si in about twenty minutes along the coast road.

## 4    Ao Luboa

Ko Jum's peaceful northernmost beach, **AO LUBOA**, feels remote. It's accessed chiefly by a loop in the main island road that circles the northeastern slopes of Khao Ko Pu and terminates at the north end of the bay, though the steeply undulating coast road from Ao Ting Rai can also be walked (about 45min from *Koh Jum Resort*). Like Ao Ting Rai, Ao Luboa's shorefront reef gets exposed at low tide, making it impossible to swim, though at high water things are fine and it's anyway a supremely quiet, laid-back beach with just a few bungalows.

### ARRIVAL AND DEPARTURE                                                                KO JUM

**To/from Krabi & Ko Lanta** During high season, usual access to Ko Jum is via the Krabi–Ko Lanta ferry (daily; 1hr 30min from Krabi, currently leaving at 11.30am, or about 45min from Ko Lanta, currently leaving at 8.30am; B400 including transfer to pier). Some bungalows, like Andaman Beach Resort, send longtails out to meet the ferries as they make two stops off the west coast: coming from Krabi, stop one is for the northern "*Ko Pu*" bungalows (on Ao Ting Rai and Ao Luboa), and the second, "*Ko Jum*", stop is for bungalows on *Ao Si*, *Golden Pearl* and *Long Beach*.

There is also a daily 9am (30min; B700) speedboat service to Ko Lanta by Muk-Anda Travel (☎82 278 5137, ⊛bit.ly/2GwTLyh), which also has boats to Phuket, Phi Phi and the deep south islands (see below). Advance booking necessary. Coming from Krabi town, you need to take a blue songthaew, passing the airport, either all the way through to Laem Kruat (B100) or changing in Nua Klong. Service is from 7am to about 3pm.

**To/from Ko Phi Phi** Muk-Anda runs a daily speedboat from Ko Jum to Tonsai beach at 9am (1hr; B800). Reserve a day before through your hotel.

**To/from Laem Kruat** From Laem Kruat, in the dry season five daily boats depart to Ban Ko Pu (45min–1hr; B100) about every two hours from 11.30am; likewise, there are five daily services to Mutu — the most used pier and the closest to most accommodation — from 10am to 5pm. At time of research, there seemed to be no direct services to Ban Ko Jum. At Mutu, if you haven't arranged a motorbike taxi with sidecar to transfer you to your resort (about B100/person), touts will offer taxi services or motorbike rental (from B200/day). You can also walk 15 minutes to the main road, where *Koh Jum Backpackers* is the closest place to rent your own wheels.

From Mutu pier, about seven boats per day return to Laem Kruat starting at 6.30am. The last service leaves at 2.30pm and should be well-timed to connect with the last blue songthaew departure to Krabi town — which passes by the airport, Tesco Lotus, Big C and the bus station.  In the rainy season you have to travel to Ko Jum by minibus on transport ferries, conveniently never having to change transport. An increasing number of visitors now use this route year-round; some bungalow operators, for example, offer transfers from

Krabi airport using this route (about B800/car to Laem Kruat), which continues to Ko Jum.

**To/from Phuket** During high season, Muk-Anda Travel runs a daily speedboat from Ko Jum to Phuket's Rassada Harbour at 2.30pm (30min; B1900).

**To/from the deep south Islands** Muk-Anda Travel runs a daily speedboat from Ko Jum to Ko Lipe at 9am (4hr 30min; B2500) in high season. It also stops at Ko Ngai (1hr 30min; B1400), Ko Mook (2hr; B1600), Ko Kradan (2hr 20min; B1800) and Ko Bulon Lae (3hr 30min; B2500).

## GETTING AROUND AND SERVICES

**Getting around** Most bungalows can arrange kayak (about B700/day) and motorbike (about B350/day) rental, while *Bo Daeng* has mountain bikes (B150/day; see below). The main island road is slowly being paved north from Ban Ko Jum, but the track on the west side of Khao Ko Pu remains a bumpy nightmare.

**Tourist information** For a comprehensive guide to life on the island, along with pictures of all the available

bungalow operations, check out the useful website at ⓦkohjumonline.com.

**Clinic** The island medical centre is on the road near *Ko Jum Lodge*, beyond the southern edge of Ban Ting Rai.

**Exchange** There's no ATM on the island, so it's best to bring all the cash you'll need with you. At a pinch, you can change money at Jum Island Travel (☎081 797 7397), next to the pier in Ban Ko Jum, at expensive rates.

## ACCOMMODATION

### LONG BEACH

**Andaman Beach Resort** ☎081 476 3689 or 089 724 1544, ⓦfacebook.com/andamanbeachresortkohjum; map p.375. You can't miss the steeply roofed concrete bungalows at this friendly, well-run place, painted like gingerbread houses in shocking pink, yellow and other "lucky" colours. Set in a pleasant garden filled with lucky-charm Chinese-style little statues, and even a giant golden *naga*, the rooms are all bright, clean and en suite, with mosquito screens and terraces, and are priced according to size and proximity to the beach (rising to B3000 for a big, a/c, beachfront pad with hot water and breakfast). Their restaurant, where free Wi fi is available, opens from 7.30am to 10pm and has good and reasonably priced Thai and Western dishes. B300

**Bo Daeng** ☎081 494 8760; map p.375. This funky, ultra-cheap and ultra-basic (no wi-fi and open-roofed shared showers encased by just four low corrugated iron walls) travellers' classic is run by a famously welcoming charismatic island *chao ley* family and has legendary food. The rudimentary bamboo huts come with or without private bathrooms, but all have nets and electricity during the evening. Open all year. B300

**Coco Bar & Bungalow** On the southern end of Long Beach, further north from Koh Jum Freedom Resort ☎081 895 6768, ⓦcocokohjum.com; map p.375. Clustered around a pretty beach-facing bar (open daily from 7.30am until late), surrounded by casuarinas and low wooden tables, the bungalows here are simple yet well equipped, with spacious verandas strewn with hammocks, plush mattresses and mosquito nets. Breakfast is served at the bar and costs about B150 extra. B900

**★ Friendly Restaurant & Bungalows** Along the tarred road between the main coastal road and Andaman Beach Resort ☎088 8209901, ⓦfacebook.com/friendlyrestaurant.kohjum; map p.375. Just five beautiful en-suite darkwood bungalows on low stilts set

in a garden full of colourful flowers, a 5min walk from the beach. The rooms are spacious and clean; across the road, the restaurant dishes up some hearty Thai and Western dishes (from B100). Breakfast is included. B900

**Koh Jum Freedom Resort** At the southernmost point of the island ☎086 239 8075, ⓦkohjumfreedomhut.com; map p.375. This popular and rustic cluster of budget bamboo huts recently received a plush makeover. The sea-facing, en-suite bungalows and two treehouses have a/c, floor tiles, dark wooden bed-frames with sturdy mattresses, thick mosquito nets, and breezy front verandas. Wi-fi is only available at their bar-restaurant. B1800

### GOLDEN PEARL BEACH

**Koh Jum Backpackers** A few metres from the turnoff to Mutu Pier ☎087 461 7175, ❸kohjumhostel@gmail.com; map p.375. The island's first bona fide hostel occupies a large white-tiled room inside of a Thai home, with just a few bunk beds and plenty of empty space. There are a couple a/c en-suite doubles (B850), motorbike (B300) and bicycle (B100) rental. Shared toilets are clean, and it's a 15min walk from the Mutu pier. B250

**Koh Jum Lodge** ☎089 921 1621, ⓦkohjumlodge.com; map p.375. This French–Thai place is one of the most upscale resorts on the island, with nineteen thatched wooden chalets designed in charming rustic-chic style. Thoughtfully constructed to make the most of the island breezes, they have doors onto the veranda to avoid the need for a/c, plus low beds and elegantly simple furniture. The resort has a small pool, a TV and DVD area, a massage service and a restaurant. Minimum stay four nights, seven in peak season. Closed in low season. Breakfast included. B4500

### AO SI

**Ao Si Bungalows** ☎081 747 2664, ⓦkohjumonline.com/aosi.html; map p.375. On Ao Si's northern

4

headland, the woven-bamboo, en-suite bungalows here are built on piles up the side of the cliff and have wrap-around verandas for soaking up the commanding views of the bay and the southern half of the island. No wi-fi. **B500**

### AO TING RAI

**Koh Jum Resort** ☎ 061 235 1332, ⓦ kohjumresort. com; map p.375. Upmarket resort set amongst well-manicured tropical gardens on a rocky slope that hugs one of Ting Rai's best stretches of coast. The thatched-bamboo spacious bungalows and teak villas – all en suite – are set on stilts and have perfect verandas to soak the sunset views. There's also an infinity pool and a restaurant. Breakfast is included; book online for discounts of up to 40%. **B7000**

### AO LUBOA

**Luboa Hut** ☎ 081 388 9241, ⓦ luboahut.com; map p.375. Friendly establishment with ten en-suite bamboo and wooden bungalows, all recently renovated, with sea views from their verandas in a well-shaded spot under shoreside trees; many of them are roomy and good quality, some have extra beds or sofas and all have mosquito nets. The owners offer free kayaks and cooking classes. 30% discounts off season. **B500**

★ **Sunset Beach Bungalows** After a rocky headland on the central part of the beach ☎ 085 797 1602, ⓦ sunsetbeachbungalow.com; map p.375. A leftover of Ko Jum's former self, set below huge trees and in metres from the water, as if it were a forlorn village of thatched-bamboo huts, most sharing bathrooms. The two tree-houses, literally built in the canopy overhead, tower above a relaxed reggae-style restaurant tstrewn with hammocks. A few concrete bungalows (B700) have en-suite toilets and offer more comfort, but all rooms are fan only. There's a well-stocked bar, a snooker table, and the friendly owner fills the place with good vibes. On a good day, Phi Phi island is visible from the bar. **B300**

### NORTHERN SHORE

**Rock View Bungalows** Down a signposted slope on Ko Jum's northernmost headland ☎ 095 916 1530, ⓦ facebook.com/rockviewterrace; map p.375. With Ko Jum's increasing development, it's no surprise that new places are starting to pop all over the coastline. Recently opened *Rock View Bungalows* chose a great spot above a secluded bay to set their bar-restaurant (with free wi-fi, and Thai mains from B80), a delightful white wooden platform perched on rocks, just metres from the waves. Right behind the vegetation are a few treehouses on stilts, and three slightly more expensive en-suite bungalows (B1100) that are sheltered by jungle and among the quieter accommodation on the island. **B500**

## EATING AND DRINKING

### LONG BEACH

★ **Bo Daeng** map p.375. For an outstanding Thai meal, at some of the cheapest prices on the island (around B100), you should join the (sometimes lengthy) queue here, whose highlights include baked fish, vegetable tempura (B90) and a southern yellow curry (B90), plus Thai desserts, home-baked bread and coconut shakes. Daily 7.30am–9pm.

**Woodland Lodge** map p.375. Delicious curries – try the Indian curry with prawns (B200) – plenty of choice for vegetarians, including tasty vegetable tempura (B90), plus Western food, including breakfast and fish and chips. Daily roughly 7am–8.30/9pm.

### BAN KO JUM

**Ban Ko Jum Seafood** ☎ 081 893 6380, ⓦ facebook. com/kohjumseafood; map p.375. The big name in the village is this very popular and very good restaurant, whose tables occupy a scenically sited jetty near the pier and enjoy fine views across the mangrove channel. Among its big menu of fresh seafood cooked any number of ways (B150–400), the juicy fat prawns barbecued with honey are a standout, and their crab and lobster dishes are famous too. Standards such as *phat thai* (B150) are here too. Daily 9am–10pm.

# Ko Lanta Yai

Although **KO LANTA YAI** can't quite compete with Phi Phi's stupendous scenery, the thickly forested 25km-long island has the longest beaches in the Krabi area – and plenty of them. There's decent snorkelling and diving nearby, plus caves to explore, kayaking and other watersports, so many tourists base themselves here for their entire holiday fortnight. The island is especially popular with families, in part because of the local laws that have so far prevented jet-skis, beachfront parasols and girlie bars from turning it into another Phuket, though there's now a long line of resorts stretching along the west coast. Lanta is also rapidly being colonised by Scandinavian expats and tourists, with villa homes and associated businesses all over the place. The majority

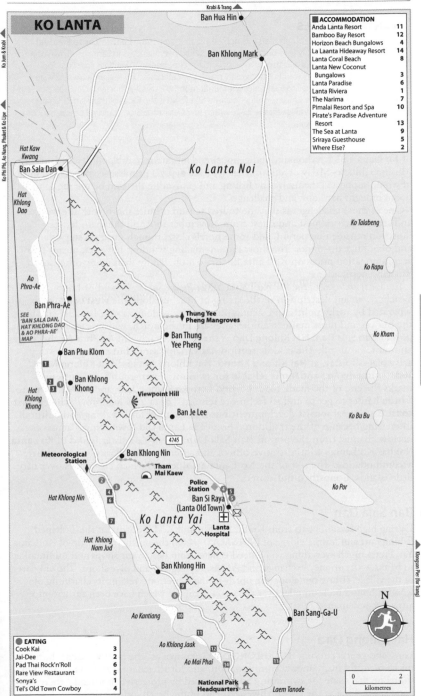

# KO LANTA

**Krabi & Trang** ◀▲▶

Ban Hua Hin ●

Ban Khlong Mark ●

Ko Jum & Krabi ◀

Ko Phi Phi, Ao Nang, Phuket & Ko Lipe ◀

*Hat Kaw Kwang*

Ban Sala Dan ●

*Hat Khlong Dao*

*Ko Lanta Noi*

Ko Talabeng

Ko Rapu

*Ao Phra-Ae*

Ban Phra-Ae ●

SEE 'BAN SALA DAN, HAT KHLONG DAO & AO PHRA-AE' MAP

Thung Yee Pheng Mangroves ▮

Ban Thung ● Yee Pheng

Ban Phu Klom ●

Ko Kham

**1**

**2** **1**
**3**

Ban Khlong ● Khong

*Hat Khlong Khong*

Viewpoint Hill

Ban Je Lee ●

Ko Bu Bu

4745

Ban Khlong Nin ●

Meteorological Station ▮

Tham Mai Kaew

**2**
**4** **3**
**6**

*Hat Khlong Nin*

Police Station ●

**4**
**5**
**5**

Ban Si Raya (Lanta Old Town)

Ko Por

Lanta ✚ Hospital

**7**

*Ko Lanta Yai*

*Hat Khlong Nam Jud*

**8**

Ban Khlong Hin ●

Klongon Pier (for Trang) ▶

**9**

**6**

Ban Sang-Ga-U ●

N

*Ao Kantiang*

**10**

**11**

*Ao Khlong Jaak*

**12**

*Ao Mai Phai*

**14**

**13**

National Park Headquarters �

*Laem Tanode*

0 ———— 2
kilometres

4

---

**LANTA FESTIVALS**

Every March, Ko Lanta Yai celebrates its rich ethnic heritage at the **Laanta Lanta Festival** (*laanta* meaning roughly "eye-dazzling"), which is held over five days in Lanta Old Town and features both traditional and modern music and entertainments, countless specialist food stalls, and crafts for sale. Traditional *chao ley* rituals are celebrated on Ko Lanta twice a year, on the full moons of the sixth and eleventh lunar months – usually June and Oct/Nov (see below). Meanwhile, the Chinese shrine in Lanta Old Town is the focus of the island's version of the **Vegetarian Festival** (see page 320), which involves processions, cultural performances and walking on hot coals.

---

of Ko Lanta Yai's ten thousand indigenous residents are mixed-blood descendants of Muslim Chinese–Malay or animist *chao ley* ("sea gypsy") peoples (see page 300), most of whom supported themselves by fishing and cultivating the land before the tourist boom brought new jobs, and challenges.

One of those challenges is that the **tourist season** is quite short, with the weather and seas at their calmest and safest from November to April; the main ferries don't run outside that period, and some hotels close, though most do stay open and offer huge discounts. The short money-making window, however, means that accommodation prices on Ko Lanta fluctuate more wildly than many other south Thailand destinations.

The local *chao ley* name for Ko Lanta Yai is *Pulao Satak*, "Island of Long Beaches", an apt description of the string of beaches along the **west coast**, each separated by rocky points and strung out at quite wide intervals. Broadly speaking, the busiest and most mainstream beaches are in the north, within easy reach of the port at **Ban Sala Dan: Hat Khlong Dao** is the family beach and **Ao Phra-Ae** the longer and more beautiful. The middle section has variable sands but some interesting, artsy places to stay, at **Hat Khlong Khong, Hat Khlong Nin** and **Hat Khlong Nam Jud**. Southerly **Ao Kantiang** is reliable for swimming year-round and currently marks the end of the made road; beyond here **Ao Khlong Jaak** and **Ao Mai Phai** are a little harder to get to and so feel more remote. Lanta Yai's mangrove-fringed **east coast** has no real tourist development but is both good for kayaking and culturally interesting because of the traditional homes in **Lanta Old Town**. North across the narrow channel from the port at Ban Sala Dan, Lanta Yai's sister island of **Ko Lanta Noi** has Ko Lanta's administrative offices and several small villages but no tourist accommodation. The rest of the Ko Lanta archipelago, which comprises over fifty little islands, is mostly uninhabited.

## Ban Sala Dan

During high season, boats from Krabi, Phi Phi and Ko Lipe arrive at the T-shaped fishing port and tourist village of **BAN SALA DAN**, on the northernmost tip of Ko Lanta Yai. Pretty much everything you'll need is here, from beachwear shops and minimarkets to banks with currency exchange and ATMs, tour agents and dive shops. The old part of the village, strung out along the north-facing shorefront, retains its charming old wooden houses built on piles over the water, many of which have been turned into attractive restaurants.

## Hat Khlong Dao

Long and gently curving **HAT KHLONG DAO** is known as "the family beach", both for its plentiful mid-range accommodation, and for its generous sweep of flat sandy shoreline that's safe for swimming and embraced by protective headlands; there's good snorkelling at the far northwestern end of the beach, off the tiny Kaw Kwang peninsula. Despite being developed to capacity, Khlong Dao is broad enough never to feel overcrowded, the sunsets can be magnificent, and the whole beach is framed by a dramatic hilly backdrop. Though Ban Sala Dan is close by, the beach supports plenty of its own minimarkets and transport outlets, both shoreside and along the main road.

## Ao Phra-Ae (Long Beach)

With its lovely long parade of soft, white sand, calm and crystal-clear water that's good for swimming and shady fringe of casuarina trees, **AO PHRA-AE** (also known as **Long Beach**) is strikingly beautiful and the best of Lanta's many long beaches. There's a little more variety and character among the accommodation options here than at Khlong Dao, a couple of kilometres to the north, and quite a development of shops, with ATMs, restaurants and tour agents along the main road. The main stretch of the beach is divided from the southern rocky extremity by a shallow, easily wadeable khlong; *Lanta Marina Resort* marks the southern reaches of the beach and is about half an hour's walk along the beach from *Sayang* at the northern end. Phra-Ae's budget enclave, with plenty of guesthouses, driftwood bars and a feelgood vibe is clustered along a network of sandy tracks behind the *Ozone Bar*.

## Hat Khlong Khong

The luxuriously long beach at **HAT KHLONG KHONG**, 2km south of Ao Phra-Ae's *Relax Bay Resort*, is peppered with rocks and in most parts only really swimmable at high tide, though the snorkelling is good. Another big draw is the traveller-oriented bungalows, among the most creatively designed places to stay on the island. There are several funky little beach bars.

## Hat Khlong Nin

About 4km south of Hat Khlong Khong the road forks at kilometre-stone 13, at the edge of the village of **Ban Khlong Nin**. The left-hand, east-bound arm runs across to Ko Lanta Yai's east coast, via the caves and viewpoint (see page 384). The right-hand fork is the route to the southern beaches and continues southwards along the west coast for 14km to the southern tip.

Just beyond the junction, the little enclave of bungalows, restaurants, bars and tour agents at **HAT KHLONG NIN** lends this beach more of a village atmosphere than the northern beaches. The beach itself is lovely, long and sandy and good for swimming, though the road runs close alongside it. There are several reasonably priced places to stay here, with the cheapest beds in some hotels located in separate little garden compounds on the inland side of the road, and a low-key collection of shoreside bar-restaurants with plenty of character and mellow vibes.

---

### YOGA AND COOKING CLASSES ON LANTA

#### YOGA

During high season there are **yoga** classes at *Cha-Ba* bungalows on Khlong Dao (ⓦcha-babungalows.com; also meditation classes and yoga and meditation retreats), but the most famous teacher is now at *Oasis Yoga* on Hat Khlong Dao (ⓦoasisyoga-lanta.com).

#### THAI COOKING CLASSES

Five-hour **cooking** classes (B2000) are offered by Time for Lime, at the south end of Hat Khlong Dao (ⓣ075 684590, ⓦtimeforlime.net).

There are minimarkets, ATMs and a clinic at the Ban Khlong Nin junction, and from here you could walk the 3km to the Tham Mai Kaew caves from Khlong Nin in about an hour.

## Hat Khlong Nam Jud (Nui Beach)

Just over 1km south of Hat Khlong Nin, the road passes the two tiny little bays known as **HAT KHLONG NAM JUD**. The northerly one is the domain of *The Narima* (see page 388). A brief scramble around the rocky point to the south, the next tiny cove is rocky in parts but enjoys a swimmable beach and is home to *Lanta Coral Beach* (see page 388).

## Ao Kantiang

The secluded cove of **AO KANTIANG**, some 7km beyond Hat Khlong Nam Jud, is an impressively long curve, backed by jungle-clad hillsides and dominated by one luxury hotel, which keeps the southern half of the beach in pristine condition. Unusually for Lanta, the bay is protected enough to be good for swimming year-round, and there's some coral at the northern end; snorkelling and fishing trips are easily arranged. The small but lively roadside village covers most necessities, including tours, onward transport, motorbike rental and internet access.

## Ao Khlong Jaak and Ao Mai Phai

The road beyond Ao Kantiang to Lanta's southern tip, about 4km away, is steeply undulating but slowly being paved. The next bay south of Kantiang is **AO KHLONG JAAK**, site of some accommodation including the lively *Anda Lanta Resort* (see page 389). Though it's not much more than a trickle, the **waterfall** inland from Ao Khlong Jaak can be reached from the bay by walking along the course of the stream for about two hours. South around the next headland, western Lanta plays its final card in the shape of handsome white-sand **AO MAI PHAI**, a peaceful getaway because of its remote position. There's good coral close to shore here, but this makes it too rocky for low-tide swimming, when you'll need to kayak or walk up to Ao Khlong Jaak instead.

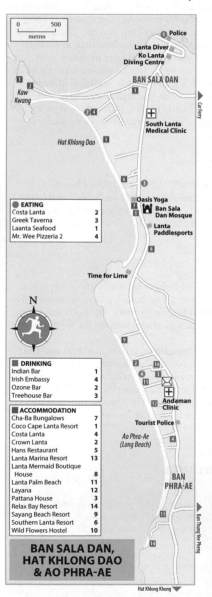

0  500
metres

Police

Lanta Diver
Ko Lanta
Diving Centre

**BAN SALA DAN**

Kaw Kwang

South Lanta
Medical Clinic

Hat Khlong Dao

Car Ferry

Oasis Yoga
Ban Sala Dan Mosque
Lanta Paddlesports

Time for Lime

N

**EATING**
| | |
|---|---|
| Costa Lanta | 2 |
| Greek Taverna | 3 |
| Laanta Seafood | 1 |
| Mr. Wee Pizzeria 2 | 4 |

**DRINKING**
| | |
|---|---|
| Indian Bar | 1 |
| Irish Embassy | 4 |
| Ozone Bar | 2 |
| Treehouse Bar | 3 |

**ACCOMMODATION**
| | |
|---|---|
| Cha-Ba Bungalows | 7 |
| Coco Cape Lanta Resort | 1 |
| Costa Lanta | 4 |
| Crown Lanta | 2 |
| Hans Restaurant | 5 |
| Lanta Marina Resort | 13 |
| Lanta Mermaid Boutique House | 8 |
| Lanta Palm Beach | 11 |
| Layana | 12 |
| Pattana House | 3 |
| Relax Bay Resort | 14 |
| Sayang Beach Resort | 9 |
| Southern Lanta Resort | 6 |
| Wild Flowers Hostel | 10 |

Andaman Clinic

Tourist Police

Ao Phra-Ae
(Long Beach)

**BAN PHRA-AE**

Ban Thung Yee Pheng

**BAN SALA DAN,
HAT KHLONG DAO
& AO PHRA-AE**

Hat Khlong Khong

## SNORKELLING TRIPS AND WATERSPORTS ON LANTA

### SNORKELLING TRIPS

The best and most popular **snorkelling** is at the islands of **Ko Rok Nai** and **Ko Rok Nok**, 47km south of Ko Lanta; these forested twins are graced with stunning white-sand beaches and accessible waterfalls and separated by a narrow channel full of fabulous shallow reefs. Also hugely popular is the "**four island**" snorkelling trip that takes in the much nearer islands off Trang – the enclosed emerald lagoon on **Ko Mook** (see page 403), plus nearby **Ko Hai** (Ko Ngai), **Ko Ma** and **Ko Kradan** – but these sites can get very crowded. Another option is the day-trip to **Phi Phi Don**, Phi Phi Leh and Bamboo Island (see page 365). The trips cost around B1300 in a speedboat or B900 in a big boat, including lunch, snorkelling equipment and national park entry fee. For a smaller, more personal experience, contact Sun Island Tours or Freedom Adventures.

### DIVING

The **reefs** around Ko Lanta are quieter and in some cases more pristine than those round Phi Phi and Phuket, and excellent for seeing whale sharks. The **diving season** runs from November to April, though a few dive shops continue to run successful trips from May to August. All dive boats depart from Ban Sala Dan, and nearly all dive courses are taught either in Sala Dan or on Hat Khlong Dao, though there are dive shops on every beach.

Some of Lanta's best **dive sites** are located between Ko Lanta and Ko Phi Phi, including the soft coral at **Ko Bidah**, where you get lots of leopard sharks, barracuda and tuna. West and south of Lanta, the **Ko Ha** island group offers four different dives on each of its five islands, including steep drop-offs and an "underwater cathedral" and other caves; visibility is often very good. Much further south, about 56km from Ko Lanta, are **Hin Daeng** and **Hin Muang** (see page 335).

The nearest recompression chambers are located on Phuket (see page 317); check to see that your dive operator is insured to use one of them (see page 51).

### KAYAKING

There are several rewarding **kayaking** destinations, rich in mangroves and caves, around Ko Lanta Yai's east coast and around Ko Lanta Noi and its eastern islands, including **Ko Talabeng** and **Ko Bubu**; a few companies also offer kayak-snorkel trips to the four islands described above.

### OPERATORS

**Easy Day Thailand** ☎062 245 1224, ⊛easyday thailand.com/koh-lanta/koh-lanta-tours. Kayaking trips to Ko Talabeng for B1300.

**Freedom Adventures** ☎084 910 9132, ⊛freedom-adventures.net. A variety of snorkelling day-trips, as well as all-inclusive overnight camping trips on Ko Rok and Ko Kradan (2D/1N B3200 including meals, camping and snorkelling gear).

**Ko Lanta Diving Centre** On the main road into Ban Sala Dan ☎075 668 065, ⊛kolantadivingcenter. com. German-run outfit charging B3000, plus B600 National Park fees for two dives, including equipment; B1500 for accompanying snorkellers; and B14,500 for the Open Water course.

**Lanta Diver** On the main road into Ban Sala Dan ☎075 684 208, ⊛lantadiver.com. Swedish-owned,

PADI Five-Star Instructor Development Centre charging from B3300 for two dives, excluding equipment, and B14,400 for the Open Water course.

**Lanta Paddlesports** On the main road in Hat Khlong Dao and on several beaches ☎082 278 8055, ⊛bit.ly/LantaPaddlesports. Paddleboard lessons, rental and tours, as well as windsurfing, kayaking, surfing and snorkelling trips.

**Pirate Kings Tour & Travel** ☎091 0369669, ⊛bit. ly/PirateKingsSpeedboat. One of the main operators of four-island snorkelling trips, which can be booked through any agent on Ko Lanta.

**Sun Island Tours** ☎086 001 6138, ⊛lantalongtail. com. Various longtail trips to the four islands, around Ko Lanta, and to Lanta's eastern islands (where there's also an overnight camping option), which come very highly rated and cost B1500, excluding national park fees.

# Tham Mai Kaew caves

3km southeast of the Khlong Nin junction • 2hr tours Mon–Thurs, Sat & Sun 9am–4pm, Fri 8–10am & 1.30–4pm • B300, including national park entry fee and head torch • ☎089 288 8954 • A motorcycle taxi costs about B200 each way from Khlong Dao or Ao Phra-Ae

The myriad chambers at **Tham Mai Kaew caves**, some of which you can only just crawl into, are Ko Lanta's biggest inland attraction. They are filled with stalactites and interesting rock formations, and there's a creepy cave pool too, as well as the inevitable bats. Tours of the cave are given by the local family who first properly explored the cave system in the 1980s; as well as the standard tour they sometimes offer longer cave tours and overnight jungle treks. Most of Thailand's countless caves are underwhelming and certainly not worth B300, but this is one of the better ones: among its star features are crystallized waterfalls, fossils and ammonites embedded in the cave walls and overhangs, stalagmites and stalactites young and old and a tangible sense of there being endless passageways to explore. Set aside three hours for getting into and out of the caves and use sensible shoes and clothes you're happy to get dirty. In the rainy season there may well be some wading involved, together with the option of a dip in the wet-season-only lagoon.

## Viewpoint Hill

3km beyond the turn-off to the Tham Mai Kaew caves • Café daily 8am–8pm

Beyond the turn-off to the caves, the eastbound road drops down over the central spine of hills and you pass Viewpoint café, where nearly everyone stops for a drink and a gawp at the stunning panorama. The **view over the east coast** is glorious, encompassing the southeast coast of mangrove-fringed Ko Lanta Noi, dozens of islets – including Ko Bubu and Ko Por – adrift in the milky blue sea, and the hilly profile of the mainland along the horizon.

## Lanta Old Town (Ban Si Raya)

The seductively atmospheric little waterfront settlement of **LANTA OLD TOWN**, officially known as **Ban Si Raya**, is Ko Lanta's oldest town. It began life as a sheltered staging post for ships and served as the island's administrative capital from 1901 to 1998. The government offices have since moved to Ko Lanta Noi, and Ban Sala Dan has assumed the role of harbour, island gateway and commercial hub, so Ban Si Raya has been left much as it was a century ago, with its historic charm intact. There's little more to the Old Town than its peaceful main street, which runs right along the coast parallel to Route 4245 and is lined with traditional, hundred-year-old a- and wind-blasted wooden homes and shops, many of them constructed on stilted jetties over the sea, their first-floor overhangs shading the pavements and plant-filled doorways. The Chinese shrine midway down the street is evidence of the town's cultural mix: Ban Si Raya is home to a long-established Buddhist Chinese–Thai community as well as to Muslims and, in its southern neighbourhood, communities of animist Urak Lawoy *chao ley* ("sea gypsies").

The **Urak Lawoy** *chao ley* (see page 300) are thought to have been Ko Lanta's first inhabitants, perhaps as long as five hundred years ago, living along the shoreline during the monsoon season and setting off along the coast again when the winds abated. They have now settled permanently in their own villages on the island, including at **Ban Sang-Ga-U**, 4km to the south of Lanta Old Town; other Urak Lawoy living elsewhere in the Andaman Sea, around Trang and beyond, consider Ko Lanta their capital and will always stop at Sang-Ga-U when making a journey. One of the accessible elements of Urak Lawoy culture is their **music**, an interesting fusion of far-flung influences, featuring violins (from the Dutch East Indies), drums (from Persia) and gongs (from China), as well as singing, dancing and ritual elements. A good time to hear their music is at one of their twice-yearly three-day full-moon **festivals**, or at the Laanta Lanta Festival (see page 380).

As an additional incentive to linger among the wooden architecture of the main street, there are several **shops** selling batik sarongs and souvenirs, plus the charming Hammock House (⚛jumbohammock.com), whose amazing range of hammocks includes ones woven by people of the endangered Mrabri tribe of northern Thailand.

### Koh Lanta Community Museum

Across the small grassy park from the pier and parking lot • Daily 9am–3pm • B40

There's an attempt to introduce the cultures of Ban Si Raya's three distinct but peaceable communities at the **Koh Lanta Community Museum**, which is housed in the attractive 1901 wooden building that used to serve as the local district office. Archive photos and one or two English-language captions describe the main occupations for the communities, including fishing and making charcoal from mangrove wood.

## Thung Yee Pheng mangroves

About 1km north of the junction of Route 4245 and the road across from Ao Phra-Ae, take the right turn for a couple of hundred metres • Daily 8am–4pm • B20

This community tourism project allows you to take a short, not very compelling stroll along a 200m boardwalk out into the **mangrove swamps** that line Ko Lanta Yai's east coast. More interesting are the one-hour longtail tours available here (B1000/person, including guide), and you can also hire a two-person kayak to have a look around (B500/2hr, B300 extra for a guide).

### ARRIVAL AND DEPARTURE        KO LANTA YAI

The principal mainland gateways to Ko Lanta are Krabi, Phuket and Trang, all of which have good long-distance bus services, and **airports**. Trang also has a train station. Flight and minibus through-tickets from Don Muang Airport in Bangkok are offered by Air Asia, Thai Smile, Thai Lion Air, via Krabi Airport; and by Nok Air, via Trang Airport. In high season, joint tickets can get you directly to Baan Sala Dan.

**By boat** In high season ferries and speedboats to Ko Lanta Yai departfrom Krabi (via Ko Jum, B480, 2hr); from Ko Jum (B800, 45min); from Phuket (ferry via Ko Phi Phi, B950, 4hr; direct speedboats B1500, 2hr); from Ko Phi Phi (B450, 1hr; speedboats B800, 30min); and from Ao Nang via West Railay (B580, 2hr15min). There are also high-season services to Ko Lanta from the Trang islands and Ko Lipe (B1700, 2hr 30min), with connections to Langkawi in Malaysia (see page 401). All of these ferries dock at Ban Sala Dan and are met by bungalow touts who usually transport you to the beach of your choice for free. If you need to use the motorbike sidecar taxi service instead, be warned that drivers will try and charge arrivals way over the normal fares; walk 250m from the pier head to the main road to get a ride at more reasonable rates. Speedboats run between Ban Si Raya at Lanta Old Town and Klongson pier in Trang (3 daily; 30min; B480), which you can book through your resort or Lanta Info (☎081 979 7947; ✉nong@lantainfo.com).

Destinations: Ao Nang, via West Railay (daily; 2hr 30min); Ko Phi Phi Don (2 daily; 1hr 30min); Krabi, via Ko Jum (daily; 2hr 30min); Phuket (1–2 daily; 4hr 30min).

**By road** The alternative to the ferries is the overland route to Ko Lanta Yai – essential during the rainy season but increasingly popular at any time of year. Access is via Ban Hua Hin on the mainland, 75km south of Krabi, from where a small ferry crosses to Ban Khlong Mark on Ko Lanta Noi, after which there's a 7km drive across to Lanta Noi's southwest tip, then a bridge over the narrow channel to the car-ferry port on Ko Lanta Yai's northeastern coast; the ferry runs approximately every 20min from about 7am to 10pm (B100 per car, plus B20 per passenger). This is the route used by a/c minibuses from Krabi town (hourly; 2hr; B250–400 depending on which beach you get dropped at, terminates in Lanta Old Town); from Phuket (9 daily; 5hr; B500); from Trang (roughly hourly; 3hr; B300); and by anyone bringing their own vehicle. From Lanta, the Krabi minibuses will make stops at Krabi bus station, airport and then town; on arrival, you'll need to call ☎081 606 3591 to ask them to pick you up at the airport. There's also a daily bus between Ban Hua Hin and Bangkok's Mo Chit bus terminal (12hr), fed by a/c minibuses to and from Ko Lanta Yai, such as the Krabi town minibuses (hourly; 30–50min depending on your pick-up point on Ko Lanta Yai), which any hotel can arrange.

### GETTING AROUND AND INFORMATION

There's no public transport on the island, but motorbikes are widely available for rent and there are jeeps too.

**By share-taxi and songthaew** A fleet of motorbike sidecar share-taxis, with drivers in numbered vests, and a few white songthaews operate out of Ban Sala Dan and will go pretty much anywhere on the island, though they usually need to be phoned (by staff at hotels or restaurants) for pick-ups from anywhere outside Sala Dan. Lanta has its share of scamming taxi-drivers, so bear in mind the approximate per-person rates for rides out of Sala Dan: B40 to Hat Khlong Dao, B60 to Ao Phra-Ae, B90 to Hat Khlong Kong, or about B50 between the above; B200 to Ao Mai Phai.

**Tourist Information** The free handbook *Lanta Pocket Guide* (download it from the website at ⍵lantapocketguide.com or pick up a copy on the island; published quarterly) has the latest information on transport and some of the best available activities, with a regularly updated list of operators and hotels. *Love Lanta* (⍵lovelanta.com) distributes a handy nightlife and accommodation pocket map.

## ACCOMMODATION

Ko Lanta Yai is extremely popular during high season (Nov–Feb), when it's worth either booking your first night's accommodation in advance or taking up the suggestions of the bungalow touts who ride the boats from the mainland. A confirmed booking also means you should get free transport from the port to your hotel. **Accommodation pricing** on Ko Lanta is disconcertingly flexible and alters according to the number of tourists on the island: bungalow rates can double between mid-December and mid-January (and some resorts extend their "peak season" to include the whole of January and February), while during the rainy season (May–Oct) rates are vastly discounted.

### HAT KHLONG DAO
There are a couple of budget-oriented places to stay on Hat Khlong Dao, but the emphasis is on accommodation for families and others looking for a/c comfort.

**Cha-Ba Bungalows** ☎ 075 684 823, ⍵ cha-babungalows. com; map p.382. There's plenty of kitsch creativity at this welcoming, idiosyncratic complex of bungalows, set among model dinosaurs and Flintstone boulders. The tightly packed bungalows are simple and flimsy, but cute, decorated with loud retro-look fabrics and wallpapers. Fan ones come with hot showers, while the a/c ones also have TVs, fridges and free breakfasts. Fan B1300, a/c B2000

**Coco Cape Lanta Resort** ☎ 062 954 1527, ⍵ coco caperesort.com; map p.382. Perched on the northwesternmost tip of the cape, the 35 sea-facing en-suite rooms mix bright colours with industrial-chic touches. There's also one swanky islet-facing honeymoon suite (B4900) and large family rooms (B4300). There's a tempting swimming pool, bar and restaurant too. Breakfast included. B2500

**Costa Lanta** ☎ 075 684630, ⍵ costalanta.com; map p.382. You're either going to love or hate this ultra-brutal minimalist grouping of 22 polished-grey concrete boxes, each bungalow consisting of an unadorned bedroom all in grey and white with a mosquito net, a similarly styled bathroom with rain shower and a large terrace. The bamboo cottages are equally minimalist, but warmer thanks to the wood and nice verandas. They're all set in a broad garden bisected by khlongs, with a big, sleek pool and a striking bar-restaurant. Breakfast included. Rooms B7100, cottages B4800

**Crown Lanta** ☎ 075 626999, ⍵ crownlanta.com; map p.382. Upmarket, German-managed resort on the island's

very northwestern tip, where crown motifs feature heavily on the rooftops. The hotel divides into two zones: standard (with very large balconies) and pool-access rooms near the lobby; up on the hill, villas and another free-form pool, plus a panoramic restaurant, a spa and steps down to a part-sandy, part-rocky private beach. B8400

**Hans Restaurant** ☎ 075 684152, ⍵ krabidir.com/ hansrestaurant; map p.382. One of the cheapest places on this beach, with over twenty huts ranged along a narrow, scruffy strip of garden behind the shorefront restaurant, next to the *Royal Lanta* resort in the heart of the beach. Choose between very simple, rickety bamboo bungalows with mosquito nets and bathrooms, and slightly better-furnished wooden versions (from B1300). Open in high season only. B700

★ **Lanta Mermaid Boutique House** ☎ 075 684364, ⍵ lantamermaid.com; map p.382. This three-storey house, set across the road from the beach, hides a sparkling-clean, high-end yet affordable boutique hotel. Rooms, all with balconies and en-suite bathrooms, have either mountain or sea views, and glamorous wooden tiles that emphasise space and comfort. Breakfast included. B3500

**Pattana House** On the road between Kaw Kang cape and Ban Sala Dan ☎ 098 674 9122; map p.382. Almost hidden behind a small café, these rooms and little bungalows set around a stone courtyard are some of the best value in northern Lanta. Preferred for long-term stays (from B7000 per month), they are mostly en suite, with large beds and wall windows. Breakfast is B100 extra. B200

**Southern Lanta Resort** ☎ 075 684175–7, ⍵ southern lanta.com; map p.382. One of the biggest hotels on the beach, offering dozens of very spacious a/c bungalows set at decent intervals around a garden of shrubs, clipped hedges and shady trees. There's a good-sized swimming pool, too. Popular with families and package tourists. Breakfast included. B2000

### AO PHRA-AE (LONG BEACH)
★ **Lanta Marina Resort** ☎ 075 684168, ⍵ lanta marina.com; map p.382. At the far southern end of Ao Phra-Ae by a rocky point, this friendly place has 23 shaggily thatched wood-and-split-bamboo bungalows, connected by wooden walkways, which circle a very pretty lawn and flower garden. All the huts have nice beds, well-designed bathrooms, high palm-leaf roofs and fans, and the larger, more expensive ones on the beach have hot showers. B800

4

**Lanta Palm Beach** ☎075 684406, ⓦlantapalm beachresort.com; map p.382. A busy, clean, central and popular spot within stumbling distance of several beach bars. The concrete bungalows and large, bright cottages sit back from the shore a little, within a garden of neat clipped hedges, and come with a/c and hot water. Has internet access and a dive centre. Breakfast included. B3000

★ **Layana** ☎075 607100, ⓦlayanaresort.com; map p.382. Located plumb in the middle of the beautiful beach, this is currently the top spot on Ao Phra-Ae and one of the best and most liked on the whole island, not least for its calm ambience (the hotel has a no-under-18s policy) and attentive service. Its 44 a/c rooms occupy chunky, two-storey villas designed in modern-Thai style and set around a tidy beachfront garden of lawns and mature shrubs. There's a gorgeous shorefront saltwater infinity pool, a spa and plenty of activities and day-trips. Breakfast included. The rack rate is one third higher than the internet rate listed here. B15,100

**Relax Bay Resort** ☎075 684194, ⓦrelaxbay.com; map p.382. On a tiny bay south around the next rocky point (and quite a hike) from *Lanta Marina*, the style of this French-managed place is affordable rustic chic. Accommodation is in forty tastefully simple thatched bungalows, all with large sea-view decks. Also has a luxury safari-style tent on a large deck with a chic outdoor bathroom. There's a pool, a dive centre and yoga classes during high season. Breakfast included. Fan B2150, a/c B5300

**Sayang Beach Resort** ☎075 684 156, ⓦsayang beachresort.com; map p.382. Welcoming, family-run place whose thirty a/c bungalows are nicely spaced beneath the palm trees in the expansive shorefront grounds. Some bungalows are designed for families and there's also a beachfront suite. Prices include buffet breakfasts and there's a very good restaurant here too. Daily free transfers to Sala Dan. B2000

★ **Wild Flowers Hostel** Opposite Treehouse Bar ☎094 258 2597, ⓦfacebook.com/wildflowershostel; map p.382. With well-manicured gardens and a sociable bamboo and driftwood bar, this Italian-run 70s-themed hostel is a notch above the rest of Long Beach's budget accommodation. The a/c dorms, set in a cosy bungalow strewn with floor pillows and bamboo carpets, have plush beds, wooden bed stands, and clean shared bathrooms. Paying a little more will get you a private cosy en-suite. Breakfast is included. Dorms B300, doubles B900

### HAT KHLONG KHONG

**Lanta New Coconut Bungalows** ☎081 537 7590, ⓦlantanewcoconut.com; map p.379. Attractive collection of bungalows flanked by coconut trees and set next to an azure free-form swimming pool. Most bungalows are wooden and en-suite, with plush double beds, TVs and pleasing wooden furnishings. There's a restaurant that serves Thai food; a simple breakfast is included. B1000

**Lanta Riviera** ☎075 667043, ⓦlantariviera.net; map p.379. There are rows and rows of good, standard-issue, comfortably furnished fan and a/c concrete bungalows here, plus a few rooms in a two-storey building, set among shady beds of shrubs and flowers at the far northern end of the beach. Many of the rooms sleep three so it's popular with families. Also has a pool and Jacuzzi near the shore. Fan B800, a/c B1360

**Where Else?** ☎075 667 173, ⓦwhereelselanta.com; map p.379. This charming collection of bungalows has a laid-back vibe and lots of personality, and their *Feeling Bar* also makes it a bit lively. The artfully and individually designed bamboo and coconut-wood bungalows all have fans, mosquito nets, hammocks and open-air bathrooms filled with plants, and there are shell mobiles, driftwood sculptures and pot plants all over the place. The pricier bungalows are larger and nearer the sea, and some even have bamboo sunroofs and turrets. B600

### HAT KHLONG NIN

★ **Horizon Beach Bungalows** ☎087 626 4493, ⓦlantahorizon.com; map p.379. A well-executed mix of sociable traveller-oriented hangout and mid-range guesthouse, *Horizon* is artfully decked out in wood and stone. Sun loungers and little tables spill out on to the beach. Rooms vary from good value budget doubles with exceptionally clean shared bathrooms, to pricier en suites, and family bungalows (B3800). The restaurant dishes up quality Thai meals; the beach bar has live bands and fire shows. B500

**Lanta Paradise** ☎075 662569, ⓦlantaparadise beachresort.com; map p.379. Though the shorefront concrete bungalows at this friendly spot are packed uncomfortably close together, they feel spacious inside and are well maintained; they lack style and are plain, but are all a/c with hot showers, and there's a pool here too. Breakfast included. B1800

### HAT KHLONG NAM JUD (NUI BEACH)

**Lanta Coral Beach** ☎088 761 2428, ⓦlantacoralresort. com; map p.379. Friendly resort with a lovely, lofty restaurant – especially nice at sunset – up on the rocky point. The twenty good-sized, plain but very clean en-suite bamboo and concrete huts here are scattered over a lawn among the palms (some of which are hung with hammocks); the concrete options, whether fan or a/c, boast hot showers. Fan B500, a/c B1200

**The Narima** ☎075 662668, ⓦnarima-lanta.com; map p.379. Very quiet but welcoming, elegantly designed, environmentally conscious resort of 32 posh but unadorned thatch-roofed bamboo bungalows set in three rows in a palm-filled garden. The bungalows all have polished wood floors, verandas with sea view, hot showers and fans as well as a/c (but no TV or wi-fi, just paid internet); there's also a three-tiered pool (with kids' level) and a dive centre, and staff rent out jeeps, motorbikes and mountain bikes. Breakfast included. **B2700**

## AO KANTIANG

**Pimalai Resort and Spa** ☎075 607999, ⓦwww. pimalai.com; map p.379. One of Ko Lanta's poshest hotels, at the southern end of Ao Kantiang, spreading over such an extensive area that guests are shuttled around in golf buggies. All rooms are luxuriously and elegantly designed in contemporary style, and there's a delightful spa, two infinity-edge swimming pools, a dive centre and lots of other watersports, tennis courts and free bicycles. However, only the more expensive accommodation gets a sea view (the pool villas and walled beach villas are particularly stunning). In high season, guests are usually transferred direct to the resort by boat, landing at the *Pimalai's* private floating jetty. Breakfast is included. **B14,500**

**The Sea at Lanta** At the beginning of Ao Kantiang's tourist village ☎075 665158, ⓦfacebook.com/ theseaatlantahotel; map p.379. This ultra-modern two-storey hotel on the hillside may not look like much value from the outside, but inside has smart en-suite a/c rooms. Some have sea views; all boast large bathrooms, plush beds, windows and LED TVs. There's also motorbike rental (B300) and a tour desk. **B1000**

## AO KHLONG JAAK

**Anda Lanta Resort** ☎075 665018, ⓦandalanta. com; map p.379. Lively, buzzing resort that offers well-furnished, well-maintained a/c bungalows and rooms (all with hot showers, balconies and DVD players), set around the shorefront garden and swimming pool. It's popular with families and has free kayaks and plenty of day-tripping options. **B5500**

## AO MAI PHAI

**Bamboo Bay Resort** ☎075 665023, ⓦbamboobay. net; map p.379. At the northern end of the bay, this welcoming and very popular Thai–Danish resort offers 21 concrete bungalows with hot showers, stepped up the cliffside above the headland. Nearly all have great sea views and interiors are spacious and of a high standard. Its *pièce de résistance* is its idyllically sited deck restaurant and bar, which jut out over the rocks just above the water. Wi-fi barely works and only near the restaurant. Fan **B1800**

**La Laanta Hideaway Resort** ☎075 665066, ⓦlalaanta.com; map p.379. Luxurious bolthole located at the far southern end, which is very well liked for its attentive, friendly staff and collection of chic, thatched, wooden-floored villas – all with a/c, hot showers, DVD players and low beds – built to a cosy, village-style layout, around two pools and a beachfront garden. Breakfast included. **B2800**

## LANTA OLD TOWN (BAN SI RAYA)

★ **Sriraya Guesthouse** 77 Moo 2 ☎075 697045 or 082 536 1781; map p.379. Beautiful conversion of a 100-year-old Sino-Portuguese shophouse, featuring wooden floors, original beams and creaking staircases. The good value fan rooms mix the house's original charm with modern plush beds, while the few a/c rooms (B1000) have en-suite bathrooms and large windows. There's a relaxing wooden veranda over the sea at the back, and a kitchen available for guests' use. **B500**

## BAN-SANG-GA-U

**Pirate's Paradise Adventure Resort** At the end of Ban-Sang-Ga-U's paved road ☎099 315 6993, ⓦfacebook.com/Piratesparadiseresort; map p.379. A clutch of good-value en-suite wooden bungalows tucked under a sloping green hill next to Lanta's southeastern tip. The sea-facing, free-form swimming pool is set right above a reef with good snorkelling and only 1km from the national park, where staff organize kayaking trips. Their *Pirasta Bar* is an ideal spot for sundowners and parties. **B1000**

## EATING

## BAN SALA DAN

Many charming old wooden houses built on piles over the water have been turned into attractive jetty restaurants, perfect for whiling away a breezy hour with great views of marine activity.

**Laanta Seafood** ☎075 684 016, ⓦbit.ly/Laanta Seafood; map p.382. The oldest restaurant in town and the most highly rated – its seafood, displayed on ice at the front, is great, including *haw mok thalay* (curried seafood soufflé; B140) and local dishes such as *nam prik kung siab*, smoked prawn dip with vegetables. Daily 11am–10pm.

## HAT KHLONG DAO

Restaurant tables fill the shoreline in the evening, illuminated with fairy lights and lanterns, which lends a nice mellow atmosphere. The formula is very similar at most of them, with fresh seafood barbecues the main attraction during the season. Clusters of little beach bars serve cocktails on deckchairs and cushions, often with chill-out music and a campfire to gather round.

**Costa Lanta** ☎075 684630 (see page 387); map p.382. The most sophisticated drinking venue on the beach is a great place for a relaxing sundowner, with sea-view daybeds, plump bolsters, cool sounds and lemon-

4

grass martinis. The food, however, doesn't match up to its hefty price tag. Daily 11am–midnight.

## AO PHRA-AE (LONG BEACH)

Most of Ao Phra-Ae's most interesting restaurants are along the main road.

**★ Greek Taverna** ☏ 083 521 6613, ⓦ bit.ly/GreekTaverna; map p.382. The authentic Greek food served here is popular and comes in big portions. There's a wide choice of vegetarian and non-vegetarian dishes, all served with delicious pitas. A meal will set you back around B800. Daily 10am–10pm.

**Mr. Wee Pizzeria 2** On the beachfront ☏ 098 618 4378; map p.382. A simple beach restaurant with tables spilling out on to the sand, ideal for a romantic but casual sunset dinner. The pizzas (from B200) are crunchy and well-baked; there's also Swedish food (from B250), burgers (B150) and Thai mains (B100/150). Daily 8am–12pm.

## HAT KHLONG KHONG

**Sonya's** On the main road, just north of 7-Eleven ☏ 075 667 055, ⓦ facebook.com/sonyahomekohlanta; map p.379. Very popular, cheap, garden restaurant with free wi-fi (and pay computers), where you can "build your own" pasta from a wide choice of pastas, sauces, meats and extras. Also has a big selection of Thai food (from B75), Western breakfasts and teas, as well as sandwiches and espresso coffees. Daily 8.30am–9.30pm.

## HAT KHLONG NIN

A dozen or so mellow little beachfront bar-restaurants make inviting places to while away a few hours, day or night, with mats and cushions on the sand, tables under the shade of the spiky shoreside pandanus trees, and appropriately chilled sounds.

**Cook Kai** ☏ 087 461 8598, ⓦ cookkairestaurant.com; map p.379. Friendly restaurant hung with shell mobiles

and lamps, dishing up hearty portions of all the Thai classics, plus famous hotplate dishes such as sizzling squid with garlic and pepper (B190) and a few Western dishes including breakfast. Daily 7.30am–10.30pm.

**Jai-Dee** North end of the beach, squeezed between the road and the beach ☏ 088 832 2664, ⓦ bit.ly/JaiDeeRestaurant; map p.379. Bar-restaurant with a lovely shady deck and hammocks, internet access and free wi-fi, plus a good menu of Thai curries and sandwiches (bacon B80), fresh coffee and breakfasts. Daily 9am–late, kitchen closes 9pm.

## AO KANTIANG

**Pad Thai Rock'n'Roll** ☏ 080 784 8729 ⓦ facebook.com/phadthairock77; map p.379. The bass player of a Thai rock band dishes up simple yet zesty Thai food in this cosy, welcoming café, furnished with musical memorabilia and boasting beautiful sea views. The *phat thai* (B90/120), green curry (B150) and freshly prepared fruit smoothies (B80) are highly recommended. Daily 11am–4pm & 6pm–9pm.

## LANTA OLD TOWN (BAN SI RAYA)

**★ Rare View Restaurant** ☏ 087 191 3353; map p.379. Shophouse converted into a seafood restaurant, with a modern indoor *sala* and an attractive long, wooden veranda that extends over the water. Try the steamed prawn in butter and garlic sauce (B280), fried soft crabs in yellow curry (B300), or just grab a cup of coffee (B60) and enjoy the views of Ko Lanta's eastern islets from the two swings perched at the back. Daily 8am–9pm.

**Tel's Old Town Cowboy** ⓦ bit.ly/TelsOldTown; map p.379. Decked out like a Wild West saloon with swinging doors, this long shophouse may try a little too hard, but draws a crowd thanks to the wisde selection of beers and whiskey shots (from B90). Open during the high season only. Daily 12pm–12am.

# DRINKING

## HAT KHLONG DAO

Clusters of little beach bars serve cocktails on deckchairs and cushions, often with chill-out music and a campfire to gather round.

**Indian Bar** Three doors south of Cha-Ba Bungalow; map p.382. One of the most genial bars on the beach, where the host, dressed as a Hollywood-style American Indian, makes a mean cocktail and does good fire-juggling shows. Claims to open 24hr.

## AO PHRA-AE (LONG BEACH)

The cluster of guesthouses and driftwood bars beyond the beach attract a steady flow of backpackers and youngsters with their dance music and cheap beers.

**Irish Embassy** On the main road near the centre of the bay ☏ 089 472 0404, ⓦ irishembassylanta.com; map p.382. Very friendly Irish bar, serving up a good selection of beers and hearty comfort food such as fish and chips (B220). Also host quiz nights and live bands. Daily 4pm–1am.

**Treehouse Bar** In front of Wild Flowers Hostel along the beach road ☏ 098 765 4321, ⓦ facebook.com/Treehouselanta; map p.382. The quintessential Long Beach party bar, perched on wooden stilts and set just off the main stretch of beach. It's all made in driftwood, with a dancefloor literally set into the thicket. It's very popular on Wednesdays and Sundays, when bands and DJs perform. Daily roughly 4pm–3am.

**Ozone Bar** On the beach ☎084 060 6244, ⓦfacebook. com/ozonebar; map p.382. One of the most famous bars on the beach, especially for its weekly DJ parties (currently Thurs), which usually draw a lively crowd. Daily roughly 11am–late.

## DIRECTORY

**Banks and ATMs** Several banks and ATMs in Ban Sala Dan, and there are ATMs beside the road at most of the beaches and in Lanta Old Town, but there are no ATMs or shops at the very southern tip at Ao Mai Phai.

**Hospitals** Nearly every beach has a clinic; **South Lanta Medical Clinic** has branches in Saladan (☎075 656134) and Hat Klong Khong (☎075 656843), while the rather basic island hospital is in Lanta Old Town (☎075 697017). However, for anything serious you'll need to go to Phuket.

**Post offices** At the south end of Hat Khlong Dao and in Lanta Old Town.

**Post offices** At the south end of Hat Khlong Dao and in Lanta Old Town.

**Tourist police** On the main road in Ao Phra-Ae (Long Beach; ☎1155).

**Travel agent** A helpful, clued-up travel agent is Otto Lanta Tour at *Otto Bungalows* on Hat Khlong Nin (☎083 634 8882, ⓔottolantatour@gmail.com).

4

# The deep south

SUGAR-WHITE BEACHES OF KO MOOK

# The deep south

The frontier between Thailand and Malaysia carves across the peninsula six degrees north of the equator, but the cultures of the two countries shade into each other much further north. According to official divisions, the southern Thais – the Thai Pak Tai – begin around Chumphon, and as you move further down the peninsula into Thailand's deep south you'll see ever more sarongs, yashmaks and towering mosques, and hear with increasing frequency a staccato dialect that baffles many Thais. Here too, you'll come across caged singing doves outside many houses, as well as strange-looking areas spiked with tall metal poles, on which the cages are hung during regular cooing competitions; and you'll spot huge, hump-backed Brahma bulls on the back of pick-up trucks, on their way to bullfights (in the Thai version, beast is pitted against beast, and the first to back off is the loser).

In Trang and Phatthalung provinces, the Muslim population is generally accepted as being Thai, but the inhabitants of the southernmost provinces – Satun, Pattani, Yala, Narathiwat and most of Songkhla – are ethnically more akin to the Malays: most of the 1.5 million followers of Islam here speak a dialect of Malay and write Jawi, an old modification of Arabic script to reflect Malay pronunciation. To add to the ethnic confusion, the region has a large urban population of Chinese, whose comparative wealth makes them stand out sharply from the Muslim farmers and fishermen.

The touristic interest in the deep south is currently all over on the beautiful **west coast**, where sheer limestone outcrops, pristine sands and fish-laden coral stretch down to the Malaysian border. Along Trang's **mainland coast**, there's a 30km stretch of attractive beaches, dotted with mangroves and impressive caves that can be explored by sea canoe, but the real draw down here is the offshore **islands**, which offer gorgeous panoramas and beaches, great snorkelling and small clusters of resorts. Apart from the tiny and remote but overcrowded honeypot of Ko Lipe, the other islands remain less developed, and scheduled boat services offer the intriguing possibility of **island-hopping** your way down from Phuket as far as Penang in Malaysia without setting foot on the peninsula. Yet, by going east from Trang, travellers find a slice of authentic rural Thailand at the lesser-visited **Thale Noi** (see page 415) protected wetland near Phattalung or decent beaches and Sino-Portuguese heritage at **Songkhla**, 30km northeast of **Hat Yai** (see page 416).

## ARRIVAL AND GETTING AROUND

As well as the usual bus services, the area covered in this chapter is served by **flights** and **trains** to Trang (see page 397), as well as by **boats** between the islands (see page 401) and from the mainland to the islands.

**By share-taxi** The deep south has traditionally been the territory of share-taxis, which connect certain towns for about twice the fare of ordinary buses. They leave when full, which usually means six passengers – charter the whole car if you're in a hurry.

**By minivan** A/c minibuses cover the same routes as share-taxis, but typically at lower prices. You'll have the advantage of a seat to yourself, with services usually running from major bus stations to a rough timetable. However, note that in town centres, the minibuses tend to leave as soon as they're full.

**By train** Hat Yay is the deep south's major train hub, with several northbound trains to the Gulf coast and Bangkok, together with the unreliable southbound services to Sungai Kolok. Trang also has two convenient evening services to Bangkok.

## Brief history

The central area of the Malay peninsula first entered Thai history when it came under the sway of Sukhothai, probably around the beginning of the fourteenth century. Islam

ENTRANCE TO EMERALD CAVE AT KO MOOK

# Highlights

❶ **Ko Hai** A variety of good resorts for all budgets and gorgeous views of the karst islands to the east, especially at sunset. See page 402

❷ **Tham Morakhot** Ko Mook's Emerald Cave, with its inland beach of powdery sand at the base of an awesome natural chimney, is best visited by kayak or chartered longtail boat. See page 403

❸ **Ko Kradan** Remote island with a long, white, east-facing strand, crystal-clear waters, a reef for snorkellers to explore and a few diverse resorts. See page 404

❹ **Thale Noi** Boat hop amidst lotus flowers in Thailand's biggest, yet undiscovered, waterfowl reserve. See page 415

❺ **Ko Tarutao** Huge national park island with mangroves, limestone caves and jungle tracks to investigate, and the most unspoilt beaches in the area along its 26km west coast. See page 408

❻ **Hat Pattaya** Though far from undiscovered, Ko Lipe's main beach is a beautiful crescent of white sand as fine as flour that squeaks as you walk along it. See page 411

HIGHLIGHTS ARE MARKED ON THE MAP ON PAGE 396

**5**

was introduced to the area by the end of that century, by which time Ayutthaya was taking a firmer grip on the peninsula. **Songkhla** and **Pattani** then rose to be the major cities, prospering on the goods passed through the two ports across the peninsula to avoid the pirates in the Straits of Malacca between Malaysia and Sumatra. More closely tied to the Muslim Malay states to the south, the Sultanate of Pattani began to **rebel** against the power of Ayutthaya in the sixteenth century, but the fight for self-determination only weakened Pattani's strength. The town's last rebellious fling was in 1902, after which it was definitively and brutally absorbed into the Thai kingdom, while its allies, Kedah, Kelantan and Trengganu, were transferred into the suzerainty of the British in Malaysia.

During World War II the **Communist Party of Malaya** made its home in the jungle around the Thai border to fight the occupying Japanese. After the war they turned their guns against the British colonialists, but having been excluded from power after independence, descended into general banditry and racketeering around Betong. The Thai authorities eventually succeeded in breaking up the bandit gangs in 1989 through a combination of pardons and bribes, but the stability of the region soon faced disruption from another source, a rise in Islamic militancy.

### The troubles: 2004 to the present

Armed resistance to the Thai state by **Muslim separatists** had fluctuated at a relatively low level since the 1960s, but in early 2004 the violence escalated dramatically. Since

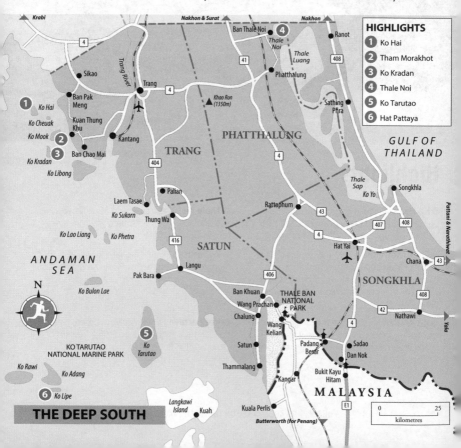

**THE DEEP SOUTH**

**5**

**TRAVEL WARNING**

Because of the ongoing **violence** in the deep south (see below), Western governments are currently advising their citizens **not to travel** to or through Pattani, Yala, Narathiwat and Songkhla provinces unless essential; following on from this, check if your insurance company covers travel in the affected areas. The four provinces encompass the city and transport hub of **Hat Yai** and several of the main border crossings to Malaysia: by rail from Hat Yai (and Bangkok) to Butterworth (near Penang in Malaysia) via Padang Besar and to Sungai Kolok; and by road from Hat Yai via Sadao, from Yala via Betong, and down the east coast to Kota Bharu. In practice, however, crossing from Hat Yay into Malaysia by train is a very popular and generally safe route used daily by many international travellers.

On the contrary, avoid the routes to Sungai Kolok, Betong and Kota Bharu as they pass through particularly volatile territory, with **martial law** declared in Pattani, Yala and Narathiwat provinces; however, martial law is only in effect in certain districts of Songkhla province, and not in Hat Yai itself.

The provinces of **Trang** and **Satun** are not affected, and it's also possible to continue overland to Malaysia via Satun: by air-conditioned minibus from Satun to Kangar, or by ferry from Thammalang to the Malaysian island of Langkawi (see page 415); or by boat from Ko Lipe to Langkawi (see page 411). For up-to-the-minute advice, consult your government travel advisory (see page 58).

then, there have been hundreds of deaths on both sides in the troubles: the insurgents have targeted Buddhist monks, police, soldiers, teachers and other civil servants, as well as attacking a train on the Hat Yai–Sungai Kolok line and setting off bombs in marketplaces, near tourist hotels and bars and at Hat Yai airport. Increasingly, they have attacked other Muslims who are seen to be too sympathetic to the Thai state.

Often writing the militants off as bandits, the authorities have stirred up hatred – and undermined moderate Muslim voices – by reacting violently, notably in crushing protests at Tak Bai and the much-revered Krue Se Mosque in Pattani in 2004, in which a total of over two hundred alleged insurgents died. In 2005, the government announced a **serious state of emergency** in Pattani, Yala and Narathiwat provinces, and imposed **martial law** here and in southern parts of Songkhla province. This, however, has exacerbated economic and unemployment problems in what is Thailand's poorest region.

A large part of the problem is that a wide variety of shadowy groups – with names like the Pattani Islamic Mujahideen, the Barisan Revolusi Nasional-Coordinate and Runda Kumpulan Kecil – are operating against the government, generally working in small cells at village level without central control. Rather than religious issues, the most likely causes of their militancy are ethnic grievances. However, it's unclear exactly who they are or what they want, and, faced with such shifting sands, so far all attempts to broker a ceasefire have failed.

# Trang town

**TRANG** (also known as Taptieng) is a popular jumping-off point for travellers drawn south from the crowded sands of Krabi to the pristine beaches and islands of the nearby coast. The town, which prospers on rubber, oil palms, fisheries and low-key tourism, is a sociable place whose wide, clean streets are dotted with crumbling, wooden-shuttered houses. In the evening, the streets are festooned with colourful lights and, from Thursday to Sunday, the central square in front of the station hosts a lively market, while during the day, many of the town's Chinese inhabitants hang out in the cafés, drinking the local filtered coffee. Trang's Chinese population makes the **Vegetarian Festival** in October or November almost as frenetic as Phuket's (see page 320). You can also take a day-trip to nearby **Kantang**, 25km south of town with its well-preserved old train station.

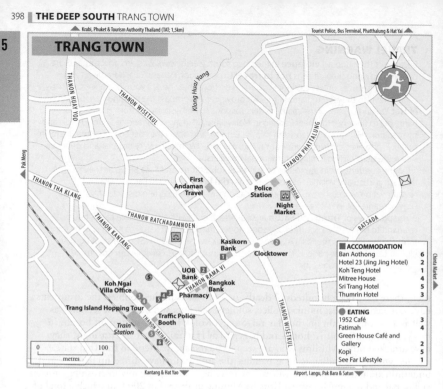

TRANG TOWN

**ACCOMMODATION**

| Ban Aothong | 6 |
|---|---|
| Hotel 23 (Jing Jing Hotel) | 2 |
| Koh Teng Hotel | 1 |
| Mitree House | 4 |
| Sri Trang Hotel | 5 |
| Thumrin Hotel | 3 |

**EATING**

| 1952 Café | 3 |
|---|---|
| Fatimah | 4 |
| Green House Café and Gallery | 2 |
| Kopi | 5 |
| See Far Lifestyle | 1 |

## ARRIVAL AND DEPARTURE

**By plane** Air Asia and Nok Air run daily flights between Bangkok and Trang airport (1hr 30min), which is 3km south of town. On arrival, a/c minibuses bring passengers downtown (B100/person), while on departure, you can charter a tuk-tuk or taxi (about B300/two people).

**By train** Two overnight trains from Bangkok (15–16hr) use a branch of the southern line to Trang and return to the capital at 1.30pm and 5.25pm. A daily third-class service (10.36am; 15min; B20) also runs to Kantang.

**By bus** Buses arrive at and depart from the new bus terminal on Thanon Phattalung (Highway 4), opposite Robinson department store, about 3km northeast of the centre, including an a/c bus service between Satun and Phuket four times daily. Shared songthaews (B20) shuttle between here and the train station.

**Destinations** Bangkok (5 daily; 12hr); Krabi (roughly every 30min; 2hr); Phuket (hourly; 5hr).

**By minibus** A/c minibuses to Pak Meng, Ban Chao Mai, Satun (via Langu), Ko Lanta (including drop-offs as far south as Hat Klong Nin; 6 daily; 3hr), Krabi, Nakhon Si Thammarat, Phattalung, Songkhla, Surat Thani and Hat Yai also use the new bus terminal on Thanon Phattalung. In high season, travel agents such as Trang Island Hopping Tour can arrange through tickets to Ko Lipe (B700–750), Ko Tarutao and Ko Bulon Lae (both B650), including an a/c minibus to Pak Bara (departing 9am) and the boat trip.

**By share-taxi** Share-taxis for Pak Bara, Satun and Krabi congregate at the old bus station on Thanon Huay Yod, on the north side of town (about 500m north of the junction with Thanon Wisetkul).

## GETTING AROUND

**By rental car** Avis (☎02 251 1131–2, ⓦavisthailand.com) and Budget (☎075 572159, ⓦbudget.co.th), both at the airport.

**By motorbike** Motorbikes can be rented from the desk at *Sri Trang Hotel* (see page 399), which is on Thanon Rama VI (B250/day).

## INFORMATION AND TOURS

**Tourist information** TAT office on Thanon Huay Yod (daily 8.30am–4.30pm; ☎075 211 058) is located out of town, but Green House Café (see below), just east of the clock tower, distributes free city maps and information.

**Tourist police** Thanon Phattalung (Highway 4), about 2km northeast of the centre ☎075 211903 or ☎1155.

**Travel agents** The best travel agent in town is Trang Island Hopping Tour, with a desk located at Fatimah, which is directly opposite the station at 28/2 Thanon Sathanee (T082 804 0583, W trang-all-tour.com, E trangalltour@gmail.com). They offer one-day boat trips around the islands (B750 excluding the B200 national park entry fee) and day-trips and camping trips to Ko Rok (B3800 for 3D/2N), and inland excursions to waterfalls and caves (B1200), as well as trekking, bird-watching, rafting and kayaking.

## ACCOMMODATION

**Ban Aothong** 25/28–31 Thanon Sathanee T075 290 192, W facebook.com/banaothongandmyfriend; map p.398. An overblown facade of multi-tiered roofs and gables announces this upmarket guesthouse, with its chunky wooden furniture, half-tester beds and rather kitsch decor. "Standard" double rooms are compact, some with no window, while the slightly pricier "superior" twins have a slice more space, though the bathrooms are still small; all come with a/c, hot showers, fridges and cable TV. **B700**

★ **Hotel 23 (Jing Jing Hotel)** 77–79 Thanon Rama VI, T075 218 077, W facebook.com/hotel23trang; map p.398. This affordable boutique hotel packs six spacious rooms that integrate modern plush beds and cute rattan furniture with the building's original wooden features. Bathrooms are clean and shared, but some of the a/c rooms (B500) come with private showers. Free coffee and tea for all guests is supplied. **B300**

**Koh Teng Hotel** 77–79 Thanon Rama VI T075 218622 or T075 218148; map p.398. This characterful 1940s Chinese hotel is a little battered and dusty, but it offers large, mostly clean, basic en-suite rooms with cold showers – some with cable TV and a/c – set above a popular restaurant and coffee shop that serves a mix of southern Thai and Chinese food and Western breakfasts. Fan **B200**, a/c **B360**

**Mitree House** 6–8 Thanon Sathani T075 212292, W facebook.com/mitreehouse; map p.398. Interesting mid-range choice opposite the train station, with a series of clean and white-tinted rooms (those with windows feel much less claustrophobic) spread over two wooden-decked floors tucked behind a spacious lounge-reception. Breakfast is included. **B750**

**Sri Trang Hotel** 22 Thanon Sathanee T075 218122, W sritranghotel.com; map p.398. Welcoming, thoroughly updated 1950s hotel offering spacious a/c rooms with some colourful decorative touches, hot water, cable TV, DVD players and fridges above a cool little café. **B550**

**Thumrin Hotel** Thanon Rama VI T075 211011–4, W thumrin.co.th; map p.398. Good-value, very central hotel offering international-standard facilities – a/c, hot water, TV, minibar – in a high-rise block above its popular bakery-cum-coffee shop. **B700**

## EATING AND DRINKING

Trang's streets are dotted with dozens of traditional cafés, which serve up gallons of **kopi** (local filtered coffee) accompanied by various tidbits and light meals. Most famous of these is the local speciality, **muu yaang**, delicious charcoal-grilled pork, which is generally eaten for breakfast. There's an excellent weekend **night market** in front of the train station, and, near Centrepoint shopping mall, the hipper **Chinta Market,** which features an upmarket food court, souvenir stalls, and live music.

**1952 Café** Opposite the train station on Thanon Sathanee T089 114 4777, W facebook.com/nineteen fiftytwocafeattrang; map p.398. Annexed to Sri Trang Hotel, this contemporary-styled Café is the place to get Western comfort foods. There are burgers (from B190), pizzas (from B200), chicken wings (B100), Thai mains and a good selection of drinks and coffee. Daily 8am–9pm.

**Fatimah** Opposite the train station on Thanon Sathanee T086 5942053, W facebook.com/FatimahHal Restaurant; map p.398. Simple Thai and Malay-style halal restaurant that's especially popular in the evenings. Buffet of southern curries, tasty *phat thai* (B40), fried rice and noodles (B40), *kopi* and tea. Tues–Sun roughly 8.30am–9pm.

★ **Green House Café and Gallery** 148/1 Rama VI, 15m east of the clocktower T075 218411, W facebook.com/greenhouseattrang; map p.398. Congenial hip café that bakes delicious goodies, including cakes and wholemeal wheat breads, serves all-day brunch, and brews strong coffee in an arty, sociable *sala*. The manager, Dear, speaks great English and is happy to share her local knowledge and tips with customers and travellers. Daily 10am–10pm.

**Kopi** Next to the train station at 25/25–26 Thanon Sathanee T075 214225; map p.398. Very popular, updated traditional café: *kopi* with dim sum and main courses (fried rice B50), or espresso, various teas and Western breakfasts. Daily 7am–5pm.

**See Far Lifestyle** 37 Thanon Phattalung (right by the entrance to Soi 3) T075 210139; map p.398. Good, inexpensive restaurant with a varied menu of carefully prepared dishes, specialising in healthy cuisine, vegetarian and local food, such as *tom som plakapong*, a light, refreshing soup of sea bass, mushrooms and cumin, and *kao yook* (B150), a Chinese-style dish of steamed pork with taro found only in Trang. Daily 10.30am–8.30pm.

**5**

# The Trang coast

From Pak Meng, 40km due west of Trang town, down to the mouth of the Trang River runs a 30km-long stretch of lovely beaches, broken only by dramatic limestone outcrops. A paved road roughly parallels this stretch of coast, but otherwise there's surprisingly little development, as the shoreline is technically part of Hat Chao Mai National Park.

## Pak Meng and Hat Chang Lang

Although it has a fine outlook to the headlands and islands to the west (with regular boats to the biggest, Ko Hai), the beach at **PAK MENG** is not the most attractive on the coast, becoming a rather muddy strip of sand at low tide. At other times, however, it offers quiet, calm swimming, and there's always the possibility of a meal at one of the many tree-shaded food stalls and restaurants that line the back of the beach.

Immediately south of Pak Meng's beach is the white sand of **Hat Chang Lang**, famous for its oysters, which shelters at its north end the finest luxury hotel in the province, *Anantara Si Kao*.

## Hat Chao Mai National Park HQ

The turning for the headquarters is 3km on from Hat Chang Lang · B200 · ☎ 075 213260, ⊛ dnp.go.th

**Hat Chao Mai National Park** covers 230 square kilometres, including parts of Ko Mook and Ko Kradan, but the park admission fee is only rigidly enforced if you visit its headquarters. From the HQ a short trail leads to the south end of the beach and a viewpoint partway up a karst pinnacle, from which you can see Ko Mook and occasionally dugongs in the bay below. At the park headquarters there's a simple café as well as accommodation.

## Hat Yong Ling and Hat Yao

About 5km south of the national park HQ, beyond Kuantunku, the pier for Ko Mook, is **Hat Yong Ling**. This quiet and attractive convex beach, which shelters a national park ranger station (entry B200), is probably the nicest along this stretch of coast, with a large cave which you can swim into at high tide or walk into at low tide. Immediately beyond comes **Hat Yao**, which is free, runs in a broad 5km white-sand strip, and is backed by casuarina trees and some simple restaurants.

## Ban Chao Mai

At the south end of Hat Yao is **BAN CHAO MAI** (also called **Ban Hat Yao**), a straggle of houses on stilts, which exists on fishing, especially for crabs. From the harbour, boats run regularly across to Ko Libong, and this is the mainland ferry stop on Tigerline's Lanta–Lipe route. Also on offer are trips by longtail and canoe through the mangroves to the nearby cave of **Tham Chao Mai** (daily 8am–5pm), which shelters impressively huge rock pillars and a natural theatre, its stage framed by rock curtains – contact Bang Wit (☎087 463 7628), who speaks English, or ask around in the village for him.

---

**ARRIVAL AND GETTING AROUND**                  **THE TRANG COAST**

Air-conditioned **minibuses**, departing roughly hourly but leaving early if already full, run from the bus station in Trang to Pak Meng (45min), as well as via Hat Yao to Ban Chao Mai (1hr), but if you want to explore the whole coastline, you'll need to rent a **motorbike** or **car** in Trang (see page 398).

**ACCOMMODATION AND EATING**

**PAK MENG**
**Lay Trang Boutique** ☎089 4744423, ⓦfacebook. com/laytrangboutique. The nicest place to stay and eat at Pak Meng, a stone's throw from the pier at the far north end of the beach. Ranged around a large, peaceful garden with lawns and orchids set back from the beach, its bright concrete chalets with huge bathrooms and smart brick rooms come with verandas, hot showers, a/c and TV. Its welcoming, reasonably priced restaurant is nationally famous for its seafood, including *nam prik kung siap* (dried shrimp relish) and *kaeng som* soup with sea bass. B1500

**HAT CHANG LANG**
★**Anantara Si Kao** ☎075 205888, ⓦanantara.com. The finest luxury hotel in the province, where the low-rise blocks of stylish bedrooms and pool suites, all with large balconies, are set behind a line of casuarina trees. Facilities encompass a beautiful, large swimming pool, Italian and international restaurants, a kids' club, a fitness centre and a spa. Watersports on offer include diving, kayaking and sailing, and there's plenty of other activities, notably cooking and Thai-language lessons and some interesting local tours. The hotel also has its own beach club and restaurant on the main strand on Ko Kradan (see page 404), reached by daily boat transfer. Breakfast included. B9000

**HAT CHAO MAI NATIONAL PARK HQ**
**National park bungalows** ⓦdnp.go.th. Fan-cooled, en-suite bungalows and rooms, most with refrigerators, for two to six people, set under the casuarinas at the back of the sandy beach, and a simple café. B1000

# The Trang and Satun islands

Generally blessed with blinding white beaches, great coral and amazing marine life, the islands off the coast of **Trang** and **Satun** provinces have managed, mostly with just a handful of resorts on each, to cling onto some of that illusory desert-island atmosphere which better-known places like Phuket and Samui lost long ago. Indeed, islands such as **Ko Hai** and **Ko Kradan** support no permanent settlements other than the bungalow concerns, while on **Ko Tarutao** and **Ko Adang** in the far south, the peace and quiet is maintained by the national parks department; at the other end of the scale, however, nearby **Ko Lipe** boasts over fifty resorts, as well as a substantial *chao ley* village (see page 300).

---

**ISLAND-HOPPING AND TOURS**

**Access** to the Trang and Satun Islands from their nearest mainland ports is described in the individual island accounts, but what sets this area apart are the enticing opportunities for **island-hopping**, thanks to regular boat services in the tourist season between Ko Lanta and Ko Lipe, or even between Phuket and Langkawi in Malaysia, which can be booked through any travel agent in the area. (Several companies on Ko Lanta that organize day-trips by speedboat to Ko Hai, Ko Mook and Ko Kradan will drop you off at any of the islands, but the cost will be about the same as with Bundhaya Speedboat, Satun Pakbara Speedboat Club and Tigerline detailed below.) If you just fancy a day exploring some of the islands, any travel agent in Trang can book you on a **boat trip** (roughly mid-Oct to mid-May only) to Ko Kradan for snorkelling, the Emerald Cave on Ko Mook, and other small nearby islands for snorkelling, for around B750/person including packed lunch and soft drinks (excluding the B200 national park fee).

**Bundhaya Speedboat** ☎074 783111, ⓦbundhayaspeedboat.com. Speedboats between Lanta and Lipe (1 daily; about 4hr; B1900) via Ko Hai, Hat Farang on Ko Mook and Ko Bulon Lae. Onward, same-day connections to Langkawi, and to Ko Phi Phi and Phuket.
**Satun Pakbara Speedboat Club** ☎081 959 2094, ⓦspcthailand.com. Speedboats between Lanta and Lipe (1 daily; about 4hr; B1900) via Ko Hai, Hat Farang on Ko Mook, Ko Kradan and Ko Bulon Lae. Onward, same-day connections between Lipe and Langkawi, and between Lanta and Ko Phi Phi and Phuket.
**Tigerline** ☎098 016 8181, ⓦtigerlinetravel. com. Ferries between Phuket and Langkawi (1 daily; about 9hr; B3500), via Ko Phi Phi, Ko Lanta, Ko Hai, Hat Farang on Ko Mook (with longtail transfers to Ko Kradan), Ban Chao Mai on the mainland (usually with a change of boat) and Ko Lipe. Hai–Lipe, for example, costs B1600.

**5**

## KO HAI ACTIVITIES

You can rent **snorkelling equipment** and **kayaks** at most of the resorts. All the resorts offer **boat trips** (B1800/boat, maximum six people, at *Ko Hai Seafood*, for example) that take in the Emerald Cave on Ko Mook, nearby islands such as Ko Cheuak and Ko Waen and some snorkelling off Ko Hai.

Towards the southern end of the beach, *Fantasy Resort* has a well-organized **dive shop**, the German-run Ko Hai Divers, which specialises in small-group trips and PADI courses (☏ 080 545 5012, ⊛ kohaidivers.com; Nov–April).

**Accommodation** on the islands, much of which is mid-priced, is now often fully booked at the very busiest times. Most of the resorts open year-round, though in practice many can't be reached out of season (roughly June–Oct) due to treacherous seas. It's sensible to get in touch ahead of time to check whether the resort you're interested in is open or has vacancies, and in many cases to arrange transfers from agents in Trang town.

## Ko Hai (Ko Ngai)

**KO HAI** (also known as **KO NGAI**), 16km southwest of Pak Meng, is the most developed of the Trang islands, though it's still decidedly low-key and much quieter than Ko Lipe down in Satun. The island's action, such as it is, centres on the east coast, where half a dozen resorts enjoy a dreamy panorama of jagged limestone outcrops, whose crags glow pink and blue against the setting sun, stretching across the sea to the mainland behind. The gently sloping beach of fine, white sand here runs unbroken for over 2km (though at low tide, swimming is not so good at the northern end, which is scattered with dead coral), and there's some good snorkelling in the shallow, clear water off the island's southeastern tip.

### ARRIVAL AND DEPARTURE
KO HAI

If you're planning to **fly** into Trang or Krabi airports, contact your resort in advance about transfers. There are also plenty of island-hopping options (see page 401). Hat Chao Mai National Park maintains a booth at Pak Meng pier, where visitors to Ko Hai will usually be charged B200 entrance fee; hang on to your ticket as this should also cover you if you take a trip to Ko Mook's Emerald Cave.

**By ferry** In high season a ferry leaves Pak Meng pier at 12pm (45min–1hr; B350), returning from Ko Hai at 10am; longtail boats come out to meet the ferries and shuttle passengers to the various resorts up and down the beach. Travel agents in Trang offer a/c minivan and boat combination tickets for B500. In high season, speedboats connect Ko Hai all the way to Ko Lipe, with stops at Ko Mook, Ko Kradan and Ko Tarutao.

**By chartered longtail** If you miss the ferries, you can charter a longtail boat for around B1500, for example through *Coco Cottage* (see below).

### ACCOMMODATION

★ **Coco Cottage** Towards the northern end of the beach ☏ 089 724 9225, ⊛ coco-cottage.com. Charming, helpful and family-friendly resort in a grassy palm grove, where most of the chic, thatched, a/c wooden bungalows (both detached and semi-detached) sport verandas and well-designed bathrooms, with outdoor bamboo hot showers, wooden basins and indoor toilets. Also has a stylish beach bar and a very good restaurant that serves creative Thai food, Thai desserts and espresso coffees. Breakfast included. B2500

**Ko Hai Seafood** Near the centre of the beach, north of Koh Ngai Villa ☏ 095 014 1853. Large, well-built, thatched, woven-bamboo bungalows with wall fans, mosquito screens and cold-water bathrooms, in a single row facing the beach across a nice lawn. B1500

**Mayalay Beach Resort** Near the centre of the main beach, south of Koh Ngai Villa ☏ 081 894 3585, ⊛ mayalaybeachresort.com. Welcoming place with nineteen deluxe, a/c, woven-bamboo bungalows with thatched roofs, day beds, fridges and capacious hot-water bathrooms. Often open all year round. Breakfast included. B3000

**Sea Camp Hostel** North end of the beach ⊛ bit.ly/SeaCamp. Basic but charming mixed dorm with mosquito nets, literally on the sand with no flooring, and facing its own private part of beach. Ideal for backpackers and nature lovers. B600

**Thanya** South end of the beach ☎ 075 206967, ⓦ kohngaithanyaresort.com. A large, very attractive beachside swimming pool with Jacuzzis, set on a spacious lawn, is the main draw here. As well as a/c, hot water and fridges, the dark-wooden villas feature verandas, big French windows and lots of polished teak, while the restaurant has a varied menu of Thai food, including some interesting seafood dishes. Breakfast included. B3600

**Thapwarin Resort** Towards the northern end of the main beach, north of Coco Cottage ☎ 081 894 3585, ⓦ thapwarin.com. Welcoming, shady resort, where you can choose between well-appointed bamboo and rattan cottages with semi-outdoor bathrooms, and large, very smart, beachfront wooden bungalows; all are thatched and have a/c, minibars and hot showers (more expensive stilted villas, with bedrooms upstairs and living area downstairs, are also planned). There's a massage spa, beach bar and good restaurant, serving Thai and Western food, including seafood barbecues in the evening. Breakfast included. B3800

# Ko Mook

**KO MOOK**, about 8km southeast of Ko Hai, supports a comparatively busy fishing village on its eastern side, around which – apart from the sandbar that runs out to the very pricey *Sivalai Resort* – most of the beaches are disappointing, reduced to dirty mud flats when the tide goes out. However, across on the island's west coast lies beautiful **Hat Farang**, with gently shelving white sand, crystal-clear water that's good for swimming and snorkelling, and gorgeous sunsets.

## Tham Morakhot

Part of Hat Chao Mai National Park • Open mid-Nov to mid-May • B200 admission fee if the park rangers are around

The island's main source of renown is **Tham Morakhot**, the stunning "Emerald Cave" north of Hat Farang on the west coast, which can only be visited by boat, but shouldn't be missed. An 80m swim through the cave – 10m or so of which is in pitch darkness – brings you to a *hong* (see page 346) with an **inland beach** of powdery sand open to the sky, at the base of a spectacular natural chimney whose walls are coated with dripping vegetation. Chartering your own longtail from the boatmen's co-operative on Hat Farang (B1000/boat, maximum four people; the boatman will swim with you to guide you through the cave) is preferable to taking one of the big day-trip boats that originate on Lanta or Pak Meng: if you time it right, you'll get the inland beach all to yourself, an experience not to be forgotten. (The boatmen also offer combined trips to Tham Morakhot, Ko Kradan and Ko Cheuak for B2500/boat.) It's also easy enough to **kayak** there from Hat Farang (from B200/hr from *Sawaddee*), and at low tide you can paddle right through to the inland beach: buoys mark the cave entrance, from where a tunnel heads straight back into the rock; about halfway along, there's a small, right-hand kink in the tunnel which will plunge you briefly into darkness, but you should soon be able to see light ahead from the *hong*. Mid-afternoon is often a good time to paddle off on this trip, after the tour boats have left and providing the tide is right.

### ARRIVAL AND DEPARTURE                                          KO MOOK

In addition to the services mentioned below, there are plenty of island-hopping options (see page 401).

**By Boat** A year-round minibus leaves Trang station at 11.30am, connecting to the local ferry at Kuan Thung Khu pier, 8km south of Pak Meng (B250 all included). Ferries disembark at the main Ko Mook jetty, off Ao Kham, a 30min walk or B50–100 motorbike-taxi ride over to Hat Farang.

Travel agents in Trang can also organise minibus-and-boat packages to Hat Farang, which costs about B350, including a 30min longtail ride direct to the beach.

In high season, speedboats depart from Hat Farang hopping all the way south to Ko Lipe (B1400), stopping at other islands en route. There are also direct services to Phi Phi (B1600) and Phuket (B2400) via Ko Lanta (B900).

### ACCOMMODATION

**Had Farang Bungalows** ☎ 087 884 4785, ⓦ facebook. com/hadfarang. The eighteen bungalows and rooms at this friendly place are simple, yet clean and with wood and bamboo furnishing and mosquito nets. Nearly all are en

suite with their own verandas and the restaurant is very good. Fan B400, a/c B1000

**Ko Mook Hostel** 400m from the boat pier ☎ 089 724 4456, ⓦ facebook.com/Kohmookhostelfanpage. This single-storey blue building, the cheapest option on the island, has three (a/c female, a/c mixed and fan mixed) six and ten-bed dorms. The clean bunk beds are equipped with wooden dividers, privacy curtains and reading lights, and the shared bathrooms are kept clean. There's free coffee and tea, and an in-house bakery-coffee-shop that makes for a perfect breakfast spot. B380

**Ko Mook Riviera Beach Resort** ☎ 087 885 7815, ⊕ riviera-resorts.com. On the south-facing shore of the sandbar that ends at *Sivalai Resort*, the bright, concrete bungalows at this sustainable, eco-friendly resort all have mosquito-screened French windows directly facing the sea, as well as a/c, satellite TV and DVD player. Bicycles, kayaks and trips to the Emerald Cave and neighbouring islands available. Breakfast and dinner included. B3000

★ **Mountain View Resort** 3min walk inland from Charlie's Beach ☎ 065 053 3077, ⊕ facebook.com/ moutainviewresortkohmook. A collection of Thai-style bungalows set in a well-tended, shady garden just minutes away from the beach. All rooms are en suite, some are graciously decked out in thatched bamboo, and all have serene wooden verandas. Breakfast is included. B1300

# Ko Kradan

About 6km to the southwest of Ko Mook, **KO KRADAN** is the remotest of the inhabited islands off Trang, and one of the most beautiful, with crystal-clear waters. On this slender, 4km-long triangle of thick jungle, the **main beach** is a long strand of steeply sloping, powdery sand on the east coast, with fine views of Ko Mook, Ko Libong and the karst-strewn mainland, and an offshore reef to the north with a great variety of hard coral; such beauty, however, has not escaped the attention of the day-trip boats from Ko Lanta, who turn the beach into a lunchtime picnic ground most days in high season. From a short way north of the *Anantara* beach club (see page 401), which is located towards the south end of this beach, a path across the island will bring you after about fifteen minutes to **Sunset Beach**, another lovely stretch of fine, white sand in a cove; a branch off this path at *Paradise Lost* leads to a beach on the short south coast, which enjoys good reef snorkelling (also about 15min from the *Anantara* beach club).

### ARRIVAL AND DEPARTURE        KO KRADAN

**By minibus-and-longtail transfer** Agencies such as Trang Island Hopping Tour (see page 401) can arrange minibus-and-longtail transfers from Trang town, via Kuan Thung Khu pier (twice daily in season; B450). There are also a number of island-hopping options available (see page 401).

### ACCOMMODATION

**Kalume** ☎ 093 650 0841, ⊕ kalumekradan.com. Eco-friendly Italian-run resort on the beach next to *Seven Seas*, with small, basic, thatched bamboo huts with mosquito nets, fans and en-suite bathrooms and smart, large, wooden bungalows with French windows and nice verandas. Good Italian food at the bar-restaurant. B1500

**Paradise Lost** ☎ 089 587 2409; for further information, go to ⊕ kokradan.wordpress.com. In the middle of the island, roughly halfway along the path to *Sunset Beach*, is Kradan's best-value accommodation, run by an American and his dogs. Set in a grassy, palm-shaded grove, it offers simple, clean, thatched rattan bungalows with mosquito nets, fans and shared bathrooms or larger, en-suite, wooden affairs (some with hot showers), kayaks, snorkels and good Thai and Western food. B700

**Seven Seas** ☎ 075 203389–90, ⊕ sevenseasresorts. com. By far the best of several resorts on the east coast, *Seven Seas* adds a surprising splash of contemporary luxury to this remote spot. Behind a small, black, infinity-edge pool, the large bungalows, villas and rooms with outdoor warm-water bathrooms are stylishly done out in greys and whites, and sport a/c, fridges, TVs and DVD players. There's a spa and a dive shop, and breakfast is included. B9300

# Ko Libong

The largest of the Trang islands with a population of six thousand, **KO LIBONG** lies 10km southeast of Ko Mook, opposite Ban Chao Mai on the mainland. Less visited than its northern neighbours, it's known mostly for its wildlife, although it has its fair share of golden beaches too. Libong is one of the most significant remaining refuges in Thailand of the **dugong**, a large marine mammal similar to the manatee, which

**5**

> ## KO LIBONG ACTIVITIES
>
> *Libong Beach Resort* (see below) runs **boat trips** to see the dugongs for B1500 per boat. To this you can add on a visit to the bird sanctuary (B1800 in total), plus a cruise around the island (B2000 in total). The resorts can also organize trips to the Emerald Cave on Ko Mook. For **diving**, ask at *Libong Beach Resort*: Yat, a dive master who works on Ko Hai, can usually arrange trips from his home island of Libong.

feeds on sea grasses growing on the sea floor – the sea-grass meadow around Libong is reckoned to be the largest in Southeast Asia. Sadly, dugongs are now an endangered species, traditionally hunted for their blubber (used as fuel) and meat, and increasingly affected by fishing practices such as scooping, and by coastal pollution, which destroys their source of food. The dugong has now been adopted as one of fifteen "reserved animals" of Thailand and is the official mascot of Trang province.

Libong is also well known for its migratory **birds**, which stop off here on their way south from Siberia, drawn by the island's food-rich mud flats (now protected by the Libong Archipelago Sanctuary, which covers the eastern third of the island). For those seriously interested in ornithology, the best time to come is during March and April, when you can expect to see brown-winged kingfishers, masked finfoots and even the rare black-necked stork, not seen elsewhere on the Thai–Malay peninsula.

The island's handful of resorts occupies a long, thin strip of golden sand at the fishing village of **Ban Lan Khao** on the southwestern coast. At low tide here, the sea retreats for hundreds of metres, exposing rock pools that are great for splashing about in but not so good for a dip.

### ARRIVAL AND DEPARTURE                                                KO LIBONG

**By public longtail** Public longtails depart daily year-round from Ban Chao Mai (see page 400) when full (most frequent in the morning and around lunchtime; B50/person), arriving 20min later at Ban Phrao on Ko Libong's north side. From here motorbike taxis (B100) transport you to Ban Lan Khao. In high season, Tigerline speedboats (wtigerlinetravel. com) stop at Hat Yao on Ko Libong and can take you to/from Phi Phi, Phuket, Ko Lanta, Ko Hai, Ko Mook, Ko Kradan, Ko Lipe and Langkawi in Malaysia.

**By private transfer** You can arrange a direct boat transfer from Ban Chao Mai through *Libong Beach Resort* for B1000/boat.

### ACCOMMODATION

**Libong Beach Resort** ☏075 225205, wlibong-beach. com. Friendly resort on the north side of Ban Lan Khao with a wide variety of accommodation set amid lawns and flowers, ranging from small, en-suite concrete and wood bungalows at the back to spacious, bright, stilted, wooden cabins with a/c and nice decks on the beachfront (B2500). Kayak and motorbike rental are available. Fan B1000, a/c B1500
**Libong Relax Beach Resort** ☏091 825 4886, wlibongrelax.com. Located on an attractive stretch of the beach, all of the bungalows here face directly onto the sea across a narrow, tree-lined lawn and sport some attractive Thai decorative touches. The "Pavilions" have Thai-style roofs, picture windows and large verandas, while the "Cottages" are more functional with smaller verandas; upgrading to a/c also snags you a hot shower. There's a massage hut and the resort can also arrange island tours on a motorcycle with a sidecar. Fan B1400, a/c B2000

## Ko Sukorn

A good way south of the other Trang islands, low-lying, ATM-free **KO SUKORN** lacks the white-sand beaches and beautiful coral of its neighbours but makes up for it with its friendly inhabitants and laid-back ambience; for a glimpse of how the Muslim islanders live and work, this is a good place to come.

The lush interior is mainly given over to rubber plantations, interspersed with rice paddies, banana and coconut palms; the island also produces famously delicious watermelons, which are plentiful in March and April. Hat Talo Yai, the main **beach** – 500m of gently shelving brown sand, backed by coconut palms – runs along the southwestern shore.

## KO SUKORN BOAT TRIPS AND OTHER ACTIVITIES

**Boat excursions** arranged through the resorts include trips out to the islands of Ko Lao Liang and Ko Takieng, which are part of the Mu Ko Phetra National Marine Park, for some excellent snorkelling. These run nearly every day from November to May; at other times of year, the sea is sometimes calm enough but you're usually restricted to fishing trips – and to looking round the island itself, which, at thirty square kilometres, is a good size for exploring. Yataa Island Resort has a handy map that marks all the sights, including the three villages and seafood market, and offers motorbikes (B250/half-day) and mountain bikes (B150/half-day) for rent.

### ARRIVAL AND DEPARTURE                                                                                    KO SUKORN

**Transfers from Trang** A songthaew-and-boat transfer to Ko Sukorn (B300/person), via the public ferry from Laem Ta Sae, can be arranged through any travel agent in Trang, leaving daily at 11.30am. The journey takes about two and a half hours. Alternatively, you can arrange a private transfer through most of the resorts for about B2000 all-in.

**Inter-island transfers** *Yataa Island Resort* c(see below) can organize pricey longtail-boat transfers to or from any of the nearby islands.

### ACCOMMODATION

**Ko Sukorn Cabana** ⓣ 089 724 2326, ⓦ sukorncabana.com. This friendly and peaceful place offers stilted, a/c bungalows with attractive bathrooms and large, well-appointed log cabins on a secluded beach to the north of Hat Talo Yai. Kayaks and motorbikes are also available. Breakfast included. B1000

**Yataa Island Resort (Sukorn Beach Bungalows)** ⓣ 089 647 5550, ⓦ sukornisland.yataaresort.com. Low-key, quiet resort under new management, where the attractively decorated bungalows and different categories of rooms – all a/c and with en-suite hot showers – are set around a lush garden dotted with deckchairs and umbrellas, and there's a small swimming pool and a good restaurant. At the resort, you can also get a good massage, and you're free to paddle around in kayaks. Breakfast included. B1400

# Ko Bulon Lae

The scenery at tiny **KO BULON LAE**, 20km west of Pak Bara in Satun province, isn't as beautiful as that generally found in Ko Tarutao National Park just to the south, but it's not at all bad: a 2km strip of fine white sand runs the length of the casuarina-lined east coast, where the two main resorts can be found (open roughly from Nov to April or mid-May), while *chao ley* fishermen make their ramshackle homes in the tight coves of the rest of the island. A reef of curiously shaped hard coral closely parallels the eastern beach, while **White Rock** to the south of the island has beautifully coloured soft coral and equally dazzling fish.

### ARRIVAL AND DEPARTURE                                                                                  KO BULON LAE

**From/to Pak Bara** Boats for Ko Bulon Lae currently leave Pak Bara (see below) daily at about 12.30pm (about 1hr; B450). As there's no pier on Bulon Lae, boat arrivals are met by longtails to transfer visitors to shore at School Beach (B50). Boats return from Bulon Lae to Pak Bara at around 9.30am. There are also island-hopping options (see page 401).

## KO LAO LIANG

The beautiful twin islets of **Ko Lao Liang**, with their white-sand beaches, abundant corals and dramatic rock faces, lie to the west of Ko Sukorn and are part of the Mu Ko Phetra National Park. They're deserted apart from a single adventure-sport camp, *Lao Liang Resort* (ⓣ 084 304 4077, ⓦ facebook.com/LaoLiangResort; open Nov to April; B1500) All-in costs at the resort comprise camping in deluxe tents on the beach, three meals, including seafood barbecues, and snorkelling gear; kayak rental, rock-climbing, bouldering and snorkelling tours are extra. The resort offers transfers from Trang for B1600 per person return.

## ACCOMMODATION

**Bulone** ☎ 081 897 9084 or ☎ 086 960 0468, ⌨ bulone-resort.net. Friendly, popular spot in a huge grassy compound under the casuarinas at the north end of the beach. Airy, en-suite stilted bungalows come with large verandas and most have a/c. The restaurant features plenty of vegetarian options and a few Italian favourites. Breakfast included. B3000

**Pansand** ☎ 081 693 3667, ⌨ pansand-resort.com; Trang office at First Andaman Travel on Thanon Wisetkul. The oldest and largest resort on the island, situated on the east-coast beach, where large, smart, peaceful cottages come with verandas, fans, mosquito screens, cold-water bathrooms and plenty of room to breathe. On the beach side of the shady, well-tended grounds, there's a sociable restaurant serving up good seafood and other Thai dishes; boat trips and snorkelling gear are also available. Breakfast included. B1700

# Ko Tarutao National Marine Park

B200 admission fee • ⌨ dnp.go.th

The unspoilt **KO TARUTAO NATIONAL MARINE PARK** is probably the most beautiful of all Thailand's accessible beach destinations. Occupying 1400 square kilometres of the Andaman Sea in Satun province, the park covers 51 mostly uninhabited islands. Site of the park headquarters, the main island, **Ko Tarutao**, offers a variety of government-issue accommodation and things to do, while **Ko Adang** to the west is much more low-key and a springboard to some excellent snorkelling. The port of **Pak Bara** is the main jumping-off point for the park and houses a **national park visitor centre** (☎074 783485), next to the pier, where you can gather information and book a room on Tarutao or Adang before boarding your boat.

The park's forests and seas support an incredible variety of **fauna**: langurs, crab-eating macaques and wild pigs are common on the islands, which also shelter several unique subspecies of squirrel, tree shrew and lesser mouse deer; among the hundred-plus bird species found here, reef egrets and hornbills are regularly seen, while white-bellied sea eagles, frigate birds and pied imperial pigeons are more rarely encountered; and the park is the habitat of about 25 percent of the world's tropical fish species, as well as dugongs, sperm whales, dolphins and a dwindling population of turtles.

The park amenities on Adang, though not on Tarutao, are officially closed to tourists in the monsoon season from mid-May to mid-November (the exact dates vary from year to year). Accommodation is especially likely to get full around the three New Years (Thai, Chinese and Western), when it's best to book national park rooms in advance (see page 39).

## Ko Tarutao

The largest of the national park's islands, **KO TARUTAO** offers the greatest natural variety: mountains covered in semi-evergreen rainforest rise steeply to a high point of 700m; limestone caves and mangrove swamps dot the shoreline; and the west coast is lined with perfect beaches for most of its 26km length. For a different perspective on Ko Tarutao, John Gray's Sea Canoe in Phuket runs multi-day **sea-kayaking** trips that include trips round the island (☎076 254505–6, ⌨ johngray-seacanoe.com).

---

### TRANSPORT TO AND FROM PAK BARA

The main port for Bulon Lae, Tarutao and Lipe is **PAK BARA**, towards the north end of Satun province. **From Trang**, you can book minibus-and-boat packages to all three islands and there are direct share-taxis to Pak Bara (see page 408); otherwise you'll need to take a Satun-bound bus (2hr–2hr 30min) to the inland town of **Langu** (also served by buses from Phuket via Krabi to Satun) and change there to a red songthaew for the 10km hop to the port. There are also direct a/c minibuses **from Hat Yai** (see page 416) Talad Kaset station, while **from Satun**, frequent buses and a/c minibuses make the 50km trip to Langu, where you'll have to change onto a songthaew.

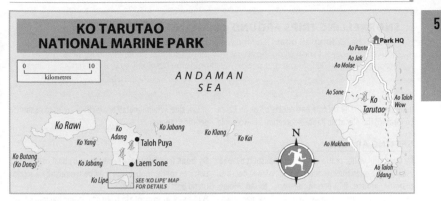

### The west coast

At **Ao Pante**, site of the **park headquarters**, you'll find the only shop on the island, selling basic supplies, as well as a visitor centre. Behind the settlement, the steep, half-hour climb to **To-Boo cliff** is a must, especially at sunset, for the view of the surrounding islands and the crocodile's-head cape at the north end of the bay. A fun ninety-minute trip by boat (B400/boat; contact the visitor centre to book) or kayak can also be made near Ao Pante, up the canal which leads 2km inland from the pier, through a bird-filled mangrove swamp, to **Crocodile Cave** – where you're unlikely to see any of the big snappers, reported sightings being highly dubious.

A half-hour walk south from Ao Pante brings you to the two quiet bays of **Ao Jak** and **Ao Molae**, fringed by coconut palms and filled with fine white sand. Beyond the next headland (a 2hr walk from Ao Pante) lies **Ao Sone** (which gets its name from the casuarina trees that fringe the beach), where a pretty freshwater stream runs past the ranger station at the north end of the bay, a good place for peaceful camping. The main part of the bay is a 3km sweep of flawless sand, with a one-hour trail leading up to **Lu Du Waterfall** at the north end, a ninety-minute trail to **Lo Po Waterfall** in the middle and a **mangrove swamp** at the far south end.

### The east coast

On the east side of the island, **Ao Taloh Wow** is a rocky bay with a ranger station, shop and campsite, connected to Ao Pante by a 12km-long road through old rubber plantations and evergreen forest. Beyond Taloh Wow, a 16km-long trail cuts through the forest to **Ao Taloh Udang**, a sandy bay on the south side where you can pitch a tent. Here the remnants of a penal colony for political prisoners are just visible: the royalist plotters of two failed coup attempts against the recently established constitutional regime – including the author of the first English-Thai dictionary – were imprisoned here in the 1930s before returning to high government posts. The ordinary convicts, who used to be imprisoned here and at Ao Taloh Wow, had a much harsher time, and during World War II, when supplies from the mainland dried up, prisoners and guards ganged together to turn to piracy. This turned into a lucrative business, which was not suppressed until 1946 when the Thai government asked the British in Malaysia to send in three hundred troops. Pirates and smugglers still occasionally hide out in the Tarutao archipelago, but the main problem now is illegal trawlers fishing in national park waters.

### ARRIVAL AND DEPARTURE                                                          KO TARUTAO

**From Pak Bara and Ko Lipe** The speedboat services between Pak Bara and Ko Lipe (see page 411) will usually call in at Ko Tarutao if requested; Tarutao is located about a 30min journey from Pak Bara (B450) and 1hr

**5**

---

### SNORKELLING TRIPS AROUND KO ADANG

You can charter **longtail boats** (and rent snorkels and masks, for B50/day) through the rangers for excellent snorkelling trips to nearby islands such as Ko Rawi and Ko Jabang (around B1500–2500 for up to ten people, depending on how far you want to go).

---

from Lipe (B450). Boats drop passengers off at Ao Pante on Tarutao; the pier at Ao Pante is sometimes inaccessible at low tide, when longtail boats (B50) are used to shuttle people to shore.

### GETTING AROUND

**By truck** The visitor centre can arrange transport by road, usually in an open truck, to several of the island's beaches, charging around B50/person one-way to Ao Molae, around B400 per vehicle to Ao Sone and B600 per vehicle to Ao Taloh Wow.

**By boat** Transfers to the same places by boat cost at least twice as much, though you may be tempted by a round-island boat trip for B3000.

**By kayak or mountain bike** Kayaks and mountain bikes are available at headquarters.

### ACCOMMODATION

**National park accommodation** At park headquarters, the rooms and bungalows (sleeping four people, or available as twin rooms), which are spread over a large, quiet park behind the beach, are for the main part national park standard issue with cold-water bathrooms, but there are also some basic mattress-on-floor four-person rooms in longhouses, sharing bathrooms, as well as a restaurant. There are also bungalows containing en-suite twin rooms and a small restaurant at Ao Molae. HQ $\boxed{B500}$, Ao Molae $\boxed{B600}$

**Camping** There are campsites at Ao Pante, Ao Molae and Ao Taloh Wow. Two-person tents can be rented from Ao Pante for B150/night (plus B50/person for bedding).

## Ko Adang

At **KO ADANG**, a wild, rugged island covered in tropical rainforest 40km west of Ko Tarutao, the park station with its accommodation and restaurant is at **Laem Sone** on the southern shore, where the beach is steep and narrow and backed by a thick canopy of pines. The half-hour climb to **Sha-do** cliff on the steep slope above Laem Sone gives good views over Ko Lipe to the south, while about 2km west along the coast from the park station, a twenty-minute trail leads inland to the small **Pirate Waterfall**.

### ARRIVAL AND DEPARTURE
KO ADANG

**By boat** To get to Ko Adang, hop aboard any boat heading to Ko Lipe (see page 411), from where a transfer to Adang by longtail boat will cost approximately B100–200 per person.

### ACCOMMODATION

**National park accommodation** At the park station at Laem Sone, there are rooms in bamboo longhouses sleeping three, bungalows of various sizes (two–six people), and two/three-person tents can be rented (B225/night plus B50/person for bedding). Rooms $\boxed{B300}$, bungalows $\boxed{B600}$

## Ko Lipe

Home to a population of around a thousand *chao ley*, tiny **KO LIPE**, 2km south of Ko Adang, is something of a frontier maverick, attracting ever more travellers with one dazzling beach, over fifty private bungalow resorts and a rough-and-ready atmosphere. It's technically a part of Ko Tarutao National Marine Park, but the authorities seem to have given up on the island and don't collect an admission fee from visitors. A small, flat triangle, Lipe is covered in coconut plantations and supports a school and a health centre in the village on the eastern side. By rights, such a settlement should never have been allowed to develop within the national park boundaries, but the *chao ley* on Lipe are well entrenched: Satun's governor forced the community to move here from Phuket and Ko Lanta between the world wars, to reinforce the island's Thai character and prevent the British rulers of Malaya from laying claim to it.

More recently, a huge, diverse influx of tourists – Westerners, Thais, Chinese and Malaysians, families and backpackers – has been enticed here by the gorgeous beach of **Hat Pattaya**, a shining crescent of squeaky-soft white sand with an offshore reef to explore on its eastern side, as well as by the relaxed, anything-goes atmosphere and mellow nightlife. Many of Lipe's *chao ley* have now sold their beachfront land to Thai–Chinese speculators from the mainland, who have increased the island's capacity to over two thousand guest rooms; with the money earned, the *chao ley* have bought the scores of longtail boats that clog up the bay at Hat Pattaya. Lipe's main drag is **Walking Street**, a paved path lined with tourist businesses between the eastern end of Hat Pattaya and the south end of the village, which lies on east-facing **Sunrise**, an exposed, largely featureless beach that gives access to some good snorkelling around Ko Gra; a few other narrow roads also radiate out from the village. A track runs from *Pattaya Song Resort* at the west end of Pattaya across to **Sunset** beach, a shady, attractive spot with good views of Ko Adang, in around ten minutes.

## ARRIVAL AND DEPARTURE                                    KO LIPE

As well as being one of the hubs for island-hopping boats (see page 401), Ko Lipe is served by **speedboats** from Pak Bara in the north of Satun province and from the Malaysian island of Langkawi. However, services to Lipe seem to change by the year, due to competition between the boat companies and local politicking; in the past, there have been boats from Thammalang near Satun town (see page 414), which may or may not resurface; for up-to-date **transport information**, contact Koh Lipe Thailand (see below). There is no pier on Lipe, so boats usually anchor at a platform off Hat Pattaya, where they're met by **longtails** (B50–100/person to any beach on Lipe); sometimes speedboats will just run ashore at Pattaya, leaving you to jump off onto the beach; in low season, all

boats tend to stop at Sunrise Beach, where there's shelter from the southwest monsoon, leaving you with a longtail trip to any of the beaches.

**Via Pak Bara** Several companies run speedboats (plus occasional ferries) between Pak Bara (see page 408) and Ko Lipe in high season (usually at 11.30am & 3.30pm; 1hr 30min; B750). In the rainy season, there's at least one crossing a day, usually heading out at 11.30am.

**Via Langkawi** Boats operate between Ko Lipe and Langkawi, the large Malaysian island situated to the southeast, several times a day in high season (1hr; B1000–1400). During the season, a Thai immigration post is set up at the far east end of Lipe's Hat Pattaya to cover this route.

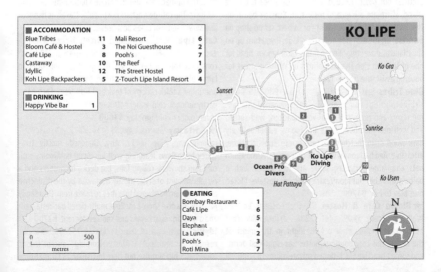

| **ACCOMMODATION** | | | |
|---|---|---|---|
| Blue Tribes | 11 | Mali Resort | 6 |
| Bloom Café & Hostel | 3 | The Noi Guesthouse | 2 |
| Café Lipe | 8 | Pooh's | 7 |
| Castaway | 10 | The Reef | 1 |
| Idyllic | 12 | The Street Hostel | 9 |
| Koh Lipe Backpackers | 5 | Z-Touch Lipe Island Resort | 4 |

| **DRINKING** | |
|---|---|
| Happy Vibe Bar | 1 |

| **EATING** | |
|---|---|
| Bombay Restaurant | 1 |
| Café Lipe | 6 |
| Daya | 5 |
| Elephant | 4 |
| La Luna | 2 |
| Pooh's | 3 |
| Roti Mina | 7 |

KO LIPE

Ko Gra

Sunset

Village

Sunrise

Ko Lipe Diving

Ocean Pro Divers

Hat Pattaya

Ko Usen

N

0    500
metres

**5**

## SNORKELLING AND DIVING AROUND KO LIPE

The prime **diving and snorkelling sites** near Ko Lipe are around Ko Adang, Ko Rawi and Ko Dong, just to the north and west in Ko Tarutao National Marine Park, where encounters with reef and even whale sharks, dolphins and stingrays are not uncommon. Further afield to the south, advanced divers head for Eight Mile Rock, a pinnacle that rises to about 14m from the surface, with soft corals, mantas, leopard and whale sharks. A handful of dive shops operate on Lipe, and there are dozens of places offering snorkelling day-trips on *chao ley* longtail boats; snorkellers are liable to pay the park admission fee of B200, though some longtail captains will try to dodge the park rangers.

**Koh Lipe Thailand** See below. This travel agent offers snorkelling day-trips to the best sites around the islands on the west side of Ko Adang for B550–650/person, including lunch and full snorkelling equipment, or a sunset trip for B450.

**Ko Lipe Diving** On Walking Street between Sunrise and Hat Pattaya ☎087 622 6204, ⓦkolipediving. com. Well-regarded SSI dive centre offering daily trips (B2800 for two dives) and SSI courses (B14,500 for the

Open Water; for PADI add B1500). Also runs snorkelling trips (B1000).

**Ocean Pro Divers** On Pattaya beach, just east of the main pier ☎089 733 8068, ⓦoceanprodivers. com. Five-Star PADI centre offering daily trips (B3000, including equipment rental and National Marine Park diving fees, for two dives) and PADI courses (B14,500 for the Open Water). Also offers diving and accommodation packages for divers.

## INFORMATION

**Koh Lipe Thailand** The best travel agent and source of information on the island is Koh Lipe Thailand (Boi's Travel; ☎089 464 5854 or ☎081 541 4489, ⓦkohlipethailand. com or ⓦthaibeachtravellers.com), which currently has two outlets on Walking Street between Hat Pattaya and the village, with the main, year-round one hard by the beach (the second, seasonal, shop, further inland towards *Pooh's*, has a book exchange). On offer are all manner of

transport tickets (including a/c minibuses in high season to Penang and other popular mainland destinations) plus accommodation bookings (including on the websites).

**Currency exchange** There are currently no ATMs on Ko Lipe (the nearest is in Pak Bara), but Koh Lipe Thailand, for instance, offers currency exchange and cash advances.

**Tourist police** Behind the immigration post at the far east end of Hat Pattaya ☎1155.

## ACCOMMODATION

The majority of Lipe's bungalows are on **Hat Pattaya**, the prettiest but most crowded and expensive beach on the island. There are a bunch of resorts on **Sunset** beach on the northwest side, while twenty or so have set up shop on **Sunrise**, on the east side near the village. If you turn up on the island and are struggling to find a vacant room, head for one of the Koh Lipe Thailand offices on Walking Street for booking assistance (see above).

**Blue Tribes** East end of Hat Pattaya ☎080 546 9464, ⓦbluetribeslipe.com; map p.411. Congenial, Italian-run resort and restaurant with very spacious, well-spread and well-designed bungalows and rooms, either in lovely dark wood or in thatched white concrete, sporting large, attractive tiled bathrooms with hot showers, fans, mosquito nets and large verandas; some are two-storey with a balcony and chill-out room/extra bedroom upstairs. Closed mid-May to July. B1700

★ **Bloom Café & Hostel** On the eastern end of Walking Street ☎095 440 2288, ⓦfacebook.com/ bloom.cafe.hostel; map p.411. Right in the midst of the action, this cosy boutique hostel has eight-bed dorms and some attractive black-tinged private rooms (B1100), all

with plush mattresses, dark wooden bed stands and floor tiles. The immaculate and chic shared bathrooms have rain showers. The cafe downstairs is a popular travellers hangout and serves some of Lipe's best brews. B600

**Café Lipe** West of Walking Street, central Pattaya ☎086 969 9472, ⓦcafe-lipe.com; map p.411. Eco-conscious, solar-powered place in a great location, offering large, old-style bamboo bungalows that are nicely spaced out under a thick canopy of teak and fruit trees. Each has a partly outdoor, cold-water bathroom, fan and mosquito net. Three-night minimum stay. B1000

★ **Castaway** Sunrise ☎083 138 7472, ⓦcastaway-resorts.com; map p.411. Airy, thatched, mostly two-storey bungalows featuring well-equipped bathrooms with cold rain showers, ceiling fans, big decks, hammocks and a certain amount of style, mostly bestowed by the distinctive red Indonesian hardwood that they're made from. On a sandy patch with a dive shop, a mellow, multi-tiered bar-restaurant and a massage spa; kayaks and snorkels for rent. B2700

**Idyllic** South end of Sunrise ☎074 750399, ⓦidyllic resort.com; map p.411. This welcoming "concept resort" comes as a big surprise out here in Thailand's far maritime corner, with its angular contemporary architecture in white, grey and wood. Set in an attractive garden, the minimalist rooms boast huge windows, a/c, hot outdoor rain showers, minibars and nice touches such as sun hats for guests' use. There are two pools – one infinity-edged and beachside, with a swim-up bar, the other with a Jacuzzi – as well as kayaks and other watersports. Breakfast included. B6000

**Koh Lipe Backpackers** West end of Hat Pattaya Ⓦkohlipebackpackers.com; map p.411. Part of Davy Jones' Locker diving centre (free stays included with a PADI course), this place offers two eight-bed dorms in plain concrete rooms with thick mattresses, hot showers and lockers, as well as plain, a/c double bedrooms with hot-water bathrooms. Wi-fi in the lobby. Dorms B500, doubles B1200

**Mali Resort** Towards the west end of Hat Pattaya ☏077 033020, Ⓦmaliresorts.com/koh-lipe/pattaya-beach; map p.411. At this shady, well-appointed luxury resort, go for one of the Balinese bungalows if you can (from B6800), thatched, dark-wood affairs with big French windows, sizeable verandas and open-air bathrooms, which are spread out around a lovely lawn and beach bar. Breakfast included. B4300

**The Noi Guesthouse** ☏094 495 4953, Ⓦfacebook. com/noiguesthouse; map p.411. Comfortable en-suite rooms with naked walls and wooden furnishings. Most rooms have little balconies facing the road that are set over the annexed restaurant, where guest can enjoy the rich included breakfast. The friendly staff are more than happy to pick up guests from the docks. B2000

**Pooh's** On Walking Street between Sunrise and Hat Pattaya ☏074 750345, Ⓦfacebook.com/poohbar

kohlipe; map p.411. Well inland behind the popular restaurant, but a good, functional choice if you get stuck for somewhere to stay. The eight, concrete single-storey rooms have small terraces, a/c, hot showers and TVs, and there's a dive centre. Breakfast included. B1800

**The Reef** In the village ☏82 733 7034, Ⓦthereef kohlipe.com; map p.411. Boutique guesthouse with a selection of homely, spacious a/c rooms, ranging from smart budget singles (B950), to charming family suites featuring wooden mezzanines (B2400) or cosy, large wooden private balconies (B3000). It's a quieter option, slightly removed from the action, but still within walking distance of all the main beaches. Breakfast included. B1400

**The Street Hostel** On Walking Street ☏099 125 9146, Ⓦthestreethostels.com; map p.411. Housed in a metallic net-covered building that opens with an arty loft filled with wooden frames, hanging bulbs and industrial chic furniture, this is a comfortable, clean and modern hostel. The white-tinged a/c rooms have private pods – some with double beds for couples (B1000) – equipped with privacy curtains, plugs and reading lights. The shared bathrooms are squeaky clean; there's free coffee and tea and a fridge for guests' house. B600

**Z-Touch Lipe Island Resort** On the West end of Hat Pattaya ☏086 292 8204, Ⓦztouchresort.com; map p.411. Clustered around gardens that face a relatively boat-free stretch of beach, the rooms, villas and cottages here have en-suite bathrooms and spacious verandas. There's an inviting free-form swimming pool; breakfast is included. B2800

## EATING AND DRINKING

There are a couple of beach bars on Sunset, but the east end of Pattaya has the biggest concentration, with low candlelit tables and cushions sprawled on the sand, fire shows and names like *Peace and Love*.

**Bombay Restaurant** On Walking Street ☏094 810 1872, Ⓦbit.ly/BombayRestaurant; map p.411. Authentic Indian food served with care and attention by the affable owner. The naan bread is particularly good, and a meal will set you back around B400. Daily 10am–10pm.

**Café Lipe** West of Walking Street, central Pattaya (see page 411); map p.411. Behind a thick screen of foliage this resort restaurant serves up decent veggie choices among its inexpensive Thai dishes, sandwiches and espressos, as well as home-made bread, fruit juices and muesli. Daily 7am–5pm.

**Daya** West end of Hat Pattaya (see page 411); map p.411. One of the most popular of half a dozen restaurants that lay out candlelit tables and seafood barbecues on the beach at night. It also offers a long menu of mostly Thai dishes, such as prawn tempura (B160), lots of tofu options for vegetarians, Thai desserts and Western breakfasts. Daily 7am–11pm.

**Elephant** Walking Street, 100m inland from Pattaya ☏088 046 8234, Ⓦfacebook.com/ElephantKohLipe; map p.411. Mellow restaurant and secondhand bookshop, where you can tuck into delicious chicken sandwiches (B180) and burgers made with Australian beef, as well as salads, breakfasts and espressos. Daily 8am–8pm.

**Happy Vibe Bar** On Sunrise beach ☏084 807 3781, Ⓦbit.ly/HappyVibe; map p.411. Welcoming Dutch-owned thatch-and-bamboo beach bar festooned with hand-painted driftwood signs. They serve cocktails (from B150), coffee and fresh fruit shakes (B120). There's a cosy upstairs veranda, and wooden tables and loungers spilling out on to the sand – a good reminder of Lipe's low-key yesterdays. Daily 10am–late.

**La Luna** ☏082 286 1910, Ⓦfacebook.com/laluna kohlipe; map p.411. An appreciated Italian restaurant set in the hotel of the same name, with an attractive wooden-decked sala and bar. Pizzas (from B200) are crunchy, and the ravioli, bruschettas and tiramisu taste authentic. A meal will set you back around B1000. Daily 6pm–11pm.

**Pooh's** On Walking Street between Sunrise and Hat Pattaya (see page 411) ☏087 392 3838, Ⓦfacebook.

**5**

com/poohbarkohlipe; map p.411. This well-run and welcoming bar-restaurant-bakery is a long-standing institution and a hive of activity, with nightly movies. Offers tasty Thai food, including chicken with cashew nuts (B150) and vegetarian dishes, as well as sandwiches, cakes, evening barbecues, DJs and live music, plus a wide choice of breakfasts and espresso coffees. Daily roughly 8.30am–10.45pm.

**Roti Mina** Walking Street, about 50m inland from Hat Pattaya on the right-hand side ☎081 397 7018; map p.411. This place serves all manner of outlandish *roti* pancakes – raisin and cheese *roti*, anyone? – as well as the more familiar varieties with curry (B100) or banana. Also does some classic southern and central Thai dishes. Daily 7am–10pm.

# Satun town

Nestling in the last wedge of Thailand's west coast, the remote town of **SATUN** is served by just one road, Highway 406, which approaches through forbidding karst outcrops. Set in a green valley bordered by limestone hills, the town is leafy and relaxing but not especially interesting, except during its small version of the Vegetarian Festival (see page 320) and its International Kite Festival at the end of February. There's little reason to come here apart from the boat service to and from Langkawi in Malaysia.

## National Museum

Soi 5, Thanon Satun Thani, on the north side of the centre • Wed–Sun 9am–4pm • B30

The **National Museum** has a memorable setting in the graceful **Kuden Mansion**, which was built in British colonial style, with some Thai and Malay features, by craftsmen from Penang, and inaugurated in 1902 as the Satun governor's official residence. The exhibits and audiovisuals in English have a distinctive anthropological tone, but are diverting enough, notably concerning Thai Muslims, the *chao ley* on Ko Lipe, and the **Sakai**, a dwindling band of nomadic hunter-gatherers who still live in the jungle of southern Thailand.

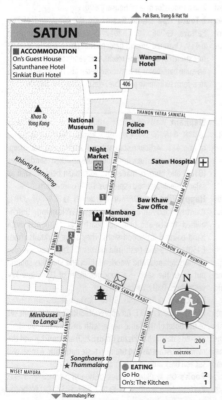

### ARRIVAL AND DEPARTURE
### SATUN TOWN

**By bus** Satun's bus station is far to the southeast of the centre on the bypass, but Trang buses usually do a tour of the town centre, stopping, for example, near *On's* on Thanon Bureewanit; incoming buses from Phuket via Krabi, Trang and Langu will set you down on Thanon Satun Thani by the *Wangmai* hotel; and you can book long-distance tickets in advance at the central Baw Khaw Saw office on Thanon Hatthakam Sueksa (for the long journey to Bangkok, it's worth shelling out a bit extra for the VIP buses that depart around 3–4pm).

Destinations Bangkok (4 daily; 16hr); Phuket (4 daily; 8hr); Trang (hourly; 2hr 30min–3hr).

**By minibus** A/c minibuses to Langu congregate on Thanon Sulakanukul.

**By ferry** There are ferries from nearby Thammalang pier to Langkawi in Malaysia (see page 415).

## CROSSING INTO MALAYSIA FROM SATUN

Two or three ferry boats a day cross from Thammalang to the Malaysian island of **Langkawi** (☎074 725294, ⓦlangkawi-ferry.com; 1hr 15min; B300). The journey from Satun town to Thammalang is covered by orange songthaews (roughly every 30min; B40) from near the 7-Eleven supermarket on Thanon Sulakanukul, as well as chartered tuk-tuks (B150) and motorcycle taxis (B60–70).

It's also possible to take an a/c minibus to Malaysia's **Kangar** (which has bus connections to Penang and Kuala Lumpur) through the Wang Kelian border and Thale Ban National Park (B400; 1 daily in the morning; about 2hr) – contact On Kongnual (see below) to book tickets.

### GETTING AROUND

**By motorbike or car** On Kongnual (see below) offers   motorbike (B250–300/day) and car rental (B1000–1500/day).

### INFORMATION

**On Kongnual** 36 Thanon Bureewanit ☎074 724133 or   restaurant, *On's: The Kitchen*, On Kongnual dispenses helpful
☎081 097 9783, ✉onmarch13@hotmail.com. From her   tourist information and sells all kinds of transport tickets.

### ACCOMMODATION

**On's Guest House** 36 Thanon Bureewanit ☎074 724133 or ☎081 097 9783, ✉onmarch13@hotmail. com; map p.414. A variety of rooms in two opposite modern, Sino-Portuguese-style buildings with wooden shutters and coloured-glass windows, one above *On's: The Kitchen*. There's a fan-cooled dorm but most have a/c, fridges and satellite TV; bathrooms with hot showers are shared but plentiful. Dorms B300, doubles B500

**Satunthanee Hotel** Thanon Satun Thani ☎074 711010; map p.414. This centrally placed, good-value,

traditional Chinese hotel offers battered but clean rooms with small bathrooms and TVs, though it suffers from noise from the road and the mosque. Fan B300, a/c B400

**Sinkiat Buri Hotel** 50 Thanon Apainuratrumluk ☎074 721055–8, ⓦsinkiathotel.com; map p.414. Higher-end hotel in Satun, offering a collection of large bedrooms in a minimalist style with lots of dark wood, a/c, rain showers, fridges, flat-screen TVs and good views over the surrounding countryside from the upper floors. Breakfast included. B1500

### EATING AND DRINKING

Satun has a slim choice of restaurants, but for a meal in the evening you can't do much better than the lively and popular night market, north of the centre on the west side of Thanon Satun Thani.

**Go Ho** Thanon Saman Pradit, opposite the Chinese temple ☎074 711018; map p.414. A cheap, busy, friendly restaurant with leafy pavement tables that serves tasty Thai and Chinese food, including plenty of seafood (according to market price), salads and southern specialities such as *kaeng som* (B120). Mon–Sat 3pm–midnight.

**On's: The Kitchen** 36 Thanon Bureewanit ☎074 724133 or ☎081 097 9783; map p.414. Very tasty Thai cuisine, including southern specialities, some interesting fish dishes and handy set menus, along the likes of green curry with prawn patties (*thawt man kung*) and rice for B120. Also offers a wide array of Western food, including good breakfasts, jacket potatoes, pies and espresso coffees. (On's bar, a couple of doors away, *The Living Room*, stays open late, depending on customers.) Daily 8am–10pm.

# Phattalung

The friendly town of **Phattalung**, strewn below the looming limestone boulder housing the **Tham Malai Caves**, sees very few visitors despite its excellent sites. The caves, a 2.5km walk north of the train station along Apaiborirak Soi 1 and up a steep staircase, are creepy and filled with bats, but the main draw here is the stunning lotus-filled **Thale Noi**, 16km to the northeast. The smallest extension of Songkhla Lake is Thailand's biggest waterfowl reserve, supporting more than 180 species of protected local and migratory birds. Boats can be chartered (RM500/hour) in Baan Thale Noi, but with your own vehicle, you can drive along scenic backroads towards the **Pak Pra Canal**, where local fishermen still use stilted Chinese fishing nets (*yor yak* in Thai).

**5**

## ARRIVAL AND DEPARTURE                                    PHATTALUNG

**By train** Phattalung is on the main Northern line, with at least five daily sleeper trains to Bangkok (15hr), and five daily to Hat Yai (3hr).

**By bus** The bus station is inconveniently located 6km out of the centre of Phattalung, off Route 41 (B40 one-way by motorbike taxi from the train station). From here, minivans travel to Baan Thale Noi roughly every 30 minutes (B70). All services dwindle after 6pm. Destinations Bangkok (at least 7 daily; 13hr); Hat Yai (every 15min; 3hr); Phuket (at least 6 daily, with stops in Trang and Krabi; 6/7hr); Songkhla (hourly; 2hr); Surat Thani (half-hourly; 3hr30min); Trang (half-hourly; 1hr).

## ACCOMMODATION

**Phattalung Thai Hotel** 14 Dissarasakarin Rd ☎074 611636. The cheapest accommodation in town is home to a clutch of old yet clean en-suite guestrooms, each with televisions and large windows, some with a/c (B500). A convenient option; it's within easy walking distance of the train station. **B300**

# Hat Yai & Songkhla

Regardless of the volatile situation in the south (see page 396), travelling to **HAT YAI**, the biggest city in the region and a major transport axis, is possible and relatively safe; check up-to-date information before setting off though. Besides a lively night market and the shopping streets around central thoroughfare Thanon Sanehanusorn, the Phra Maha Chedi Tripob Trimongkol, set on a hilltop in the south of town and better-known as the **Stainless Steel Temple**, is worth a visit for its unique futuristic design, especially when illuminated after sunset. It's about B300 in a taxi, including a short wait. For beaches and a livelier atmosphere, you are better off moving to **SONGKHLA**, 30km northeast of Hat Yai.

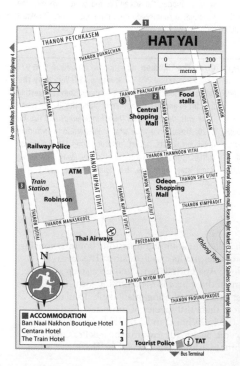

## Songkhla

Set on a narrow peninsula separating the Gulf of Thailand from the coastal lake of the same name, breezy **Songkhla**, with accessible beaches and a Sino-Portuguese Old Town, makes for a rewarding stop. The main beach, **Samila**, has a popular **Golden Mermaid Statue** perched on the easternmost tip of the cape. Swimming is possible, but **Chalathat Beach** directly to the south is quieter. The atmospheric **Old Town** extends around the **City Pillar Shrine**, on the eastern side of Songhkla's peninsula. Nakhorn Nok, Nakhorn Nai and Nang Ngam roads are filled with street art and relaxed shop house cafés where Chinese-Thais dish up the best of their town's mixed culinary heritage.

## ARRIVAL AND DEPARTURE       HAT YAI

**Travel agency** The helpful Cathay Tour (93/1 Thanon Niphat Uthit 2 ☎074 235044, ⊕ cathaytourthailand. com), a travel agency on the ground floor of the guesthouse of the same name, handles onward

## CROSSING INTO MALAYSIA FROM HAT YAI

Two daily trains leave Hat Yai station at 7.30am and 13.05pm to Padang Basar KTM station in Malaysia (☎603 2267 1200, ⌨ktmb.com.my/ktmb_ui; 30min; B70), where there is an immigration checkpoint. Malaysian trains proceed to Butterworth (for Penang; RM10.20), departing roughly hourly from 6am to 9.30pm; at least five high-speed trains also leave daily to Kuala Lumpur (4/5hr; from RM56).

You can also reach Padang Besar using local buses (roughly every 30min; B30) and a/c minivans (B100): both leave from Hat Yai's train station or the clock tower and will drop you opposite the Thai immigration checkpoint. From there, it's a 500m walk to the Malaysian border, which is about 300m to the left of Padang Besar's train station.

As another option, direct a/c minibuses to Penang (several daily; 5hr; B500/700) can be booked from most travel agents in Hat Yai's Thanon Sanehanusorn, and use the Sadao/Bukit Kayu Hitam border, connecting to Malaysia's North-South Expressway E1.

flight, bus, share-taxi, a/c minibus and ferry bookings, both within Thailand and into Malaysia, as well as offering car and motorbike rental.

**By plane** Situated about 5km south of town, Hat Yai airport is connected to the downtown area by a/c minibuses (B80) and has Avis (☎02 251 1131, ⌨avisthailand.com) and Budget (☎074 227268, ⌨budget.co.th) car rental desks.

**By train** The train station is on the west side of the centre at the end of Thanon Thamnoon Vithi, and has useful late

afternoon departures to Bangkok, stopping in Surat Thani, Chumpon and Hua Hin.

**By bus or minibus** Hat Yai bus terminal is southeast of the centre on Thanon Kanchanawanit, while the a/c minibus terminal at Talat Kaset is about 5km west of town, both leaving you with a songthaew ride to the centre. Minibuses for Songkhla depart from the main bus terminal and the clock tower until about 7pm and cost B30, returning from the Anuban Songkhla School on Ramwithi Road, just south of Songkhla's clock tower.

### INFORMATION

**Tourist information** The TAT office is at 1/1 Soi 2, Thanon Niphat Uthit 3 (daily 8.30am–4.30pm; ☎074 243747, ✉tatsgkhl@tat.or.th).

**Tourist police** Thanon Niphat Uthit 3, near the TAT office ☎074 246733 or ☎1155.

### ACCOMMODATION

**Baan Nai Nakhon Boutique Hotel** 166 Nang Ngam Rd, Songkhla ☎095 438 9323, ⌨facebook.com/baannainakhon; map p.416. Absorb Songkhla's old town vibe in these dark crimson-tinged, Sino-Thai-inspired wooden-floored rooms, equipped with plush queen beds, handmade quilts, and en-suite bathrooms with rain showers. Breakfast included. __B1500__

**Centara Hotel** 3 Thanon Sanehanusorn ☎074 352222, ⌨centarahotelsresorts.com; map p.416. Luxury hotel in a central location next to the Central Department Store,

featuring contemporary-styled rooms with a spa, fitness centre, sauna, swimming pool and Thai, Chinese and Japanese food at its several restaurants. __B3000__

**The Train Hotel** Hat Yay Railway Station ☎074 221 133–35, ⌨bit.ly/TrainHotel; map p.416. Modern bunk bed dorms and spacious, smart en-suite rooms located inside of Hat Yai station, right next to the ticket booth. It's cleaner than most nearby budget hotels and convenient for early departures, but it gets noisy when trains come and go late at night or early in the morning. Dorms __B300__, doubles __B700__

MURALS

# Contexts

# History

Thailand's history is complex and fascinating, but what follows can be only a brief account of the major events in the country's past. For more detailed coverage, read David Wyatt's excellent *Thailand: A Short History* (see page 437).

## Early history

The region's first distinctive civilization, **Dvaravati**, which encompassed city-states in central and northern Thailand, was established around two thousand years ago by an Austroasiatic-speaking people known as the Mon. One of its mainstays was Theravada Buddhism, which had probably been introduced to Thailand during the third century BC by Indian missionaries. In the eighth century, peninsular Thailand to the south of Dvaravati came under the control of **Srivijaya**, a Mahayana Buddhist state centred on Sumatra, which had strong ties with India.

From the ninth century onwards, both Dvaravati and Srivijaya Thailand succumbed to invading **Khmers** from Cambodia, who took control of northeastern, central and peninsular Thailand. They ruled from Angkor and left dozens of spectacular temple complexes throughout the region. By the thirteenth century, however, the Khmers had overreached themselves and were in no position to resist the onslaught of a vibrant new force in Southeast Asia: the **Thais**. The earliest traceable history of the Thai people picks them up in southern China around the fifth century AD, when they were squeezed by Chinese and Vietnamese expansionism into sparsely inhabited northeastern Laos. Their first significant entry into what is now Thailand seems to have happened in the north, where, some time after the seventh century, the Thais formed a state known as Yonok. Theravada Buddhism spread to Yonok via Dvaravati around the end of the tenth century, which served not only to unify the Thais themselves, but also to link them to the wider community of Buddhists.

By the end of the twelfth century, they formed the majority of the population in Thailand, then under the control of the Khmer empire. The Khmers' main outpost, at Lopburi, was by this time regarded as the administrative capital of a land called "Syam".

## Sukhothai

Some time around 1238, Thais in the upper Chao Phraya valley captured the main Khmer outpost in the region at **Sukhothai** and established a kingdom there. When the young Ramkhamhaeng came to the throne around 1278, he seized control of much of the Chao Phraya valley, and over the next twenty years gained the submission of most of Thailand under a complex system of tribute-giving and protection – the political system that persisted in Thailand until the end of the nineteenth century.

Although the kingdom of Sukhothai extended Thai control over a vast area, its greatest contribution to the Thais' development was at home, in cultural and political matters. A famous inscription by Ramkhamhaeng, now housed in the Bangkok National Museum, describes a prosperous era of benevolent rule, and it is generally agreed that Ramkhamhaeng ruled justly according to Theravada Buddhist doctrine. A

| **6800 BC** | **3rd century BC** | **6th–9th centuries AD** |
| --- | --- | --- |
| Date of earliest pottery found in Thailand | Theravada Buddhism probably first enters Thailand | Dvaravati civilization flourishes |

further sign of the Thais' growing self-confidence was the invention of a new script to make their tonal language understood by the non-Thai inhabitants of the land.

## Ayutthaya

After the death of Ramkhamhaeng around 1299, however, Sukhothai's power waned, and **Ayutthaya** became the most powerful Thai city-state. Soon after founding the city in 1351, the ambitious King Ramathibodi united the principalities of the lower Chao Phraya valley, which had formed the western provinces of the Khmer empire. When he recruited his bureaucracy from the urban elite of Lopburi, Ramathibodi set the style of government at Ayutthaya, elements of which persist to the present day. The elaborate etiquette, language and rituals of Angkor were adopted, and, most importantly, so was the concept of the ruler as *devaraja* (divine king).

The site chosen by Ramathibodi for an international port was the best in the region, and so began Ayutthaya's rise to prosperity, based on exploiting the upswing in trade in the middle of the fourteenth century along the routes between India and China. By 1540, Ayutthaya held sway over most of the area of modern-day Thailand. Despite a 1568 invasion by the Burmese, which led to twenty years of foreign rule, Ayutthaya made a spectacular comeback, and in the seventeenth century its foreign trade boomed. In 1511, the Portuguese had become the first Western power to trade with Ayutthaya, while a treaty with Spain in 1598 was followed by similar agreements with Holland and England in 1608 and 1612 respectively. European merchants flocked to Thailand, not only to buy Thai products, but also for the Chinese and Japanese goods on sale there.

In the mid-eighteenth century, however, the rumbling in the Burmese jungle to the north began to make itself heard again. After an unsuccessful siege in 1760, February 1766 saw the **Burmese** descend upon the city for the last time. The Thais held out for over a year but, finally, in April 1767, the city was taken. The Burmese savagely razed everything to the ground, led off tens of thousands of prisoners to Myanmar and abandoned the city to the jungle.

## From Taksin to Rama III

Out of this lawless mess emerged **Phraya Taksin**, a charismatic general, who was crowned king in December 1768 at his new capital of **Thonburi**, on the opposite bank of the river from modern-day Bangkok. Within two years, he had restored all of Ayutthaya's territories and, by the end of the next decade, had brought Cambodia and much of Laos under Thai control.

However, by 1779 all was not well with the king. Taksin was becoming increasingly irrational and sadistic, and in March 1782 he was ousted in a coup. Chao Phraya Chakri, Taksin's military commander, was invited to take power and had Taksin executed.

With the support of the Ayutthayan aristocracy, Chakri – reigning as **Rama I** (1782–1809) – set about consolidating the Thai kingdom. His first act was to move the capital across the river to what we know as Bangkok, on the more defensible east bank. Borrowing from the layout of Ayutthaya, he built a new royal palace and impressive monasteries in the area of Ratanakosin within a defensive ring of two (later expanded to three) canals. In the palace temple, Wat Phra Kaeo, he enshrined the talismanic Emerald Buddha, which

| 1278 | 1351 | 1511 | 1767 |
|---|---|---|---|
| Ramkhamhaeng "the Great" comes to the throne of Sukhothai | Ramathibodi founds Ayutthaya | The first Western power, Portugal, begins trading with Ayutthaya | Ayutthaya is razed to the ground by the Burmese |

he had snatched during his campaigns in Laos. Trade with China revived, and the style of government was put on a more modern footing: while retaining many of the features of a *devaraja*, he shared more responsibility with his courtiers, as a first among equals.

The peaceful accession of Rama I's son as **Rama II** (1809–24) signalled the establishment of the Chakri dynasty, which is still in place today. This Second Reign is best remembered as a fertile period for Thai literature; indeed, Rama II himself is remembered as a famous poet.

By the reign of **Rama III** (1824–51), the Thais were starting to get alarmed by British colonialism in the region. In 1826, Rama III was obliged to sign the Burney Treaty, a limited trade agreement with the British, by which the Thais won some political security in return for reducing their taxes on goods passing through Bangkok.

## Mongkut and Chulalongkorn

Rama IV, commonly known to foreigners as **Mongkut** (in Thai, *Phra Chom Klao*; 1851–68), had been a Buddhist monk for 27 years when he succeeded his brother. But far from leading a cloistered life, Mongkut had travelled widely throughout Thailand, and had taken an interest in Western learning, studying English, Latin and the sciences. Realizing that Thailand would be unable to resist the military might of the British, the king reduced import and export taxes, allowed British subjects to live and own land in Thailand and granted them freedom of trade under the Bowring Treaty. Within a decade, similar agreements had been signed with France, the United States and a score of other nations. Thus, by skilful diplomacy the king avoided a close relationship with just one power, which could easily have led to Thailand's annexation.

Mongkut's son, **Chulalongkorn**, took the throne as Rama V (1868–1910) at the age of only fifteen, but was well prepared by an education which mixed traditional Thai and modern Western elements – provided by Mrs Anna Leonowens, subject of *The King and I*. One of his first acts was to scrap the custom by which subjects were required to prostrate themselves in the presence of the king. In the 1880s, he began to restructure the government to meet the country's needs, setting up a host of departments – for education, public health, the army and the like – and bringing in scores of foreign advisors to help with everything from foreign affairs to railway lines.

Throughout this period, however, the Western powers maintained their pressure on the region. The most serious threat to Thai sovereignty was the Franco-Siamese Crisis of 1893, which culminated in the French sending gunboats up the Chao Phraya River to Bangkok. Flouting numerous international laws, France claimed control over Laos and made other outrageous demands, which Chulalongkorn had no option but to agree to. During the course of his reign, the country ceded control over huge areas of tributary states, and forewent large sums of tax revenue in order to preserve its independence. However, by Chulalongkorn's death in 1910, the frontiers were fixed as they are today.

## The end of absolute monarchy and World War II

Chulalongkorn was succeeded by a flamboyant, British-educated prince, **Vajiravudh** (Rama VI, 1910–25), and by the time the young and inexperienced **Prajadhipok** – 76th child of Chulalongkorn – was catapulted to the throne as Rama VII (1925–

| 1782 | 1893 | 1932 |
| --- | --- | --- |
| A grandiose new capital, Bangkok, is established, modelled on Ayutthaya | The Franco-Siamese Crisis obliges Thailand to give up its claims to Laos and Cambodia | A coup brings the end of the absolute monarchy and introduces Thailand's first constitution |

35), Vajiravudh's extravagance had created severe financial problems, which were exacerbated by the onset of the Great Depression.

On June 24, 1932, a small group of middle-ranking officials, dissatisfied with the injustices of monarchical government and led by a lawyer, **Pridi Phanomyong**, and an army major, Luang Phibunsongkhram (**Phibun**), staged a coup with only a handful of troops. Prajadhipok weakly submitted to the conspirators, and a hundred and fifty years of **absolute monarchy** in Bangkok came to a sudden end. The king was sidelined to a position of symbolic significance, and in 1935 he abdicated in favour of his ten-year-old nephew, Ananda, then a schoolboy living in Switzerland.

Phibun emerged as prime minister after the decisive elections of 1938, and a year later officially renamed the country Thailand ("Land of the Free") – Siam, it was argued, was a name bestowed by external forces, and the new title made it clear that the country belonged to the Thais rather than the economically dominant Chinese.

The Thais were dragged into **World War II** on December 8, 1941, when, almost at the same time as the assault on Pearl Harbor, the Japanese invaded the east coast of peninsular Thailand, with their sights set on Singapore to the south. The Thais resisted for a few hours, but realizing that the position was hopeless, Phibun quickly ordered a ceasefire.

The Thai government concluded a military alliance with Japan and declared war against the United States and Great Britain in January 1942, probably in the belief that the Japanese would win. However, the Thai minister in Washington, Seni Pramoj, refused to deliver the declaration of war against the US, and, in cooperation with the Americans, began organizing a resistance movement called Seri Thai. Pridi Phanomyong, now acting as regent to the young king, secretly coordinated the movement, smuggling in American agents and housing them in Bangkok. By 1944, Japan's defeat looked likely, and in July, Phibun, who had been most closely associated with them, was forced to resign by the National Assembly.

## Postwar upheavals

With the fading of the military, the election of January 1946 was the first one contested by organized political parties. Pridi became prime minister, a new constitution was drafted, and the outlook for democratic, civilian government seemed bright. Hopes were shattered, however, on June 9, 1946, when King Ananda was found dead in his bed, with a bullet wound in his forehead. Three palace servants were tried and executed, but the murder has never been satisfactorily explained. Pridi resigned as prime minister, and in April 1948, Phibun, playing on the threat of communism, took over the premiership again.

As **communism** developed its hold in the region with the takeover of China in 1949 and the French defeat in Indochina in 1954, the US increasingly viewed Thailand as a bulwark against the red menace. Between 1951 and 1957, when its annual state budget was only about $200 million a year, Thailand received a total of $149 million in American economic aid and $222 million in military aid.

Phibun narrowly won a general election in 1957, but only by blatant vote-rigging and coercion. After vehement public outcry, General Sarit, the commander-in-chief of the army, overthrew the new government in September the same year. Believing that Thailand would prosper best under a unifying authority – an ideology that still

| 1939 | 1941 | 1946 |
|---|---|---|
| The country's name is changed from Siam to the more nationalistic Thailand | The Japanese invade, and Thailand forms an alliance with them | Rama VIII is mysteriously shot dead, to be succeeded by Rama IX (Bhumibol) |

has plenty of supporters today – Sarit set about re-establishing the monarchy as the head of the social hierarchy and the source of legitimacy for the government. Ananda's successor, **Bhumibol** (Rama IX), was pushed into an active role, while Sarit ruthlessly silenced critics and pressed ahead with a plan for economic development.

## The Vietnam War and the democracy movement

Sarit died in 1963, whereupon the military succession passed to General Thanom. His most pressing problem was the **Vietnam War**. The Thais, with the backing of the US, quietly began to conduct military operations in Laos, to which North Vietnam and China responded by supporting anti-government insurgency in Thailand. By 1968, around 45,000 US military personnel were on Thai soil, which became the base for US bombing raids against North Vietnam and Laos. The effects of the American presence were profound. The economy swelled with dollars, and hundreds of thousands of Thais became reliant on the Americans for a living, with a consequent proliferation of prostitution – centred on Bangkok's infamous Patpong district – and corruption. Moreover, the sudden exposure to Western culture led many to question traditional Thai values and the political status quo.

Poor farmers in particular were becoming increasingly disillusioned with their lot, and many turned against the Bangkok government. At the end of 1964, the Communist Party of Thailand and other groups formed a broad left coalition which soon had the support of several thousand insurgents in remote areas of the northeast and the north. By 1967, a separate threat had arisen in southern Thailand, involving Muslim dissidents and the Chinese-dominated Communist Party of Malaysia.

Thanom was now facing a major security crisis, and in November 1971 he imposed repressive military rule. In response, **student demonstrations** began in June 1973, and in October as many as 500,000 people turned out at Thammasat University in Bangkok to demand a new constitution. Clashes with the police ensued on October 14, during which over 350 people were reported killed, but elements in the army, backed by King Bhumibol, refused to provide enough troops to crush the demonstrators. Later that day, Thanom was forced to resign and leave the country.

In a new climate of openness, **Kukrit Pramoj** formed a coalition of seventeen elected parties and secured a promise of US withdrawal from Thailand, but his government was riven with feuding. In October 1976, the students demonstrated again, protesting against the return of Thanom to Bangkok. This time there was no restraint: supported by elements of the military and the government, the police and reactionary students launched a massive assault on Thammasat University. On October 6, hundreds of students were brutally beaten, scores were lynched and some even burnt alive; the military took control and suspended the constitution.

## "Premocracy"

Soon after, the military-appointed prime minister, Thanin Kraivichien, forced dissidents to undergo anti-communist indoctrination, but his measures seem to have been too repressive even for the military, who forced him to resign in October 1977. General Kriangsak Chomanand took over, and began to break up the insurgency with

| 1973 | 1976 | 1980–88 |
|---|---|---|
| Bloody student demonstrations bring the downfall of General Thanom | The brutal suppression of further student demos ushers the military back in | Period of Premocracy, General Prem's hybrid of military rule and democracy |

shrewd offers of amnesty. He in turn was displaced in February 1980 by **General Prem Tinsulanonda**, backed by a broad parliamentary coalition. Untainted by corruption, Prem achieved widespread support, including that of the monarchy. Overseeing a period of rapid economic growth, Prem maintained the premiership until 1988, with a unique mixture of dictatorship and democracy sometimes called **Premocracy**: although never standing for parliament himself, Prem was asked by the legislature after every election to become prime minister. He eventually stepped down (though he remains a powerful privy councillor) because, he said, it was time for the country's leader to be chosen from among its elected representatives.

## The 1992 demonstrations and the 1997 constitution

The new prime minister was indeed an elected MP, Chatichai Choonhavan. He pursued a vigorous policy of economic development, but this fostered widespread corruption. Following an economic downturn and Chatichai's attempts to downgrade the political role of the military, the armed forces staged a bloodless coup on February 23, 1991, led by Supreme Commander Sunthorn and General Suchinda, the army commander-in-chief, who became premier.

When Suchinda reneged on promises to make democratic amendments to the constitution, hundreds of thousands of ordinary Thais poured onto the streets around Bangkok's Democracy Monument in **mass demonstrations** between May 17 and 20, 1992. Suchinda brutally crushed the protests, leaving hundreds dead or injured, but was then forced to resign when King Bhumibol expressed his disapproval in a ticking-off that was broadcast on world television.

Elections were held in September, with the **Democrat Party**, led by Chuan Leekpai, a noted upholder of democracy and the rule of law, emerging victorious. Chuan was succeeded in turn by Banharn Silpa-archa – nicknamed by the local press "the walking ATM", a reference to his reputation for buying votes – and General Chavalit Yongchaiyudh. The most significant positive event of the latter's tenure was the approval of a **new constitution** in 1997. Drawn up by an independent drafting assembly, its main points included: direct elections to the senate, rather than appointment of senators by the prime minister; acceptance of the right of assembly as the basis of a democratic society and guarantees of individual rights and freedoms; greater public accountability; and increased popular participation in local administration. The eventual aim of the new charter was to end the traditional system of patronage, vested interests and vote-buying.

### Tom yam kung: the 1997 economic crisis

In February 1997 foreign-exchange dealers began to mount speculative attacks on the **baht**, alarmed at the size of Thailand's private foreign debt – 250 billion baht in the unproductive property sector alone, much of it accrued through the proliferation of prestigious skyscrapers in Bangkok. Chavalit's government defended the pegged exchange rate, spending $23 billion of the country's formerly healthy foreign-exchange reserves, but at the beginning of July was forced to give up the ghost – the baht was floated and soon went into free-fall. Thailand was obliged to seek help from the **IMF**, which in August put together a $17-billion **rescue package**, coupled with severe austerity measures.

| 1991 | 1992 | 1997 |
|---|---|---|
| The military launch a coup, protesting the corruption of the recently democratically elected government | Mass demonstrations lead to bloodshed – and the return of democracy | *Tom yam kung*: Thailand is ravaged by economic crisis |

In November, the inept Chavalit was replaced by Chuan Leekpai, who immediately took a hard line in following the IMF's advice, which involved maintaining cripplingly high interest rates to protect the baht and slashing government budgets. Although this played well abroad, at home the government encountered increasing hostility from its newly impoverished citizens – the downturn struck with such speed and severity that it was dubbed the **tom yam kung crisis**, after the searingly hot Thai soup. Chuan's tough stance paid off, however, with the baht stabilizing and inflation falling back.

## Thaksin

The general election of January 2001 was the first to be held under the 1997 constitution, which was intended to take vote-buying out of politics. However, this election coincided with the emergence of a new party, **Thai Rak Thai** ("Thai Loves Thai"), which was formed by one of Thailand's wealthiest men, **Thaksin Shinawatra**, an ex-policeman who had made a personal fortune from government telecommunications concessions.

Thaksin duly won the election but, instead of moving towards greater democracy, as envisaged by the new constitution, he began to apply commercial and legal pressure, to try to silence critics in the media and as his standing became more firmly entrenched, he rejected constitutional reforms designed to rein in his power – famously declaring that "democracy is only a tool" for achieving other goals.

Thaksin did, however, maintain his reputation as a reformer by carrying through nearly all of his election promises. He issued a three-year loan moratorium for perennially indebted farmers and set up a one-million-baht development fund for each of the country's seventy thousand villages – though many villages just used the money as a lending tool to cover past debts, rather than creating productive projects for the future as intended. To improve public health access, a standard charge of B30 per hospital visit was introduced nationwide.

Despite a sharp escalation of violence in the Islamic southern provinces in early 2004 (see page 396), Thaksin breezed through the February 2005 election, becoming the first prime minister in Thai history to win an outright majority at the polls but causing alarm among a wide spectrum of Thailand's elites. When Thaksin's relatives sold their shares in the family's Shin Corporation in January 2006 for £1.1 billion, without paying tax, tens of thousands of mostly middle-class Thais flocked to Bangkok to take part in protracted demonstrations, under the umbrella of the **People's Alliance for Democracy** (**PAD**). After further allegations of corruption and cronyism, in September 2006 Thaksin was ousted by a military government in a **coup**, while on official business in the United States.

## ... and the spectre of Thaksin

Thaksin set up home in London, but his supporters, now the People's Power Party (PPP), won the December 2007 general election. In response, the PAD – its nationalist and royalist credentials and its trademark **yellow shirts** (the colour of King Bhumibol) now firmly established – restarted its mass protests.

Matters came to a head in November and December 2008: the PAD seized and closed down Bangkok's Suvarnabhumi airport; the ruling People's Power Party was

| 2001 | 2004 | 2006 |
|---|---|---|
| Thaksin Shinawatra, loved and hated in roughly equal measure, wins the general election | The violence in the Islamic southern provinces sharply escalates | Thaksin is ousted in a military coup and goes into exile |

declared illegal by the courts and **Pheu Thai**, the PPP's swift reincarnation, found itself unable to form a new coalition government. Instead, led by the Eton- and Oxford-educated **Abhisit Vejjajiva**, the Democrat Party jumped into bed with the Bhumjaithai Party, formerly staunch supporters of Thaksin, to take the helm.

This in turn prompted Thaksin's supporters – now **red-shirted** and organized into the **UDD** (United Front for Democracy against Dictatorship) – to hold mass protest meetings. In March 2009, Thaksin claimed by video broadcast that Privy Council President, Prem Tinsulanonda, had masterminded the 2006 coup and Abhisit's appointment as prime minister, and called for the overthrow of the *amat* (elite).

Amid a clampdown by the Democrat government on free speech, including heavy-handed use of Article 112, the *lèse majesté* law, much more violent protests took place early the following year. Calling on Abhisit to hold new elections, thousands of red-shirts set up a heavily defended camp around the **Ratchaprasong** intersection in central Bangkok in early April. On May 19, Abhisit sent in the army to break up the camp by force; altogether 91 people died on both sides in the two months of protests.

Mass popular support for Thaksin, however, did not wane, and in the general election of May 2011, Pheu Thai – now led by his younger sister, **Yingluck Shinawatra** – romped home with an absolute majority. Yingluck proposed an amnesty bill for all those involved in the political turmoils of the last ten years, which would have included wiping out Thaksin's corruption convictions, thus allowing him to return to Thailand. However, in late 2013 this prompted further mass protests on the streets of Bangkok: thousands of nationalists – no longer wearing yellow shirts, but now blowing whistles as their trademark – occupied large areas of the city centre for several months, in an attempt to provoke the military into staging a coup. In May 2014, this duly happened, Thailand's twelfth **coup d'état** in the period of constitutional monarchy since 1932. The army chief, **General Prayut Chan-ocha**, installed himself as prime minister, at the head of a military junta known as the National Council for Peace and Order (NCPO).

All political gatherings and activities have been banned, politicians, journalists, academics and activists have been imprisoned or fled abroad and censorship of the media and social media has been greatly tightened (which in turn has fostered broad self-censorship). General elections were initially promised for 2015, but have been postponed repeatedly; the latest proposal is for February 2019, but at the time of writing that too seems about to slip.

In October 2016, the much-revered King Bhumibol passed away, to be succeeded by his 64-year-old son Vajiralongkorn, who spends much of his time in Germany. A year-long nationwide period of mourning followed, until the funeral was held in October 2017; a date for King Vajiralongkorn's coronation has not yet been set. The new king seems to favour a return to traditional ways and intervened in the drafting of the new constitution (Thailand's twentieth charter since 1932) to take direct control of the immense holdings of the Crown Property Bureau (the equivalent of the Royal Household). This constitution also reduces the power of elected politicians while bolstering the power of the military, with provisions for a strong appointed Senate of 250 members and for a prime minister who is not an elected representative. In 2017, Yingluck Shinawatra fled abroad just before she was sentenced to five years in prison for negligence.

| **2011** | **2014** | **2016** |
|---|---|---|
| Thaksin's sister, Yingluck, wins the general election | Thailand's twelfth military coup since 1932 | The much-loved Rama IX dies, succeeded by Vajiralongkorn (Rama X) |

# Religion: Thai Buddhism

Over 85 percent of Thais consider themselves Theravada Buddhists, followers of the teachings of a holy man usually referred to as the Buddha (Enlightened One), though more precisely known as Gautama Buddha to distinguish him from lesser-known Buddhas who preceded him. Theravada Buddhism is one of the two main schools of Buddhism practised in Asia, and in Thailand it has absorbed an eclectic assortment of animist and Hindu elements.

**Islam** is the biggest of the minority religions in Thailand, practised by between five and ten percent of the population. Most Muslims live in the south, especially in the deep-south provinces of Yala, Pattani and Narithiwat, along the Malaysian border, whose populations are over eighty percent Muslim. The separatist violence in this region (see page 396) has caused great tension between local Buddhist and Muslim communities, which have traditionally co-existed peacefully; it has not, however, obviously affected inter-faith relationships elsewhere in Thailand. The rest of the Thai population comprises Mahayana Buddhists, Hindus, Sikhs, Christians and animists.

## The Buddha: his life and beliefs

Gautama Buddha was born as **Prince Gautama Siddhartha** in Nepal, in the seventh century BC according to the calculations for the Thai calendar, though scholars now think it may have been a century or two later. At his birth, astrologers predicted that he would become either a famous king or a celebrated holy man, depending on which path he chose. Much preferring the former, the prince's father forbade the boy from leaving the palace grounds, and set about educating Gautama in all aspects of the high life. Most statues of the Buddha depict him with elongated earlobes, which is a reference to this early pampered existence, when he would have worn heavy precious stones in his ears.

The prince married and became a father, but at the age of 29 he flouted his father's authority and sneaked out into the world beyond the palace. On this fateful trip he encountered successively an old man, a sick man, a corpse and a hermit, and thus for the first time was made aware that pain and suffering were intrinsic to human life. Contemplation seemed the only means of discovering why this was so – and therefore Gautama decided to leave the palace and become a **Hindu ascetic**.

For several years he wandered the countryside leading a life of self-denial and self-mortification, but failed to come any closer to the answer. Eventually concluding that the best course of action must be to follow a "Middle Way" – neither indulgent nor overly ascetic – Gautama sat down beneath the famous riverside bodhi tree at **Bodh Gaya** in India, facing the rising sun, to **meditate** until he achieved enlightenment. For 49 days he sat cross-legged in the "lotus position", contemplating the causes of suffering and wrestling with temptations that materialized to distract him. Most of these were sent by **Mara**, the Evil One, who was finally subdued when Gautama summoned the earth goddess **Mae Toranee** by pointing the fingers of his right hand at the ground – the gesture known as **Calling the Earth to Witness**, or *Bhumisparsa Mudra*, which has been immortalized by thousands of Thai sculptors. Mae Toranee wrung torrents of water from her hair and engulfed Mara's demonic emissaries in a flood, an episode that's also commonly reproduced, especially in temple murals.

Temptations dealt with, Gautama soon came to attain **enlightenment** and so become a Buddha. As the place of his enlightenment, the **bodhi tree** (*bodhi* means "enlightenment" in Sanskrit and Pali; it's sometimes also known as the bo tree, in Thai *ton po*) has assumed special significance for Buddhists: not only does it appear in many

Buddhist paintings, but there's often a real bodhi tree (*Ficus religiosa*, or sacred fig) planted in temple compounds as well. In addition, the bot is nearly always built facing either a body of water or facing east (preferably both).

The Buddha preached his **first sermon** in the deer park at Sarnath in India, where he characterized his doctrine, or **Dharma**, as a wheel. From this episode comes the early Buddhist symbol the **Dharmachakra**, known as the Wheel of Law, which is often accompanied by a statue of a deer. Thais celebrate this first sermon with a public holiday in July known as **Asanha Puja**. On another occasion 1250 people spontaneously gathered to hear the Buddha speak, an event remembered in Thailand as **Makha Puja** and marked by a public holiday in February.

For the next forty-odd years the Buddha travelled the region converting non-believers and performing miracles. One rainy season he even ascended into the **Tavatimsa heaven** (Heaven of the 33 Gods) to visit his mother and to preach the doctrine to her. His descent from this heaven is quite a common theme of paintings and sculptures, and the **Standing Buddha** pose of numerous Buddha statues comes from this story.

The Buddha "died" at the age of eighty on the banks of a river at Kusinari in India – an event often dated to 543 BC, which is why the **Thai calendar** is 543 years out of synch with the Western one, so that the year 2019 AD becomes 2562 BE (Buddhist Era). Lying on his side, propping up his head on his hand, the Buddha passed into **Nirvana** (giving rise to another classic pose, the **Reclining Buddha**), the unimaginable state of nothingness which knows no suffering and from which there is no reincarnation. Buddhists believe that the day the Buddha entered Nirvana was the same date on which he was born and on which he achieved enlightenment, a triply significant day that Thais honour with the **Visakha Puja** festival in May.

Buddhists believe that Gautama Buddha was the five-hundredth incarnation of a single being: the stories of these five hundred lives, collectively known as the **Jataka**, provide the inspiration for much Thai art. Hindus also accept Gautama Buddha into their pantheon, perceiving him as the ninth manifestation of their god Vishnu.

## The spread of Buddhism

After the Buddha entered Nirvana, his **doctrine** spread relatively quickly across India, and probably was first promulgated in Thailand in about the third century BC, when the Indian emperor, Ashoka (in Thai, Asoke), sent out missionaries. His teachings, the *Tripitaka*, were written down in the Pali language – a then-vernacular derivative of Sanskrit – in a form that became known as **Theravada**, or "The Doctrine of the Elders".

By the beginning of the first millennium, a new movement called **Mahayana** (Great Vehicle) had emerged within the Theravada school, attempting to make Buddhism more accessible by introducing a pantheon of **bodhisattva**, or Buddhist saints, who, although they had achieved enlightenment, postponed entering Nirvana in order to inspire the populace. Mahayana Buddhism spread north into China, Korea, Vietnam and Japan, also entering southern Thailand via the Srivijayan empire around the eighth century and parts of Khmer Cambodia in about the eleventh century. Meanwhile Theravada Buddhism (which the Mahayanists disparagingly renamed "Hinayana" or "Lesser Vehicle") established itself most significantly in Sri Lanka, northern and central Thailand and Myanmar.

## Buddhist doctrine and practice

Central to Theravada Buddhism is a belief in **karma** – every action has a consequence – and **reincarnation**, along with an understanding that craving is at the root of human suffering. The ultimate aim for a Buddhist is to get off the cycle of perpetual reincarnation and suffering and instead to enter the blissful state of non-being that is **Nirvana**. This enlightened state can take many lifetimes to achieve so the more realistic goal for most is to be reborn slightly higher up the karmic ladder each time. As Thai Buddhists see it, animals are at the bottom of the karmic scale and monks at the top, with women on a lower rung than men.

Living a good life, specifically a life of "pure intention", creates good karma and Buddhist doctrine focuses a great deal on how to achieve this. Psychology and an understanding of human weaknesses play a big part. Key is the concept of *dukka* or **suffering**, which holds that craving is the root cause of all suffering or, to put it simplistically, human unhappiness is caused by the unquenchable dissatisfaction experienced when one's sensual, spiritual or material desires are not met. The concepts concerning suffering and craving are known as the **Four Noble Truths** of Buddhism. The route to enlightenment depends on a person being sufficiently detached from earthly desires so that *dukka* can't take hold. One acknowledges that the physical world is impermanent and ever changing, and that all things – including the self – are therefore not worth craving. A Buddhist works towards this realization by following the **Eightfold Path**, or **Middle Way**, that is by developing a set of highly moral personal qualities such as "right speech", "right action" and "right mindfulness". Meditation is particularly helpful in this.

A devout Thai Buddhist commits to the **five basic precepts**, namely not to kill or steal, to refrain from sexual misconduct and incorrect speech (lies, gossip and abuse) and to eschew intoxicating liquor and drugs. There are **three extra precepts** for special *wan phra* holy days and for those laypeople including foreign students who study meditation at Thai temples: no eating after noon, no entertainment (including TV and music) and no sleeping on a soft bed; in addition, the no-sexual-misconduct precept turns into no sex at all.

## Making merit

**Merit-making** in popular Thai Buddhism has become slightly skewed, so that some people act on the assumption that they'll climb the karmic ladder faster if they make bigger and better offerings to the temple and its monks. However, it is of course the purity of the intention behind one's **merit-making** (*tham buun*) that's fundamental.

Merit can be made in many ways, from giving a monk his breakfast to attending a Buddhist service or donating money and gifts to the neighbourhood temple, and most **festivals** are essentially communal merit-making opportunities. Between the big festivals, the most common days for making merit and visiting the temple are **wan phra** (holy days), which are determined by the phase of the moon and occur four times a month. The simplest **offering** inside a temple consists of lotus buds, candles and three incense sticks (representing the three gems of Buddhism – the Buddha himself, the Dharma or doctrine, and the monkhood). One of the more bizarre but common merit-making activities involves **releasing caged birds**: worshippers buy tiny finches from vendors at wat compounds and, by liberating them from their cage, prove their Buddhist compassion towards all living things. The fact that the birds were free until netted earlier that morning doesn't seem to detract from the ritual. In riverside and seaside wats, fish or even baby turtles are released instead.

For an insightful introduction to the philosophy and practice of Thai Buddhism, see ⓦ thaibuddhism.net. A number of Thai temples welcome foreign students of Buddhism and meditation (see page 50).

# The monkhood

It's the duty of Thailand's 200,000-strong **Sangha** (monkhood) to set an example to the Theravada Buddhist community by living a life as close to the Middle Way as possible and by preaching the Dharma to the people. The life of a monk (*bhikkhu*) is governed by 227 precepts that include celibacy and the rejection of all personal possessions except gifts.

Each day begins with an alms round in the neighbourhood so that the laity can donate food and thereby gain themselves merit, and then is chiefly spent in meditation, chanting, teaching and study. As the most respected members of any community, monks act as teachers, counsellors and arbiters in local disputes, and sometimes become spokesmen for villagers' rights. They also perform rituals at cremations, weddings and other events, such as the launching of a new business or even the purchase of a new car. Many young boys from poor families find themselves almost obliged to become either a *dek wat* (temple boy) or a **novice monk** because that's the only way they can get accommodation, food and, crucially, an education. This is provided free in exchange for duties around the wat, and novices are required to adhere to ten rather than 227 Buddhist precepts.

Monkhood doesn't have to be for life: a man may leave the Sangha three times without stigma and in fact every Thai male (including royalty) is expected to **enter the monkhood** for a short period, ideally between leaving school and marrying, as a rite of passage into adulthood. Thai government departments and some private companies grant their employees paid leave for their time as a monk, but the custom is in decline as young men increasingly have to consider the effect their absence may have on their career prospects. Instead, many men now enter the monkhood for a brief period after the death of a parent, to make merit both for the deceased and for the rest of the family. The most popular time for temporary ordination is the three-month Buddhist retreat period – **Pansa**, sometimes referred to as "Buddhist Lent" – which begins in July and lasts for the duration of the rainy season. (The monks' confinement is said to originate from the earliest years of Buddhist history, when farmers complained that perambulating monks were squashing their sprouting rice crops.)

## Monks in contemporary society

Some monks extend their role as village spokesmen to become influential activists: Wat Tham Krabok near Lopburi and Wat Nong Sam Pran in Kanchanaburi are among a growing number of temples that have established themselves as successful drug rehabilitation centres; monks at Wat Phra Bat Nam Pu in Lopburi run a hospice for people with HIV/Aids as well as a famously hard-hitting AIDS-awareness museum; monks at Wat Phai Lom near Bangkok have developed the country's largest breeding colony of Asian open-billed storks; while the monks at Wat Pa Luang Ta Bua Yannasampanno in Kanchanaburi hit the headlines for the wrong reasons, with their controversial, now closed tiger sanctuary. Other monks, such as the famous Luang Pho Khoon of Wat Ban Rai in Nakhon Ratchasima province who died in 2015 aged 91, have acquired such a reputation for giving wise counsel and bringing good fortune to their followers that they have become national gurus and their temples now generate great wealth through the production of specially blessed amulets and photographs.

Though the increasing involvement of many monks in the secular world has not met with unanimous approval, far more disappointing to the laity are those monks who **flout the precepts** of the Sangha by succumbing to the temptations of a consumer society, flaunting Ray-Bans, Rolexes and Mercedes (in some cases actually bought with temple funds), chain-smoking and flirting, even making pocket money from predicting lottery results and practising faith-healing. With so much national pride and integrity riding on the sanctity of the Sangha, any whiff of a deeper scandal is bound to strike deep into the national psyche. Cases of monks involved in drug dealing, gun running, even rape and murder, have prompted a stream of editorials on the state of the Sangha and the collapse of spiritual values at the heart of Thai society. The inclusivity of the monkhood – which is open to just about any male who wants to join – has been highlighted as a particularly vulnerable aspect, not least because donning saffron robes has always been an accepted way for criminals, reformed or otherwise, to repent of their past deeds.

Interestingly, back in the late 1980s, the influential monk Phra Bodhirak (Photirak) was defrocked after criticizing what he saw as a tide of decadence infecting Thai

Buddhism. He now preaches his ascetic code of anti-materialism through his breakaway **Santi Asoke** sect, famous across the country for its cheap vegetarian restaurants, its philosophy of self-sufficiency and for the simple blue farmers' shirts worn by many of its followers.

### Women and the monkhood

Although the Theravada Buddhist hierarchy in some countries permits the ordination of **female monks**, or *bhikkhuni*, the Thai Sangha does not. Instead, Thai women are officially only allowed to become **nuns**, or *mae chii*, shaving their heads, donning white robes and keeping eight rather than 227 precepts. Their status is lower than that of the monks and they are chiefly occupied with temple upkeep rather than conducting religious ceremonies.

However, the progressives are becoming more vocal, and in 2002 a Thai woman became the first of several to break with the Buddhist authorities and get **ordained** as a novice *bhikkhuni* on Thai soil. Thailand's Sangha Council, however, still recognizes neither her ordination nor the temple, Watra Songdhammakalyani in Nakhon Pathom, where the ordination took place. The Watra (rather than Wat) is run by another Thai *bhikkhuni*, Dhammananda Bhikkhuni, the author of several books in English about **women and Buddhism** and of an informative website, Ⓦ thaibhikkhunis.org.

# Hindu deities and animist spirits

The complicated history of the area now known as Thailand has made Thai Buddhism a confusingly syncretic faith, as you'll realize when you enter a Buddhist temple compound to be confronted by a statue of a Hindu deity. While regular Buddhist merit-making insures a Thai for the next life, there are certain **Hindu gods and animist spirits** that many Thais – sophisticated Bangkokians and illiterate farmers alike – also cultivate for help with more immediate problems; and as often as not it's a Buddhist monk who is called in to exorcize a malevolent spirit. Even the Buddhist King Bhumibol employs Brahmin priests and astrologers to determine auspicious days and officiate at certain royal ceremonies and, like his royal predecessors of the Chakri dynasty, he also associates himself with the Hindu god Vishnu by assuming the title Rama IX – Rama, hero of the Hindu epic the *Ramayana*, having been Vishnu's seventh manifestation on earth.

If a Thai wants help in achieving a short-term goal, like passing an exam, becoming pregnant or winning the lottery, he or she will quite likely turn to the **Hindu pantheon**, visiting an enshrined statue of Brahma, Vishnu, Shiva or Ganesh, and making offerings of flowers, incense and maybe food. If the outcome is favourable, the devotee will probably come back to show thanks, bringing more offerings and maybe even hiring a dance troupe to perform a celebratory *lakhon chatri*. Built in honour of Brahma, Bangkok's Erawan Shrine is the most famous place of Hindu-inspired worship in the country.

### Spirits and spirit houses

Whereas Hindu deities tend to be benevolent, **spirits** (or *phi*) are not nearly as reliable and need to be mollified more frequently. They come in hundreds of varieties, some more malign than others, and inhabit everything from trees, rivers and caves to public buildings and private homes – even taking over people if they feel like it.

So that these *phi* don't pester human inhabitants, each building has a special **spirit house** (*saan phra phum*) in its vicinity, as a dwelling for spirits ousted by the building's construction. Usually raised on a short column to set it at or above eye-level, the spirit house must occupy an auspicious location – not, for example, in the shadow of the main building. It's generally about the size of a doll's house and designed to look like a wat or a traditional Thai house, but its ornamentation is supposed to reflect the status of the humans' building, so if that building is enlarged or refurbished, the spirit house should be improved accordingly. And as architects become increasingly bold in their designs, so modernist spirit houses are also beginning to appear, especially in Bangkok where an eye-catching new skyscraper might be graced by a spirit house of glass or polished concrete. **Figurines** representing the relevant guardian spirit and his aides are sometimes put inside, and daily offerings of incense, lighted candles and garlands of jasmine are placed alongside them to keep the *phi* happy – a disgruntled spirit is a dangerous spirit, liable to cause sickness, accidents and even death. As with any religious building or icon in Thailand, an unwanted or crumbling spirit house should never be dismantled or destroyed, which is why you'll often see damaged spirit houses placed around the base of a sacred banyan tree, where they are able to rest in peace.

# The coastal environment

Spanning some 1650km north to south, Thailand lies in the heart of
Southeast Asia's tropical zone, its southern border running less than seven
degrees north of the Equator. Coastal Thailand's climate is characterized by
high temperatures and even higher humidity, a very fertile combination
that nourishes a huge diversity of flora and fauna in the tropical rainforests,
mangrove swamps and coral reefs that constitute the region's main habitats.

## Habitats

Some of Thailand's most precious habitats are protected as **national park**, including the
steamy jungles of Khao Sok; the coastal mud flats of Khao Sam Roi Yot, a favourite haunt
of migrating birds; and the island shorelines and reefs of Ko Surin, Ko Similan, plus Ko
Tarutao, Ang Thong, Khao Luang, parts of Phang Nga bay, Ko Lanta and Ko Chang.

### Tropical rainforests

Thailand's **tropical rainforests** occur in areas of high and prolonged rainfall in the
southern peninsula, most accessibly in the national parks of Khao Sok, Tarutao and
Khao Luang. Some areas contain as many as two hundred species of tree within a single
hectare, along with a host of other flora. Characteristic of a tropical rainforest is the
multi-layered series of **canopies**. The uppermost storey sometimes reaches 60m, and
will often have enormous buttressed roots for support; beneath this, the dense canopy
of 25–35m is often festooned with climbers and epiphytes such as ferns, lianas, mosses
and orchids; then comes an uneven layer 5–10m high consisting of palms, rattans,
shrubs and small trees. The forest floor in tropical rainforests tends to be relatively open
and free of dense undergrowth because the upper three layers shade much of the light.

The family **Dipterocarpaceae** dominate these forests, a group of tropical hardwoods
prized for their timber – and as nesting sites for hornbills and lookout posts for
gibbons. Also very common are the many different species of **epiphytes**, plants that
usually grow on other plants, but aren't parasitic, obtaining their nutrients from the
atmosphere instead, and from decaying plant and animal matter. Among the most
famous, and most beautiful, epiphytes are Thailand's countless species of wild **orchids**,
many of them gratifyingly common in the forest and prized as houseplants in the
West, including the golden spiky petalled *Bulbophyllum picturatum*, the bright yellow
members of the genus *Dendrobium*, the flame-red *Ascocentrum curvifolium*, and the
blue *Vanda coerulea*.

For the early years of its life, the **strangling fig** (*Ficus* sp) is also an epiphyte, often
using a dipterocarp as host while it drops its distinctive lattice of roots to the ground. It
can then feed normally, so well in fact that, after many years, the fig's roots and crown
completely enshroud the support tree and hasten its death. As the host decomposes, it
leaves a hollow but structurally sound strangling fig. Strangling figs are excellent places
to observe birds and mammals, particularly when in fruit, as they attract hornbills,
green pigeons, barbets, gibbons, langurs and macaques.

### Mangrove swamps and coastal forests

**Mangrove swamps** are an important habitat for a wide variety of marine life (including
two hundred species of bird, seventy species of fish and fifty types of crab) but, as
with much of Thailand's inland forest, they have been significantly degraded by
encroachment, as well as by large-scale prawn farming. Huge swathes of Thailand's
littoral used to be fringed with mangrove swamps, but now they are mainly found only

along the west peninsular coast, between Ranong and Satun, though Chanthaburi's Ao Khung Kraben is a notable east-coast exception. A great way of **exploring the swamps** is to paddle a kayak through the mangrove-clogged inlets and island-lagoons of Ao Phang Nga. Not only do mangrove swamps harbour a rich and important ecosystem of their own, but they also help prevent coastal erosion; in certain areas of the tsunami-hit Andaman coast intact mangrove forest absorbed some of the waves' impact, protecting land and homes from even worse damage.

**Nipa palms** share the mangrove's penchant for brackish water, and these stubby-stemmed palm trees grow in abundance in the south, though commercial plantations are now replacing the natural colonies. Like most other species of palm indigenous to Thailand, the nipa is a versatile plant that's exploited to the full: alcohol is distilled from its sugary sap, and its fronds are woven into roofs (especially for beach huts and village homes), sticky-rice baskets and chair-backs.

The hardy **coconut palm** is also very tolerant of salty, sandy soil, and is equally useful. On islands such as Ko Kood, it's the backbone of the local economy, with millions of coconuts harvested every month for their milk, their oil-producing meat (copra), and their fibrous husks or coir (used for making ropes, matting, brushes and mattress stuffing); the palm fronds are woven into roof thatching and baskets, and the wood has an attractive grain.

**Casuarinas** (also known as she-oaks or ironwoods) also flourish in sandy soils and are common on beaches throughout Thailand; fast-growing and tall (up to 20m), they are quite often planted as wind-breaks. Though its feathery profile makes it look like a pine, it's actually made up of tiny twigs, not needles.

## Wildlife

Thailand lies in an exceptionally rich "transition zone" of the Indo-Malayan realm, its forests, mountains and national parks attracting wildlife from both Indochina and Indonesia. In all, Thailand is home to three hundred species of mammal (37 of which are considered to be endangered or vulnerable), while 982 species of bird have been recorded here (49 of them globally threatened). For a guide to Thailand's spectacular array of **marine species**, check out the "Underwater Thailand" section (see page 20).

### Mammals

In the main national parks like Khao Sok, the animals you're most likely to encounter – with your ears if not your eyes – are **primates**, particularly macaques and gibbons.

The latter are responsible for the distinctive hooting that echoes through the forests. Chief noise-maker is the **white-handed** or **lar gibbon**, a beige- or black-bodied, white-faced animal whose cute appearance, intelligence and dexterity unfortunately make it a popular pet. The poaching and mistreatment of lar gibbons has become so severe that a special Gibbon Rehabilitation Project has been set up in Phuket (see page 340).

Similarly chatty, macaques hang out in gangs of twenty or more. The **long-tailed** or **crab-eating macaque** lives in the lowlands, near rivers, lakes and coasts, including around Ao Phang Nga, Krabi, Ko Tarutao, Ang Thong and Khao Sam Roi Yot. It eats not only crabs, but mussels, other small animals and fruit, transporting and storing food in its big cheek pouch when swimming and diving. The **pig-tailed macaque**, named for its short curly tail, excels at scaling tall trees, a skill which has resulted in many of the males being captured and trained to pick coconuts.

Commonly sighted on night treks in Khao Sam Roi Yot, the **civet** – species of which include the common palm and small Indian – is a small mongoose-type animal which hunts smaller mammals in trees and on the ground; it's known in the West for the powerful smell released from its anal glands, a scent used commercially as a perfume base. Far more elusive is the **Indochinese tiger**, which lives under constant threat from both poachers and the destruction of its habitat by logging interests, both of which have reduced the current population to probably fewer than one hundred; it's thought that some still live in Khao

---

**THE GECKO**

Whether you're staying on a beach or in a town, chances are you'll be sharing your room with a few **geckos**. These pale-green tropical lizards, which are completely harmless to humans and usually measure a cute 4cm to 10cm in length, mostly appear at night, high up on walls and ceilings, where they feed on insects. Because the undersides of their flat toes are covered with hundreds of microscopic hairs that catch at even the tiniest of irregularities, geckos are able to scale almost any surface, including glass, which is why you usually see them in strange, gravity-defying positions. The largest and most vociferous gecko is known as the **tuukae** in Thai, named after the disconcertingly loud sound it makes. *Tuukae* can grow to an alarming 35cm but are welcomed by most householders, as they devour insects and mice; Thais also consider it auspicious if a baby is born within earshot of a crowing *tuukae*.

---

Sok, however. Khao Sok is also potentially one of the easier places to encounter wild, small-eared Asian **elephants**, of which around two thousand now remain in Thailand.

### Birds

Even if you don't see many mammals on a trek through a national park, you're certain to spot a satisfying range of birds. The **hornbill** is the most majestic, easily recognizable from its massive, powerful wings (the flapping of which can be heard for long distances) and huge beak surmounted by a bizarre horny casque. The two most commonly spotted species in Thailand are the plain black-and-white **oriental pied hornbill**, frequently sighted on the little islands of Ko Phayam and Ko Chang in Ranong province, among other places, and the flashier **great hornbill**, whose monochromic body and head are broken up with jaunty splashes of yellow. Thailand is also home to the extremely rare **Gurney's pitta**, found only in Khlong Thom national park, inland from Ko Lanta.

**Coastal areas** attract storks, egrets and herons, and the mud flats of Khao Sam Roi Yot are breeding grounds for the large, long-necked **purple heron**. The magnificent **white-bellied sea eagle** haunts the Thai coast, nesting in the forbidding crags around Ao Phang Nga, Krabi and Ko Tarutao and preying on fish and sea snakes. The tiny **edible nest swiftlet** makes its eponymous nest – the major ingredient of the luxury food, bird's-nest soup – in the limestone crags, too (see page 370).

For information on specific **bird-watching** locations throughout Thailand see ⓦ thaibirding.com; for guided birding tours contact Thailand Bird Watching (ⓦ thailandbirdwatching.com); bird-watching guidebooks are listed in the "Books" section (see page 437).

### Snakes

Thailand is home to around 175 different species and subspecies of **snake**, 56 of them dangerously venomous. Death by snakebite is not common, however, but all provincial hospitals should keep a stock of serum.

Found everywhere and highly venomous, the 2m, nocturnal, yellow-and-black-striped **banded krait** is one to avoid, as is the shorter but equally venomous **Thai** or **monocled cobra**, which lurks in low-lying humid areas and close to human habitation and sports a distinctive "eye" mark on its hood. The other most widespread venomous snake is the 60cm **Malayan pit viper**, which has an unnerving ability to camouflage its pinky-brown and black-marked body. The **mangrove snake** lives in the humid swamps south of Chumphon: arboreal, nocturnal and mildly venomous, it can grow to about 2.5m and is black with thin yellow bands.

## Environmental issues

Thailand's rapid economic growth has had a significant effect on its environment. Huge new infrastructure projects, an explosion in real-estate developments and the constantly expanding tourist industry have all played a part, and the effects of the subsequent **deforestation** and pollution have been felt nationwide. Such was the devastation caused by floods and mud slides in Surat Thani in 1988 that the government banned commercial logging the following year, though land continues to be denuded for other purposes. There is also the endemic problem of "influence" so that when a big shot wants to clear a previously pristine area for a new property development, for example, it is virtually impossible for a lowly provincial civil servant to reject their plan, or money.

**Flooding** has always been a feature of the Thai environment, crucial to the fertility of its soil, and its worst effects are obviated by the stilted design of the traditional Thai house. However, there is now an almost annual inundation in certain riverside town centres, and of roads and railways, particularly along the Gulf coast, with especially severe floods in 2011, when towns in the central plains, including the World Heritage Site of Ayutthaya and many suburbs of Bangkok, were under metres of water for weeks on end. And in recent times, far more dangerous **flash floods** have recurred with depressing frequency, most dramatically around the northern town of Pai in 2005, where many homes and guesthouses were washed away. The link between deforestation and floods is disputed, though encroaching cement and tarmac on Thai flood plains surely play a part, as does the clogging of exit channels by garbage and other pollutants, and of course climate change.

### Reefs and shorelines

A number of Thailand's **coral reefs** – some of which are thought to be around 450 million years old – are being destroyed by factors attributable to tourism, most significantly the pollution generated by coastal hotels with inadequate sewage systems. Longtail boats that anchor on reefs, souvenirs made from coral, and the use of harpoon guns by irresponsible dive leaders all have a cumulative effect, dwarfed however by the local practice of using dynamite to gather fish, including reef fish for sale to aquariums.

The 2004 **tsunami** also caused significant damage to coastal and marine environments the length of the Andaman coast. Reefs close to shore were crushed by debris (furniture, machinery, even cars) and buried under displaced soil; the sea was temporarily polluted by extensive damage to sewage systems; and tracts of shorefront farmland were rendered unusable by salt water. In 2010, a mass **coral bleaching** event occurred in all of the world's oceans, damaging especially shallow-water reefs in Thailand, such as Ko Surin's; the event was caused by sudden, steep rises in sea temperatures, and has been interpreted as dramatic evidence of the effects of climate change.

### National parks

Although Thailand has since the 1970s been protecting some of its natural resources within **national parks**, these have long been caught between commercial and conservationist aims, an issue which the government addressed in 2002 by establishing a new National Park, Wildlife and Plant Conservation Department (DNP; ⓦnps.dnp.go.th), separate from the Royal Forestry Department and its parent Ministry of Agriculture.

With 140 national parks and marine parks across the country, as well as various other protected zones, over thirteen percent of the country is now, in theory at least, protected from encroachment and hunting (a high proportion compared to other nations, such as Japan at 6.5 percent, and the US at 10.5 percent).

However, the touristification of certain national parks endures; Ko Phi Phi and Ko Samet in particular have both suffered irreversible environmental damage as a direct result of the number of overnight visitors they receive. While most people understand that the role of the national parks is to conserve vulnerable and precious resources, the dramatic hike in entrance fees payable by foreigner visitors to national parks – from B20 up to B200 in 2000 and up again to B400 or B500 for a few special parks – was greeted with cynicism and anger, not least because there is often little sign of anything tangible being done on site with the money.

# Books

We have included publishers' details for books that may be hard to find outside Thailand, though some of them can be ordered online through ⓦdcothai.com, which sells e-books on ⓦebooks.dco.co.th. Other titles should be available worldwide. Titles marked ★ are particularly recommended. There's a good selection of Thai novels and short stories in translation, available to buy as e-books, on ⓦthaifiction.com.

## CULTURE AND SOCIETY

**Michael Carrithers** *The Buddha: A Very Short Introduction.* Accessible account of the life of the Buddha, and the development and significance of his thought.

★ **Philip Cornwel-Smith and John Goss** *Very Thai.* Why do Thais decant their soft drinks into plastic bags, and how does one sniff-kiss? Answers and insights aplenty in this intriguingly observant, fully illustrated guide to contemporary Thai culture. In similar vein is Cornwel-Smith's *Very Bangkok*, an insider's view of the city covering its full ethnic diversity.

**James Eckardt** *Bangkok People.* The collected articles of a renowned expat journalist, whose encounters with a varied cast of Bangkokians – from construction-site workers and street vendors to boxers and political candidates – add texture and context to the city.

**Sandra Gregory with Michael Tierney** *Forget You Had A Daughter: Doing Time in the "Bangkok Hilton" – Sandra Gregory's Story.* The frank and shocking account of a young British woman's term in Bangkok's notorious Lard Yao prison after being caught trying to smuggle 89g of heroin out of Thailand.

**Sebastian Hope** *Outcasts of the Islands: The Sea Gypsies of Southeast Asia.* Unusual insight into the lives of the *chao ley* people from a British traveller who spent several months in various sea gypsy communities.

★ **Erich Krauss** *Wave of Destruction: One Thai Village and its Battle with the Tsunami.* A sad and often shocking, clear-eyed account of what Ban Nam Khem went through before, during and after the tsunami. Fills in many gaps left unanswered by news reports at the time.

**Father Joe Maier** *Welcome to the Bangkok Slaughterhouse: The Battle for Human Dignity in Bangkok's Bleakest Slums* and *The Open Gate of Mercy.* Catholic priest Father Joe shares the stories of some of the Bangkok street kids and slum-dwellers that his charitable foundation has been supporting since 1972 (see page 55).

**Cleo Odzer** *Patpong Sisters.* An American anthropologist's funny and touching account of her life with the prostitutes and bar-girls of Bangkok's notorious red-light district.

**James O'Reilly and Larry Habegger** (eds) *Travelers' Tales: Thailand.* Absorbing anthology of contemporary writings about Thailand, by Thailand experts, social commentators, travel writers and first-time visitors.

★ **Phra Peter Pannapadipo** *Little Angels: The Real-Life Stories of Twelve Thai Novice Monks.* A dozen young boys, many of them from desperate backgrounds, tell the often poignant stories of why they became novice monks. For some, funding from the Students Education Trust (see page 56) has changed their lives.

**Phra Peter Pannapadipo** *Phra Farang: An English Monk in Thailand.* Behind the scenes in a Thai monastery: the frank, funny and illuminating account of a UK-born former businessman's life as a Thai monk.

**Pasuk Phongpaichit and Sungsidh Piriyarangsan** *Corruption and Democracy in Thailand.* Fascinating academic study, revealing the nuts and bolts of corruption in Thailand and its links with all levels of political life, and suggesting a route to a stronger society. Their sequel, a study of Thailand's illegal economy, *Guns, Girls, Gambling, Ganja*, co-written with Nualnoi Treerat, makes equally eye-opening and depressing reading.

**Tom Vater and Aroon Thaewchatturat** *Sacred Skin.* Fascinating, beautifully photographed exploration of Thailand's spirit tattoos, *sak yant.*

**William Warren** *Living in Thailand.* Luscious gallery of traditional houses, with an emphasis on the homes of Thailand's rich and famous; seductively photographed by Luca Invernizzi Tettoni.

## HISTORY

**William Warren** *Jim Thompson: the Legendary American of Thailand.* The engrossing biography of the ex-intelligence agent, art collector and Thai silk magnate whose disappearance in Malaysia in 1967 has never been satisfactorily resolved.

★ **David K. Wyatt** *Thailand: A Short History.* An excellent, recently updated treatment, scholarly but highly readable, with a good eye for witty, telling details. Good chapters on the story of the Thais before they reached what's now Thailand, and on recent developments.

## ART AND ARCHITECTURE

★ **Steve Van Beek** *The Arts of Thailand*. Lavishly produced and perfectly pitched introduction to the history of Thai architecture, sculpture and painting, with superb photographs by Luca Invernizzi Tettoni.

**Sumet Jumsai** *Naga: Cultural Origins in Siam and the West Pacific*. Wide-ranging discussion of water symbols in Thailand and other parts of Asia, offering a stimulating mix of art, architecture, mythology and cosmology.

**Steven Pettifor** *Flavours: Thai Contemporary Art*. Takes up the baton from Poshyananda (see below) to look at the newly invigorated art scene in Thailand from 1992 to 2004, with profiles of 23 leading lights, including painters, multimedia and performance artists.

★ **Apinan Poshyananda** *Modern Art in Thailand*. Excellent introduction which extends up to the early 1990s, with very readable discussions on dozens of individual artists, and lots of colour plates.

**William Warren and Luca Invernizzi Tettoni** *Arts and Crafts of Thailand*. Good-value, large-format paperback, setting the wealth of Thai arts and crafts in cultural context, with plenty of attractive illustrations and colour photographs.

## NATURAL HISTORY AND TRAVEL GUIDES

**Ashley J. Boyd and Collin Piprell** *Diving in Thailand*. A thorough guide to 84 dive sites, plus general introductory sections on Thailand's marine life, conservation and photography tips.

**Oliver Hargreave** *Exploring Phuket & Phi Phi: From Tin to Tourism*. Fascinating, thoroughly researched guide to the Andaman coast's big touristic honeypots; especially good on Phuket's history.

★ **Thom Henley** *Krabi: Caught in the Spell – A Guide to Thailand's Enchanted Province* (Thai Nature Education, Phuket). Highly readable features and observations on the attractions and people of south Thailand's most beautiful region, written by an expat environmentalist.

**Boonsong Lekagul and Philip D. Round** *Guide to the Birds of Thailand*. Unparalleled illustrated guide to Thailand's birds. Definitely worth scouring secondhand sellers for.

**Craig Robson** *A Field Guide to the Birds of Thailand*. Expert and beautifully illustrated guide to Thailand's top 950 bird species, with locator maps.

**Eric Valli and Diane Summers** *The Shadow Hunters*. Beautifully photographed photo-essay on the bird's-nest collectors of southern Thailand, with whom the authors spent over a year, together scaling the phenomenal heights of the sheer limestone walls.

## LITERATURE

**Alastair Dingwall** (ed) *Traveller's Literary Companion: Southeast Asia*. A useful though rather dry reference, with a large section on Thailand, including a book list, well-chosen extracts, biographical details of authors and other literary notes.

★ **Chart Korbjitti** *The Judgement* (Howling Books). Sobering modern-day tragedy about a good-hearted Thai villager who is ostracized by his hypocritical neighbours. Lots of interesting details on village life and traditions and thought-provoking passages on the stifling conservatism of rural communities. Winner of the S.E.A. Write award in 1982.

★ **Rattawut Lapcharoensap** *Sightseeing*. This outstanding debut collection of short stories by a young Thai-born author now living overseas highlights big, pertinent themes – cruelty, corruption, racism, pride – in its neighbourhood tales of randy teenagers, bullyboys, a child's friendship with a Cambodian refugee, a young man who uses family influence to dodge the draft.

**Nitaya Masavisut** (ed) *The S.E.A. Write Anthology of Thai Short Stories and Poems* (Silkworm Books, Chiang Mai).

Interesting medley of short stories and poems by Thai writers who have won Southeast Asian Writers' Awards, providing a good introduction to the contemporary literary scene.

**S.P. Somtow** *Jasmine Nights*. An engaging and humorous rites-of-passage tale, of an upper-class boy learning what it is to be Thai. *Dragon's Fin Soup and Other Modern Siamese Fables* is an imaginative and entertaining collection of often supernatural short stories, focusing on the collision of East and West.

★ **Khamsing Srinawk** *The Politician and Other Stories*. A collection of brilliantly satiric short stories, crammed with pithy moral observation and biting irony, which capture the vulnerability of peasant farmers in the north and northeast, as they attempt to come to grips with the modern world. The stories were written by a local insider who came from a peasant family, gained an eduction at Chulalongkorn University, became a hero of the left, and then joined the communist insurgents following the 1976 clampdown.

## THAILAND IN FOREIGN LITERATURE

**Dean Barrett** *Kingdom of Make-Believe*. Despite the clichéd ingredients – the Patpong go-go bar scene, opium smuggling in the Golden Triangle, Vietnam veterans – this novel about a return to Thailand following a twenty-year absence turns out to be a rewardingly multi-dimensional take on the farang experience.

**John Burdett** *Bangkok 8*. Riveting Bangkok thriller that takes in Buddhism, plastic surgery, police corruption, the *yaa baa* drugs trade, hookers, jade-smuggling and the spirit world.

**Alex Garland** *The Beach*. Gripping cult thriller (later made into a film, shot partly on Ko Phi Phi Leh) that explores the way in which travellers' ceaseless quest for "undiscovered" utopias inevitably leads to them despoiling the idyll.

**Andrew Hicks** *Thai Girl*. A British backpacker falls for a reticent young beach masseuse on Ko Samet but struggles with age-old cross-cultural confusion in this sensitive attempt at a different kind of expat novel.

**Michel Houellebecq** *Platform*. Sex tourism in Thailand provides the nucleus of this brilliantly provocative (some would say offensive) novel, in which Houellebecq presents a ferocious critique of Western decadence and cultural colonialism, and of radical Islam too.

**Christopher G. Moore** *God of Darkness*. Thailand's best-selling expat novelist sets his most intriguing thriller during the economic crisis of 1997 and includes plenty of meat on endemic corruption and the desperate struggle for power within family and society.

## FOOD AND COOKERY

**Vatcharin Bhumichitr** *The Taste of Thailand*. Another glossy introduction to this eminently photogenic country, this time through its food. The author runs a Thai restaurant in London and provides background colour as well as about 150 recipes adapted for Western kitchens.

**Jacqueline M. Piper** *Fruits of South-East Asia*. An exploration of the bounteous fruits of the region, tracing their role in the likes of cooking, medicine, handicrafts and rituals. Well illustrated with photos, watercolours and early botanical drawings.

★ **David Thompson** *Thai Food and Thai Street Food*. Comprehensive, impeccably researched celebrations of the cuisine with hundreds of recipes, by the owner of the first Thai restaurant ever to earn a Michelin star.

# Language

Thai belongs to one of the oldest families of languages in the world, Austro-Thai, and is radically different from most of the other tongues of Southeast Asia. Being tonal, Thai is very difficult for Westerners to master, but by building up from a small core of set phrases, you should soon have enough to get by. Most Thais who deal with tourists speak some English, but once you stray off the beaten track you'll probably need at least a little Thai. Anywhere you go, you'll impress and get better treatment if you at least make an effort to speak a few words.

Distinct dialects are spoken in the north, the northeast and the south, which can increase the difficulty of comprehending what's said to you. **Thai script** is even more of a problem to Westerners, with 44 consonants and 32 vowels. However, street signs in touristed areas are nearly always written in Roman script as well as Thai, and in other circumstances you're better off asking than trying to unscramble the swirling mess of letters and accents. For more information on transliteration into Roman script, see the box in this book's introduction.

Among **dictionaries**, Paiboon Publishing's (ⓦ paiboonpublishing.com) *Thai-English, English-Thai Software Dictionary* (also available as an enhanced app), lists words in phonetic Thai as well as Thai script, with sound recordings for each word.

The best **teach-yourself course** is the expensive *Linguaphone Thai* (including eight CDs and an alphabet book), which also has a shorter, cheaper beginner-level *PDQ* version (with CDs or available as a downloadable coursebook and audio files). *Thai for Beginners* by Benjawan Poomsan Becker (book with CDs or app; Paiboon Publishing) is a cheaper, more manageable textbook and is especially good for getting to grips with the Thai writing system. For a more traditional textbook, try Stuart Campbell and Chuan Shaweevongse's *The Fundamentals of the Thai Language*, which is comprehensive, though hard going. The **website** ⓦ thai-language.com is an amazing free resource, featuring a searchable dictionary with over seventy thousand entries, complete with Thai script and audio clips, plus lessons and forums; you can also browse and buy Thai language books and learning materials. There are also plenty of **language classes** available in Thailand (see page 65).

## Pronunciation

Mastering **tones** is probably the most difficult part of learning Thai. Five different tones are used – low, middle, high, falling, and rising – by which the meaning of a single syllable can be altered in five different ways. Thus, using four of the five tones, you can make a sentence from just one syllable: "mái mài mâi ma˘i" meaning "New wood burns, doesn't it?" As well as the natural difficulty in becoming attuned to speaking and listening to these different tones, Western efforts are complicated by our habit of denoting the overall meaning of a sentence by modulating our tones – for example, turning a statement into a question through a shift of stress and tone. Listen to native Thai speakers and you'll soon begin to pick up the different approach to tone.

The pitch of each tone is gauged in relation to your vocal range when speaking, but they should all lie within a narrow band, separated by gaps just big enough to differentiate them. The **low tones** (syllables marked `) middle tones** (unmarked syllables), and **high tones** (syllables marked ´) should each be pronounced evenly and with no inflection. The **falling tone** (syllables marked ^) is spoken with an obvious drop in pitch, as if you were sharply emphasizing a word in English. The **rising tone** (marked ˘) is pronounced as if you were asking an exaggerated question in English.

As well as the unfamiliar tones, you'll find that, despite the best efforts of the transliterators, there is no precise English equivalent to many **vowel and consonant sounds** in the Thai language. The lists below give a simplified idea of pronunciation.

## VOWELS

**a** as in dad
**aa** has no precise equivalent, but is pronounced as it looks, with the vowel elongated
**ae** as in there
**ai** as in buy
**ao** as in now
**aw** as in awe
**ay** as in pay
**e** as in pen

**eu** as in sir, but heavily nasalized
**i** as in tip
**ii** as in feet
**o** as in knock
**oe** as in hurt, but more closed
**oh** as in toe
**u** as in loot
**uu** as in pool

## CONSONANTS

**r** as in rip, but with the tongue flapped quickly against the palate – in everyday speech, it's often pronounced like "l"
**kh** as in keep
**ph** as in put

**th** as in time
**k** is unaspirated and unvoiced, and closer to "g"
**p** is also unaspirated and unvoiced, and closer to "b"
**t** is also unaspirated and unvoiced, and closer to "d"

## GENERAL WORDS AND PHRASES

### GREETINGS AND BASIC PHRASES

When you speak to a stranger in Thailand, you should generally end your sentence in *khráp* if you're a man, *khâ* if you're a woman – these untranslatable politening syllables will gain goodwill, and are nearly always used after *sawàt dii* (hello/goodbye) and *khàwp khun* (thank you). *Khráp* and *khâ* are also often used to answer "yes" to a question, though the most common way is to repeat the verb of the question (precede it with *mâi* for "no"). *Châi* (yes) and *mâi châi* (no) are less frequently used than their English equivalents.

**Hello** sawàt dii
**Where are you going?** pai năi? (not always meant literally, but used as a general greeting)
**I'm out having fun/ I'm travelling** pai thîaw (answer topai năi, almost indefinable pleasantry)
**Goodbye** sawàt dii/la kàwn
**Good luck/cheers** chôhk dii
**Excuse me** khăw thâwt
**Thank you** khàwp khun
**It's nothing/ it doesn't matter** mâi pen rai
**How are you?** sabai dii reŭ?
**I'm fine** sabai dii
**What's your name?** khun chêu arai?
**My name is...** phŏm (men)/diichăn (women) chêu...
**I come from...** phŏm/diichăn maa jàak...
**I don't understand** mâi khâo jai
**Do you speak English?** khun phûut phasăa angkrìt dâi măi?
**Do you have...?** mii...măi?
**Is...possible?** ...dâi măi?
**Can you help me?** chûay phŏm/diichăn dâi măi?

**(I) want...** ao...
**(I) would like to...** yàak jà...
**(I) like...** châwp...
**What is this called in Thai?** nîi phasăa thai rîak wâa arai?

### GETTING AROUND

**Where is the...?** ...yùu thîi năi?
**How far?** klai thâo rai?
**I would like to go to...** yàak jà pai...
**Where have you been?** pai năi maa?
**Where is this bus going?** rót nîi pai năi?
**When will the bus leave?** rót jà àwk mêua rai?
**What time does the bus arrive in...?** rót theŭng... kìi mohng?
**Stop here** jàwt thîi nîi
**here** thîi nîi
**there/over there** thîi nâan/thîi nôhn
**right** khwăa
**left** sái
**straight** trong
**north** neŭa
**south** tâi
**east** tawan àwk
**west** tawan tòk
**near/far** klâi/klai
**street** thanŏn
**train station** sathăanii rót fai
**bus station** sathàanii rót mae
**airport** sanăam bin
**ticket** tŭa
**hotel** rohng raem

post office praisanii
restaurant raan ahăan
shop raan
market talàat
hospital rohng pha-yaabaan
motorbike rót mohtoesai
taxi rót táksîi
boat reua
bicycle jàkràyaan

## ACCOMMODATION AND SHOPPING

How much is...? ...thâo rai/kìi bàat?
I don't want a plastic bag, thanks mâi ao thŭng khráp/khâ
How much is a room here per night? hâwng thîi nîi kheun lá thâo rai?
Do you have a cheaper room? mii hâwng thùuk kwàa măi?
Can I/we look at the room? duu hâwng dâi măi?
I/We'll stay two nights jà yùu săwng kheun
Can you reduce the price? lót raakhaa dâi măi?
Can I store my bag here? fàak krapăo wái thîi nîi dâi măi?
cheap/expensive thùuk/phaeng
air-con room hăwng ae
ordinary room hăwng thammadaa
telephone thohrásàp
laundry sák phâa
blanket phâa hòm
fan phát lom

## GENERAL ADJECTIVES

alone khon diaw
another ìik...nèung
bad mâi dii
big yài
clean sa-àat
closed pìt
cold (object) yen
cold (person or weather) năo
delicious aròi
difficult yâak
dirty sokaprok
easy ngâi
fun sanùk
hot (temperature) ráwn
hot (spicy) phèt
hungry hiŭ khâo
ill mâi sabai
open pòet
pretty sŭay
small lek
thirsty hiŭ nám
tired nèu-ay
very mâak

## GENERAL NOUNS

Nouns have no plurals or genders, and don't require an article.

bathroom/toilet hăwng nám
boyfriend or girlfriend faen
food ahăan
foreigner fàràng
friend phêuan
money ngoen
water/liquid nám

## GENERAL VERBS

Thai verbs do not conjugate at all, and also often double up as nouns and adjectives, which means that foreigners' most unidiomatic attempts to construct sentences are often readily understood.

come maa
do tham
eat kin/thaan khâo
give hâi
go pai
sit nâng
sleep nawn làp
walk doen pai

## NUMBERS

zero sŭun
one nèung
two săwng
three săam
four sìi
five hâa
six hòk
seven jèt
eight pàet
nine kâo
ten sìp
eleven sìp èt
twelve, thirteen... sìp săwng, sìp săam...
twenty yîi sìp/yiip
twenty-one yîi sìp èt
twenty-two, twenty-three... yîi sìp săwng, yîi sìp săam...
thirty, forty, etc săam sìp, sìi sìp...
one hundred, two hundred... nèung rói, săwng rói...
one thousand nèung phan
ten thousand nèung mèun
one hundred thousand nèung săen
one million nèung lăan

## TIME

The most common system for telling the time, as outlined below, is actually a confusing mix of several different systems. The State Railway and government officials use the

24-hour clock (9am is *kâo naalikaa*, 10am *sìp naalikaa*, and so on), which is always worth trying if you get stuck.

**1–5am** tii nèung–tii hâa
**6–11am** hòk mohng cháo–sìp èt mohng cháo
**noon** thîang
**1pm** bài mohng
**2–4pm** bài săwng mohng–bài sìi mohng
**5–6pm** hâa mohng yen–hòk mohng yen
**7–11pm** nèung thûm–hâa thûm
**midnight** thîang kheun
**What time is it?** kìi mohng láew?
**How many hours?** kìi chûa mohng?
**How long?** naan thâo rai?
**minute** naathii
**hour** chûa mohng
**day** wan
**week** aathít
**month** deuan
**year** pii

**today** wan níi
**tomorrow** phrûng níi
**yesterday** mêua wan níi
**now** diăw níi
**next week** aathít nâa
**last week** aathít kàwn
**morning** cháo
**afternoon** bài
**evening** yen
**night** kheun

## DAYS
**Sunday** wan aathít
**Monday** wan jan
**Tuesday** wan angkhaan
**Wednesday** wan phút
**Thursday** wan pháréuhàt
**Friday** wan sùk
**Saturday** wan săo

## FOOD AND DRINK

### BASIC INGREDIENTS
**kài** chicken
**mŭu** pork
**néua** beef, meat
**pèt** duck
**ahăan thalay** seafood
**plaa** fish
**plaa dùk** catfish
**plaa mèuk** squid
**kûng** prawn, shrimp
**hŏy** shellfish
**hŏy nang rom** oyster
**puu** crab
**khài** egg
**phàk** vegetables

### VEGETABLES
**makĕua** aubergine
**makĕua thêt** tomato
**nàw mái** bamboo shoots
**tùa ngâwk** bean sprouts
**phrík** chilli
**man faràng** potato
**man faràng thâwt** chips
**taeng kwaa** cucumber
**phrík yùak** green pepper
**krathiam** garlic
**hèt** mushroom
**tùa peas, beans or lentils**
**tôn hŏrm** spring onions

### NOODLES
**ba mìi** egg noodles
**kwáy tiăw (sên yaì/ sên lék)** white rice noodles (wide/ thin)
**khanŏm jiin nám yaa** noodles topped with fish curry
**kwáy tiăw/ba mìi haêng** rice noodle/egg noodles fried with egg, small pieces of meat and a few vegetables
**kwáy tiăw/ba mìi nám (mŭu)** rice noodle/egg noodle soup, made with chicken broth (and pork balls)
**kwáy tiăw/ba mìi rât nâ (mŭu)** rice noodles/egg noodles fried in gravy-like sauce with vegetables (and pork slices)
**mìi kràwp** crisp fried egg noodles with small pieces of meat and a few vegetables
**phàt thai** thin noodles fried with egg, bean sprouts and tofu, topped with ground peanuts
**phàt siyú** wide or thin noodles fried with soy sauce, egg and meat

### RICE
**khâo** rice
**khâo man kài** slices of chicken served over marinated rice
**khâo mŭu daeng** red pork with rice
**khâo nâ kài/pèt** chicken/duck served with sauce over rice
**khâo niăw** sticky rice
**khâo phàt** fried rice
**khâo kaeng** curry over rice
**khâo tôm** rice soup (usually for breakfast)

## CURRIES AND SOUPS
**kaeng phèt** hot, red curry
**kaeng phánaeng** thick, savoury curry
**kaeng khîaw wan** green curry
**kaeng mátsàman** rich Muslim-style curry, usually with beef and potatoes
**kaeng karìi** mild, Indian-style curry
**hàw mòk thalay** seafood curry soufflé
**kaeng liang** peppery vegetable soup
**kaeng sôm** tamarind soup
**tôm khà kài** chicken, coconut and galangal soup
**tôm yam kûng** hot and sour prawn soup
**kaeng jèut** mild soup with vegetables and usually pork

## SALADS
**lâap** spicy ground meat salad
**nám tòk** grilled beef or pork salad
**sôm tam** spicy papaya salad
**yam hua plee** banana flower salad
**yam néua** grilled beef salad
**yam plaa mèuk** squid salad
**yam sôm oh** pomelo salad
**yam plaa dùk foo** crispy fried catfish salad
**yam thùa phuu** wing-bean salad
**yam wun sen** noodle and pork salad

## OTHER DISHES
**hâwy thâwt** omelette stuffed with mussels
**kài phàt bai kraprao** chicken fried with holy basil leaves
**kài phàt nàw mái** chicken with bamboo shoots
**kài phàt mét mámûang** chicken with cashew nuts
**kài phàt khîng** chicken with ginger
**kài yâang** grilled chicken
**khài yát sài** omelette with pork and vegetables
**kûng chúp paêng thâwt** prawns fried in batter
**mǔu prîaw wǎan** sweet and sour pork
**néua phàt krathiam phrík thai** beef fried with garlic and pepper
**néua phàt nám man hâwy** beef in oyster sauce
**phàt phàk bûng fai daeng** morning glory fried in garlic and bean sauce
**phàt phàk ruam** stir-fried vegetables
**pàw pía** spring rolls
**plaa nêung páe sá** whole fish steamed with vegetables and ginger
**plaa rât phrík** whole fish cooked with chillies

**plaa thâwt** fried whole fish
**sàté** satay
**thâwt man plaa** fish cake

## THAI DESSERTS (*KHANǑM*)
**khanǒm beuang** small crispy pancake folded over with coconut cream and strands of sweet egg inside
**khâo lǎam** sticky rice, coconut cream and black beans cooked and served in bamboo tubes
**khâo niǎw daeng** sticky red rice mixed with coconut cream
**khâo niǎw thúrian/ mámûang** sticky rice mixed with coconut cream and durian/mango
**klûay khàek** fried banana
**lûk taan chêum** sweet palm kernels served in syrup
**sǎngkhayaa** coconut custard
**tàkôh** squares of transparent jelly (jello) topped with coconut cream

## DRINKS (*KHREÛANG DEÙM*)
**bia** beer
**chaa ráwn** hot tea
**chaa yen** iced tea
**kaafae ráwn** hot coffee
**kâew** glass
**khúat** bottle
**mâekhǒng (or anglicized Mekong)** Thai brand-name rice whisky
**klûay pan** banana shake
**nám mánao/sôm** fresh, bottled or fizzy lemon/orange juice
**nám plào** drinking water (boiled or filtered)
**nám sǒdaa** soda water
**nám taan** sugar
**kleua** salt
**nám yen** cold water
**nom jeùd** milk
**ohlíang** iced black coffee
**thûay** cup

## ORDERING
I am vegetarian/vegan **Phǒm (male)/diichǎn (female) kin ahǎan mangsàwirát/jeh**
Can I see the menu? **Khǎw duù menu nóy?**
I would like… **Khǎw…**
with/without… **Sài/mâi sài…**
Can I have the bill please? **Khǎw check bin?**

# Glossary

**Amphoe** District.

**Amphoe muang** Provincial capital.

**Ao** Bay.

**Apsara** Female deity.

**Avalokitesvara** Bodhisattva representing compassion.

**Avatar** Earthly manifestation of a deity.

**Ban** Village or house.

**Bang** Village by a river or the sea.

**Bencharong** Polychromatic ceramics made in China for the Thai market.

**Bhumisparsa mudra** Most common gesture of Buddha images; symbolizes the Buddha's victory over temptation.

**Bodhisattva** In Mahayana Buddhism, an enlightened being who postpones his or her entry into Nirvana.

**Bot** Main sanctuary of a Buddhist temple.

**Brahma** One of the Hindu trinity – "The Creator". -Usually depicted with four faces and four arms.

**Celadon** Porcelain with grey-green glaze.

**Changwat** Province.

**Chao ley/chao nam** "Sea gypsies" – nomadic fisherfolk of south Thailand.

**Chedi** Reliquary tower in Buddhist temple.

**Chofa** Finial on temple roof.

**Deva** Mythical deity.

**Devaraja** God-king.

**Dharma** The teachings or doctrine of the Buddha.

**Dharmachakra** Buddhist Wheel of Law (also known as Wheel of Doctrine or Wheel of Life).

**Doi** Mountain.

**Erawan** Mythical three-headed elephant; Indra's vehicle.

**Farang** Foreigner/foreign.

**Ganesh** Hindu elephant-headed deity, remover of obstacles and god of knowledge.

**Garuda** Mythical Hindu creature – half man, half bird; Vishnu's vehicle.

**Gopura** Entrance pavilion to temple precinct -(especially Khmer).

**Hamsa** Sacred mythical goose; Brahma's vehicle.

**Hanuman** Monkey god and chief of the monkey army in the *Ramayana*; ally of Rama.

**Hat** Beach.

**Hin** Stone.

**Hinayana** Pejorative term for Theravada school of Buddhism, literally "Lesser Vehicle".

**Ho trai** A scripture library.

**Indra** Hindu king of the gods and, in Buddhism, -devotee of the Buddha; usually carries a thunderbolt.

**Isaan** Northeast Thailand.

**Jataka** Stories of the Buddha's five hundred lives.

**Khaen** Reed and wood pipe; the characteristic musical instrument of Isaan.

**Khao** Hill, mountain.

**Khlong** Canal.

**Khon** Classical dance-drama.

**Kinnari** Mythical creature – half woman, half bird.

**Kirtimukha** Very powerful deity depicted as a lion-head.

**Ko** Island.

**Ku** The Lao word for prang; a tower in a temple complex.

**Laem** Headland or cape.

**Lakhon** Classical dance-drama.

**Lak muang** City pillar; revered home for the city's guardian spirit.

**Lakshaman/Phra Lak** Rama's younger brother.

**Lakshana** Auspicious signs or "marks of greatness" displayed by the Buddha.

**Lanna** Northern Thai kingdom that lasted from the thirteenth to the sixteenth century.

**Likay** Popular folk theatre.

**Longyi** Burmese sarong.

**Luang Pho** Abbot or especially revered monk.

**Maenam** River.

**Mahathat** Chedi containing relics of the Buddha.

**Mahayana** School of Buddhism now practised mainly in China, Japan and Korea; literally "the Great Vehicle".

**Mara** The Evil One; tempter of the Buddha.

**Mawn khwaan** Traditional triangular or "axe-head" pillow.

**Meru/Sineru** Mythical mountain at the centre of Hindu and Buddhist cosmologies.

**Mondop** Small, square temple building to house minor images or religious texts.

**Moo/muu** Neighbourhood.

**Muang** City or town.

**Muay thai** Thai boxing.

**Mudra** Symbolic gesture of the Buddha.

**Mut mee** Tie-dyed cotton or silk.

**Naga** Mythical dragon-headed serpent in Buddhism and Hinduism.

**Nakhon** Honorific title for a city.

**Nam** Water.

**Nam tok** Waterfall.

**Nang thalung** Shadow-puppet entertainment, found in southern Thailand.

**Nielloware** Engraved metalwork.

**Nirvana** Final liberation from the cycle of rebirths; state of non-being to which Buddhists aspire.

**Pak Tai** Southern Thailand.

**Pali** Language of ancient India; the script of the -original Buddhist scriptures.

**Pha sin** Woman's sarong.

**Phi** Animist spirit.

**Phra** Honorific term – literally "excellent".

**Phu** Mountain.

**Prang** Central tower in a Khmer temple.

**Prasat** Khmer temple complex or central shrine.

**Rama/Phra Ram** Human manifestation of Hindu deity Vishnu; hero of the *Ramayana*.

**Ramakien** Thai version of the *Ramayana*.

**Ramayana** Hindu epic of good versus evil: chief -characters include Rama, Sita, Ravana, Hanuman.

**Ravana** see Totsagan.

**Reua hang yao** Longtail boat.

**Rishi** Ascetic hermit.

**Rot ae/rot tua** Air-conditioned bus.

**Rot thammadaa** Ordinary bus.

**Sala** Meeting hall, pavilion, bus stop – or any open-sided structure.

**Samlor** Three-wheeled passenger tricycle.

**Sanskrit** Sacred language of Hinduism; also used in Buddhism.

**Sanuk** Fun.

**Sema** Boundary stone to mark consecrated ground within temple complex.

**Shiva** One of the Hindu trinity – "The Destroyer".

**Shiva lingam** Phallic representation of Shiva.

**Soi** Lane or side road.

**Songkhran** Thai New Year.

**Songthaew** Public transport pick-up vehicle; means "two rows", after its two facing benches.

**Takraw** Game played with a rattan ball.

**Talat** Market.

**Talat nam** Floating market.

**Talat yen** Night market.

**Tambon** Subdistrict.

**Tavatimsa** Buddhist heaven.

**Tha** Pier.

**Thale** Sea or lake.

**Tham** Cave.

**Thanon** Road.

**That** Chedi.

**Thep** A divinity.

**Theravada** Main school of Buddhist thought in -Thailand; also known as Hinayana.

**Totsagan** Rama's evil rival in the *Ramayana*; also known as Ravana.

**Tripitaka** Buddhist scriptures.

**Trok** Alley.

**Tuk-tuk** Motorized three-wheeled taxi.

**Uma** Shiva's consort.

**Ushnisha** Cranial protuberance on Buddha images, signifying an enlightened being.

**Viharn** Temple assembly hall for the laity; usually contains the principal Buddha image.

**Vipassana** Buddhist meditation technique; literally "insight".

**Vishnu** One of the Hindu trinity – "The Preserver". -Usually shown with four arms, holding a disc, a conch, a lotus and a club.

**Wai** Thai greeting expressed by a prayer-like gesture with the hands.

**Wang** Palace.

**Wat** Temple.

**Wiang** Fortified town.

**Yaksha** Mythical giant.

**Yantra** Magical combination of numbers and letters, used to ward off danger.

# Small print and index

## A ROUGH GUIDE TO ROUGH GUIDES

Published in 1982, the first Rough Guide – to Greece – was a student scheme that became a publishing phenomenon. Mark Ellingham, a recent graduate in English from Bristol University, had been travelling in Greece the previous summer and couldn't find the right guidebook. With a small group of friends he wrote his own guide, combining a contemporary, journalistic style with a thoroughly practical approach to travellers' needs.

The immediate success of the book spawned a series that rapidly covered dozens of destinations. And, in addition to impecunious backpackers, Rough Guides soon acquired a much broader readership that relished the guides' wit and inquisitiveness as much as their enthusiastic, critical approach and value-for-money ethos. These days, Rough Guides include recommendations from budget to luxury and cover more than 120 destinations around the globe, from Amsterdam to Zanzibar, all regularly updated by our team of roaming writers.

Browse all our latest guides, read inspirational features and book your trip at **roughguides.com**.

## Rough Guide credits

**Editors:** Joanna Reeves, Tom Fleming and Rachel Mills
**Cartography:** Katie Bennett
**Managing editor:** Rachel Lawrence
**Picture editor:** Aude Vauconsant

**Cover photo research:** Marta Bescos
**Senior DTP coordinator:** Dan May
**Head of DTP and Pre-Press:** Rebeka Davies

## Publishing information

Seventh edition 2019

**Distribution**
*UK, Ireland and Europe*
Apa Publications (UK) Ltd; sales@roughguides.com
*United States and Canada*
Ingram Publisher Services; ips@ingramcontent.com
*Australia and New Zealand*
Woodslane; info@woodslane.com.au
*Southeast Asia*
Apa Publications (SN) Pte; sales@roughguides.com
*Worldwide*
Apa Publications (UK) Ltd; sales@roughguides.com
**Special Sales, Content Licensing and CoPublishing**
Rough Guides can be purchased in bulk quantities
at discounted prices. We can create special editions,
personalised jackets and corporate imprints tailored to
your needs. sales@roughguides.com.

roughguides.com
Printed in China by CTPS
All rights reserved
© 2019 Apa Digital (CH) AG
License edition © Apa Publications Ltd UK
All rights reserved. No part of this publication may be
reproduced, stored in or introduced into a retrieval system,
or transmitted in any form, or by any means (electronic,
mechanical, photocopying, recording or otherwise) without
the prior written permission of the copyright owner.
A catalogue record for this book is available from the
British Library
The publishers and authors have done their best to ensure
the accuracy and currency of all the information in **The
Rough Guide to Thailand's Beaches & Islands**, however,
they can accept no responsibility for any loss, injury, or
inconvenience sustained by any traveller as a result of
information or advice contained in the guide.

## Help us update

We've gone to a lot of effort to ensure that the seventh
edition of **The Rough Guide to Thailand's Beaches
& Islands** is accurate and up-to-date. However, things
change – places get "discovered", opening hours are
notoriously fickle, restaurants and rooms raise prices
or lower standards. If you feel we've got it wrong or
left something out, we'd like to know, and if you can
remember the address, the price, the hours, the phone
number, so much the better.

Please send your comments with the subject line
**"Rough Guide Thailand's Beaches & Islands Update"** to
mail@uk.roughguides.com. We'll credit all contributions
and send a copy of the next edition (or any other Rough
Guide if you prefer) for the very best emails.

## Photo credits

(Key: T-top; C-centre; B-bottom; L-left; R-right)

**Alamy** 2, 9B, 13T, 271, 385, 405
**Donyanedomam/Dreamstime.com** 223
**Getty Images** 11TL, 12M, 16B, 16T
**iStock** 4, 10, 12T, 12B, 14T, 15T, 17C, 17B, 18, 21, 23, 25, 205, 283, 392/393, 418
**Karen Trist/Rough Guides** 73, 177, 353
**KatjaKreder/AWL Images** 7

**Martin Richardson/Rough Guides** 11C, 11B, 15BR, 17T, 26, 70/71, 89, 107, 127, 202/203, 251, 325
**Michele Falzone/AWL Images** 1
**Shutterstock** 9T, 11TR, 13B, 14B, 15BL, 146/147, 149, 280/281
**SuperStock** 395
**Cover:** Kam Tok island **Getty Images**

## ABOUT THE AUTHORS

After twenty years of toing and froing, **Paul Gray** has recently settled down in Thailand. He
is author of the *Rough Guide to Bangkok* and co-author of the *Rough Guide to Thailand*, as well
as the *Rough Guide to Ireland*, and has edited and contributed to many other guidebooks,
including an update of his native Northeast for the *Rough Guide to England*.

**Marco Ferrarese** first came to Thailand in 2007 and since then has kept visiting the country's
well-trodden and most obscure corners from his home base of Penang, Malaysia. Besides
writing for Rough Guides, he covers Southeast Asia, the Indian subcontinent and the Middle
East for a number of publications, including *Travel + Leisure Southeast Asia, Nikkei Asian Review,
the Guardian*, BBC Travel and Adventure.com. Find out more at Ⓦmarcoferrarese.com and
Ⓦmonkeyrockworld.com.

SMALL PRINT | 449

## Readers' updates

Thanks to all the readers who have taken the time to write in with comments and suggestions (and apologies if we've inadvertently omitted or misspelt anyone's name):

Evgeny Bobrov; David Cunningham; Bénédicte de Decker; Jamison Firestone; Posy Harvey; Andrew J. Hebert; Monica Mackaness and John Garratt; William Peskett; Mila Rodriguez.

## Acknowledgements

**Marco Ferarrese** Thanks to Andy Turner who commissioned me on this guide, Helen Abramson who picked it up when he left, and Joanna Reeves and Tom Fleming who edited it. A special thanks with hugs goes to my wife Kit Yeng Chan, who offered her car, was my co-pilot, and a perfect moral booster during this umpteenth research trip. At last, a strong heads-up to all the people who helped me out in a way or another during the different legs of the research trip, in particular Maneenuch Assavanichakorn at Centara.

**Paul Gray** Thanks to Anne Bachmann, Mike Barraclough, Lucy Ridout, Josep Marti Romero and Ron Emmons; Marion Walsh in Bangkok; Evelien in Kanchanaburi; Tan and Michel in Sukhothai; Fhu and Ung in Nan; Kung in Chiang Khong; Suda in Chumphon; and Tuppadit Thaiarry and all the staff at Avis. Big thanks to Gade and Stella, who make everything possible.

# Index

# Map symbols

The symbols below are used on maps throughout the book

| | | | | | |
|---|---|---|---|---|---|
| | International boundary | | Tourist information | | Lighthouse |
| | Provincial boundary | | Post office | | Viewpoint |
| | Chapter division boundary | | Telephone office | | Wildlife park |
| | Expressway | | Internet access | | Arch |
| | Pedestrian road | | Bank/ATM | | Park HQ |
| | Road | | Embassy/consulate | | Museum |
| | One-way street | | Hospital/clinic | | Statue |
| | Steps | | Market | | Temple |
| | Unpaved road | | Landmark hotel | | Mosque |
| | Path | | Landmark restaurant | | Hindu temple |
| | Railway | | Point of interest | | Chinese temple/pagoda |
| | Ferry route | | Border crossing | | Church |
| | Wall | | Peak | | Building |
| | Cable car & station | | Mountains | | Stadium |
| | International airport | | Cave | | Park/forest |
| | Transport stop | | Waterfall | | Beach |
| | Airline office | | | | |

## Listings key

■ Accommodation

● Eating

■ Drinking/nightlife

● Shopping

# ESCAPE
# THE EVERYDAY

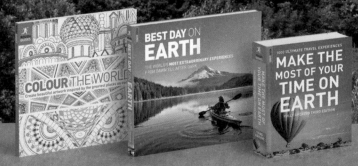